1980

Theories and
Models of Personality

Desmond S. Cartwright

Theories and
Models of Personality

wcb
Wm. C. Brown Company Publishers
Dubuque, Iowa

Acknowledgments

The author is grateful for permission to use excerpts
and illustrations from the following sources:

Page 21: from D. O. Hebb, "What Psychology Is
About." In *American Psychologist,* 1974, no. 29,
p. 74. Copyright 1974 by the American Psychological Association. Reprinted by permission of
the author and the publisher.
Page 29: from S. R. Maddi, *Personality Theories: A
Comparative Analysis* (3rd ed.), Dorsey Press,
1976. Reprinted by permission of the author and
the publisher.

(*Continued on page 567*)

To Sat Rattan, Viriam, Carolyn, and Theophilus

Contents

Preface ix

Chapter 1: A Practical Theory of Personality: Maslow 2

Chapter 2: What Is Personality? 26

Chapter 3: Personality as Thematic Dispositions: Murray 48

Chapter 4: Personality as Behavior: Skinner 72

Chapter 5: Personality as Subjective Experience: Rogers 106

Chapter 6: The General Nature of Scientific Theories 126

Chapter 7: A Theory with Explicit Empirical Assumptions: Miller and Dollard 148

Chapter 8: Types of Theory and Theoretical Models 178

Chapter 9: A Theory of Personality Structure: Freud 206

Chapter 10: A Causal Theory of Personality: Freud 234

Chapter 11: A Pattern Theory of Personality: Freud 264

Chapter 12: Carl Jung's Theories: Structure, Cause, and Pattern 288

Chapter 13: Comparing Two Models of the Unconscious: Freud and Jung 320

Chapter 14: Erickson's Pattern Theory of Personality Development 338

Chapter 15: Cattell's Functional Theory of Personality Structure and Causal Dynamics 360

Chapter 16: Ego, Self, Identity: Five Competing Models? 398

Chapter 17: Eysenck's Functional Theory of Personality Structure and Causal Dynamics 422

Chapter 18: Comparing Four Theories: Freud, Cattell, Jung, Eysenck 446

Chapter 19: Lewin's Functional Theory of Personality Structure and Dynamics 462

Chapter 20: Rotter's Social Learning Theory of Personality Functions 482

Chapter 21: A Competing Social Learning Theory of Personality: Bandura and Walters 502

Chapter 22: Looking Back and Thinking Ahead 524

Appendix A: The Lie-detector: Trying to Find When Experience and Behavior Are Inconsistent 542

Appendix B: Use of Statistics Procedures for Test Analysis 544

Appendix C: The Correlation Coefficient 547

Appendix D: Estimating the Heritability of a Trait 549

References 551

Name Index 571

Subject Index 575

Preface

Theories and Models of Personality is written for the student who wishes to do more than simply follow a cafeteria line of one personality theory after another. It assumes that the student is interested in personality as a live topic that is relevant to his or her own quest for understanding. It assumes that theories of personality contain models that can facilitate individual understanding of self and of others. It also assumes that the student wishes to develop a personal, critical, scientific approach to considering, appraising, and testing any of these models that appears promising. Accordingly, this book is as much an introduction to ways of evaluating and comparing theoretical models in personality science as it is a presentation of particular theories of personality.

It is surprising to realize that we are actually unsure what the word *personality* really means. How can you have a theory of something when you are not sure what the something is! Each theorist, of course, knows the meaning of personality that his or her theory addresses. But such meanings differ from theorist to theorist. Nevertheless it is possible to find order in this chaos, and chapter 2 suggests that there are just three main definitions

of personality in actual use among theorists. Each theorist offers a variation on one or another of these three themes. Putting them all together and filling out the picture a bit, it becomes possible to discern the reality behind these three major meanings of personality. This reality is more complex than any one of the separate meanings and, in fact, includes all of them and then something more.

Chapter 1 presents Maslow's personality theory, which is practical and interesting, and gives the reader some initial common reference points. Maslow's implicit definition of personality can be compared with others in chapter 2. Chapters 3, 4, and 5 each present a single theory of personality (Murray, Skinner, and Rogers) that exemplifies one of the three main definitions discussed in chapter 2 Some of the contrasts between these three theories become very obvious.

With four current examples of personality theory now placed in view, it is possible to consider the general nature of scientific theories in chapter 6. Chapter 6 discusses, among other things, the tricky question of how to evaluate a theory and, from a large number of possible criteria, recommends four as being the most important for evaluating a theory of personality: accuracy, power, fruitfulness, and depth.

From this point on it is possible to use the conceptual tools of analysis and evaluation developed in chapters 2 and 6. However, one of the most important components of a scientific theory, as studied in chapter 6, consists of the empirical assumptions made by the theorist. Although examples of these assumptions are offered in chapter 6, it seemed desirable to illustrate their use more fully by presenting a theory of personality in which empirical assumptions are made especially clear. This goal is accomplished in chapter 7 with a discussion of the theory formulated by Miller and Dollard.

Each overall theory of personality is found to contain several different types of theory. For example, Eysenck's theory, like Freud's theory, contains both a theory of structure (of personality) and a theory of cause (of causal relations between, say, brain and behavior). The types described in chapter 8 are theories of structure, cause, pattern, function, system, and priority.

Subsequent chapters now use the many concepts of analysis, evaluation, and classification developed in previous chapters. Chapters 9, 10, and 11 each take one of the types of theory found in Freud's overall theory of personality: his theories of structure, of cause, and of pattern. This procedure enables the reader to develop a fuller understanding of each type of theory at the same time as portions of Freud's monumental work are studied. In chapter 12, Jung's theories of structure, cause, and pattern are presented; and Jung's theory of structure is compared with Freud's theory of structure in the next chapter, with special focus upon a comparison of the two models of the unconscious. Later chapters present examples of the various types of theories. Theories and particular theoretical models are compared at suitable points so that the reader

has an opportunity to acquire skills of analysis and comparative evaluation.

One mark of this book, then, is its goal of leaving the reader with much more than a knowledge of who said what in personality theories. The chapters are sequenced to build increasing skills in the critical evaluation of theories and in comparative analysis, including empirical testing of theoretical models. As will be evident to the reader, the later chapters draw increasingly upon the conceptual tools of analysis and evaluation developed in the early part of the book. Workshops are provided at the end of each chapter, with exercises in conceptual analysis, theory construction, data gathering, development of research instruments, hypothesis testing, and designs for survey, psychometric, or experimental tests of theoretical models. A final emphasis is placed on the design of *confrontation experiments* in which genuinely competing theoretical models are made to confront each other in one and the same experimental arena.

Many persons have provided helpful comments and critiques of early drafts of the manuscript for this book. My thanks go especially to Professor Juris I. Berzins of the University of Kentucky, Professor Robert Kessler of the University of Massachusetts, Professor Kathryn M. Krogh of Brooklyn College of the City of New York, Professor Martin Manosewitz of the University of Texas at Austin, Professor David E. Silber of George Washington University, Professor Harold E. Vetter of Loyola University in New Orleans, and Professor Robert A. Zucker of Michigan State University. These reviewers provided constructive feedback on the entire structure of the book as well as on particular chapters. Many of the book's strong points would not be included had they not made the initial suggestions for them and, in some cases, shown me how to present them. I am likewise indebted to Professor Hans J. Eysenck of the

University of London, Professor Raymond B. Cattell of the University of Illinois and the University of Hawaii, Professor Eldon Whipple of the University of California at San Diego, and Anne De Vore of Seattle University. These persons read drafts of one or more chapters and gave me valuable suggestions and criticisms. I wish to express my deep appreciation to each one of these reviewers and readers.

I am grateful to Professor P. Polson, Terry Spear, and the staff of the Computer Laboratory in Psychological Research at the University of Colorado for making available to me extensive amounts of editor processing space on the computer and a private terminal to compile the indexes. I greatly appreciate also the assistance of Dr. Gideon Weisz in the preparation of the Name Index.

I am grateful also to members of my immediate family, Carol and Jacqueline Cartwright, who helped me with a continuing informal critique of tentative ideas and with numerous suggestions for specific new directions and emphases in the text, and with the arduous tasks of reading and correcting galley proofs and preparing the indexes.

I should also like to thank as a group the many authors and publishers who kindly gave me permission to reproduce selected passages and diagrams from their own publications, thereby facilitating my task and enabling me to present a more complete picture of relevant theories, models, and methods. I am grateful for the valuable assistance of Elaine Catalano, who handled the large amount of correspondence involved in obtaining permission for use of this material.

Theories and
Models of Personality

INTRODUCTION

Overview of the book
Introduction to Maslow's life and work
   Maslow's life and professional career
   The meaning of humanistic psychology
   Maslow as a humanistic psychologist
The hierarchy of needs
   Instinctoid nature of needs
   Classes of needs
      Physiological needs
      Safety needs
      Needs for love, affection, and belongingness
      Needs for esteem
      Needs for self-actualization
   A model of the hierarchy
Needs and the formation of syndromes
   The meaning of a syndrome
   The syndrome of insecurity
   Persistence and change in syndromes
The self-actualization syndrome
   Three core characteristics
      Spontaneity
      Acceptance of self and others
        Deeper personal relations
        Quality of detachment
      Efficiency of perception
        The peak experiences
   Metamotivation
Accomplishments of Maslow's theory
   Humanistic psychology
   Industrial psychology
   Potentials and possibilities
   How to develop a child's potentials
   How to develop our own potentials
Critique of Maslow's theory
   As a humanistic theory
   As related to empirical research
   Accuracy and other characteristics of the theory
Workshop 1 Self-actualizing people
Summary

A Practical Theory of Personality: Maslow

In this first chapter we shall discuss one of the most influential of modern personality theorists, Abraham Maslow. As we shall see, Maslow's influence has been felt not only in psychology but also in a number of other fields, notably in business management. The reason for this wide influence is no doubt the essential practicality of Maslow's theory of personality. This theory accurately describes many realities of personal experience. People find they can understand what Maslow says; they can recognize with delight some feature of their experience or behavior which is true and significant but which they have never put into words.

Before going on with our formal introduction to Maslow and his theory I must say a word about why this first chapter starts off so abruptly with a specific theory of personality; why the book does not open with the study of personality in general, the definition of personality, and the nature of a scientific theory. The reason is that it will be much easier to talk about these things after we have gone over at least one theory of personality, for that will provide a living instance for reader and writer alike to point to. Chapter 2 will take up the question of what personality is and how it has been defined. Actually, per-

sonality has been defined in so many different ways as to be confusing. But it is possible to organize the definitions into three groups: those that focus upon *conscious experience;* those that are concerned primarily with the person's *overt behavior;* and those that emphasize the *underlying causes* or tendencies within the person that determine experience and behavior. Chapters 3, 4, and 5 each provides an example of these different definitions of personality. Chapter 6 then discusses the general nature of scientific theories, and chapter 7 gives an example of a personality theory in which the part played by the scientist's assumptions is made very clear.

In chapter 8 we shall lay the groundwork for comparing different theories of personality. Theories differ not only in their definition of personality but also in exactly what they try to deal with, whether it be the underlying structure of personality, the dynamic or causal forces within personality, or the patterns found in personality characteristics. In the typical case a theory will include one or more models of how the personality works in some particular respect, how dreams are formed, for example, how anxiety develops, or how people find their real identity. Chapters 9 through 22 will present several different theories of personality, making a number of comparisons among them regarding exactly what they deal with and their particular models.

The point of writing a book like this is not only to describe and compare essential features of several theories of personality but also to stimulate an understanding of how theories are made and what they are good for. In addition to giving us some useful particular insights into ourselves and other people, the study of personality theories can equip us with a more general new skill. This skill lies in building our own theories and models as we cope with the daily tasks presented to each one of us by social change: meeting new friends, discovering how strangely different people can be from one another, or finding unexpected new limits to our own capabilities. At some point in life for example, we are likely to learn that many people suffer from feelings of inferiority, and they often react by pretending to be superior. So when we come across a person who seems very conceited we suspect that underlying the conceit are secret feelings of inferiority. This observation is an example of a theoretical model we can use in understanding another person or ourselves. Almost any trait we see in another person or in ourselves could be produced in an attempt to make up for some lack, and we call this *compensating*. For instance, a person who seems very bold, always doing exceptionally daring stunts, might actually be very timid underneath. This person would be compensating for an inner fearfulness by acting courageously. Another personality model is seen in the difference between introverts and extraverts. When we first observe that distinction, a light goes on in our heads: "Oh! So that's why [so-and-so] is such an oddball. She's an introvert!" As we learn more about these and other theoretical models we get a clearer picture of personality and its variety of manifestations. We learn also some-

thing of the limitations and special conditions of each model. For example, only an extravert would think that an introvert is an "oddball."

With this preamble about the book as a whole, we can now get on with the main topic of this chapter, Maslow's theory of personality.

Introduction to Maslow's Life and Work

Maslow was born in Brooklyn, New York, in 1908. By his own account (1968, p. 37) he was "the little Jewish boy in a non-Jewish neighborhood . . . isolated and unhappy." He said it was like being the first black child enrolled in an all-white school, and the effect was to encourage him to spend time reading in libraries. Later, at the University of Wisconsin, he studied under Harry Harlow, specializing in the study of primate behavior. Maslow's interest in primates never vanished completely, and as late as 1960 he published a paper on dominance and sex behavior in monkeys (Maslow, Rand, & Newman, 1960).

Although all of his graduate training was in behaviorism, several forces in Maslow's life converged to move him away from that approach to psychology. He relates that he did not question behaviorism until he began reading Freud and gestalt psychology. The works of Ruth Benedict, Alfred Adler, Erich Fromm, and Max Wertheimer were especially influential. He wrote a paper on "Personality and Patterns of Culture" as early as 1937 (Maslow, 1937). But his personal experiences in psychoanalysis and in marriage appear to have had the greatest influence in shifting him beyond the horizons of behaviorism. At the age of twenty he married the girl he had fallen in love with at sixteen. He and his wife Bertha had two children, Ann and Ellen. Maslow writes: "Then when my baby was born that was the thunderclap that settled things. . . . I was stunned by the mystery. . . . I felt small and weak and feeble before all this. I'd say that anyone who had a baby couldn't be a behaviorist" (Maslow, 1968, p. 56).

In 1938 he took a position as associate professor at Brooklyn College, where he taught until 1951. He became increasingly interested in human personality, and his first book, in 1941, was on abnormal psychology (Maslow & Mittleman, 1941). The outbreak of World War II had a dramatic effect on Maslow, according to his own recollection (Maslow, 1968, p. 54). He asked himself: Why is it that psychology is unable to contribute anything to world peace, to the solution of major human problems? He concluded that psychology had been failing to pay attention to such issues. It had focused upon animal behavior and upon the study of human beings who were mentally ill. But neither of these topics could help bring nations together in a peace conference. And so he set himself the task of studying the very best examples of humanity, with the hope of discovering the highest potentials for good in human beings and developing ways to nurture such potentials. His work produced the concepts of *self-actualization* and *self-actualizing people,* which we shall study in the course of this chapter.

In 1951 Maslow became professor and chairman of the Department of Psychology at Brandeis University, a position he held until 1969. In 1968 he was president of the American Psychological Association. In this and many other ways Maslow was highly honored by his colleagues. He was named Humanist of the Year by the American Humanist Association, and he received an honorary doctorate of law from the University of Cincinnati. Maslow's best known books deal with topics of optimal personality development: *Motivation and Personality;* (1954; second edition, 1970a); *Religions, Values, and Peak Experiences* (1964; reissued in 1970b); and *The Farther Reaches of Human Nature* (completed in 1970 just before his death, and published posthumously under the direction of Bertha Maslow in 1971).

Maslow began his career as a biological psychologist and ended it as a humanistic psychologist. But, as we shall see, he did not abandon the fruits of his early training and work in biological psychology. Rather, he integrated the biological and the humanistic view of human nature. What is the difference between the two? What is "humanistic psychology" all about? James Bugental, the first president of the American Association for Humanistic Psychology, has set forth six distinguishing characteristics of the humanistic psychologist (1967, p. 9). The humanistic psychologist believes that:

1. Descriptions of human psychology based upon animal research are inadequate and misleading.
2. Meaningfulness is more important than methodology in the choice of research topics in psychology.
3. Subjective experience is more important than behavior.
4. Pure and applied research studies are equally important and should be seen as mutually supportive.
5. The individual, unique, exceptional, and unpredicted aspects of human beings should be studied with equal emphasis as is given the universal, regular, or conforming and expectable aspects.
6. Reducing human experience to simple mechanical concepts (like stimulus-response habits) is a dangerous activity. It is dangerous because it encourages people to treat others as if they were machines. Rather, those ways and concepts should be explored which will widen and enrich human experience.

Humanistic psychology, then, is concerned with topics that are meaningful to human beings, focusing especially upon subjective experience and the unique, unpredictable events in individual human lives. Moreover, humanistic psychology is devoted to the aim of improving human experience. As Buhler and Allen describe it in their book *Introduction to Humanistic Psychology* (1972), a deep philosophical commitment characterizes the humanistic psychologist. There is a philosophy of humankind and a philosophy of science.

In its relationship to humanity, humanistic psychology is deeply aware of the relativity imposed by rapidly changing cultural conditions. Confronted with realities of war, the ecological crisis, and political corruption, human beings find themselves without foundations of faith, without individual purpose. Traditional values seem no longer adequate. Humanistic psychologists acknowledge these factors of relativity, dislocation, and crisis as fundamental facts about the nature of human beings today. To survive despite a disintegrating ecology and an inadequate set of social systems, the human race must understand its own potentials for transcendence. Individuals must be enabled to transcend the conflicts of their time and achieve meaningfulness in their own lives. Humanistic psychologists are dedicated to helping them do this.

In its philosophy of science, humanistic psychology asserts that science is a product of human inventiveness under the constraints of contemporary culture and conditions. Modern technological society has produced two major theories of personality, behaviorism and psychoanalysis, both of which are technological. Both these theories of personality present human beings as pushed and pulled by mechanical forces, either of stimuli and reinforcements (behaviorism) or of unconscious instinctual impulses (psychoanalysis). This representation is in error, the humanists believe, because human beings are most importantly characterized by their possession of subjective experience, inner purposiveness, and the ability to rise above and even change any forces in the environment or in their own given nature.

Humanistic psychology focuses upon *potentials*. By studying exceptional individuals, it tries to understand the upper limits of human capability. It seeks the frontiers of creativity, the highest reaches of consciousness and wisdom. Each of the humanistic psychologists specializes in a particular way of looking at this phenomenon. Rogers, for example (see chapter 5), describes the "fully functioning person" as the ideal of what the human may become. Rogers obtains this insight from observing the ways people change as they grow in personal maturity. Jourard (1974) describes the "healthy personality" as the ideal. Maslow describes the characteristic features of "self-actualizing people" and points beyond self-actualization to even higher levels of consciousness and being.

In one typical statement, Maslow wrote (1971, p. 194): "Man is a hierarchy of needs, with the biological needs at the base of the hierarchy and the spiritual needs at the top." We shall begin our study of Maslow's theory with this hierarchy of needs. Then we shall consider some syndromes or patterns of personality, such as insecurity and self-actualization. Finally we shall examine some social and personal implications of Maslow's theory, focusing especially upon what he had to say about helping people achieve self-actualization.

The Hierarchy of Needs

Maslow says that we are born with weak instincts which become specific needs in the context of our culture. These needs, if unsatisfied, dominate our personality. In *Motivation and Personality* (1970a), he has set forth a complete statement of his theory of personal motivation. He holds that previous theories have been too biased by animal data, too eager to list specific needs or instincts or drives, too prone to consider physiological needs like hunger as the prototype for all needs, and too unaware of the complexities of human motivation especially as it is consciously experienced. Even worse, all other theories of motivation have failed to recognize one of the most obvious facts of human motivation: When a need is satisfied it is no longer a need. When people are basically well-fed, housed, clothed, and free of most physical threats and other sources of insecurity, they do not often experience hunger, thirst, safety, or security as real needs. In fact these are not real needs precisely because they are satisfied.

Maslow does not accept the idea that there are some basic needs out of which or upon which all other needs develop. He does not believe, as the behaviorists do, that the need for love develops as a result of conditioning—that the baby will love the caretaker who gratifies its hunger, for example. On the contrary, Maslow asserts, the need for love is in itself a separate need, just as instinctive in origin as the hunger need.

Maslow thinks psychologists have spent too much time setting up dichotomies, particularly on the question of nature versus nurture. All of Maslow's basic needs are *instinctoid;* they are the human equivalent of instincts in animals. Very weak dispositions, given by heredity, must then be fashioned fully by the growth of the organism. In happy circumstances benevolent needs develop; in ugly circumstances brutish needs develop. If the environment is right, as the humanists define it, people will grow straight and beautiful, actualizing the potentials they have inherited. If the environment is not "right" (and mostly it is not) they will mostly not grow tall and straight and beautiful.

Classes of Needs

Maslow's hierarchic theory holds that certain *classes* of needs are stronger than others.

Laid down in weak tendency by heredity, these classes of needs are activated and control behavior and experience when they are not satisfied. The characteristic stamp of the theory is that there is a certain *pattern* of relative strength, a *hierarchy,* among the different classes of basic needs. It is a pattern of *prepotency,* in which the person does not feel the second need until the demands of the first have been satisfied, nor the third until the second has been satisfied, and so on. Physiological needs (hunger, thirst, sex) are strongest; safety needs are next, then needs for belongingness and love, then needs for esteem, and finally, needs for self-actualization. These are the basic needs. Beyond them come needs for understanding, esthetic appreciation, and also more purely spiritual needs. We shall deal with these later. For the present, we shall discuss what Maslow has called the hierarchy of basic needs.

Physiological Needs. The first of the five classes of basic needs is physiological. It comprises all the needs for oxygen, acid-base ratio, salt, vitamins, and so on; as well as the needs for food, water, and sex. Elimination would also be included, as would the need to maintain a comfortable ambient (external) temperature and relatively constant body temperature. It is perhaps a paradox that these are the strongest needs. For as Maslow points out, the typical day in the life of the average citizen of the United States will not include much reveries about oxygen, acid-base ratios, salt, or the like. Their heads are more likely to be preoccupied with thoughts of a new auto, another person, or a World Series game.

So why are physiological needs the strongest? What makes them so prepotent? Maslow's answer is that the physiological needs *must* be met before others can be met. On the rare occasions when persons in our civilization are deprived of all needs for any length of time, the physiological ones take precedence.

The starving cross-country skier trapped in an avalanche is primarily concerned with finding food. Plane-crash victims trapped in the Andes eventually ate their dead friends. The diver who has run out of air thinks little of getting a new TV; one gasp of air is the only thing he wants. Physiological needs are prepotent in the sense that if all needs were deprived, the physiological ones would come first in the person's search for satisfaction. This seems to be both a biological and a subjective fact.

Safety Needs. When all physiological needs are satisfied and are no longer controlling thoughts and behaviors, the needs for security can become active. Maslow points out that many adults have little awareness of their security needs except in times of emergency or periods of disorganization of the social structure (such as widespread rioting). Children, however, display the signs of insecurity readily enough. Infants react as if endangered when they are dropped, startled, or handled roughly. Children have a similar reaction when they become sick or when their family routines are disrupted or their parents fight, and so on.

Nevertheless some symptoms of the need for safety do appear in adults: safety programs on the job; the desire for tenure; or the security of a savings account, insurance, or pension programs. Inflation can threaten many of these so the need for safety may be seen a bit more clearly even among adults in times of economic instability.

Needs for Love, Affection, and Belongingness. When the needs for safety and for physiological well-being are satisfied, the next class of needs in the hierarchy can emerge. These are the needs for love, affection, and belongingness. Little scientific evidence supports the need for belongingness, Maslow says, although

there is some evidence that moving to a new home often affects children adversely and that being a transient or a loner is not good for mental health.

Maslow does cite the increase in growth centers, communal living, T-groups, encounter groups, and so on, as evidence that people are seeking more and more to overcome feelings of loneliness and alienation. He notes that the need for love is not the same as sex, since the latter can be studied solely as a physiological need. Nevertheless, he says sexual behavior is ordinarily determined by many needs, primarily those for love and affection. These factors involve both giving and receiving.

Needs for Esteem. The needs for esteem can become dominant when physiological needs, safety needs, and the needs for love, affection, and belongingness are satisfied. These needs involve both self-esteem and the esteem a person gets from others. Everyone in our society, Maslow contends (1970a, p. 45), has a need for a stable, firmly based, high level of self-respect, and respect from others. There are two components: the need for competence and confidence; and the need for prestige, fame, recognition, and so on. When these needs are satisfied, the person feels self-confident and valuable as a person in the world. When these needs are frustrated, the person feels inferior, weak, helpless, and worthless.

Needs for Self-actualization. When all the foregoing needs are satisfied, then and only then (in most cases) are the needs for self-actualization activated. What is self-actualization? Maslow describes it as a person's need to be and do that which that person was born for. "A muscian must make music, an artist must paint, a poet must write" (Maslow, 1970a p. 46).

Like all needs, the need for self-actualization makes itself felt in signs of restlessness.

The person feels on edge, tense, lacking something, in short, restless. With hunger we can see very easily what we are restless about—the lack of food. Likewise if we are very lonely we know what we need—the company of friends. But it is not always clear what we want when the need is for self-actualization. And so very often in such a state of restlessness people say they don't know what it is that is bothering them. They simply feel restless, want a change, want to go away, want to go off and *do* something, though what that might be exactly they are unable to say.

We can observe these feelings in many modern housewives, who have devoted themselves to home and family for twenty or more years. When the last teenager is in high school, the mother at last has time to breathe and take stock. Then she becomes restless. Neither husband nor children can understand. Her husband might say: "You have a nice home, plenty of food and clothing. You are well protected, and I have good insurance that will keep you going if I should die. You are loved by all of us here and you have your friends, too. We all think very highly of you and you are a respected member of your social group. What can possibly be wrong with your life?" Given such a list of blessings can anyone reasonably still feel restless? Maslow says yes. For the statements above represent satisfaction of physiological needs, safety needs, love needs, and esteem needs; only when these needs are satisfied can the needs for self-actualization emerge and produce the restlessness the housewife feels.

A Model of the Hierarchy

As Maslow says, there is intuitive appeal to the hierarchic theory of needs. We all know the intensity and compelling quality of some need at some time—how it obliterates our awareness of all else and becomes prepotent or dominant. There is no time for writing poetry or painting a picture when the house is on fire.

The hierarchic theory is often represented as a pyramid, with the larger, lower levels representing the lower needs, and the peak layer representing the need for self-actualization. This representation of the theory seems inadequate to me because it does not show that a lower need must be satisfied before a higher need can become active. The higher need can be felt and attended to as a need to be filled *only* after the next lower need has been already filled and satisfied. This connection between prior satisfaction of the lower need and activation of the next higher one seems to me to be essential in Maslow's theory. The pyramid simply represents the fact that classes of needs are arranged in a pattern of higher and lower; it fails to represent the triggering action effected by a lower need's satisfaction upon the activation of a higher need. I have shown a more satisfactory model in figure 1.1: an electromechanical model which attempts to capture the stepwise activation principle.

Needs and the Formation of Syndromes

Maslow points to both empirical research and clinical experience in saying that gratification of a need allows the organism to move on unpreoccupied with that need. By contrast, if a need is frustrated it tends to persist and become increasingly active (Maslow, 1970a, p. 64): "The best way to teach a child to go seeking in all directions for affection and to have a constant craving for it is partially to *deny* him love" (Maslow, 1970a, p. 65). Clinical observation, Maslow says, shows that when safety needs have been frustrated, the person becomes apprehensive and nervous, living like a spy behind enemy lines. By contrast, the person in whom safety needs have been gratified is assured, confident, secure. The same holds

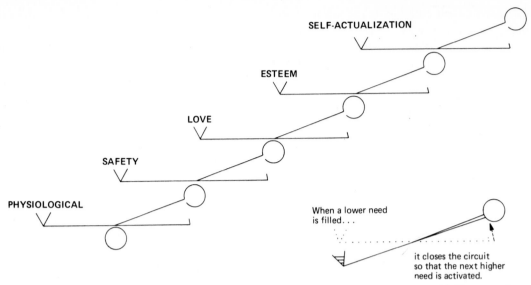

Figure 1.1. Electromechanical model of Maslow's need hierarchy. The model illustrates how each need is activated by satisfaction (filling) of the immediately lower need.

true for the needs for love and belongingness or for esteem; when these needs are gratified the person can develop affection and self-respect.

The frustration or gratification of needs thus leads to definite kinds of character formation, or the development of what Maslow calls a *syndrome*. A syndrome—such as insecurity, self-esteem, or self-actualization—"is a general flavor which can be detected or savored in practically everything that the person does, feels, or thinks" (Maslow, 1942b, p. 331). It is also a grouping of characteristics "that are usually found to occur together and that are therefore given a unifying name" (Maslow, 1970a, p. 302). As a more formal definition, Maslow offers the following tentative statement that a personality syndrome is "a structured, organized complex of apparently diverse specificities (behaviors, thoughts, impulses to action, perceptions, etc.) which, however, when studied carefully and validly are found to have a common unity that may be phrased variously as a similar dynamic

meaning, expression, 'flavor,' function, or purpose" (Maslow, 1970a, p. 303). Box 1.1 presents a particular illustration of the personality syndrome of insecurity.

From his studies of several different kinds of syndromes in many people, Maslow concludes that a well-developed syndrome tends to maintain itself. It is hard to change it, even despite major changes in the environment. Maslow cites the example of a man who had lost all his wealth and had been exposed to many horrors of persecution. He emigrated to the United States and was found to have retained his dignity, self-respect, and positive view of human nature despite experiences which could have turned others bitter (Maslow, 1970a, p. 309). But if a syndrome changes at all it tends to change as a whole: changes are seen in all parts of the syndrome. A patient of Maslow's was instructed to behave aggressively in a number of specific, trivial situations. Three months later her dreams had changed, she had bought clothes that made her more attractive, her sexual behavior had

From an initial study of sixty persons judged to be very insecure or very secure, Maslow (1942b) selected thirty-six for intensive clinical study, addressing both unconscious and conscious aspects of the personality. His final formulation of the insecure person presents essential, common characteristics (in Maslow's terms, **static** characteristics) and also some different ways in which insecure people react to these characteristics (the **dynamics** of insecurity). The static and dynamic patterns together make up a **syndrome** of insecure personality.

Static Characteristics

The insecure person feels rejected, unloved, treated without affection, even hated or despised. Feeling alone and out of ordinary social life, the person sees the world as dangerous and threatening and sees other human beings as basically evil, selfish, and hostile. Understandably, the person feels constantly endangered and experiences continuous anxiety. Expecting the worst, pessimistic, the insecure person is also suspicious of others, mistrusts them, is envious, jealous, prejudiced, and hateful toward others. Unhappy, discontented, conflictive, irritable, this person craves for power over others and for status and strives continually for means to ensure his or her own safety and security.

Dynamic Characteristics

To each of the static characteristics "there is always a reaction, a drive, a motivation which sets processes going . . . reactions to the reactions, and reactions to the reactions to the reactions, and so on" (1942b, p. 336). When a person feels unloved, for example, almost invariably the reactions include attempts to regain love, feelings of anger, and a lowered self-esteem. Real love and affection are the only things that can truly satisfy the need for love; the person may instead settle for various substitutes such as belonging to clubs or ensuring safety. Safety may be sought either through finding someone strong upon whom the person can become dependent, or through the accumulation of power and/or money.

The insecure person who fails in the attempts to find security is likely to experience very deep discouragement and then to engage in various defense reactions. For instance, the person might avoid all situations in which such attempts can be made and in which failures might ensue. Rationalization may be employed ("Too many friends can be a burden"). If he or she is still struggling, has not yet given up, then the conscious feelings of rejection may be less apparent than the unconscious ones. Such a person may not notice or may overlook slights and snubs; but then these rejections will show up in a dream the following night or in other obscure ways. Although the person adopts an optimistic air, the clinician can sense its shakiness. When an insecure person has given up, then the pessimism is clear for all to see. Ten compliments may be forgotten, but the one snub will be remembered and dwelt upon.

become more spontaneous to the point that her husband noticed the change, and she was doing other things she had never done before, such as going swimming with a group of people. She also *felt* more confident; in general, there was a rise in her overall level of self-esteem (Maslow, 1970a, p. 311). Maslow points out in a footnote that his work with this particular patient would today be called

behavior therapy, although it had actually taken place more than forty years ago, in 1935. The suggestion is clear that if behavior therapy succeeds in effecting helpful personality change, it may well do so as a result of changes in an entire syndrome brought about by some specific, even trivial, change in behavior. For as Maslow says, a personality syndrome is very hard to change, but if even one part is successfully changed then changes will follow in all other parts.

We turn now to the syndrome of self-actualization, the pattern of static and dynamic characteristics found in persons who have received gratification in all of their lower needs and in whom the need for self-actualization is now active.

The Self-actualization Syndrome

What precisely is the need for self-actualization? It is the need to become more fully and more truly what we have the potential to be. In the analogy of boxing which Maslow offers, it is as though we are all like Joe Doakes, who tested out pretty well when he boxed to show a prospective trainer his capabilities. The trainer took him on and devoted his attention to making Joe the very best boxer in the Joe-Doakes style he could be. It would be useless to try and make him into a boxer like Louis or Dempsey; he might only weigh one hundred twenty pounds, for instance. He might be a left-hander. He might have a thunderous uppercut, yet a poor right cross, but superb jabbing potential because of his arm length and shoulder speed. The best training would actualize these potentials and take him to the heights of his *own* capabilities.

Three Core Characteristics

A few people are self-actualizing, but many or most are not. For those who are not we must presume they are struggling to satisfy needs for esteem and perhaps for love and affection.

Maslow undertook a prolonged research study of exceptional people, both living and dead (the latter through biographies). Included were Samuel Johnson, Abraham Lincoln, Thomas Jefferson, Eleanor Roosevelt, Jane Addams, George Washington Carver, and others. As the study progressed, he was able to formulate some of the essential characteristics of these people, whom he called self-actualizing. Figure 1.2 presents sixteen main characteristics he found, with some indication of the relationships among them. The three core characteristics of self-actualizing people, as may be seen in the figure, are acceptance of self and others, spontaneity, and efficiency of perception.

Self-actualizing people accept their own natures as they are, without guilt or shame for their own human and animal qualities and processes. They have no unrealistic guilt or disgusts. They tend to be hearty eaters and hearty sex partners; they sleep well. Likewise they accept the failings and weaknesses of others. They accept human nature as simply that: part of nature. One does not have contempt for a thunderstorm or think it ought to be ashamed of itself even if it produces damaging floods. Self-actualizing people treat human nature the same way they would treat a thunderstorm or any other part of nature.

Their acceptance of nature enables them to see other people more clearly, and, indeed, to have a more *efficient perception* of many other areas of life. They seem to see the essence of a confused political situation more quickly and more accurately than other people. Hence their predictions of the future turn of events are correct more often than are those of most persons. Most of us have perceptions of the world which are severely colored by our wishes and fears, or by the characteristic pessimism or optimism we bring to things. We see darkly through our own personality encumbrances. Self-actualizing people are far less encumbered in their perceptions.

As a result, Maslow says, self-actualizing persons are more likely to see what is actually there to be seen and less apt to "see" what they wish or fear might be there. This surely is an important contribution to their being more accepting of others: they actu-

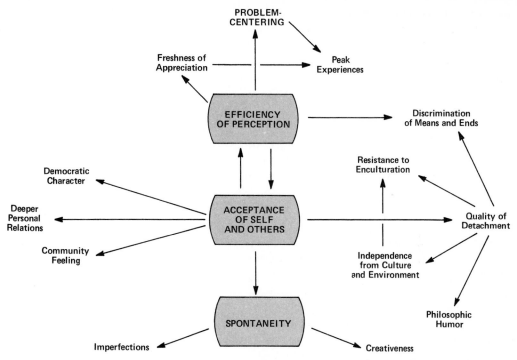

Figure 1.2. Characteristics of Maslow's self-actualizing person

ally see more of what is there. For this reason, efficiency of perception influences acceptance, as shown by an arrow in the figure. Acceptance influences and is influenced by perception. The influence seems to be facilitative and mutual, so that the two help each other to grow.

Maslow tells us that self-actualizing people are more *spontaneous* than most, especially in their inner thoughts but also in their behavior. The reason for greater conventionality in behavior than in thoughts is apparently that these people have no wish to hurt others who *are* bound by conventions. The self-actualizing person will be as conventional as seems necessary in a given social situation, but will not hesitate to do whatever he or she considers important even if it is not conventional. We may take an example from the life of Dr. Samuel Johnson. At a formal dinner party he

bit into a very hot potato. Immediately he spat it out, all over the tablecloth. Just as quickly he glared around the table and announced that a fool would have swallowed it.

Spontaneity. Arrows in figure 1.2 show spontaneity, one group of core characteristics, leading to imperfections and creativeness. The *imperfections* of self-actualizing people abound. They are not angels. Their very spontaneity often lets them be wasteful, thoughtless, even vain. They often have temper outbursts. Sometimes, due to their ability to concentrate on some topic of interest, they become absent-minded and inattentive to ordinary social niceties. Although their guilts and anxieties are not neurotic, they still have them, as well as conflicts and self-blame. Mostly such rumblings occur in connection with missed opportunities to achieve a good end; but they are rumblings nonetheless. It may seem paradoxical to find that self-actualizers have imperfections, but the paradox is only apparent, not real. Most of us expect too much of human nature because we do not accept it. These self-actualizers—these seers, saints, sages, and creators, as Maslow calls them—can also be "boring, irritating, petulant, selfish, angry, or depressed." Like everybody else, they are not all of one piece. Their pieces merely seem to work better.

Spontaneity leads to *creativeness* as well. Maslow says this is a universal characteristic of self-actualizing people, with no exceptions. In some the creativeness is in the usual forms of art, music, and so on. But in others it appears in a creative way of living and relating; or in creative work other than in the arts. For example, it might be creative shoemaking or leatherwork. Their creativeness has a special "catching" effect, so that anything they touch is handled creatively.

Acceptance of self and others. This core characteristic leads to two main personality groups: the quality of detachment on the one hand and, on the other, deeper personal relations, a feeling of community with others, and a democratic character.

All of the subjects are of a deeply *democratic character,* Maslow generalizes. Their friendships extend toward all people of like nature, regardless of social class, political persuasion, color, race, and so on. They seem to give "a certain quantum of respect to *any* human being just because he is a human individual." Not at all prejudiced, they will not try to humiliate another person. They can and do learn from anyone. They try to maintain the dignity of others as well as of themselves. They will respond with full anger against evil behavior, but they do not carry that emotion beyond what is minimally necessary.

Maslow believes that self-actualizing people have *deeper personal relationships* with others, deeper than those of other adults, although perhaps not deeper than children have. These relationships, however, tend to be selective. They do not have greater love and greater identification with others indiscriminately; the people they love deeply tend to be other self-actualizing people. This makes sense, since we know that a profound relationship calls for complementarity of involvement. Someone who has deep feelings cannot really have deep relationships with shallow people, for the very good reason that shallow people cannot have deep relationships with anybody.

The notion of community in this sense was introduced by Alfred Adler (1927) to refer to a sense of general kindliness toward the human race. Self-actualizing people have this *community feeling,* Maslow reports. They tend to have a deep feeling of sympathy, even affection, for most human beings. They are likely to think of the whole human race as one family. Often they seek to improve the lot of humankind in general. Nevertheless they can become angered at the weakness of human beings whom they judge could be stronger. They are likely to take the attitude of an older brother or sister toward other people in the world.

The self-actualizing person accepts self and accepts others as parts of nature. That gives this person an ability to stand back, to be uninvolved, to be above the roar of prejudice and confusion—maintaining a *quality of detachment.* These are the people who keep their heads when all about them are losing theirs. It is not merely an ability, however. They also seem to *need* detachment, according to Maslow. They like to be alone and to be off in a private place far more than do most people.

Self-actualizing people extend their detachment into decision-making. They do not look to others to make decisions for them; they arrive at conclusions independently. They tend to be self-disciplined, personally responsible, in control of their own lives, self-starters, and self-stoppers. They are, in Maslow's words, possessed of more "free will" than average people.

Detachment leads to a number of other characteristics: independence from culture, resistance to enculturation, discrimination of means and ends, and philosophic humor, as shown in figure 1.2. Self-actualizing people tend to be *independent of their culture and environment*. They do not depend on either for their main satisfactions; rather they are internally motivated. They are growth-motivated, Maslow says, and not deficiency-motivated. Their activities are driven not by lacks that must be filled, but by strivings for growth which they decide to fulfill. This makes them relatively impervious to the hard knocks and frustrations that life deals. They maintain serenity in the midst of adversity.

Their inner detachment, as I have said, is something they cherish, and it reinforces their *resistance to enculturation*. They resist being completely made over into a creature of a given culture. They are above particular cultures. This does not mean they are rebels. On the contrary, they tend to live lives well within the bounds set by their own particular culture. Nevertheless they are "ruled by the laws of their own character rather than by the rules of society."

Self-actualizing people *discriminate clearly between means and ends,* and they give more attention to ends than means. They are strongly ethical in the sense that they do what they believe to be right and they avoid doing what they know to be wrong. Their notions of what is right and what is wrong, of course, do not always coincide with beliefs of society at large. Their detachment, inde-

pendence, and resistance have led them to formulate their own value system on a firm basis. In part, this development of clear values and clear discrimination between means and ends results from the greater efficiency of perception that self-actualizing people have, as suggested by the arrow connecting these two characteristics in figure 1.2. They see things more clearly; they see more of reality than others; they have more information on which to base their value judgments.

Self-actualizing people also display what Maslow calls a *philosophic type of humor.* While many jokes are based upon sex or hostility, theirs never are. They do not laugh at the usual jokes, and so might be considered sober or serious people by their contemporaries. Their jokes tend rather to be humorous commentary upon human nature. For instance, when Abraham Lincoln became president many people came to him seeking office, and most of them left disappointed. About this time, he caught a mild form of smallpox. He remarked to a visitor that there was one good thing about his sickness: now he had something he could give to everybody.

Efficiency of Perception. We come now to the last of the three groups of characteristics, those stemming from the core characteristic of efficiency of perception. Maslow says that self-actualizing people have a continuous *freshness of appreciation.* They do not tire of the basic good things in life. Again and again they enjoy the beauties of the world around them and feel gratitude. They have a sense of awe, of wonder. Some are thrilled mainly by the scenes of nature, others by the wonders of children's play, or by great music. They do not get the same thrill out of the manufactured entertainment of nightclubbing or cocktail parties that scores of people do. Their appreciation of the natural good things in life tends to be healthful. They derive refreshment and strengthening from these experiences. Not only do they see more clearly, they also appreciate more fully and they prosper more completely from the beauty and wonder of the world around them.

Self-actualizing people are *problem-centered.* That is, they tend to focus on some mission in life, some task that needs to be accomplished and that absorbs much of their energy. They tend not to be introspective, although they have a rich inner life. But they do not brood over themselves as so many average people do. Rather they brood over questions of eternal importance when they do brood. They think about basic issues in as broad a framework as may be conceived. Even smaller issues are placed in a broader framework if suitable.

The principal of a school I attended manifested this quality. Seniors asked him whether he thought they should join the army right away (during World War II) or spend a year at college first. He replied after a brief moment: "It depends on what happens at Stalingrad." The seniors waited until that distant battle's conclusion became clearer. Had the Germans won, it would have required everyone to join the Allied forces immediately in order to even hope for a future in which college would have any significance. Thus he brought the current international scene into the career decisions of a few young persons in high school.

Self-actualizing persons also tend to have *peak experiences,* intense forms of subjective experiences. A peak experience occurs in a moment of intense feeling, coupled with an especially clear awareness of some profound truth. Maslow called it a "mystical" experience. It is partly emotional, partly intellectual. The emotional part appears as an experience of ecstasy, of being transported out of the ordinary realms of feeling and emotion into a sublime and higher experience. The intellectual part is one of being enlightened, of seeing things even more clearly, of darkness dropping away.

Self-actualizing people tend to lose themselves in such peak experiences. Not all do. But Maslow says that most of them do, and there are important differences between those who are "peakers" and those who are not. Peakers tend to live in a world of symbols, poetry, essences, and esthetic qualities, as well as in the everyday world of practicalities. Nonpeakers stay within the practical world. Peakers are more likely to become philosophers or poets or composers. Nonpeakers are more likely to become reformers, politicians, crusaders. On the contemporary scene we might expect that Ralph Nader is a nonpeaker; Maharishi Mahesh Yogi is probably a peaker.

It is obvious that Maslow himself was a peaker, as his own remarks reveal. In his investigations of peak experiences he would ask people if they had had moments of special joy, moments of transcendence, moments of sensing the immensity of the universe, the meaning of eternity. He found that women frequently have such experiences during childbirth, essentially a religious or deeply spiritual experience. He also found that many people cannot easily recall ever having had a peak experience. These would be weak peakers who only after considerable prompting are able to recognize some previous experience as an approximation of a peak experience.

It seems possible that many people actually do have peak experiences which are not exactly like those of the self-actualizers, but which are nevertheless qualitatively similar. For example, many people lose themselves in the course of watching a good movie; others get caught up in the intense excitement of sports events. Such intense moments may not have the important aspect of changing the person's insight into essential truth, but they may well be accompanied by a deep realization of the supreme accomplishments that some can reach. From my own experience, such a realization came once in 1976, when one of the Cincinnati Reds leaped several feet into the air to catch a ball that was really impossible to catch—but he caught it!

It seems quite likely also that those engaged in a sporting event or certain other activities may have an intense subjective experience which comes close to being a peak experience. Skiers report that they are exhilarated in mind and body as they sweep at high speed down the slopes, slicing through crisp mountain air, small clouds of snow swirling like surf around them. Perhaps there are moments of exquisite joy for all who achieve advanced skills, whether in skating or dancing, painting or carpentry, music or mechanics.

Certain moments in national life have the capacity to arouse a peak experience in every citizen. Such moments may be joyful, as in national triumph, a declaration of peace, or news of a heroic rescue of hijack victims. They may be moments of unbelievable despair, or tragedy, as was the day President Kennedy was shot; all the citizens were plunged into grief. At such times the individual participates in a historic moment. No longer is it all just in the history books. Now a page of history unfolds before the person's very eyes and ears, and everyone suddenly knows that time and history are real and that human life is finite. At such times great leaders speak to the people with feeling so intense and new awareness so profound that all who hear them have right there and then a peak experience. So it was when Abraham Lincoln addressed the people at Gettysburg, or when Winston Churchill vowed to his people that they would have nothing but blood, toil, tears, and sweat —and victory.

Maslow reported (1970b, pp. 84-90) that he had tried many ways to bring to the awareness of nonpeakers some experience which could be considered the beginning of a peak experience. He felt that peak experiences were tremendously important because they add freshness and vitality to life. He felt that peak experiences were probably very helpful in furthering any person's growth toward self-actualization. He provided a list of questions which might trigger a subject's memory of a peak experience they had not noticed before, and so help him or her understand its meaning and know what to look for in the future. Box 1.2 provides a comparable list of trigger questions.

Metamotivation

In Maslow's view, self-actualizing people are not motivated in the usual sense. How could they be? All their basic needs are satisfied, including self-actualization, which they are continually in the process of satisfying. So what does make them tick? Maslow's theory— the latest and last of his theories—is that self-actualizing people are what he calls *metamotivated* (1971, pp. 299-340). Metamotives are beyond ordinary motives. They are actually eternal values: truth, beauty, justice. It is the pursuit of these values that propels self-actualizing people, Maslow says. Though they may be immersed in their professions or other missions, it is the underlying value which really constitutes the object of their efforts. The self-actualizing lawyer, for instance, is really concentrating upon the pursuit of justice.

Maslow calls these metamotives *B-values*, values of Being, the ultimate goals of advanced varieties of human beings. He suggests a somewhat larger list of these values than might ordinarily be expected, each value or goal being made possible by one or more of the characteristics he observed in self-actualizing people. Thus all the characteristics of efficiency of perception would be utilized in the appreciation of the values of *truth* and *beauty*. And spontaneity would foster the values of *effortlessness, playfulness,* and *aliveness.* With deeper personal relations and acceptance of others would come appreciation for the values of *goodness* and *justice.* From the quality of detachment would come a valuing of *self-sufficiency,* and of *uniqueness.* Other B-values, such as *meaningfulness* and *unity or wholeness* are not obviously linked in a direct way with just one group of personal characteristics. In the self-actualizing person, they would emerge from blends or perhaps from newly created qualities.

Accomplishments of Maslow's Theory

Maslow's theory epitomizes what he himself called a "third force" in psychology (Buhler & Allen, 1972, p. v). In 1962 he provided leadership in the formation of a new organization to represent this third force, the Association of Humanistic Psychology. National and regional meetings of the association attest to its growing strength. In 1975 over five thousand members attended the national annual meeting in Estes Park, Colorado. Maslow's thrust toward a psychology of growth and personal development continues to be strongly represented in the programs of the association and in the *Journal of Humanistic Psychology.*

Outside of the immediate circle of humanistic psychologists Maslow's theory has provided new insights for a number of disciplines such as personnel psychology, industrial psychology, and group dynamics. Lyman Porter has been particularly responsible for the application of Maslow's theory of needs to the study of job satisfaction in industry. He began by constructing a questionnaire (Porter, 1961) to assess deficiencies people felt in the satisfaction of needs they experienced in their jobs. Characteristics of job positions referred specifically to one another of Maslow's need classes. The physiological level was omitted because it would not be expected to show much variation in satisfaction among normal citizens. The esteem needs were divided into kinds, those concerned with recognition and those concerned with autonomy, which reflects the "competence" component envisaged in these needs by Maslow. Each respondent was asked to indicate how much each item does characterize the present job and how much it *should* characterize that job. These ratings were both made on a 7-point scale, with 1 equaling *minimally characteristic* and 7 equaling *maximally characteristic*. A deficiency score was calculated for all subjects for each item by taking each one's rating for *should* characterize and subtracting from it the rating for *does* characterize the job. The larger the discrepancy, the more deficiency the person must feel in regard to that need. Typical items for each need referred to a feeling of security (safety need), opportunity to make friends (social or belonging needs), prestige inside the company (needs for esteem), opportunity to participate in goal-setting (the autonomy part of esteem needs), and feeling of valuable accomplishment (needs for self-actualization). Studying two samples, one of lower-management and one of middle-management personnel, Porter found that the lower-management personnel experienced significantly more deficiencies in need fulfillment than did the middle-management people. This was true primarily in the needs for esteem and autonomy in which category roughly 60 percent of the lower-management personnel experienced deficiencies.

Further work by Porter and his associates led to the position by 1968 in which Maslow's theory of need satisfaction constituted one of the only two viable theories of management motivation (Cummings & ElSalmi, 1968). This continues to be true, and developments continue to be published. For example, Slocum (1971) confirmed Porter's results and also found that first-line supervisors experience more deficiencies than middle- and top-management personnel do in the self-actualization group of needs as well as in the esteem and autonomy groups. A special purpose of Slocum's study was to test the hypothesis that need-satisfaction is correlated with performance. Using ratings of performance by supervisors and by peers, he found that performance was indeed significantly correlated with need-satisfactions for most of the items in the Porter scale for both groups, supervisors and managers. The strongest correlations (.33-.42) were found among the autonomy and self-actualization needs for the management personnel.

The research by Porter and others shows clearly that there are important rewards in work besides money, and that worker satisfaction and productivity are related to these other rewards, identified in Maslow's theory of need hierarchy. The research shows that if management is more sensitive to the hierarchy of needs, then the workers will be happier and more productive. Such a theory, with such obviously practical results, could perhaps only have come from a theorist who was himself a plant manager for many years. Thus the theory of needs has provided for breakthroughs in the important applied field of work motivation.

Maslow's theory of self-actualization has special application to the field of education, as Maslow himself made clear. We saw earlier the great emphasis placed by humanistic psychologists upon the *potentials* of men and women. We saw that they mean the potentials that are inherent in being human, the potentials that are laid down as potentials in the very beginning of life. But the word "potential" has two meanings. One meaning refers to what exists ready to be actualized, like the potential energy in physics or the genius that lay in Mozart even before he was born. Another meaning refers to possibilities. It is possible that someday we shall derive all of our energy needs from the sun. It is possible that we will build a bridge from San Francisco to Hawaii. It is possible that someone will run a mile in two minutes. Possibilities are things that might be done, could conceivably be done. They are not impossible. But neither are they already present in potential form.

Maslow purposely set out to find the good things in human beings, both potential and possible. Moreover he is very explicit about his mission. Science is not and should not be without values, he says. Social psychology in particular should be *normative*, he believes. It should tell people how to live better. Personality theory should show people how to become better and how to help others become better. In Maslow's view, the characteristics of the self-actualizing person describe not merely a portion of the human race. They describe what *all* people can aspire to become.

Everyone can be on the road to self-actualization. (Maslow does say, however [1970a, p. xx], that you cannot expect young people to be self-actualizing. Self-actualization takes experience, patience, development, and, above all, time. But the young can begin the long process, and will be different young persons from those who have not begun.) Maslow believes that the only reason that people would not move well in the direction of self-actualization is because of hindrances placed in their way by society. The institutions of education serve an especially important function here. And so he recommends ways education can switch from its usual person-stunting tactics into person-growing approaches. Maslow says that most educators respond to society's needs for certain numbers of engineers or accountants. They *should* respond to what potential an individual child or youth has for growing into a self-actualizing person of his own kind. Maslow recommends ten points (1971, pp. 180-195) in his prescription for a nation of self-actualizing persons:

We should teach people to be *authentic:* to be aware of their inner selves and to hear their inner-feeling voices.

We should teach people to *transcend their own cultural conditioning,* and become world citizens. This will require an awakening of the sense of brotherhood in young children so that they will hate war when they are adults and do everything possible to avoid it.

We should help children and youth *discover their vocation in life,* their calling, fate, or destiny, if you like. This is especially focused upon finding the right career and the right mate.

We should teach people that *life is precious,* that there is joy to be experienced in life, and if people are open to seeing the good and joyous in all kinds of situations it makes life worth living.

We must *accept the child* and help him or her learn their inner nature. From real knowledge of aptitudes and limitations we can know what to build upon, what potentialities are really there.

We must see that the child's *basic needs are satisfied.* That includes safety, belongingness, and esteem needs.

We should *refreshen consciousness,* teaching the child to appreciate beauty and the other good things in nature and in living.

We should teach people that *controls are good,* and complete abandon is bad. We all know that a well-cooked meal at a well-prepared table is superior and more enjoyable than a slovenly served piece of hash. It takes control to improve the quality of life in all areas.

We should teach our children and young people to transcend the trifling problems and *grapple with the serious problems in life.* These include the problems of injustice, of pain, suffering, and death.

We must teach them to be *good choosers.* They must be given practice in making choices, first between one goody and another; later between one god and another.

Maslow writes further about how we can grow toward greater self-actualization (1971, pp. 45-50): We need often to close our eyes and find out if we really like something, not just take for granted what it says on the label or what our friends tell us. We should try to express our real views about matters of importance rather than trotting out some cliché we have heard. We should throw ourselves into some enterprise, work for some cause we consider valuable, and involve ourselves completely in it, to the point of being forgetful of ourselves and absorbed in the work. We should take responsibility for our real thoughts and avoid pretense. We should take a good look at ourselves, who we are, what we like, what our mission in life is. We should come to know fully some of the unpleasant facts about ourselves as well as the good ones, facts about our fears and our cruelties to others as well as our strengths and our contributions. We should look for joy and welcome peak experiences. We should renew within us a sense of the mystery of life, its grandeur, its sacredness, its constant worthiness to call forth our gratitude.

With such recommendations the practical implications of Maslow's theory can reach into the lives of each one of us and suggest the paths we might take toward greater actualization of our potentials.

Critique of Maslow's Theory

Maslow's theory is not all of humanistic psychology, but it certainly makes up a large and central portion of the ideas of humanistic psychology. Thus D. O. Hebb's recent critique of humanistic psychology (1974, p. 74) is a critique of Maslow's theory. Hebb notes that scientific psychology "leaves much to be desired in the understanding of man and has little to tell us about how to live wisely and well." But Hebb says that the situation cannot be remedied by trying to turn a science into one of the humanities. He says: "Humanistic psychology . . . confuses two very different ways of knowing human beings and knowing how to live with self-respect. One is science; the other is literature." He describes literature as a "valid and deeply penetrating source of light on man, going directly to the heart of the matter." But literary giants like Conrad or Austen are "telling us things that are not on science's program," for science "imposes limits on itself and makes its progress by attacking only those problems that it is fitted to attack by existing knowledge and methods." Hebb concludes, "Trying to make over science to be simultaneously scientific and humanistic (in the true sense of the word) falls between two stools. Science is the servant of humanism, not part of it."

Of course Maslow knew very well that he would receive such criticism. But he believed that intuition was an appropriate method of discovery. Henry Geiger wrote about this matter and Maslow as follows: "all through his work one finds exposed nodes open to intuitive verification . . . 'insights,' we call them— that make people keep on reading Maslow. . . . There are two ways to arrive at a difficult but valuable conclusion. You can climb up a ladder of related syllogisms, tightening the rungs as you go by the use of precise language. The other is simply to *be* up there . . . freely able to look in all directions. . . ." (Geiger, 1971). He goes on to suggest that Maslow often seems to have "been" there for a long time. "Well," he asks, "has a *scientist* any business getting to where he gets by such private or inexplicable means? Maybe; maybe not. But if the subject of his inquiry—man— moves forward in that way when he is at his best, how could you practice human science without yourself performing or at least attempting such exploits?" In Geiger's view also, then, Maslow's kind of humanistic science is not only possible but necessary.

Beyond that, it would be quite wrong to assume that Maslow's work was somehow basically different from what a majority of psychologists do in their research. Although he relied primarily upon clinical impressions in his study of self-actualizing people, this was a chosen strategy. He was in fact very able in the conduct of controlled experiments and in the pursuit of sound statistical analysis of important psychological constructs such as the syndromes of insecurity (Maslow et al., 1945) or self-esteem (Maslow, 1942a). In fact one should conclude that he was a psychological scientist of the kind that Hebb would approve—up to a point. But Maslow went beyond; he added to the usual run of psychological research techniques a rare intuition, a rare willingness to reach beyond the data given, a new purpose to seek for the best in mankind's potentials. That is not in competition with science. That is not being less than a scientist, it is being a scientist *par excellence*. For who will discover something new without looking beyond the obvious?

Maslow's work has stimulated the empirical research of a great many other psychologists. Even so complex a notion as self-actualization has been subjected to psychometric measurement by Shostrom (1966). His test is a questionnaire which calls for the respondent to choose between 150 pairs of alternative statements. It covers ten of the main characteristics of self-actualized people, including self-acceptance, spontaneity, and inner-directedness. Very extensive studies made with this test have recently been summarized and critiqued by Tosi and Lindamood (1975).

How does Maslow's theory stand up to objective tests of its accuracy? It has made possible a number of accurate predictions in the fields of personnel and industrial psychology, as we have seen. Also in group dynamics,

Messe and colleagues (1972) predicted that groups composed of people who are safety-oriented would tend to choose males as their leaders, while groups composed of people who are esteem-oriented would tend to choose leaders on the basis of competence, regardless of sex. In these and other fields the theory of needs developed by Maslow has proven accurate. There have also been a few direct tests of the accuracy of the theory. For example, Gourevitch and Feffer (1962) did a study suggested by Maslow with respect to differences between age groups in our society, predicting that older age groups would have increasingly stronger needs in the higher categories of the hierarchy. They studied children, adolescents, and adults; the results supported the predictions. Again, Maslow's own work on the syndromes of self-esteem (1940, 1942a) and insecurity (1942b, 1945) showed the accuracy of those syndrome constructs.

So far as certain syndrome constructs and the hierarchic theory of needs are concerned, Maslow's hypotheses appear to be quite accurate. No research, however, bears directly on such issues as the instinctoid nature of needs in human beings, on whether a higher need cannot (strictly) be activated until lower needs are filled, on whether the satisfaction of all but one of lower needs would still keep the next higher level of needs from being activated, and so on. In short, a vast realm of scientific uncertainty still surrounds the need theory. This is true also of many other aspects of Maslow's theory. With so rich and practical a theory it is perhaps surprising that no one has yet mounted a comprehensive study of its many hypotheses. Nevertheless it has been fruitful, inspiring a good deal of applied research with respect to patterns of motivation, and setting in motion the humanistic movement in psychology.

Self-actualizing People

It is often true that we learn best by doing. If we recite what we have just read we are likely to retain it better; if we rehearse it again, or paraphrase it, we are likely to learn it more thoroughly. But if we actually take the ideas and work with them, building something new for ourselves and others, then the ideas tend to sink into our nervous system in some way so that they are never forgotten. Obviously the ideas have to be worth something to put that much effort into!

If you agree with me that Maslow's ideas about self-actualization are worth putting effort into, perhaps you will enjoy this workshop. The aim is to repeat Maslow's study of self-actualizing people for ourselves. However, for a workshop we must do our job in much less time. We can begin with the characteristics listed by Maslow, and make sure we know their meanings. Write your definitions for each characteristic:

1. Acceptance of self = _____

2. Acceptance of others = _____

3. Efficiency of perception = _____

4. Spontaneity = _____

5. Detachment = _____

6. Independence of culture = _____

7. Resistance to enculturation = _____

8. Discrimination of means and ends = _____

9. Philosophic humor = _____

10. Deeper personal relations = _____

11. Community feeling = _____

12. Democratic character = _____

13. Freshness of appreciation = _____

14. Problem centering = _____

15. Peak experiences = _____

16. Creativeness = _____

17. Imperfections = _____

18. _____ = _____

19. _____ = _____

20. _____ = _____

You may need more than twenty items—if not now, then after you have studied awhile.

The suggestion is that you pick one person you believe is truly self-actualizing. To make this judgment you must already know quite a lot about the person, either from personal acquaintance or from reading biographies, news stories, and so on. Take your list of items and think hard about each one in relation to the person you have selected. For example, number 1: Does this person show acceptance of self? In what way? Can you give an example? Number 2: Does this person accept others? In what way? Give an example.

Your Code Name for the Person

Is the item true of the person?	If so, in what way?	Give an example
1. Accepts self _____	_____	_____
2. Accepts others _____	_____	_____
3. Efficient perception _____	_____	_____
4. Spontaneity _____	_____	_____
5. Detachment _____	_____	_____
6. Independence _____	_____	_____
7. Resistance _____	_____	_____
8. Discrimination _____	_____	_____
9. Philosophic humor _____	_____	_____
10. Deep relations _____	_____	_____
11. Community feeling _____	_____	_____
12. Democratic _____	_____	_____
13. Fresh appreciation _____	_____	_____
14. Problem-centered _____	_____	_____
15. Peak experiences _____	_____	_____
16. Creativeness _____	_____	_____
17. Imperfections _____	_____	_____
18. _____ _____	_____	_____
19. _____ _____	_____	_____
20. _____ _____	_____	_____

If you found this part of the workshop interesting and if you have time, it would be quite revealing now to select someone you think is definitely **not** self-actualizing and go through the same procedure for this person. What are some outstanding contrasts?

Summary

Maslow's theory of personality stresses the importance of human needs and states that satisfaction or frustration of needs produces particular patterns of personality characteristics. These patterns, called *syndromes*, include insecurity, self-esteem, and self-actualization. Maslow tried to discover the best potentials in human nature and to urge that people strive to reach these potentials and to educate their children toward them. He discovered these potential characteristics by studying self-actualizing people who see things clearly, are spontaneous and independent, yet fully accept others and themselves.

Maslow says human needs are *instinctoid,* yet do not exist until activated. Needs exist in five main categories: physiological, safety, love, esteem, and self-actualization. The pattern of the needs is hierarchical; lower needs (physiological) must be satisfied before higher needs can be activated (safety before love, love before esteem, and so on).

First among the accomplishments of Maslow's theory must be the origin and continuing inspiration of the Association for Humanistic Psychology. His theory of needs has been extremely influential in applied fields such as personnel and industrial psychology (see the extensive bibliography prepared by Roberts for *Research in Education*, 1973).

Maslow's theory has been criticized along with all of humanistic psychology as attempting to make an impossible union between science and humanism. But Maslow believed that that is precisely what must be done, at least for the science of psychology. Some parts of the theory of needs appear to be quite accurate on the evidence; and at least three syndrome constructs have been validly measured: insecurity, self-esteem, and self-actualization. A great deal of research still needs to be done on this theory, however.

In anticipation of the material in the next chapter on defining personality, I include here as figure 1.3 a diagram which attempts to summarize the kind of definition of personality that is implicit in Maslow's theory. It

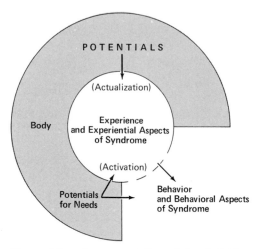

Figure 1.3. A representation of the definition of personality implicit in Maslow's theory

emphasizes the body's natural potentials both as talents to be actualized and as needs to be activated. The responses to talents and needs result in what he called *feelings* (e.g., of self-esteem or of insecurity) and in behaviors. Maslow distinguished very sharply between subjective experience of such things as feelings and outward behaviors. For example, he emphasized (1942a) that his test of self-esteem measured dominance-*feeling* and not dominance behavior. Dominance-feeling, he said, would be only one thing contributing to dominance behavior, which would also be affected by the person's status relative to others in the same situation, and by other factors. The diagram illustrating Maslow's implicit definition of personality makes an appropriate transition to our next topic, the question of what is personality, which is taken up in chapter 2.

INTRODUCTION

Personality contrasted with other specialties in
  psychology
Personality
  Everyday and scientific meanings
  Three groups of definitions of personality
    Personality as an organization of systems within
      the individual
    Personality as behavior
    Personality as inner experience and the sense
      of identity
Toward an integrative definition of personality
  Possible reasons for the different definitions
  Behaviorists' denial of existence of inner causal
    systems of personality
  Behaviors and experiences
  The record of behaviors and experiences
  Causal interaction of experience and behavior
  Structure and process in psychological and
    physical causation
  Importance of the body
  A definition of personality
Workshop 2A   Ordinary knowledge of experience
  and behavior
Workshop 2B   Some aspects of your own
  personality
Summary

2

What Is Personality?

In this book we examine several theories of personality which have contemporary significance for psychology and related scientific fields. We will try not only to understand each theory but also to examine similarities and differences between theories. Comparisons should sharpen our view of each theory we examine and should also lead us closer to an understanding of the common ground these theories share. When the theories differ we shall try to discern whether they differ in their interpretation of the same set of facts, and therefore are strictly competing theories, or whether their difference stems from their focusing upon different sets of facts—different parts of reality.

Human personality is precisely the kind of complex subject matter upon which theorists can easily disagree, both in interpretation of facts and selection of facts to interpret. Psychologists generally agree that personality science is concerned with the person as a whole. This subject matter may be contrasted with the more partial concerns of other specialties in psychology. Physiological psychology, for example, is interested in the structure and function of the nervous system and how they relate to particular kinds of behavior. Studies in perception focus on the mechanisms where-

by human beings acquire organized knowledge of their immediate environment: how they see shapes and colors; how they discriminate different tones of voice; or how they know when an object is large but distant and when it is small but near. The study of memory concerns itself with basic topics such as exactly how an item of information, once perceived, comes to be recalled at a later date, either as an image of the original scene or in the form of some verbal representation. Is it stored as an exact replica of the original perception like a photo in an album, or is it more like a line of symbols in a stenographer's record? Social psychologists are interested in the nature of groups and of social influences upon the individual. Clinical psychologists study abnormal behaviors, how they are created, and how they may be ameliorated. Specialists in child development focus on the course and causes of development in particular patterns of perception or behavior, such as motor behavior, conceptual skills, or moral judgment. But only personality psychologists are concerned with the whole person, the sum and product of all the physiology, perception, memory, social interaction, clinical history, and developmental trends.

In the present chapter we shall consider

in more detail the nature of personality and how scientists have defined this complex phenomenon. In the following three chapters we shall study three different theories, each representing a quite different approach to defining personality.

Personality

In everyday discourse we use the notion of personality in two ways, first as the salient, characteristic features of a person, and second as the impact a person's presence has upon us. In the first sense we might describe a person as the kindest man we know or as a woman of exceptionally sunny disposition. Or we might say that so-and-so is a Scrooge, thereby summing up his essential miserliness and miserable disinterest in the welfare of others. In the second sense, the notion of personality refers to a strong impression made upon us by someone. For example, movie stars like Barbra Streisand and Paul Newman or John Wayne and Katharine Hepburn have very distinctive personalities; they affect us strongly, each in a different way.

Scientists have taken both of these everyday usages and expanded them. A scientific concern for characteristics of individuals is addressed to establishing the fact of salience, or the relation of a salient trait to other features of the person. It might be asked, for instance, whether miserliness is part of a more general personality picture which features obstinacy and fear of untidiness as well as excessive frugality. Scientific interest might raise the question of how such miserliness came to be characteristic of the person: Was it modelled upon equally miserly parents or does it serve a deeper adjustive purpose in the person, such as guarding against a threatened mental illness in some way?

Again, a scientific concern with the impact of a person upon others might well turn attention away from the mere fact of that individual's impressiveness and ask questions about the impressionability of the audience. Indeed the impact of person A upon the others might be studied more readily as a function of their perceptions of person A. It would thus fall in the domain of social psychology, of person-perception, as this topic is technically named.

In daily life, moreover, we use words like *temperament* and *character*. Temperament refers to a person's typical moods and emotions, and these are assumed to be related to the physiological functioning of glands and the nervous system. Character, on the other hand, is assumed to be developed by social training and by individual willpower; it refers to the consistency with which a person follows certain rules of life, especially moral and disciplinary rules. Both of these terms have a long history in human thought and writing, but in recent times it has become customary to treat both emotional and moral features as part of the total *personality*.

Many psychologists have offered definitions of personality. Most of them seem to fall into three main groups: 1) those that define personality as an organization of systems within the individual that causally determine that person's behaviors and experience; 2) those that focus upon the behaviors only and seek for causes within the environment; and 3) those that focus upon the inner experience itself, emphasizing the subjective awareness and sense of personal identity.

Personality as an Organization of Systems Within the Individual

The most exhaustive consideration of definitions of personality was given by Gordon Allport. He studied some 50 different definitions that had been offered since Graeco-Roman times and, after careful evaluation of them, Allport proposed the following definition as the one that seemed most accurate in capturing the notion of personality: Personality is the dynamic organization within the individual of those psychophysical systems that determine his unique adjustments to his environment (Allport, 1937, p. 48). Nearly 25 years later Allport revised this definition slightly to clarify exactly what those psychophysical systems determine. They are, he wrote, "systems that determine [one's] characteristic behavior and thought" (Allport, 1961, p. 28).

According to Allport's definition, then, to understand someone's personality you have to find out about his or her most important underlying traits or motives, and how these are organized on the inside. Inner organization of psychophysical systems is the essence of personality. These systems determine behavior, thought, or unique adjustments to the environment, which means that they are causally related to the thought and action of the individual. Allport made very clear his position that personality is causal: "Personality *is* something and *does* something. It is not synonymous with behavior or activity. . . . It is what lies *behind* specific acts and *within* the individual" (Allport, 1937, p. 48).

Other authors who essentially follow Allport's approach include Maddi, Pervin, and Stagner. Maddi gives the following definition: "Personality is a stable set of characteristics and tendencies that determine those commonalities and differences in the psychological behavior (thoughts, feelings, and actions) of people that have continuity in time and that may not be easily understood as the sole result of the social and biological pressures of the moment" (Maddi, 1976, p. 9). Pervin has given a working definition: "*Personality represents those structural or dynamic properties of an individual or individuals as they reflect themselves in characteristic responses to situations*" (Pervin, 1970, p. 2). Noting that Allport did not spell out the nature of the psychophysical systems, Stagner has formulated the following definition of personality:

> Personality is the organization within the individual of those perceptual, cognitive, emotional, and motivational systems which determine his unique responses to his environment (Stagner, 1974, p. 13).

The definitions in this group, then, all stress the inner organization of determining or causal systems. These systems determine not only the behaviors but also the thoughts or inner experiences of the individual. The other groups of definitions are in sharp contrast. They focus precisely upon behaviors and thoughts, not upon underlying causal systems.

Personality as Behavior

The second group of definitions stresses the position that observable behaviors are the only available evidence upon which scientific theories of personality can be based. A moderate version of this position holds simply that all we can know about personality must be inferred. One such definition is given by Liebert and Spiegler (1974, p. 9): "*Personality is an abstraction and is not observed directly; instead, it is inferred from behavior which is observed.* 'Personality' is an example of a *theoretical construct*. Theoretical constructs do not actually exist, nor can they be seen or touched." Personality is a construct; constructs do not exist; therefore. . . .

Inference may be necessary, but Liebert and Spiegler assert that because inference is necessary, personality is an abstraction. What they mean by *abstraction* is made very clear on another page of their book (p. 7): "It is obvious that our direct knowledge of others is limited to what we can see of their behavior and that we can never directly know what is (inside) a person. We may say that Tom is happy in order to provide a summary label for his smiles, jovial conversation, or his invitation to take us all out for a beer, but we are speaking of his overt behavior and not necessarily of any private, internal state that he is experiencing." By abstractions, they mean *summary label*. Again, they say (p. 9): "Theoretical constructs are often shorthand summaries of relationships among many different variables, and they therefore serve to facilitate communication about these relationships." Once again, personality as an abstraction is a shorthand summary; this time it is a summary of relationships among variables.

We may note that this moderate version of the view that behavior is the central concept in a definition of personality argues essentially as follows: we must start with behavior and infer personality from it. This view allows that the theoretical constructs refer to conditions "inside" the person. Another recent definition is that of Lundin, who similarly proposes that, although the focus is upon behavior, the notion of personality refers to something presumably located within the individual. Lundin has proposed the following definition: *"Personality is that organization of unique behavior equipment an individual has acquired under the special conditions of his development"* (Lundin, 1974, p. 7). In this definition it is an "organization of unique behavior equipment" that is inferred to exist within the personality. That which underlies behavior as observed is some "equipment" the individual has acquired in the course of development.

A more radical version of this type of definition may be traced to the pioneering work of B. F. Skinner (1938), in which he proposed that the science of behavior has no need to appeal to underlying structures and processes within the organism. It is sufficient if laws can be established which relate behaviors to contingencies in the environment. An example of a contingency in the life of a pigeon might be as follows: given that the green light is on, a peck at the target will be followed by food in the hopper; but given that the red light is on, it will take 25 pecks at the target before food will appear in the hopper. The red or green light would be a signal or discriminative stimulus. The food in the hopper would be a reinforcing stimulus. The connection between green and one peck per food delivery (and also between red and 25 pecks per food delivery) is called a *contingency*. Skinner proposes that all behaviors are under that sort of control by contingencies, not only behaviors of pigeons and rats, but of humans as well. Contingencies for humans may be more complex and subtle, but they are contingencies nonetheless. The development and maintenance of complex contingencies can be said to explain completely the organism's behavior. Thus behavior is seen to be determined by environmental stimuli, and not by any structures or systems assumed to be operative within the individual.

Two recent theorists who adopt this more radical approach to personality are Krasner and Ullmann, who criticize Lundin's definition as given above. They argue that it postulates a personality structure, a set of enduring properties within the individual, namely one's "behavior equipment." Krasner and Ullmann, 1973, do not offer a summary definition of personality; however, they make quite plain their position on this matter. They write:

> *Rather than dealing with behavior in a vacuum as a characteristic of the person, we wish to deal with behavior in situations* (p. 138). We will suggest . . . *behavior influence* as an alternative, or as a new theory of "personality". . . . The very word *personality* is focused on an individual, the regularities of his behavior, and the hypothesized "enduring structures" *within him* that mediate between environmental stimuli and subsequent responses. We prefer behavior influence . . . because it em-

phasizes that the person acts within a physical and social environment. We wish to emphasize that 1) *the necessary interaction is between the person and his social situation* and 2) *the focus should be on measurable activity rather than hypothesized internal constructions* (p. 21).

The behavioral point of view, then, defines personality as behavior and looks for causes in the environment. According to this view it is useless to look for the causes of behavior in some inner psychological organization. There is no such organization there, certainly no causal "personality" inside the skin. The person is simply the sum of his or her behaviors. If you want to understand a person you must understand the environmental conditions which cause that person to behave in particular ways. The less radical behaviorist holds merely that personality is a theoretical construct, an abstraction based on observed behavior. The more radical behaviorist holds that even that theoretical construct is unnecessary. All you need is to see the behaviors and understand the conditions which control them.

Personality as Inner Experience and the Sense of Inner Identity

One of the earliest expressions of this third point of view in definitions of personality was given by William James, who wrote the following passage about our personal stream of consciousness and our inner assurance that it is *our* stream and not someones else's:

> On waking from sleep we usually know that we have been unconscious. . . . The result of it, however, is that the consciousness . . . remains sensibly continuous and one. What now is the common whole? The natural name for it is *myself, I,* or *me.*
> When Peter and Paul wake up in the same bed, and recognize that they have been asleep, each one of them mentally reaches back and makes connection with but *one* of the two streams of thought which were broken by the sleeping hours. . . . Peter's present instantly finds out Peter's past, and never by mistake knits itself onto that of Paul. . . . The past thought of Peter is appropriated by the present Peter alone. He may have a *knowledge,* and a correct one too, of what Paul's last drowsy states of mind were as he sank into sleep, but it is an entirely different sort of knowledge from that which he has of his own last states. He *remembers* his own states, whilst he only *conceives* Paul's. Remembrance is like direct feeling; its object is suffused with a warmth and intimacy to which no object of mere conception ever attains. This quality of warmth and intimacy and immediacy is what Peter's *present* thought also possesses for itself . . . whatever past feelings appear with those qualities must be admitted to receive the greeting of the present mental state, to be owned by it, and accepted as belonging together with it in a common self. This community of self is what the time-gap cannot break in twain, and is why a present thought, although not ignorant of the time-gap, can still regard itself as continuous with certain chosen portions of the past.
> Consciousness, then, does not appear to itself chopped up in bits. Such words as "chain" or "train" do not describe it fitly. . . . It is nothing jointed; it flows. A "river" or a "stream" are the metaphors by which it is most naturally described. *In talking of it hereafter, let us call it the stream of thought, of consciousness, or of subjective life* (James, 1890/1950, pp. 238-239).

Every reader knows what James is talking about: the sense of personal continuity resides at first in the sense of continuity in consciousness despite time gaps like those of being asleep. Later on (p. 333) James adds that there are certain other features of the qualities of "warmth and intimacy": "We feel the whole cubic mass of our body all the while, it gives us an unceasing sense of personal existence. Equally do we feel the inner 'nucleus of the spiritual self,' either in the shape of yon faint physiological adjustments, or (adopting the universal psychological belief), in that of the purer activity of our thought taking place as such."

On the modern scene there is a very strong movement toward defining personality almost exclusively in terms of the self, consciousness, striving for an ideal. The theory developed by Rogers (see chapter 5) is one that stresses the subjective, experiential viewpoint in defining personality. A related approach is that of George Kelly, whose theory of personality is explicitly based upon inner thoughts. Indeed, the first fundamental assertion in Kelly's theory is that "A person's processes are psychologically channelized by the ways in which he anticipates events" (Kelly, 1963, p. 46). Kelly calls his personality theory a "psychology of personal constructs," where "constructs" means the ways in which a person interprets whatever is experienced.

For this third group of approaches to defining personality, then, emphasis is placed upon *subjective experience*. To understand a person you must try to understand how the world seems to that person, how that person sees his or her own identity, or what it is like to have the kinds of conscious experience of the world and of the self that that other person has. To do this you would probably have to be very aware of your own stream of consciousness and then try to put yourself in the other person's stream.

Toward an Integrative Definition of Personality

The three groups of definitions emphasize quite different subject matters: (1) causal systems within the person; (2) the person's behaviors; (3) the person's thoughts, feelings, and other kinds of inner experience. How is it possible that such different viewpoints could arise with respect to one and the same subject matter, personality? One way to suggest an answer to this question is to consider the different kinds of working conditions that different theorists have been in while their theory was developing. Perhaps a definition of personality reflects whatever makes sense to a theorist under the conditions he or she most commonly has to deal with. For example, a psychologist who spends a majority of time involved in laboratory experiments may be so used to solving problems through the manipulation of environmental conditions that it seems only natural to define personality as the totality of an individual's behavior as controlled by environmental stimuli. This psychologist would find a behavioral definition of personality most meaningful. By contrast, a counseling psychologist who works with people in face-to-face psychotherapy may find it more natural and more readily meaningful to define personality in terms of subjective experience. This psychologist comes to understand those he or she works with primarily through listening to what they have to say and trying to understand their feelings and thoughts.

There may be many other reasons for a scientist's adopting a particular definition of personality; and the study of these reasons is of interest to those who are concerned with the history of ideas. But for the present purposes we are primarily interested in the differences between the three main groups of definitions as they are found in modern writings. As we try to formulate a definition of personality which will be useful in this book it becomes clear that we need a definition which allows us to include all three major approaches. Our definition might go beyond that, of course; but at least it ought to include those approaches since all three are actively employed in personality study at the present time. In order to make this integrative effort toward definition, however, it will be necessary to consider some issues which appear to make such integration impossible. For example, the behavioral definition of personality is accompanied by a denial that definitions of personality as an organization of systems within the individual have validity.

Behaviorists' Denial of Existence of Inner Causal Systems of Personality

Whereas Allport and many others think that personality is an organization of inner systems which are causal, scientists in the behaviorist group deny that such inner systems can have any causal influence. The most radical viewpoint states that inner personality systems do not even exist, let alone have causal influence.

Here we have a direct contradiction, and we must study the behavioral viewpoint more carefully in order to decide whether it should be sustained. It is argued that either inner causal systems are pure inferences and must be so accepted, or that actually the only causal relationships are those that exist between environmental stimuli and behavioral responses. In the view of the radical behaviorist there can be no *personality structure* in the sense of a set of causal systems providing the individual with enduring dispositions and properties. It is claimed that thinly spun inferences about internal structures and states of "mind" or "personality" are scientifically untenable. Science, it is held, rests upon observable data and manipulable or otherwise reproducible phenomena. It rests upon the ability to provide complete control over the set of phenomena under investigation. Such control can be established in the laboratory with relative ease and in field situations it needs close attention to the total stimulus environment of the individual. Once this control has been fully described, the behaviorists propose, then it is possible to determine the precise stimuli and contingencies which control any piece of behavior. The argument states that if complete control can be established in the laboratory through manipulation of the stimulus-response contingencies, then it is reasonable to suppose that unsuspected stimulus-response contingencies control human behavior under natural life conditions. Careful study seems to suggest that this is true to a certain extent. In the natural settings of hospitals and reformatories it has been possible to modify inmate behaviors substantially by making the receipt of reinforcements such as candy or a weekend pass contingent upon performance of certain operant behaviors.

But the truly crucial question for the present discussion is whether such demonstrations justify the claim that persons do not have enduring dispositions or that there are no inner causal systems. In my judgment the claim is not substantiated. It can be shown that military drill sergeants modify the behavior of recruits regularly. This does not justify a claim that military drill is the only cause of behavior. It can be shown that physical education and coaching in athletics substantially modifies student behavior. This does not justify a claim that physical education and coaching are the only causes of behavior or behavior change. It can be shown that surgery can often cause a permanent change in behavior; this obviously does not justify a claim that surgery is in general an exclusive cause of behavior change.[1] Human beings are remarkably adaptive organisms. It is well known also that they learn in a great variety of ways, including by rote, by observations of models, by simple associations of contiguous experiences, and even by listening to professors for

---

1. Of course neither behavior nor changes in behavior must necessarily be taken as the only or even the most important criterion of causal efficiency. And, as Maslow emphasized more than once, behavior may be relatively misleading with respect to the true nature and direction of a given personality. But behaviorists do assume the criterion value of behavior, and so the present argument meets them on their own ground.

an hour at a time! Doubtless they also learn some contingencies in more or less the way described by radical behaviorists. But the establishing of one kind of learning does not preclude the possibility of another kind of learning. The demonstration that one set of causal relationships with behavior exists does not deny the possibility that other sets of causal relationships exist. Thus I submit that even if the existing evidence for stimulus control of behavior were fully accepted it would not justify the claim that such control is the only possible cause of behavior. (As a matter of fact the evidence for stimulus control of adult human behavior has recently been seriously questioned. Careful experiments suggest that such control is illusory [see chapter 4].) It seems that the behaviorists' denial of the existence or effectiveness of causal systems within the personality cannot be sustained.

Behaviors and Experiences

Before considering whether we should include both the behavioral and the experiential groups of definitions, we must face another challenge from the radical behaviorists. They have argued that even so-called subjective mental experiences like thoughts and feelings are really behaviors of the same kind that walking and eating are. For example, Krasner and Ullmann write: "what would be implied by thoughts and feelings that neither classify as behavior (as defined by measurable changes in some form of corporeal activity) nor are subject to behavioral formulations(?). Such a view implies that there is a dualism between mind and body—a notion that psychologists do not find acceptable" (1973, p. 15).

Actually such a view does not imply a dualism between mind and body without a good deal of philosophical extrapolation. It merely implies a dualism between thoughts and feelings on the one hand and behavior on the other. Many psychologists accept this sort of dualism. Liebert and Spiegler, for example, write as follows.

In defining personality and developing a theoretical description of it, we must decide whether our interest will be limited to overt behavior or whether we can talk about internal events as well. . . . Psychologists who subscribe to the *behavioral* view (which holds that our primary concern should be with observable responses rather than presumed internal states . . .) argue that the scientific study of personality can be no more than an examination of observable responses. Others, though, have argued that personality must refer to some private experiences as well.

Tom, who *appears* happy, may in fact be miserable inside; a prim and proper girl may be seething with sexuality; and, in general, a man's behavior may not reflect his "real" personality. Although this orientation has a good deal of intuitive appeal, the problem of measuring private experiences is a thorny one. (1974, p. 7.)

Clearly some psychologists believe that private experiences exist and are different from overt behaviors, especially in regard to ease of measurement. One might wonder whether it really makes much difference to speak of "behavior and thought" as Allport or Liebert and Spiegler do, or to speak of "behavior and behavior" as Krasner and Ullmann do. It seems to me that it makes a great deal of difference in that many phenomena in psychology cannot be adequately described (let alone explained) unless the distinction between behavior and thought is made. Phenomena such as lying, diplomacy, and intrigue could not be adequately described without reference to two diffferent kinds of events, namely outward behavioral events and inner secret thoughts and intentions, so-called *contents of consciousness*.

The notion of consciousness or awareness has returned to experimental psychology in recent years. Studies include topics such as subliminal *perception* (perception without awareness; see Dixon, 1971), and *encoding process* for words (storing the meanings and other aspects of words). Here subjects can be shown to use categories which nevertheless do not enter consciousness (Wickens, 1970). Consciousness has also received new attention from neurophysiologists. Sperry (1970, p. 585) states that consciousness is "something different from and more than" its neural basis, and that it can "actively govern the flow pattern of neural excitation." Consciousness, in Sperry's view, is inseparably tied to the brain processes, but nevertheless is itself a dynamic emergent property that may exert influence in its own right, even upon the course of brain processes themselves.

The contents of consciousness such as thoughts cannot be described by overt indicants such as physiological responses, even though some related happenings might be indicated by deflections on a galvanometer or other equipment in a lie-detector system. The widespread acceptance of lie-detection devices (*millions* currently in use; see Lykken, 1974) suggests that the distinction between truth and falsehood is widely understood. This distinction rests upon the difference between private thoughts and public utterances, a distinction that would be ill described by referring to private behaviors and public behaviors. For the present it seems reasonable to reject the radical behaviorist challenge and accept the distinction between thoughts and behaviors.

The Record of Experiences and Behaviors

We must now ask how thoughts and behaviors are to be incorporated into our definition of personality. In order to achieve this goal we must introduce another technical term: the *record*. For many years it has been customary in psychology to distinguish between thoughts and other *cognitions* on one hand, and feelings and emotions, or *affects*, on the other. In this text we shall consider both cognitions and affects as *experiences*, and shall therefore from now on speak of *experiences* and behaviors. The *record* is the sequence of actually occurring experiences and behaviors in a person's life. A close approximate representation of the record could be obtained by such devices as a diary, biography, work record, medical record, and so on. Over shorter spans of time, a videotape and sound track augmented by the person's continuous report of inner events into a tape recorder would provide a good approximation of the record. Such records have been kept in experiments for periods of a few days, and similar records are kept during space flights.

It has also been discovered by Wilder Penfield (Penfield, 1975, pp. 20-27) that the brain keeps a record of all conscious experiences. This record can be reactivated by a brain surgeon's electrode. When the brain is so stimulated the patient "relives" the particular portion that is stored where the electrode makes contact.

Box 2.1 provides a number of excerpts from records of experience and of behavior, and study of this box should provide a deeper understanding of both types of record.

Causal Interaction of Experience and Behavior

So far, then, our definition of personality will refer to the record of experiences and behaviors and to the psychophysical systems that determine the record. However, the experiential group of definitions includes the notion that experience itself contains some causal properties, as for instance when a person imagines swimming in a blue lagoon and plans all the details of getting there. This planning may be followed by actions of saving money, making travel arrangements, and finally arriv-

Box 2.1
Portions of Behavioral and of Experiential Records

In this box are presented a number of published records of behavior and experience. First is part of a stream of behaviors as observed by a trained psychologist studying one boy's behaviors throughout an entire day:

8:34. He announced, "I'm going to take my belt," as though this were something very important. Then he put on the belt. This completed the dressing. Roy said proudly and with definiteness, "I'm going to take my gun, too." He looked at me and said, "The gun is still under my pillow." He then looked toward his pillow (Barker & Wright, 1951).

A record of behaviors can be provided by the person through verbal report. Notice that the verbal report is sometimes said to be simply behavioral. But that which the verbal report refers to or describes can be behavioral, and, as will be seen in later excerpts, it can also be experiential. To say that a written report is behavior is not to say that what the report is about is necessarily behavior. It might be about the Grand Canyon. In the present case it is about a sequence of behaviors, as told by a gang member:

We met Mike and went to the "Boy." I do not know his name, but Eddie had seen him out in South Chicago. The Boy, who was about sixteen, had been in St. Charles [a reformatory]. When we met him he was working in a wienie shop on Sixty-third. We were about twelve and thirteen then.

The Boy brought us some buns, and then we went to Jackson Park. On the way back we went to a show. When we came out, we bought some candies. We slept that night with the Boy, in a little shed. The next day we spent in the park. About four o'clock that afternoon, we helped the Boy, but we left the door of the store open so we could come back later. In the evening we went to a show. About midnight we met the Boy and came back and robbed the store (Thrasher, 1963, p. 71).

Gang members also report on their imaginative inner experiences:

My pal and I belonged to the Silent Three. The third member, who made us a gang, was a very terrible and mysterious personage. He was really the dominant figure in our triumvirate although he was entirely imaginary. . . . To protect our secrets we developed a series of symbols and writings which nobody else could possibly fathom (Thrasher, 1963, p. 86).

Next we have a report of repeated experiences of worry on the part of a call girl, who describes her career as:

a hell of a life . . . when you're afraid you're slipping. Some days you sit and sit by the telephone, smoking and smoking, and nobody rings, and you think: "Look out, kid, you're slipping." What have I done? WHAT HAVE I DONE? Are they telling each other I'm no good? (Young, 1970, p. 76).

What she imagines, her assertion that that is not what she is afraid of, her identification of the trouble in her work, and her thoughts about herself when nobody calls, all of these would be called cognitive experiences, as would the implied feelings of despair.

Our next report is from a young woman at the time of going to bed but before going to sleep. The images that come to her are described as follows:

There was no light in the room. I closed my eyes, and had the feeling of waiting for something that was about to happen. Then I felt a great relaxation come over me, and I remained as completely passive as possible. Lines, sparks, and spirals of fire passed before my eyes, symptoms of nervousness and ocular fatigue, followed by a kaleidoscopic and fragmentary review of recent trivial events. Then an impression that something was on the point of being communicated to me. It seemed as if these words were repeating themselves in me—"Speak, Lord, for thy servant heareth—Open thou mine ears." The head of a sphinx suddenly appeared in the field of vision, in an Egyptian setting: then it faded away. At that moment my parents called to me, and I immediately answered them in a perfectly coherent way, a proof that I was not asleep. . . .

Suddenly, the apparition of an Aztec, complete in every detail: hand open, with large fingers, head in profile, armoured, with a head-dress resembling the plumed crests of the American Indians, etc. . . . The name "Chiwan-to-pel" forms itself bit by bit, and it seems to belong to the previous personage, son of an Inca of Peru. . . . Then a swarm of people. Horses, a battle, the view of a **dream-city.** . . . A strange conifer with knotty branches, lateen sails in a bay of purple water, a perpendicular cliff. A confusion of sounds resembling Wa-ma, Wa-ma. . . . (Jung, 1907/1967, p. 458).

This young woman's record refers chiefly to **hypnagogic** images, those that occur just before going to sleep. They occur quite often and are well known as one class of images (dream images form another class). Here is another example, with features similar to the young woman's imagery but lacking the audio components:

When I close my eyes I see darkness but then it lightens to gray. Next I see colored lights and sometimes very complex geometric forms that dance, rotate, or sparkle about. Soon a succession of images of people and scenes parades before me. I find these quite interesting and often go to sleep watching them. At times, however, I get vivid hallucinations which may frighten me awake. For instance, once all of a sudden I saw a spider on my pillow; another time a crab. They were ugly and scary and caused me to start up in bed thinking they were real (Horowitz, 1970, p. 11).

Creative imagery does not depend on going to sleep. Sometimes it proceeds while the person is engaged in some behavior such as driving an automobile or doing the dishes. Sometimes it is used in planning a course of behaviors such as moves in chess or a vacation. Sometimes it affects ongoing perceptions as in the following experience of a patient responding to the therapist who had just reminded him that psychotherapy is difficult and the outcome cannot be guaranteed:

I feel right now as though I were 20 feet farther from you . . . and suddenly you become very bright . . . your image in my eyes becomes much brighter . . . you . . . just you, nothing else, will become lustrous, almost as though a light were placed in you . . . and burned . . . (Shands, 1973, p. 431).

It seems appropriate to return to behaviors. The record of behaviors can be lively and informative, especially when told with artistry and referring to many people, as in anthropologist Margaret Mead's account of an evening with the Arapesh:

A party of visitors from another locality asks first for fire, which their hosts immediately give them; then a low-voiced, excited conversation begins. Then men cluster about an open fire; the women cook nearby, often in the open, supporting their tall, black cooking-pots on huge stones; the children sit about in sleepy contentment, playing with their lips, sucking their fingers, or sticking their sharp little knees into their mouths. Someone relates a slight incident and everyone laughs uproariously and happily, with a laughter that stirs easily at the slightest touch of humor. As the night falls and the damp mountain evening drives them all closer to the fire, they sit around the embers and sing songs imported from far and wide (Mead, 1963, p. 6).

The same anthropologist who relates the above description of behaviors does not hesitate to place individual experience on record:

Young Alis was slowly dying of anxiety. . . . Two years before, at a feast in Yimonihi, a far-away village on the road of the setting sun, he had met a Plainswoman who had seduced him. . . . Alis had yielded and then, his nerve failing him, he had fled back to Alitoa without her. He had remembered his young wife Taumulimen, whom he liked very much and who had not yet borne him a child. If he brought this tall avid stranger into their

Continued

home, Taumulimen would probably run away. . . he shuddered, partly in thought of Taumulimen and partly in remembrance of his skill as a hunter, which would surely suffer if he brought such a turbulent woman into his home. A month after he deserted her, he heard that she was dead. He did not doubt for one moment that she had placed a small bit of his personality in the hands of some sorcerer relative . . . they would be satisfied only with his death . . . (Mead, 1963, pp. 102-103).

Margaret Mead's empathic understanding of the feelings, memories, anticipations, fears, doubts, and certainties that flowed through the inner experience of this young man, Alis, provides us with a deep insight into the nature of Arapesh culture, as well as a three-dimensional view of one personality.

---

ing at the lagoon and swimming. Had the imagery and planning referred to a safari in the jungle or a snowmobile trip through northern Alaska, the relevant behaviors would have been different. Thus imagery and planning (which are parts of the record of subjective experience) can causally influence various actions like saving money, making arrangements, and swimming (which are part of the record of behavior).

So, as the experientialists believe that subjective experience can cause actions (or behavior), the behavioralists believe that behavior has a causal effect. For example, behavior therapy rests upon the notion that a *symptom* of illness or neuroticism is behavioral, and if that behavior is changed then the person is "better." This means that some behaviors are seen as producing undesirable consequences for the person; changes in these behaviors can produce more desirable consequences. For example, the symptom of *phobia*, which is extreme anxiety or fear of a certain kind of object (like snakes) or place (like open spaces or high places), has the consequence of keeping the person in a condition of restricted movement. The person avoids situations where the feared object or place might cause an anxiety attack. Persons afraid of open spaces would always stay inside the house. This would deprive them of sunlight and many other necessities and advantages of living. So if the fearful behavior of the phobia can be changed, the person's condition will be improved, regardless of whether or not there might have been deep psychophysical inner causes of the phobia.

In a more general vein, it is not unusual to recognize that some behaviors have causal effects upon other behaviors and upon experiences. For example, if you trip suddenly on the sidewalk you immediately engage in activity designed to reestablish your balance. Again, you cannot take shorthand at high speed (one behavior) unless you have previously done a lot of studying and practicing (other, necessary, behaviors). Similarly, many people are suddenly surprised and embarrassed to find that they have behaved inappropriately on some occasion. They might be ashamed of their actions. The feeling of shame thus is caused in part by their shameful deed. So behaviors can be causally related both to other behaviors and to experiences.

It becomes obvious that the record of behaviors and experiences contains some of its own determinants. Not every detail of the record is attributable to the psychophysical systems within the person. Indeed Allport and others stressed the view that the psychophysical systems should be held accountable for *characteristic* aspects of thought and behavior, namely those that are repeated and reflect enduring dispositions or properties of the individual. But other theorists would suggest that even one-time occurrences can be attributable to some complex feature of psychophysical systems, as when a female neurotic patient's disgust reaction to the first sexual advance ever made to her is seen to be quite strictly determined by the particular conflicts involved in her neurosis.

We must recall also that the record of behaviors and experiences contains many events which can be shown to depend upon contingencies and other types of causal relationships with the environment. A startle response, for example, is often produced by a sudden loud noise. Like other features of the environment, the noise itself would not be included as part of our definition of personality. Nevertheless, special sensitivities to such environmental occurrences might well be an important part of personality and would be included within the notion of psychophysical systems.

Structure and Process in Psychological and Physical Causation

What do we mean exactly when we use the term *psychophysical system?* The concept has four parts. *Psycho* refers to psychological; *physical* refers to the body, including the nerves and muscles, organs, sense organs, lymph, blood, glands, ligaments, and bones. The word *system* refers to a number of parts in relatively complex interaction. That is, there are *structures* within the system and there are *processes* or regular sequences of events occurring between the structures. Thus there is a heart in the body (one structure) which pumps (a process) blood throughout the

arteries, veins, and other vessels (structures). This entire set of structures and the process is referred to as the *vascular system.*

In psychophysical systems, then, there must be physical and psychological structures. The physical structures are the organs of the body, especially the brain and nerves. Psychological structures include *innate* nervous pathways and connections which provide for survival, and also *acquired* bodies of skill and memory. When someone returns from a period of training we recognize the difference, for now that person can do things that previously he or she could not do. Skills and habits have been developed which previously were not there. New attitudes and the potentials for new inner experience may have been acquired. There would have been structural change.

The relationship between physical and psychological structures is of course immensely complex. It can be seen first that the new skill or habit (psychological structure) must be stored somewhere in the body, presumably in the brain (physical structure). But new skills typically involve also some structural changes in muscles and tendons, strengthening, enlarging, providing for more rapid response and less fatigability, and so on. This is common knowledge among those who take on the task of acquiring a new skill such as skiing or horseback riding or wrestling or singing or dancing or golf. The more we study and practice, building our knowledge and ability (psychological structures) the stronger and better coordinated our muscles (physical structures) become.

Similar interrelationships must exist between psychological and physical processes, the sequences of events linking structures. At the level of nerve tissue it becomes especially clear that the transmission of information is associated with chemical exchanges across the nerve membrane. The actual functioning of a new habit such as typing must flow through information transmitted from head to fingers via nerve and muscle fibers. The new skill in action (psychological process) flows along channels of excitation and inhibitory control based upon chemical changes (physical processes) in nerve and muscle and physical movements of muscles, tendons and bones.

Importance of the Body

Although the involvement of the body is implied in the notion of psychophysical structures, it is not often made explicit in definitions of personality. Allport did say that the psychophysical systems are within the person; but he could have said *within the body* of the individual. In everyday life a person's face, build, voice, and posture are judged to be important in the individual's personality. But some authors have explicitly excluded the body from the definition of personality as such. For example, Holt (1971, p. 8) distinguishes the personality from the physique, anatomy, and physiology on one hand, and from the person's social role and status on the other. The personality, for Holt, is simply an observable pattern of ongoing behaviors or traits, with no inferences as to dispositions implied by the word "trait." Thus Holt focuses upon what we have called the *record* and excludes the body as well as psychophysical causal structures.

Other authors, by contrast, have made a point of including the body in their definition of personality. For example, Eysenck (1947, p. 25) defines personality as a set of actual and potential behavior-patterns organized into four sectors: intelligence, character, temperament, and constitution. The latter refers to the body. Throughout the ages thinkers have assumed some connection between temperament and body build, and a number of prominent theories have been advanced suggesting that certain types of personality are associated with certain types of physique (e.g., Kretschmer, 1926; Sheldon, 1942).

The body determines behavior (you can't walk with a broken leg) and experience (a broken leg gives you pain). Behavior affects the body (eating and exercise) and experience also affects the body (self-hypnosis for anaesthesia; relaxation imagery).

The Definition

We may now formulate our definition of personality in terms of the four major components discussed above: psychophysical systems, record of experience, record of behavior, and the body:

> *Personality is the record of an individual's experience and behavior, together with the psychophysical systems contributing causal determination to the record, and the individual body within and through which the systems and record exist and function. Some causal determination is found within the record itself.*

A diagram showing the four main components of the definition is shown in figure 2.1. Through the arrows it may be seen that some effects are exerted by each one of the four main components on all the other three. Throughout the remainder of the book it will be possible to compare each theory we study

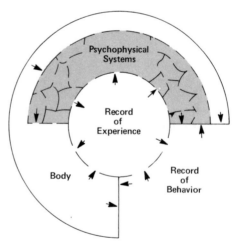

Figure 2.1. Some components of personality and their interrelationships

with the definition given here and represented in figure 2.1. As an example of the use of the diagram's components in illustrating definitions of personality, the three main groups of definitions we examined earlier are represented in figure 2.2. It is obvious that each alternative in figure 2.2 focuses upon selected components represented in figure 2.1. The behaviorist definition in figure 2.2 makes explicit the relation between behavior and the environment, whereas the other definitions, including that of figure 2.1, leave the relations with environment implicit, or at least not in focus when *defining* personality.

Looking back to Maslow's theory (chapter 1, especially figure 1.3) it is clear that his conception of personality syndromes, collections of characteristic thoughts and behaviors, would refer to an important part of the record. It is also clear that Maslow did not include a component of psychophysical systems in his definition, since needs and other characteristics emerge directly from the body.

It is of interest to consider briefly a theory that does refer to all of the components in our definition of personality: the theory of psychosomatic disorders formulated by Alexander, French, and Pollock (1968). This is part of modern psychoanalytic theory of personality. They write, for example, about certain skin disorders (neurodermatitis) as follows.

In general, such patients lacked close physical contact in early life and now try to get attention by the means of infantile exhibitionism (the attempt to induce adults to cuddle the child).

The early exhibitionistic techniques for getting attention and love are aimed at winning one parent's attention away from the other parent or a sibling. If the child is successful, he may suffer from feelings of guilt which later manifest themselves in a tendency to put the wrong foot forward, to appear in a bad light, to make embarrassing faux pas. The sexual impulse in these patients, in which skin eroticism is accentuated, is deeply linked with guilt feelings.

The disease, as a rule, is precipitated after the patient achieves some form of exhibitionistic victory. The victory arouses guilt and creates a need for suffering in the precise part of the body that is involved in the exhibitionistic success. By scratching, which is a substitute for autoerotic masturbation, the patient both relieves sexual tension and at the same time inflicts pain upon himself. Some patients vividly describe the pleasure that they derive from scratching, referring to it as a *vicious* kind of pleasure. In these scratching orgies, they attack their bodies mercilessly, experiencing pleasureful pain or painful pleasure of a high order (pp. 14-15).

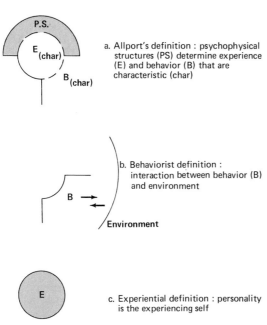

a. Allport's definition : psychophysical structures (PS) determine experience (E) and behavior (B) that are characteristic (char)

b. Behaviorist definition : interaction between behavior (B) and environment

c. Experiential definition : personality is the experiencing self

Figure 2.2. The three primary groups of definitions of personality formulated prior to 1976:

a. Allport's definition. Psychophysical structures (PS) determine experiences (E) and behaviors (B) that are characteristic (char) of the personality.
b. Behaviorist definition. Personality is interaction between behavior (B) and environment.
c. Experiential definition. Personality is the experiencing self.

Ordinary Knowledge of Experience and Behavior

So far we have considered the entire matter of behavior and experience from an academic point of view. As ordinary people, however, we know certain things about our own nature and existence. As twentieth-century people we inherit from the past a store of knowledge about our bodies and our experience. Most of this we can check against the evidence of current living.

Consider each of the following ten points carefully. Write whether it refers to behavior or to experience, to both, or to neither.

Propositions	Your comments

1. There exists a body composed of head, trunk, and limbs which often move around in space.

2. In the body there are nerves, muscles, glands, bones and other tissues, most of which are in some condition of activity most of the time.

3. The body makes sounds through the mouth or in other ways.

4. Parts known as sense organs receive stimuli from the outer world and also from within the body, producing sensations.

5. Head, trunk, and limbs often move in **meaningful** ways such as gestures or dancing.

6. Muscles, nerves, and other tissues often are active in meaningful ways, as in facial expressions, tensing when angered, and so on.

7. Sounds are often made meaningfully, as in a conversation.

8. Our memory holds traces of previous sensations, so that we remember how warm it is in the sunshine, for instance. We learn that there are things out there like sunshine and sun. We say we perceive things in the world.

9. We remember things as they are out there even when we are away from them. We have something stored in our memory so that pictures of those things and people can come flashing back in our dreams and in our daydreams. (It is a fact that no subject ever studied by dream researchers fails to dream, even though some subjects while awake insist that they never dream. Also, 95 percent of persons asked if they daydream say that they do. See Singer, 1966.)

10. We are able to put memories together and compare them. We can put perceptions together and compare them (as in comparing a photo and a portrait of the same person). Many similar operations go on in our heads, and we call them **thinking.**

_____

_____

_____

_____

This is what I think about these items. I think that numbers 1, 2, and 3 are not experience; they are either behaviors or else merely movements, depending on what else is true. For example, in number 1, a boxer's head might jerk as he is punched unconscious. Most people would not call that behavior. But a similar jerk, if selected for reinforcement in an operant conditioning study, would be considered to be a piece of behavior.

A glandular secretion (number 2) would not ordinarily be called behavior. Such a thing is probably going on somewhere in your body and mine right this very minute. Likewise the blood is continuously flowing in our bodies. This is neither behavior nor experience. But a glandular secretion could be transformed into a piece of behavior in a laboratory study of salivary responses, for example.

Many sounds would not be considered either experience or behavior (number 3). Take a belch as an example. If a person is asleep and gas escapes through the mouth, that sound would probably not be considered a piece of behavior. In some social situations, however, it might be considered to be behavior and judged either good or bad, depending on local customs.

Number 4 would most likely be considered experience; or at least as functions of the body closely associated with experience—a sensation of heat, for example.

Numbers 5, 6, and 7 are all meaningful movements or sounds and seem to me to be clear examples of behavior.

Numbers 8, 9, and 10 seem to me to be clear examples of experience.

Now we should try to see how these differences affect our daily living. A good way to do this is to consider the implications for someone who is actually experiencing each of the ten points and someone who is merely observing the first person. The doctor and the patient make a convenient example. Make a short reference list of the ten points so that you can rapidly identify them by number. For example: 1. body motions; 2. tissue activity; 3. sounds; 4. sensations; 5. meaningful movements; 6. meaningful tissue activity; 7. meaningful sounds; 8. perception; 9. memory; 10. thought. Now in the following account of exchanges between doctor and patient, put in the number of the relevant point for each statement. For instance, in the first space in the first sentence following, you would write (1) for body motion. (Answers below).

> With a broken arm, both the doctor and the patient can see it fall, swinging at a point where it ought not to swing (Number ..). With an open wound, both doctor and patient can see the blood flow out (Number ..); they can both hear the escaping flatus (Number ..). They both see the gesture of greeting (Number ..), although the patient also intended it (Number ..) and feels it (Number ..). They both see the goose pimples of fear (Number ..)although the doctor only sees it and the patient also feels it (Number ..). They both hear what the patient says to the doctor (Number ..). The patient remembers the needle (Number ..) but the doctor does not see or hear this memory; **if** the patient gives a wince or says something to the effect, then the doctor finds out that the patient remembers the needle. The patient recalls a scene in a hospital during a war (Number ..); but the doctor knows nothing of this recollected image unless the patient tells him. The doctor might suspect that something was preoccupying the patient if the eyes went into a fixed and glassy stare; but at best the doctor would have to imagine what it was unless the patient told him. The patient notes that doctors are better equipped now than they were during the war (Number ..). Again the doctor knows nothing of this comparison unless the patient tells him (Answers 1, 2, 3, 5, 10, 4, 6, 4, 7, 8, 9, 10)

There are those situations in which the doctor and the patient (the observer and the experiencer) obtain knowledge in the same way: Numbers 1, 2, 3, 5, 6, and 7. However, in some of these (Numbers 5, 6, and 7) the patient has additional channels of information. But in Numbers 4, 8, 9, and 10 the doctor and the patient obtain their knowledge in quite different ways; and often the doctor is dependent on the patient's verbal report for any knowledge at all. However, the doctor can imagine the realities of Number 4, 8, 9, and 10, since in other times and places he has been a patient and an experiencer himself. He uses "empathic introspection."

The points on which the doctor and the patient obtain knowledge in the same way are those which most people would probably classify as body motions (points 1, 2, and 3). The points on which the doctor and the patient would share at least some of the ways in which they obtain knowledge would probably be classified by most people as meaningful behaviors or actions (points 5, 6, and 7). Finally, the points on which the doctor and the patient obtain knowledge in different ways are those which would probably be classified by most people as experience (4, 8, 9, and 10).

Workshop 2B

Some Aspects of Your Own Personality

Here are some matters that could be important to you in the way you think about your own personality. Think about each item and check those that are important for your personality:

Leadership ability	Creative potential	Trustworthiness
Innermost convictions	Subjective feelings	Secret plans
Behavior in groups	Recreational activities	Work habits
Shape of your body	Physical energy	Nervous system
Popularity	Social position	Reputation

How do these items fit our definition of personality? I would classify leadership **ability** as a **psychophysical structure, secret plans** as **subjective experience, recreational activities** as part of the **record of behaviors,** and **nervous system** as part of the **body. Reputation** would be one of the ways in which a person's presence has an impact upon other people: it would not be included in the definition of personality developed in this chapter.

Here are the items again. Please think about each one carefully and classify it as to which aspect of personality in our definition it most readily represents:

	Psychophysical structure	Record of experience	Record of behavior	Body	Other
Leadership ability	_____	_____	_____	_____	_____
Innermost convictions	_____	_____	_____	_____	_____
Behavior in groups	_____	_____	_____	_____	_____
Shape of your body	_____	_____	_____	_____	_____
Popularity	_____	_____	_____	_____	_____
Creative potential	_____	_____	_____	_____	_____
Subjective feelings	_____	_____	_____	_____	_____

Recreational activities	_____	_____	_____	_____	_____
Physical energy	_____	_____	_____	_____	_____
Social position	_____	_____	_____	_____	_____
Trustworthiness	_____	_____	_____	_____	_____
Secret plans	_____	_____	_____	_____	_____
Work habits	_____	_____	_____	_____	_____
Nervous system	_____	_____	_____	_____	_____
Reputation	_____	_____	_____	_____	_____

By comparing your earlier responses with the classifications you have just made you can perhaps reach a decision on the following question: What was your implicit **definition** of personality before you started reading this chapter? For example, if all the matters you had checked as important were classified as either **Record of experience** or **Body,** then your implicit definition of personality probably emphasized physical body characteristics and subjective experiences as the heart of personality.

As a result of these considerations, perhaps you would find it interesting to write down the nature of your **definition** of personality as it was before starting this chapter, and the nature of your **definition** now after completing the chapter. They might be exactly the same, or they might be quite different.

My definition of personality before reading this chapter.

_____

_____

_____

_____

My definition of personality now.

_____

_____

_____

This theory makes clear reference to behaviors (such as scratching), to experiences (such as experiencing painful pleasure), to psychophysical structures (such as the continued infantile exhibitionism) and processes (such as the link between sexual impulses and guilt feelings). The body is also clearly implicated (the skin, for example), as is also the environment (lack of close physical contact, for instance).

Summary

There have been three main definitions of personality, emphasizing respectively behaviors, subjective experiences, and the psychophysical systems (structures and causal processes) which are assumed to determine behaviors and experiences. It can be argued that each has validity to a limited extent. A more complete and general definition would include all three. One such definition is offered here, stressing the record of actually occurring experiences and behaviors. Since experiences and behaviors occur through the physical body and since the body has independently important characteristics for personality as well as causal influences on both experiences and behaviors, it therefore seems appropriate to include the body explicitly in the definition. The resulting definition of personality, then, refers to these four components: (1) the *body,* (2) *psychophysical systems;* (3) *record of subjective experience;* and (4) *record of behavior.* Our considerations lead us to conclude that each component exerts causal influence on all other components.

Using the suggested definition of personality, we see that it is possible to characterize each of the original main definitions in terms of the component or components it emphasizes. In the next three chapters we shall take up three theories, each of which exemplifies one of the three main approaches to defining personality. We begin with Murray's theory, which exemplifies Allport's kind of definition, emphasizing psychophysical systems.

INTRODUCTION

A theory which defines personality as an
organization of psychophysical systems within
the individual
Introduction to Murray's life and work
  Murray's life and professional career
  The importance of psychoanalytic insights
  Researches on normal personality
  The central thema and complexity of personality
The theory of needs
  Needs as forces
  Fusion and combination of needs
  Four groups of needs
    Ascendance
    Deference
    Orderliness
    Sensuous expression
Environmental pressures
  The press of the environment
  Press and needs
  Alpha and beta press
  Transmittors and receptors
Thema, thematic disposition, and complex:
  organization of need and press
  Thema
  Thematic disposition
  Complex
    The claustral complex
Accomplishments of Murray's theory
  Personnel assessment
  The Thematic Apperception Test (TAT)
    Nature of the test
    Examples of interpreting stories told to the
      TAT
  Questionnaires
    Edwards' Personal Preference Schedule
    Stern's Activities Index
    Jackson's Personality Research Form
  Traditions of research into special constructs: the
    need for achievement
      The work of McClelland and associates
      Atkinson's and Feather's mathematical model
        of achievement motivation
      Current status of both traditions
Critique of Murray's theory
  Criticism that the theory is too complex

Criticism of relation between theory and research
Replies to the criticisms: complexity, reality, and
  formalism
The meaning of "simplicity" (the opposite of
  "complexity")
Accuracy and fruitfulness of Murray's theory
Workshop 3   Stimulus-influenced apperception
  study
Summary

Personality as Thematic Dispositions: Murray

In this chapter we shall explore one of the most productive and creative theories of modern psychology, the personality theory of Henry Murray. The theory emphasizes that human personality is a complex organization of needs, preferred patterns of action to satisfy the needs, and subjective appraisals of the various situations within which needs arise and are satisfied. The essence of personality is a set of *thematic dispositions,* each of which organizes needs of a particular kind around situations of a particular kind (such as needs for achievement in competitive situations). The theory thus defines personality essentially in terms of the *psychophysical systems* discussed in chapter 2; although, as we shall see, the *records* of subjective experience and of behavior are both prominent in Murray's theory of personality.

Henry Murray was born in 1893 in New York City, where he lived for most of his childhood. The family was wealthy, Murray tells us (1967), so that he went to a private school, spent some vacations on Long Island, and also traveled in Europe several times, visiting its treasures of the past in museums, art galleries, and cathedrals. Nevertheless, Henry Murray had his problems. The middle of three children, he suffered from strabismus, a muscle

imbalance in the external eye muscles, causing deficient depth vision. This made it hard for him to compete in sports, a fact for which he compensated by working harder for success in athletic activities than in class. As a result, in school he did well in football (playing quarterback) and in boxing (he won the featherweight championship). At Harvard College he rowed for the college team. But all this athletic effort cost him something; his grades were below average.

That his poor grades were due to insufficient effort rather than low ability became clear when Murray later graduated from the Columbia College of Physicians and Surgeons, where he achieved outstanding grades. After receiving his M.D. he went on to study biology and obtained a master's degree in that field. He then spent two years on an internship in surgery, followed by work as a research assistant at the Rockefeller Institute for Medical Research, studying the biochemistry of chick embryos. Following that he went to Cambridge University in England, where he received a Ph.D. in biochemistry.

After this extensive background in medicine, surgery, biology, and biochemistry, how was it that Henry Murray finally found his niche in psychology? His own account (1967, pp. 290-291) tells us that he had for a long time been deeply interested in people, especially the people behind the illnesses he had treated as physician and surgeon. Moreover he had read some of Freud's works, and when Carl Jung's book *Psychological Types* was published in 1923 the young Murray obtained a copy immediately. He was profoundly influenced by its insights into human nature. Though still immersed in the biological sciences, Murray managed, during his stay in England, to spend three weeks visiting Jung in Zurich, Switzerland. He describes his visits with Dr. Jung in 1925 as "revolutionary sessions." He felt that much of his own inner emotional and artistic strivings had been blocked by concentration on chemistry, surgery, and biological research. When he was invited to take a position as research assistant to the famed psychiatrist Morton Prince, at Harvard University in 1926, Murray felt that this was precisely the opportunity for which he really had been preparing all these years without knowing it. And so he became an academic psychologist and helped found the Harvard Psychological Clinic. He believed that Freud's psychoanalytic theories were the most appropriate for understanding human personality and he underwent further training in psychoanalysis, including a personal analysis. He was one of the founders of the Boston Psychoanalytic Society.

In 1928 Murray became director of the clinic and brought together a large number of psychologists and other social scientists who worked together in a project to devise measurement procedures for assessment of normal human personality in accordance with psychoanalytic insights, and in accordance with a new theory built by Murray and his associates on the basis of Freud's theory. Why should one study human personality "in accordance with psychoanalytic insights?" Murray answered that question many times. On one occasion he compared it to normal vision as against myopia, and continued:

> Instead of seeing merely a groomed American in a business suit, traveling to and from his office like a rat in a maze, a predatory ambulating apparatus of reflexes, habits, stereotypes, and slogans, a bundle of inconsistencies, conformities, and allegiances to this or that institution—a robot in other words—I visualize (just as I visualize the activity of his internal organs) a flow of powerful subjective life, conscious and unconscious; a whispering gallery in which voices echo from the distant past; a gulf stream of fantasies with floating memories of past events, currents of contending complexes, plots and counterplots, hopeful intimations and ideals. . . . A personality is a full Congress of orators and pressure-groups, of children, demagogues, communists, isolationists, war-mongers. . . . And a psychologist who does not know this in himself, whose mind is locked against the flux of images and feelings, should be encouraged to make friends, by being psychoanalyzed, with the members of his household (Murray, 1940, pp. 160-61).

Through grants from The Rockefeller Foundation, extensive researches on normal human personality were carried out at the Harvard Psychological Clinic. During World War II Murray was called to head up an extensive program of personality assessment in the selection of personnel for the Office of Strategic Services. As a result of his work, he received the Legion of Merit. More recently the American Psychological Association recognized him through a Distinguished Scientific Contribution Award. The American Psychological Foundation honored his long years of signal contributions to psychology with the Gold Medal Award.

Psychoanalysis was not the only source of inspiration. A number of psychologists influenced Murray, especially Lewin through his emphasis upon the meaningful environment (see chapter 19). The conception of environment that Murray gradually developed was also much influenced by the work of sociologists and cultural anthropologists. As early as 1938, he wrote, "the individual is always embedded in his culture. He assimilates it, is changed by it, conserves it, represents it, conveys it, modifies it, creates it. The culture is expressed through personalities, and personalities are expressed in the culture" (Murray, 1938, p. 609). Murray found Lewin's form of representing the environment insufficient for the level of complexity at which he wanted to study personality. A mere account of particular stimuli and reinforcement events would likewise be inadequate. Murray's aim was higher, his intent more profound.

"What is personality?" he asked over and over again. His answer was that personality is the whole organization of needs and characteristic tendencies of a person, integrated at any moment and continuing over time. In one sense it is the person's entire biography. Murray strove continuously to find the best means of formulating biography, and probably came closest to it in his concept of *unity-thema*, which was conceived to be an "underlying reaction system" that provided the key to an individual's uniqueness. He defined it as follows:

> A *unity-thema* is a compound of interrelated —collaborating or conflicting—dominant needs that are linked to *press* (environmental pressures) to which the individual was exposed on one or more particular occasions, gratifying or traumatic, in early childhood . . . it repeats itself in many forms during later life (Murray, 1938, p. 60).

The notion of unity-thema was indeed a new key. For particular behaviors reflect the personality, and since the unity-thema is the key to the personality, it follows that many behaviors cannot be understood except in relation to the unity-thema. It signifies the essential thrust and purpose of the personality.

Also it is a complex *psychophysical structure* as described in chapter 2.

If behavioral responses cannot be understood without reference to the central theme, much less can particular environmental stimuli. What meaning do they have to this unique individual? In our account of Murray's theory we shall see how he handled this problem and provided a systematic way of conceptualizing the environment so that its many-sided meanings for particular individuals could nevertheless be understood in a coherent theoretical framework. Ninety pages into writing his text about the variables of personality, Murray observed (1938, p. 230), "No one who has had the patience to read through this section can be expected to come away from it now with a clear head." He knew what an overwhelming array of ideas he had put on paper.

But, what is the alternative to profusion? If life *is* complicated, if personality *is* made up of numberless events, each event formed through the convergence of myriad influences, then how can any simple account of it be adequate? Murray observed that many people find comfort when an author explains all personality or all behavior as a result of some one single factor. Those same people, he said, become disinterested and bored if too many things are mentioned. He defended his own approach by saying that life is even more complicated than his theory. He said that people who are serious about the study of personality must be prepared to work hard at memorizing and comprehending the many concepts required; they should study to the point where the concepts are simply part of their nervous systems, concepts which pop into consciousness appropriately without effort.

The richness of Murray's theory accounts for the wide use to which it has been put. Clinical and experimental psychologists all over the world continue to use profitably both the ideas and the instruments of assessment which flowed from Murray's theory. But he was right about the reader's head. No one can keep a clear head about *all* the concepts in his theory, particularly at an introductory level. So the description given in this chapter will be greatly condensed and simplified. Instead of describing every single need and press that Murray distinguished we shall examine just four groups of needs, with greater attention to just two needs in each set. Following the discussion of needs we shall look at the theory of press, thema, and complex. Then we shall examine an array of applications.

The Theory of Needs

Murray believed even more strongly than Freud did that a person's major motivating forces consist of needs. A need is a force which influences a person to see things and do things in such a way that an unsatisfying situation is changed into a satisfying one. An example is the case of Earnst, an engineering student who ran out of money before he could complete his training. Earnst had a strong need to be autonomous, which overrode his desire for education (Murray, 1938, p. 617), and he refused to seek help from anyone.

A need is not active all the time. Commonly it becomes active only under certain stimulation. The stimulation may come from within the person's body, as when stomach contractions let us know we are hungry. Or it may come from the outside, as in those instances where someone puts us down and we need to defend or reassert ourselves. An aroused need causes us to look for ways of satisfying it. It activates thoughts and imagination, and triggers actions. If we are hungry we might head for a restaurant or make a peanut butter and jelly sandwich. If somebody puts us down, we might lie awake at night thinking about it all and dreaming up

ways to get even or to put ourselves back up again.

Needs often rise up, are satisfied, and then subside, only to rise up again later. The need for food is obviously one good example, stimulated by internal changes. Needs stimulated by outer events usually are less rhythmic and can often be repeated. For example, you might be in an environment where you are constantly challenged to put forth your best performance possible, whether in athletics, school work, or whatever. Such pressures would then frequently arouse your need to achieve something, to excel. So this need would rise and subside and rise again, perhaps irregularly.

Needs may *fuse* together. That is, in the course of living, a particular person may always have two or more needs rising or subsiding together—both able to be satisfied by a single situational event. For example, many people satisfy their need to be looked after and their need for a sexual relationship through marriage or living together. Two needs are fused in the sense that satisfaction of the one also provides satisfaction of the other. Those who make a living doing something that others acclaim (acting, music, art, professional boxing, golfing, football, and so on) probably have their needs to make money and to obtain recognition in a state of fusion. Other needs would sometimes be fused also as, for instance, the need to excel, the need for esthetic expression, or the need to express aggression or to dominate others.

Needs may be connected through a process Murray called *subsidiation*—that is, one need (a subsidiary goal) serves another need (the determining goal). Murray gives the example of a politician who needs to win friends (need for affiliation) in order to be elected to office (need for achievement). In our own lives we know how one need subsidiates to another. We need to achieve on this test in order to get into college. We need to get into college in order to make friends. We need friends in order to find a place in life. Or we need college in order to get to graduate school. We need graduate school in order to get a Ph.D. We need a Ph.D. in order to get a job as a research scientist. We need the job to satisfy our curiosity. . . .

We have mentioned numerous needs. Is there a separate need for every little goal in life? Murray believed that there were twenty main needs, several lesser needs, and several general attributes which, he said, "may be variously described as dimensions, functions, vectors, modes, or traits of personality" (1938, p. 25). An example of attributes would be the tendency to be impulsive about things rather than being deliberate. In regard to needs, Murray proposed that quite a few needs function at an unconscious level. He called these *latent* needs.

Four Groups of Needs

The latest research (using the methods of factor analysis described in chapter 11) shows that several needs are linked in the ways Murray suggested. In listing the main needs, Murray grouped them according to various associations. For example, he grouped together (1938, p. 151):

n Dominance	n Deference
n Autonomy	n Abasement
n Aggression	

The three on the left, he said, are in some way opposed to the two on the right. Thus those who need to dominate others must find others who need to be deferent. Leaders must find followers. Those who do not wish to be led or even to lead have a strong need to be on their own, a need for autonomy (n Autonomy). When dominance is insufficient to achieve its goals, aggression is aroused to supplement it; n Aggression may easily fuse with

n Dominance. But the opposite of aggression is seen in the need to submit passively to the force of others: n Abasement. Those traits on the left seem to form a group different from those on the right, although n Autonomy drops out. Elsewhere, however, (1938, p. 242) Murray linked n Dominance and n Aggression with n Exhibition, the need to show off. These three form the essential components of the broad trait of *ascendance*, he said.

In regard to deference and abasement, Murray suggested that there is something adaptive about them. He pointed out that quite often people are deferent to those above them and dominant toward those below them in some hierarchy of authority. Moreover, he wrote that "the average subject is deferent only when the action suggested by the leader conforms to his own system of needs" (1938, p. 152). This quality of adaptiveness is also found in the grouping of deference and abasement found in recent research. The need to help and look after others (n Nurturance) is also found in this group; and there is no doubt adaptive significance in this need.

Murray grouped a number of needs and general attributes together under the notion of stability, rigidity, or organization. These included the need to keep things in order (n Order), the tendency to prefer sameness as against change, the tendency to be coherent and well organized versus being disorganized and confused, the tendency to be deliberate rather than impulsive, and the tendency to be calm or placid rather than emotional about things. Murray believed that these factors quite often go together, the more orderly person being more placid, for example. Research in recent years supports his conclusion.

Another collection of needs that Murray proposed has also found some support recently. He suggested that the needs for erotic attachment (n Sex), for play (n Play), for sensuous pleasures (n Sentience), and for showing off (n Exhibition) formed a loosely connected group. We shall refer to this group as *sensuous expression.*

We shall deal, then, with these four groups of related needs: ascendance, deference, orderliness, and sensuous expression.

Ascendance. Murray states that the trait of ascendance breaks up into three needs: n Dominance (to lead and guide), n Exhibition (to show off in public), and n Aggression (to attack or overcome opposition).

Need for dominance is more fully described as a need to control and influence others. The more dominant person has feelings of confidence as he or she directs others, tells them what to do, decides arguments, and so on. The dominant person is always a top dog, or at least wants and tries to be. According to Murray the most common fusion of n Dominance is with n Aggression, as in forcing someone to do something under threat, or in enforcing the law. But it may also fuse with n Exhibition (as in being very forceful in public), or with n Achievement when the individual seeks to achieve results as a group leader.

The n Exhibition involves a desire to make an impression, to show off and entertain or intrigue other people. The very exhibitionistic person tends to be vain and feel exceptionally self-confident. This need may fuse with n Achievement as in striving for excellence in some public performance; also with n Sentience in, for example, the display of beauty.

Deference. Murray defines n Deference as a wish to give admiration and support to a superior, as well as obedience and praise. The very deferent person may feel respectful and be compliant and obliging. When fused with n Abasement, the deference becomes a need to serve someone who is very dominant. Fused with the need to help other people,

n Nurturance, it becomes a need to give praise in order to help someone get over a bad feeling.

It is not easy to understand how people would have a real need to abase themselves. But apparently many do. Murray said that n Abasement is a wish to submit to external force, to surrender, to admit defeat. It is also a need to lower oneself, to blame or belittle oneself; and also to receive blame and even punishment. Have you ever known anyone like that? Sometimes persons like that are said to be gluttons for punishment.

The person who is high on n Abasement is likely to have feelings of being very humble, helpless, or hopeless. Such people also are quite likely to feel guilty before they are accused and whether or not they have done anything to be guilty about. When fused with n Sex, of course, n Abasement becomes very clearly masochism, the tendency to need punishment and pain before being able to experience sexual gratification. Such were some of the men who came to the brothel in Steinbeck's *East of Eden.* Apparently some liked to be trampled on by sharp-heeled boots.

Orderliness. This large group includes the need for order and other general attributes: preferring sameness over change, being organized versus being confused, being deliberate rather than impulsive, and being placid rather than emotional.

Murray defines n Order as a need to keep things in order and to set them straight if they are in disorder. The person high in this need likes to keep everything clean and tidy, precisely arranged, just so. Disorder produces feelings of disgust in this person. It may fuse with several other needs, but it is particularly related to n Construction, which includes building and organizing things and even creative writing (Murray, 1938, p. 354). It is also related to conscience and scrupulousness, the

Freudian concept of superego (see chapters 9, 10, 11).

The contrast between being organized and being confused is called *Conjunctivity versus Disjunctivity* in Murray's theory. The conjunctive person has it all together—is organized, coordinated, sticks to a plan once chosen, is methodical and systematic in everyday living. By contrast the disjunctive person lacks clear purposes in life and the ability to stay with one line of thought or activity. This person is likely to go from one thing to another during the day without much plan or concerted action.

Sensuous Expression. Murray thought that sensuous expression included a rather loose grouping of needs. In the group is n Sentience, which is defined as the wish for sensuous impressions and pleasures, including erotic and esthetic feelings and experiences. These can be in the perception of beautiful landscapes, pictures, paintings, and so on; the experiencing of music and poetry; or of delicious foods and fragrant perfumes. The erotic component is evidenced in the need for sexual intercourse and an erotic relationship, but shows itself also in sheer enjoyment of the opposite sex, delight in parties, dancing, and so on. Sensuous pleasure can also be sought through movement, as in dancing, skating, or diving.

There is a wide range of possible fusions: with n Affiliation (for romantic love), with n Aggression (for sadism), with n Cognition (for sexual curiosity or Peeping Tom tendencies in excessive cases), with n Nurturance (for nurturant love), with n Sex, and so on. Need for Sentience may also fuse with n Exhibition to provide joy in giving an artistic performance of some kind, or joy in looking and feeling beautiful. Many people like to dress up at least occasionally and to go out looking and feeling their best.

Environmental Pressures

Murray did not conceive of needs as existing in a vacuum, but rather as existing within the context of the environment. Every person in the world is in an environment, and adaptation to that environment is a necessary condition of existence. Many of our needs arise directly in response to events in the environment, such as a change of temperature or a sudden threat. Murray conceived of the environment as exerting pressures on the individual. He called these pressures *press*. Murray referred to press as follows (press is indicated by p):

p Inferior person
p Coercion, physical restraint
p Opposition, ridicule

p Superior person
p Aggressive, dominant person

These press are likely to arouse relevant needs:

p Inferior	$\rightarrow$	n Dominance
p Coercion	$\rightarrow$	n Autonomy
p Opposition	$\rightarrow$	n Aggression
p Superior person	$\rightarrow$	n Deference
p Aggressive person	$\rightarrow$	n Abasement

The first instance (p Inferior $\rightarrow$ n Dominance) means, of course, that a person with high n Dominance, say, an army officer, is likely to have that need triggered by the appearance of an inferior. For example, when a captain encounters a private, he expects the enlisted man to salute and to be deferential; the officer's need for dominance is aroused at the sight of the private. Similarly a man's need for autonomy is apt to be aroused especially when someone is trying to coerce him. A woman's aggressive need is likely to be activated when some opposition or frustration blocks her intentions. Someone with a high need for deference is likely to respond readily to a new acquaintance who has a commanding air. Great leaders presumably command their followers largely through the needs for deference that those followers have.

But the followers themselves are not entirely passive. With high needs for the expression of deference, they are likely to seek out a social or a job situation in which their need can be gratified. They are not simply passively receiving the press of whatever environment they happen to be in. In the fulfilling of almost all needs people do partly arrange for the press they encounter, as when one goes to a party hoping that some attractive person of the opposite sex will stimulate the need for sex.

Alpha and Beta Press

Murray makes an important distinction between the environment as it may be objectively described by social scientists, and the press that come to affect individuals in a special way. Some individuals are unmoved by the force of a great orator; it is likely that they have a very low need for deference. Some people manage to accept opposition calmly, as if it is nothing more than they expected on a fine summer's day. They do not react aggressively. Presumably they have very low need for aggression, and do not see the opposition as frustrating. Yet it is one and the same orator; one and the same opposition. Other thousands flock to hear the famed speaker, other millions would fight the opposition.

Murray analyzed this problem in the following way. The objective environment is determinable in some way that would be agreed to by independent observers. For example, the thermometer might read 95 degrees F. in the shade. That would be the objective pressure upon all individuals present. Murray called this the *alpha press*. But some individuals feel oppressed by the heat; others find it tolerable. That is, individuals experience heat differently. Murray called the press as experienced by an individual the *beta press*. For all possible press in the environment there would be an alpha aspect which is objectively determinable and a beta aspect which must be determined separately for each individual.

Social stimuli are especially subject to differences in interpretation. That is, the beta press may have much greater range for social stimuli than for physical stimuli. For example, at a hotel, you call to reserve a tennis court. They answer: "We'd love to have you come play." How would you see this remark? Is it an act of endearment, expressing a great need for affiliation by being especially nice to you? Assuming the tone of voice was truly enthusiastic, would you believe it reflected pride in the hotel's beautiful court which the management is eager to have people see (high n Exhibition)? Would you perhaps find the remark a bit overdone and therefore vaguely threatening? However you would see this remark, that would be the beta press for you.

Social stimuli are what other people do to us. Much of the press that we experience day in and day out comes from persons. Early in the morning people rise up and begin complaining, ordering, asking, demanding, threatening, pleading, impressing, showing off, telling, teaching, helping, supporting, nursing, fixing, deceiving, enticing, seducing, chasing, attacking, defending, admiring, loving, and obeying other people. Some of these *proceedings* (as Murray, 1959, calls them) extend over long periods of time. The long-drawn-out trial is an example, in which one group is attacking one or more others, who are in turn defending themselves or their interests, prosecution versus the defense.

The environment of each one of us, then, is filled with press from other people. But we in turn exert demands and other pressures upon *them*. Even as we go forth at dawn (or whenever we go forth) filled with our needs for dominance, abasement, achievement, nurturance, or whatever, so must there be going forth some other person toward whom we can express our need. Each need must find its appropriate press. If we are filled with n Affiliation one morning we must find someone else who is likely to respond favorably or even press us to give them affiliation. To be friendly you have to find someone who needs a friend. If you have high n Abasement you will have to find someone who will provide the appropriate press of putting you down.

Murray suggests (1959) that there are two kinds of people: transmittors and receptors. The transmittors are those who bring more press to bear upon others. The receptors are those who are more likely to be simply responsive to the press that others bring. As an example, there are those who actively seek out persons who are in need of help; others simply respond helpfully if someone comes along needing it.

Thema, Thematic Disposition, and Complex: Organizations of Need and Press

Need and press, the most elementary units in Murray's theory, are commonly found to be organized in higher-order structures of dispositions. The simplest of these structures are called themas. A *thema* is a unit which consists of one need meeting one press. Here are some examples. Joe smelled the apple pie cooking (press) and realized he was hungry (need). Ann was feeling lonely (need) and she found a friend in Erika who was lonely too (press). The general exhorted his troops to fight harder for victory (press) and they obeyed (need for deference). Toni likes to speak in public (need) and was delighted when the class asked her to be the leader in their debate with an opposing team (press). Each of these four proceedings has just one unit, one thema, a junction of a press and a need.

Thematic Disposition

Some persons are always being asked to speak in public. Others are always exhorting others to try harder. Yet others are always feeling lonely. Murray says that such characteristics of a person's encounters with the environment are the essential building blocks of personality. He calls them *thematic dispositions*. The person has a disposition to be engaged in a particular kind of thema, a particular kind of need-press exchange. Murray says that these thematic dispositions are the most important "energic components of personality" (1959, p. 34), and in the section on the accomplishments of Murray's theory, below, we shall see a number of examples of thematic dispositions as evaluated by a psychological testing device specially designed for such assessment.

Complexes

Murray described an organization of two or more thematic dispositions as an integration of the component needs. A *need-integrate*, he wrote (1938, p. 747), is "a complex of one or more needs with the images that depict the common objects and actones associated with these tendencies." *Actone* is Murray's term for patterns of action, both motor actions and verbal ones. Thus the *integrate* is a connected set of needs plus images (thoughts, inner representations) of the objects and actions typically associated (in the individual's mind) with satisfaction of the needs. Elsewhere Murray (1938, p. 363) gave a special meaning to the term *complex,* saying that it is the kind of *need-integrate* that is unconscious and is derived from one of the five major sources of infantile pleasure as described by Freud and other psychoanalysts: 1) the security of the womb, 2) sucking at the breast, 3) freely enjoyed defecation, 4) the sensations of urinating, 5) the excitations of genital friction. According to psychoanalytic theory (see chapter 11) the interruption of such pleasures (for example, by birth, or by weaning) is liable to produce permanent consequences in the personality. In Murray's treatment of these consequences they are seen as enduring *integrates* of needs, *actones,* and a certain type of object.

For example, without implying that there is a wish to return to the womb as such, Murray notes that some individuals continue as adults to prefer womb-like places. He calls this the *claustral complex,* the word *claustra* referring to places that are "small, warm, dark, secluded, safe, private, or concealing" (1938, pp. 383-384). A person with this complex finds such objects attractive or tends to build them if they are not otherwise available. They may enter into the person's dreams as a castle, a cave, a secret place, a cabin, and so on. As a child such a person might like to spend time hiding in a closet, under a table or bed, and so on. As an adult, the individual with a claustral complex is likely to seek a home which is secluded. And whatever home the individual lives in is likely to be an object of such great attachment that he or she cannot bear to give it up and move. In addition, there is likely to be an attachment to the mother in a dependent way. These persons are commonly homesick when away from home, particularly if they are extraverts.

The needs active in the claustral complex are n Passivity, n Harmavoidance, n Seclusion, and n Succorance. Satisfaction of passivity is achieved by sleeping a lot, and the actones involved include curling up as in the fetal position. The need for Harmavoidance is the need to avoid shock, danger, loud noises, and to be free from pain and guaranteed against loss of support. Murray says that n Harmavoidance uses n Succorance as a subsidiary since the presence of another,

supportive, human being can mediate satisfaction for n Harmavoidance. Such a supporting other person can even help gratify the need for Seclusion by serving as a barrier between the individual and others, thereby protecting the individual's privacy.

Accomplishments of Murray's Theory

We have already mentioned the wide range of applications to which Murray's theory has been put, including assessments for selection of personnel for the Office of Strategic Services (1948) and a variety of uses in clinical, personality, and experimental psychology. Many of these uses have involved the original form or some variation of the Thematic Apperception Test (TAT), which Murray originated in collaboration with Christiana Morgan (Morgan and Murray, 1935; Murray, 1943). It will be recalled that needs stimulate not only actions but also thoughts and imagination, and this principle is used to study the needs and press experienced by a person through the medium of imaginative stories that the person makes up.

Figure 3.1. A picture like one of those in the TAT series

The TAT

In the Thematic Apperception Test, the subject is presented with a series of pictures, something like the one shown in figure 3.1. For each picture the person must tell a story about what led up to the present situation, what the persons involved are thinking and feeling, and how it will all turn out. From the stories it is possible for the trained inter-viewer to begin to interpret the major *thematic dispositions* which characterize the storyteller. It is assumed that the storyteller projects his or her own personality onto the characters in each story.

Box 3.1 presents two stories told by a patient in the course of taking the TAT. The predominant theme is that of n Aggression, in response to the press of failure to express

---

Box 3.1

Two Stories Told for TAT Cards by a Hospitalized Patient, Mrs. T., in Response to Cards 1 and 14 of the TAT Series, and their Interpretations.

TAT 1—Boy with Violin

Reaction Time 12"   Total Time 52"

Uh—this child—uh—[sigh] has been study-ing music for a few years. He can hear it—hear lovely sounds in his head, but he can't get them to come out of his violin. At the time of this picture, he's sitting there very unhappy, because he can hear the sounds, but he can't create anything himself. And—uh—so he gets up and he—and very frus-trated, he smashes his violin.

Interpretation. One of the most striking con-tent features of this story is the passivity and lack of action at the outset of the response. It is not until the very end that there appears an impulsive eruption of affect and aggression. As was suggested earlier in the WAIS [Wechsler Adult Intelligence Scale], here too we see an initial passivity and inaction which is followed by strong action. In this instance, however, there is an indication that this activity can have a strong aggressive quality. Whether she is likely to act in an openly aggressive manner is as yet not clear. But this theme seems to be persistent.

The statement, "has been studying music for a few years," is an indication of a broader time dimension and concern with the past than one commonly sees on this card, on which the boy is usually described as having gotten the violin recently. But the extended time span is accom-panied by an emphasis on the lack of accom-plishment: "he can't get them to come out of his violin," which has a noteworthy depressive qual-ity. The juxtaposition of the unhappiness about

hearing the sounds but not being able to get them out of his violin reflects a state of tension and a longing for an active role which is finally and only expressed through violent, volcanic ac-tivity.

TAT 14—Silhouette of a Person Against a Window

Reaction Time: 2"   Total Time: 46"

This man is an artist and he has studied art for many years, but he can't—he's very rest-less, very unhappy. He can't paint like he wants to. He's standing near the window watching the sun go down. And he's very dissatisfied with the slovenly way in which he's living. And—uh—he jumps out of the window. That's it.

Interpretation. The story on this card is almost a repetition of what she told to Card 1. Again we hear of somebody who has studied hard for many years, but is unable to produce in the way he wishes to. The depressive quality is striking in her description of the man as standing near the window watching the sun go down, and es-pecially in the culmination of the story when he jumps out of the window.

In these [first four] stories, there has not been a single comment about a good, warm re-lationship between people. Two of the four stories have had direct themes of death and suicide. Her TAT stories are becoming somewhat monothe-matic, which indicates the extent to which these issues preoccupy her and represent her limited ability to employ fully her current skills, and creative capabilities. (Allison, Blatt & Zimet, 1968, 115-116)

---

personal abilities. It should be emphasized that the TAT is designed to reveal unconscious needs and associated thematic dispositions or complexes.

In box 3.1 the use of the TAT is shown in a clinical application: the understanding of a patient's dynamic problems. The TAT has often been used also in the scientific study of normal personality, and this was its original application by Murray and Morgan.

In the case of Earnst (Murray, 1938, pp. 673-680), Morgan was responsible for administering and interpreting the TAT to a young engineering student who had come from a hard, impoverished background. He suffered from lack of money and had to drop out of school before completing studies in order to get a job. His TAT stories were filled with lacks: of water, food, support, and so on. In his early life he had been forced to work long hours on the farm and, for this and other reasons, he deeply resented his father. He also feared his father, who was a powerful man. Earnst said that he and all the other children were afraid of what their father might do to them when he got drunk.

Four of Earnst's stories contained the theme of p Dominance (Coercion) → n Aggression. In one story a little boy, the son of a factory worker, feels there is something wrong at the factory and he wants to get out and get an education. He manages to become educated and returns to teach the workers that they are oppressed and that the financiers who control them must be overthrown. The boy said that the owner of the factories had great power and exploited the workers, made them do anything he wanted them to do, and they could not fight back. In this story the thematic p Coercion appears in the power of the owner and his forcing of the workers. The n Aggression is seen in the hero's instigation of revolt.

In another story, Earnst told about a hyp-notist who got a young man in his power and then sought to extract from him the combination to a safe in which large amounts of money were kept. Here again, the older man is forcing the younger man (p Coercion). But the story continues with the older man being apprehended and arrested for robbery. Earnst's n Aggression shows this time in the arm of justice.

A third story told by Earnst for a TAT picture has a young bank clerk in debt to an older man. The latter tries to get the young man into some shady deal, but is resisted. The young man will find some way to get out of the old man's power, perhaps by strangling him and throwing the body into the water somewhere. Once again there is p Dominance via p Coercion and this elicits n Aggression, namely murder. Yet another story showing the same theme tells of an old miser who employs a young man to help him bilk an old lady of some money. Somehow she sees through the plan and calls the police. This is the second time that n Aggression is realized through law enforcement.

All through his early life, then, Earnst had lived with the thema of p Dominance (p Coercion) → n Aggression. The press came especially from his father. In the course of telling a few stories for TAT pictures this same theme is repeated four times in various guises. Murray would say that it had become one of the main energic components of Earnst's personality: a thematic disposition.

Like every other subject in the study, Earnst was given a large number of other psychological tests and interviews. All of the results were pooled in a final conference. The thematic disposition of p Coercion → n Aggression was believed to be part of a *predator* thema, in which Earnst unconsciously thought that his father had robbed both Earnst and his mother of food and adequate sustenance, as a result of which his mother had died when

Earnst was young; Earnst himself was under-nourished. This was one of four unconscious themes that formed an overall unity-theme which seemed to be characteristic of Earnst at the time of assessment: Deprivation press produce lacks in his life (of food, water, comfort, and interesting entertainment); these lacks give rise to anxiety; Earnst strives to solve it through aggression and isolated self-sufficiency. In his daily life he has no communication with any of his family, lives alone, and spends almost all his time working.

Questionnaires

Murray and his co-workers used a number of questionnaires in their 1938 study. They found, however, that subjects often gave desirable answers rather than accurate ones. Murray found that Earnst, for example, "marked himself *up* on 'desirable' variables" (1938, p. 650). In subsequent years investigators have attempted to construct questionnaires that would be free of this problem.

In the Edwards Personal Preference Schedule (EPPS), fifteen needs are measured, including Achievement, Dominance, and Nurturance (Edwards, 1959). Each need is measured by a series of items which ask the subject to choose between two statements. For example,

A. I try to do the best I can in whatever I do.
B. I like to help people whenever I have the opportunity.

Alternative "A" would indicate a preference for Achievement, "B" a preference for Nurturance. Each pair of items in the EPPS was selected so that the value of "desirability" was roughly equal in the two items.

The scores obtained on the EPPS tend to be quite stable over a one-week interval, with estimates of reliability for the separate scales ranging between .74 and .88. Validity seems good in many cases. For example, Bernadin

and Jessor (1957) showed that subjects who scored high on n Deference and low on n Autonomy (and were therefore dependent personalities) were very much more likely to ask for assistance and reassurance in an experimental situation, and critical comments about their performance tended to interfere with their learning ability.

Milton and Lipetz (1968) questioned whether the needs measured by the EPPS are grouped together meaningfully. They studied males and females separately and found similar groupings in each study. Their methods were correlation and factor analysis (a technique described in chapter 11). They found the ascendance group clearly present: n Dominance, n Exhibition, and n Aggression. They found the deference group, with n Deference, n Abasement, and n Nurturance going together. The orderliness group comprised n Order and n Endurance. This latter need, as measured by the EPPS, refers to finishing jobs, persisting until a task is completed, and so on. It thus comes close to the meaning of Conjunctivity, namely being well-organized. Milton and Lipetz also found a group which consisted of n Sex, n Aggression, and n Succorance, the latter being the need to have people care for you. Since n Sentience is not one of the needs measured by the EPPS, the Sensuous Expression grouping could not be proved. Thus three of the patterns of needs appear to have confirmation in recent research with the EPPS: ascendance, deference, and orderliness.

Another questionnaire recently developed is the *Activities Index* (AI), as reported by Stern (1958, 1970). The subjects indicate simply whether they like or dislike various activities. The items are scored in terms of 30 variables, most of which are derived from Murray's theory. Among the variables of the AI Stern reports the following groupings, based on a sample of more than 1,000 male and female students. The ascendance group appears in the variables of n Dominance, n Exhibition, and n Aggression. The deference group appears in the linkage of n Deference, n Abasement, and n Nurturance. Stern also has a measure of *adaptiveness*, which correlates .60 with the deference group, thereby emphasizing what Murray had suspected, namely that deference is often adaptive. The orderliness group appears in Stern's results (1970, p. 48), and includes almost all of the needs and general attributes Murray had suggested: n Order, Sameness, Conjunctivity, and Deliberateness. The sensuous expression group likewise appears well substantiated, but it is indeed a loose grouping, as Murray had supposed. In Stern's results it comprises n Sex, n Sentience, n Play, and n Exhibition, along with the attribute of Emotionality. Some other needs also join this grouping (technically known as a "second-order factor"): n Narcissism, n Supplication (similar to n Succorance), and n Affiliation.

There may be some advantages to Stern's groupings. For one thing, they are easier to handle than Murray's because they are fewer in number. Also, when such groupings can be found and measured repeatedly, the measurements tend to have greater reliability and validity. One set of results with groupings will be of special interest to all who are involved in the women's movement. On the EPPS, Edwards (1959, p. 10) reported that a sample of nearly 5,000 women and 4,000 men had the following mean scores in the ascendance group, indicating a consistent pattern of differences:

	Women	Men
n Dominance	10.2	14.5
n Exhibition	11.5	12.8
n Aggression	10.2	13.1

Many of the analyses reported by Stern (1970) were originally carried out by Saunders (1969). Saunders calculated a combined score on the ascendance group for each subject. There were roughly 500 males and 500 females. He found a statistically significant difference between the sexes, with the males higher on ascendance.

Yet another questionnaire, the *Personality Research Form,* has recently been developed in accordance with Murray's theory (Jackson, 1967). This test has items which describe the self, and the subject simply checks whether each item truly describes himself or herself. This test also shows males higher on ascendance. Samples of more than 1,000 men and 1,000 women showed the following results (Jackson, 1967, p. 30):

	Women	Men
n Dominance	8.7	11.1
n Exhibition	9.7	10.8
n Aggression	5.9	7.9

In the years to come it will be interesting to see whether the women's movement changes this consistent difference between the personalities of men and women as revealed in the measured constructs of Murray's theory.

Tradition of Research: The Need for Achievement

We single out the need for achievement to illustrate the development of a research tradition based upon just one of Murray's need constructs. Murray stated that n Achievement (n Ach) may fuse with any other need, since it is "the desire to do things as rapidly and/or as well as possible" (Murray, 1938, p. 164). It means also the desire to accomplish something difficult, to master problems and situations, to excel, and especially to compete successfully with others.

David C. McClelland was responsible for much of the beginning work aimed at intensive measurement of n Ach (1951). The first objective was to obtain a measure which would be reliable and have straightforward scoring. Four pictures were used. Two were from the TAT and two were new ones, showing respectively a child studying and two men working. Subjects were shown the pictures one at a time by slide projection; thus whole groups of subjects could be tested at one time. They were given instructions similar to those for the TAT and told to write a brief story about the picture—what was happening, what led up to the present situation, what people were thinking, and how it would turn out. These points were preprinted on the response sheets to guide subjects, and five minutes was allowed per story. Within thirty minutes the entire measurement procedure could be completed. The experimenters would then have four written stories from each subject under standard conditions. To score the stories for n Ach they developed a definition: Any statement in a story which suggested that someone was trying to excel or compete with some standard of excellence would receive one point for achievement imagery. In other words, stories were regarded as collections of indicators of fantasy or imagery, and so the score obtained was one of n Ach as revealed in the subject's fantasy productions.

If the measure of n Ach really reflects motivation to achieve, then it should be responsive to conditions which invite the subject to strive for excellence. It was found repeatedly that subjects taking the test under neutral conditions ("to obtain normative data") scored significantly lower than subjects taking the test under *ego-involving* conditions ("This is a test of intelligence" or "of leadership ability").

Once a sound measure had been developed it was possible to investigate numerous hypotheses concerned with the effects of different strengths of achievement motivation. Lowell (1952) showed that subjects with higher n Ach not only solved more anagrams than did those with lower n Ach, but they also improved their performance over a series of four-minute periods of working at this task. This suggests strongly that the high n Ach subjects looked for and found ways to improve their performance, while the others did not. It might be expected that school grades would similarly reflect achievement motivation, and this has been found for high school students (Ricciuti and Sadacca, 1955; Rosen, 1956), but not for college students (Cole et al., 1962). Of course, intellectual capability would also determine grades, and quite likely would overshadow differences in n Ach, especially if the group were highly selected in the first place; everyone has to go to high school, but probably most of those who go on to college are quite high in n Ach.

Birney (whose excellent review of research on achievement motivation, 1968, should be consulted) has pointed out that the research began to divide into two different traditions around 1960. One group continued to study the characteristics of high achievers (see McClelland, 1961); the other group probed further into the nature of the need and of the processes involved in its arousal (see Atkinson and Feather, 1966). In this latter tradition, the emphasis has been upon deeper understanding of the total motivational process, especially in situations involving risk. When people are confronted with a challenge and asked to estimate their chances for success, what factors influence the estimate? Atkinson and Feather say that no less than six factors are involved. The first three are strength of n Ach, the incentive value of succeeding, the person's subjective judgment of the likelihood of actually succeeding; the last three are strength of the person's motivation to avoid failure (a kind of negative n Ach), the negative incentive value (or amount of displeasure) in failing, and the person's subjective judgment of the probability of failing. The first three factors are multiplied together and the last three factors are multiplied together; the product of the last three is then subtracted from the product of the first three. This means the first three factors define a tendency to approach success (T_s) and the last three factors define a tendency to avoid failure (T_{-f}); subtracting yields a resultant achievement-oriented tendency (T_r):

$$T_r = T_s - T_{-f}$$

These formulations allow some quite unexpected predictions. For example, it is predictable that persons whose T_{-f} is stronger than T_s for a particular range of tasks (and therefore in whom T_r is *negative* in value) will tend to avoid intermediate degrees of risk. Such people will always give either a very low estimate of their chances or an unrealistically high estimate. Among other tests of this prediction, the study by Inkson (1971) showed that English high school students who scored low on the TAT measure of n Ach gave their aspirations for occupational achievement in accordance with the hypothesis: they selected either low-status occupations or "celebrity" occupations (such as astronaut or auto racer). By contrast those with high n Ach selected middle-status occupations such as business or engineering.

Neither the *high-achiever* tradition of research nor the *motivational process* tradition shows any sign of passing into the annals of history. Indeed the most recent factor-analytic work of Jackson et al. (1976) shows clear evidence for no less than *six* different kinds of achievement motivation: *status with experts, acquisitiveness* (money as a symbol of achievement), *achievement via independence* ("doing it my way"), *status with peers, competitiveness,* and *striving for excellence.* Each kind of achievement motivation was measured by five different methods, including questionnaire and

self-rating methods. Accordingly we may expect yet another broadening of research on achievement motivation as these different well-measured varieties of n Ach are studied in relation to risk-taking, learning, performance, grades, and other important criteria. It is as though Henry Murray started a small high mountain spring that has grown in size until it is now streaming down in a system of several major rivers.

Critique of Murray's Theory

Two main criticisms have been directed at Murray's theory. The first is that it is too complex; the second holds that the research stimulated by Murray and by his theory does not follow as a direct consequence of that theory.

Is Murray's theory too complex? One needs a yardstick against which to measure what is too complex and what is too simple. Murray himself believed that a complex subject matter deserves a complex treatment. Thus he used the yardstick of human personality itself against which to evaluate his theory. If personality is nothing less than an entire human life (as he once defined personality), then obviously a complex theory is appropriate. Anything simpler would probably be an oversimplification. Murray believed that a simple account of personality is inadequate, no matter how popular it might be.

As to the second criticism, it seems to require the possibility of strict logical derivation from theory to research. This can only be achieved if the theory is set out in a completely formal manner, with primitive terms, basic postulates or assumptions, definitions, hypotheses, and theorems all stated in explicit logical form, preferably with mathematical symbolism. But hardly any psychological theories are formulated with this degree of formal specification. In a poll of major theorists done by Sigmund Koch in the late 1950s (Koch, *Psychology: A Study of a Science*, 1959), it was found that a majority of the theorists opposed attempts to formalize their theories. Murray was one of them. The task of writing a formally exact statement of theory, he said, "calls for meticulous criticism of one's own speech, semantic niceties, over-elegant definitions. Should not criticism and refinement be in balance with spontaneity, exploration, and invention if a science is to grow in a way and at a pace appropriate to its age?" (Murray, 1959, p. 8). Thus Murray himself rejected the suggestion that his theory ought to be more formally stated.

What position should we take on these two criticisms and the answer that Murray gives? I would answer as Murray did, that a complex subject matter deserves a complex theory. On the other hand, if science cannot achieve some simplification through theoretical work, it will wallow forever in a welter of complex facts. Nevertheless it is important that whatever simplification is introduced should not distort the account of reality provided; it should not be inaccurate. Thus accuracy, not simplicity, is the first criterion of importance. If you cannot be accurate without being complex, then you have to be complex. Oversimplification is precisely the achievement of simplicity at the expense of accuracy. It was to such efforts that Murray was opposed.

On the matter of formalizing theories, it is once again a question of whether the formalism is purchased at the price of accuracy. A highly formal, mathematical theory is not thereby guaranteed to be accurate. Indeed Laplace formulated an elegant mathematical theory of "caloric" (see Brush, 1965), which was supposed to be a substance responsible for the phenomena of heat. Laplace's fine work, however, did not demonstrate the ac-

curacy of the theory of caloric, nor did it delay the abandonment of the theory once it was clearly found to be inaccurate.

The requirement for formal, logical derivations from theory to research also can conflict with the requirement of simplicity. In psychology, for example, a notable instance of strictly formal development of a theory was that of Clark Hull and his associates (Hull et al., 1940) who formulated an elegant mathematico-deductive theory of rote learning. At the time it was hailed by many as the model of the future. But it is now generally recognized that it was too complicated despite its elegant logic. Marx and Hillix say: "The postulational structure that was necessary to encompass the area of rote learning was so formidable that the model has aroused more amazement than interest on the part of psychologists. The model was too complex and unwieldy to be of much use, even if it had provided significant predictive advances over those possible from simpler empirical generalizations" (1973, p. 434). Yet another effort at formal development of theory was made by Lewin (see chapter 19), and it, too, failed to be of especial utility in its formal aspects.

Formalism can be appropriate for some topics and not others; it can be a definite hindrance, if not irrelevant. Not all criteria for evaluating theories should be taken seriously; some are ill-conceived. It is not intended here to criticize the use of formalism in theory-construction wherever that might be appropriate, as indeed it is in a number of areas of psychology such as signal-detection theory. The point to be made is that some theories do not lend themselves to formalism.

Bunge (1963) has examined carefully all the meanings of the word "simplicity" as used in science, and finds that for the most part the word has lost all usefulness. In particular it is useless to apply it to scientific theories and evaluate their simplicity or complexity without regard to their accuracy. A theory may be very simple and very wrong. A theory may also be very elegant from a formal point of view and yet be inaccurate. Its degree of formalism does not affect its accuracy, although in some cases it might make it easier to test whether the theory is accurate or not in crucial respects. But if formalism gets to the point of being a source of amazement rather than assistance to scientists, it can detract from the fruitfulness of a theory.

It appears, then, that *accuracy* and *fruitfulness* are the most important criteria for evaluating theory. In chapter 6 we shall take up this question of criteria more fully. But for the present it seems reasonable to evaluate Murray's theory primarily on these two criteria.

When we consider the criterion of accuracy, it appears that Murray's theory is accurate in terms of identifying needs, groups of needs, and relationships among need constructs and other variables. The research cited above gives ample testimony to this effect. Yet some of the most central constructs such as thematic dispositions, complexes, or unity-themes have not yet been properly tested. Although there is clinical evidence for such constructs (as in the case of Earnst) there has been no experimental evidence. The reason for this no doubt lies in the fact that such constructs refer to characteristics of the record of experience and behavior extended over very long periods of time. A unity-theme characterizes a personality during an entire lifetime. One would need to obtain data over significant portions of an individual's life in order to evaluate such a construct. Alternatively, one could carry out assessments which seek to describe an entire span of life through the data gathered in one session. An autobiography, for example, might be written in one week. Murray indeed advocated the use of interviewing and autobiographies in research. Sim-

ilarly the Thematic Apperception Test can reveal underlying thematic dispositions and conflicts that presumably have existed for a long time. By repeating such wide-lens assessments at intervals of a person's life it is possible to put together a picture of the entire course of development. This has been done by White (1975) and his collaborators for a number of subjects, with the first assessments starting at college age and proceeding to late middle age. This research was begun under Murray's direction at the Harvard Psychological Clinic. The results are rich in interest but they have not yet been analyzed from the specific point of view of determining the accuracy of Murray's theory.

Rather, Murray's theory has been used to guide data collection and to understand the life-history materials. The theory thus provides a research framework and specific pointers toward the collection of certain kinds of data. For example, White and his colleagues specifically look for thematic dispositions in the interview, TAT, and other data they collect. Thus they find a connection between Hartley Hale's (a patient) productivity as a scientist and the presence in his life of another person who is deeply interested in him and his work. When such a person is there (e.g., a girl friend or an interested teacher), Hale can become absorbed in scientific work. The press of another deeply interested person triggers or releases his need for Cognizance, for scientific search and discovery: "Whenever he felt assured of some respected person's esteem . . . his productiveness sprang into high gear" (White, 1975, p. 59). To find such a connection one must search over a long period in a person's life, establishing the occasions in question and also noting the concurrent rise in n Cognizance. Without the construct of thematic dispositions it is unlikely that anyone would make such a search; without the interview, TAT, autobiographical material, and so on, the researcher would not find the relevant information in a reasonable amount of time. This is what is meant when we say that Murray's theory has been used to guide data collection and to understand life-history materials. This is also part of the evidence for saying that Murray's theory has been immensely fruitful: it has stimulated and made possible the research of many other scientists.

Murray's theory has been built upon the psychoanalytic theory of Freud (see chapters 9, 10, and 11). It includes also a number of constructs and insights derived from Jung's theory (see chapter 12), such as the distinction between introverts and extraverts, or the notion of differentiation of functions (Murray, 1938, p. 395). Yet the most distinguishing and creative features of the theory pertain to the constructs of needs, press, and the various forms of need-integrate, such as thematic dispositions, complexes, and unity-themas. In this respect Murray's theory is much like Maslow's. Indeed, in the example above, one might suggest that Hartley Hale's surges of scientific interest occur only when the lower need of esteem is satisfied, an observation that fits Maslow's conception of the need hierarchy rather well. Likewise, Maslow's constructs of the various syndromes bear a close resemblance to Murray's constructs of complex or unity-thema. Maslow does not have constructs which match Murray's press or thematic disposition, however; and Murray does not have a concept to match Maslow's model of the hierarchical relation among groups or classes of needs. There are other differences. Most crucially, perhaps, Murray's conception of the needs falls into the category of psychophysical structures and processes, and the need-integrate includes images of objects and actones, the images being a definite part of ongoing subjective experience. These features give Murray's basic construct of need a much more purely psychological flavor as compared with Maslow's conception of need as a way in which the body naturally functions.

Murray's conceptions fit more readily into the framework of Freud's theory, notably of the ego, that structure in Freudian theory which seeks to express and gratify instinctual drives as well as possible under the limitations and opportunities of reality. Such reality factors are not necessarily contemporaneous, but rather may have molded the need expression at an earlier time in the person's history. They are of course molded partly in response to the press of the environment, which constitute the inner texture of "reality" as it impinges upon the ego, notably through the *beta press*—the individual's interpretation of current stimuli. The construct of thematic disposition refers to the existence within the ego of long-term tendencies to perceive certain kinds of press and to react to them in a certain kind of way. It is as though the ego developed particular "press-related" structures of need-expression and need-satisfaction. Likewise the unity-thema refers to an organization of collaborating and conflicting thematic dispositions which enduringly characterizes the ego.

Thus Murray's theory has been fruitful not only in stimulating research but also in advancing the psychoanalytic theory of the ego. These contributions to psychoanalytic theory are perhaps the most important reason why the Thematic Apperception Test continues to be found meaningful and helpful in the practical work of diagnosis by clinical psychologists as well as in pure research.

Stimulus-Influenced Apperception Study

Figure 3.1 was drawn specially for this book and is not part of the TAT. Some obvious features of the picture are important in considering a psychological test like the TAT. First, the two people are apparently male and female and about the same age, somewhere between 25 and 50. They are looking at either pictures in a brochure or photos in an album. The background might be a window scene or it could be a painting on the wall. The setting might be an office or a home. We do not know the relationship between the two people. We do not know what led up to the present scene, what they are thinking or feeling, or how it will turn out. So it fits the requirement of being ambiguous and yet presenting enough structure in the stimuli to give the respondent a start in imagining a story.

In order to make a brief study of the effects of the picture on the story we need a second picture, which we can obtain from the first by changing one major stimulus component in figure 3.1. We can change the age of the female figure quite easily; this has been done in figure 3.2. We may reproduce both pictures and thereby have two illustrations for a Stimulus-Influenced Apperception Study (SIAS). Question: What effect does the age of the female (stimulus) have upon the pattern of needs expressed by male and by female respondents? When the female stimulus is younger does the male respondent project to the male stimulus needs of nurturance, or needs of ascendance? Does the female respondent project needs of succorance or submission when the female stimulus is younger? Ask several volunteers to give you a story under the regular TAT instructions to each of three pictures. Make up a first picture yourself, and give it as a warm-up exercise. Then give figures 3.1 and 3.2. In accordance with your institution's provisions regarding privacy, assure respondents of anonymity, and debrief them at the end. Have at least two male and two female respondents. Score and tabulate. What conclusions can you draw? Could you design a totally new series of pictures that would systematically elicit thematic dispositions involving the major groups of needs?

Figure 3.2. A second picture for use in a study of stimulus-influence in apperception tests

Summary

The central construct in Murray's theory is *need*, which is defined as a force that influences a person to see and do things in such a way that some unsatisfactory state of affairs is changed. Four main groups of needs are: ascendance (including n Dominance and n Autonomy), deference (including n Deference and n Abasement), orderliness (including n Order and the general attribute of Conjunctivity), and sensuousness (including n Sex and n Sentience). Needs may fuse together or one may serve the other by subsidiation. The environment exerts influence through *press*, which are of two kinds, *alpha* and *beta*. The alpha press can be observed by independent judges; beta press reflect the individual subject's particular interpretation of the external stimulus. Each person develops particular connections between certain press and certain needs, called *themas*. When a particular thema characterizes a person over a long period of time it is called a *thematic disposition*. Murray regards these thematic dispositions as the basic energic components of personality. A *need-integrate* or *complex* is an organization of two or more needs plus the images of goal objects and action patterns which satisfy the needs.

Murray has always emphasized the importance of obtaining measurements of the needs and thematic dispositions. The Thematic Apperception Test (TAT) is one of the instruments he designed (with Morgan) for such assessments. It consists of twenty cards with quite complex social stimuli to which the subject responds by telling an imaginative story. The story is analyzed for the various themes reflecting needs and dispositions. The TAT is widely used in clinical and others types of assessment. Several questionnaires have also been devised following Murray's own lead. These instruments offer substantial confirmation for the existence of the needs and for the accuracy of the hypothesized groupings. Among the many developments which show the fruitfulness of Murray's theory is the tradition of research on the need for achievement, measured by a special short form of the TAT.

Murray's theory has been criticized for its complexity and lack of formalism, but Murray himself argues strongly against formalism and for complexity. In addition to being very fruitful, Murray's theory appears to be accurate as far as research has demonstrated so far. But his conceptions of higher-order structures (like need-integrates or unity-thema) have not so far yielded to research techniques other than interviewing or the Thematic Apperception Test, and have not so far been brought to the tests of more general empirical research. Nevertheless they continue to produce results in guiding life-history research and clinical diagnosis.

Recognizing that Murray employed Freud's theory as the major framework upon which he constructed his own theory, it is not easy to disentangle the portions of Murray's theory which are his own and which imply the definition of personality implicit in his unique contributions, which figure 3.3 at-

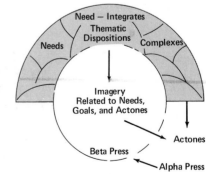

Figure 3.3. Diagram illustrating the definition of personality implied in the unique parts of Murray's theory

tempts to illustrate. For a full description of all that personality means to Henry Murray, one must add most of Freud's theory and some of Jung's.

Murray's theory presents us with a fine example of a theory which defines personality primarily in terms of psychophysical structures and processes. In the next chapter we shall study the contrasting theory formulated by B. F. Skinner, a theory which defines personality solely in terms of behaviors and their contingent interactions with environmental stimuli of several kinds. Comparing it directly to Murray's definition as represented in figure 3.3, Skinner's definition would include only the actones (behaviors) and alpha press (environmental stimuli). We turn now to this remarkable approach to defining personality.

INTRODUCTION

A theory which defines personality as behavior
  No causes of human behavior inside the person
  All causes of behavior exist in the environment
  Personality is the pattern of behaviors found in the
    record
Introduction to Skinner's life and work
  Skinners' life and professional career
  Only behavioral conceptions appropriate for
    behavioral explanations
  A behavioral conception of the reflex
  Control environmental conditions and you control
    behavior
  The case of Anne, a truant
  The case of Rick, a bed-wetter
Activity, behavior, conditioning, and the nature of
  the scientific task
  Behavior is that part of activity that interacts with
    the environment through conditioning of
    reflexes
  Type S conditioning
    Unconditioned and conditioned stimuli and
    responses
    Reinforcing stimuli
    Reflex strength and its measures
    Extinction
    Laws of conditioning in Type S .
  Type R conditioning
    Respondent contrasted with operant responses
    The Skinner box
    Discriminative stimuli
    Contingencies
    Chains
    Rate of responding and the cumulative record
    Conditioning and extinction in Type R
    Periodic reconditioning
    Spontaneous recovery
Skinner's theory of structure of behavior
  The Law of Chaining in Type R conditioning is a
    law of composition, how elements are
    composed into a structure
  Other laws of composition in Skinner's theory of
    structure of behavior
    Law of Compatibility
    Law of Algebraic Summation
    Law of Spatial Summation

    Law of Blending
    Law of Induction: generalization as a special
      case; and an experimental example
Refinements of behavior: Cognitive events are
  responses to discriminative stimuli
  Discrimination training
Motivation: Changes in strength of groups of
  reflexes
  The meaning of "drive" or "need"
The control of behavior
  Schedules of reinforcement
    Fixed ratio
    Fixed interval
    Variable ratio
    Variable interval
    Weekly pay as a fixed-interval schedule
Behavior out of control: Emotional behaviors
  "Anxiety states" so-called
  Studying and test anxiety
Praise and punishment
  Aversive stimuli produce emotional behaviors
Accomplishments of Skinner's theory
  Applications to human personality: conceptual
    reanalysis
  Behavior modification
Critique of Skinner's theory
  Five main classes of criticisms
    Behaviorism neglects important facts of human
      personality
    Behaviorism is limited to stimuli and responses
      of captive animals
    Behaviorism is sterile, oversimplified
    Behaviorism is immoral
    Behaviorism is paradoxical
  Evaluations of each class of criticisms
    Neglect—criticism may be justified in modified
      form
    Limited—criticism unjustified
    Sterile—criticism unjustified
    Immoral—criticism unjustified
    Paradoxical—criticism can be sustained
  Commentary on the criticisms
  A twenty-first criticism
    Chomsky's critique
    Brewer's critique
    Humans only **appear** to be conditionable
Workshop 4   Self-directed behavior modification
Summary

CHAPTER

4

Personality as Behavior: Skinner

In earlier chapters we have seen that many psychologists feel that behavior is somehow produced by forces inside the person. Maslow (chapter 1) sees these forces as *needs* that become active within the body, producing relevant subjective experiences and associated behaviors. For Murray (chapter 3), the forces are primarily associated with long-term links, called *thematic dispositions,* between particular needs and particular environmental pressures. These dispositions are thought to be psychophysical structures which produce characteristic portions of the record of subjective experience and behavior whenever relevant environmental conditions and states of need arise. The environmental situation is important, according to Murray, because it is closely connected with some thematic disposition. The importance is subjective; it is attributed chiefly to the person's inner appraisal or interpretation of the external situation. The effective environment for a person is the *beta press,* the environment as that person sees it. Moreover, in Murray's analysis the person's subjective experience may contain images of the environment, especially of goal objects that can satisfy a need, and these images influence the person's subsequent behavior. Thus

all or most of the truly important causes of human behavior reside within the human person, inside the skin.

The present chapter considers a very different approach to personality. According to B. F. Skinner's approach none of the causes of human behavior are within the person. All causes lie outside the person, in the connections between the behaviors as such and various conditions in the environment. In this view personality is simply the *pattern of behaviors* found in the record of a given individual.

B. F. Skinner was born in 1904 in Susquehanna, New York, a railroad town. According to his autobiography (1976) he had a happy childhood, playing many of the ordinary childhood games. Early in life he wanted to study law, but later his interests turned to literature and he majored in English as an undergraduate.

Nevertheless, he was fascinated by the writings of the behaviorist John Watson, and also by the newer work of Ivan Pavlov. Having decided he would go to Harvard to study psychology, he spent the intervening months in Greenwich Village enjoying the bohemian life there. After receiving the Ph.D. degree from Harvard in 1931, he spent some years at the University of Minnesota and a short period at Indiana University. Finally he returned to Harvard where he has remained as professor of psychology. In 1958 he received the Award for Distinguished Scientific Contribution from the American Psychological Association.

Skinner wrote his first book, *The Behavior of Organisms,* while at the University of Minnesota, and although his theory has undergone much development since then, many important principles were advanced in that first book which has remained influential. There he first set down the view that conceptions of entities existing at any other than the purely behavioral level are inappropriate for behavioral explanation. He noted that psychologists had always been more interested in these supposed causes of behavior than in behavior itself. They had postulated, as the basis of causal explanations, a "mind" with "mental faculties"; a "personality" with an "id," "ego," and "superego"; and even a nervous system. They had done so, moreover, at the expense of direct description of the behavior under study. Scientists were following the folkways of their culture, Skinner maintained, tending to seek causes, to formulate hypotheses, and to advance "explanations" before they had a proper description of what was to be explained.

As an alternative and superior approach Skinner proposed the method of simply describing the observed behavior and its relation to observed stimuli. He cited the neurological construct of reflex in which a particular stimulus elicits a particular immediate response, by apparently inborn arrangements. The knee jerk is one example; the eye blink to a bit of grit is another. In neurology, a reflex is thought of as a pathway. A stimulus excites a sense organ, which sends excitation along a sensory nerve to the spinal column.

The excitation is then transmitted to a motor nerve, travels along that nerve, and finally stimulates a muscle, producing action. A purely descriptive approach, Skinner said, has no need to refer to nerves at all. It simply records the fact that this external stimulus elicits that action or response. Actually even the notion that a stimulus *elicits* a response has some causal implication, and so Skinner proposed that science should speak simply of a *correlation* between the occurrence of the stimulus and the occurrence of the response, avoiding the causal inference.

Science does not need to use constructs referring to hidden causal entities, but it must observe and describe its subject matter, according to Skinner. If you search for causes in the world of the spirit, in the mind, in the nervous system, or in some inner personality, you come up with an idea you cannot substantiate. But a search for causes in the environment is simply a matter of manipulating the conditions and observing what happens. For example, to speak of a person's drinking lots of water because of thirst is to explain the drinking behavior as a function of some unobservable inner cause. But to deprive an animal of water for thirty hours and then observe it drinking much water is to know, see, and manipulate the conditions which produce drinking behavior. If you think about the problem carefully, Skinner said, and search for relevant environmental conditions which can be manipulated to produce, change, or maintain a given behavior, then you have no need to posit hidden causes.

Is it possible to study human personality solely in terms of the record of behaviors and their relationship to environmental conditions? Is it possible to define personality by the record of behaviors alone, omitting all reference to the body (nerves, muscles, glands, and so on), taking no account of the record of subjective experiences (thoughts, feelings, images), and denying any hypothesized psycho-physical structures (needs or thematic dispositions)? It certainly is possible to do so. Modern procedures of behavior modification demonstrate this. For example, the following cases are described by Tharp and Wetzel (1969, p. 88).

Anne was frequently absent from school. Her mother was on welfare and could not afford to reward Anne for attending school. So the behavior modification project sent Anne a note with a dollar bill, saying it was a reward for having attended school on a certain day. The note was anonymous. After she had attended school for four more days another note and dollar bill were sent. After seven more days of attendance she received another. No more notes were sent, but Ann continued to attend school for four more weeks.

In another case Rick was still wetting his bed at the age of seven. He did not respond to rewards of being allowed to go swimming or take part in other activities. Praise and approval from the parents, however, were found to be effective rewards. So the plan was instituted that whenever Rick got through a night without wetting his bed he was rewarded by their letting him sit in bed and talk with them for a short time. Bed-wetting and recurrent disobedience vanished in three months.

Note that in Anne's case attending behaviors were *increased* by the rewarding conditions, while in Rick's case bed-wetting and disobedient behaviors decreased in frequency and were eventually eliminated by the rewarding conditions. In neither case was any reference made to inner problems, needs, neuroses, willfulness, rebellious feelings, syndromes, complexes, or anything connected with nervous disorder or glandular disturbance. No reference is made to the body, to subjective experience, or to psychophysical systems. Only the target behaviors (missing school, bed-wetting) and rewarding conditions (money; family talk) are mentioned.

We will now consider how Skinner explains these simple relationships between the record of behaviors and the conditions of the environment. The relationships *are* simple. But the scientific explanation of those relationships is not at all simple; it is *not easy* to understand. The reader must expect to do some very hard work in this chapter.

Activity, Behavior, Conditioning, and the Nature of Scientific Data

In Skinner's view behavior is part of an organism's activity. It is that part of the activity which is "engaged in acting upon or having commerce with the outside world" (Skinner, 1938, p. 6). But simply by recording all the behavior in an organism's history we would not gain an understanding of its relation to the environment, so attention must be paid to those features or changes in the environment which are correlated with particular behaviors. The *reflex* refers to two types of correlations that arise from *conditioning*. In the next section we will consider these two types, Type S and Type R.

Type S Conditioning

Drawing upon the work of Pavlov (1927) and others (but rejecting any neurological theorizing) Skinner describes Type S conditioning, as that in which a new stimulus comes to elicit a particular response. Presentation of meat powder, an *unconditioned stimulus* (US) to a hungry dog elicits salivation, an *unconditioned reponse* (UR). But if a bell is sounded just before the powder is presented and continues to sound while the powder is presented, then the bell is described as a *conditioned stimulus* (CS). The pairing of CS and US sufficiently often will gradually result in the tendency for the CS to elicit the response.

The response then becomes a *conditioned response* (CR). When the bell is first rung, it does not elicit salivation, but gradually, as it is rung with the giving of the powder, it gains in probability of eliciting salivation. Finally it elicits salivation regularly.

Today we call this process *acquisition,* the development of the tendency for the UR to occur in response to the CS and thereby become a CR. Figure 4.1 illustrates the process Skinner calls *Type S conditioning.*

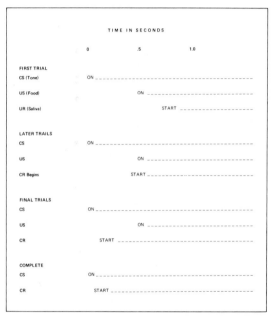

Figure 4.1. Illustration of the process of Type S conditioning

In Skinner's analysis of Type S conditioning the unconditioned stimulus is a reinforcing stimulus, one which has the "power to produce the resulting change" (Skinner, 1938, p. 62). What Skinner is underlining here is the formation of the *new reflex* leading to the CR.

More precisely, the change is in the *strength* of the new reflex. At first the bell sound did not elicit salivation; the reflex consisting of sound stimulus and salivation response was nonexistent. As pairings of CS and US continue, the likelihood increases of some salivary response to the CS prior to presentation of the US. Two indications of the strength of the reflex would be a greater *magnitude* of response (more drops of saliva collected in a tube) or a shorter *latency* (first drop occurs at a shorter interval after initiation of the CS). Two further measures of the strength of the reflex are *threshold* (intensity of stimulus that will elicit a response) and *after-discharge* (amount of activity taking place after cessation of the stimulus.

These measures of reflex strength primarily involve a *relationship* between stimulus and response—a relation between behavior and environment. For example, latency is a measure of the time elapsing between onset of stimulus and onset of response; threshold is that point on the intensity scale of the stimulus (for example, the degree of loudness of the bell) at which there is a 50 percent chance of the response being elicited. Thus these measures pertain to the reflex as a whole, the connection between stimulus and response. Reflex strength refers to this connection or contingency between environmental events (stimuli) and behavioral events (responses). The overall strength of a reflex can be expressed as a function of the measures employed:

$$RS = f(T, L, M, A)$$

where RS is reflex strength, T is threshold, L is latency, M is magnitude, and A is after-discharge. (RS would be greater for smaller T, shorter L, larger M and more A.)

Measurements taken repeatedly may be plotted over trials. Figure 4.2 illustrates such a plot over trials, indicating the gradual increase in strength of the conditioned reflex. Brogden (1951, p. 576) notes that many different forms of the curve have been found in studies of acquisition of conditioned reflexes,

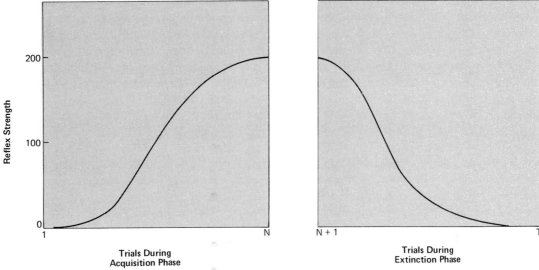

Figure 4.2. Curves illustrating acquisition and extinction of a conditioned reflex

because many factors affect the strength or the rate of acquisition. Nevertheless it is possible to provide examples: the curve in figure 4.2 represents a *curve of acquisition* that might be obtained from pooling the data for several animals in the conditioning process illustrated in figure 4.1.

Figure 4.2 also shows the *curve of extinction,* the reduction of reflex strength to zero, or continued failure of the reinforcing stimulus to occur upon presentation of the conditioned stimulus. In other words, extinction would occur if the situation represented as "complete" in figure 4.1 were to continue for an indefinite number of trials.

The values which indicate the degree of reflex strength (latency, magnitude, threshold, after-discharge) are called *static properties* of the reflex. *Dynamic laws* describe ways in which the values of these static properties change as a result of various operations. For example, the *Law of Reflex Fatigue* states that strength declines if the reflex is repeatedly elicited; strength recovers during a period of inactivity. The rate at which strength declines

is a positive function of the rate at which the reflex is elicited. This law is based upon extensive demonstrations by neurologists; notice, however, that in Skinner's formulation it refers only to operations of elicitation at varying rates and only to measurements of reflex strength. The *Law of Type S Conditioning* states that a reflex having zero or very small strength (e.g., a bell *does not* elicit salivation) develops greater strength (a bell *does* elicit salivation) as a result of repeated pairing of CS with US. (bell with meat powder).

If conditions are changed, and the CS is no longer followed by the US, the strength of the reflex will gradually diminish, reverting eventually to zero or very small strength. This process, known as *extinction,* is also illustrated in figure 4.2.

Summarizing, in Type S conditioning two stimuli are presented. The US (meat powder) elicits a response (salivation); the CS (bell) does not at first elicit that response but it is repeatedly followed by presentation of the US. Gradually the CS comes to elicit the response. The connection between the CS and the response is called a *conditioned reflex*. The strength of this reflex is measured by static properties, such as the number of drops of saliva produced in any one response. Repeated presentation of the US shortly after the CS *reinforces* the conditioned reflex, changing its strength from zero to some positive quantity. This process is referred to as the *Law of Type S Conditioning*. The *Law of Type S Extinction* is demonstrated after the reflex strength has been built up. The experimenter stops presenting the US after the CS and the strength of the conditioned reflex declines, eventually going to zero again.

Type R Conditioning

In Type R conditioning the experimenter does not manipulate the occurrence of the response directly, as in Type S conditioning. That is, the organism's response is not provoked. Rather, the experimenter waits until the subject (animal or person) makes a particular response, (as in the target response for Anne, attending school, and then delivers a reinforcing stimulus, like the note and the dollar bill.

Skinner distinguishes two kinds of responses. The evoked or provoked response in Type S conditioning is called a *respondent*. The unprovoked response in Type R conditioning, is called an *operant*. In Type S conditioning the reinforcing stimulus is presented immediately after the conditioned stimulus (right after the tone, for example). Type S is so named because reinforcement follows the conditioned *stimulus* (S for stimulus). In Type R conditioning reinforcement follows the *response* (R for response). Operants are responses emitted "spontaneously" by the organism. When this type of response occurs no correlated eliciting stimulus can be identified. The operant is simply a piece of behavior which is studied "as an event appearing spontaneously with a given frequency" (Skinner, 1938, p. 21).

A conditioned reflex involving an operant has no static properties, since these require a prior eliciting stimulus. There is no way to measure latency in an operant since there is no prior stimulus against which to calculate latency. Nevertheless Skinner uses the same construct of reflex strength for conditioning of both respondents and operants. This is justified even though an operant is not elicited by a stimulus; it may nevertheless develop a connection with some prior stimulus. A pigeon's peck is an operant, yet we may teach a pigeon to peck at a food tray only when a green light is on and not when the light is red. Thus, although the peck is not elicited by the green light, it has come under the control of the green light; the pigeon emits the pecking operant only when the green light is on.

Despite the fact that under certain circumstances both respondents and operants can be called *conditioned reflexes*, there is a difference between them with respect to the meaning of reflex strength. Strength of respondents is assessed through values of the static properties, but the strength of operants is assessed through rate or frequency of response; the dynamic laws are expressed in terms of changes in that frequency.

The *Law of Conditioning* for operants states that presentation of a reinforcing stimulus following occurrence of an operant increases its reflex strength. The *Law of Extinction* states that failure to present a reinforcing stimulus upon occurrence of an already conditioned operant will result in a decrease of its reflex strength. Discussion of other dynamic laws for operants must be delayed until we have considered the basic procedures of Type R conditioning. Figure 4.3 reproduces a schematic drawing of the kind of experimental apparatus, developed by Skinner, that has become known as a "Skinner box."

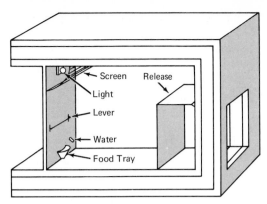

Figure 4.3. Schematic drawing of Skinner's experimental apparatus. From B. F. Skinner, **The Behavior of Organisms: An Experimental Analysis,** © 1938, 1966, p. 49. Reproduced by permission of Prentice-Hall, Inc., Englewood Cliffs, N. J., and by permission of the author.

Consideration of the rat's behavior in the Skinner box will give us an insight into the way complex behavior or personality can be described solely in terms of the record of behaviors and the connections between behaviors and environmental conditions.

A rat placed in a box as shown in figure 4.3 will typically explore its surroundings and may be expected to depress the lever in its normal movements. An untrained rat depresses the lever anywhere from one to ten times an hour. A mechanism may be attached to the lever to operate a food dispenser, which drops a pellet of food into the food tray. A more complete description of the rat's behavior begins when the animal is placed in the compartment at the rear of the box. The release mechanism lets the animal into the main chamber. Sooner or later the rat encounters the food tray; eating the food will constitute a reinforcement if the rat is hungry. The probability of the rat's approaching the tray can be increased by depriving it of food beforehand. They tray is called a *discriminative stimulus* (S^D); it is said to be correlated

with an approach response (R). Notice that the tray as a stimulus does *not* elicit the approach response in the same manner that meat powder elicits a salivation response in a dog. The S^D serves chiefly to direct the operant or guide it.

Once the animal makes reliable approaches to the tray upon being placed in the box, it is possible to make food appear there only on condition that the lever has just been depressed. That is, the experimenter can make food *contingent* upon bar-pressing. The fuller description of this contingency requires that the food-dispensing mechanism make a "click" sound when a pellet is released. This constitutes another S^D, so that now the animal must learn to approach the tray only when the "click" S^D has sounded. This means that a combined stimulus now serves to guide the response of approaching the tray: S^{DI} (tray) S^{DII} (click). But note that S^{DII} occurs only as a result of the lever-pressing. The reader will immediately note that the lever itself is a discriminative (visual) stimulus (S^{DIII}), which must lead to the response of rearing up and pressing. So we have an entire *chain* S^D's and responses:

$$S^{DIII} \cdot R^{III} \rightarrow S^{DII} \, S^{DI} \cdot R^I \rightarrow S^1 \cdot R^1$$

The lever stimulus (S^{DIII}) directs the rearing and pressing response (R^{III}) which leads to ($\rightarrow$) the click stimulus (S^{DII}), which is followed by the tray stimulus (S^{DI}), which directs the response of approaching the tray (R^I). The last part of the expression states that a reinforcing stimulus (S^1) is correlated with ($\cdot$) an eating response (R^1).

In a later section we shall return to this important matter of chaining. For the moment we must continue with an exploration of Skinner's approach to scientific data. We have already noted the importance he places upon frequency of response: In Type R conditioning the strength of a reflex is evaluated in

Box 4.1
Skinner's Invention of the Cumulative Recorder: A Case History

Skinner's story of how he developed one of his most successful technological items (1959, pp. 363 ff) also illustrates five principles of scientific method which, he says, are normally overlooked by philosophers and others who try to formulate methodology of science. The five principles are: 1) When you come across something really interesting, drop everything else and turn your whole attention to it. 2) If you can find an easier way of doing a particular piece of research, do it. 3) Some investigators are lucky. 4) Experimental apparatus sometimes fails. 5) While looking for one thing, an alert investigator may stumble across something entirely different and make a totally unexpected discovery.

Starting from the single assumption that order may be found in behavior if conditions are controlled, Skinner was observing rats and their babies emerging from a dark tunnel. As he watched the young rats crawl about and sit up, he turned to studying their postural reflexes. A pull on a young rat's tail, he noticed, made the rat pull forward in resistance, even losing its tail in the process. To study this systematically he placed a rat on a platform that he mounted on tight piano wires. Movement in the wires was translated into the motions of a stylus on a **kymograph,** a rotating drum with smoked paper on it. As the stylus moved up and down it scratched a record of these motions onto the smoked surface of the rotating paper. This record could then be fixed with shellac and stored.

Next Skinner decided to apply the recording technique to adult rats also, so he released them one by one from a tunnel onto a runway from which tremors could be recorded on a kymograph. At the end of the runway he fed them. Every so often he made a click stimulus and observed whether it interfered with their running (it did). The effect of the interference (hesitation or cessation of motion) was recorded automatically on the kymograph. The task of feeding the rat each time and carrying it back to the starting place was tedious, so Skinner added to the runway. This made it possible for the rat to reach the end of the runway, turn left to receive food, return along another runway, and eventually come down the first runway again.

It was a rectangular frame, all four sides of which were runway.

The next step was to have the rat obtain its own food instead of being fed by hand. Skinner built the new piece of apparatus shown in figure 4.4. The rectangular runway was now pivoted at

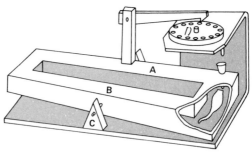

Figure 4.4. Runway apparatus in which the rat's own response (running down alley A) produces release of food. Reproduced by permission of author and publisher from B. F. Skinner, A case history in scientific method. In S. Koch, ed., **Psychology: A Study of a Science,** Vol. 2. New York: McGraw-Hill, 1959, pp. 365-366.

point C. As the rat runs up alley A after eating its weight causes the runway to tilt. The tilting movement causes a notched food wheel to turn one notch, bringing a piece of food over a chute to drop into the food dish. The rat, continuing down runway B, eventually arrives at the food dish again and eats the food. Another response up runway A sets the process in motion again.

Each tilt of the runway was recorded on a kymograph. As Skinner watched the procedure one day he noticed that the food wheel, which he had made out of an old piece of apparatus, had a spindle sticking up through its center. It occurred to him that if he wound a piece of string around the spindle at the beginning of an experimental session the string would unwind a little each time the food wheel turned a notch. The string, properly attached to the stylus on the kymograph, would provide a different kind of record, a curve. The arrangement is shown

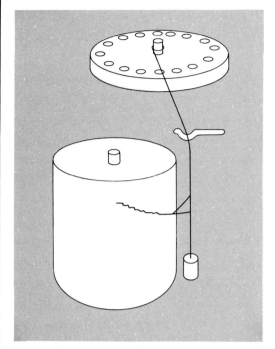

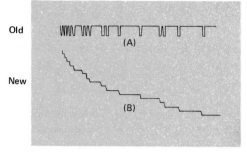

Figure 4.6. The old and the new types of record. Reproduced by permission of author and publisher from B. F. Skinner, A case history in scientific method. In S. Koch, ed., **Psychology: A Study of a Science,** Vol. 2. New York: Mc-Graw-Hill, 1959, p. 366.

Figure 4.5. Weighted string moves the stylus down on the kymograph every time the food wheel turns a notch. Reproduced by permission of author and publisher from B. F. Skinner, A case history in scientific method. In S. Koch, ed., **Psychology: A Study of a Science,** Vol. 2. New York: McGraw-Hill, 1959, p. 366.

in figure 4.5, with the difference between the old and the new type of record illustrated in figure 4.6.

The old record is simply a series of blips; the new record is a **cumulative record,** since it keeps on dropping a given amount every time a response is made. If no responses were made the kymograph would keep turning and the stylus would draw a straight line. In the old method each response would produce a simple blip in the straight line, but in the new method each response carries the line lower to produce a curve. Between each response the horizontal line continues as before. If responses are rapid the curve drops at a faster rate, as in the beginning of the "new" curve in figure 4.6. A slower rate of response produces a flatter curve. Thus the shape of the curve on the cumulative record reveals important characteristics about the frequency of responding per unit time, the **rate** of response.

Although the original equipment allowed only for the curve to descend it seemed more useful to have an ascending curve. So the kymograph was replaced by a solenoid, which activated a pen making an ink mark upward on a sheet of moving paper. Soon the runway seemed unnecessary; it would be simpler to have the rat operate a lever which would release food into the dish. So the box shown in figure 4.3 was built, and the new electrically operated cumulative recorder was activated by each press on the lever.

terms of frequency. Box 4.1 describes one of Skinner's most ingenious inventions, the *cummulative record,* a technique for recording the

rate of responding (frequency per unit time) in such a way that a steeper slope to a curve reflects a higher rate of responding; a flatter slope represents a lower rate of responding; a horizontal line represents no responding at all for that period of time.

In the earliest experiments with the box shown in figure 4.3 Skinner studied the rate of conditioning. Animals were first accustomed to the box and to the fact that the click sound preceded release of a food pellet into the dish. During this time the lever did not operate the food magazine, since it was precisely this operant of lever-pressing that would be the object of conditioning. Skinner writes: "On the day of conditioning the rat is placed in the box as usual. The lever is present, and for the first time in the history of the rat its movement downward will operate the magazine" (1938, p. 67). The drama is obvious. The results are no less dramatic: twenty out of seventy-eight rats were instantaneously conditioned as they made their first response to the lever. Others responded four or five times, receiving reinforcement each time, before becoming conditioned (responding at maximal rate). Only three rats failed to become conditioned within three hours. Of those who required several reinforced responses before becoming conditioned, most accomplished the goal within thirty minutes. The slowest one took a little over two hours. Examples of the cumulative records are shown in figure 4.7.

Extinction in Type R is accomplished simply by not letting the response be followed by the usual stimulus. After conditioning as described above, for example, the magazine would be disconnected from the lever; so that the lever-press no longer releases food. When first placed in the box under these conditions the rat emits responses at a high rate, responses then taper off irregularly. As can be seen in figure 4.8, however, it is possible to draw a smooth curve (dashed lines) which represents the course of the animal's behavior under extinction. Deviations from this ideal

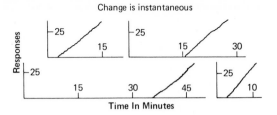

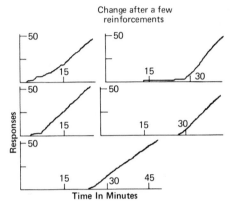

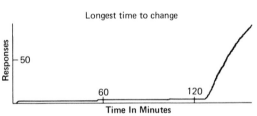

Figure 4.7. Examples of cumulative records in conditioning. From B. F. Skinner, **The Behavior of Organisms: An Experimental Analysis,** © 1938, 1966, pp. 67, 68, 69. Reproduced by permission of Prentice-Hall, Inc., Englewood Cliffs, N. J., and by permission of the author.

curve occur: after slacking off for a while each rat seems to start in at a higher rate and the actual curve catches up with the ideal curve.

Conditioning can be reinstituted after extinction if the reinforcing stimulus is again provided after the response. It is found that after one such reinforcement the rate of responding increases sharply. If no further reinforcements follow then the rate falls off in

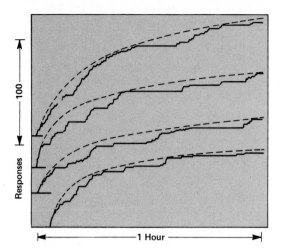

Figure 4.8. Examples of cumulative records under extinction. From B. F. Skinner, **The Behavior of Organisms: An Experimental Analysis,** © 1938, 1966, p. 75. Reproduced by permission of author and Prentice-Hall, Inc., Englewood Cliffs, N. J., and by permission of the author.

the curve typical of extinction. But if another reinforcement is given before the extinction curve flattens out completely, then the conditioning curve takes over again. When this process is repeated the behavior soon takes on a steady high rate. Such alternation of conditioning, extinction, and reconditioning, called *periodic reconditioning,* effectively *maintains* the behavior.

In one series of experiments on periodic reconditioning a lever-pressing response had been conditioned and subsequently extinguished in each rat. On the day after extinction, a rat placed in the box typically showed some renewed activity in lever pressing, even though no reinforcement was present. This renewal after a period of delay following extinction is known as *spontaneous recovery from extinction.* Recovery activity rapidly shows the typical extinction curve, however, as may be seen in the curve (from A to B and

A' to B') in figure 4.9. At points B and B' in figure 4.9 reinforcement was introduced for the first time. Thereafter, every five minutes a response was reinforced but responses in between were not reinforced. As may be seen, after the first reinforcement at B and B' the curve follows the usual pattern for extinction but does not flatten completely. Following the reinforcement at C and C' the curve is steeper and takes longer to reach the typical extinction pattern. Shortly after that the curve no longer looks like an extinction curve at all but rather follows essentially a straight line, which represents a steady rate of responding.

The schedule of reinforcing a response only once every five minutes is known as a *fixed-interval (FI) reinforcement.* The notation FI 5 indicates the time of five minutes. We shall return later to consider this and other schedules of reinforcement in greater detail. For the moment we must note that Type R conditioning has built up a new reflex in the

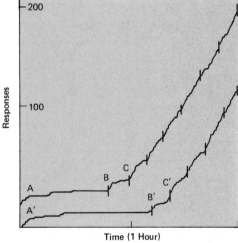

Figure 4.9. Examples of periodic reconditioning and the maintenance of a steady rate of responding. From B. F. Skinner, **The Behavior of Organisms: An Experimental Analysis,** © 1938, 1966, p. 118. Reproduced by permission of author and Prentice-Hall, Inc., Englewood Cliffs, N. J., and by permission of the author.

animal and that periodic reconditioning has maintained that reflex at a steady high rate. Similar high rates were maintained in four rats for a period of twenty-four hours, one hour per experimental day, by periodic reconditioning; it was shown also that a shorter interval (roughly 3 minutes) produced responses at a higher rate, while longer intervals (roughly 6, 9, and 12 minutes) produced progressively lower rates of responding (Skinner, 1938, p. 119).

We have now described the most basic operations in Skinner's system of behavior. How do these basic operations on elementary reflexes combine to produce complex behavior? Skinner's statement of these principles amounts to a theory of the structure of behavior.

Skinner's Theory of Structure of Behavior

Earlier we saw an example of a chain of reflexes in Type R conditioning. Now we can examine the associated *Law of Chaining* (Skinner, 1938, pp. 32, 52), which states that the response of one reflex may produce a stimulus (eliciting or discriminative) for a second reflex. Skinner says that this law describes a "principle of extraordinarily wide application in the integration of behavior. Most of the reflexes of the intact organism are parts of chains" (1938, p. 52). It is this law, then, which provides a means whereby elementary reflexes are built into complex behaviors. Since the law refers to both Type S and Type R conditioning it embraces all the behaviors which come under environmental stimulus control. It appears to be a *law of composition,* specifically related to a theory of structure (see chapter 8). A composition law states the principles whereby the finer elements discerned by a theory of structure are brought together to form the whole whose

structure is under examination. In this case the whole in question is any piece of complex behavior. The structural theory formulated by Skinner states that this kind of whole is made up of component reflexes. The Law of Chaining explains how component reflexes are linked together to form the whole. In Skinner's phrase, it specifies how the *integration* of behavior takes place, specifically the integration of reflexes into complex behaviors.

In relation to personality as defined in chapter 2, Skinner's theory focuses on connections between environmental conditions and the record of behavior, connections between three kinds of stimuli (eliciting, reinforcing, and discriminative) and chained responses. His theory of structure states that the behavioral part of a person's record is composed of wholes that implicate aspects of the environment. The elements of these wholes are reflexes; they are integrated by chaining.

Chaining is not the only principle of composition in Skinner's theory. Skinner states at least five additional laws of composition:

1. *The Law of Compatibility.* Two or more responses which do not occur in the same place may occur simultaneously. For example, a person when shocked may withdraw the hand and at the same time gasp. When driving a person may obey a traffic signal (discriminative stimulus) by braking, looking in the mirror, and responding verbally to a companion, all at the same time. In each case the several responses occurring simultaneously do not interfere with each other because they occur in different places. The total behavior at that point is composed by co-occurrence. The old-fashioned "one-man band" is a good example.

2. *The Law of Algebraic Summation.* Two reflexes which share the same effector muscles, but in opposite directions, may occur at the same time and produce an algebraic

resultant. Skinner gives the example of a squirrel responding to a novel stimulus with both approach and avoidance responses. If either reflex has relatively much greater strength only that response will occur, but if both reflexes are more or less equal in strength, then an oscillation takes place; partial approach is followed by a partial withdrawal, followed by a partial approach, and again a partial withdrawal, and so on. Interesting modifications appear if the strengths are different but not overwhelmingly so. For example, if a strong approach reflex is coupled with a slightly weaker avoidance reflex the resultant behavior may be a definite but slow approach.

3. *The Law of Spatial Summation.* Two reflexes which share the same effector muscles in the same direction may occur at the same time and produce an increase in magnitude and decrease in latency. Skinner gives the example of a slight sound combined with a movement of the hand in front of the baby's eyes. Each alone is insufficient to elicit a blink but the two together may succeed in making the baby blink.

4. *The Law of Blending.* Two responses which share *some* of the same effector muscles may occur together, but if they do, each modifies the form of the other. One example would be playing the piano while balancing a glass on the back of your hand. "Most of the normal behavior of an organism shows blending of this sort," Skinner believes (1938, p. 31).

5. *The Law of Induction.* If two reflexes share some stimulus properties or some effector muscles, a change in the strength of one reflex may lead to a smaller degree of change in the other reflex. One special case is known as *generalization* (Tarpy, 1975, pp. 184ff). In a typical test of generalization by Guttman and Kalish

(1956), pigeons developed a chain as follows. When a disc was lighted for sixty seconds (S^{DIII}) it directed a pecking response onto itself (R^{III}), which led to a stimulus of food being released (S^{DII}) into a tray (S^{DI}), which directed the response of approaching the tray (R^{I}), whereupon the food reinforcing stimulus (S^1) was correlated with an eating response (R^1). In between each 60-second period of S^{DIII} there was a period of 10 seconds without light.

Recall the formula for chaining:

$$S^{DIII} \cdot R^{III} \to S^{DII} \; S^{DI} \cdot R^I \to S^1 \cdot R^2$$

As the chain shows, pecking at the disc during dark time would not be followed by food release. Once the pigeon had acquired the total chain of reflexes it was possible to introduce an extinction trial in which pecking did not result in the release of food even though S^{DIII} was present. In the experiment by Guttman and Kalish 132 such extinction trials were given, in only 12 of which the original S^{DIII} was actually employed. In the remaining 120 trials light stimuli varied systematically from the original in color, measured in millimicrons (m_u). For instance, if the original S^{DIII} was at 580 m_u (roughly chrome yellow), then the ten other stimuli presented were at intervals from 520 (bright green) to 640 (reddish). Each stimulus was presented in random order for a total of 12 trials each. About 300 pecking responses were emitted to 580 m_u (the original stimulus) during these extinction trials. About 280 responses were emitted to 590 m_u and 250 to 570m_u. Thus substantial generalization occurred to stimuli + or − 10 m_u distant from the original S^{DIII}. Nearly 150 responses each were emitted to stimuli + or − 20 m_u from the original. About 70 responses were emitted to + or − 30 m_u. Thus some degree of generalization occurred even to stimuli quite different from the original chrome yellow, namely to chrome green (roughly 550) and English vermillion (roughly 610). Note that, as the stimuli become increasingly different from the original, the number of responses emitted during extinction decreases. There is thus a *range* of induction or generalization, high at points close to the original and gradually diminishing as the difference from the original stimulus increases. The typical curve is shown in figure 4.10.

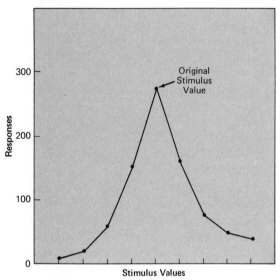

Figure 4.10. Typical shape of a generalization curve

One important implication of figure 4.10 is that conditioning does not appear to be a highly specific correlation. Conditioning to one stimulus produces a number of reflexes of varying strength depending upon the similarity of the stimulus component of each reflex to the stimulus component of the originally conditioned reflex. Thus the Law of Induction recognizes a kind of fuzziness in the composition rules

whereby reflexes are chained or otherwise integrated into complex behavioral wholes.

Refinements of Behavior: Cognitive Events Are Responses to Discriminative Stimuli

Looking at figure 4.10, the everyday observer might conclude that the animal "knows" when a stimulus is similar to the original. When the stimulus is very different the animal "can tell" that it is different and so does not emit the conditioned response. In between the animal is "uncertain." All these statements imply some inner process of knowing, certainty, telling the difference, or discriminating between situations. If we think of our own social behavior we know that we tend to behave quite differently in different situations. We recognize the difference between a cocktail party and a classroom. Skinner rejects such *cognitive* theorizing. It is not necessary to propose any such knowing, telling, or recognizing processes inside the organism. Rather, we can describe the operations the experimenter employs or the stimulus conditions existing in the natural environment. First, as the similarity between the original stimulus and the new stimulus is made smaller, so the probability of evoking a conditioned response by induction decreases. Second, other contingencies begin to narrow the range of stimuli that will evoke the response. Manipulation of these various conditions is called *discrimination training*, or training the organism to respond to one stimulus and not to the other. *Discrimination* in Skinner's view does not refer to another process but simply means the progressive conditioning of one reflex and the extinction of those others which have been produced by induction; such discrimination must always occur in Type S conditioning (1938, pp. 176-177). Suppose the animal is in an experimental apparatus. Salivation is the

UR being measured. The CS is a tone of 1000 cycles per second; the US is meat powder. When conditioning is complete the CS elicits the UR, which becomes a CR:

$$CS^1 \cdot CR^1$$

This is an oversimplified picture of what has happened during Type S conditioning. Other stimuli were present during the trials—for example, the experimental apparatus or the room itself. Referring to these as CS^2 we have a second conditioned reflex formed to the same UR (salivation):

$$CS^2 \cdot CR^1$$

But the copresence of CS^2 with CS^1 also forms a third, composite stimulus $CS^3 = CS^1CS^2$:

$$CS^3 \cdot CR^1$$

Skinner suggests that responses to the experimental situation only (CS^2) tend to disturb the experiment and therefore no reinforcing stimulus is produced, which tends to produce extinction of that particular reflex. But conditioning to the combined CS^3 cannot be wholly avoided. Of course, changing the apparatus significantly but maintaining the CS^1 simultaneously with UR would tend to weaken CS^3. In situations outside the laboratory, Skinner suggests, some discrimination must take place in the establishment of conditioned reflexes, since every CS must be correlated with a US in the presence of many other stimuli. "Consequently the reinforcement has a broader effect than the actual correlation implies and extinction of the extra effect eventually follows" (Skinner, 1938, p. 177).

Discrimination training in Type R follows the same essential pattern. One S^D, a discriminative stimulus, is correlated with reinforcement; another, S^Δ, is not correlated with reinforcement. In one experiment described by Skinner (1938, p. 184) rats were first brought to a high steady rate of reponding via periodic reconditioning with FI 5 (a fixed interval of 5 minutes). Then a change was introduced by connecting a light as well as the magazine to the lever. When the animal was put into the box the light was on and its first lever-pressing response produced reinforcement (food). Then both light and food magazine were switched off for five minutes. During these five minutes lever-pressing did not produce reinforcement. Then the light was switched on again and the magazine connected until the next responses had been made and reinforced. This was repeated twelve times on each experimental day. As expected, the rats learned to press when the light was on and not to press when the light was off. A high steady rate had been established under periodic reconditioning without the light. After the change, responding without the light is never reinforced and therefore this reflex should become extinguished. The absence of light is now the alternative discriminative stimulus, S^Δ. But the new stimulus of the light, S^D, is now correlated with reinforcement and so conditioning of the lever-pressing response to that stimulus should take place. By induction the reinforcement of S^D should strengthen the reflex associated with S^Δ; correspondingly, by induction, the extinction of S^Δ should weaken the reflex associated with S^D. The result should be a compromise between maintenance of the high rate of responding previously established under periodic reconditioning and a declining rate of response as found in a typical extinction curve. The results (1938, p. 186) were exactly in accordance with these expectations.

Since the cumulative record changes systematically upon introduction of a new discriminative stimulus there is no need to invoke a discrimination process in the animal. The scientist, according to Skinner, has obtained a complete description of the animal's behavior when the change in the record is found to be systematically related to the change in the discriminative stimulus. If the old and the new discriminative stimuli have different contingent relations to reinforcement, and if these relations are revealed in differences in the cumulative record of responses, and if these differences in the record are lawfully produced whenever we change the discriminative stimulus from new to old or vice versa; then that is all that needs to be known. To add the ideas that the animal "can tell the difference between the two colors" is superfluous if it means that there is some unseen "cognitive process" going on.

Motivation: Changes in Strength of Groups of Reflexes

Most theories of personality include a theory of motivation, that is, of what instincts, drives, needs, impulses, wishes or other forces impel the organism into action. Maslow and Murray both employ a construct of need which propels behavior and produces experiences of a certain kind. For example, a need for love produces an experience of longing when it is not satisfied and an experience of deep satisfaction when it is finally satisfied. At the same time the need for love, when aroused, leads the person to seek out someone who will satisfy that need. A lonely student might go to a party and try to find someone with whom to develop a love relationship. Or the student might go home for a week. It is assumed that such experiences and behaviors are produced by the activated need for love.

It is to be expected that Skinner takes a different position, contending that it is unnecessary to look for an inner need or drive. Rather, one should look for the conditions and contingencies existing in the environment. Everything that the word *drive* means can be accounted for by external operations and certain patterns of results in reflex strength. If any one of several operations can affect the strength of an entire group of reflexes, then that is all that is meant by saying that the "drive" has changed. An animal deprived of water and then placed by a water dispenser will make more drinking responses than one not deprived of water. If now you have trained the animal to press a lever for water reinforcement, when it is deprived of water it will depress the lever more frequently than if it is not deprived of water. Thus a group of reflexes (lever-pressing to lever, and drinking response to water) has been strengthened by depriving the animal of water (one operation). The relationship between the operation (water deprivation) and the change in strength of the group of reflexes is all that can be described or known scientifically, according to Skinner. If one were to speak of the animal's being thirsty it would add nothing to one's knowledge. All you can say is that you deprived the animal of water and it emitted more lever-pressing and drinking responses.

To study the influence of different intensities of so-called drive or need, Skinner studied their effects on extinction. He first let rats be fed a fixed amount for one hour each day. The experimental period came just before feeding time, so that all rats would have a high level of hunger. In order to vary the degree of drive the experimenter placed each rat in a separate cage prior to the experiment and allowed each one to eat a different amount of food: 0, 2, 4 or 6 grams. The more a rat ate, the lower would be its resulting drive level. All the rats had been equally conditioned prior to this test of extinction. Now upon entering the box, and with the lever not activating the food-release, extinction curves were obtained as in figure 4.11, showing clear effects of the different levels of drive strength. Rats who had just eaten nothing (had highest drive strength) pressed the lever at a high rate, emitting many responses before they

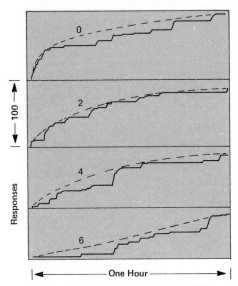

Figure 4.11. Extinction curves under different levels of drive strength, measured by intake of 0, 2, 4 or 6 grams of food before the experimental session. From B. F. Skinner, **The Behavior of Organisms: An Experimental Analysis,** © 1938, 1966, p. 388. Reproduced by permission of Prentice-Hall, Inc., Englewood Cliffs, N. J., and by permission of the author.

began to taper off (show extinction). The others began at a lower rate of responding, the lowest rate being for the rats with the lowest level of drive strength (ate 6 grams just before the trial). They also tapered off after emitting fewer responses, thus beginning extinction more rapidly. The result: The higher the drive the more delayed is extinction.

What would this result mean about human behavior in natural situations? It might mean, for example, that someone who is very highly motivated to talk to a friend on the telephone will keep on calling and calling even though there is no answer. Someone with little motivation will forget it after the first attempt.

The Control of Behavior

The fact that different contingencies can be arranged and different reflexes are thereby

strengthened or weakened is summarized in the statement that behavior is controlled by the situation in which it occurs (the particular discriminative stimulus) and by the consequences of the behavior (the reinforcing stimuli). Skinner introduced the idea of a schedule of reinforcements and showed that different schedules exert different kinds of control. A *schedule* is the particular spacing of reinforcing stimuli over time or in relation to the number of responses emitted prior to delivery of a reinforcement.

In the four typical patterns or *schedules of reinforcement* shown in figure 4.12 it is seen that different schedules typically produce different types of curves in the cumulative record. For example, fixed interval schedules (lower left) produce a kind of scalloping effect as the rate of response slows directly after a reinforcement and gradually speeds up as the time approaches for the next reinforcement. In the fixed interval schedule shown in the figure a reinforcement is given every five minutes (FI 5) provided a response has been emitted in the intervening period. In the fixed ratio schedule (upper left) reinforcement is given for a fixed number of responses (in this case, for 20 responses, hence FR 20). Variable ratio (VR) and variable interval (VI) schedules (upper right and lower right) vary either the number of responses required (ratio) or the time that must elapse (interval) before reinforcement is given.

The figure shows that the variable schedules produce a more constant rate of responding. The difference is explained by Ferster and Skinner (1957, p. 326). In the fixed schedules there is a correlation between responses and reinforcements, so that certain properties of the animal's behavior gain discriminative stimulus value. In fixed interval schedules, for example, no reinforcements are given for a fixed period of time after a given response has been reinforced. Thus a response

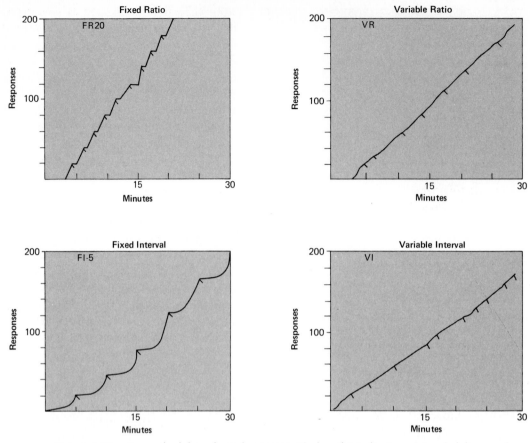

Figure 4.12. Four schedules of reinforcement. Slashes (\) indicate points of delivery of reinforcement

which is followed by a reinforcement becomes a discriminative stimulus. It signals that for a little time now further responses will not be followed by a reinforcement.

In everyday life such schedules are plainly seen in work situations. Payment of employees each Friday, for instance, constitutes reinforcement on a fixed interval schedule.

Behavior Out of Control: Emotional Behaviors

Skinner has always recognized that some responses have glandular or autonomic origin;

like salivation, increase in heart rate, change in electrical resistance on the skin, and so on, are the reactions most commonly associated with an emotional state. Certain skeletal behaviors are also commonly associated with emotion although, as Verplanck points out (1957, p. 4), the particulars are different for different species. In the rat, for example, emotional behavior includes urinating, defecating, standing still, squeaking, trembling, and so on. Because the behavioral definition of emotion requires that two or more reflexes be affected simultaneously by a given operation, such behaviors are not necessarily called *emotional behaviors* unless at least two of them are observed to increase or decrease in reflex strength together.

Typical procedure in operant conditioning requires that such emotional behaviors be eliminated either before training begins or while the animal is being accustomed to a change in stimulus conditions. For example, Ferster and Skinner (1957, p. 376) established stable performance in a pigeon on VI 3. Then they lowered the level of illumination for thirty seconds. This dimming was to become a new discriminative stimulus. But the change slowed the rate of responding on the VI 3 schedule, so they repeated the dimming every five minutes until it no longer affected the pigeon's response rate. Although the slowing effect of the new stimulus was gradually allowed to wear off, that very effect would be considered an effect of an "emotional state." Indeed Skinner considers such an effect to be among the most important features of "emotion," namely, the disruption of steady response rates under stimulus control. As such the "emotion" no longer has properties of fuzzy feelings and disturbed inner experience associated with various autonomic and glandular reactions. The word emotion comes to refer almost exclusively to emotional behaviors as defined above, and to disturbances in the control of an operant by a schedule. It refers essentially to behaviors which are out of control.

A classic example is provided by Estes and Skinner (1941) who studied two groups of twelve rats, one under high drive and the other under low drive. Periodic reinforcement was given to condition a lever-pressing response. After two weeks of daily one-hour trials, stable rates of responding had been established. Then a tone was turned on for three minutes; at the end of that period a shock was delivered and the tone was turned off. On the first day, neither tone nor shock disrupted performance. But as successive days went by the presentation of the tone began to interfere more and more with the response rate, causing it to decline until, after the fourth day, the rats stopped responding as soon as the tone came on. Thus the rats came to "anticipate" the shock, a condition Estes and Skinner called an "anxiety state." It developed with both high and low drive.

Many students will recognize the similarity between this experiment and their own behavior preceding an examination of importance. The anxiety state is sufficient to prevent them from studying. Whereas during the earlier weeks they might have established a steady rate of studying responses, when the examination is announced as being set for next week, their rate of studying drops off. They "just can't study." For other students the rate of studying goes up sharply when the examination is announced. In this case it is the rate of not-studying responses which is depressed by the emotional state.

Praise and Punishment

The shock mentioned in the previous experiment would be technically known as an aversive stimulus, or sometimes as punishment. An *aversive stimulus* is a stimulus which, if delivered following a response, tends to lower the strength of the reflex involving that response so that the likelihood of that response occurring on the next occasion is reduced. By contrast a reinforcing stimulus of food delivered to a hungry rat is called a *positive reinforcing* stimulus; if delivered following a response (such as lever-pressing) it tends to strengthen the reflex involving that response.

On the human scene praise or a money reward would typically be positive reinforcing stimuli. Saying "That's wrong," "That's bad," or "Yuck!" would probably be aversive stimuli. Physical punishment or a fine would also be aversive stimuli.

As we saw above, and as is commonly the

case, use of aversive stimuli produces emotional behavior. Emotional responses frequently interfere with conditioning and moreover often have consequences which are quite unforeseen. By contrast positive reinforcing stimuli do not typically produce emotional behavior, nor do they usually produce any other unexpected consequences. Accordingly, Skinner recommends that positive reinforcing stimuli be used for every human and animal training attempt where it is possible to do so. Praise works better than punishment.

Accomplishments of Skinner's Theory

In *The Behavior of Organisms* Skinner noted that almost no extensions of the constructs had been made to human behavior (1938, p. 441). He felt that this was appropriate for a science of behavior in the early stages of its development but that its true significance "derives largely from the possibility of an eventual extension to human affairs."

All other theories in this book have been concerned from the beginning with human personality or human behavior. Only Skinner's theory has been addressed initially to simple behaviors of simple organisms. Therefore only Skinner's theory has had to receive the special treatment of demonstrating its applicability to human affairs. Other theorists have taken the applicability of their theories for granted, since human personality was precisely the object of their formulations. As it turns out, this need to demonstrate applicability has worked to Skinner's advantage since it has provided incentive for a number of well-designed books on the subject (Skinner, 1953, 1971, 1974).

In *Science and Human Behavior* (Skinner, 1953) topics treated include emotion, anxiety, thinking, the self, and self-control, as well as many others in the areas of social behavior

and social control. Much complex behavior is described as under the control of discriminative stimuli: $S^D \cdot R^1 - S^1$. Education is almost completely carried out through control of such chains, Skinner tells us:

> We set up contingencies which generate behavior as the result of which children will look before crossing streets, will say "Thank you" upon the proper occasions, will give correct answers to questions about historical events, will operate machines in the proper manner, will buy books, attend concerts, plays, and moving pictures identified in certain ways, and so on (1953, p. 110).

The "G" in a "G-rated" movie is an S^D that is correlated with letting children go to it and finding that they have a rewarding experience. The "X" in an "X-rated" movie is correlated with taking a child to the movie and finding that they will not let the child in. So "G" is correlated with a positive reinforcing stimulus, and "X" is correlated with an aversive stimulus.

Skinner has put a great deal of emphasis upon translating the language ordinarily used to describe mental events into the language of objective behaviorism. We have seen above the results of such translations in the realm of cognitive events (knowing, discriminating), motivation (needs, drives), and emotion. These translations have been important precursors to practical attempts to deal with a variety of "mental" issues in strictly behavioral terms. Some of the other issues so treated include thought processes, imagery, and self-control.

Thought processes, Skinner says, are nothing more or less than fictions invented to account for certain responses related to certain "problems," where a problem means essentially that "the organism has no behavior immediately available which will reduce the deprivation or provide escape from aversive stimulation" (1953, p. 246). More generally, such a problem is present when *"a response exists in strength which cannot be emitted"* (1953, p. 246). The hungry person has a problem only if no food is available: Eating responses exist in strength but cannot be emitted. The appearance of a solution to the problem, however, does not require the existence of "thought processes." It merely requires that the strength of the problem-solving response was weak but grows stronger. When the response is emitted which "solves the problem," Skinner states, what we need to know is that "variables change automatically during a period of time. Variables which have interfered with a solution may grow weak, and supporting variables may turn up" (1953, p. 252). In other words, while the person or the animal is having a problem of this kind, certain reflexes are strong in which the responses are actually interfering with responses which would reduce deprivation. For example, when hungry, you might be looking in the refrigerator, having forgotten that it was just cleaned out and all available food is now stored in the cupboard. You might keep going back to the refrigerator to make sure, checking every compartment. Gradually these interfering responses diminish in strength. The response of going to the cupboard increases in strength. Finally you do look in the cupboard; this response solves the problem. Notice that no discussion of "thought processes" has been necessary in this account.

The most unlikely application of Skinner's system of behavior may be to daydreams, dreams, imagery, and fantasy. Indeed, Skinner writes: "Perhaps the most difficult problem in the analysis of behavior is raised by responses beginning 'I see . . . ,' 'I hear . . . ,' and so on, *when the customary stimuli are lacking.* Here an accurate formulation of responses which describe one's own discriminative behavior is essential" (1953, pp. 265-266).

When the customary stimuli are present (the tree in the garden is really there or the auto outside is really honking), the "discriminative behavior" referred to in Skinner's statement is likely to be described by psychologists as sensation, perception, or recognition. Described by the perceiver in ordinary language it would appear as "I see the tree in the garden," "I hear the auto honking," or "I recognize Uncle Joe's car—that's the way it sounds when he honks the horn." But when the customary stimuli are absent, the psychological description of such discriminative behavior would be in terms of imagery, memory, dreaming, or fantasy. Described by the person in ordinary language it might appear as "I can see the tree in the garden now, just the way it was when I was a child," or "I remember the tree in the garden," or "I can just imagine the tree in the garden," or "In my dream I could see the tree in the garden." Skinner's analysis of these statements is that they are Type S conditioned responses.

At some point in the person's history a tree was an actual stimulus. As an unconditioned stimulus it produced a response of "seeing a tree." Other people said such things as "see the tree." This would serve as a conditioned stimulus. Later the person might say "I see the tree," and this behavior would gain the same value as a conditioned stimulus. Notice that the external stimulus "See the tree" (CS) precedes the external stimulus of the actual tree (US) which elicits the response of actually seeing the tree (UR). In accordance with the Law of Type S Conditioning "See the tree" (CS) will eventually come to evoke the response of actually seeing the tree (UR) in the absence of the actual tree (US). This is exactly what happens in all Type S conditioning: the conditioned stimulus comes to evoke a conditioned response in the absence of the original unconditioned stimulus.

How had the child also learned to respond

with appropriate words such as "I see the tree" when actually confronted with a tree? Skinner's analysis of this learning is summed up in the following statement from his work on *Verbal Behavior* (1957, p. 31): "A child acquires verbal behavior when relatively unpatterned vocalizations, selectively reinforced, gradually assume forms which produce appropriate consequences in a given verbal community." For example, English-speaking parents would emit positive reinforcement when the child first vocalizes "ma-ma" or "spoon." Thus the learning of language is conceived as the operant conditioning (Type R) of vocalizing responses. The use of language in describing discriminative behavior such as "I see the tree" is more closely tied to respondent conditioning (Type S) of perceptual or sensory responses. Thus imagery, dreams, and similar cognitive phenomena are treated as conditioned sensations or perceptions.

One of the remaining bastions of mentalistic theory is the concept of free will. Most people believe that they have thought processes, inner imagery, and the ability to use these processes and imagery to choose freely what they will do. Not only do they solve problems in a spontaneous way, actively thinking through the issue, but they can decide whether or not to implement the solution once found. More generally, people believe they control their own behavior. (The Constitution and the United States Statutes also assume that the individual has control over his or her own behavior.)

How does Skinner deal with this matter of self-control or free will? He argues (1953, pp. 230ff.) that self-control is accomplished through a number of relatively simple operations upon stimuli and responses. For example, one physical response is used to control another, as when we shut our mouth tightly and swallow in order to control a belch response at table. Such control is reinforced

by avoiding the aversive stimuli (punishment, embarrassment) which otherwise would follow if we did not control our behavior. We may remove discriminative stimuli that are correlated with a response which is to be controlled. For example, we can remove all objects associated with a particular unpleasant event in order to control our conditioned responses of "thinking" about the event whenever we see the objects. We may reduce unwanted emotional responses by going away for a rest or by concentrating on stimuli which elicit happy emotional responses. In these and other cases, however, the ultimate source of the control lies not with the individual but with the community which is that individual's social environment. The community teaches the need for control by arranging for aversive consequences to follow certain behaviors; and it often teaches precisely the responses required to exert the control, such as placing the hand over the mouth in case of a yawn or cough in public.

Thus there is only a semblance of free will. In fact there is nothing inside our skin that is an uncaused cause; there is no central psychic entity which "thinks," "solves problems," "forms images," has "free will," or exerts "self-control." Each of these phenomena is illusory. Each can be described adequately in terms of stimuli and responses and conditioning. Several of these matters are illustrated in an interesting discussion provided by Skinner and reprinted in box 4.2.

In this section we have emphasized what might be called the "conceptual" accomplishments of Skinner's approach. We have taken for granted that many applications have been made in the area of therapy and education, as exemplified in the cases of Anne and Rick mentioned at the beginning of this chapter. Many advances in applied psychology have been contributed by Skinner and his coworkers, and many of these developments are well known, as in teaching (Skinner, 1968), modifying the behavior of psychotic patients (Allyon and Azrin, 1965), or in reducing the use of aversive discipline in correctional and detention facilities by improving conformity responses (Gambrill, 1976). Many other relevant applications can be found in edited collections of articles such as that by Honig (1966) or McGinnies and Ferster (1971), and of course in original sources such as the *Journal of the Experimental Analysis of Behavior.*

Critique of Skinner's Theory

Skinner's system has been one of the main targets of criticism by humanistic psychologists, since his views appear to threaten cherished ideals of individuality and seem to deny the real complexity of human personality. In his view behavior is *all* that we should study, all we need to study, all there *is* to study. What is more, in Skinner's approach, behavior is simply behavior. The peck of a pigeon is no different from the verbal response of a politician: Both can be brought under stimulus control, both will show characteristic response rates as a function of particular reinforcement schedules, and so on. Behavior up and down the phylogenetic scale can be studied in precisely the same way, with the same set of concepts. A green light can be just as good a discriminative stimulus for a chicken as it can for a truck driver. But is there no difference then between animals and people?

Storms of criticism have often gathered around Skinner's theory. He has summarized these recently (1974 pp. 4, 5), listing no less than twenty criticisms that are commonly made about behaviorism and about the science of behavior or its associated technology of behavior modification. It seems possible to group these twenty criticisms into five main classes as follows:

1. Behaviorism *neglects* important facts of human personality such as consciousness, feelings, intentions, purpose, cognitive processes, the sense of self, the uniqueness of individuals, and so on.
2. Behaviorism is *limited* to formulations about stimuli and responses, notably in connection with animals, whose behaviors it can predict and control so long as they are captive in the laboratory.
3. Behaviorism is *sterile* in its oversimplified, naive, superficial, and pseudoscientific treatment of human behavior, and any facts it presumes to have discovered or technologies it presumes to have invented either are trivial, are already known, or could just as easily have been made or made known by common sense.
4. Behaviorism is *immoral* in its reduction of human personality to elementary reflexes, in its antidemocratic advocacy of manipulative control of human behavior, and in its mistreatment of traditional virtues such as morality or justice.
5. Behaviorism is *paradoxical*, because if behavior is controlled by contingencies of reinforcement due to conditioning, then the behavior of the behaviorist or behavioral scientist must itself be similarly controlled; therefore his statements are simply the result of conditioning and cannot be taken as true propositions. This criticism seems to claim that if the statements of behaviorists are true, then those statements are conditioned responses; but conditioned responses can neither be true nor false, and therefore the statements of behaviorists cannot be true (and cannot be false). Collapsing the sequence of propositions we find that if the statements of behaviorists are true then they cannot be true, which is a paradox.

We shall take up these criticisms in turn and consider briefly their justification.

Neglect

Skinner states that this criticism, like all the others, is based upon misunderstandings of behaviorism and is wrong. As we have seen in this chapter, his system does not neglect experience, purpose, feelings, or cognitive processes; it simply translates the words referring to these matters into the language of behavioral science. As Skinner says (1974, p. 19), the behaviorist translates verbal expressions with mentalistic meanings into phrases which do not implicate a ghostly world of completely inaccessible "psychic" experiences. But of course it is not completely and simply a *translation* in the sense of trying to keep the original meaning, for "what is felt or introspectively observed is not some nonphysical world of consciousness, mind, or mental life but the observer's own body" (Skinner, 1974, p. 17). And therefore the translation also does in fact omit something—namely "mind" and similar concepts—and does neglect what it omits. But Skinner justifies this omission as being a contribution to science and to human affairs, for "In this way we repair the major damage wrought by mentalism . . . education, politics, psychotherapy, penology, and many other fields of human affairs are suffering from the eclectic use of a lay vocabulary" (Skinner, 1974, pp. 17, 18). Some mentalistic expressions "can be 'translated into behavior,' others [must be] discarded as unnecessary or meaningless" (Skinner, 1974, p. 17).

Limited

The criticism that Skinner's system of behavior is limited to the conditioned responses of captive animals is apparently unjustified. As we saw in the previous section, conceptual and practical applications have been made to human behavior and continue to be made.

Sterile

The charge that behaviorism is sterile or superficial seems to address the criterion of *depth* in the evaluation of a theory. Probably it is connected with the charge of neglect, for what is neglected is perhaps the essence of what would constitute "depth" in the opinion of these critics: Such matters as will, feelings, unconscious motives, and the like. Instead Skinner's system treats of stimuli and conditioned responses, the details of lever-pressing or eye blinks, and their relations to stimulus contingencies. But this surely is only one meaning of "depth," a meaning of personal, psychic, subjective, or unconscious forces. No one would seriously charge that the theory of atomic physics is superficial because it attempts to account for the constitution of all matter in terms of combinations of atoms. Skinner's system of behavior attempts to account for complex behaviors in terms of combinations of reflexes and their associated contingencies. When "depth" is interpreted as theoretical penetration, then a mere listing of events in the record would be shallow; an analysis of the composition of those events from elementary components would be deep. It seems that Skinner is correct in his view that the criticism of sterility is wrong.

Immoral

The criticism that Skinner's system of behavior and associated technologies are immoral rests upon his reductionistic analysis of human behavior and upon his advocacy that established principles for the scientific control of behavior be applied in human affairs, especially government. This advocacy entails rejection of a number of traditionally held virtues and convictions—for example, that citizens have free will rather than being determined by contingencies of reinforcement in their votes and other behaviors. The argument seems to involve questions of social philosophy, and although important in that context, it seems remote from questions of personality theory as such. One of the chief arguments against Skinner's advocacy has come from Rogers (Rogers, 1974; Rogers and Skinner, 1976), who is very explicit about the philosophical nature of these issues. Rogers writes for example: "the basic difference between a behavioristic and a humanistic approach to human beings is a *philosophical* choice. . . . Choosing the humanistic philosophy, for example, . . . leads to a deeply democratic political philosophy rather than management by an elite" (Rogers, 1974, pp. 118-119). Skinner responds to this argument by asserting that "No one steps outside the causal stream. No one really intervenes" (Skinner, 1974, p. 206). In other words, even the "elite" are causally determined in their behaviors and are just as much subject to control by contingencies as anyone is. To fear a dictatorship is to assume that some individuals (the dictators) do step outside the causal stream and have free will and (evil) intentions. The very statements of a "philosophical choice" implies such stepping outside the causal stream. The criticism, then, is based upon a misunderstanding of Skinner's entire system of behavior, which applies to all organisms alike, governors as well as governed.

Paradoxical

We already found that the criticism of paradox in the behaviorist's position can be sustained. But like most paradoxes it probably will be resolved by proper philosophical analysis. There is little we can do about it except to say that it exists. However it provides absolutely no warrant for disbelieving the empirical findings or the scientific theories of behaviorism. These exist also, and their truth-values must be ascertained quite independently of the truth-values to be assigned to particular utterances of a particular behaviorist.

Commentary on the Criticisms

Where the criticisms are scientific rather than philosophical, then, they are generally found to be weak when subjected to scrutiny from a scientific point of view. One exception is the charge that behaviorism neglects feelings and intentions and consciousness, not as terms in the English language, but as realities of an order different from stimuli and responses. The attempt to treat them all the same yields some important modifications in the scientific meaning of the constructs of stimulus and response.

We all know, for example, that we have intentions which have not so far resulted in overt behavior. Indeed some of our best intentions never get translated into behavior! How does Skinner deal with these phenomena? He offers several alternative interpretations, such that if one does not seem to apply then "one of the other interpretations may well be preferred" (Skinner, 1953, p. 264). One interpretation is that when a person expresses an intention of doing something he or she is actually "describing a history of variables which would enable an independent observer to describe the behavior in the same way if a knowledge of the variables were available to him" (Skinner, 1953, p. 263).

Another interpretation suggested is that the individual who "describes unemitted behavior" (expresses an intention) may actually have created the relevant stimuli for that description response by emitting the responses so described in a reduced form. "Sometimes it is said that the reduced form is merely the beginning of the overt form—that the private event is incipient or inchoate behavior" (Skinner, 1953, p. 263). For instance, if I am at the office and make the statement "I'm going home in half an hour," then my statement is a descriptive response to stimuli produced by covertly emitting the "going home" behavior.

But we read in Skinner's 1938 book (p. 6) that "Behavior is only part of the total activity of an organism. . . . Behavior is what an organism is *doing*—or more accurately what it is observed by another organism to be doing . . . behavior is that part of the functioning of an organism which is engaged in acting upon or having commerce with the outside world." Can it be seriously supposed that an observer could detect the covert "going home" behavior even with the most sensitive of conceivable instruments? Is that covert action really acting upon the outside world? It seems improbable. It appears that the meanings of the constructs of *behavior* and of *response* and even of *stimuli* have changed in the transition from descriptions of overt to interpretations of covert behavior. This change has gone unacknowledged by Skinner (and others).

Although in most respects the twenty criticisms levelled at Skinner's theory seem to be adequately answered (with the exception noted), there is a twenty-first criticism that has not so far been dealt with satisfactorily. This is a criticism that behaviorism (as applied to human beings) is predicated on the empirical assumption that human beings are subject to conditioning of Types S and R as demonstrated in animals. This assumption has come under serious question in recent years.

A major critic is Noam Chomsky, a specialist in the study of language, who has reviewed Skinner's work on verbal behavior

(Chomsky, 1959). The available evidence, he says, makes it very unlikely that language develops in children through the conditioning of specific verbal responses, under reinforcement control by the child's language community. In Chomsky's view, the development of language in children occurs largely without any such reinforcement, and indeed without specific training from adults. On the positive side Chomsky states, "it is beyond question that children acquire a good deal of their verbal and nonverbal behavior by casual observation and imitation of adults and other children" (Chomsky, 1959, p. 41). Chomsky cites evidence that points to children's forming very early in life a grammar which then allows them to generate new sentences and to recognize completely new sentences when they occur. For example, we recognize immediately when a statement is a sentence and when it is not, even though the same words may be used. Chomsky gives the example of the sentence "friendly young dogs seem harmless," compared with "harmless seem dogs young friendly." He notes that every adult reading a newspaper has no trouble understanding large numbers of sentences which are completely new to the reader and indeed he or she will note distortions from good sentence structure, misprints, and so on. Chomsky rejects the learning-theorist's construct of *stimulus generalization* as a useful explanation for these abilities, saying, "Talk of 'stimulus generalization' in such a case simply perpetuates the mystery under a new title. These abilities indicate that there must be fundamental processes at work quite independently of 'feedback' from the environment" (Chomsky, 1959, p. 42).

Skinner has made an idiosyncratic reply to Chomsky. He notes (1967, p. 408) that he has always paid much less attention to the reactions of other scientists than to the reactions of the rats and pigeons he studies. Posi-

tive or negative criticisms by his contemporaries, he says, make him wary, especially because they are likely to cause him to take time away from work. And so he admits that he has never read more than a few pages of Chomsky's critique. Skinner relates that Clark Hull used to accuse him of not making hypotheses because he was afraid of being wrong. (Remember that Skinner prefers descriptions of conditions and consequences, and avoids making hypotheses about "inner" entities and processes.) In some sense, he admits, he wants his own statements to be right rather than wrong, but he is more interested in "measures for the control of a subject matter" (Skinner, 1967, p. 409). Such measures "are not so much right or wrong as effective or ineffective, and arguments are of no avail." For the same reason he is "not interested in psychological theories . . . in mathematical models, in hypothetico-deductive systems, or in other verbal systems which must be *proved* right."

It seems that Skinner's reply to Chomsky is that verbal conditioning procedures are effective, and if the implied description of *how* they work (through the various laws of induction, conditioning, and so on) is wrong in some sense—inaccurate, for example—it is of little importance. Skinner's position appears to be pragmatic: Whatever works or is effective is scientifically acceptable.

Another body of research has been gradually accumulating since the 1940s. This research is aimed at determining whether conditioning takes place in human subjects in the same way that it takes place in animals.

Brewer (1975) has reviewed a large number of studies involving what he calls "dissociation experiments." These experiments all are designed to provide information as to whether conditioning takes place in an unconscious, automatic way, or whether it takes place only under conditions in which the human subject is aware of relationships between CS and US (in Type S) or of the contingency between response and reinforcement (in Type R). Thus the issue is concerned with the interpretation of conditioning results in humans. One explanation (that of Skinner and other behaviorist theorists) states that the conditioning occurs in humans in the same way that it does in animals. An alternative explanation is precisely the mentalistic (cognitive) sort of explanation that Skinner has opposed. It states that if conditioning appears to take place among humans it is because the subject either correctly *guesses* the connection between CS and US (Type S) and responds accordingly or correctly *infers* the contingency (Type R) and what the experimenter wants the subject to do. If willing to be compliant, the subject behaves as expected, but not otherwise. Thus in many instances cognitive theory and conditioning theory generate opposite predictions. For instance, the cognitive theory would say that only those subjects who are aware of the relationship (contingency) between response and reinforcement will give the results expected by conditioning theory. Subjects who are not aware of the contingency will not show those results. As an example, subjects might be presented with a series of adjectives ("Brown; Strong; Hard; Famous," and so on.) To each such stimulus the subject is to respond with a noun. The experimenter might reinforce (praise) each response involving a *plural* noun ("brown–gloves; strong–women; hard–exams; famous–men"), and not reinforce other nouns ("brown–dog; strong–drink"). In this experiment, conditioning theory would predict that the rate of plural nouns will increase if the reinforcement is positive. But cognitive theory would predict that, if the subject is aware of the contingency and if the subject is hostile to the experimenter (or to psychology experiments in general), then the rate of plural nouns will decrease under positive reinforcement. Knowing what the experimenter wants, the hostile subject will do just the opposite!

Brewer examined thirteen studies by various investigators, most of them conducted after 1960. In each study the subjects, after conditioning, were simply told that the US would no longer follow the CS. Conditioning theory would predict that under these circumstances a straightforward extinction curve would be obtained (as in figure 4.2). Cognitive theory would predict that extinction would be very rapid, and that, in those cases where the subject really believes the experimenter, extinction would be immediate and complete. In twelve of the studies rapid extinction did take place; in those studies which examined subjects' beliefs it was found that those who believed the experimenter showed almost complete extinction immediately. These results support the theoretical model proposed by cognitive theory.

Seven studies of original conditioning of the GSR (a response measured on the skin surface) were examined by Brewer. In these studies the subjects were simply told that the CS was supposed to elicit the GSR. It did so in all cases. In some of these studies control subjects were actually given the CS-US pairings and it was found that the amplitude of GSR responses was greater for the subjects given verbal information than for those who went through the actual pairings.

Studies with heart rate and other autonomic responses similarly tended largely to support the cognitive model and not the conditioning model. Studies with operant responses, such as marble dropping in children, likewise found conditioning only in children who were aware of the contingency. The clear effects of different schedules of reinforcement (see figure 4.12) were also found in four studies in which subjects were told the contingency; when subjects were not told, the usual findings (such as scallops in FI) were not obtained. Although a few types of studies apparently do yield expected conditioning without awareness (such as operant conditioning of GSR), Brewer points out that in such designs it is difficult for the experimenter to know whether or not some cognitive activity is being inadvertently reinforced. The balance of well-controlled studies of diverse kinds by many different investigators, Brewer concludes, is clearly in favor of the cognitive model: "Conditioning" occurs when the human subject is aware and wants to comply with the experimenter's wishes.

For years I have accepted the results of human conditioning experiments and the reports of behavior modification in field situations (such as in schoolrooms, correctional institutions, mental hospitals, and so on). It has seemed sensible to conclude that human subjects *can* be conditioned in much the same way that animal subjects are conditioned. Scattered reports of variations in human conditioning based upon awareness of the subject or the subject's personality type have seemed to me to indicate that, like everything else in psychology, there are individual differences in the phenomena of conditioning. This position is also that taken by several other researchers, notably Eysenck (see chapter 17), who says that the ease of conditioning depends in part on how neurotic and how introverted the subject is. But the evidence so carefully assembled by Brewer, based upon a wide range of studies, suggests that we have all been deceived by thinking too little about the nature of human subjects. They do not walk into a laboratory experiment without some sort of reflection or concern or curiosity about that situation. Many presumably have some hypotheses in their mind as to what it's all about. Perhaps some feel inclined to

identify with the experimenter, hoping some day to be psychologists themselves. At any rate, they are presumably quite different from animals in regard to their actual or potential social relationship with the experimenter and with regard to the contents of their problem-solving processes as they sign up for and enter an experiment. The result is that human subjects have *appeared* to be conditionable: They have simulated the expected results whenever they were aware enough of the contingencies and wanted to comply for some reason.

It can be argued that, as in the cases of Anne and Rick described above, behavior modification based upon Skinner's principles has proven successful in teaching, in corrections, and in treatment of the mentally ill and that therefore it must be accurate despite the results cited by Brewer. This line of reasoning is certainly cogent, since something satisfactory and real is presumably happening in these events of behavior modification. But the question now before us is whether it is simply behavior modification as an automatic result of stimulus "control" or whether the subjects change their behavior as a result of cognitive factors and willingness to comply. If the subjects are adult humans, the evidence strongly suggests that the cognitive model is the correct one. If the subjects are children we must now at least entertain the hypothesis that apparent modification through conditioning is actually due to cognitive strategies and compliance. This means that the attempt to do away with all reference to inner events of experience—thoughts, feelings, ideas, wishes, and so on—has so far not succeeded. There is another and more sinister implication to be drawn from the results surveyed by Brewer, but since it refers to personality theory in general it will not be discussed here but at the end of the book.

Self-directed Behavior Modification

Behavior modification is a generic name for a variety of treatment methods that depend on learning theories or behavior theories such as Skinner's for their rationale. In recent years interest has turned to the possibility of persons' directing their own behavior modification (Watson and Tharp, 1972). Trying out one of these procedures may give the reader a personal insight into what is really going on. For if the underlying scientific theory is actually inaccurate but some of these procedures are effective anyway, then presumably they are effective for reasons which no one at present understands. It is all very well to call upon "cognitive theory," but it too will have to be checked for error and the concurrent effectiveness of other plausible factors such as suggestion, redirected accountability, or revitalized interest. Setting all such possibilities aside for the moment, the reader is invited actually to modify some piece of unwanted behavior, using Skinner's technology, and then write up an account of what really happened.

First, select some piece of your own behavior that bothers you. Watson and Tharp (1972, p. 103) give two examples which probably are common. A student spends hours studying but gets little done; a professor tells people when he thinks they are not acting intelligently and then they get mad at him. What is reinforcing each behavior? For the student, his nonattending behavior while studying was found to be due to his attending too much to girls in the environment. After analyzing his situation from a behavioral viewpoint the student decided to study for one hour at a time in his room and then reward himself by going out to watch girls full-time for a period. For the professor, it was found that the reinforcer for his behavior was a feeling that **he** was intelligent. The authors suggested that he could get that same feeling by making an intelligent positive remark instead of a negative one.

An initial procedure followed by the student was to log his study times exactly for a period, and note also whether or which part was actually paying attention to his work. This simple record provided a baseline. Then he began noting what else he was doing and what other stimuli were in his environment. That was how he discovered the girl-watching behaviors. It was fortunate that he subsequently could arrange to use this same reinforcer for longer periods of concentrated study behavior in his room.

After you have isolated a behavior you wish to modify, you may be able to get a baseline count on it by keeping a record. Then try to isolate the reinforcer for that behavior. Then try to get that reinforcer for some appropriate substitute behavior. If this does not work and you still wish to extinguish the original behavior, then one way is to find a stronger reinforcer and use it to reinforce **avoidance** of the original behavior. For example, suppose you are a pinball addict and you decide it's time to quit. After making a record and obtaining a baseline, you search for the reinforcer. You find it is a certain thrill at beating the game. There probably is no substitute behavior that will give you the same thrill exactly. But perhaps there are stronger reinforcers. For example, you might have a favorite breakfast food. Make that your reinforcer. Now suppose you play pinball at least once a day five days a week. You decide that every relevant day you **avoid** playing pinball you get to have your favorite breakfast food next morning; otherwise you do **not** get it. If the favorite breakfast food does not work, find a stronger reinforcer and make **it** contingent on avoidance of pinball games.

Do not forget to keep a diary of what is going on inside yourself all the time: your interest, determination, resentment, hope, and so on as well as actual avoidances and reinforcements (or behaviors and nonreinforcements). After you have completed your experiment (keep it short—say three weeks), analyze the entire process from your notes and see if you can formulate some general principles as to why you did or did not manage to modify the behavior.

Report on an Experiment in Self-directed Behavior Modification

Code name of behavior: _____

Summary of baseline observations: _____

_____

Reinforcer(s) currently maintaining behavior (code if necessary): _____

_____

Substitute behavior tried (code again if desired): _____

_____

Decrease in frequency of original behavior? _____

If no, or if no substitute, stronger reinforcer(s) tried: _____

_____

Schedule selected: _____

Note that a variable ratio may be instituted by opening a different book each time the avoidance is successfully accomplished and noting the page number so opened without looking. If the number is even you get your reinforcement; if it is odd you do not. Or use a table of random numbers if you have one. Describe record of avoidance behaviors, failures, reinforcements and nonreinforcements:

_____

_____

From your notes, describe what really went on in modifying (or not modifying) your behavior:

_____

_____

_____

Summary

One of the most important assumptions made in B. F. Skinner's approach is that the causes of behavior, whether physical or mental, should not be sought inside the organism. Naming Pavlovian conditioning *respondent*, Skinner introduced the construct of *operant* as an emitted response and *operant conditioning* as the strengthening of a response through reinforcement produced by the response. He has invented many new pieces of apparatus for more effective conditioning (such as the Skinner box) and automated recording of responses (such as the cumulative recorder).

Use of these devices and variation of the ratio or timing of reinforcements relative to responses has shown that there are important differences in the curves of conditioning and extinction as a result of different schedules of reinforcement. Skinner's theory of the structure of behavior includes a number of laws of composition whereby component reflexes are built up into complex behaviors. These include the laws of conditioning, summation, chaining, induction, and others.

Skinner's theory has had widespread influence on psychology and has yielded many important applications, both conceptual and actual—in teaching and rehabilitation. The most important criticism of the theory comes from evidence which suggests that language development and human conditioning are based upon processes quite different from those proposed by Skinner. The definition of personality implicit in this theory is illustrated in figure 4.13.

In the next chapter we turn to the work of Carl Rogers, whose work has most often been cited as representing an approach completely opposed to that of B. F. Skinner. Rogers' theory represents the third of the three main ways of defining personality we dis-

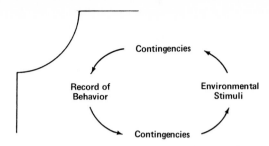

Figure 4.13. The definition of personality implicit in Skinner's theory

cussed in chapter 2, the definition of personality in terms of subjective experience.

INTRODUCTION

A theory which defines personality as subjective
   experience
Introduction to Rogers's life and work
   Rogers's life and professional career
   Rogers and humanistic psychology
   The central hypothesis
   Experience is the highest authority
   Caring about clear communication
Rogers's theory of the structure of experience
   The meaning of experience
   Awareness
   Self
      Self-concept
      Self-structure
      Q-sort methods for describing the self
   Openness to experience
Rogers's theory of motivation
   The actualizing tendency
   Need for positive regard
   Need for positive self-regard
   Organismic valuing process
   Introjected values
   Conditions of worth
Personality consequences of conditions of worth
   Incongruence
   Vulnerability
   Anxiousness
   Psychological maladjustment
The fully functioning person
   Unconditional positive regard
   Empathic understanding
Accomplishments of Rogers's theory
   Client-centered psychotherapy
      A theory of therapy
      Empirical support for the theory
   Other applications
   Developments in theory
   New developments in psychotherapy
   Marriage and other relationships
   Parent effectiveness training
Critique of Rogers's theory
   Rogers as a humanistic psychologist
   Accuracy of the theory as determined by
      empirical research
      Example of research on "denial to awareness"
Research on psychotherapy; conflicting
   evidence for the basic hypothesis
Logical analysis of the theory by Krause
Fruitfulness of the theory
The theory as a theory of the structure of
   experience only
Workshop 5   An exercise in empathic
   understanding
Summary

Personality as Subjective Experience: Rogers

In this chapter we study a theory which represents the third main approach to defining personality, namely the approach through subjective experience. This is Carl Rogers's theory of personality.

Carl Rogers was born in Oak Park, Illinois, in 1902. It was a farm family, with five other children. Rogers intended to study scientific farming when he entered the University of Wisconsin. His experience in Christian youth work, however, led him to go on to Union Theological Seminary in New York. There he came to appreciate the possibilities of professional psychology as a means of helping individuals, and so he transferred to Teacher's College, Columbia University, where he received his doctoral degree. In 1928 he moved to Rochester, New York, to work in the Child Study Department of the Society for the Prevention of Cruelty to Children. Out of this department grew the Rochester Guidance Center, of which he became the first Director.

From 1940 to 1944 he was professor of psychology at the Ohio State University, and there began the first formal development of theory and practice in client-centered psychotherapy. This innovative body of thought gradually came to influence large numbers of clinical psychologists, educators, and others

concerned with the facilitation of personality growth and of interpersonal relations. The first systematic presentation of the new approach came in 1942 with the publication of Rogers's book *Counseling and Psychotherapy,* containing among other things some of the earliest transcriptions of recorded interviews between counselor and client.

In 1945 Rogers moved to the University of Chicago to establish a counseling center. This center proved to be a source of highly productive research and theoretical development, funded in large part by the Rockefeller Foundation. In 1951 Rogers published the book *Client-centered Therapy,* in which he developed a systematic theory of personality. This was soon followed by an even more rigorous formulation prepared for the prestigious volumes of *Psychology: A Study of a Science,* edited by Sigmund Koch. Rogers's contribution was published in volume 3 of this study, under the title of "A Theory of Therapy, Personality, and Interpersonal Relationships, as Developed in the Client-centered Framework" (Rogers, 1959).

Together with the 1951 book, this 1959 paper constitutes the essential statement of Rogers's theory of personality, and these are the two main sources for the present chapter.

After leaving the University of Chicago in 1957 Rogers spent some years at the University of Wisconsin, where he and colleagues undertook an extensive project on the application of client-centered therapy to schizophrenic patients. Following that he spent some years as a Fellow of the Western Behavioral Sciences Institute. In 1968 he took a position as Fellow at the Center for Studies of the Person in La Jolla, California, where he still works.

Rogers has been highly honored in psychology. He was president of the American Association for Applied Psychology in 1944 and President of the American Psychological Association in 1946. In 1956 he received the first Distinguished Scientific Contribution Award (along with Wolfgang Kohler and Kenneth W. Spence); in 1972 he received the first Award for Distinguished Professional Contribution. Both awards were made by the American Psychological Association.

As Rogers notes in a retrospect, his work has had its greatest impact in the area of humanistic psychology (Rogers, 1974). The study of "the whole person" constitutes the essential basis of humanistic psychology (Buhler and Allen, 1972); and the Citation accompanying his 1972 Award began: "His commitment to the whole person has been an example which has guided and challenged the practice of psychology in the school, in industry, and throughout the community." What does it mean to be committed to the whole person? Negatively, it means not being committed to some part of the person, like the midbrain, or the memory, or the intelligence. Positively, it provides the central hypothesis from which client-centered therapy was founded: "that the individual has within himself vast resources for self-understanding, for altering his self-concept, his attitudes, and his self-directed behavior—and that these resources can be tapped if only a definable climate of facili-

tative psychological attitudes can be provided" (Rogers, 1974, p. 116).

In following the implications of this hypothesis Rogers and his colleagues have developed a form of psychotherapy which requires the therapist to open his or her mind as wide as possible and listen fully to what the client is saying. Rogers believes that this is the reason his hypothesis has such broad impact upon so many fields of research and practice. Not only does such listening have beneficial effects upon the client, but in addition it provides the listener with the clearest possible picture of the workings of the human mind. Laying aside all preconceptions the therapist listens to the client and learns what it is really like to be that client, to look at the world as that client does, and to suffer life's slings and arrows as that client suffers them. New insights into human personality have been gained from such therapeutic listening, and Rogers and his colleagues have always followed up these insights with objective research to determine their general validity.

The hypothesis has had its impacts upon Rogers as a person. In a delightful chapter entitled "This Is Me" (1961, pp. 3-27), Rogers tells some of the things he has learned from "thousands of hours . . . spent working intimately with individuals in personal distress." He has found that it doesn't help to pretend to be something he is not. He is more effective with clients when he can also listen to himself and be himself. It can be enormously helpful to the other person when Rogers allows himself fully to understand what the person is saying, rather than only half understanding and half reacting critically. When channels are open so that others communicate their real feelings to him, Rogers feels personally enriched. The more open he is to whatever realities of thought, feeling, attitude, opinion, or behavior may be in himself or the other person, the more Rogers finds himself accepting of those realities and the less he feels any need or obligation to try to change them. He finds he can trust his own experience and not be guided by the opinions and evaluations that others have toward himself, his work, and his ideas. *"Experience is, for me, the highest authority"* (Rogers, 1961, p. 23), he says, and reinforces this view by saying that nothing in heaven or earth can take precedence over his own direct experience, not even scientific research. He finds that *"facts are friendly,"* that life is good, and that people are basically good and tend to grow in positive directions.

The facts Rogers and his colleagues have learned about people are not at all limited by being confined to some small or specialized segment of the population. The therapists deal with people in all walks of life. The list of persons with whom Rogers has personally worked reads like a cross section of our society: men, women, children, business executives, hospitalized patients, students, teachers, administrators, factory workers, black militants, members of opposing political factions or minority groups, religious leaders, housewives, and others.

Looking back over the years of his professional career Rogers sees one "overriding theme": that he has cared deeply about clear communication, trying to make himself understood and to understand others, and trying to help other people understand themselves as well as their friends and enemies. "I have worked," he writes (1974, p. 121), "for better communication between groups whose perceptions and experiences are poles apart: strangers, members of different cultures, representatives of different strata of society."

Behind all distortions in communication and all misunderstandings, Rogers believes, lie distortions in the personality. If the person were fully functioning such distortions would not exist. The theory of personality and its nature and functioning which Rogers formulated suggests very clearly how such distortions arise; his theory of therapy suggests how they may be corrected and how the person will grow as a result toward full functioning.

In this chapter we shall first examine Rogers's basic theory of structure, which deals with the nature and organization of experience, awareness, and the self-concept. Then we shall describe his theory of motivation and his construct of the fully functioning person. Finally we shall consider both the accomplishments of Rogers's theory and some critiques of it.

Rogers's Theory of the Structure of Experience

Experience

The central construct in Rogers's theory of personality is *experience*: everything that is going on inside a person of which he or she could become conscious. That includes everything that is conscious, everything that is in the focus of attention or awareness, and everything that is only on the periphery of awareness—in the back of your mind, so to speak. Moreover it includes everything that might enter awareness but momentarily does not, as, for example, feelings of hunger when you are completely preoccupied with winning a contest—only afterwards do you realize that you are ravenous.

Experience does not include physiological happenings such as blood flow or changes in the blood's composition, because these things would not potentially enter awareness. Experience does include events which are perceptions of the environment, memories returning, current feelings and thoughts, and so on. Experience happens in the here and now. It refers to the present moment of experiencing.

Awareness

Awareness is consciousness. To be aware of some part of your experience is to be conscious of it. Rogers says that awareness arises from symbolization of a portion of experience. The symbol can be verbal, as a thought formulated in words in your head, or it might be some other kind of symbol, like a visual image, Morse code, or a memorized bit of music.

Self

Important parts of experience involve the person's own body and relationships to the environment. A baby, for example, may see its own toes and hear its own babbling noises. You may see your face in the mirror. Most people respond readily to their own names. The perceptions of self and self-in-relationship come to form a single whole part of experience, a gestalt. The self is usually available to awareness but we are not necessarily conscious of it at any given time. Rogers speaks of the *self-concept* when it is looked at from the point of view of the person. He speaks of the *self-structure* when thinking about the self from an objective or scientific viewpoint.

The self is a changing gestalt, but at any one moment it has a particular set of characteristics. Hence appropriate assessment devices can capture the self-structure of a person at a particular point in time. One technique is the *Q-sort* method of self-description, in which a person sorts numerous statements according to which ones best describe his or her self at this moment. For example, you might arrange the following items in the order that best describes you right now:

a. I am a happy person
b. I am emotionally mature
c. I get on well with most people I know
d. I tend to be quite anxious much of the time

e. I feel driven and overworked most of the time
f. People don't seem to give me the respect I deserve.

Which item best describes you and which is least descriptive of your present self? Which item is the next best? In this way you can arrange the items from most descriptive to least descriptive. If there were 100 items the arrangement would provide an objective approximate picture of your present concept of self.

The self-concept also includes the values attached to these various perceptions. Some of these items may be true of you and you like that fact. Other things may be true of you but you dislike that fact and wish it were not so. Still other things may be not true of you. You may have put item *c* at the bottom of your list, for instance, and yet you approve of that characteristic and wish it were true of you. Not only do we evaluate our actual characteristics, then, but also we know to some extent what we would like to be, what we would wish to be true of our self. Rogers refers to such wishes as elements of the *ideal self*. It may be quite similar to the actual self-concept or very different from it.

Openness to Experience

Awareness does not necessarily include all portions of experience. For various reasons which we shall discuss later, there can be blocks against the symbolization of some experiences; or some experiences can be distorted in symbolization. Rogers gives the examples of someone who thinks of himself as a poor student, but who then gets a very good grade. He symbolizes this as pure luck, a mistake, or the stupidity of the professor. It is not symbolized straightforwardly as evidence of being a good student. This person would be described as not *open to the experience* of being a good student.

If all the experience that *could* become conscious actually did become conscious, we would say that person was completely open to experience. If none of it did, the person would be completely closed to experience. Between these two extremes lies a wide range of possibilities.

This wide variation in openness to experience, Rogers says, occurs because certain portions of experience may be threatening to the person. These portions may be threatening because they are inconsistent with the self-concept; that is, they go against or fail to confirm some element of the concept of self. A person who is fully open to experience would accept even inconsistent experiences, and would accept the change in the self-concept such experiences would produce. For example, a young man who thought he was really tough might feel like crying on the death of his friend. If open to experience, the young man would then change his ideas about how tough he is and acknowledge that he has tender spots as well; if not he would deny that he felt like crying and continue to believe in his total toughness. What would motivate the need to hang on to an inaccurate concept of self? Rogers's answer to this question is given in his theory of motivation and conditions of worth.

Rogers's Theory of Motivation

Rogers assumes that organisms have one dominant motivation, to *actualize* the potentialities and needs within them. In human beings this tendency becomes specialized in two ways. The person can develop and grow both as a physiological, anatomical entity and as a psychological and social being. The *self-actualizing tendency* involves, among other things, a need to be liked and respected by others—the *need for positive regard*—and the parallel need to like and think well of oneself—the *need for positive self-regard*.

The infant and child knows well what is good for it to do and be. It possesses a built-in, natural set of mechanisms for choosing what is helpful and nutritious, Rogers asserts, and avoiding what is harmful. Rogers calls this the *organismic valuing process*. But we are all exposed at an early age to the judgments of other people as to what is good for us to be and do. If we follow those judgments we receive their positive regard and can think well also of ourselves. When the values we place upon different elements of our experience and behavior reflect what other people have demanded, then we have *introjected* their values into ourselves. Following Standal (1954) Rogers calls these introjected values *conditions of worth*—the conditions under which we see ourselves as worthy to receive positive regard from others and from ourselves. They become the values we live by and our criteria for feelings of acceptability, of adequacy, of worthiness. If an unthinking parent, teacher, or peer group has persistently refused to treat us well unless we admit to being stupid, then it is highly likely that we shall carry that assumed stupidity with us as a condition of worth. We believe we are acceptable and deserve a place in life only so long as we are stupid and a poor student.

Personality Consequences of Conditions of Worth

The person who has accepted these conditions of worth is said to have been given *conditional positive regard*. Feelings of anxiety and a sense of being threatened result whenever some experience contradicts an element of the self-concept maintained under a given condition of worth. That experience threatens the person's feelings of worth because it contradicts this element of the self-concept.

But life goes on regardless, and new happenings occur each day. Our experience in life must therefore contain changes from day to day. If the self-concept does not change along with changing experiences of the self, if awareness of such new and different experiences is denied or distorted, then *incongruence* develops, widening the gap between one's self-concept (as symbolized in awareness) and those portions of experience pertaining to the self. This incongruence between real experience and the self-concept increases the likelihood that the person will have new experiences which threaten some condition of worth. The person is more *vulnerable* to threat; as a consequence, the person becomes more *anxious*. The more anxious the person becomes, the more the person is *psychologically maladjusted*. From incongruence, the basic abstract condition of the personality, all these other features—vulnerability, anxiety, maladjustment—may be said to follow.

Figure 5.1 illustrates several of these relationships. Note that the ideal self is *not* directly implicated in incongruence, represented by the shaded portion. All elements of the ideal self are assumed to be in awareness, as is the self-concept; but portions of self-experiences *denied to awareness* are not in the self-concept. The self-concept, therefore, is only partially congruent with relevant experience. Also it only partially overlaps the ideal self. The person represented in the diagram would be somewhat maladjusted, not fully functioning.

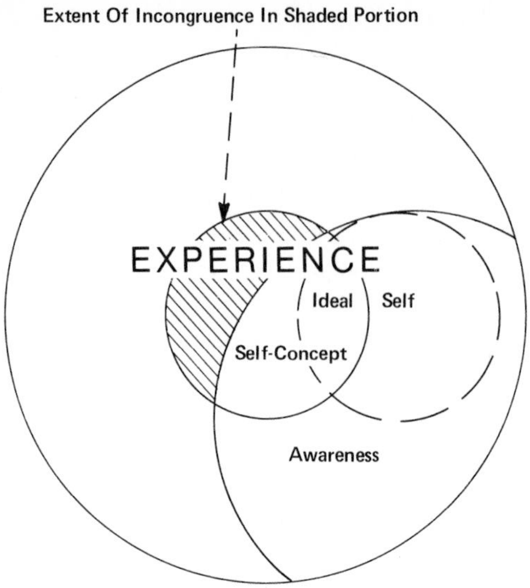

The Fully Functioning Person

All of the maladjusted person's incongruence, we have seen, flows from the fact that conditions of worth were implanted by people who offer only conditional positive regard. If all of the important, significant people around

Extent Of Incongruence In Shaded Portion

EXPERIENCE
Ideal Self
Self-Concept
Awareness

Figure 5.1. Relationships between experience, awareness, self-concept, and ideal self in Rogers's theory

one at an early age offer their positive regard unconditionally, Rogers says, one can become *fully functioning*. When the client-centered therapist gives unconditional positive regard to the client, it releases the client's growth potentials. So if parents and other family and important people would give the child only unconditional positive regard, it would allow the child to grow up fully functioning. What kind of person would that be?

The fully functioning person is one in whom there is congruence between experience and self-concept. The person is fully open to experience, having no conditions of worth. All evaluations of experience are based solely on an organismic valuing process, not upon introjected values.

Because the person is open to experience, therefore the self-concept will change with new experiences about the self. For in the fully functioning person all experiences are symbolized just as accurately as the experience itself makes possible. There is no distortion, no denial. Hence the self-concept can change as new experiences of the self occur. Rogers states (1959, p. 234) that the degree to which a person approximates full functioning depends upon two factors. First, it depends upon the extent to which the person experiences unconditional positive regard from those people who are important in his or her life. Second, this unconditional positive regard must be communicated through *empathic understanding* of the person's *internal frame of reference.*

These two new concepts must be clarified further. *Empathic understanding* is simply the full, untouched, appreciative understanding of another person's internal frame of reference. An individual's *internal frame of reference* is "all of the realm of experience which is available to the awareness of the individual at a given moment. It includes the full range of sensations, perceptions, meanings, and memories which are available to consciousness" (Rogers, 1959, p. 210).

Rogers adds that only the individual can know the internal frame of reference completely. It is that person's subjective world. Another person can only achieve some degree of empathic understanding, an inference which depends upon seeing the world through the individual's eyes.

It is not enough for the important people in an individual's life (*significant others* is the term Rogers used) to have unconditional positive regard; they must also communicate it to the individual. What they communicate must be based upon empathic understanding and must as far as possible match the reality of the individual's internal frame of reference. It must be communicated as unconditionally accepting and prizing the way the person conceives of himself or herself. If a woman does not see herself as beautiful then telling her how much you appreciate her beauty would not be unconditional positive regard.

Empathic understanding, furthermore, does not include a penetrating diagnostic comprehension of what is really right or wrong or true about a person regardless of what that person thinks about it. It does not mean being able to interpret causes and characteristics of people that they have not seen before—to "psych them out." It does not mean having a deep insight into another person's motivation. It does mean humbly trying to understand and even feel the way a person at this moment consciously feels, what they think about self and others, what they want.

Person A may have unconditional positive regard for everything about Person B, including body, manners, and experience. But Person A *communicates* unconditional positive regard through empathic understanding of Person B's *conscious* experience. No conditions are set up. No changes are required, but if they occur they are equally accepted. No part of the person is questioned or doubted or diminished. All of it is accepted and prized and respected, as it is now and as it may change later.

When these conditions hold true, Rogers says, then the person can become fully functioning. The person can be fully open to all experiences. The person is not vulnerable, or anxious, or maladjusted.

Accomplishments of Rogers's Theory

The first and most important accomplishment of Rogers's theory of personality is *client-centered psychotherapy.* Rogers has formulated a specific theory of therapy that follows almost precisely from his theory of personality. The theoretical description of the therapeutic process, for example, includes the following conditions:

1. The client is in a state of incongruence, being anxious and vulnerable

2. The therapist experiences unconditional positive regard for the client
3. The therapist experiences empathic understanding of the client's internal frame of reference
4. The client perceives at least minimally the unconditional positive regard and the empathic understanding which the therapist gives.

Another condition described by Rogers is *genuineness*—the congruence of the therapist in the relationship. What the therapist actually experiences in the relationship with the client is accurately symbolized in the therapist's awareness; the therapist is not faking positive regard or empathy. The therapist who actually feels revulsion toward the client's thoughts and feelings does not try to delude himself or herself and pretend to value those thoughts and feelings.

An analogy is found in all of our relationships with some people at some time. We strongly believe we like someone when in fact we are deeply disturbed by something about him or her. Rogers (1971) described those incongruent feelings. He would wake in the middle of the night feeling furious anger with someone he had been dealing with a day or so before. But *at the time* he did not recognize his anger. This is incongruence in the relationship; it is being unaware of one's true feelings about another.

In everyday life we may block awareness of our own annoyance or anger because we are supposed to be "nice," or kind and helpful. We may perhaps be controlled by a condition of worth requiring us to be "masculine," hostile, and brutal, never feeling a pang of sympathy for someone who is hurt. But in the night we may weep in our dreams for that person. Machismo, bravado, the cool front, or the tough-guy pose hides even from ourselves any true feelings of tender compassion which

well up in our experience. We block them from awareness because they do not meet our conditions of worth. This will not do for psychotherapy, says Rogers. The therapist must be genuine, must be congruent in the relationship.

There is much support for this theory. Barret-Lennard (1959) was able to measure the extent to which clients perceived their therapists as genuine, empathic, and unconditional in positive regard. It was found that the therapists who more fully displayed these three characteristics were able to facilitate greater progress in their clients. Van der Veen (1970) demonstrated the same result with therapists treating schizophrenic patients in hospital. Truax and Mitchell (1971) surveyed a number of studies in several fields of counseling and psychotherapy and concluded that therapists with these three characteristics are effective regardless of their specific type of training and regardless of the specific kinds of problems faced by patients. Several later studies of the effects of warmth, empathy, and genuineness, however, have not provided similar support for their importance in therapy. While these qualities do appear to be important in client-centered therapy, it is becoming clear that they have less importance in affecting the outcomes of other kinds of treatment (Bergin and Suinn, 1975). In one study (Mitchell et al., 1973; quoted by Bergin and Suinn, 1975, p. 515) the authors studied 75 expert non-Rogerian therapists and 120 patients; it was found that warmth and empathy had no relationship to outcome.

A vast array of other applications and accomplishments includes: client-centered play therapy, student-centered teaching, group-centered leadership, encounter groups, parent-effectiveness training, leaderless discussion groups, business executive training, conflict resolution, and others. From the viewpoint of scientific psychology one of the strongest accomplishments of Rogers's theory has been its amenability to research, both on purely theoretical issues and also on the process and outcomes of psychotherapy. It is fair to say that Rogers led the way in research on psychotherapy, having pioneered the recording of interviews and the use of objective psychological tests in the evaluation of therapeutic outcomes.

Rogers has always given the same encouragement and freedom to his colleagues that he gives to his clients. So it is not surprising that new developments in theory, research, and even in therapy, have sprung from the work of Rogers's associates. For example, Butler, Rice, and Wagstaff (1961) developed a new approach to naturalistic research in which the investigator categorizes all the hypotheses of the research. Such a category system might consist of ten classes of emotional reaction by a client and eight classes of response by the therapist. Client reactions include "Verbally expressed anger; anger evident in voice only but not put into words; verbally expressed anxiety; anxiety evident in voice only but not expressed in words; [and so on]". Responses include "Therapist simply accepts, saying (e.g.) 'I see,' or 'Mm-mm'; therapist asks for clarification, further details, etc.; therapist reflects client's feelings, saying (e.g.) 'You feel really mad at him. . . .' or 'Is this it, that you know you'll do O.K. on the exam, because you always have, but still you always feel a bit anxious about it, more than you'd like to feel. Is that how it is. . . ?'" Each exchange of statements throughout a whole interview or throughout the entire course of therapy can be studied. If the category system works all the statements can be classified into one or other of the relevant categories. Repeating for several client-therapist pairs, the researcher obtains a rich body of material, ordered into successive sets of categorical data. These sets

may then be analyzed by specially designed quantitative techniques to reveal the main trends throughout an interview, or throughout therapy as a whole. It might be found, for example, that anger is increasingly expressed verbally by the client if such expressions are steadily followed by a therapist response of simple acceptance, but not if followed regularly by a request for clarification. In an important sense this approach to research is client-centered (or data-centered) in that once the category system is constructed any relationships found are those presented spontaneously by the data. The researcher does not embark upon his study with preconceived notions set up as hypotheses to be tested (for example, that acceptance of client anger will produce a rise in client anxiety as evidenced only in the voice). Given the category system (the "listening equipment") the researcher simply listens to the successive sets of data and tries to understand fully whatever they reveal.

Several of Rogers's associates have been in the forefront of new developments in psychotherapy practice. Axline (1947) developed the practice and theory of play therapy with children within the client-centered framework and wrote a now famous case history of one young client's dramatic recovery (*Dibs: In Search of Self*, 1964). Lewis and others (1959) introduced the interesting concept of time-limited therapy, in which a definite number of interviews (usually 20) is established before therapy begins. Client and therapist, rather than working toward a therapeutic goal to be achieved in an indefinite number of interviews, are committed by the concept of time-limited therapy to anticipate achieving results in the allotted time. Research on time-limited therapy suggests that outcomes are about as good as with unlimited therapy (Shlien, 1965).

During the last ten years Rogers has devoted his time primarily to activities outside of direct counseling and psychotherapy. In one of these projects (Rogers, 1972) he explored the meaning of relationships between young men and women through nondirective interviewing of couples. One couple had lived together for a number of years and then decided to get married. Another couple wrote each other notes in which each could freely express true feelings about their marriage, even when one's free expression caused some hurt or deprivation to the other. Young people from a commune where free exchange of partners was accepted reported experiencing jealousy and other hurts even in this open environment. One couple's particularly long marriage passed through many different phases over the years; the crises they experienced sometimes seemed to be the saving factor of the marriage. An interracial couple noted that race problems simply were added to difficulties that would exist anyway; they maintained a good relationship by accepting and prizing each one's color.

What does Rogers conclude from all of this? His conclusion rests in part upon statistical evidence, such as higher divorce rates, that existed independent of his own investigation. He concludes that our present institutions of marriage and the family are failing. It has often been observed that throughout history any civilization in which the family institutions broke down was doomed to collapse.

Rogers also concludes that many couples across the land are experimenting with alternative types of relationships such as trial marriage, living in communes, freely expressive marriage, marriage that is open to encounters between the mates and other partners; and so on. Rogers points out that our nation is experimental throughout, from medicine to industry and the schools, and this new type of experimentation in relationships is entirely consistent with the character of this country. He concludes that our society should respect this new laboratory. It might save our civilization from extinction.

From his studies, Rogers believes that young couples should have the opportunity to be educated explicitly in the arts of human relationships. Many young couples start out too confident of their abilities to relate to each other—to understand, share, and overcome problems. Almost all find out later that they were not as mature as they had thought. Encounter groups for teachers and students in high schools, for example, could offer a great deal of the necessary learning. Above all it is important to maintain honest and open communication in a marriage.

Parent Effectiveness Training, written by Thomas Gordon (1970), must be mentioned at this point as an application of client-centered theory. It addresses the very same problems, but in regard to the relationships between parents and their children; it aims to help both parents and children to communicate more effectively with each other. Gordon was for many years a close associate of Rogers.

On a quite different front, Rogers has recently conducted some pioneering efforts to mediate reduction of conflict between warring parties. For example, Protestants and Catholics met with him in encounter group sessions in Northern Ireland (Rogers, 1974).

Critique of Rogers's Theory

Rogers is one of the leaders of the humanistic movement in psychology, and his theory is similar to Maslow's (chapter 1), though with much greater emphasis on subjective experience. Like Maslow, Rogers emphasizes purposive striving (through self-actualization) as a primary aspect of personality, and rejects analysis of human personality in categories appropriate to lower animals. Rogers emphasizes the wholeness of the self-concept, rather than the thousands of conditionings or perceptions which have gone to make up that whole. He emphasizes the role of the body in presenting "visceral" experience. Rogers comes closer to embracing the humanistic concept of the *whole person* than many other humanistic psychologists.

Rogers meets the criteria of a humanistic psychologist in many ways. He believes that the study of the individual case is of central importance and that direct experiential knowledge of the person must be given prime importance. He thinks of the self-concept as an experiential gestalt with two alternative perspectives, that of the *self-concept* (emphasizing the subjective view of the self) and that of the *self-structure* (emphasizing the view that another person may have of the individual's self). Perhaps Rogers's construct of *experiencing* (the ongoing aspect of experience) is closest to the humanistic construct of the self as subject. Like many humanistic psychologists, including Maslow, Rogers emphasizes the importance of creativity as an aspect of human personality. He emphasizes the importance of delineating the characteristics of healthy personality and especially of ways to help individuals achieve a healthier personality or, as he would call it, a more fully functioning personality. Rogers's theory includes a prescription: It would be better if everybody could grow toward being more fully functioning.

Research performed under experimental conditions has led to confirmation of his hypotheses. For example, Chodorkoff (1954) studied two categories of people: those whose conscious self-description using items like those listed earlier matched the descriptions of them given by trained clinicians using psychological test data, and those whose self-description was discrepant from that given by clinicians. The former were thought to show more congruence between self-concept and experience, the latter less. It was assumed that the clinicians' descriptions reflected the true experience of the persons fairly accurately. It could be predicted from Rogers's theory that the less congruent persons would also be more defensive, more likely to deny or distort threatening experiences. To test this prediction, threatening experiences were presented to subjects in the form of personally threatening words, using a device which varied the length of exposure of the words. Subjects were initially shown words at speeds too fast for recognition, and then at successively slower speeds until they could be recognized. Chodorkoff presented both neutral words and threatening words. The results were as predicted. The less congruent subjects took much longer to recognize threatening words than neutral words. For the more congruent subjects the average recognition time difference was not as great.

Chodorkoff, for this experiment, interpreted Rogers's construct of *denial to awareness* as increased time required for word recognition. Other researchers have interpreted denial to awareness as failure in memory, either in immediate recall (Cartwright, 1956) or in two-day recall (Suinn et al., 1962). In both cases consistent and inconsistent self-descriptive adjectives were used, and the results showed that subjects recalled the consistent adjectives better. Suinn and colleagues also showed that the degree of failure in recall increased with the degree of inconsistency. Both Chodorkoff and Cartwright also found that the degree of cognitive failure for inconsistent stimuli was greater for persons with greater degrees of maladjustment, as independently measured. Thus the full circle of relationships predicted by Rogers's theory in this respect has been confirmed: greater incongruence is related to more denial or distortion in awareness, which is related to more maladjustment.

Like the basic theory, Rogers's theory of therapy has been subjected to extensive research, much of which has supported the theory. Some data, however, have suggested that Rogers's basic hypothesis is inaccurate as a generalization. The basic hypothesis states that "the individual has within himself vast resources [for beneficial change] . . . and that these resources can be tapped if only a definable climate of facilitative psychological attitudes can be provided" (Rogers, 1974, p. 116). The statement of the hypothesis leaves little doubt but that "the individual" means any individual, or all individuals. What is the evidence?

We have already reviewed evidence concerning the "definable climate of facilitative psychological attitudes": genuineness, empathy, and unconditional positive regard of the therapist for the client. A crucial question remains unanswered by those researches, however: Is it possible that the therapist's actual display or experience of these three positive qualities might be dependent upon behaviors of the client? Is the display of these qualities actually initiated by the therapist, or is it perhaps initiated by the client? Which comes first? Certain kinds of client behavior or characteristics might well liberate or trigger such qualities in the therapist while also liberating a curative process in the client. It is plausible that the client who will show most improvement is the client who will also generate these beneficial qualities in the therapist. Indeed, many researchers have examined the possibility that certain clients enter treatment with personality characteristics that allow for the prediction of greater success in therapy. In connection with client-centered therapy, Kirtner and Cartwright (1958) presented evidence that the way the client behaves during the initial interview is predictive of both length

of treatment and degree of successful outcome. Gendlin (1966) presented evidence that the extent to which, at the beginning of treatment, schizophrenic patients in client-centered treatment became involved in the process of therapy was predictive of the degree of successful outcome. Noting that the genuineness of the therapist could be produced by the client, Gendlin reports that one part of the study with schizophrenics involved the same therapist meeting with different patients, thereby allowing the effects of patients on therapists and of therapists on patients to be separately evaluated. The results showed that both kinds of effect were in operation, although the effect of therapist variables upon clients was the stronger of the two.

By contrast, Fiske and colleagues (1964) showed that more experienced therapists had no better effect on their clients than did less experienced therapists. On the other hand, replicating earlier findings, their work showed that clients differed sharply among themselves in the way they behaved during the first interview, and that these differences did have an effect upon the outcome of therapy. For example, clients who immediately discuss their feelings and problems in an important relationship (such as with a parent or fiancé) are usually found to have a very successful outcome in therapy; clients who list various features of the people and places they encounter and discuss their problems as if they were someone else's problem ("My main trouble is that my wife is an alcoholic.") are not likely to make much progress in therapy (see Kirtner and Cartwright, 1958).

So it seems that the manner in which the client approaches therapy in the very first interview determines to some extent the amount of change that will occur during the course of treatment. Similarly, Gendlin (1966) reports that clients with a higher initial involvement in the process of therapy made more beneficial changes in general psychological health during treatment, although the level of involvement did not change much. Involvement in the therapy process therefore seems to be a fairly constant catalyst for therapeutic change, but it is a catalyst that resides in the client, not the therapist.

These results have important implications for Rogers's basic hypothesis, that the client has the tendency and the capacity to develop self-understanding and ameliorative change "if only" an appropriate "climate" is provided; these results suggest that not all clients have these tendencies and capacities to the same degree. Moreover, the results obtained by Gendlin suggest a complex interaction between characteristics of the client's initial behavior and the therapist's manifested level of genuineness, empathy, and unconditional positive regard. Thus it may be that the client with greater initial involvement in the process of therapy stimulates in the therapist a higher level of empathy, which keeps the client going at a high level of involvement, which yields beneficial change. By contrast, the client with lower involvement or less propitious patterns of behavior in initial interviews may lower the therapist's empathy, with resulting lack of facilitation for change. Moreover, Gendlin's results in combination with those of Fiske and colleagues (1964) suggest that the level of the three beneficial qualities actually displayed by a given therapist in a given case may be high or low regardless of the therapist's number of years of experience; this variation is closely related to variation in initial client characteristics and behavior.

Rogers has himself noted variations in degree of success in outcomes of therapy, especially in his publication of the transcripts of one successful case and one case of failure in the same book (Rogers and Dymond, 1954). Since the therapist is the same the difference must lie either wholly in the clients, in the effects that clients had on the therapist, or in some combination of these. Any of these alternatives would seem to require some revision of the basic hypothesis, for the mere presentation of an appropriate climate of acceptance does not always allow the client's self-healing processes to come into play. Insofar as the basic hypothesis of client-centered therapy is a scientific hypothesis it is presented as a generalization applicable to all individual cases. But it is found not to be correct in all cases; therefore, some revision is needed in terms of those conditions or characteristics which make it not correct in some cases.

The most thorough critique of a theory of personality is one which considers all of the constructs, assumptions, and hypotheses as a logical system. Few theories have received the kind of careful analytic attention that has been given Rogers's theory by Krause (1964). In a 50-page monograph Krause first summarizes the essential constructs in the theory as Rogers himself presented it in its most developed form (Rogers, 1959). Krause notes that *experience* is the most encompassing construct in the theory, and that it is not equivalent to *consciousness*, although it includes reference to awareness in the present moment. Experience also refers to those matters that are potentially "available to awareness" and therefore to what we might call the memory. But in addition, the very notion of those matters that are potentially available to awareness implies that some matters are not available to awareness, and presumably these matters are also part of experience, namely that part of experience which is not symbolized and cannot be. Krause notes that, in Rogers's theory, the construct of consciousness or awareness refers to a "selection from experience" (Krause, 1964, p. 57).

In the second part of the monograph Krause formulates Rogers's theory as a system of interrelated propositions something like Euclid's geometry. He establishes terminology, postulates, and theorems. (We shall be discussing these matters more fully in chapter 6). The postulates cluster around four main constructs: *Regard, Defense, Failure of Defense,* and *Changes in the Self.* In connection with Regard, for example, Postulate IV states: *"The level of Self-Regard varies monotonically with that of Regard of others"* (Krause, 1964, p. 75). Postulate V states: *"Conditionalities in the Regard of others become conditionalities in Self-Regard and are the latter's only source."* Theorems are derived from one or more postulates. Theorem 15 states: *"There are no Conditions of Worth which were not once conditions for another's Regard.* This is a corollary of Postulate V and suggests biographical data as an aid to discovering a client's Conditions of Worth" (p. 89).

Krause recommends that several important theorems be tested experimentally; for example: *"Theorem 62.* Providing another with Regard conditional upon the same experiences as are his Conditions of Worth will increase the likelihood of the occurrence in Consciousness and the assimilation of experiences incongruent with these, and other, Conditions of Worth: A positive monotonic function" (p. 96).

Krause notes very few logical inconsistencies in the theory. One of these is occasioned by the fact that positive regard satisfactions are "associated with particular self-experiences." When self-experiences are implicated in the definition of *unconditional positive regard* it appears that no self-experience can be discriminated as more or less worthy of positive regard if the state of unconditionality is to hold. But this can be true only if all the positive regard satisfactions are equal, which places a conditionality upon them. Krause suggests that the inconsistency be removed by revising definitions so that positive regard is

not defined as being "associated with particular self-experiences." Such redefinition, however, would doubtless have further logical consequences in other parts of the theory, and Krause does not develop the implications further.

One matter of some importance concerns Rogers's construct of *actualization,* which is the only motive in Rogers's theory. The separate needs for positive regard and for positive self-regard are included as part of this actualization tendency. Krause suggests that Rogers intends the construct of actualization to convey the idea that all behaviors of the organism or person represent some actualization of potentials. However, such a notion is too broad to be useful. As a construct, it "tells us, in effect, that the organism is self-directing, that it only fails of its course when it is impeded . . ." (Krause, 1964, p. 70). But Krause points out that the impediment itself is attributed indirectly to the actualization tendency, because the latter contains the needs for positive regard and self-regard; Rogers states (1959, p. 224) that it is precisely these needs which allow for conditions of worth (the impediments) to arise. In the same work Rogers adds that expressions of positive regard by significant social others can become "more compelling than the *organismic valuing process,* and the individual becomes more adient to the *positive regard* of such others than toward *experiences* which are of positive value in *actualizing* the organism" (p. 224). Hence the actualizing tendency is a notion which tells us that the organism is self-directing and that it only fails to direct itself when it is impeded, but that this impediment is also produced by the actualizing tendency. Krause concludes that the construct of the actualizing tendency "appears to explain too much too vaguely for any differential predictions to derive from it" (Krause, 1964, p. 70). Accordingly he does not employ this construct in his reformulation of the theory.

Krause does contrast Rogers's use of actualization with Maslow's use of self-actualization, however; since Maslow's construct is placed as only one part of a total hierarchical theory of motivation, he observes, it therefore is more useful than its counterpart in Rogers's theory.

Few theories of personality can stand up to this kind of penetrating logical analysis, and it is a tribute to the soundness of Rogers's theory that so few basic changes seem to be called for after Krause's analysis. Indeed, removing the construct of the self-actualizing tendency seems to be no loss at all if Krause's judgment is correct.

If logically sound, then, does Rogers's theory also seem to be empirically accurate? So far as the research has gone, the theory does seem to be accurate, except for its failure to account for the kind of individual differences among clients described above, which contribute so heavily to the outcome of therapy. As a theory of personality, however, many of its hypotheses are still in need of empirical research, hypotheses about the actual development of conditions of worth, for example, or about the role of parents' conditional regard in creating incongruence in the child. Nevertheless, Rogers's theory of personality has been tremendously fruitful in stimulating new developments in theory, research, and therapeutic practice among his many associates and other scientists (such as Chodorkoff) who have been influenced by the client-centered approach.

Although we have called Rogers a humanistic psychologist, does this mean that his definition of personality in fact includes the whole individual, all aspects of the personality as defined in chapter 2? For instance, does he include the body in his definition of personality? The question seems to be debatable.

Certainly the body does not exert any independent causal influences according to his theory. Rather, Rogers seems to *refer* to the body in such constructs as the *actualizing tendency* and the *organismic valuing process*. Neither of these constructs, however, plays a really significant role in his theory. Rather it is the *self*-actualizing tendency which plays a crucial role through its constituent needs for positive regard and self-regard. And the organismic valuing process appears to function only as part of experience, a part that is either symbolized in awareness or denied to awareness. Despite its presence in the theory, then, the body component is given at best a background function. Although Rogers includes the actualizing and self-actualizing tendencies as motivational principles, along with the needs for regard, he does not seem to consider them as part of psychophysical systems. Insofar as they function as causes they do so within experience, and they do not appear to have any structural basis. Rogers insists that it is "the organism as a whole, and only the organism as a whole, which exhibits" the actualizing tendency; there are ". . . no other sources of energy or action in the system" (Rogers, 1959, p. 196.) It does not appear that there is some well-spring of energy waiting to force its way into behavior. Rather, as Rogers formulated it in *Client-centered Therapy* (1951, pp. 483 ff.), the organism's actualizing tendency is directed at actualizing, maintaining, and enhancing *"the experiencing organism,"* as it *"reacts to the field as it is experienced and perceived."* And again, *"Behavior is basically the goal-directed attempt of the organism to satisfy its needs as experienced, in the field as perceived"* (Rogers, 1951, p. 491.) Thus it seems that Rogers does not consider the tendencies and needs as latent structures and forces, but rather as whole-characteristics of the organism. Even behaviors incongruent with the self actualize the organism as a whole, or actualize "those aspects of the experience of the organism which are not assimilated into the *self-structure*" (Rogers, 1959, p. 227). Even these behaviors (which might seem alien to the self) nevertheless do not stem from an independent well spring of energy. They express total organismic experience even if, once expressed, they do not gain clear symbolization as self-experiences.

Experience thus has the central part in Rogers's theory and definition of personality. Even the environment works through it: "The field as perceived" is Rogers's terminology. Behavior is an outcome of attempts to satisfy "needs as experienced, in the field as perceived." Behavior as such is not part of Rogers's definition of personality.

Rogers's theory subordinates all else to experience. He develops a theory of the structure of experience, not of personality as a whole: The parts are divisions of experience. First there is a division of experience into that which is symbolized and that which is not; next there is a cross-division into those experiences that are self-related and those that are not. Those experiences that are both self-related and symbolized are the constituents of the self-concept. His theory of cause is likewise confined to experience: conditions of worth, for example, produce incongruence between symbolized and unsymbolized self-experiences. Even the conditions of worth are also part of experience.

Workshop 5 •

An Exercise in Empathic Understanding

In this workshop you are invited to test your own ability to understand empathically. Study once again the passages in the text that describe empathic understanding and its relationship to the other person's internal frame of reference. Note here the major characteristics of such understanding:

_____

_____

_____

_____

It is important that you make your attempt at empathic understanding in a context where it can be truly manifested. This must be a context in which the other person is truly concerned, feels deeply, and perhaps is personally involved. You might ask a friend to tell you about his or her religious convictions, political views, career aspirations, or feelings toward parents. Explain that you simply want to understand how they feel and think, as fully as you possibly can. Try to listen with all ears and understand as deeply as possible.

You might wish to make a personal note of every departure from the internal frame of reference; every time you interject one of your own thoughts or feelings, approvals or disapprovals; or even times when your attention wanders away from focusing upon what your friend is telling you.

One way to check out how accurately you have captured what your friend thinks and feels is to ask him or her to write it all down first, before you have your talk. Then you write down what you have learned afterwards; and compare the two.

Summary

The most important construct in Rogers's theory is *experience,* the ongoing thoughts, feelings, perceptions, and other aspects of experiencing. If experience is symbolized we are conscious of it, the experience has entered our *awareness.* Some experiences refer to the self, and such self-experiences form the *self-concept* if they are in awareness. The sole motivation construct in the theory is the *actualizing tendency* with its counterpart in the tendency toward *self-actualization* and the component *needs for positive regard* and *positive self-regard.* Because of the need for positive regard human beings develop *conditions of worth.* These are conditions they must fulfill in order to obtain positive regard from others and eventually to obtain positive self-regard. Because of these conditions, if an experience of the self contradicts an element of the self-concept that is controlled by a condition of worth, that experience may be denied to awareness or distorted in awareness. For this reason one's actual self-experiences and the self-concept may not be congruent. The more *incongruence* there is, the more likely it is that the person will be threatened by some inconsistent self-experience and have to defend by denial or distortion. The more threat that is possible, the more *vulnerable* the person is; the more vulnerable the person is, the more *maladjusted* also. These hypotheses have been confirmed by research.

Rogers extends these notions to consider what a *fully functioning person* would be like. Such a person would be completely *open to all experiences,* including those inconsistent with an element of the self-concept; and the concept would then change accordingly. Thus the self-concept as a whole would be in continual flux as new experiences come along, but at any given time it would be congruent with experience. In order for a person to become fully functioning, however, it is necessary that the significant other people in that person's life give him or her *unconditional positive regard.* Since this rarely happens outside therapy, people can at best only hope to move toward that goal without actually attaining it. But Rogers makes it clear that people should be helped to become more fully functioning as defined.

The theory has proven accurate in the main, limited only by a relatively restricted range of research applications so far. The theory is very fruitful in research and in stimulating new therapeutic approaches. The associated theory of therapy has considerable support but also seems to need some basic revision. The theory of personality developed by Rogers is mainly a theory of experience, including both structure of experience and causal relations within experience. Other components of personality (body, psychophysical systems, behavior) are given scanty treatment as background or no treatment at all. A diagram illustrating the definition of personality implicit in Rogers's theory is given in figure 5.2.

With Rogers's theory we have completed

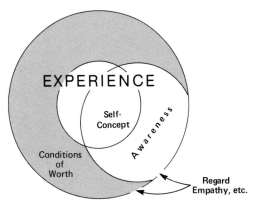

Figure 5.2. The definition of personality implicit in Rogers's theory

our presentation of theories exemplifying the three main approaches to defining personality: in terms of psychophysical systems (dispositions and the like), in terms of behavior, and in terms of experience. We have studied four theories of personality: those of Maslow, Murray, Skinner, and Rogers. We are now ready to move beyond the matter of defining personality. It is time to consider what some of the general features and requirements of a scientific theory are, and to this task we turn in chapter 6.

INTRODUCTION

Components of a theory
 Facts
  Particular facts
  General facts
  Generalizations
  Theories constructed to explain facts
  Scientists both gather and generate facts
 Constructs
  Constructs distinguished from concepts
 Hypotheses
  Trend hypotheses
  Generalization hypotheses
  Causal hypotheses
 Laws
  Laws as well-substantiated hypotheses
  Examples of laws in psychology and physics
 Assumptions
  Empirical assumptions: examples in physics
   and psychology
  Methodological assumptions: examples from
   Lewin's theory and humanistic psychology
 The nature of scientific theories: a summary
Criteria for evaluating theories
 Functions of a theory
  Prediction of useful factual information
  Deep penetration of reality
  Directing extensions of research
 Criteria for evaluation related to functions
  Accuracy
  Depth
  Fruitfulness
 An absolute criterion for evaluating scientific
  theories: the empirical basis
  Meanings of empirical:
   confirmable by observation, or
   testable by experiment
 Comparative criteria and the empirical basis
  Accuracy and the empirical basis
  Depth and the empirical basis
  Fruitfulness and the empirical basis
  Power of a theory as a fourth criterion
Application of the criteria to personality theories
 Hard and soft sciences
 Contrast in clinical, experimental and personality
  psychology
 Criteria in relation to personality theories

Workshop 6   Uranian scientists do preliminary
   work on data concerning Namwons
Summary

The General Nature
of Scientific Theories

It is widely accepted among scientists that a scientific theory must be *empirical*. As we shall see in more detail later in the chapter, this means that a scientific theory is one which contains concepts and hypotheses that can be confirmed or disconfirmed by observation or tested by experiment. Although great changes have been seen in recent years in the philosophy of science (Suppe, 1974), these changes have served to make us more aware of the great complexity, the enormous variety of types of thought that go into the making of scientific theories. It is no longer possible to say that a theory is simply a set of formal axioms and theorems which attempts to map reality. A theory may be valuable even though it is quite informal and has no mathematical formulation at all. Although the ideal of simplicity in theoretical formulation is no longer supported (Bunge, 1963), other criteria have become increasingly recognized: *accuracy* in accounting for reality, *depth* of understanding provided, and *fruitfulness* in directing further research are a few

Despite the complexity it is possible to see a few essential components in all scientific theories: constructs, hypotheses, laws, and assumptions. In the present chapter, then, we shall try to describe these components as

clearly as possible. When that is understood we shall examine the most important criteria for evaluating a theory.

Components of a Theory

Facts

A scientific theory is a set of related constructs and hypotheses which offers descriptions and explanations for a wide range of facts of a certain kind. A theory of heat describes and explains all the known facts about heat. A theory of learning describes and explains all the known facts about learning. These facts may be particular or general, and it is this notion we must now clarify.

Particular Facts. A particular fact refers to some particular time and place and event or characteristic. My name is Des. This sheet of paper is white. The gerbil is scratching at its piece of cardboard. These and similar facts are particulars about me, the paper, or the gerbil. Some particular facts are quite important. For example, the sun exists; or, the sun is farther from earth than the moon is; or, the wind is very cold now. In scientific work it is often essential that a particular fact be determined with accuracy. In an experiment, for example, we might determine that: This gallon of liquid is at 212° Fahrenheit as measured by this thermometer; or, these five gerbils all displayed five hours or more of wheel-running on this thirtieth day after being placed in the new environment.

General Facts. Those facts pertaining to all or most of a certain class of events or entities or characteristics are general facts. In logic they are called *universals*: all swans have long necks; all men are mortal; and so on. But in science we speak of *generalizations* because we often really do not mean *all,* we mean *most.* For example, human beings are born weighing between four and ten pounds in most cases; or, on the average human babies grow from roughly 50 centimeters to roughly 75 centimeters in length during the first twelve months after birth. These statements are generalizations.

Many of the general facts of interest to science concern *correlations*: relationships between two or more measured characteristics. Based upon a sample of 17,523 observations of height and weight of males ranging from infancy to old age, for example, it is found that heavier people also tend to be taller: there is a positive correlation between height and weight. While this is a particular fact about the sample of 17,523 people, we accept it as a general statement about height and weight. It becomes a general fact when we say that, in general, and regardless of the particular sample of people studied, height and weight are correlated positively.

Scientists construct theories in order to explain facts, and the explanation of general facts is usually considered to be the more important accomplishment because it implies that there are many facts of the same or a related kind which can be understood through one explanation. One explanation for many particular facts, all encompassed in the general fact, represents the ideal of *parsimony* in scientific theory.

We should note that science does not simply receive facts and then try to explain them. While the process may start this way, it rapidly develops new facts which need explanation. For example, Saunders (1973) has described the collection of reports of sightings of unidentified flying objects (UFOs) and the subsequent division of the reports into categories of highly reliable and questionable. Plotting dates, times, and locations of reliable reports, he then found that bursts of reports occur in a definite cycle of time and at systematically changing locations around the globe. The time cycle and the global path are new facts found by the scientist after studying the given facts. The new facts are found through application of special techniques of investigation.

Constructs

Psychologists have not been clear about the difference between a *concept* and a *construct* (see Marx & Hillix, 1973, pp. 62-63). One clear distinction seems to be that the word *concept* is used in everyday English, but the word *construct* is used only in the technical language of philosophy and psychology. A *concept* is defined in Webster's *Third Edition* as a general idea; a *construct* is a general idea which has been carefully formulated by a scientist to refer to a class of objects or events or relationships. A construct is a technical representation of a general fact. Fiske (1971, p. 98) points out that a construct should refer to a unique quality and the core or essence of the construct should be spelled out. He gives some examples as follows: "The core of dominance can be identified as acting overtly so as to change the views or actions of another . . . the core of affiliation can be stated as sharing experiences with another. The sharing may be as casual as remarks to a seatmate on a plane or as intimate as disclosing disturbing private experiences to a loved one."

Hypotheses

Hypotheses are the scientist's guesses about reality. The guess may refer to continuation of an observed trend, as for example in predicting that many UFO sightings will be made in 1984. Often a few particular facts of the same kind are observed; the scientist then guesses that there is a general fact behind them and makes a hypothesis accordingly. For example, Jacqueline Cartwright (1976) observed several instances in which a child's nose became very red and slightly swollen, and in each case the child developed chicken pox shortly thereafter. She hypothesized that the appearance of a red swollen nose is always a premonitory symptom of chicken pox, and she proceeded to gather as much further observational evidence and relevant retrospective report data as possible. The results were consistent with the hypothesis.

Many hypotheses are of the causal variety: they seek to explain some descriptive generalization. For example, Boyle (1660, in Brush, 1965) proposed a now famous hypothesis to explain the fact that air, when compressed, exerts pressure against the compressing surface. His hypothesis was that air consists of "a heap of little bodies, lying upon one another, as may be resembled to a fleece of wool. For this . . . consists of many slender and flexible hairs; each of which may indeed, like a little spring, be easily bent or rolled up; but will also like a spring, be still endeavoring to stretch itself out again" (p. 44). Boyle referred to his idea precisely as a "hypothesis" (p. 46).

Most scientific explanation can be seen to consist of offering one or more hypotheses from which the fact in question can be deduced (Braithwaite, 1960, pp. 53ff).

Take Boyle's hypothesis, for example. From the hypothesis that air consists of a heap of springy little bodies like the hairs of a fleece of wool, we could deduce the fact that compressed air exerts pressure against the compressing surface. As another example, consider the relational fact that height and weight are correlated over a population of humans ranging in age from infancy to old age. An explanatory hypothesis might invoke the construct of a general bodily growth factor which steadily puts out the ingredients necessary for bodily growth to occur, whether in height or weight. That is, the hypothesis would explain the fact of correlation between height and weight as a result of some third cause which produces increments in height and in weight more or less simultaneously. Another way of saying the same thing is that, from the statement of the hypothesis as premise, we could logically derive the conclusion that height and weight are correlated.

Laws

A *law* is a well-substantiated and widely accepted hypothesis. Bunge has given the following description of a law:

> A proposition is a law statement if and only if it is general in some respect (i.e., does not refer to unique objects), has been empirically corroborated in some domain in a satisfactory way (for the time being), and belongs to some theory (whether adult or embryonic) (Bunge, 1963, p. 178).

An example of a law in psychology is the well-known Weber's Law, which states that if a stimulus has intensity I, then the increase in intensity which is needed to produce a just noticeably different sensation is some constant proportion of the original intensity. Letting dI be the necessary increment, we would write:

$$dI = kI$$

where k is a constant. In other words, no matter what the intensity of a stimulus, the increase needed for us to notice it is a constant proportion, *k*, of that given intensity. Like many laws it was accepted at first, but later questioned. The law failed at very low intensities. Nevertheless Stevens (1951) has pointed out that in vision and hearing (where measurement is probably most accurate) Weber's law holds over 99.9 percent of the usable stimulus intensities.

Scientists often use laws when they formulate testable hypotheses. Newton's Law of Gravity might thus be used in a model of quasistellar radio sources which assume that such sources consist of great mass and thereby exert gravitational pull upon all surrounding particles. (This example will be more fully described in the next chapter.) The law itself is not considered to be under test, but it is being used to help in providing a tentative explanation: Given the law, and assuming the great mass, then a force would be exerted upon all surrounding particles, drawing them toward the mass. Thus laws and empirical assumptions play a similar role in facilitating hypotheses. But there are important differences between laws and assumptions. In the first place a law is generally accepted to be valid and has typically been formulated only after a good deal of confirmation has been found for it. That is, a law is a well-established hypothesis, established in terms of observation and experiment, and also established in the sense of receiving widespread acceptance by the scientific community. But assumptions, although they may be widely used by scientists, are not ordinarily established by observation and experiment.

Assumptions

We shall find it necessary to describe two quite different sorts of assumptions scientists make in constructing theories. The first is an assumption about facts. Like a law, this kind of assumption is not actually going to be tested: it is not like the hypotheses of a given theory. On the other hand it is not a well-established form of hypothesis like a law. But it is needed by the theory in order to allow testable hypotheses to be formulated. We shall call this kind of assumption an *empirical assumption,* and give several examples. (The second kind, the *methodological assumption,* will be described below.)

Empirical Assumptions. In his treatise on air as an elastic fluid, Daniel Bernoulli made several explicit assumptions:

> Proceeding now to elastic fluids, we may assume that they have the same characteristics as everything else we have so far examined. . . .
> Now let us find a weight π sufficient to compress the air ECDF into the space eCDf (a smaller space) assuming that the particles of the air have the same velocity before and after compression (Bernoulli, 1738, in Brush, 1965, pp. 58-59).

Bernoulli first assumes that elastic fluids have the same characteristics as certain other forms of matter. This assumption is remote from the mere fact of pressure exerted by air when compressed, which he ultimately hopes to explain. The second assumption is more particular to the explanatory hypothesis he develops. By assuming that the particles of air do not change in velocity, Bernoulli is able to explain the increased pressure under compression as a result of two causal processes: "first because the number of particles is now greater in proportion to the smaller space in which they are confined, and secondly because any given particle makes more frequent impacts" (Bernoulli, in Brush, 1965, p. 59). His hypothesis holds that air pressure is increased under compression because now a smaller space confines the particles, thus making the number of particles impinging on a square meter of surface relatively greater; and also because, given the reduced space, the average distance between a particle and the compressing surface must be reduced also. This means that any particle has a smaller distance to travel and so hits the surface more frequently.

A seemingly simpler assumption would hold that the particles *do* change velocity during compression; the increased speed would account for increased frequency of impacts and, hence, increased pressure. But this assumption would not generate the precise hypotheses about more particles per square meter and greater average frequency of impact. Bernoulli's precisely formulated hypotheses, by contrast, led to further formulation as follows: with infinite weight, a piston would travel a distance down the cylinder, shrinking the volume so that all particles touch each other. Letting the remaining distance be some value *m*, Bernoulli deduces equations which lead to the following hypothesis (in which *P* is the weight applied to the piston, and *s* is the volume containing the air):

> Putting $m = 0$, we have $\pi = P/s$, so that the force of compression is approximately inversely proportional to the volume occupied by the air. This is confirmed by a variety of experiments (Brush, 1965, p. 61).

In this way we see that Bernoulli's assumption of constant velocity made it possible for him to formulate a strictly testable hypothesis. Indeed the hypothesis was so well confirmed by experiments that it could be described eventually as a law.

In psychology we have found that assumptions are particularly complex and varied in nature. In one monumental study a few years ago (Koch, 1959) a panel of eminent psychologists sought to survey the state of psychology as a science. Major theorists in all phases of psychology were asked to formulate their views in a systematic and relatively standard way. Among other features of formal

theory, it was requested that the assumptions of each theory be spelled out, along with initial evidence for those assumptions. This request implied that an assumption is made initially on the basis of some empirical observations. Many of the theorists, especially those in personality and social psychology, did not comply with this request; and many objected to such formalization of their theory. Formalization, they felt, should come much later in the development of a science, even as modern physics rests upon work done by Newton, Galileo, and even those living hundreds of years earlier, such as Archimedes. Of course formal development of theory includes far more than a statement of assumptions: it must include explicit description of postulates of all kinds, of hypotheses, and of the modes of deriving the hypotheses. It was argued then that formalization of a theory could be premature and could distract the scientist from giving due attention to the complexity of raw data and its tendency to produce the unexpected. It was held that informal theories are better because they leave the scientist more open and responsive to new events (Koch, 1959, Vol. 3, pp. 776 ff.).

Nevertheless, for Koch's volume many theorists did not state their assumptions even informally, which suggests either that the theorist considered them so obvious he would not bother to make them explicit; or that they are buried so deeply within the context of contemporary scientific beliefs that they cannot readily be brought to light; or, as B. F. Skinner argued (Koch, p. 369), that the scientist needs only one basic assumption—that there is order in behavior if you can only discover it.

Among the contributors who did spell out the assumptions of their theory was David Rapaport. He stated that Freud's theory (see chapters 9, 10, and 11 below) rests upon one basic assumption and three special assumptions. The basic assumption is that all behavior (including thoughts and feelings) is determined by psychological causes. Rapaport writes that the initial evidential ground for assuming purely psychological determinism was "the observation that apparently meaningless hysterical symptoms, previously attributed to a somatic [bodily] etiology, disappeared when the patient, in hypnosis, related them to past experiences, thoughts, feelings, or fantasies, and thus endowed them with meaning and psychological 'cause'" (Rapaport, 1959, pp. 112-113). The first special assumption is that there are *unconscious* psychological *processes*. The essence of this assumption is that "it refuses to treat the nonconscious as somatic and the nonlogical as nonpsychological. It rejects both consciousness and logical relations as necessary criteria of psychological processes, and thus arrives at the concept of unconscious psychological processes abiding by rules other than those of conscious processes" (Rapaport, 1959, p. 112). The second special assumption was that there are unconscious psychological *forces;* these forces were thought to be responsible for the creation of unconscious fantasies the patients mistook for memories. The third special assumption was that there are psychological *energies;* they originate in instinctual drives and, when blocked, may seek discharge in unexpected ways.

While the basic assumption of psychoanalytic theory, then, represents a scientist's general credo, the three special assumptions appear to be more evidently about facts, and therefore to qualify as *empirical assumptions.* That they are not expected to be tested is clear from Rapaport's view that the theory is at present stated too informally to permit precise tests. Nevertheless he also says that the assumptions of psychoanalytic theory permit *clinically* testable hypotheses to be made about the causes of particular symptoms in individual patients. It is also clear from Kline's recent review of the evidence (1972) that the assumptions of psychoanalytic theory have made possible the formulation of many testable research hypotheses of a more general scientific nature than those associated with clinical treatment of particular individual patients.

One of the clearest examples of an empirical assumption is that used by Chodorkoff (1954) in his test of Rogers's theory concerning congruence. Recall that Chodorkoff assumed that trained clinical psychologists would be able to provide a description of the person which would represent the totality of the person's experience more accurately than the person's own self-description which would reflect only those portions of experience the person had symbolized in awareness. Whatever had been denied to experience would not appear in the person's self-description at all. By assuming that the clinicians' descriptions would be more accurate it was possible to determine who was more and who was less *congruent,* and then to test the hypothesis that more congruent persons would be less defensive, more open to awareness of threatening experiences.

In chapter 7 we shall study a theory of personality which is especially clear with regard to the role played by empirical assumptions: the theory advanced by Neal Miller and John Dollard.

Methodological Assumptions. In his contribution to the Koch volumes (1959), B. F. Skinner stated his basic assumption that there is order out there to be discovered. This is not an empirical assumption, but it is more like a credo or belief about the nature of ultimate reality. Nevertheless it provides an incentive and general direction for the scientist's work, and in this way it contributes to the beginnings of method. Many of the assumptions which are not empirical may be described as either broadly or more pointedly methodological in that they guide the scientists or motivate them in a certain way. Examples from psychology may be found in the work of Dorwin Cartwright in his contribution to the Koch volumes. In his presentation of Lewin's theory of personality, Cartwright described three basic assumptions (1959, p. 21): 1) That "the most important task of psychology is to devise ways of treating the full empirical reality of human experience and behavior in a scientific manner without doing violence to them." 2) That "the language of psychologists should be psychological . . . psychology will be deterred in fulfilling its basic task if it assumes that it must describe human experience in physical or physiological terms." 3) That " 'only what is concrete can have effects' . . . [with several consequences including the consequence that] causation must be viewed as contemporary with the event caused."

These assumptions appear to be quite different from those of Bernoulli or of psychoanalytic theory as described above. The assumptions lying behind Lewin's theory sound more like decisions (as to the goals of the scientist), preferences (for one language representation over another), and a highly abstract belief about the nature of reality (causes are concrete and contemporaneous with effects). It seems clear that such decisions, preferences, and beliefs have more to do with guiding the scientists' behavior than with offering an unproven statement of general fact. It therefore seems reasonable to put all of these kinds of assumptions into one class and call them *methodological assumptions.*

The importance of methodological assumptions in controlling the final output of theory and research may be judged from the fact that these methodological guides determine what problems will be studied, or at least what kinds of problems will and will not be addressed by the scientist. Humanistic psychologists have been especially concerned with the methodological assumptions of mechanistic psychology and of their own alternative "Third Force" psychology. One leader in the field, J. F. T. Bugental, has expressed this concern:

the issue between mechanomorphic and humanistic psychologies may be reduced to a contrast in their views of the nature of man and the orientation of their sciences. Mechanomorphic psychology . . . views man as an object acted upon from the outside by various forces or driven from within by other forces which are to be characterized chiefly by their relation to the outside (e.g. thirst, hunger, sexual appetite). The regularities in man thus most attract the mechanomorph: instincts, reflexes, conditioned responses, habits, learning. It is all too easy for such an orientation to slip into dismissing irregularities and individual differences as annoying artifacts, chiefly to be accounted for as experimental errors or inadequacies of control and certainly not felt to be ultimately significant. Such thinking soon evolves into a nothing-but orientation in which the intent is to show that all human phenomena are nothing but a minimum number of response processes (e.g., conditioned responses) (Bugental, 1967, p. 8).

Clearly Skinner's theory (chapter 4) is one of Bugental's targets.

In contrast, the humanistic view is perhaps best given in the statement found in the brochure of the Association of Humanistic Psychology, as cited by two other leaders of this approach:

1. A centering of attention on the experiencing *person,* and thus a focus on experience as the primary phenomenon in the study of man. Both theoretical explanations and overt behavior are considered secondary to experience itself and to its meaning to the person.

2. An emphasis on such distinctively human qualities as choice, creativity, valuation, and self-realization, as opposed to thinking about human beings in mechanistic and reductionistic terms.
3. An allegiance to meaningfulness in the selection of problems for study and of research procedures, and an opposition to a primary emphasis on objectivity at the expense of significance.
4. An ultimate concern with and valuing of the dignity and worth of man and an interest in the development of the potential inherent in every person. Central in this view is the person as he discovers his own being and relates to other persons and to social groups (quoted in Buhler & Allen, 1972, pp. 1-2).

There can be no doubt that a scientist espousing these humanistic assumptions would select suitable problems for research and avoid unsuitable ones. The humanist would study emotions not through establishment of conditioned emotional responses, for example, but as they are experienced by individual human beings. The humanistic scientist would be more like Rogers than like Skinner. Maslow, of course, in his work on self-actualizing people, gave us a prime instance of point 3, above: deliberately choosing to study a meaningful problem and deliberately choosing significance over objectivity.

Some authors have claimed that the humanistic approach violates the presuppositions of science as such, and that it is impossible to be both scientific and humanistic in the same theory and approach (compare Hebb, 1974). It is argued that because science is self-limiting and narrow by design it should be used by humanism but not confused with it. My own interpretation of the argument is that it centers upon methodological assumptions of such generality that they are prior to any actual scientific theory and do not enter into it. They simply place constraints on the

kinds of concepts, hypotheses, and investigations the scientist will use. Unlike the empirical assumptions, methodological assumptions do not contribute intrinsically to the theory. They do not, for instance, make it possible to formulate testable hypotheses. So we might conclude that while empirical assumptions are an actual part of a scientific theory, methodological assumptions precede the formulation of any theory and are more a part of the scientist as a person than of the theory as a product.

Summary: The Nature of Scientific Theories

We have said that scientific theories are systems of ideas directed at the explanation of particular and general facts. The components are constructs, hypotheses, laws, and empirical assumptions. The elements are linked together into a more or less coherent system of conceptually related ideas. Braithwaite has summarized the nature of scientific theory as "a deductive system in which observable consequences logically follow from the conjunction of observed facts with the set of fundamental hypotheses of the system" (1960, p. 22). We should add that the deductive logic is not always quite as tight as Braithwaite implies, since many theories, especially in psychology and other social and behavioral sciences, are developed without the formalization necessary for strict deductive inferences.

Criteria for Evaluating Theories

In this section we shall consider some of the ways in which scientists and philosophers of science evaluate scientific theories. Before describing the criteria that are used it will be helpful to consider what theories are expected to accomplish. In the previous section we tried to understand the nature of a scientific theory in terms of its component hypotheses, laws, and assumptions. It was stated that a scientific theory seeks to explain some factual generalizations. Actually, the theory may be responsible for even making the generalizations in the first place. This will become clearer as we now look first at the functions that a theory performs in science.

Functions of a Theory

Kuhn (1970, pp. 23-34) has described the normal scientific process as consisting of three main factual activities and three related theoretical functions. The first activity is that of making detailed descriptions and measurements of a particular domain of facts. In physics, for example, scientists once had to establish the specific gravities or electrical conductivities of different materials. In chemistry, the study of solutions involved determining their boiling points or acidity levels. Scientists also do research into ways and means of improving the reliability and accuracy of their instruments and procedures for making these descriptions and measurements. The related function of theory is "to predict factual information of intrinsic value. The manufacture of astronomical ephemerides [almanacs of the positions of stars, used in navigation], the computation of lens characteristics, and the production of radio propagation curves, are examples of problems of this sort" (Kuhn, 1970, p. 30). Here the theory is *used to predict useful factual information.*

The second activity of science is gathering facts to test the theory. Experiments, made at the direction of theory and designed specifically to provide a test of the theory, yield facts that otherwise would not have been observed or, if observed, would not have had particular meaning. An unusual but revealing example is provided by the prediction from Einstein's general theory of relativity concerning the angular distance between two stars. According to the theory a gravitational field can deflect light rays, and hence it may be predicted that the apparent angular distance between two distant stars will increase if the sun (with its huge gravitational field) comes between the rays from the two stars. Photographs taken when the sun is in such a position and when it is not confirm the prediction. The crucial photograph can only be taken during a total eclipse, so that the observation of the relevant facts must necessarily be rare. In this second activity of normal science, then, *new facts are sought under guidance from the theory's deeper penetration of reality.* The new fact itself may not be especially useful, but its discovery lends indirect support for the insight provided by the theory into the hidden nature of matter or of mind.

The third normal activity of science is what Kuhn calls *articulation*: "It consists of empirical work undertaken to articulate the paradigm theory [the theory generally accepted at the time], resolving some of its residual ambiguities and permitting the solution of problems to which it had previously only drawn attention" (Kuhn, 1970, p. 27). One kind of articulation is the establishment of constants, such as the speed of light or the force between two unit masses at unit distance. A second form of articulation is the establishment of quantitative laws, such as Boyle's Law that pressure is inversely related to the volume of gas. A third form of articulation takes a given theory and attempts to apply it in a slightly different situation. Alternative formulations and experiments are required to determine just how the theory is to be applied in the new setting. A great deal of theoretically relevant work in psychology seems to be of this kind. One programmatic example is provided by the work of the Yale group who articulated the theory of behavior developed by Hull (1943). This theory was formulated in terms of basic learning processes in the context of experiments primarily on the white rat. Neal Miller articulated the theory in regard to conflict (1944) and displacement (1948); Dollard and Miller articulated the theory's application to psychotherapy (1950). In all forms of articulation the theory *directs the extension of research*: into new instances (constants), into precise formulation and experimental measurement of important relationships between variables (laws), and into new situations which can be illuminated by application of the theory.

Criteria for Evaluation

The three functions of theories as described by Kuhn (and I think his description would be supported by most scientists), imply three parallel criteria for the evaluation of theories. The value of a theory may be measured by its accuracy, depth, and fruitfulness.

Accuracy. The factual information predicted from a theory must turn out to be actually useful. If the theory predicts positions of stars which are inaccurate, then the almanac will at best be useless for navigation, and may be disastrous. Because usefulness of a theory in this sense depends upon its accuracy in predicting states of the real world, the first criterion is *accuracy* in describing and predicting reality. Note that prediction is a form of describing an event before it actually takes place.

In earlier chapters of the book we have repeatedly commented upon the accuracy of particular theories of personality, and in each case our estimate of accuracy has been based largely upon the results of research. Much research was begun with the intention of testing a prediction concerning the relationship between two or more variables in a particular setting. For example, it would be predicted that needs among factory workers will show the hierarchical order proposed by Maslow's theory (see chapter 1). A prediction of

the positions of stars is basically similar: Star Alpha is predicted to have a certain position in relation to Star Beta and to Earth at some particular time.

Depth. Second in the list of criteria is the depth of insight into reality a theory provides.

Going beyond ordinary understandings in a given state of a science, a deep theory offers a view of reality which penetrates accepted appearances. Its assumptions and hypotheses convey a new grasp upon hidden structures and causal processes. By contrast, a theory which sticks to accepted generalizations and does little more than summarize existing knowledge would provide little depth of insight or new understanding. A deep theory, of course, takes some risks in hypothesizing the existence of things unseen. If a specific prediction can be made and tested on the basis of such a theory, then it might prove to be inaccurate. By contrast, a shallow theory takes little risk, for the only kind of prediction it can make is to facts of a generally well-known kind: It guarantees accuracy by sacrificing depth. Recall that Clark Hull charged Skinner with trying to guarantee accuracy by sticking to description and not making hypotheses about the inner workings of organisms.

Murray's theory offers examples of deep theorizing. For instance, he proposed that characteristics of the claustral complex are produced in very early childhood and have profound unconscious meaning for the person. This proposition has depth, especially by contrast with an alternative proposition that might have been made: that people who like small, enclosed spaces also tend to resist moving to a new home.

It is probably easier for a shallow theory to be accurate, because depth implies going beyond the surface. Nevertheless a deep theory may also prove to be accurate, and when it does its achievement is all the greater. The greater risk of a deep theory may be rewarded with higher achievement. For to be accurate about a new kind of fact requires an insight into reality which goes beyond the usual, and thus pushes back the frontier of ignorance along an entire stretch of territory. Our second criterion for evaluating a theory can be called simply *depth*, meaning depth of insight into reality.

Fruitfulness. The third function of a theory, according to Kuhn, is articulation or directing extensions of research: solution of constants, establishment of laws, and applications to new problems and areas of study. Not all of these kinds of articulation can be expected of all theories. Many theories, especially in psychology, are not formulated in a way that would lead to solution of constants (no constants are proposed) or the establishment of quantitative laws (no quantities are employed). Nevertheless any theory may be expected to stimulate applications to new problems and otherwise guide research. We might call this latter criterion the *fruitfulness* of a theory, meaning the extent to which it provides helpful suggestions for understanding or studying new empirical matters.

In personality theories we often find fruitfulness of another kind. Going back to Maslow (chapter 1) or Rogers (chapter 5), for instance, we find that their theories have been usefully applied to far-ranging situations such as business, education, or marriage relationships. Their theories have stimulated the development of new research techniques (such as Porter's assessment of the Maslow needs hierarchy) or of new approaches to psychotherapy (such as Shlien's development of time-limited therapy). This fruitfulness is found not only in guidance of research but also in development of instruments and practical technologies.

An Absolute Criterion: The Empirical Basis

Criteria for evaluating theories may be either comparative (like the three we have discussed so far) or they may be absolute. A comparative criterion is one which allows us to compare one theory with another. Thus we might conclude that theory A is more accurate than theory B, has greater depth than theory C, and is more fruitful than theory D. However all of the theories compared would have to be *empirical* if they were to qualify as scientific. This means that theories which are not empirical are not scientific theories. Hence the property of being empirical is an absolute criterion for a scientific theory. But what does *empirical* mean?

According to Carnap (1954) the word *empirical* can be defined in at least two different ways. The first requires that an empirical sentence be *confirmable by observation;* this means that a person could, in principle, actually examine the relevant matters and conclude that the sentence is confirmed. For example, the sentence might be "This cherry is red." You could look and see and decide whether the sentence is true or false. Or the sentence might be "All cherries are red"; again you could look and see; but you could never be absolutely sure. At best, having examined half a million cherries and found them all red you might conclude that the sentence is very probably true. You would have given strong confirmation to the hypothesis contained in that sentence. Alternatively, on the basis of your observations you might conclude that the sentence definitely is false; you have seen many red cherries but also many yellow cherries. Therefore you would disconfirm the sentence. Summarizing, in the first definition according to Carnap (1954, pp. 33-34 and 456-457), an empirical theory must contain confirmable concepts.

Carnap's second definition requires that

an empirical sentence be either observable or *testable by experiment*. Philosophers of science have pointed out that a theory with any degree of real depth must go beyond matters that can be immediately observed by human beings. They have stressed the difference between observation and experiment. For example, we can observe the temperature of a liquid by putting our hands in—if the temperature is within some usual range from, say, −40° to 120° Fahrenheit. But suppose we need to measure the boiling-point temperatures of water ($+$ 212°F.) or oxygen (−361.35°F.). We cannot directly observe these temperatures because of the limitations of our physical characteristics. So we must produce a device which will measure the temperature and provide us with a recording. We might use a mercury thermometer or a helium-gas device or something else. Then we would say something like this: We have a suitable thermometer inserted in the liquid; and its mechanism has completed the work of measurement and shows 212° Fahrenheit; we conclude that this liquid (which is water bubbling and changing to steam) has a temperature of 212° Fahrenheit.

Note that while 212° Fahrenheit is not an observable characteristic for human organisms it is nevertheless a testable characteristic. It is testable because we know how to set up an experiment, how to read the results, and what those results mean about the temperature of the substance being studied. We have so arranged it that when we say "This liquid has a temperature of 212° Fahrenheit" we mean that the measuring device was properly applied to the liquid and that its readings showed the value 212.

In Carnap's second definition, then, empirical theories are those which contain at least some sentences which are *testable;* and *testable* means "either observable or introduced by a test chain" (Carnap, 1954, p. 459); *introduced by a test chain* means precisely the

events we described above: a suitable thermometer is applied, its reading shows such and such, and therefore the liquid has a specified value on the temperature scale.

The broadest meaning of *empirical* appears to be Carnap's second definition, and this is the one accepted in this book. An empirical theory, then, is one which contains testable sentences, using either observations or experiments. Not all the sentences need to be testable, however; only some sentences, through which the theory is anchored, so to speak, to the domains of knowledge that other scientists can share. An empirical theory does not have to contain sentences which are already tested but it must contain some sentences that in principle can be tested. Einstein's theory mentioned above, for example, contained a statement about the bending of light waves which was not tested until the eclipse made it possible. Still, it was an empirical theory all along because it was testable.

In summary, an empirical theory is one which can be tested, either by controlled experiments in the laboratory or by careful observations.

Comparative Criteria and the Empirical Basis

Until a theory is provided with at least one test it cannot be either accurate or inaccurate. Accuracy is determined by correspondence between prediction and observation, between hypothesis and the outcome of the experiment. A theory may generate numerous predictions and hypotheses, some of which turn out as expected while others do not. And so a theory may be only partially accurate. Moreover, some particular tests may be quite far removed from the main assumptions and hypotheses, and so their outcome is not that important for the theory one way or the other. There are degrees of accuracy, then, made up of the number of accurate versus inaccurate predictions, each weighted by its importance. A so-called *crucial experiment* is one that provides a definite decision as to the accuracy or inaccuracy of an important hypothesis.

Bunge (1963, pp. 100-106) provides an organized evaluation of many criteria for evaluating theories. He uses the criterion of *depth* essentially as we have described it, and makes its relationship to the empirical basis of a theory very clear. He writes that a theory should be applicable to specific situations and should preferably go to the essences rather than simply describing and predicting without understanding. His contrast is reminiscent of the distinction made by Cronbach and Meehl (1955) between construct validity and predictive validity in psychological tests. For example, if you have a score on a test that predicts performance in college but you have no idea why or how it does so, then that score would have *predictive validity*. But if you had a measure of scholarly ability, meaning the ability to read, grasp concepts, integrate ideas, and extend their application to new topics; and if this measure showed clear differences between acknowledged scholars and persons who preferred and excelled in other pursuits but not scholarship; and if it distinguished between persons who spend much time in the library and those who spend no time there; and so on; then this measure would have *construct validity*. Predictive validity means predicting accurately without knowing why or how; construct validity means measuring a construct with some evidence and assurance that that construct is actually being measured. If then you can predict performance in college with this measure of scholarly ability you can do so for some well-understood reasons, since presumably college performance depends upon the exercise of scholarly ability.

Thus construct validity goes to the essences. The full meaning of a construct is given only by its full set of relationships with the laws, assumptions, and other constructs in the theory. A test with good construct validity is a test whose scores are deeply understood: You know not only what they predict in terms of future performance, but also why that prediction is possible, what causal structures (like scholarly ability) are responsible for the predicted outcome. The theory in which a construct is embedded thus provides the boundaries of understanding which can be attained through measurement of that construct. Bunge writes: "Theories accounting for the 'mechanism' of events and processes afford a deeper understanding, take greater risks, and are more fertile. . . ." (1963, pp. 101-102.) Thus a theory which offers an explanation of how things work or how certain phenomena are composed of other events and processes (such as Boyle's spring of the air) are deeper than theories which simply classify events and objects on the basis of observable characteristics. But deeper theories are less amenable to confirmation by simple observation and often require very complicated experiments, frequently with new, specially designed apparatus (such as the spaceship *Viking's* biological probes). Sometimes it is years (or even centuries) before the appropriate apparatus is invented. This means that a deeper theory, while providing us with greater insight into the nature of reality, may require a much longer time before adequate testing can determine its accuracy. This suggests that depth and accuracy are independent dimensions of theories, and up to a point they are. That is the point at which sufficient evidence is obtained to determine the balance of accuracy or inaccuracy of the theory. Up to that point either a deep or a shallow theory may be retained; beyond that point it must be rejected regardless of its depth if it is inaccurate on balance.

We turn now to the *fruitfulness* of a theory and the relationship of this criterion to the empirical basis. Fruitfulness is the indirect productivity of a theory, the extent to which it stimulates research on other empirical problems than those initially encompassed, or the extent to which it guides new research. Again, up to the point at which the balance of a theory's accuracy is determined, the fruitfulness criterion appears to be independent of accuracy and depth. Beyond that point a theory can retain its degree of fruitfulness only if its balance is in favor of accuracy. But of course, the more fruitful a theory, the more applications will be attempted. Their success or failure will in many cases reflect upon the accuracy of the theory. This will not always be true, however, as the theory of caloric showed. What this means is that a theory can be fruitful even if it is eventually found to be inaccurate.

Bunge has drawn attention to a crucial fact about accuracy. A theory may be either accurate or inaccurate with respect to a large number of facts or phenomena or a smaller number. Bunge suggests that a theory which is accurate about more phenomena should be described as having greater *power*. Thus a theory about the development of one mental disorder such as schizophrenia might be accurate within that limited domain; another theory, dealing with the development of all mental disorders, including schizophrenia and also depression and neurosis, might be accurate over a much larger domain of phenomena. The latter theory would be said to have greater power than the former.

Power is obviously dependent upon accuracy, since only instances of accuracy enter into the calculation of power. Yet the results of that calculation are very important in evaluating a theory, even as a diamond ring with three half-carat diamonds is worth more than a diamond ring with only one half-carat diamond.

Bunge has described several other criteria for evaluating theories, including the extent to which a theory is compatible with other theories in related fields or with currently accepted knowledge, its originality, and the extent to which it is technically possible to actually test the theory properly and within a reasonable time frame. Our considerations in this text, however, will be restricted to the four criteria of *accuracy, power, depth,* and *fruitfulness.*

Application of the Criteria to Personality Theories

Accuracy, power, depth, and fruitfulness are criteria by which all scientific theories may be judged. In actual application, however, there may be differences between different sciences such that one of the criteria becomes more important. For instance, in a completely new science where little systematic observation or testing had been done, it would be impossible to evaluate a theory on the basis of accuracy at that time, hence power would be inapplicable also; nevertheless fruitfulness and depth would be viable criteria even in the beginning stages of a science.

Sciences differ in terms of how "hard" or "soft" they are. A natural science like physics or chemistry is considered "hard." Social or political science is considered relatively "soft." Usually the percentage of statements in the science that can be backed up by hard, clear evidence is an important determiner of how "hard" the science is. Another determinant is the extent to which the theories of that science can be expressed and tested in quantitative form, thereby harnessing the "hard" force of mathematical analysis. In a hard science a theory is just expected to be accurate. But in a "soft" science it is a pleasant surprise if a theory's hypotheses are shown to be accurate.

Within any one science some areas may be "harder" than others. For example, in psychology experimental study of cognition is "harder" than the typical study of clinical problems. Because clinical psychology must concern itself with the entire personality of the subject, both inside and outside of the laboratory or clinic, its facts tend to be fuzzier, its hypotheses less clearly demonstrable, and its accuracy less obvious. The clinician must deal with cases of hysteria or depression as they are found in real life, part of the warp and woof of a person's entire life experience and personality. The clinical researcher cannot produce a depression or a hysterical attack in the laboratory (except by using animal subjects). Hence fewer important variables can be controlled, and hypotheses cannot be as precisely tested as would be possible if all relevant variables could be controlled.

By contrast, such reference to individual personality beyond a test session is of little concern in experimental cognitive psychology. Nor do cognitive psychologists rely much on observation. Almost all such research is conducted by experiments. For example, suppose one is studying memory for verbatim materials (remembering the exact words of each sentence) in contrast to memory for meaning (remembering the essential information contained in each sentence and expressing it in any suitable words). The experimenter would not have to wait for subjects to come along who happen to be good at verbatim memory and for others who are good at meaning memory. Rather, the experimenter randomly assigns volunteer subjects to two or more groups, one receiving materials to be remembered verbatim and the other receiving the same materials to be remembered for meaning. Thus the researcher in cognitive psychology can produce the phenomena of interest right there in the laboratory. Unlike the clinical researcher, the experimenter in cognitive psy-

chology can control most important variables and obtain clear tests of hypotheses. A theory in cognitive psychology can be more obviously accurate or inaccurate because that area of our science is "harder."

Personality science embraces both "soft" (more like clinical) and "hard" areas (more like experimental cognitive psychology). In our consideration of theories of personality, then, we shall apply the criterion of accuracy, having in mind a mix which gives equal weight to confirmation through observation and testing through experiment. It is recognized that the psychology of personality has in recent years received a considerable impetus in the direction of experimental testing of hypotheses, more so than clinical psychology. However, personality psychology shares with clinical psychology the concern for reference beyond the immediate observational or experimental setting. The *particular* personality characteristics brought by a subject to a research session are of direct importance; as for example when a study in personality examines the difference between extraverts and introverts in immediate or delayed memory performance. The essential point of doing such a study in personality research is that differences in the patterns of performance are predicted on the basis of hypotheses about the structure and dynamics of personality among introverts as contrasted with extraverts. These two contrasting groups cannot be created in the laboratory by assignment on a random basis to different manipulative treatments. Extraverts and introverts already exist out there in the general population. All the experimenter can do is use the best psychological test possible to select members of each group without error. This means that each subject's personality (outside the experimental setting as well as in it) is of direct and immediate importance for the data of the study, at least insofar as the characteristics of extraversion versus introversion are concerned.

The study of personality encompasses a wide range of different subject matters, including topics in clinical psychology like bedwetting or fearfulness (compare Maslow's work on the syndrome of insecurity, as described in chapter 1; or Murray's work on the claustral complex, described in chapter 3). Personality studies also include topics in cognitive psychology (like the experiment on memory among introverts and extraverts; or like Chodorkoff's experiment in which he tested Rogers's hypothesis that less congruent subjects would tend to deny awareness of threatening experiences, as described in chapter 5).

Related to the varieties of subject matter are varieties of method. Maslow, for example, relied mainly on informal observation and interviewing, although he did also develop very carefully controlled procedures for psychological testing, as in his work on the insecurity syndrome. Rogers relied primarily on deep sharing in the course of counseling with distressed individuals, later phrasing his conclusions from these observations as tentative hypotheses to be tested by laboratory experiments. Skinner relied from the outset on tightly controlled experimental studies (of animals) and then generalized conclusions to human beings. As we shall see in chapter 15, R. B. Cattell has worked from the beginning with careful measurement data, further strengthened by mathematical analysis.

Thus within personality study we find a range of science, from quite "soft" (Maslow) to quite "hard" (Skinner, Cattell). This diversity accounts for the richness of our field. Skinner would never discover "peak experiences" as Maslow did, simply because he would not be looking in that direction. Rogers would never discover the typical effects of fixed interval schedules of reinforcement be-

cause he would not be studying schedules of reinforcement at all. We must remember that it is easier to show the accuracy (or inaccuracy) of a "hard" area of our science. But both "hard" and "soft" areas *can* be accurate. They differ mainly in ease and clarity of showing the accuracy.

So as we comment upon theories of personality we shall rely mainly on the criterion of accuracy and the related criterion of power, which refers to the range of topics about which a theory is accurate. The criterion of depth of understanding is extremely important, as one reviewer of this manuscript noted. He writes that depth refers to:

> How well a theory provides insight into the totality of personality—that is how well a theory enables us to make sense of the complexity of a human being. . . . A theory that provides depth of understanding no doubt should square with empirical findings [should turn out to be accurate], but . . . while empirical validity is necessary, it is not sufficient grounds for appraising a theory. . . . An important theory frequently will generate testable hypotheses that are in themselves quite trivial, and which, while providing *indirect* support for the theory as a whole, do not directly bear upon the depth of understanding provided by the theory. . . . Depth of understanding has more to do with the adequacy of the theory in providing insight. . . .

I have made several attempts to define more closely what is meant by depth of understanding, but each has been unsatisfactory. At present it seems best to leave it without further definition and let each reader judge what depth a particular theory has. In one sense this might be the most accurate way of evaluating depth anyway, since a theory which gives me a deeper insight may not do the same for you because you knew more about that sort of thing than I did in the first place.

Uranian Scientists Do Preliminary Work on Data Concerning Namwons

Please imagine you are a scientist living on the planet Uranus. Your space probes have recovered photographic data of people-like objects on Alpha-3, a distant planet in another solar system. You are presented with representations of these objects as shown in figure 6.1a. Your first action is to label each observation, using the letters shown in figure 6.1b. Put the appropriate letter in the center of each object in figure 6.1a.

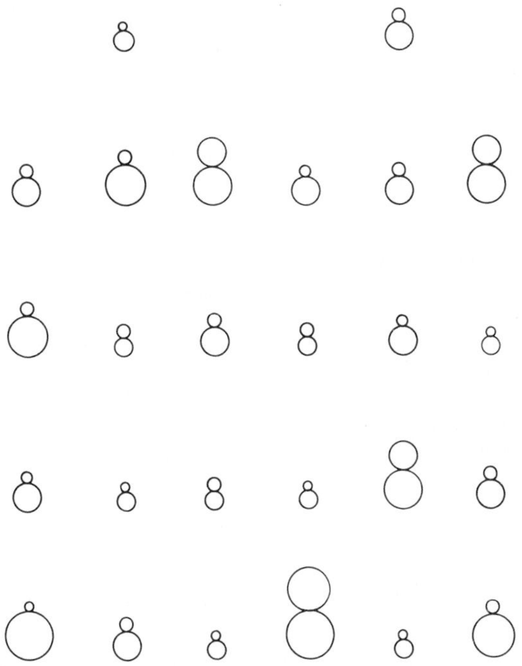

Figure 6.1a. Representations of all Namwons observed

Figure 6.1b. Labels identifying each Namwon by location in figure 6.1a

In your approach to these observations you first name them: Namwons. Now you should ascertain some facts about them.

How many Namwons are represented in figure 6.1a? _____

Are they all different or are some similar to each other? _____

Although all have **some** similarity, can you find some groups of Namwons that appear to be **very closely** similar? For convenience, list these groups of individuals by letter here:

Group 1: _____

Group 2: _____

The General Nature of Scientific Theories   143

Group 3: _____

Group 4: _____

Group 5: _____

Group 6: _____

Are there any individuals who do not fit such groups? _____

Now ask whether some of the groups might be somewhat similar to each other.

Groups _____

Groups _____

Groups _____

Your results might look like the classification system shown in figure 6.2, which shows six basic similarity groups and two individuals (U, X). Also shown is the similarity of group D, I, Z, and group F, M, O, with respect to shape.

Actually all the groups have an overall similarity. For example, a very general fact about Namwons is that each has a certain number of major segments in the body: How many? _____

Another general fact is that all segments of a Namwon's body are similar in shape. What is the shape?

_____

Another general fact about Namwons in all groups is that the two segments are joined at the circumference, there being apparently no connecting part, such as a neck, as Uranians have. From Uranian theory of cosmic forms we have the assumption that all segments of a given organism do interact. What inner structure of the Namwons could be hypothesized to allow for interaction between the two segments? Perhaps

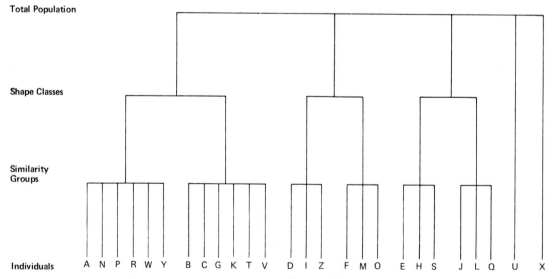

Figure 6.2. Pattern of classifications of Namwons

you would draw a diagram indicating a model of the inner structure of Namwons which would permit interaction between the two segments:

Model of Inner Structure of Namwons:

In Uranians the index of relative arael size of upper to lower segments is roughly .20 on the average (the same as for humans). This index is computed by taking the radius of a circle with center on the centerpoint of the body segment and calculating the area of that segment as

$$A = 3.1416 \times r^2$$

where r is the radius. The ratio of A for the upper segment over A for the lower segment gives the index. A distribution of values for this index taken on the sample of observed Namwons is shown in figure 6.3. (The index has been multiplied by 10 to eliminate decimal points.)

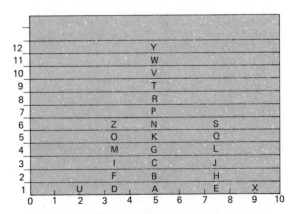

Index of Relative Size of Upper to Lower Segments

Figure 6.3. Distribution of indices of body proportionality for Namwons

In later work it will be necessary to have available a representation of each group of Namwons. So now please draw the leading member of each group on page 146.

A	B	D	F	E	J	U	X
___	___	___	___	___	___	___	___
___	___	___	___	___	___	___	___

You will need to refer to this diagram in the workshop at the end of chapter 8.

Summary

A scientific theory seeks to explain general facts through its constructs, hypotheses, laws, and empirical assumptions. All scientific theories are *empirical,* which means that they are expressed in sentences some of which could be confirmed by observation or tested by experiment.

Four important criteria for evaluating theories are: 1) *accuracy,* the degree of correspondence between theoretical descriptions and predictions on the one hand and the actual outcomes of observations or experiments on the other; 2) *power,* the extent or range or number of different facts which the theory accurately explains or predicts; 3) *depth,* the depth of insight into reality or the depth of understanding provided by a theory; and 4) *fruitfulness,* the amount of stimulation and guidance of research the theory produces.

In evaluating a theory we must recognize its historical stage of development and also some of the constraints imposed by the inherent characteristics of its subject matter. Personality theories typically are aimed at topics that go beyond the boundaries of knowledge that can be gained in a single laboratory session. Although there are exceptions, for most theories there is insufficient evidence to make a thorough judgment as to accuracy. Judgments of depth are best left to the individual reader, who alone will know whether a particular theory contributes to his or her understanding and insight.

Because assumptions are so important but often seem mysterious, in the next chapter we shall study a theory of personality in which empirical assumptions are given very close attention. It is hoped that a fuller concrete example will illustrate more clearly what empirical assumptions are and how they work.

Then we shall return to the general nature of scientific theories in chapter 8, where we shall examine the ways in which theories deal with particular small sets of facts concerning a defined, small segment of reality. They do this through generating *theoretical models,* which are like word pictures of how something works, where the language the words come from is the set of laws, assumptions, hypotheses, and constructs of a given theory.

INTRODUCTION

A social learning theory of personality
  Intellectual origins of the theory: Hull and Freud
Introduction to the life and work of each theorist
  Neal Miller
  John Dollard
  Personality is the sum of learned habits
Social learning and imitation
  Basic constructs
    Drive
    Cue
    Response
    Reward
  Other principles
    Learning and extinction
    Spontaneous recovery
    Generalization
    Discrimination
    Gradient of reward
    Anticipatory response
  Three kinds of imitation
    Same behaviors
    Copying
    Matched-dependent behavior
      Theory of matched-dependent learning
      Case of Bobby: An illustration
      An experiment on matched-dependent
        learning
      Personality is acquired by learning to imitate
        the behaviors of other people via matched-
        dependent learning
Conflict and displacement
  Conflict
    Gradients of approach and of avoidance
    Empirical assumptions required for the model
  Displacement
    Empirical assumptions required for the model
    Hypotheses derived from assumptions
    Experiments testing the hypotheses
    Work of Miller, Murray, Kraeling, Berkun
    Implications for personality dynamics
Higher mental processes
  Cue-producing responses
    Paying attention
    Counting
    Classification
Foresight
Language and thought
The instructor's dilemma: a case illustration
Chains of cue-producing responses;
  reversibility in direction
Higher mental processes and neurosis
Accomplishments of the theory
  Conceptual and technical applications to
    psychotherapy
  Case illustration of self-study
  Use and development of the theory by other
    scientists
    Epstein's theory and research on drive and
      conflict
Critique of the theory developed by Miller and
  Dollard
  Faults of intellectual origin
  The critique by Bandura and Walters: Miller
    and Dollard fail to consider truly **social** context
    of human learning
    Critique of the critique
  The extreme liberalization of S-R theory
  Possible advantages of the liberalization
  Chomsky's criticisms
  Criticisms by Breger and McGaugh
  The theory began with responses but ends with
    subjective experience
  The theory as psychodynamic and cognitive
  Accuracy, fruitfulness, power, and depth
Workshop 7 Does matched-dependent learning
  require awareness of the contingency?
Summary

A Theory with Explicit Empirical Assumptions: Miller and Dollard

The theory we shall study in this chapter is one of several known as *social learning theories* of personality. Others include the theories of J. B. Rotter (chapter 20) and Albert Bandura and Richard Walters (chapter 21). All these theories are similar in their view of personality as learned by the individual in a social context, but they differ regarding exactly what is learned and how it is learned. Rotter believes, for example, that personality consists of two learned factors: (1) expectations regarding the probable success or failure of one's own efforts to secure desired rewards; (2) values an individual places upon different kinds of rewards. Bandura and Walters believe that personality consists of behaviors that have been acquired through observational learning in imitation of other people. Miller and Dollard believe, like Skinner (chapter 4), that personality consists of learned habits. Unlike Skinner, they believe that drives exist within the person and that the habits are part of the inner make-up of the person. For them, the habits and also the drives are real structures and processes occurring within the individual.

My own first encounter with social learning theory took place many years ago, although at the time I was unaware of its name. The story is significant here because it illustrates the use of empirical assumptions in everyday life, and shows continuity between shrewd thinking on the part of an ordinary citizen and scientific thinking on the part of psychological theorists.

I used to mess about with boats a good deal while I was a student in England. One day my friend George Knight looked across from the boathouse and saw two men walking slowly up the road. They had just come out of the Queen's Arms, a nearby pub. "Look at those two!" he said. "They're both walking in that same funny way." The two men were not swaying or anything like that, but as they walked each swung his head and shoulders from side to side in rhythm with the stride. "What do you make of it?" asked George. I replied that it seemed like an odd way to walk. "I'll bet you," said George, "that the bigger guy is the smaller chap's boss; and the smaller one is imitating his boss without knowing it." I thought this showed remarkable insight on George's part. He was a carpenter by trade, and often understood what was going on with people much better than I did. That incident has remained vivid in my memory, partly because it illustrated the power of empirical assumptions in everyday life. George's underlying empirical assumption seems quite evident: We are likely to imitate the behavior of someone who can reward us for doing so. The idea that we learn to imitate another's behavior if it is rewarding to do so lies at the heart of the theory of personality developed by Neal Miller and John Dollard.

Miller and Dollard were among the first scientists to take the learning theory developed by Clark Hull (1943) and apply it to the understanding of human personality and behavior. As defined in chapter 6, they *articulated* Hull's theory for personality and modified it as necessary to deal with human learning in social situations. They studied a number of socially important topics such as imitation (Miller & Dollard, *Social Learning and Imitation,* 1941), frustration and aggression (Dollard et al., *Frustration and Aggression,* 1939), and personality (Dollard & Miller, *Personality and Psychotherapy,* 1950.) Particularly in their work on frustration and on neuroses they used clinical insights obtained by Freud and coordinated these where possible with constructs in Hull's theory. Freud referred to basic motives in personality as *instincts;* basic motives in Hull's theory are called *drives.* In Freud's theory, instincts can become *attached to* particular objects; drives, in Miller's and Dollard's formulations, can become acquired or *learned in response to* particular objects. In Freud's theory *conflict* between motives lies at the root of all neuroses; Miller and Dollard (as we shall see below) deal with *conflict* between two behavior tendencies, the tendency to approach a goal and the tendency to avoid it.

Miller and Dollard are among the most distinguished of American psychologists. Neal Miller was born in 1909 and obtained his undergraduate training at the University of Washington. He received a master's degree from Stanford University in 1932 and a Ph.D. from Yale in 1935. With the exception of a four-year period during which he directed a project for the Army Air Force, Miller taught at Yale University for thirty years. He was a professor of psychology there from 1952 until 1966 when he became professor of psychology at Rockefeller University. He received the Award for Distinguished Scientific Contribution from the American Psychological Association in 1959, and several other high honors including the President's Medal of Science in 1965.

John Dollard was born in 1900, did undergraduate work at the University of Wisconsin, and received an M.A and Ph.D. in sociology from the University of Chicago in 1930 and 1931 respectively. In 1932 Dollard went to Yale University where he taught first as assistant professor of anthropology, then sociology, and finally as professor of psychology. Apart from his collaboration with Miller, Dollard wrote a number of important books in the field of social anthropology, such as *Caste and Class in a Southern Town* (1937), and also in clinical psychology, such as *Victory Over Fear* (1942).

The theory of personality developed by Miller and Dollard states that an individual's personality is the sum of his or her learned habits. The basic elements of personality, then, are habits, learned connections between environmental stimuli (or *cues*), inner drives, and behavioral responses. Many of these habits are automatic in the sense that they operate without the individual's conscious thought. Dollard and Miller give the example (1950, p. 98) of a driver. Seeing a child run in front of the car, the driver automatically presses the brake. Even the passenger presses hard on the floorboards without thinking about it. *Child* is the cue, *protection* is the drive, *hitting the brake* is the response in this automatic habit. How do people learn the habits that become the building blocks of their personality? One way is through imitation of other people—through *social learning.*

Social Learning and Imitation

Basic Constructs

Miller and Dollard (1941) begin their analysis of imitation with an account of Hullian learning theory's four basic constructs: *drive, cue, response,* and *reward.* The construct of *drive* refers to any stimulus which serves as an impulse to action. Usually it would be internal, like a hunger pang or a definite wish for something. A drive can be thought of as an internal stimulus that impels a person to respond. By contrast, a *cue* is defined as a stimulus that guides behavior. Cues determine which *response* (among several alternatives) is to be made, and when and where the response will occur. Dollard and Miller (1950, p. 32) give several examples. Traffic lights determine which response will occur, stepping on the accelerator or pushing on the brake. The highway sign indicating *Food and Lodging Next Exit* determines where a hungry traveler will go. The morning school bell determines when the children enter the building to begin classes. Traffic lights, highway signs, and school bells are all examples of external cues.

In a demonstration experiment, for example, it was ascertained that a six-year-old girl was momentarily hungry for some candy, thus ensuring that *drive* was present (1941). Certain cues were provided for her. She was told that a piece of candy had been hidden under one of a whole shelf of books and that she could look for it by searching under one book at a time until she found it, and then she could eat it. These instructions, together with the array of similarly sized and colored books, constituted the *cues* in this experiment. The little girl began removing books; this was her *response.* Under the thirty-seventh book she removed she found the piece of candy. With an exclamation of delight she ate the candy, her *reward.* After she left the room the experimenter placed another piece of candy under the same book and the entire sequence was repeated. On this second trial she removed only twelve books before she found the candy. By the ninth trial she went to the right book immediately. Thus errors were gradually eliminated and *learning,* a systematic change in instrumental behavior, had taken place.

According to Miller and Dollard (1941, p. 17), this change, called *learning,* is specifically due to the fact that the error responses (picking out a wrong book) are not rewarded by an event which reduces the drive, and therefore tend to drop out, or *extinguish.* But if a response is followed by a reward, "the connection between the cue and this response is strengthened, so that the next time the same drive and other cues are present, this response is more likely to occur" (Miller & Dollard, 1941, p. 17).

Other Principles

The essential nature of the learning process for Miller and Dollard is the strengthening by reward of the connection between cue and response. Among the major principles of learning employed in their theory are several we have discussed at length in chapter 4: *extinction,* the dropping out of unrewarded responses; *spontaneous recovery,* the tendency of an extinguished response to recur after a lapse of time; *generalization,* the innately given tendency for the organism to respond to cues similar to the original cues in the presence of which reward was received following a response; *discrimination,* the elimination of generalized responses to cues which are so far from the original cues that responses in their presence are not followed by reward; a *gradient in the effects of reward,* such that rewards which are delayed after the response have lesser tendency to strengthen the connection between cue and response; and *anticipatory response.* They describe the principle of anticipatory responses in the following way (Miller & Dollard, 1941, p. 49): "responses near the point of reward tend wherever physically possible to occur before their original time in the response series. . . . When the little girl was looking for candy, the response of selecting the correct book moved forward in the series and crowded out the originally prior response of selecting the wrong book." The response made just prior to reinforcement tends to be made sooner and sooner as trials progress. Another example comes from thinking about breakfast when you are hungry. You tend to salivate even before you sit down to the meal.

Imitation

Miller and Dollard (1941, pp. 91 ff.) describe three different kinds of imitation not typically distinguished in everyday discussion of imitation: *same behaviors, copying*, and *matched-dependent behavior*. In all cases two or more persons' behaviors are similar but the similarity can arise in three quite different ways.

First, the behaviors of the two might simply be the *same* because both are independently responding to the same cues under the same drive. For example, two people might both flee from a forest fire, impelled equally by a fear drive and both cued independently by the smell of smoke.

Second, the similarity can arise as a result of *copying*, in which a *model* of behavior to be imitated is present as one cue and the *similarity or differences* between the copier's behavior and the model serve as additional cues. The cues of similarity or difference are often made distinctive by a critic or coach who points out the deficiencies of the copier's behavior relative to the model. Sometimes the critic is also the model, as when a master guitarist demonstrates a piece to a student, then requests the student to play the piece, and then comments on the points of difference between what the student did and what

the master did. The model is often behavior by a teacher or other exemplar, but it may also be a product, as when children learn to copy cursive writing. The essential feature of this kind of imitation is that the similarity or difference between the copier's behavior and the model is a crucial cue. As it happens, this kind of imitation is often also described as conscious imitation or purposeful imitation, since the copier must already be aware of the general nature of similarity and difference in behavior as constituting a cue for which responses can be rewarded. In social life conformity and upward striving depend upon copying as defined; persons who wish to remain members of a community in good standing must conform to the customs and norms of the community; deviance (too great a difference from model) is punished. Likewise, acceptance by the community as a person of higher rank depends upon the ability to behave in ways that are similar to those of higher-ranked models.

Matched-dependent Behavior. In this third kind of imitative behavior a leader can discriminate certain cues which the follower cannot. In everyday life examples are plentiful. People behave as experts do, or as experts tell them to, because the experts have access to or awareness of cues not available to others. People take their raincoats when the weather experts forecast rain. People take pills when told to by their doctors. Children imitate their parents and older siblings, and the less skilled must depend upon the more skilled to respond adequately to cues which they cannot discriminate themselves. Because they depend on the leader or expert, this kind of imitative behavior is called *dependent;* because it is imitative, the behavior is called *matched.*

A detailed account of one child's learning of matched-dependent behavior (Miller & Dollard, 1941, pp. 93-97) will provide a clear picture of their theory.

Two children, aged five and two, played daily near the back entrance to their home about the time when the father returned home from work. As he came home he stepped up the outside staircase. The older boy heard his father's footstep, ran to meet him, and received a piece of candy the father always brought home. Bobby, the younger child, did not notice the father's step and usually kept on playing, until one day he happened to be running in the same direction as his brother when the father arrived. He too received a piece of candy. Subsequently, the younger child often ran when he saw his brother running, and consequently received his piece of candy. Still he was not running to his father's footstep; his cue was his brother's running.

Some time later the children were told to look for two pieces of candy that were hidden in the living room. The older boy looked in several places and eventually found his piece under a cushion. The younger one followed everywhere the older brother looked, looking there too, but when the older one got his candy and stopped looking further the younger one was helpless, and kept looking again under the cushion. In this case his matched-dependent behavior did not receive a reward. But this situation illustrates the important principle that the younger child had generalized his matched-dependent behavior to many situations other than the original one of running when father came home. Now he matched his behavior to that of his older brother in many different situations.

Miller and Dollard present a diagram clearly depicting the relationships among the various elements of the original matched-dependent behavior in this case. It is reproduced in figure 7.1. The diagram brings out the facts that the imitator's behavior is matched to the behavior of the leader but it is cued by the leader's behavior also. Thus the imitator is dependent upon the leader to provide the cue for behavior. Miller and Dollard clarify the important role played by each element of the learning process (drive, cue, response, and reward) in this case of matched-dependent behavior as follows:

If Bobby (the younger child) had had no drive—that is, if he had not been hungry for candy—it would have been impossible for reinforcement to occur, and the connection between the response and the cue of the leg-twinkle would not have been fixed. If he had been unable to perceive his brother's cue—if, say he had been blind—it would have been impossible for the learning to occur. If he had been unable to make the response of running—if, for instance, he had been kept in the room

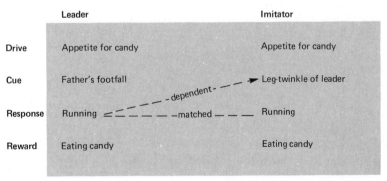

Figure 7.1. Relationships of learning factors in a case of matched-dependent behavior. From Miller, N.E., and Dollard, J. **Social Learning and Imitation.** New Haven: Yale University Press, 1941, p. 96. Reprinted by permission of author and publisher.

A Theory With Explicit Empirical Assumptions: Miller and Dollard   153 by a barrier which only his brother could leap —it would have been impossible to learn the imitative responses. If he had not been rewarded on the occasions when he did follow his brother, he could not have learned to imitate (Miller & Dollard, 1941, p. 97).

Miller has also pointed out that *"once the child had learned to imitate,* he might imitate in a specific case without making the overt, motor response" (Miller, 1976), which suggests that he would acquire many habits from his brother which would not be immediately obvious.

It must be added that Miller and Dollard employed such case examples primarily for purposes of illustration, not for proof of their theory. Tests of the theory were carried out in numerous experiments on animals and on children. In one representative study first-grade children were paired. Candies were hidden in one of two boxes. One child in each pair was told in which of the two boxes to find the candy. This child became the leader. Both were then told there was candy in one of the boxes (see diagram, figure 7.2); the leader would look first. The leader was instructed to open the box in such a way that the second child (imitator) could not see whether candy was in it or not. Then the imitator was given a turn. The imitator who followed the leader was rewarded by finding a piece of candy in the box. The one who did not received no reward but was taken out of the room until the next trial. The leader thus had access to the relevant cue and the imitator did not. The imitator would receive a reward by matching the leader's behavior. It was expected that under these conditions the imitators would learn matched-dependent behavior, and the results showed that 100 percent of the subjects did learn to match their behaviors to those of the leader. Later, seventy-five percent generalized this learning to a new situation in which four boxes were placed at the four corners of a room and subjects started

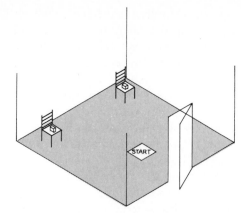

Figure 7.2. The two-box experiment for the study of matched-dependent behavior in children. From Miller, N.E., and Dollard, J. **Social Learning and Imitation.** New Haven: Yale University Press, 1941, p. 124. Reprinted by permission of author and publisher.

their turns in the center of the room (Miller & Dollard, 1941, pp. 127, 130).

In the original two-box situation a control group was given exactly the same instructions and conditions except that there was one piece of candy in each box. When the leader removed the piece of candy from the cued box it was empty; a matched response by the second child would not be rewarded, but a nonmatched response would be followed by reward. Under these conditions it was expected that the children would learn to be nonimitators. In a test trial after training it was found that none of the control group made imitative responses.

The theory of matched-dependent learning, and its confirming experiments, point the way to an explanation of how personality is acquired. Each person finds it rewarding to imitate the behaviors of one or more other people in his or her immediate environment. At home one imitates parents or brothers and sisters. In the street one imitates other children. At school one imitates teachers and students. Such learning can begin with one or a few habits acquired directly in the way that Bobby learned to run for candy. Generalization to other responses and associated habits then takes place. Some habits may be acquired even without the overt response being made, and a wide range of habits can be acquired, only some of which may be immediately apparent. Later that habit might be overtly expressed in some combination of suitable circumstances. Parents may stand back in amazement and say, "Why, she threw that ball just like her older sister used to!"

Acquired Personality Traits. We have all noticed how personality characteristics often seem to be shared by members of a family. Also we often note that geographic areas seem to have certain prevailing personal characteristics, at least within a certain socioeconomic or ethnic group. People from the eastern part of the United States are generally more bound by rules of dress and of relationships with strangers. They tend to be more formal. I recall one Philadelphian who came to Boulder, Colorado, as a consultant. When he was picked up at his hotel the next morning he announced that a very unpleasant thing had happened to him. While waiting outside the hotel some complete stranger had walked by and greeted him. In the Rocky Mountain region of the United States such greetings are commonplace. People tend to be friendly and open toward strangers. They tend to be less formal in dress, and jeans worn with a denim work jacket is known locally as "Boulder tux." Similar variations in personal characteristics may be found in different countries of the world, Germans being reputedly stern and businesslike, Italians being reputedly more fun-loving and emotional.

Many theories of personality cannot readily explain such group differences in personality characteristics. Indeed the whole problem of "national personality" or "national character" has remained in the hands of compe-tent sociologists or cultural anthropologists primarily. But Miller and Dollard have no problem accounting for such commonalities of personality among members of family, regional, or national groups. Since personality is composed of learned habits, and since many learned habits are the product of matched-dependent learning (or other forms of imitation), it is to be expected that the members of a family or cultural group will learn from each other and thereby develop similarities of personality.

Conflict and Displacement

Freud (1905) proposed that the first five years of a child's life are the most crucial in development of personality. For during those years the child's instincts (of sex, hunger, anger, and so on) are blocked from natural expression by the parents, who want to raise the child in the ways of society. The child inevitably experiences conflict between instinctual impulses seeking expression on the one hand, and fear of punishment or of losing the parents' love on the other hand. The manner in which the child attempts to resolve these conflicts (by keeping the impulses under control or by expressing them in devious ways) lays the foundations for the adult personality. Miller and Dollard sought to account for these hypotheses in their learning-theory framework. Hence an account of *conflict* was of major importance. So also was a treatment of *displacement*, which was the process which made devious expression of impulses possible, according to Freud.

Conflict

In their analysis of the social conditions producing conflict, Dollard and Miller (1950, pp. 127 ff.) identified four critical areas in the early training of children: feeding, cleanliness, sex, and the control of anger. In each of these areas, when the child's drives are met with opposition from the parents in the form of punitive measures, conflict is produced in the child between the original drive and the new fear or anxiety associated with punishment or loss of love. In his previous work on basic theory, Miller (1944) analyzed this conflict in terms of *gradients of approach and of avoidance*. The gradient of approach was the response equivalent of the gradient of the effects of reward mentioned earlier. A gradient of avoidance was assumed for the effects of punishment. These empirical assumptions were made by Miller in his model:

1. The gradient of approach represents a stronger tendency to approach when the person is nearer to a goal than when farther away from it.
2. Likewise, the gradient of avoidance reflects a stronger tendency to avoid a source of punishment when the person is nearer to it than when farther from it.
3. With increasing nearness to the goal or source of punishment, there is a more rapid increase in the strength of tendencies to avoid than the strength of tendencies to approach, resulting in a steeper gradient of avoidance than of approach.

4. The average strength of a tendency to approach or to avoid is directly related to the strength of the relevant drive, so that a higher level of drive raises the entire gradient.

Figure 7.3 illustrates these four assumptions.

Displacement

In many experiments using animal subjects Miller showed that hypotheses derived from these empirical assumptions were confirmed. In one experiment rats were placed in a harness so that the strength of their pull could be measured. Rats deprived of food for forty-eight hours were then placed at different distances from a food dish; the strength of their approach responses to the food was measured. Rats also were given a strong shock at one end of an alley and then placed at different distances from the shock point; the strength of their avoidance responses was measured. The resulting curves closely approximated those shown in figure 7.3.

Empirical Assumptions and Hypotheses. Relating his model of conflict to Freud's the-

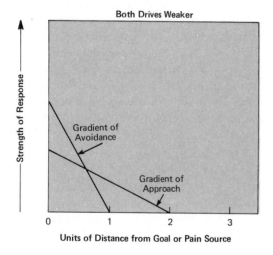

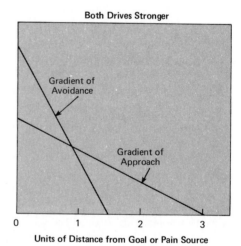

Figure 7.3. Miller's theoretical model of conflict

ories (see chapter 10 especially), Miller went on to provide a theoretical model of *displacement,* a psychoanalytic construct referring to the shift of affect from one object to another due to conflict surrounding the first object. To develop a model of displacement Miller proposed (1948b) six main assumptions:

1. The gradient of approach generalizes to stimuli similar to the original stimulus, so that not only distance from the goal but also *stimulus difference* from the goal constitutes a dimension along which the strength of approach tendencies declines.
2. The gradient of avoidance also generalizes to other stimuli along a dimension of stimulus dissimilarity.
3. The gradient of avoidance is steeper than the gradient of approach when the gradients are taken along the dimension of stimulus dissimilarity just as it is when the gradients are taken along a dimension of distance from the goal or source of shock.
4. When the situation elicits an avoidance and an approach response simultaneously the one that actually occurs is the one with the greatest net strength at the moment.
5. The net strength of a response is a sum-

mation of its strength minus the strength of a momentarily incompatible response.
6. A higher drive level for approach raises the overall gradient of approach when based on generalization as well as when the gradient is based on distance, and likewise for the effect of drive level for avoidance upon the gradient of avoidance.

Figure 7.4 illustrates these six assumptions.

Miller deduces a number of hypotheses from the assumptions. First, in the absence of both the original stimulus and a conflicting response tendency, *displaced responses will be directed toward similar stimuli,* the more strongly to the more similar stimuli. If only one such stimulus can be responded to it will most likely be made to the most similar stimulus. For example, if one's sweetheart died one would most likely choose another sweetheart who closely resembled the first. In figure 7.4 if the original sweetheart was at point A and there was no conflicting response at all, then the new sweetheart would be at point B, the most similar. The second hypothesis is that if approach is prevented by conflict, *dis-*

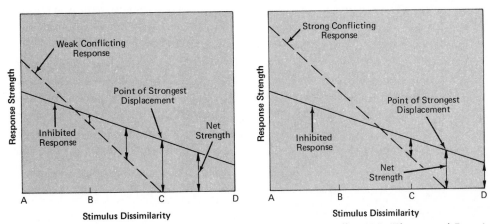

Figure 7.4. Miller's theoretical model of displacement. From Miller, N.E. "Theory and Experiment Relating Psychoanalytic Displacement to Stimulus-response Generalization. **Journal of Abnormal and Social Psychology,** 1948, **43,** p. 169, figure 9b. Copyright 1948, the American Psychological Association. Reprinted by permission of author and publisher.

placed responses will be directed to stimulus objects having a medium degree of similarity to the original. For example, a girl who broke up with her lover after discovering some repulsive characteristics in him would be expected to choose another lover who was not completely like the first one but not completely different either. The new lover would fall at point C in figure 7.4.

Several experiments with animals yielded confirmations of these hypotheses (Miller, 1948b; Miller and Kraeling, 1952; Murray and Miller, 1952). In an application to psychotherapy, however, Edward Murray (1954) found that displacement appeared to have some features he could not account for. For instance, statements made by a patient in therapy (see figure 7.5) expressing hostility to mother, aunt, and other people in general seemed to follow a reverse order to that expected from Miller's theory. It would be expected that the most conflict would center on hostility to mother, the next most on conflict regarding the aunt, and the least on conflict toward other people in general; then it would be reasonable to find the patient first expressing hostility to other people in general (who would be most dissimilar from mother), then expressing hostility to the aunt (who would be more similar to mother), and finally expressing hostility to mother. But exactly the reverse order appeared in the data, as depicted in figure 7.5.

In the sixteenth hour of therapy, as figure 7.5 shows, there is a return to a high number of statements expressing hostility toward the mother. Interpreting these results, Murray and Berkun (1955) pointed out that the first set of hostility statements toward the mother were relatively mild but the second set were relatively strong, as indicated by tone of voice, loudness, and the fact that they tended to be about more recent events. Murray and Berkun offer the following explanation:

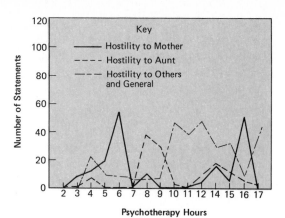

Figure 7.5. One patient's statements indicating hostility to various people, plotted over time. From Murray, E.J. "A Case Study in a Behavioral Analysis of Psychotherapy." **Journal of Abnormal and Social Psychology,** 1954, **49,** pp. 305-310. Figure 3. Copyright 1954, the American Psychological Association. Reprinted by permission of author and publisher.

The patient was afraid to express strong hostility about his mother. He gradually came *nearer* to expressing strong hostility, but finally reached the point where anxiety was too great. This is the conflict point: Hour 6. At this point, the conflict was resolved by displacement to statements about the aunt, who was similar but less anxiety arousing. Eventually, the conflict point with respect to the aunt was reached, and again the conflict was resolved by displacement (Murray & Berkun, 1955, p. 48).

Murray and Berkun proposed a model comprising both the *nearness* (of expressing strong hostility) and the *similarity* between the original target and the person to whom the hostility is actually expressed. This model would thus employ Miller's assumptions in the conflict model and assumptions in his displacement model. This new model assumes that conflict is itself subject to displacement along the dimension of similarity. As stimuli become less similar to the original source of conflict, they evoke that conflict at a later and later point in time, until eventually they evoke no conflict at all and the displaced response may be expressed. Figure 7.6 gives a graphic illustration of the intersection of the conflict model (nearness) and the displacement model (similarity).

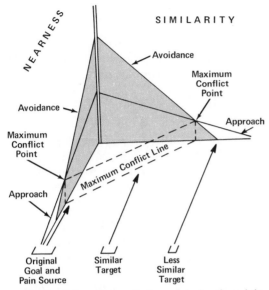

Figure 7.6. Theoretical model developed by Murray and Berkun

Murray and Berkun's model, depicted in figure 7.6, shows the point of maximum conflict for both the nearness and the similarity dimensions. The intersection of these two dimensions produces a plane for avoidance, a plane for approach, and a plane representing points having values on both nearness and similarity dimensions. For example, the boxes at the foot of the diagram show *Original goal and pain source, Similar target,* and *Less similar target.* The boxes are placed at maximum distance from the goal. The line arrows are moving toward points on the similarity dimension. Thus the line arrow for the original goal moves closer and closer to the original goal; but the line arrow for similar target moves closer and closer to a goal that is similar

to the original but displaced in the direction of dissimilarity. The line linking the maximum conflict point for nearness and the maximum conflict point for similarity is the locus of maximum conflict points in the intersection of the avoidance plane with the approach plane. When this line (*maximum conflict line*) is projected onto the floor plane it represents those junctions of nearness and similarity which will be accompanied by maximum conflict.

Using this theoretical model Murray and Berkun (1955) constructed experimental apparatus, shown in figure 7.7, consisting of three alleys in which rats may run: A wide white

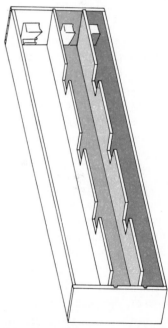

Figure 7.7. Experimental box constructed by Murray and Berkun for testing their theoretical model of conflict and displacement. From Murray, E. J., and Berkun, M. M. "Displacement as a Function of Conflict." **Journal of Abnormal and Social Psychology,** 1955, **51,** p. 50, Figure 5. Copyright 1955, the American Psychological Association. Reprinted by permission of author and publisher.

alley, adjacent to a medium-width gray alley, which is adjacent to a narrow black alley. Windows between alleys can be opened to allow the rat to move between alleys. After the rats became accustomed to all alleys they were placed in the white alley with the windows closed. They were trained to approach the goal box for food. After this training was complete they began to receive shock at the goal box. This condition established an avoidance tendency as well as an approach tendency to the goal box. The situation at this point can be represented by the panel of gradients for nearness in figure 7.6. As expected, rats with this conflict would go only a little way down the alley toward the goal box before vacillating and stopping as the conflict increased. Then the windows were opened.

It was predicted from the model that the rat would enter the gray alley and move closer toward the goal before reaching a point of maximum conflict, then it would move into the black alley and proceed even farther down it toward the goal, possibly as far as the actual goal box. Upon reaching the goal box the rat would be rewarded with food. Since no shock would be given, it was expected that fear would be reduced, and the (displaced) conditioned avoidance reaction would be somewhat extinguished. This slight extinction of the conditioned avoidance response in the black alley would generalize to the gray alley, so that on the next trial the rat would progress nearer to the goal in the gray alley. Finally, the extinction of fear would generalize to the white alley and the rat should once again approach the goal in that alley.

This entire set of predictions was confirmed. Applying the illustration of the theoretical model in figure 7.6 to these experiments, the line of movement when the animal is in a less similar target (the black alley) progresses farther toward the goal before reaching conflict, and not as far when the target is more similar (the gray alley). Figure 7.8 shows the record of one rat's trials after conflict was established in alley 1. As may be seen, the rat's behavior matches the predictions very closely, both within trials and from one trial to the next. In trial 3 the behavior is almost an exact tracing of the movement in figure 7.6 along the arrow for the original goal to the maximum conflict line, then over to the arrow for the similar target and along to the maximum conflict line, and then over again to the arrow for the less similar target and all the way to the goal box. The model and the experimental data all seem to follow the same pattern of movement as that displayed by the patient from whose therapy data the initial stimulation arose for the construction of this theoretical model.

Personality Implications. What insight into personality dynamics can we gain from this experiment? Let us review what has happened. First, Murray found some interesting data in the sequences of patient statements of hostility toward different persons. Second,

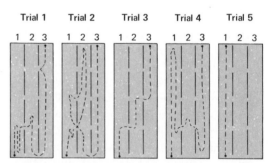

Figure 7.8. Record of one rat's behaviors in the experiment on conflict and displacement by Murray and Berkun. From Murray, E. J., and Berkun, M. M. "Displacement as a Function of Conflict." **Journal of Abnormal and Social Psychology,** 1955, **51,** p. 51, figure 6. Copyright 1955, the American Psychological Association. Reprinted by permission of author and publisher.

these data could not be explained by Miller's model of displacement. Third, Murray and Berkun constructed an alternative model, combining assumptions related to Miller's model of conflict with assumptions relating to his model of displacement. This model allowed for an explanation of the data found in the psychotherapy records. In order to test the model Murray and Berkun deduced hypotheses concerning the behavior of rats under suitable conflict conditions. These hypotheses were supported by the experimental results.

Now we need to reverse the chain of events. Instead of saying which event followed which, we can say what is implied by each event. Since the experimental hypotheses were supported by the rats' behavior patterns (as in figure 7.8), we conclude tentatively that the hypotheses are valid in general. This means that, given suitable conditions of conflict, displacement will occur along a dimension of stimulus dissimilarity, and behavior indicating conflict is more likely to occur at points nearer to substitute goals the more dissimilar those goals are to the original. Support for the hypotheses implies support for the model (that is, it seems to be accurate). Support for the model implies support for the assumptions.

Now we can draw some conclusions about personality dynamics. Assuming that results from animal experiments imply validity for models about human behaviors as well, the experiment supports the idea that people tend to attack objects (or other people) sufficiently different from the real source of their hostility to produce no conflict. Short of that degree of difference, people are likely to experience conflict in relation to other people who are similar to original targets of approach (including aggression) who were also sources of fear. This means that many times when we meet some new person who reminds us vaguely of such an original target we will feel a growing uneasiness and tension. We get tense around certain kinds of people, the tension reflecting the conflict between our (generalized) tendencies to approach and tendencies to avoid people who are sufficiently similar to someone who was a potent source of conflict earlier in our lives.

Higher Mental Processes

Miller and Dollard (1941, pp. 54ff.) point out that a person can be stimulated by his or her own responses. Just as responses can serve as cues for other people in matched-dependent behavior, so they can serve as cues for oneself. If the stimuli so produced are very strong they can serve as drives; reduction of those drives can then also serve as reward. For example, pain experienced by a child at the dentist's office elicits a number of responses aimed at escaping from the situation, including efforts to get out of the chair and also all of the internal physiological responses associated with fear, such as increased heart rate, tensing of muscles, and so on. The latter responses produce strong stimuli such as feelings of goosepimples and a tight, slightly sick feeling in the stomach. These are the stimuli involved in anxiety. In subsequent visits to the dentist the child will react to the previously neutral cues of the waiting room with anxiety as an anticipatory response producing the stimuli of anxiety feelings. Any response which results in a reduction of this anxiety would thus be rewarded and learned, for anxiety has become an acquired drive.

Cue-producing Responses

Responses may produce stimuli which are weak and distinctive enough to serve as cues, but not strong enough to serve as drives. In this case the responses serve to guide more complex behavior. For example, a junior officer encountering a senior officer must learn to notice the often quite small cues distinguishing the senior from all others. Miller and Dollard stress (1941, pp. 71 ff.) how complex is the total cue situation provided by a soldier in uniform. A junior officer must go through a number of cue-producing responses in order to meet the ceremonial requirements of saluting a superior. The junior officer must learn to direct special looking responses in the small area where special insignias are located (such as an eagle or stars or pips on the shoulder). Given the appropriate number of such symbols the junior officer then responds with a salute. So the sequence is: general set of cues of approaching officer → response of paying attention to insignias → cues of definite insignia → appropriate response (salute or no salute). Notice that *paying attention* has been described as a cue-producing response. As we shall see, Miller and Dollard make use of the construct of *cue-producing responses* in their account of higher mental processes.

Counting is one of the most important types of cue-producing responses. It is the simplest and yet also one of the most fundamental of the human's higher mental processes. By actually counting (making responses) we can distinguish very small differences in amounts or make very precisely adjusted movements. The counting makes this possible by producing fine cues. By counting, for example, we can tell if our change is one dollar short; merely looking at a heap of bills would probably not be sufficient to discern that one is missing. Miller and Dollard suggest that the child who took several trials to learn exactly under which book the candy was hidden (in the experiment described above) would probably have learned after one trial if she had been old enough to count the number of books to the left of the book where the reward was found.

Another important cue-producing response, *classification* is a response whereby we group objects into classes even though the objects are not exactly alike. For example, apples and cheese are quite different in appearance and taste, yet we often treat them alike as "dessert." Miller and Dollard (1941, pp. 74ff.) describe this kind of generalization (across unlike objects) as *acquired equivalence of cues*. The equivalence is accomplished by making a similar response to different objects and thereby giving each of them one important cue in common, the cue produced by the response. For example, when the hostess says "Would you like apples or cheese for dessert?" she is using a response of "dessert" toward both items and thereby eliciting a common cue for her guests. Similarly, parents teach their children that bread, meat, and potatoes are "food," which gives them all a common cue toward which reaching and eating responses may be directed.

Foresight may be described in terms of cue-producing anticipatory responses. In one experiment rats were trained to go down an alley, through a curtain, and then into a special box with a narrow passage, where by turning sharply right they could receive food. In the second stage of the experiment the rats were taken to a different location and placed directly in front of the special box, but here they received a shock when they turned to the right. In the third stage of the experiment the rats were returned to the original alley. Would they go down it to the reward as before? Or would the cues of the alley itself produce anticipatory right-turning responses, which now would be expected to elicit anxiety? Actually they ran partway down the alley and then stopped. Miller and Dollard (1941, p. 80) suggest that some foresight in humans "seems to be mediated by nonverbal anticipatory responses similar to those present in the rat. It is often difficult for the individual to explain in words the basis of such foresight." They believe that it is much easier for people to explain their foresight when it is based on language mediating responses, however, and they offer the following amusing possibility. Imagine a human being in the same experiment the rats were in. Asked to give a verbal report of the experience, the subject might say (Miller & Dollard, 1941, p. 80), "On my way down the alley, I started to say to myself how good the food would taste in the reward device; then I remembered the shock, a cold shudder ran down my spine, and I stopped."

Language and thought are also cue-producing responses. Among humans the responses of talking are particularly likely to move forward in the series and become anticipatory responses, even as a child begins to say "Ball!" prior to actually reaching for it. Miller and Dollard treat thinking as even more abbreviated (*fractional*) anticipatory responses. Each such response is also a cue-producing response. If you think of lemon juice, for instance, that thought produces a cue which then elicits another response: perhaps a little actual salivation, perhaps the thought "sour." Chains of responses—that is, response → cue → response → cue → response —offer a model of thinking. Each of these responses is a fractional anticipatory response, a "thought." Miller and Dollard note that in wrestling with a problem we often try one sequence after another, abandoning each in turn, very much as in trial-and-error learning. They propose that a sequence is abandoned as a result of response-producing cues which arouse anxiety. If a response produces a cue which has acquired reward value (solving a problem, making progress, reducing some need), then the sequence containing that response tends to be strengthened; if it produces cues having acquired anxiety value then it tends to be weakened or abandoned. Miller and Dollard write (1941, p. 85), "The individual learns to cease making responses which

produce cues arousing anxiety; stopping such responses is rewarded by reduction in anxiety." Box 7.1 gives a case illustration of these processes.

In a later discussion, Dollard and Miller emphasize again the role of anticipatory goal responses in reasoning (yielding cues having acquired reward value or anxiety value), but they add another important principle, namely the reversibility of the sequence of response → cue → response → cue, and so on. They write (1950, p. 111), "A similar but more radical possibility is for the chain of cue-producing responses to begin at the goal and unreel backward step by step till the correct response in the problem situation is reached." They suggest that when the chains can run both forward and backward, true reasoning and creative thought can take place.

Higher Mental Processes and Neurosis

Miller and Dollard propose that the higher mental processes are implicated in the creation of neuroses. They follow Freud's hypothesis that neuroses are produced in part by an automatic withdrawal of consciousness from dangerous impulses. Such impulses involve a conflict; for example, between sex and anxiety. How may such a hypothesis be formulated in learning theory terms? If responses of thinking and talking about sex produces cues which elicit anticipatory fear responses, and if stopping thinking about sex produces a reduction in the anticipatory fear responses, (that is, a reduction in anxiety), then the person is rewarded for stopping thinking about sex. But "stopping thinking about" is essentially the same as "a withdrawal of consciousness from." The neurotic thus is disabled, because important internal drive stimuli (like sex or aggression) are not given verbal labels (cue-producing responses). So they are not brought under the control of higher mental processes. The

Box 7.1
The Instructor's Dilemma

An instructor was to give a paper at a seminar which would be about one hour in duration. Previously he had been embarrassed by reading papers that were either too long or too short. How many pages should he write in preparation this time? Miller and Dollard continue the case as follows:

His initial response in this dilemma was one which had often been rewarded in other similar dilemmas. He said to himself, "I'll ask Professor Smith." This response . . . produced a stimulus pattern which was a cue to a number of further responses. At first, these responses produced a temporary relaxing sense of reassurance, which seemed to reward and strengthen the response of saying to himself, "I'll ask Professor Smith." But in the past experience of this instructor, permanent relaxation after thinking of an idea had never been rewarded. He had learned that one cannot afford to tarry too long at a sub-goal. In such situations he had been rewarded for tensing again to spur himself to greater action. The additional drive produced by this tension, together with the cue of saying to himself, "I'll ask Professor Smith," resulted in a slight tendency to get up out of his chair and go downstairs. As soon as he raised his head, however, he became aware of cues indicating the lateness of the hour. Previously, in the presence of such cues, he had tried to look for people in similar situations and had discovered that persons of professional status, including this professor, were rarely to be found in their offices at night. As a result of these experiences, the responses of pulling at locked doors and saying to himself, "He is not in," had become anticipatory to the cue of lateness of the hour. Instead of continuing downstairs, therefore, he tended to stop, almost before starting, and to say, "He is not in."

The occurrence of these responses, however, produced cues which had been connected with further responses. He had frequently been rewarded by getting information from homes over the telephone when he had found that people were not in their offices. He said to himself, "I'll telephone him." The cue produced by this response immediately touched off a twinge of anxiety. Punishment had long since taught him not to telephone people too late at night. The anxiety was a cue and a drive to terminate this response sequence.

With these responses stopped, the cue of the work on his desk again caused him to say to himself, "How many pages for the paper?" This response produced cues which elicited first the association of a paper for the meetings of the American Psychological Association. Then he said to himself, "An APA paper is fifteen minutes, and six pages." To these cues were attached in this context strong anticipatory responses originating from experiences of ultimate success with other similar problems; a triumphant instant of anxiety reduction was followed by additional motivation to continue (Miller and Dollard, 1941, pp. 86-87).

cue-producing responses of labeling and thinking about such stimuli do not occur. Hence problem solving related to those drives cannot go forward, and the neurotic appears to be "stupid" in certain respects associated with these drives, although remaining intelligent about other things.

Neurotic symptoms are learned just like other responses, according to Miller and Dollard. In one case of phobia, for example (Dollard & Miller, 1950, pp. 157 ff.), a military pilot was on a difficult bombing mission. In the course of this mission he was exposed to anti-aircraft fire which killed several crew members and damaged the plane, which eventually came down in open sea. Although the survivors were rescued, the pilot became intensely afraid of airplanes, even of thinking about them. In the theory developed by Dollard and Miller, fear-provoking stimuli like the anti-aircraft shells, deaths of crew members, and so on, "reinforce fear as a response to other cues present at the same time . . . from the airplane, its sight and sound, and thoughts about flying" (Dollard & Miller, 1950, p. 158). Fear would be learned in response to these cues and would generalize to similar cues of other airplanes. By looking away from airplanes or by walking away from them the pilot was able to reduce his fear responses, and this drive reduction served to reinforce these avoidance responses. "Similarly, he felt anxious when thinking or talking about airplanes and less anxious when he stopped thinking or talking about them. The reduction in anxiety reinforced the stopping of thinking or of talking about airplanes; he became reluctant to think about or discuss his experiences" (Dollard & Miller, 1950, p. 158).

Thus Miller and Dollard are able to explain the development of complicated disturbances of personality in terms of drives, cues, responses, rewards, and cue-producing responses. Chains of cue-producing responses constitute the elements of thought sequences, whether normal or pathological.

Accomplishments of the Theory

The two main kinds of accomplishments that have been achieved by Miller and Dollard through their theory of social learning are in its application to psychotherapy and in its use by other theorists.

First, they have been able to give an account of therapeutic processes and to make sound recommendations. They suggest, for example, that an important part of psycho-

therapy consists in changing the basis for the apparent "stupidity" of neurotics—the inability or failure to cope rationally with problems touched by the conflict or phobia. In specific conflict-related areas the neurotic is unable to bring to bear his or her usual problem-solving skills precisely because such skills require that the relevant matters be thought about. You cannot solve a problem in chess by stopping thinking about chessmen and chessboards and moves. On the contrary the very elements of the problem must be given clear discriminative labeling (cue-producing responses). Dollard and Miller show that a great deal of what a psychotherapist does is to assist the patient by providing labels for previously unlabeled emotions and other internal matters about which the patient had stopped thinking. Thereby it becomes possible for the patient once again to employ higher mental processes in the solution of emotional and interpersonal problems.

Box 7.2 presents a very good example of the kinds of activity that Dollard and Miller recommend for normal adults in what they call *self-study*. It can be formal and time consuming, with a carefully developed plan of work, or it can be spontaneous and hardly time consuming at all, as in the case of box 7.2. However, it is necessary that the basic units, *recognition of emotion* and *labeling of emotion*, be learned well beforehand.

The second kind of accomplishment achieved by social learning theory is the great stimulation provided to other scientists who have used the theory in analyzing a wide variety of topics in personality psychology. Edward Murray, for one, has recently completed an interesting analysis and experiment on complex decisions using the basic model of conflict developed by Miller and Dollard (Murray, 1975). Fitz (1976) has conducted an experiment with human subjects which sup-

Box 7.2
Labeling and Other Higher Mental Processes on a Date

Self-study can be spontaneous and hardly time consuming at all.

An analyzed youth reports the following example: He had invited a girl whom he particularly liked but did not know very well to a formal dance. The girl had declined the invitation but said she would be glad to go to dinner before the dance. Trapped by her suggestion and his attraction to her he had agreed to take her to dinner. The boy found the dinner rough going. He was immediately attacked by a stomach-ache so severe that he thought he would be forced to leave the table. He was thus urgently motivated to understand his situation. One of the units learned in his analysis came flying to mind. He recalled that aggression against a woman frequently took gastric form in his case. Could it be that he was angry at the girl, and if so, why? He realized immediately that he **was** angry and had repressed his anger. He had felt exploited by her suggesting dinner when she could not go with him to the dance. He was just being used to fill in a chink of time before the dance. When these thoughts occurred, ones contradictory to them came up also. The girl did not seem like an exploitative type. Maybe she wanted to show that she really liked him. There would, after all, be another dance, so why not ask her then and there for another date. This he did, and she accepted with evident pleasure. The combination of this lack of cause for aggression and hope of the future brought relief; the stomach-ache disappeared.

It is interesting to note that the whole reaction occurred under the cover of a social situation and was invisible to his partner. She could have noted only a change from glumness to spontaneity. The incident shows, however, that units of self-study can be performed swiftly, without formal measures, when the subject has learned well some of the needed responses, and the solution involves chiefly a transfer of these units from past to present situations. Once the stomach-ache was labelled as aggression-produced, the rest of the solution appeared rapidly (Dollard & Miller, 1950, p. 443).

---

ports Miller's theoretical model of displacement of aggression.

An exemplary program of theory development and research stimulated by the work of Miller and Dollard was carried out by Seymour Epstein (Epstein, 1962). Epstein was interested in the measurement of drive and conflict in humans. He defines *drive* as a force having a direction and a degree of activation, and makes several assumptions about drive:

1. A drive is a multiplicative function of an internal state and of cues related to the drive (for example, hunger drive is stronger if you have gone longer without eating, thus intensifying the internal state of activation; it is made stronger still if you smell a favorite food).

2. Drive can be measured by both direction of the force (what the drive is driving at) and by the degree of activation (how intense the internal state is).

3. In particular, drive can be measured in humans by inferences from the contents of their thoughts (the direction of the drive) and from physiological measures of arousal (activation).

4. The gradients of approach and avoidance (see figure 7.3) proposed by Miller and Dollard may be represented as gradients of drive.

Using these assumptions Epstein proposes an alternative model of conflict. First he takes Miller's model of displacement (see figure 7.4) and replaces the dimension of stimulus dissimilarity with a dimension of *cue relevance*. His model of conflict is then represented as an intersection of approach and avoidance gradients similar to Miller's model (figure 7.3), except that "strength of response" becomes "strength of drive" and "units of distance" becomes "cue relevance."

Epstein makes one further assumption pertinent to the measurement of conflict:

> 5. The total activation (intensity of internal arousal state) produced by conflict is the sum of the separate activation levels of the drives in conflict, and hence can be measured by the addition of the strength of the approach drive and the strength of the avoidance drive at any point along the stimulus dimension.

This means, for example, that if you are *eager* to dive off the top board and also *afraid* to dive off the top board, then the total amount of conflict you experience is the sum of both degrees of eagerness. If your amount of activation associated with conflict is measured by the galvanic skin response (GSR) it would show a low degree if you were just reading a book at home; a bit higher if you were looking at a picture of some people swimming; a bit higher if you saw a picture of someone getting ready to dive off the spring board; higher still if you came across a picture of a person about to dive off the top board; and highest if you were just coming up the steps to the top board yourself!

Epstein reports an experiment with parachutists in which predictions of amount of conflict were made. It was predicted that they would experience least conflict in telling a story to a picture without a parachute; medium conflict to a picture about a boy seeing a parachutist in the sky; most conflict in telling a story to a picture about a parachutist getting ready to jump. The pictures used were similar to the Thematic Apperception Test (TAT) pictures described in chapter 3. Each

picture was specially constructed to have increasing *cue relevance* for the conflict-producing event of actually jumping. Thus the TAT cards provided the stimulus dimension of cue relevance in this experiment. Measures of GSR were taken to estimate the degree of activation associated with conflict. It was found that each of the sixteen parachutists showed the expected gradient of activation (sum of the gradients of approach and avoidance) as the cue relevance of the pictures increased.

It was also assumed that getting nearer and nearer to an event in time has effects similar to those of nearness in space. Accordingly, a model reflecting the influence of both a cue relevance dimension and a time dimension was constructed. This model is essentially similar to the one developed by Murray and Berkun, as represented in figure 7.6. It was predicted that as the time for a scheduled parachute jump draws near, so the steepness of the gradient of conflict will increase. Tests of parachutists on the day of a scheduled jump and on a day two weeks prior to such a jump showed that there was indeed a steeper gradient of activation. On both days each parachutist showed the expected gradient of activation (GSR) as he responded to the TAT pictures of increasing cue relevance, but this gradient had a much steeper slope on the day of the jump.

It might be wondered whether any subject would show gradients. Of course Epstein and his colleagues were careful to test control subjects, namely nonparachutists. They found no gradients. The hypotheses receive specific support, therefore, and it may be concluded that the additional assumptions introduced by Epstein are valid. This means we can understand people's responses to approaching stress events and also the changes they undergo as the event draws nearer. Specifically, as the time draws near, they are more and more likely to be aroused by anything which reminds them of the conflict-producing event. And the more relevant the cue is, the more arousal of a conflict activation state it will produce. For example, the closer you get to final examinations, the easier it is for you to be reminded of them and the more you will react with a mixture of wanting to take them and get a good grade and wanting to skip the whole thing and avoid a bad grade.

Many other applications and extensions of the learning theory developed by Miller and Dollard have been made, including many more by Epstein and his colleagues. Enough have been reported here to provide an indication of the accuracy and power of this theory. We have also seen, particularly in the case of Edward Murray's work and that of Epstein and his colleagues, that Miller and Dollard stimulated other scientists not only in the content of their theory, but also in its methods. All of these scientists have employed the explicit statement of empirical assumptions to good advantage.

Critique of the Theory Developed by Miller and Dollard

Hilgard and Bower (1975, p. 177) have characterized the theory developed by Miller and Dollard as a "liberalized version of the stimulus-response-reinforcement" theory. Certainly their willingness to address problems that ordinarily preoccupy clinicians but not learning theorists is evidence of that liberalization. Nevertheless, their willingness to use Freudian concepts and to attempt to translate them into learning theory terms has not met with unequivocal support and admiration. Notably Bandura and Walters (1963) objected strongly to this aspect of the work done by Miller and Dollard, insisting that social learning principles can explain whatever facts there might be in the matters

addressed by such concepts, and that no new special principles are required.

The Social Context of Learning

Bandura and Walters (1963, pp. 19-20) have criticized the theory for at least one other reason. Although it employs learning theoretical constructs, they say, it does not adopt a properly *social* treatment of the relevant facts. The theory simply takes animal learning as a starting point and applies it to human learning, and they criticize this approach as inadequate. For example, according to the theory, one needs to know only three variables in order to predict the targets and strength of displaced responses: 1) the *strength* of the approach tendencies to the original target; 2) the *severity* with which these responses were punished (the strength of the avoidance tendencies); and 3) the *position* of the new targets on a stimulus dimension of similarity-dissimilarity to the original. Bandura and Walters argue that knowledge of these three variables is nowhere near enough. In the case of aggressive responses toward parents who also administered punishments, for example, the entire range of more complex behaviors by the parents is ignored by Miller and Dollard. Parents typically train their children also in how to behave toward other people in society. "In fact, parents often, through precept, example, and control of reinforcement contingencies, determine rather precisely the kind of displaced responses that a child will or will not exhibit" (Bandura & Walters, 1963, pp. 19-20). In addition, the so-called targets of displaced responses of aggression are not passive, and in fact are likely to deter aggression against themselves by threat of retaliation.

All these additional complexities of the reality of social life render the theory formulated by Miller and Dollard powerless to make successful predictions of actual behaviors, Bandura and Walters claim. The problem, as they see it, lies in the very assumptions of the theory, which omit considerations of a truly social context.

How shall we view this criticism? Is it true that the theory is inadequate for the reasons claimed by Bandura and Walters? Bandura (1962, pp. 207-208) makes a similar criticism of the theory of conflict developed by Epstein, stressing that the construct of *cue-relevance* is probably much less important than that of reinforcement patterns by parents and others in affecting the displacement of aggression. But of course Epstein's work had little to do with aggression among children. It had to do with conflict among parachutists, among persons deprived of sleep or of sex, and other matters. Possibly the particular complexity surrounding the socialization of aggression does not extend to all other drive situations. In short the criticisms leveled by Bandura and Walters may be valid only for the particular case they selected as an example.

But are those criticisms valid even for aggression? Do they invalidate the work of Miller himself, and of Murray, and of Murray and Berkun? In my opinion they do not. These criticisms do not assert that the models derived from the theory are inaccurate; they do not deny that supporting experimental data have been obtained. They assert only that, *probably,* in "real life," the models of conflict and displacement would not be able to predict the targets or strength of displaced aggressive responses on the part of children because these models fail to take into account other, more potent factors in real social life. Cogent as this argument may sound, it is actually only a supposition, not a criticism. Miller and Dollard did not explicitly address their models to all possible factors of importance. If called upon to do so, no doubt they would make a good showing. For example, the supposed complications due to retaliation from targets of displaced aggression would be treated in terms of an avoidance gradient directly connected to such targets; complications due to parental precepts and control of reinforcement contingencies would be treated in terms of additional cues and additional chains of cue-producing responses. To charge that Miller and Dollard did not do that is merely a proposition about history; it is not a valid criticism of their theory.

Liberalization of S-R Theory

Since Miller and Dollard eventually allowed their basic constructs to serve in the explanation of higher mental processes, including language and reasoning, we can appreciate in a very specific way the extent to which they "liberalized" the S-R approach. They hereby introduced constructs which go far beyond the simple stimulus-response-reinforcement sequences of traditional S-R theory. Indeed, the construct of *fractional anticipatory response*, which produces cues to which subsequent fractional responses are attached, which enables chains of thought and reasoning to take place (see box 7.1), is a departure so marked that it is fair to say that Miller and Dollard thereby joined the ranks of cognitive theorists who maintain that internal sequences of cognitive operations can yield causal effects on behavior. Indeed, since stimuli can be produced by fractional responses, and since the response of anxiety is also a drive, and since it can be reduced by a further fractional response (like thinking of a solution to a problem), we arrive at a situation in which neither drive, nor cue, nor response, nor reinforcement are events which take place in the world observable to experimenters or to anyone other than the subject. Such a position is very far indeed from that proposed initially by Hull, in which every construct was tied to some manipulable antecedent events and some response consequences. In the theory as developed by Miller and Dollard it is possible to conceptualize a human subject as being confronted with a situation that is not observable to anyone else. The subject may respond to the cues of that situation in ways which may be barely observable to anyone else, through fractional anticipatory response sequences. These responses may produce cues which elicit anxiety. The anxiety may be reduced by stopping thinking. All of this goes on without any real influence from the environment at all, and without effect upon it either. Indeed, the problem faced by the young man at dinner (box 7.2) was unknown to his date. The behavior he did finally emit (asking for another date) had nothing at all to do with the initial problem situation and its associated sequence of inner fractional responses, and the cues they produced, and the drives they aroused. Thus Miller and Dollard have so far liberalized S-R theory as to make it unrecognizable.

Language Formation

This departure from strict S-R theory might be a blessing in disguise, however. For S-R theories of language (including that of Miller and Dollard) are open to severe criticism. For example, Chomsky (1959) shows that language develops through formation of a "generative grammar," not through the learning of specific verbal responses (see also the critique section of chapter 4). The grammar allows people to read and speak sentences which are totally new to them and to know what is and what is not a sentence even when the two strings contain exactly the same set of words ("Cat a that is" versus "That is a cat").

Of course Miller and Dollard did insist that learning cannot occur without drive reduction (compare the commentary on Bobby above; if he had no drive he would not learn to imitate his brother). Presumably this applies equally to language learning. However, Chomsky (1959) points to numerous results showing that language learning and other kinds of learning (even learning by some lower animals) can occur without drive reduction.

However, Miller and Dollard do not specify that particular verbal responses are rewarded by drive reduction. They say that the effect of reward is felt all the way down an entire chain of responses. That is how anticipatory responses come to move forward in the series. When the chain is unobservable, as in the cue-producing response chains of inner thought, there seems to be no way of telling which of innumerable unseen responses might be receiving reward from some slight reduction in anxiety or other drive. Perhaps even the ordering of words by a "generative grammar" may be treated as chain of cue-producing responses. Groups of such chains may then be subject to classification, with some classes labeled "OK" and others labeled "Not OK" in accordance with rewards and punishments emitted by the community. In short, perhaps the theory formulated by Miller and Dollard can be wrongfully criticized for its S-R features; when actually it has abandoned many of those strict features and been liberalized to the point where it can give a very good account of language behavior. Certainly the model of thinking provided by chains of cue-producing responses is one which has intuitive appeal, since we all experience such chains of one thought leading to (cueing) another.

Use of Mediational Constructs

Breger and McGaugh (1965) have also pointed out the extent to which Miller and Dollard have departed from S-R theory. They suggest that Miller and Dollard were successful in extending the stimulus-response account as far as simple symptom formation was concerned (such as the pilot's phobia of airplanes, above). Beyond that, however, Breger and McGaugh feel that the extensions to more complex behavior such as psychoneuroses (or problem solving) were made possible only by departing from S-R theory. More and more Miller and Dollard had to rely upon constructs that were not directly connected with stimuli and responses, they say. These new constructs are called *mediational* constructs by Breger and McGaugh. Chains of fractional anticipatory cue-producing responses would be one example of a mediational construct. In more usual words, they would be called thoughts, feelings, and images. Indeed the writings of Miller and Dollard, Murray, and particularly Epstein quite often contain references to thinking and feeling. Epstein indeed proposed that "the same response tendencies manifested in animal behavior are present at some level of *thought and imagery* in humans" (Epstein, 1962, p. 135; italics mine). This assumption motivates his use of the Thematic Apperception Test as a device for revealing such thoughts and imagery. The commitment to such mentalistic concepts is not complete, however. All of these authors continue also to use the langue of the S-R laboratory. For example, Epstein assumes that "approach can be measured by goal-relevant *verbal responses*" (Epstein, 1962, p. 139; italics mine).

The Theory as Psychodynamic and Cognitive

In summarizing our critique of the theory of personality developed by Miller and Dollard, it seems appropriate first to characterize the nature of their implicit definition of personality. Habits are the basic building blocks, and these are basically connections between cues and responses that have been strengthened by drive reduction. Habits are therefore dispositions to respond in particular ways to particular cues; they are *psychophysical structures*, to use the terms of chapter 2. The drives also seem to be psychophysical structures. The *body* is directly implicated as the source of primary drives and of emotional arousal. Miller and Dollard refer both to cue-producing response chains and also to thoughts and feelings and anticipatory images; there can be little doubt but they define personality partly in terms of *subjective experience*. Of course *behavior* plays an important role in their theory, although not in the sense of the record of behavior. Rather, responses are seen primarily as instrumental to drive reduction, or to cue production, so the emphasis lies upon behavior as involved in habit formation and expression.

Miller and Dollard treat psychophysical structures and processes as the main definers of personality. This emphasis is revealed not only in the constructs of habit and drive, but also in the more complex models of conflict and displacement. These models assume the simultaneous activity of several psychophysical structures, as in the interaction of two or more response *tendencies* (for example, approach and avoidance tendencies). Miller and Dollard are quite explicit also about the important role of subjective experience, especially conscious trains of thought in problem solving. In their work on psychotherapy they stress the importance of therapist intervention to help neurotic patients attach verbal labels to their previously unlabeled drives and associated emotions. While labeling is described as a cue-producing response, it is expected to proceed normally without overt verbal expression, thereby expanding the patient's awareness and restoring control to higher mental processes. Overall, it is clear that Dollard and Miller see such aspects of subjective experience as playing a directive role over behavior: The patient cured of neurosis is expected to be able to think about problems effectively and make sensible decisions and choices among alternative courses of action.

The theory's definition of personality thus rests upon both psychophysical systems and upon subjective experience. While it may have started out with primary apparent emphasis upon stimuli and responses it certainly does not end up that way. It seems reasonable to suggest that the theory developed by Miller and Dollard is not even a liberalized S-R theory. While it uses S-R language, it is so heavily oriented toward concepts it shares with Freudian theory (psychophysical system concepts such as habit, drive, conflict, displacement) that it seems reasonable to think of it as a *psychodynamic* theory, a theory which postulates underlying psychological structures and processes as the basic determinants of experience and behavior. On the other hand Miller and Dollard have emphasized the role of higher mental processes, so much so that their theory also seems to be what nowadays would be called a *cognitive* theory, stressing memory, thoughts, images, and problem solving (or, more generally, subjective experience) in determining behavior. Altogether it seems best to consider the theory of Miller and Dollard as primarily a combination, psychodynamic-cognitive theory. Its connection with environmental stimuli and behavioral responses is guaranteed by its origin and continued attention to such matters. But stimuli and responses have certainly moved away from the center of the personality stage in this theory.

Evaluation of the Theory

Accuracy. We have often mentioned that experiments conducted by Miller and Dollard or by others have provided supporting evidence for their theory. It seems to be accurate. However, we have not yet considered the results summarized by Brewer (1975) and reported in chapter 4 above. These results suggest that conditioning does not occur among adult humans in the way that previously has been supposed. Rather, subjects must be aware of the contingencies and willing to simulate appropriate behavioral trends before the appearance of conditioning curves is obtained. What do these results mean for the accuracy of the theory formulated by Miller and Dollard? What are the implications for matched-dependent learning, for example? To my knowledge no experiments have been performed to determine whether children must be aware of the contingencies in order for matched-dependent learning to occur. It would not be surprising if it were found to be necessary. But how would it affect the theory? Is there anywhere in the theory an assumption stating that human learning requires a concurrent cue-producing response of *labeling* the connection between cue, response, and reward? There is not at present, although there seems to be no important hindrance to the development of such an assumption. Unlike Skinner's theory (see chapter 4), which seeks to avoid all reference to processes inside the organism whether physiological or mentalistic, the theory of Miller and Dollard recognizes not only the existence of such inner processes but their central importance in personality. The theory therefore has all the equipment it needs to formulate a modifying assumption about the need for awareness in human learning. This element of inaccuracy in the theory as it stands at present, then, although fundamental in nature can be quickly corrected without the invention or importation of new constructs.

If the constructs of conditioning are inaccurate for adult humans, it might be asked, how can the more complex constructs involved in models of conflict and displacement yield hypotheses which are found to be accurate by experimental results? This is indeed a puzzling question. Perhaps an answer lies in the following considerations about conflict: Regardless of *how* a particular approach tendency came to be attached to a particular goal object, that tendency may still conflict with another tendency to avoid that same object. In other words, assumptions about conflict may be valid whether or not prior assumptions about conditioning are valid.

Power. A theory's power is measured by the extent of accurate hypotheses or predictions it makes possible. The theory of Miller and Dollard has permitted development of testable models for a wide variety of topics, as we have seen; and a large number have been supported experimentally (for matched-dependent learning, conflict, and displacement particularly). The theory has considerable power.

Fruitfulness. The extent and value of its use in applied settings and in stimulating or facilitating the work of other scientists determines its fruitfulness. It is apparent that this theory has been very fruitful, even if considered only in relation to the applications and stimulations that have been mentioned in this chapter. There have actually been many, many more.

Depth. The depth of this theory is a matter for each person to decide. In my opinion the theory is deep; it discloses the hidden mechanisms of many important topics in personality.

All in all, Miller and Dollard have provided a theory of personality which contributes a good deal of accurate understanding and also provides exemplary use of the tools of theory construction.

Workshop 7

Does Matched Dependent Learning Require Awareness of the Contingency?

In this workshop you are invited to design an experiment which would test the hypothesis that—

Matched-dependent learning does not take place without the subject's awareness of the contingency between cue, response, and reward.

You could use the basic design and setting described by Miller and Dollard for the experiment reported above in connection with Figure 7.2.

First, however, some assumptions should be made explicit. You could go through earlier statements of assumptions by Miller and Dollard and others in the chapter and copy down those you wish to use in preparing a model through which the hypothesis may be tested. Consider Figure 7.1 and ask yourself whether the following preliminary assumptions are necessary:

1. The imitator has a drive which can be reduced by the reward given the leader; (necessary _____ ?)

2. The imitator has within his or her response repertoire a response which can match the response of the leader; (necessary _____ ?)

3. The response of the leader can produce a cue for the imitator; (necessary _____ ?)

4. The contingency in question is that the leader's response produces a cue which elicits a matched response from the imitator which is rewarded; (necessary _____ ?)

5. Reward strengthens the habit of matched-responding to the leader's cue; (necessary _____ ?)

6. Now think carefully about the issue of awareness. How should awareness be defined in the terms of the theory? (Hint: Consider labeling)

    _____

7. Do you need to make any assumptions about awareness?

    _____

8. How might you **ensure** that some subjects will be aware of the contingency?

    _____

9. Do you need a control group of subjects who are not aware of the contingency?

    _____

10. How might you **ensure** that some subjects will not be aware of the contingency?

    _____

    _____

11. Do any of these procedures raise additional problems for interpretation?

    _____

    _____

12. Do you need to make any more assumptions (e.g. about how awareness is measured)?

    _____

13. Please now show how your assumptions can be used to derive the original hypothesis.

    _____

    _____

14. Summarize your research design and indicate how exactly the results are expected to either support the hypothesis or fail to support the hypothesis:

    _____

    _____

Summary

Miller and Dollard develop their theory of social learning and personality from Hull's theory of learning as a basis. They emphasize constructs of *drive, response, cue,* and *reinforcement.* More complex behaviors develop through *generalization* and *discrimination.* Generalization takes place over both similarity and spatial dimensions, and useful summary constructs are offered by Miller and Dollard in their notions of *gradients*: gradients of approach, of avoidance, and so on. Their constructs are employed in formulation of theoretical models of psychodynamic processes such as conflict and displacement of aggression. Through internalization via *fractional anticipatory responses,* drives, cues, responses, and reinforcements can go forward in chains of covert events inside the person. With such constructs Miller and Dollard account for higher mental processes of thinking, planning, and even solving personal problems in psychotherapy.

Although it began as a stimulus-response theory, it has become so liberalized that it is no longer recognizable as such. More properly, although some of the language of S-R theory is used, the personality theory developed by Miller and Dollard is oriented mainly to a psychodynamic and cognitive account of personality. Both stimuli and responses occur within the individual in chains unseen by external observers. Such chains of "cue-producing responses" lead to problem solutions, decisions, choices, and other determinations of behavior emanating from the realm of cognitive events or, more generally, from subjective experience. Thus Miller and Dollard, while accepting the role of stimuli and responses as externally observable events, actually place psychophysical systems and subjective experience in the center of their definition of personality. This implicit definition is illustrated in figure 7.9 on page 176.

In much of the discussion in the present chapter we have referred to theories and to models. It is time to clarify the distinction and this is done in the next chapter.

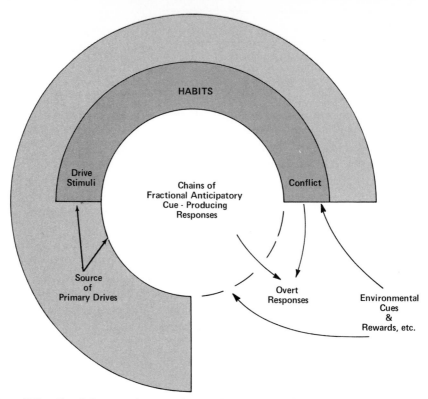

Figure 7.9. The definition of personality implicit in the theory of Miller and Dollard.

INTRODUCTION

Meanings of "model"
Meanings of "theory"
  Problems and disagreements in describing a
    particular theory of personality
  Any one theorist's theory is often a collection of
    theories
  Any one theorist's theory contains different types
    of theory and different types of theoretical
    model
Theoretical models
  A theoretical model is a selection of constructs,
    assumptions, hypotheses, and laws from a
    given theory, addressed to a narrow set of
    phenomena
  Examples of different theoretical models
    addressing the same set of phenomena
  An intuitive idea of theoretical model building
    We all do it some time
    Reconstruction of a crime
Types of theories and of theoretical models
  Theories of cause
    Examples from biology and psychology
    Independent and dependent variables
  Theories of function
    Examples from physics and psychology
  Theories of structure
    Examples from biology, physics, and
      psychology
  Theories of pattern
    Examples from history, anthropology, botany,
      and psychology
  Theories of priority
    Examples from psychology
  Theories of system
    Examples from economics
    General systems theory
    Theories of system in psychology
  Overview of types of theory
Theories and models which combine constructs of
  different types
  Examples in psychology and physics
  Structural and causal theories a frequent
    combination
Competing theories
  One general theory cannot be put into
    competition as a whole with another general
    theory as a whole
  Theories can be put into competition only through
    the theoretical models they generate
  Examples of competing theoretical models
  Can a theory ever be disproved? No. But it may
    not survive long
Changes in theory: changes in model objects and
  in theoretical models
  Model objects and theoretical models
  Nature of a model object
    Various types of model objects
  Theoretical models
  Changes in model objects
  Changes in theoretical models
  Conclusion
Workshop 8 Theories of structure, cause, and
  pattern concerning the Namwons
Summary

son going through a series of medical specialist examinations, with varying opinions on the diagnosis of some difficult symptoms of disease: some opinions are more encouraging, some are more dire; some threaten to require more expensive or painful or prolonged treatments; some promise a speedy or spontaneous recovery. In Lazarus's model the person's cognitive processes of appraisal and reappraisal serve to arouse or to reduce emotion appropriately.

Horowitz notes that neither of the foregoing models, nor others he considers, are able to offer an adequate explanation for the fact that reactions to stress frequently continue long after the stressing events have terminated. People keep on "reliving" the events; images of the horrifying scenes rise up in their minds arousing once again the terror originally experienced. In between these episodes, the same people are often completely unaware of such memories, and it seems that they alternate between phases of *intrusion* (the recurring images of stressful events) and of *denial* (lack of awareness and emotional numbness with respect to those experiences). Horowitz develops his own model to account for these cyclic phenomena with the following assumptions (1976, pp. 90-106): A second source of internal information exists, namely, an "active memory." While similar to the modern view of "short-term" memory, Horowitz says it is capable of moving its contents into long-term memory only after the latter has developed frameworks (schemata) into which the contents of the active memory will fit. A stressful event by definition is not familiar; therefore there will be no ready schemata into which memory information of such events can be assimilated. These memories exert an active pressure toward renewed cognitive processing in the form of imagery and working through so that gradually the memories become modified and the schemata in long-term memory also become modified. Then the stressful memories finally can find a suitable assimilating schema in long-term memory. At that point they can pass out of the active memory and into the long-term memory, where they remain in relative quietude.

In the meantime, while the active pressure toward cognitive processing is in force, the memories of the stressful events keep intruding upon the person's awareness in the form of visual and other imagery and of other cognitive contents. This new arousal of cognitive elements of stress tends to evoke emotional reactions such as anxiety. These once again threaten to disrupt the psychic apparatus and so motivate the working of controls in the form of denial. Once denial has sufficiently done its job of calming, the way is open for intrusions to begin again. In this manner the sequence of denial followed by intrusions followed by denial followed by intrusions (and so on) is determined until such time as the relevant contents of active memory can pass into long-term storage.

In Horowitz's model we see a new construct of *active memory* in a model which uses several constructs—anxiety, denial, imagery, long-term memory—from general psychoanalytic theory (compare the formulation of Peterfreund & Schwartz, 1971).

An Intuitive Idea of Theoretical Model Building

It will probably be helpful for the reader to recognize that most of us do some model building at some time. A model is a representation of some part of reality, and a theoretical model represents a part of reality and also tries to explain, interpret, or characterize some central features in that reality. If we focus our attention for a moment upon the human being who is creating or using a theoretical model we shall be able to obtain a deeper intuitive understanding of the objectives involved. Marx and Hillix (1973, p. 607) have suggested that the usefulness of a theory lies in the fact that it allows for ". . . generalizations beyond the data, which are used to bridge gaps in knowledge and to generate research." Such gaps are those which exist in the mind of a particular human being who is struggling to understand some set of phenomena. The theory allows the person to formulate a theoretical model of those phenomena and to bring in ideas that are not immediately given by the data.

One widely understood use of theory is in criminal investigation. A detective studies the facts of a crime in order to determine the method of operation employed by the criminal. If the crime was skillfully carrried out, the detective reasons that someone with plenty of practice in this method of operation must have been responsible. It is inferred that the list of names of such persons may be found from previous arrest records. These names are then placed in a list of suspects, thus bridging a gap in knowledge. Research is generated immediately as investigating officers are dispatched to establish the whereabouts of all suspects at the time of the crime.

But how did the detective know that the crime had been carried out skillfully? From the facts as given, the detective must *reconstruct the crime*. Assembling all the clues, he must think hard to form in his mind a moving picture of exactly what went on. Reconstructing the scene of the crime and its action is very similar to building a theoretical model of the crime. Indeed the particular model the detective builds will include a selection of constructs and assumptions from his general theory of criminal events. That theory would perhaps contain constructs about scenes, such as unguarded property, use of force, victim alone, and so on. Its constructs of actions might include those of skill as a structural characteristic of persons, and practice as a determi-

nant of the skill; it might include an assumption that more frequent practice raises the probability of being caught.

But suppose the detective's theory contained no constructs about psychological causes, about motivation. And suppose that accordingly his model of the crime did not include a construct referring to motivation. Then he would have no reason to propose a particular hypothesis about the motive of the crime and no further research on this matter would be done. If the culprit were nevertheless apprehended, that would be an end to it. But suppose the crime remained unsolved and required bringing in an outside specialist who held to a different theory, one which included individual motive as a central construct. In formulating a new model, the specialist hypothesizes that the crime was committed with a motive of revenge. His search of suspects would then focus upon persons having both reason for revenge and the necessary skills (or connections to hire them). The new model might result in solving the case.

Since we have all thought along with famous real or fictional detectives in the solution of interesting cases in the news or in novels, we can all recognize the sort of thinking that goes on when we formulate a model of a crime. In the previous paragraph we have seen also how a model built according to one theory can be inaccurate, while a model of the same situation built according to another theory can be accurate. In the example given, the first theory ignored motivation and focused upon the structure of the criminal (in terms of skill). The second theory included a focus upon motivation, and thereby allowed the specialist to formulate a model of the crime which was different in content and which had different consequences for further research and problem solution. The lesson to be learned is that if two theories differ in the constructs they include, then the theoretical models generated from those theories will probably be different too, even in accuracy.

Types of Theories and of Theoretical Models

In the hypothetical example of modeling a crime we saw the difference between a theory that contained a construct of motivation and a theory that did not. It was not possible for the theory which had no construct of motivation to generate a model containing a hypothesis as to motive.

As we consider the entire spectrum of scientific theories we are able broadly to discern different types of theory, types which differ in terms of the kinds of constructs they include and the kinds of hypotheses they can therefore yield in the generation of theoretical models. Some theories contain constructs and hypotheses suited to theoretical models of the *causes* of events. Some are specialized in the formulation of *functions,* which are quantitative relationships between constructs. Others are concerned with the *structure* of entities, which means the parts that go to make up the whole entity. Some theories have constructs especially designed to describe the *pattern* in a series of events or in the changes of an entity. Some theories have constructs which refer mainly to a *system* of several entities and related events, and some aim chiefly to specify some order of *priority* upon a set of events or entities or qualities. In the following sections we shall take up each of these six types of theories in turn.

Theories of Cause

Theories of cause contain constructs and hypotheses that make it possible to explain certain facts by suggesting relevant causes. For example, Louis Pasteur's germ theory contained the construct of *microorganism,* existing in ordinary air but invisible. Under cer-

tain conditions of time and temperature, it was hypothesized, these organisms would invade certain organic substances such as milk and produce the characteristic changes in that substance known as fermentation. A competing theory (of spontaneous generation) held that such organisms developed spontaneously within the substance. Thus Pasteur's theory allowed a model of fermentation in milk to be formulated which proposed that there existed an invisible cause (microorganisms) in the surrounding air. He tested this model in two ways. He exposed substances to filtered air and to air at very high altitudes, in which cases, as predicted, no fermentation occurred. In addition he actually inserted microorganisms from already fermented substances into unfermented milk, in which case, as predicted, the milk fermented in a short time.

An example from psychology is Freud's theory of psychological causes. Freud proposed the construct of an unconscious wish, unconscious because it was forbidden. He made the empirical assumption that such wishes seek expression in behavior or in bodily symptoms of such a kind that they evade the forbidding censor, and indeed the person is not consciously aware that the wish is being so expressed. His model of hysterical disorders (in which, for example, a person develops stomach sickness without there being any detectable physical disease) proposed that forbidden sexual wishes were expressing themselves in a transformed guise by means of the symptoms.

In both of the previous examples of a causal theory, the model proposes that there exists a *hidden* cause. A second form of a theory of cause does not include a construct referring to a possible hidden cause, but rather contains constructs referring to properties and relations among known entities or events. An example from psychology is H. J. Eysenck's model of introversion-extraversion. This construct refers to a very broad set of traits as measured by questionnaire and other psychological tests. Many people seem to be mainly introverts, others are primarily extraverts. Eysenck's theory contains the empirical assumption that individuals differ in their overt behavioral traits as a result of differences in the functioning of their nervous systems. The theory contains also constructs of *excitatory* and *inhibitory potentials* in the brain. These are electrical potentials; an excitatory potential in one neuron tends to make an adjacent neuron fire; an inhibitory potential tends to prevent an adjacent neuron from firing. In an area of the brain where excitatory potentials predominate there will be more activity. Eysenck's model says that, among introverted persons, the excitatory potentials in the cerebral cortex are stronger than the inhibitory potentials; the opposite is true for persons who are more extraverted. In this model, then, it is hypothesized that particular levels of introversion are caused by a certain balance of excitatory and inhibitory potentials in the cortex (Eysenck, 1967). Note that no new causal entity such as a microorganism, and no new hidden process such as a forbidden wish have been proposed. What has been hypothesized is that certain properties of one set of known events are causally connected to another set of known events. We might call such hypothesized connections *unrecognized causes.*

A theory of cause, then, is one from which it is possible to generate causal explanatory models of specific phenomena. This does not mean that a theory which permits the formulation of causal models is *only* a theory of cause. We saw above that both Murray's theory (chapter 3) and the theory of Miller and Dollard (chapter 7) contain causal constructs (*need* and *press*, for example; or *drive* and *reinforcement*). That fact does not prevent Murray's theory from containing also a theory of pattern, namely a theory of complexes, like

the claustral complex. When we speak about a theory of cause we mean that the general theory involved has a causal component; it might have other components as well. Freud's general theory, for example, has a theory of cause, a theory of structure, and a theory of pattern, as we shall see in later chapters.

From time immemorial, the notion of cause has been complicated. In Aristotle's four main meanings we find cause as either 1) the matter or material from which something is made; 2) the form it must take; 3) the purpose for which it is made; and 4) the agent that made it. In the modern scientific sense mainly the last of Aristotle's four causes is pertinent. He spoke of cause as that which acts upon something else—bringing it into being, changing its state, or pushing it into motion. Such a "source of motion" was a *dynamis* (Preuss, 1975, p. 18). The *dynamis* is the origin of the term dynamic which is used in chapter 10, referring to Freud's theory of personality dynamics. It is widely used in such expressions as *psychodynamic psychology and psychotherapy.* Its meaning in such expressions would indicate that psychological causes of behavior and experience are being studied or treated. We might stress that these are active causes (also called *acting causes* by Von Wright, 1974, p. 83.)

The reader may wish to consult Rychlak (1968, especially chapters 4 and 5) for further general discussion of the meaning of *cause.* For now it seems sufficient to accept the notion of an *acting cause* as our working conception.

Klein and Krech (1952, p. 17) have stated this position and meaning as follows: "For if it is true that a legitimate working conception of 'cause' is that it consists of links among events within the organism, then the ultimate objective of psychology is to know or to state the intimate web of all of these *interrelationships* (among 'causes' and 'effects')." I believe that such a working conception of cause is legitimate. It is perhaps phrased too narrowly, however: within psychology, causal analyses are found in studies of the relationships *between* organisms and environment (as well as *within* organisms). Indeed, Skinner's approach to personality (see chapter 4) emphasizes such causal relationships exclusively.

As in Skinner's work, so in many investigations using the experimental method the experimenter manipulates one variable (the *independent variable*) in order to see the effects upon another variable (the *dependent variable*).

Whenever an experimenter manipulates an independent variable and finds consequent changes in the dependent variable, there are two kinds of causal action taking place. The first is the experimenter's action; the second is whatever "natural" causal action produces the changes in the dependent variable as a result of changes in the independent variable. It is easy to become confused about which is which and also easy to believe that the natural cause has the same kind of effectiveness that the experimenter's action does. Von Wright (1974) stresses the great difference between these two kinds of causality and considers only the "natural" kind in his book. This is complicated enough.

It is often desired to express the relationship between an independent variable and a dependent variable in mathematical terms. This is then called a *functional relationship*. Variable D varies as a function of Variable I (where I is independent and D is dependent). But not all functional relationships in scientific theories express *causal* relations. Many do not, in fact. Consider the functional relation between the volume of a gas and the pressure exerted upon it from the outside. Let v be the volume, p the pressure, and c some constant quantity. Then we have the functional relation

$v \cdot p = c$ (the volume multiplied by the pressure is a constant value). Von Wright (1974, pp. 68-70) points out that this functional relationship does not express a causal law; but it does contains terms between which a causal relationship holds, namely, between pressure and volume. If we change the external pressure (the independent variable), then the volume will change (the dependent variable). Thus functional relations may or may not express causal relations; and a theory of function may or may not contain or be associated with a theory of cause.

Theories of Function

The second sort of theory is one of *function,* in the sense of a functional relationship. In Newton's theory of gravity, for example, there are constructs of *force, mass,* and *distance.* Newton's law of gravitation states that bodies attract each other with a force directly proportional to the product of their masses and inversely proportional to the square of the distance between them. All kinds of functional models may be generated from this theory: apples and meteors falling to earth, Earth moving around the sun, and so on. As we shall see in a later example, the theory is used to construct a model of the "black holes" in space by positing a body of intense mass at the center of the hole and a body of intergalactic gas being attracted toward it. Because of its applicability to any pair of bodies whatsoever the theory has great power.

The theory is a theory of function in that it merely specifies functional relationships among constructs. When these constructs are formulated in measurable terms, the relationships can be spelled out in mathematical form. Although a causal theory might be associated with a functional theory the two are not the same. For example, it might be thought that the *force* is the cause of mutual attraction between bodies, and that would be one way to conceptualize it. But it is not the way of a functional theory, which simply specifies the relationship. In this case the idea of force is completely defined by the product of the two masses and the reciprocal of the squared distance:

$$Force = \frac{K \ (Mass_1 \times Mass_2)}{Distance^2}$$

It is hard to imagine how a product of masses or the square of a distance could be the cause of anything. Such imagining is not necessary in a theory of function, however, which simply states functional relationships among constructs.

There have been several theories of function in psychology. Hull's theory of learning (1943) is an outstanding example. For example, Hull wrote:

> Whenever an effector activity $(r - R)$ and a receptor activity $(S - s)$ occur in close temporal contiguity . . . and consistently associated with the diminution of a need (G) . . . , there will result an increment to a tendency $(\Delta \ _sH_r)$ for that afferent impulse on later occasions to evoke that reaction. The increments from successive reinforcements summate in a manner which yields a combined habit strength $(_sH_r)$ which is a simple positive growth function of the number of reinforcements (N). (Hull, 1943, p. 178).

Simplifying, a *reinforcement* is defined as the co-occurrence of a stimulus (s) and a response (r) and the reduction of a need (G). Each time such a reinforcement occurs there is an increase (Δ) in strength of habit (H) linking that stimulus to that response $(_sH_r)$. If we start from zero strength, then, the habit will be 1 after one reinforcement, 2 after two reinforcements, 3 after three reinforcements and so on. Letting $N =$ the number of reinforcements, we have the habit strength at any given point expressed as a function of N:

$$_sH_r = f \ (N)$$

Lewin's theory (1935, 1951) offers another fine example of a theory of function in psychology. Lewin made the empirical assumption that a need, when aroused, sets up a state of tension in the person; and that this tension corresponds to a force toward locomotion in the environment (Lewin, 1951, p. 10). If a goal is attractive it is said to have a positive valence (Va), otherwise it is negative or neutral. The strength of the force toward that goal (G) is expressed as a function of the attractiveness or valence of the goal, $Va \ (G)$, and also the psychological distance, e, between the person (P) and the goal (G). Letting the strength of the force be denoted by $f_{P,G}$ we have (Lewin, 1951, p. 258):

$$f_{P,G} = f \ [Va \ (G), e_{P \cdot G}]$$

which states that the force propelling the person toward the goal is some function of the valence of that goal and the psychological distance between person and goal.

The most general statement of Lewin's theory was also proposed in functional terms as:

$$B = f \ (P, E)$$

meaning that behavior is some function of the person *and* the environment, neither of the latter alone being sufficient to specify a functional relationship with behavior. We may note Lewin's explicit statement that the functional relation does not involve a causal statement, even in so likely a construct as force. Lewin wrote (1951, p. 256): "The construct *force* characterizes, for a given point of the life space, the direction and strength of the tendency to change. This construct does not imply any additional assumptions as to the 'cause' of this tendency."

In chapter 19 of this book we shall see a number of theoretical models generated by Lewin's theory: models of aspiration and of conflict, for example. Needless to say, a theory of function generates theoretical models which are also functional.

Theories of Structure

In the physical and biological sciences theories of structure have played an extremely important role. A theory of structure postulates a finer grain, different component parts, or other forms of deeper reality than appears to our senses or to previous tools of observation. In a theory of structure there are some statements of fact about observed objects. It is hypothesized that some entities exist and are the more basic constituents of the observed objects. Part of the theory may include some proposed laws of composition which deal with how the constituents are supposed to come together to produce the objects which have been observed.

The cell theory in biology held that one organism (animal, plant, or person) is actually composed of many individual cells, linked together in some way. The invention of the microscope made it possible to check this theory.

Dalton's atomic theory in physics provides another example. According to his theory, the matter in a given element is composed of atoms, each identical to its fellow in weight. However, the weight in one element is different from that in another element. Atoms of the same kind are combined to form the element because they attract each other. An alternative theory was proposed by Avogadro who accepted the proposition that elements are composed of atoms, but argued that they are combined in two stages: first the atoms combine into molecules and then the molecules combine to form the matter.

A recent example of a structural theory in psychology concerns mental images in the process of cognition. One widely held theory is that mental representations of outer events can be of two kinds: mental word (such as thinking "there was a bull in that field") or mental images (such as a visual image of the bull in the field (compare Paivio, 1971). Pylyshyn (1973) argues that mental words and images are known by introspection only: "no consideration is given to the possibility that cognition may be 'mediated' by something quite different from either pictures of words, different in fact from anything which can be observed either from within or from without" (Pylyshyn, 1973, p. 4). He suggests that these mediating processes might be of the same general kind as those involved in information processing carried out by computers. Thus the entire theory of information processing may now be employed in the theoretical analysis of words and images.

Pylyshyn refers to certain of these processes as "propositions." Propositions can be made to yield a picture-like entity, however. They are abstract in nature and can be made over into patterns of signals. The analogy of television is helpful here, since it is well known that the image we see on the TV screen is made up of 150,000 elements produced by an electron beam sweeping across the screen from left to right and from top to bottom. At each point the beam has a strength proportional to the brightness of the original image element in the studio of the TV station. What we see is an integrated and lifelike image; but the real structure of the image is made up of these thousands of points of light. In a similar way, Pylyshyn is proposing that our mental images are actually made up of resultants of more abstract processes. It would be interesting indeed to follow up this line of theory and inquire into the exact nature of the proposed processes. Are there intermediating carrier waves that carry the signals? Do alternating currents have to be cut in half to produce pulsations of direct current? Why is there no *flicker* in mental images as there often is in TV images? And so on. But we must continue with our present task. It is clear that the theory proposed by Pylyshyn is a theory of structure.

Theories of Pattern

A theory of pattern proposes that a certain kind of order may be found in what previously had appeared to be a confusing, unordered array of facts. Theories of history provide a good example.[1] A pattern theory of history is aimed at meaningful interpretation and even generalization and prediction. Toynbee's theory (1946), for example, holds that all civilizations proceed through a cycle of challenge and response. Each response, if successful, produces a new challenge because it tends to go too far and end up in an overbalanced state. If a challenge continues to be met by unsuccessful responses the civilization disintegrates.

Another example of a theory of pattern may be found in anthropology. Ruth Benedict (1935) proposed that different cultures have not merely different collections of cultural traits, haphazardly brought together by randomly impinging influences. Rather, she states, in many instances the traditions of a culture select some traits and reject others according to their suitability for an overriding motivation or ethos. In one culture, moderation, self-effacement, and sober ritual pervades the lives of citizens; in another, individualism, rivalry, and ostentation are typical. Each develops according to its own patterns, accepting additional culture traits only if they are in harmony with the prevailing pattern.

Toynbee's theory relates a pattern of events to progression in time. Benedict's theory proposes rather a constellation of culture

traits as the pattern which prevails at a given period of time for a given society. This is very similar to the more general work of classification carried on in botany and other natural sciences. Usually these classifications consist of a set of classes, all arranged in a hierarchy with more general groups higher than (and including) more specific groupings. The general schema for a classification system is shown in figure 8.1.

Botany provides us with good examples. A rose, for instance, is characterized as a flowering plant (Class), with two seed leaves (Subclass), with petals forming a cup around the pistil but not touching it (Order), with fruit seeds not splitting open (Family), and seeds packed together in the "hip" (Subfamily), with prickles or thorns on the stem (Genus *Rosa*), which are straight and long (Species *Rosa spithamea,* or ground rose) (relevant details may be found in Benson, 1957, pp. 239-255).

The basically theoretical nature of classification systems may be seen in the case of botany also. For centuries various attempts at systematic classification were made, each failing to provide a satisfactory resolution for one reason or another. In the eighteenth century the famed Swedish botanist Linnaeus invented a system which classified all plants into one of twenty-four classes, based on the number and arrangement of the stamens. This system was very popular because it provided clear bases for classification, and it stimulated a great deal of research. But it was recognized even by Linnaeus himself to be an artificial basis of classification, one that did not take into account fundamental characteristics of relationship between species. For instance, it brought lilies and barberries together in one order but separated sage from mint. Modern methods depend upon natural evolutionary groupings primarily. Even so there are many debates among botanists concerning the proper

---

1. Carol I. Cartwright directed my attention to the existence of temporal pattern theories, and to the example from Toynbee's work. I am grateful to her for this insight.

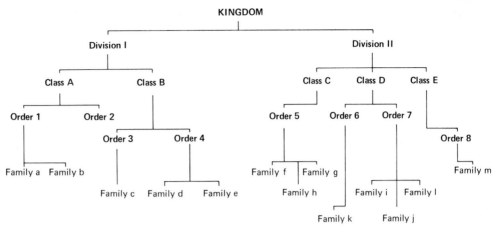

Figure 8.1. Diagram showing the schematic form of a hierarchical classification system

membership of this or that species in this or that family. Hence the theoretical bases of classification remain in dispute to some extent and can still be radically changed.

The extent to which classification systems are theoretical is evidenced by the very serious questioning of classifications of mental disorders in recent years (see Lazarus, 1976). Figure 8.2 presents an abbreviated version.

The class of schizophrenias, for example, is characterized as follows: Thought processes are disturbed, especially in representing reality; behavior and ideas are bizarre, the patient reporting hallucinations (perceptions of things that are not there, such as hearing "voices"), and manifesting delusions (beliefs having no foundation in reality).

This description of schizophrenia is particularly well suited as an example of many pattern theories in psychology such as the syndromes of insecurity, dominance, or self-actualization proposed by Maslow or the complexes proposed by Murray. Like the proposed class of schizophrenias, the syndromes and complexes describe a constellation of experience and behavior features which are found occurring together in some noteworthy frequency. As with the class of schizophrenias,

doubts about any such classifications are raised most often on the basis that precisely those features are only very rarely found together. Most cases appear to have only some of the features of any one classification and almost as many of another classification, so that little agreement can be found among experts as to which category best fits a particular case. Such debate seems to be more frequent in regard to classification systems dealing with behavioral and experiential characteristics than in those dealing with physical characteristics like leaves and petals of flowers. Nevertheless the basically theoretical nature of all classification systems is evident at both extremes.

Many psychologists have formulated pattern theories representing an order of characteristics emerging over time. Theories of personality development are good examples. For instance, Erikson's (1968) theory of psychosocial stages in personality development specifies a pattern in which the stages emerge. Following the stage of trust versus mistrust in the first year of life, a period of one to two years follows in which the issue of autonomy versus doubt is the central issue; then initiative versus guilt during the years from three to five; and so on. We shall examine this the-

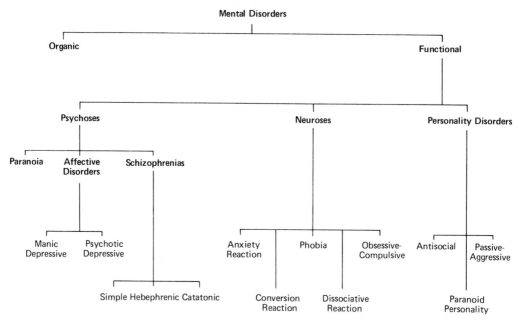

Figure 8.2. Brief classification of mental disorders

ory in detail in a later chapter, with special focus on its model of identity formation.

In summary, there are two main types of pattern theories. One type proposes a system of classification (more or less explicitly) and delineates the collection of characteristics which go together to form a particular class (of plants or people or whatever). The other type proposes a pattern of characteristics developing over time, an order of emergence or appearance. We shall call the first type theories of *classification pattern* and the second type theories of *temporal pattern*.

Theories of Priority

Closely related to some forms of pattern theory is a kind of theory which stipulates that order *ought* to be imposed upon a previously unordered array of facts. Whereas the theory of pattern claims to discern an order that already exists in the data, a theory of priority proposes an order in terms of importance or value. The importance may be for understand-

ing, as when Frankl (1970, 1973) asserts that the will to meaning is more important for our understanding of human personality than is either the will to pleasure or the will to power. The importance may be for the happiness or character or fulfillment of persons, as when Maslow proposes that persons should be helped to become more self-actualizing or when Rogers proposes that people should be helped to move toward being fully functioning. Murray does not seem to have a theory of priority in his overall theory; nor do Miller and Dollard. Skinner's theory of priority refers not to the characteristics of human personality, but to the greater desirability of positive reinforcement over other kinds.

A relationship is often found between a theory of pattern and a theory of priority. This may be seen especially in Maslow's theory of needs, according to which physical needs and safety needs must be met first; then social and status needs must be met; only when these are all met can needs for self-actualization and cognitive understanding rise to prominence within the person's motivations. This is a theory of pattern, stating that a certain ordering of temporal satisfactions *exists* among the six sets of needs in human beings. But in Maslow's search for ways to help improve the lot and destiny of mankind, he proposes that people who manifest satisfaction of self-actualization needs most fully are also the kind of people we should all emulate. He theorizes that satisfaction of the self-actualization needs is of greatest importance. St. Paul stated (I Corinthians 13:13), "And now abideth faith, hope, charity, these three; but the greatest of these is charity." Similarly Maslow states that there are six sets of needs, but the greatest of these is self-actualization. In so doing, Maslow proposes a theory of priority which is combined with his theory of pattern.

Theories of System

Today everything seems to be called a system: a computer is a system, the stockmarket is a system, the justice administration is a judicial system, all the little bits and pieces of a satellite are separate systems (and it is hoped that all systems are "go"). Interactions between organism and environment occur within an ecosystem, the military deploys a new weapons system; even the local garbage collector is now a part of some company's waste disposal systems! New professions are associated with the new entities: systems analysts and systems engineers. It is natural that scientists have attempted to develop theories of the relationships within and between systems, and of the inherent nature of systems.

In a theory of system it is assumed that all the constructs have some direct or indirect consequences for each other. These consequences are not really causal, and very often they depend upon human reactions. For example, in U.S. cities the number of manufacturing establishments is found to be quite highly correlated with the number of wholesaling establishments. Obviously neither causes the other. Quite likely wholesalers build their establishments where manufacturers produce goods in need of distribution; or perhaps manufacturers build their factories where good wholesalers already exist to distribute the manufactured products. It is within the realm of such economic facts that theories of system seem to have their most natural utility.

For example, Keynes (1936) formulated an economic theory in which a system model of inflation and unemployment was developed. The model proposed that inflation and unemployment were determined by the demand for consumer goods in relation to the supply of goods, and by the demand for producers' goods in relation to supply. According to this model, a rise in interest rates would lower demand for producers' goods (new machinery, capital construction, and so forth), and lower interest rates would raise the demand for such goods. Additional taxation on income would reduce available money in the hands of consumers and thereby reduce demand for consumer goods. Reduction of taxation would have the opposite effect.

General systems theory, first proposed by Ludwig von Bertalanffy in 1937, has been developed extensively by many workers in biology, cybernetics, systems engineering, and mathematics. The theory insists that dynamic interacting sets of parts which make up an organism have characteristics above and beyond those describable by physical science in its classical formulation. The theory emphasizes such constructs as *organization, purpose,* guided *growth,* and so on. Von Bertalanffy writes (1968, p. 12): "If we look at a living organism, we observe an amazing order, organization, maintenance in continuous change, regulation and apparent teleology. Similarly in human behavior goal-seeking and purposiveness cannot be overlooked, even if we accept a strictly behavioristic standpoint."

With specific reference to personality theory, von Bertalanffy has stated that general systems theory rejects mechanistic concepts such as those of stimulus-response theories in which all origination of behavior stems from the environment. "Even under constant external conditions and in the absence of external stimuli the organism is not a passive but a basically active system" (von Bertalanffy, 1968, p. 25). It also rejects psychoanalytic principles of homeostasis, the tendency to seek equilibrium, as the sole basis for human motivation. "One may call mountain climbing, composing of sonatas or lyrical poems 'psychological homeostasis'—as has been done—but at the risk that this physiologically well-defined concept loses all meaning" (von Bertalanffy, 1968, p. 25). Thus von Bertalanffy emphasizes the "spontaneous activity of the psychophysical organism," and notes the relationship of this construct to similar ones developed by Maslow and other humanistic theorists.

General systems theory is a clear example also of what we have called theories of system. Above all it assumes that there are many interactive relationships within an organism and between the organism and its environment; it assumes that a proper scientific analysis of such data will require simultaneous treatment of many variables. Important developments in analyzing the organism as a general system with information-processing subsystems have been made by Miller (1973), who recognizes nine such subsystems: input (sensation), internal transmission, decoding (from neural impulses into mental images, for example), association (of ideas, for example CANDY-SWEET, LEMON-SOUR), memory, decision-making, encoding (putting ideas into words, for example), and output (talking, moving). Royce and Buss

(1976) have recently proposed that decision-making and other subsystems in Miller's theory can be related to individual performance on psychological tests. The main factors measured by psychological tests include abilities, needs (like those proposed by Murray), and general personality characteristics (like Dominance, as described and measured by Maslow). Royce and Buss thereby link up two important bodies of personality theory: general systems theory and the theory of personality traits (see chapters 15 and 17).

Overview of Types of Theory

Many authors have noted the existence of structural, causal (dynamic), and pattern (developmental, typological) theories of personality (see Hall & Lindzey, 1970; Sanford, 1970). Theories of function are the classical form of scientific theory, of course, and theories of system now prevail in economics, information science, and so on. Theories of priority are found in ethics, healing arts, and in theories of optimal personality or psychological health. In the chapters which follow we shall characterize theories in terms of their type (structure, cause, pattern, and so on), but it must be understood that this characterization is not intended to be exclusive. Intermingling is frequently found between a theory of pattern and a theory of priority; so also we shall find that a theory of structure is often closely associated with a theory of cause, and a theory of function often includes a theory of structure and of cause. Nevertheless it is often possible to characterize a theory by its major type. For example, Maslow's is a theory of system overall; yet it also has a theory of cause (needs), two theories of pattern (hierarchy and syndromes), and one theory of priority (self-actualization).

Theories and Models Which Combine Constructs of Different Types

Many theorists have actually produced encompassing theories which include different types of theory. Freud, for example, developed a theory which had within it a theory of personality structure, a theory of causes, and a theory of pattern in temporal development. Many particular theoretical models take some structural constructs and some causal constructs. In physical sciences it is often found that a theoretical model employs both functional and causal constructs. For example, in the theoretical model of quasi-stellar radio sources (quasars) a causal hypothesis is combined with some functional laws.

Quasars are astronomical objects emitting great quantities of energy at all frequencies. Every known element has a characteristic pattern of radiation, so it is known what elements are emitting the energy from quasars. In the visible range, hydrogen emits radiation at wavelengths of 4101, 4340, and 4861 angstroms approximately. Studies of a particular quasar, however, may show that pattern (as recorded on Earth) shifted toward the red end of the spectrum by a factor of 1.1706, that is, at about 4801, 5080, and 5690 angstroms. This phenomenon is known as the red shift.[2]

Two laws and a hypothesis were offered to provide a theoretical model of these quasar phenomena. The first law is that the wavelength of radiation from a source is always preserved when the radiation passes through a receiving system (such as space, atmosphere, and spectrometer which analyzes the wavelengths). The second law states that if a source of radiation is moving away from a receiver the crests of the radiation waves will reach it at longer intervals than if the source is at a constant distance from the receiver. The hypothesis is that the quasar is moving away from Earth. Already one billion light years away, its speed of receding must be enormous to produce the red shift. It is truly an "expanding universe."

Note that the causal hypothesis refers to a condition which is hidden, the receding movement of the quasar. The theoretical model of quasars joins this hypothesis with two functional laws of radiation.

Combinations of Structural and Causal Theories

Structural theory combined with causal theory is singled out for special attention here because it so frequently appears in psychological theory. In everyday language, we might say that many psychological theories attempt to say what the mind or behavior is made of, and how those components work to produce the personality phenomena we observe. The older theory that mind is made of ideas which can be connected through associations is an example of such a combination. The theory that complex behavior is made up of elementary habits (Miller & Dollard, Skinner) is a theory of structure; the associated theory of reinforcement is a theory of cause.

Competing Theories

Much of the excitement of scientific investigation is generated by competing theories. It will be especially helpful in our overall understanding of theories of personality to have a preliminary idea of what is involved in the competition between theories. In this way we shall be ready to evaluate whether two theories that are claimed to be in competition really are.

Actually we shall find that two general

---

2. I am indebted to Professor E. C. Whipple, Department of Physics, University of California, San Diego, for critical comments on this and other points in the chapter.

theories cannot be put into strict competition with each other, at least not directly. The reason is that a theory as a whole cannot be tested. Bunge has written on this topic, as we saw earlier, to the effect that only theoretical models are empirically testable, because general theories do not yield a particular conclusion and hence do not yield a precisely testable conclusion.

Since neither of two theories can yield a precisely testable conclusion they cannot enter into direct competition, for there is no way to state or test the nature of the competition. It is therefore only through their respective theoretical models that two theories can be placed into competition. That is, two general theories can be compared with respect to some specific, narrow set of phenomena. For this small set of phenomena each theory generates a theoretical model. The accuracy of the models may then be compared through appropriate testing. Obviously each theoretical model must be dealing with precisely the same set of facts in order for the comparison to be sensible.

It will be instructive for us to consider some examples of competing models. Very recently a competing theoretical model of the red shift in quasars has been advanced by Whipple and Holzer (1974a,b). In this new theoretical model the causal hypothesis is changed by postulating that another entity, a gas, exists and that the gas is moving toward the center of the quasar, drawn by great mass. The gas is first cooled and then heated as it falls closer to the center. In this process light would be emitted by the separation and recombination of electron particles. In the line of sight between Earth and the quasar the gas falling toward the center of the quasar must be moving away from Earth (unless the quasar is moving toward Earth!). Therefore by the same laws that applied in the first model, the light coming from the gas will produce a red shift in the receiver on earth.

Let us notice very carefully what makes it possible for these two models to be in competition. First, all the statements of fact are common to both: the quasars exist, they emit radiation, there is a red shift. The crucial laws are common to both models. The Whipple-Holzer model uses certain other laws which deal with gravity, heat, separation and recombination of particles, laws which are not questioned by the other model, but are not directly invoked. One hypothesis statement is common to the two models, namely that a source of radiation is moving away from the earth. The essential difference between the two models is that part of the causal hypothesis which specifies exactly what kind of entity is supposed to be moving away: the quasar itself or a body of intergalactic gas.

Perhaps the most important point that must be learned from this example is that no statements of fact are in dispute: the relevant statements of fact are common to both models. When this is the case the models can be truly competitive.

An example from psychology is provided by Gray's (1973) theory of extraversion, which competes with the theory advanced by Eysenck. In Gray's theory, the crucial brain functions proposed to underlie extraversion and introversion are the "Go" system associated with the hypothalamus, and the "Stop" system associated with the septum and hippocampus. The balance of sensitivity to signals of reward ("Go") in contrast to signals of punishment ("Stop") controls the balance of extraversion and introversion. Eysenck's model, it will be recalled, proposes that excitatory and inhibitory potentials in the cortex are responsible. Gray's model proposes that systems in the midbrain are responsible. Thus there are three statements of fact, none in dispute. The competition lies in whether functions in the cortex or in the midbrain are causally related to individual differences in extraversion.

Disproving a Theory

If a general theory cannot be tested directly then very likely it can never be disproved. This seems to be the conclusion reached by most thinkers today. However, it is clear that a theory which generates models that fail cannot expect to survive very long. According to Bunge, "A theoretical model lives as long as experience tolerates it. On the other hand a general theory lives as long as it can generate reasonably true theoretical models. Being special purpose devices, theoretical models are transient and disposable as compared to general theories. The latter, being more adaptable, last longer" (Bunge, 1973, p. 113).

As long as a theory generates models which are "reasonably true" then, it will survive. It does not have to be perfect. But obviously if another general theory generates competing theoretical models which are more accurate, that may cause the earlier theory to be abandoned. Unfortunately, scientific actualities are not so clear cut. For theory A may generate more satisfactory models of phenomena P1, P2, and P3; but theory B may generate a more satisfactory model of P4.

Moreover, as we saw in the Whipple-Holzer model, it is possible to introduce a new construct or hypothesis so that one and the same general theory can be made to generate alternative models of the same set of phenomena. In addition to that, theories change! As Toulmin has recently noted, the classical idea of a static theory with a given, unchanging structure, has been very seriously questioned by philosophers of science during the past few years (Toulmin, 1974). By contrast, many now believe that the central questions should focus upon the *development* and

change of theories. Toulmin suggests that such topics would include questions of how constructs change when they fail to accomplish all they were expected to; how novel ideas are evaluated and perhaps incorporated in a theory; and so on. As we study Freud's theory of personality we shall see a good example of such changes in response to new facts and new ideas. It is difficult to say when a changed theory actually should be treated as a different theory; but perhaps when a majority of constructs have been changed or reorganized, then it is appropriate to call it a new theory. At any rate, in chapter 9 we will see no less than *three* theories of personality structure developed by Freud.

Changes in Theory

Theories do not exist forever. They are changed by experience with their models. Bunge (1973) has argued that, although the word "model" has a very large number of meanings in science, only two meanings are significant for the analysis of scientific method: the notion of a model as a *representation* of some object or set of events to be explained and the notion of a model as the *theoretical explanation* itself. He has used the terms *model object* and *theoretical model* to refer to these two different meanings.

It is the purpose of this section to explore the characteristics and implications of Bunge's distinction between the model object and the theoretical model; and particularly to study how changes in these two kinds of models occur.

Model Objects

A *model object* is a representation of an object, event, process, or state of affairs. It represents the facts of some narrow set of phenomena. It is the starting point of scientific investigation. A model object may be portrayed through a description in words or by a drawing or other suitable medium of representation.

A less obvious but common type of model object is found in the results of observations or experiments. The experimental results are recorded in some way and subsequently represented in either extended or compact form. For example, in a study by Howarth and Eysenck (1968) two groups of subjects learned paired associate nonsense syllables. One group was previously established as having high scores on a test of extraversion; the other group had high scores for introversion. Each group learned a list of seven pairs of associates to a criterion of one perfect recall (anticipation method). Each group was then divided into five experimental treatment subgroups, differentiated according to whether they waited zero minutes, one minute, five minutes, thirty minutes, or twenty-four hours before a test of retention was administered. The results were presented in terms of mean number of syllables recalled (maximum fourteen). For extraverts, the means were 11.8, 9.3, 8.9, 7.0, 7.0 for delay periods of increasing length respectively; corresponding means for introverts were: 7.0, 7.9, 8.1, 10.0, 11.0. The decreasing gradient for extravert subgroups and the increasing gradient for introvert subgroups constituted the data of salient interest for the researchers, and these patterns differed significantly at the .001 level. The fact of difference in gradients; the fact that extraverts show a decreasing gradient and introverts the opposite; the fact that these two gradient patterns are different in statistically significant amounts; these constitute the essential parts of the model object to be explained.

We must note all that is not included in the model object: the names of the subjects, their heights, weights, and other personality or intellectual characteristics; the color of the experimental room, the mood or disposition of the experimenter; the incidental remarks or utterances made by subjects during the experiment; the attitude toward the experimenter and psychological experiments in general; the shapes of the curves in distributions of data; the particular syllables recalled or not recalled by each subject; whether subgroups differed in the set of syllables recalled or not; and so on. It is abundantly clear that the physical and social realities of individual lives and interactions are not well represented by the model object. Nor, in general, is it desirable that they should be represented. If they were represented then the representation would not be a model, it would be a recording.

Thus the "results" of a particular experiment constitute also an example of a model object. The "facts" that may be stated from a review of research data from a large number of studies similarly constitute a model object, though usually one with even greater degrees of abstraction from physical and social realities. A model object is a likeness without a richness; the more abstract the model object the less its descriptive richness, the farther away it is from a complex recording.

Theoretical Models

Studying a model object, we may attempt to account for it or explain it in some way that goes more or less beyond the facts as given in the model object. This may be done in ordinary everyday language, using concepts of various kinds. Our own guesses about some reported crime would exemplify such ordinary efforts at use of concepts to account for a model object. The criminal instance would have a model object consisting of all the facts of the crime as known to us. Our accounting would appeal to concepts like "motive," "modus operandi," or the dispositions of persons in certain categories or certain types of relationship to a victim. We might throw in a bit of folklore like "never trust anyone with close-set eyes."

Faced with general facts or facts derived from experiment, our attempt to explain would more likely involve the use of technical concepts. When these are used systematically in connection with a particular theory then we may call them *constructs* to signify our transition from everyday theorizing to scientific theorizing. Folklore will not do here. Our statement of laws, assumptions, and hypotheses must be more explicit, not to mention appropriate and deductively sound. The explanation we tentatively formulate for some narrow set of phenomena would then be called a *theoretical model*. (If it happens to be formulated in mathematical terms then it would be a *mathematical model;* I shall not deal with the particulars here, since such a model is simply a numerized version of a theoretical model.)

Howarth and Eysenck (1968) formulated precisely such a theoretical model to account for the data of their experiment. First they adopted the conceptual nervous system theoretical model developed by Kleinsmith and Kaplan (1963). In this model, when paired associates are learned under high arousal there is much general neural activity in the brain, and therefore the reverberating circuits which hold incoming information continue their reverberation for a longer period, thereby strengthening consolidation of the memory trace. At the same time the prolonged reverberation makes immediate retrieval less possible, because the stored information is tied up in circuits which are still active. Thus, under high arousal, consolidation leads to better long-run retention, but momentary interference leads to worse immediate recall. By contrast, low arousal leads to good immediate recall and poor long-run retention.

Howarth and Eysenck noted that the data obtained by Kleinsmith and Kaplan were based upon differences within subjects: high arousal was defined by emotional words such as *rape;* low arousal was defined by unemotional words. In accordance with Eysenck's theory of extraversion (Eysenck, 1967), extraverts are distinguished from introverts in the ratio of excitatory potentials to inhibitory potential in the cortex. Specifically, introverts have a balance in favor of excitation. The constructs of excitation or inhibition are essentially those of Pavlovian and Hullian theory. Assuming that the construct of arousal as used by Kleinsmith and Kaplan is equivalent to the construct of excitation, Howarth and Eysenck reasoned that extraverts would be typically low in arousal, and introverts high. Therefore, using a between-subjects design, separating a group of extraverts and a group of introverts, they predicted that the data patterns obtained by Kleinsmith and Kaplan would also be found in their own experiment.

Of course the entire scientific interest of the experiment by Howarth and Eysenck lies in its meanings for the theoretical model being tested and for the theory which generated that model. Nevertheless, the test of that theoretical model was made using the model object of their experimental data. We must note that the model object faced by Kleinsmith and Kaplan was not exactly similar to that faced by Howarth and Eysenck: the former was a within-subject design using English words of varying emotionality; the latter was a between-subjects design using predetermined levels of extraversion versus introversion and nonsense syllables. The central similarity to be found is in the pattern of results.

Changes in Model Objects

Since a model object is an abstraction from physical and social reality it leaves out many features of that reality. A critic may decide that some omitted feature should be incorporated in the model object; or that some included feature should be omitted from the model object.

For example, in the report by Howarth and Eysenck (1968) it is stated that the two groups differed nonsignificantly in trials to criterion: 15.9 for extraverts, and 18.3 for introverts. Nevertheless this might be a trend which becomes significant only in the test trials. For the data of a rising pattern for introverts and a decreasing pattern for extraverts are consistent with a view of retrieval as a cyclic process, rising to a maximum and then falling. On this view the introverts would still be rising in that twenty-four-hour period of tests, and the extraverts falling. Thus the data points for introverts would not be construed as representing a basically different pattern from that of the extraverts; but simply the same pattern at a different point in time, the introverts being slower than the extraverts.

In the general literature such changes in model object are constantly reported. For example, Battig (1975) has reported that, contrary to previous views of the process of paired-associate learning, individuals use highly idiosyncratic sets of strategies, switching in presently unaccountable ways from one strategy to another. In psychotherapy research the view of the object has recently changed sharply so that the process of psychotherapy is no longer thought to be one process but many different processes depending upon particular therapists interacting with particular patients (Bergin, 1971). It used to be thought that the cerebral cortex merely received sensory impulses; Pribram has now shown that it also controls sensory input (1969).

To return to the example of a reported crime, it is a commonplace that our entire view of the facts can change with the advent of a new piece of information; for example, that a key witness had been bribed. Our model object of the crime is thus transformed.

Changes in Theoretical Models

With a change in the model object there would very likely have to be a change in the theoretical model previously formulated. But even without a change in the model object there can be a change in the theoretical model. In the first place, for one given model object there might well be two competing theoretical models offering an explanation. The long controversy between response-learning versus place-learning theorists of maze-learning behavior in rats offers a good example. Another example is provided by Horowitz's cognitive model for the facts of behavior therapy (1976).

Nevertheless the most common basis for change in a theoretical model or for the formulation of a competing model is probably the introduction of new features in the model object. Quite often, of course, such new features are brought to light by new research. One well-known example is the series of studies on conflict in rats. Maier (1939) reported that rats placed on a jumping stand and forced to jump by means of an airblast, in some cases developed seizures, with convulsions followed by a waxy inertness. The rats appeared to have been put into a state of seizure by the conflict of being unable to both avoid jumping and avoid the noxious blast of air. Morgan and Waldman (1941) subsequently reported that such seizures can be induced in rats simply by any high-pitched noise such as accompanies the air blast; no conflict is needed. Thus the theoretical model for such seizures changed from assigning the chief causal property to a construct of conflict. Now the causal property was assigned to noises of high pitch, and the seizures were accordingly renamed *audiogenic seizures.* Later work showed that the avoidance-avoidance conflict actually makes it more likely that rats will have seizures in response to high-pitched sounds. Thus the picture of the model object changed once again; and so did the theoretical model.

Conclusion

The distinction between model object and theoretical model is clearly most important. A model object is our representation of the set of facts confronting us; a theoretical model is our more or less formal attempt at explanation of those facts, using the components of a theory. Science grows by additions and refinements of facts as well as by development and improvement of theory, and it is helpful to differentiate clearly between the two. If we do not make this distinction we are liable to fall into the trap of believing that our theoretical model is also our representation of the facts. Some authors do not consider this a trap, however, but rather an inevitable state of affairs in personality science. One reviewer of an earlier draft of this manuscript felt that this is the way it is: The so-called facts are actually defined by the theory employed, and all so-called factual description is theoretical in the first place.

I would agree only that in description we use language referring to general concepts: "This is a tall man"; "Tall men tend to be better players at basketball"; "Many young women today refuse to be limited by traditional role expectations"; and so on. "Tall" is a concept; "man" is a concept; "better" is a concept; "players" is a concept; and so on. The fact that some term like "role-expectations" happens to occur in somebody's theory does not make the description of women's rightful claims *theoretical*. It remains a description of the facts.

Personality science is not different in such matters from other sciences. In botany, for example, one fact is that certain flowers have two seed leaves, a floral cup round the pistil, fruit seeds that do not split and that are packed together in the cup, with thorns on the stem which are straight and long. These flowers exist along with all other flowers regardless of the theory employed in classification. They existed before modern pattern theory in botany placed them in a species category and named them *Rosa spithamea.*

Likewise Abraham Lincoln, Florence Nightingale, and George Washington Carver existed before Maslow developed a pattern theory of self-actualization which places those persons together as self-actualizing people. The people, like the ground roses, existed before the pattern theory was invented. Also, their characteristics existed as facts before the pattern theory gathered them together. Those facts could be represented as part of a model object describing all "flowers" or all "people." The pattern theoretical model would then group certain characteristics together, and hence certain persons together as *self-actualizing*, or certain flowers together as *Rosa spithamea.*

If we could agree on the proper representation of *selected* facts (could agree on one model object), would we still differ regarding our theoretical models? If Maslow and Skinner agreed on the model object of self-actualizing persons, would their theoretical models also be the same? Most likely not. Maslow would refer to the influences of characteristics such as spontaneity upon other characteristics such as creativity or imperfections. He would also stress the importance of all of the characteristics as manifesting the satisfaction of a general need, namely the need for self-actualization. Skinner would emphasize the importance of reinforcement history and the continuing effective contingencies of reinforcement in maintaining each of the several reflexes denoted by such terms as "spontaneity" or "imperfections." Actually "imperfections" would most likely be rendered as "emotional behaviors" in Skinner's theory.

So I shall let my case rest. It is possible to agree on a model object and differ on theoretical models. This means that our representation of the facts can be quite independent of our theory. In my opinion it should be.

Fiske (1974, p. 1) has written that "The conventional science of personality is close to its limits. No major, generally accepted advances have been made in recent years. In fact, neither investigators nor theorists have much consensus on anything." But it seems clear that there could be consensus as to model objects, and perhaps such consensus should be our next major objective.[3]

3. It may be rightly asked how in fact such consensus is to be achieved. Obviously there is no immediately available channel, but there are some precedents, as for instance in the agreements formed by the APA Committee on Psychological Tests, 1950-1954 (see *Technical recommendations, 1954*) which had far-reaching effects on consensus among psychologists about *reliability, validity,* and other properties of tests and test construction. A leaf out of the botanist's book might be helpful too, namely the publication of catalogues of descriptions of portions of the record of experience and behavior, along with such other properties or events as may be pertinent. The sections in reports on experiments which describe *subjects, methods, and procedures* provide another kind of precedent which might be suitably refashioned to serve the purpose of developing consensus on model objects.

Workshop 8

Theories of Structure, Cause, and Pattern Concerning the Namwons

In this workshop you are asked to continue to imagine yourself as a Uranian scientist. Recall that photographic data of people-like objects on Alpha-3 have been provided, as shown in Figure 6.1a of the chapter before last.

You already proposed one theoretical model of structure, in Workshop 6. Without a theory to guide you, you might now propose another model of structure. For example, one model might be that the lower segment actually contains seven smaller circles. Or again it might be made of a hundred sausage-shaped organs.

State your new model: _____

_____

Now let us see what difference it makes to have a theory to guide you in generating a model. Let us suppose that our theory of cosmic forms assumes that the shape of the external surface of an organism's segment is the same as the shape of its internal organs in that segment. Then our model of seven circles would have been better than the model of sausage-like shapes, since the shape of Namwon segments is circular.

Our general theory of cosmic forms makes the empirical assumption that organism segments farther from the planet's surface are more complex than segments closer to the planet's surface. Given that assumption, offer now another structural model for Namwons that fits all aspects of the general theory as you now know it.

New structural model of Namwons: _____

_____

_____

It is reported that Namwons move by hopping. The motion has not been well described yet, but essentially it resembles the movement of a bouncing ball. Propose a causal hypothesis for this form of movement. What mechanism inside the Namwon body would cause such a hopping movement to appear?

Causal model for Namwon movement: _____

_____

_____

Now consider the array of representative members of groups of Namwons which you prepared at the end of chapter 6. Think in terms of the general pattern theory of cosmic forms, which states that as a form grows it retains its shape but changes its size. Given this law, is it possible that a member of group A could change into a member of group E?

Using the theory, propose a model of development among Namwons, allowing for different groups.

Temporal pattern model for Namwons: _____

_____

_____

Now look at figure 8.3. It represents a theoretical model of temporal pattern for three subsets of Namwons, the Ihcahs, Amucahs, and Amurads.

There are three generations of Ihcahs, according to this model in figure 8.3: groups J, E, and X. There are just two generations of Amucahs: A and B groups. There are two generations also of Amurads, F and

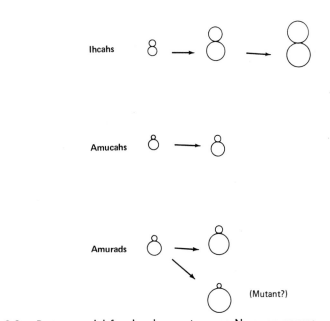

Figure 8.3. Pattern model for development among Namwon groups

D. But U appears to be a mutation in which only the lower segment grew. If we draw further upon the genetic theory of cosmic forms, we would propose also that Amucahs have resulted from a cross between Ihcahs and Amurads. Or do you have an alternative model for relationships between the different types?

In order to sharpen your awareness of a model object and its difference from a theoretical model, try now to state what would be a model object for the Namwons as far as we have facts at the present time. Consult the photographic data obtained and be sure to include also the reported fact of movement by hopping.

Model object of Namwons: _____

_____

_____

Compare your statement of the model object with your theoretical model of structure and with your theoretical model of temporal pattern.

Summary

A general theory can be tested only in application to specific, narrowly bounded phenomena. The accuracy of a theory, for example, can be estimated only by comparing a theory's explanation of a set of events with some facts which would follow from the explanation. The depth of understanding provided by a theory can be judged only in regard to understanding some particular set of phenomena such as the bending of light rays in a gravitational field or the recurrent presentation of unbidden images following a stress event. Such applications of a general theory to specific phenomena are made through the construction of theoretical models.

We may distinguish six different kinds of theories by the different subject-matters for which they generate theoretical models: causes, functional relations, structure and composition, patterns, priorities, and systems. These types are commonly intertwined in any one scientist's overall theory. When two theories enter into competition they usually are of the same type, both offering a causal explanation for example. Also they must be dealing with the same set of facts, otherwise they cannot be in competition. As a result of the application of theoretical models to delimited sets of facts theories change in their constructs and assumptions, and sometimes these changes are so major that it is necessary to speak of two theories, the one before and the one after the major changes. An example of this will be given in chapter 9.

Two meanings of "model" must be distinguished to comprehend changes in theory properly. A "model object" is a representation of a set of facts to be explained, and a "theoretical model" is the explanation of those facts in the terms provided by a theory. Model objects change as it is realized that additional facts about a given situation must be included in the model, or that some previously included fact should be omitted. These changes in a model object require changes in the theoretical model in terms of new selections of constructs and assumptions, or in the creation of new assumptions or constructs. When only a new *selection* from the theory's terms is made in order to change a particular theoretical model the theory itself does not change. But when new assumptions and constructs must be created in order to provide an adequate theoretical model, then the theory is changed. It must be emphasized that the model object is not itself described in theoretical terms. The language of description uses terms referring to general concepts, but this does not mean that such concepts are necessarily part of some particular theory. It can be shown that a model object such as a representation of flowers or people is independent of a particular theory since two or more theoretical models can be addressed to one given model object. It would seem to be a desirable objective for personality scientists to reach consensus on relevant model objects.

In the next chapter we shall concentrate upon one type of theory, namely Freud's theory of structure, or rather his three theories of structure, since the changes he made over a period of several decades were sufficiently great to justify speaking of three theories. It is hoped that this concentration upon a single type of theory will make it easier for the reader to develop understanding not only of Freud's theory, but also of the nature of a theory of structure in general so far as personality is concerned.

INTRODUCTION

Freud's component theory of structure
  Introduction to Freud's life and work
    Freud's life and professional career
    What he learned from Charcot
    Freud and Breuer
    The technique of **free association**
    His self-analysis
    Dreams and sexuality
    A modern example of dream interpretation
      in psychoanalysis
    Freud's work on theory; three theories of
      structure
Early neuropsychological theory
  Three types of neurones
  The riddle of consciousness
  Main points in Freud's first structural theory
  Commentary on the first structural theory
Conscious, preconscious, and unconscious: the
  second structural theory
  Evidence from the clinic
  Conscious ideas
  The preconscious system
  The unconscious system
Ego, id, and superego: the third theory of structure
  Development of the theory; some new clinical
    evidence
    Transference
    Repetition compulsion
    Resistance
  The id and the ego
    Differentiation
    Oedipus and the superego
    The qualities of consciousness and the
      unconscious
  Summary of the theory of structure
  Accomplishments of Freud's theory of structure
    Influence on culture
    Influence on academic disciplines
    Influence on treatment
Critique of Freud's theory of personality structure
  Allport's critique
  The divisions are arbitrary
  Comments on these criticisms
  Eysenck's critique
  Comments on Eysenck's criticisms

Accuracy, depth, and fruitfulness
Workshop 9A   Freud's theoretical model of
  consciousness
Workshop 9B   A brief experiment to test Freud's
  model of consciousness
Summary

9

A Theory
of Personality Structure: Freud

In chapter 8 various *types* of theories were described. It was argued that a personality theory often contains many component theories, each of which can generate particular sorts of theoretical models. The component theories may deal with the structure or composition of the subject matter, with causal relations, or with patterns of phenomena. The patterns may be of two kinds, either a pattern of characteristics which are presumed to go together (a classification), or a pattern of characteristics which follow in sequence over time (a temporal pattern). Other types of theories are theories of system, of priority, and of function. We begin more detailed study of particular types of component theory in the present chapter, starting with Freud's theory of personality structure. In chapters 10 and 11 respectively we shall take up two other components of Freud's overall theory, his theory of cause and his theory of temporal (developmental) pattern.

Sigmund Freud was born in 1856 in Freiberg, Moravia. He died in 1939 in London. Most of his life he lived in Vienna, where his family moved when he was four years old. He attended university, studied medicine, became a research physiologist in Ernst Brucke's

famous laboratory, and finally, with Brucke's blessing, became a medical practitioner in 1882.

Freud's lifelong friend and biographer, Ernest Jones, relates that the six years in Brucke's laboratory were spent chiefly in microscopic research upon the nervous tissues of primitive fish, including crayfish (Jones, 1961, pp. 27-36). Freud made a number of fundamental discoveries. It seems that he would have continued his career as a research physiologist had he not fallen in love with Martha Bernays, and decided to marry. It was impossible to get married on a research scientist's salary in those days in Vienna, and Freud had no savings, so he went into practice as a physician and soon settled down into the specialty of psychiatry. Even so his engagement to Martha lasted four years. Even by Victorian standards this seems like a very long engagement, and Jones tells us that it was passionate and stormy (Jones, 1961, pp. 68-92).

After leaving Brucke's laboratory, Freud started practice in surgery, then went on to internal medicine, psychiatry, dermatology, nasolaryngology, nervous disease, and ophthalmology. During this period he continued to do neurological research on the medulla, as a result of which he was appointed a Lecturer in Neuropathology in 1885.

Also in 1885 Sigmund Freud won an award for special travel to the laboratory of Jean Charcot in Paris. This was a momentous opportunity for Freud. Jean Charcot was then the world's leading psychiatrist. Jones says (1961, p. 123), "to Charcot must be ascribed the most important influence in turning Freud from a neurologist into a psychopathologist." Freud himself said that Charcot was having a dramatic effect upon him, changing him. He wrote to Martha Bernays about Charcot, calling him "one of the greatest of physicians," with a common sense that "borders on genius." Charcot's lectures challenged and changed Freud's ideas and even shook up some of his previous goals in life. He wrote:

> I sometimes come out of his lectures . . . with an entirely new idea about perfection. But he exhausts me; when I come away from him I no longer have any desire to work at my own silly things . . . no other human being has ever affected me in the same way (Freud, 1885/1960, pp. 184-185). (Letter 86).

Charcot specialized at that time in the study and cure of *hysteria*: a psychological disorder marked by loss of motor or sensory functions without discoverable damage to the physical bases in nerve and muscle tissue (Kolb, 1968, pp. 471-475). The prevailing opinion in medical circles was that such disorders were willful on the part of the patient: they were pretend disorders, or *malingering*. For example, a patient might become blind without obvious change in the eye or optic tracts. It was widely believed that the patient was simply faking blindness in order to get out of some unpleasant obligation. No doubt this did occur at times. But Charcot showed that the true hysteric patient had no idea of the reasons for the disorder, that the patient was not consciously producing the symptoms at all.

Rather, Charcot said, ideas in the patient's head were responsible for the symptoms; ideas which were not accessible to the rest of the patient's mind. These ideas were isolated but powerful. Charcot proved his point by the classic method of actually producing the phenomenon of interest. He put such ideas into a patient's head through hypnosis, observed the symptom resulting from those ideas, and then removed the ideas and observed the "remission" of the symptom. For example, in his demonstrations, Charcot would place a patient in hypnotic sleep and then give her the idea that her legs were paralyzed, whereupon the patient's legs would give way.

What would you have thought if you had seen such a demonstration? Freud later wrote his opinion that Charcot "succeeded in producing a faultless demonstration and proved, thereby, that these paralyses were the result of specific ideas holding sway in the brain of the patient, at moments of special disposition" (Freud, 1893a/1959, p. 22). Freud was specializing in neuropathology then, especially the paralyses of children. Freud's medical training and research experience could have led him to insist that there must be a physiological explanation, using the accepted terms of physics and chemistry. Alternatively, he could have ascribed to the view that the patient "was doing it on purpose," a sort of malingering on command. Instead he drew a conclusion of great theoretical importance. Combining the mental construct *idea* with the neurological construct *brain*, he hypothesized the existence of "moments of special disposition." At such a moment, he explained, there exists a state of mind in which "impressions or memories are no longer all linked up with another, and in which it is possible for one memory to express its effect by means of bodily phenomena, without the other mental processes—the ego—knowing about it or being able to interfere. . . ." (Freud, 1893a/1959, pp. 19-20).

Freud referred to this special mental condition as a state of *dissociation of consciousness.* Later this idea developed into the concept of an *unconscious mind,* a part of the mind which is not ordinarily accessible to waking consciousness, but which nevertheless exerts powerful influence over behavior and the bodily condition of the person.

Returning from his six months in Paris with Charcot, Freud took a position as clinical neurologist in a children's hospital. He wrote on the subject of *aphasia* (loss of ability to use language; see English and English, 1958) and cerebral paralyses in children, a field in which he became a recognized leader (Jones, 1961, p. 145). He remained at the hospital for a number of years but increasingly devoted his time to private practice. He used electrotherapy, baths and massage, and various other currently popular techniques. In 1888 he began using hypnosis, and a year later went for special training to Bernheim's famous clinic in Nancy, France, where he saw remarkable cures achieved through the use of suggestion. But later he found these cures to be quite transitory, and the suggestions themselves boring to repeat time after time. Also Freud found that he could not use the method of hypnosis reliably: often he was unable to put a patient into deep enough trance.

For many years he collaborated with his friend Breuer, a physician who discovered a "cathartic" method in which the patient tells all he or she can about the origins of symptoms of hysteria. So telling, Breuer found, the patient was apt to be cured. Freud began using this method in conjunction with hypnosis. But with patients whom he could not hypnotise he used a kind of suggestion in which he would press their forehead and assure them that some memory would come to mind. Then he learned that often a patient would have some memory or thought but not tell him about it because he or she "didn't think it was what you wanted" (Jones, 1961,

p. 158). And so Freud began encouraging his patients to hold nothing back, no matter how trivial it may seem. Thus he attempted to control for what has recently been called *selective therapist reinforcement* (Waskow, 1962). He developed the method of *free association*: no suggestions are given, no hands are placed on the forehead, and the single but imperative rule is that the patient must speak about whatever comes to mind, regardless of how unimportant, silly, unacceptable, or even offensive or disgusting it may seem to be. This method became the basic procedure of psychoanalytic treatment.

In 1897 Freud began the study of his own unconscious mind, employing on himself the same technique of free association, and adding to it the interpretation of his dreams. He found this so revealing of long forgotten but active emotional conflicts that he incorporated dream interpretation as another basic procedure in psychoanalysis. He carried on his self-analysis for four years. At the end of that period, according to Jones, he was much more normal than he had been four or five years earlier, yet he ". . . never ceased to analyze himself, devoting the last half hour of his day to that purpose" (Jones, 1961, p. 215).

In 1900 Freud's famous and seminal work *The Interpretation of Dreams* was published. Earlier he had found the recollections of his patients invariably going back to experiences of seduction. But later he discovered that these "recollections" were actually unconscious wishful fantasies during childhood. He formulated his theory of infantile sexuality, and published his *Three Essays on the Theory of Sexuality* in 1905. His views polarized the medical world. The famous Swiss psychiatrist Eugen Bleuler instructed his staff to study and apply Freud's principles; and Carl Jung, who was Bleuler's assistant at that time, became an ardent and innovative student. Ernest Jones in England, Sandor Ferenczi in Hungary, Karl Abraham in Berlin, and A. A. Brill in the United States joined in the leadership of the psychoanalytic movement and an International Association was founded in 1910. In 1909, at the invitation of G. Stanley Hall, Freud and other psychoanalysts gave a series of lectures at Clark University, where Freud was awarded an honorary doctoral degree.

In Vienna, however, his work received little recognition. There and elsewhere many scientists and physicians greeted Freud's theories with derision. How could anyone take seriously the idea that infants have sexual wishes! Or the idea that inhibitions produce anxiety!

But Freud continued to develop his theories in the light of accumulating clinical evidence. Psychoanalytic societies were established in many countries. Other leading psychoanalysts contributed to the advance of theory and to the detailed reporting of clinical cases. Freud himself continued to see patients and to work on his research and writing until shortly before he died. He received honors at home and abroad. In 1930 he received the Goethe Prize, and in 1936 he was honored by the Royal Society of London, England. When the lives of all Jews were threatened by the Nazi occupation of Austria in 1938, President Roosevelt and Sir Samuel Hoare, the British Home Secretary, intervened to secure passage for Freud and his immediate family to England (Jones, 1961, pp. 512-525).

London continues to be the main intellectual center for psychoanalysis. Freud's daughter, Anna, directs the Hampstead Child Therapy Clinic and continues to contribute to research and theory. A professorial chair established in memory of Sigmund Freud in the University of London is currently occupied by Professor Roy Schaefer, an outstanding psychoanalytic theorist and diagnostician. Other important centers of psychoanalysis are in Paris, New York, Chicago, Denver, and San Francisco. Psychoanalysis is practiced in every major capital of the noncommunist world. Box 9.1 gives some examples of dreams, associations, and dream interpretation in psychoanalytic practice.

The dreams in box 9.1 reveal some of the most important phenomena of human per-

---

Box 9.1
Dreams, Associations, and Dream Interpretations in Psychoanalysis

In one of Freud's early cases a young woman dreamed that the house was on fire and that her father woke her up. Her mother wanted to stop and save her jewel case, but the father said he refused to endanger himself and the two children for the sake of a jewel case.

Freud asked the patient to associate to each part of the dream and tell him what occurred to her. She replied that something did occur to her but that it had nothing to do with the dream. Freud urged her to talk about it anyway. She told of a recent argument between her mother and father over her mother's habit of locking the dining-room door at night. Her father objected because the only access to her brother's bedroom was through the dining room, and it seemed wrong for her brother to be locked in like that at night. Something might happen so that he would need to get out of the room (Freud, 1905a/1959, p. 79).

Freud asked if that had made her think of the risk of fire, and she replied that it had. But notice that she was not previously conscious of that connection, for she introduced the report of this argument by saying that it had nothing to do with the dream. In chapter 10 we shall return to this particular dream and show how Freud eventually interpreted the whole dream in terms of its sexual meanings.

Illustrations of recent work with dreams in psychoanalysis are taken from a book by the practicing psychoanalyst Leon Altman (1969). He relates that dreams occurring early in psychoanalytic treatment often reveal basic problems of the patient's relationship to the analyst and to the prospect of treatment. The first example is of this kind, the dream of a man in his mid-thirties:

> I was in a room of the house I lived in until I was six. I saw my old Teddy bear, one whose eyes lit up. It seemed to float in the air and then come right up to my face and look me right in the eye. I woke up.

He could remember having been very fond of the Teddy bear and of taking it to bed with him every night. He then recalled how miserable he had been when it somehow disappeared.

In the absence of further associations and with my limited knowledge of the patient, I [the analyst] could only surmise that the dream, with its evocation of childhood, had to do with starting analysis and possibly with his feelings about me.

Months later, when the transference had been established, I had occasion to tell the patient I noticed he had trouble meeting my eyes when I greeted him. In response, he recalled how his mother used to put her face close up to his and say, "Look me straight in the eyes and tell me the truth and I won't punish you." He had taken her at her word only to discover she hadn't meant it. After several unhappy experiences, he had learned not to trust her.

I remembered his early dream of the Teddy bear peering intently into his eyes. . . . (It) helped me to understand . . . the patient's ambivalence with respect to trusting people, including myself (Altman, 1969, p. 50).

During treatment, dreams commonly refer to unresolved conflicts over sexual wishes directed toward parents, as in the following dream:

> I wandered through an old house like a barn. It was full of old, broken-down furniture. On the second floor, I saw a table. When I came close, I saw it was an old sewing table. I thought I might be able to use it. Then I saw the top was gone, but

the legs were still holding on with screws. I thought it a shame. It was well made. I knew I couldn't put it together again. It had been done by a skilled man who should have handed down his skill to his son.

He reflected ruefully that he was not doing nearly so well as his son. . . . Why was it other people could marry, stay together, while all he ever seemed to do was spend his time with beat-up, run-down types? Other people had "well-made" marriages, they could talk to each other; he couldn't. . . . Had his father and mother?

"You must have always wanted to do what your father and mother did," I said, 'but your father could and you couldn't.' . . . The rich symbolism in the . . . dream pointed clearly to its oedipal sources" (Altman, 1969, pp. 179-180).

Toward the close of psychoanalytic treatment the dream is apt to reveal growing strengths in the patient's personality, as seen in this very short dream:

> Out of a wooded place came a pig with bristles all over.

For the first time in a long while, he somehow felt less irritable with me. . . . Money, money, money. . . . Last night he gave a hatcheck girl a quarter to retrieve two coats. She demanded two quarters, one for each coat. At first he was incensed, then thought "Ah, why be a stingy bastard, I can afford it and she needs it." The prospect of a better-paying job had come up and he decided to discuss this and other financial matters with his wife instead of excluding her as he usually did. . . . He was beginning to realize as never before that, for all his good manners, he was "a very hostile type," even with me.

While the dream condensed a host of ideas that included sexual aggression and guilt, nothing in the context or associations warranted an interpretation on that level. Paul's growing self-awareness was reflected in the dream: his superego recognized and would no longer give way to that other aspect of himself, the dirty selfish pig who masturbated and had sadomasochistic fantasies (Altman, 1969, pp. 193-94).

sonality that Freud discovered. Imagine yourself sitting with a nice, well-behaved, well-groomed man who has a stable marriage, goes to church on Sundays, and does volunteer work for the community. You ask him to free associate, say whatever comes into his head. He is your patient, and you have seen him more than fifty times. He began by complaining about his lack of motivation, feelings of fatigue, and various aches and pains in his back and stomach. But now he reports dreams quite frequently. A recent dream was about a kind of royal, kingly figure sitting on a throne, and some soldiers came in and hacked the king to pieces. There was blood all over the floor. It began to spill over and change color and cascade down into a pool below. Then he woke up in a sweat. Well, what do you make of that? Just a dream? Today he arrived late for his appointment, flung himself on the couch, and remained completely silent for ten minutes or so. What should you think about that? What should you say? What is going on? A psychoanalyst might remind him of the rule that he must say whatever comes into his mind. Or the psychoanalyst might say: "You are furious with me this morning."

Freud encountered just such events. He heard such dreams as those in box 9.1. Listening and observing and thinking about all of these phenomena, he formulated his theory of personality structure. Some of a person's ideas and feelings are unconscious. Such ideas and feelings tend to be either savagely destructive or else sexually lustful. In normal civilized life such ideas and feelings do not appear or are not acknowledged by the person. They exist nevertheless in the unconscious and make themselves felt in dreams, in symptoms of poor health and nervous disorders, and also in relationship to the psychoanalyst. The nice, well-groomed man in front of you has an inferno of animalistic impulses locked within him, hidden even to his own conscious mind.

Freud spent fifty-four years in actual clinical practice of psychoanalytic treatment, finishing only one month before his death. As a result of this prolonged observation his theories changed substantially as he endeavored to formulate an ever more accurate understanding of human personality. We shall try to see how his theories changed on the basis of new facts that had to be added to the relevant model object.

One of the most dramatic changes in Freud's theories relates to his basic methodological assumption. As we saw in chapter 6, a methodological assumption is one that motivates and guides the scientist's work. Freud's earliest basic assumption was that all the phenomena of personality can be traced back to physical and chemical causes. Accordingly, his first theory of personality structure invoked constructs of different kinds of neurones and their different chemical and electrical properties. It proved impossible to pursue this line of theory and research because techniques available for studying the brain were inadequate. He then developed the basic assumption of *psychological* determinism: that the phenomena of personality can be traced to causes of purely psychic or mental origin. When the evidence of the clinic required yet another major change in theory, his basic assumption of psychological determinism remained untouched, but the set of constructs was changed, as we shall see. We shall now turn to the development of each of these three theories in turn.

Freud's Early Neuropsychological Theory

One of Freud's first major drafts of personality theory was written in 1895, entitled *Project for a Scientific Psychology*. It was essentially a neurological theory, based upon quantitative concepts of energy in discrete neurones. With increases in the energy quantity a neurone would discharge across the *contact-barrier* between itself and the next neurone.

Three Types of Neurones

Freud conceived of three kinds of neurones, distinguished by their *permeability*, or the ease with which energy could be discharged across the contact-barrier.[1] The most permeable neurones of all were those responsible for the conscious part of the personality. The next most permeable were those involved

---

1. The "contact-barrier" is now called a *synapse*. See Schlesinger and Groves, 1976, chapter 3.

in perception, the receiving of stimuli from the outer world. The relatively impermeable neurones were those associated with memory and other psychological functions.

These three kinds of neurones were to be found in three relatively separate parts or system of the personality: the *conscious system,* the *perceptual system,* and the *nuclear system* respectively. Thus Freud's first theory of structure proposed three major parts, each composed of a different type of neurone (fig. 9.1).

Neurones transmitting information from the external and internal sense organs must be very permeable, he argued. The information (in the form of quantity of energy and frequency of firing) must readily cross the con-

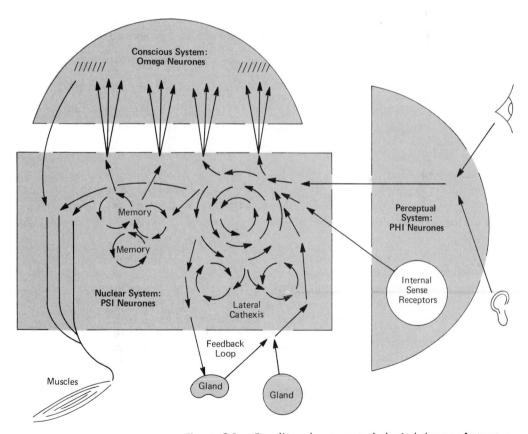

Figure 9.1. Freud's early neuropsychological theory of structure

tact-barriers. He called this the system of *phi* neurones (Freud, 1895/1966, p. 300). It is represented in figure 9.1 as the *perceptual system.*

Then he argued that a second kind of neurone is required to account for the facts of memory. These neurones must hold back the energy, must store it, except under special excitation for recall. These neurones, he reasoned, would also be the ones involved in general psychological processes (recognition, association), which rest upon the functions of memory. These neurones would be relatively impermeable, except for one class of stimuli that would probably go directly to them: the stimuli arousing emotional experience and coming physically from the glands of the body via the *autonomic nervous system* (see Schlesinger and Groves, 1976, ch. 3). Freud hypothesized the core of this system was a *sympathetic ganglion* (1895/1966, p. 303). He referred to the entire system as the *nuclear system* of *psi* neurones.

Freud was a scientifically exacting theorist. "A psychological theory deserving any consideration," he said, "must furnish an explanation of 'memory'" (1895/1966, p. 299). He began a tentative explanation with his concept of relatively impermeable neurones, the psi neurones in the nuclear system. His concept of the phi neurones already offered an explanation of certain features of perception, namely that information is readily transmitted, not stored in the relevant pathways.

Laying down yet another fundamental requirement for a psychological theory, he wrote,

> . . . every psychological theory, apart from what it achieves from the point of view of natural science, must fulfill yet another major requirement. It should explain to us what we are aware of, in the most puzzling fashion, through our "consciousness"; and since this consciousness knows nothing of what we have so far been assuming—quantities and neurones

—it should explain this lack of knowledge to us as well (Freud, 1895/1966, pp. 307-308).

The Riddle of Consciousness

How shall we explain consciousness? Is it part of the material world, no different perhaps than the internal state of a computer? Is our individual consciousness part of a separate reality, a spiritual or mental reality? Is the mental reality perhaps parallel to physical reality? Or could it be that physical reality is simply one manifestation of mental reality? Each of these positions have been put forward by philosophers. The problem is known as *the body-mind problem.* To focus better on the issues think of the brain in your head. And then think about the fact that you can *see* this page and *know the meanings* of these words and *become aware* of your bodily position (in a chair?) and location (in an apartment?). How does the pattern of matter in motion become translated into your conscious experience of black letters on a white page? Given that the physical energies are translated into the firings of nerve cells, how do those firings actually produce your state of consciousness? This was the question Freud asked himself.

His answer was that there must be yet a third kind of neurone, with the very special properties needed to make consciousness possible. He called these the *omega* neurones. He put forward the idea that somehow these neurones were responsive only to the frequency aspects of the nerve impulses that connected to them. Somehow the quantitative aspects were screened out by certain processes in the nuclear system. Freud pointed to a number of salient characteristics of consciousness: it changes quickly in content, it is fleeting, and different qualities perceived at the same time may easily be linked (Freud, 1895/1966, p. 309). Such features can only be sustained by neurones which are completely permeable.

When excited they must also be able to return immediately and completely to their former state; that is, there is no room for memory in these neurones.

Freud made quite clear what he thought about the relation of consciousness to physical processes in the nervous system. Consciousness, he wrote (1895/1966, p. 311) "is the subjective side of one part of the physical processes in the nervous system, namely of the (omega) processes. . . ." I have represented his view as the *conscious system* in figure 9.1.

Careful study of Figure 9.1 will show that no sensory stimulation reaches consciousness directly. Rather, it all goes through some part of the nuclear system first. Nevertheless, Freud's model states that no less than four kinds of input go to make up conscious experience: *immediate stimulation* coming from some external or internal sensory source; *memories of earlier exposures* to such stimulation; the *emotional reaction* currently associated with the present stimulus; and the *memories of emotional reactions* that occurred when the earlier exposures to the stimulus occurred.

You can make this concrete in your own experience. When you pick up a photo of someone you love, you look at it and have some emotional reaction to the sight of the loved person. These are two current sources of input to your conscious experience. Now think for a moment of the last time you saw the person; perhaps you can also recapture the feeling you had at that time. These two would be memory sources of input to your conscious experience. The four sources are illustrated in figure 9.1 by the four clusters of inputs going from the nuclear system to the conscious system. Two come from memory, one comes from current emotion (from glands via the nuclear system), and one comes from the perceptual system via the screening apparatus of the nuclear system.

We have not spoken about the motor side, the discharge into action via the machinery of the body's muscles. This too is represented in figure 9.1. Freud says explicitly (1895/1966, p. 311) that the omega neurones must have some very small discharge of excitation, and that this will go into the motor system.

Figure 9.1 really summarizes the main points in the structural theory developed by Freud in this early neuropsychological model. Karl H. Pribram, one of the world's leading physiological psychologists, has examined Freud's model and finds that it is detailed and sophisticated by today's standards (Pribram, 1969, p. 395).

Commentary on the First Structural Theory

Freud's neurophysiological theory of structure says that our experience is made up of energy discharges between neurones. Three major kinds of neurones are postulated: *phi, psi,* and *omega.* These have energy transactions which constitute respectively perception, memory, and consciousness. While the main part of the psi neurone system is taken up with memory it also handles many other energy transactions, such as *lateral cathexis,* a kind of defense against overwhelming amounts of emotional energy (see figure 9.1 and further discussion in chapter 10).

While satisfying to his earlier interests in neurology, this theory did not satisfy Freud's later need to understand his patients' symptoms. As he listened to their free associations he found it necessary to postulate a part of memory that was available to their conscious experience and another part that was not available in the usual sense but yet could influence the content of conscious thought. It must have seemed to him that such complications in the experience of patients required more complicated theorizing about the nervous system than was warranted either by existing knowledge or by the prospect of payoff in insight into neurosis.

Conscious, Preconscious, and Unconscious

The Second Theory of Structure

In Freud's second theory of structure, personality has three parts, the conscious, the preconscious, and the unconscious. Each part is composed of ideas of a certain kind and each has distinctive capabilities. Thus the *unconscious* is composed of instinctual ideas but lacks abilities to cope with reality; the *preconscious* is composed of memories that are available to consciousness and has the ability to relate such ideas to time and to reality; the *conscious* is the seat of our awareness, and is composed of fleeting perceptions, memories, and feelings.

Evidence from the Clinic

Studying his patients' symptoms, Freud consolidated ideas that had been in the making since his visit to Charcot's clinic in Paris. Not only was it evident that hypnosis produced ideas that actively affected the patient's behavior without the patient's being conscious of them. It was also plain from everyday experience with hysterical patients that their symptoms arose from ideas of which they were not conscious. The vomiting of a hysterical woman could arise from the idea that she was pregnant; if a woman goes into a "fit" with all the proper jerky movements, "analysis will show that she was acting her part in the dramatic reproduction of some incident in her life, the memory of which was unconsciously active during the attack" (Freud, 1912/1959, p. 24).

One boy had convulsive movements, vomiting, and headaches. When Freud asked what ideas or pictures came into his mind, he replied that he was thinking of a game of checkers in which there were forbidden moves. He saw a dagger lying on the board, then a sickle, then a scythe; and finally the image changed and he saw a peasant mowing grass outside his father's house in the distance. Upon analysis Freud found that the boy was enraged at his father but not conscious of this fury. The dagger represented his father's penis (it did in fact belong to his father). The sickle represented the boy's wish to castrate his father, as Zeus had done in the Greek myth. Much of the fury was due to the father's having forbidden the boy to masturbate as a child; the checkerboard represented masturbation, with its "forbidden moves" (Freud, 1900/1953, p. 619.)

In another case a mother brought her intelligent daughter for consultation. The girl was untidily dressed, with stockings down and blouse buttons undone. She complained of pains in her leg and a feeling that something was sticking into her body, moving back and forth, and shaking her throughout her whole being. Neither the mother nor the girl were in the least aware of the symbolic meaning of her symptoms (Freud, 1900/1953, p. 618.)

In each case the patient suffered from bodily symptoms produced by the unconscious ideas. Although the ideas were obviously very active, the patients were quite oblivious to the ideas so far as their conscious awareness was concerned. These ideas appeared to form a separate part of the mental life. There was evidence that very complex processes could go forward without the patient's awareness (as in the boy's furious resentment of his father). It appeared that these processes could nevertheless have some distorted representation in symbolic ideas of which the patient *could* become aware (the sickle and the dagger on the checkerboard). Sometimes the symbolic ideas would be manifested in the physical symptom, as in the case of the girl with something sticking into her.

Freud pointed out (1915c/1959, p. 99)

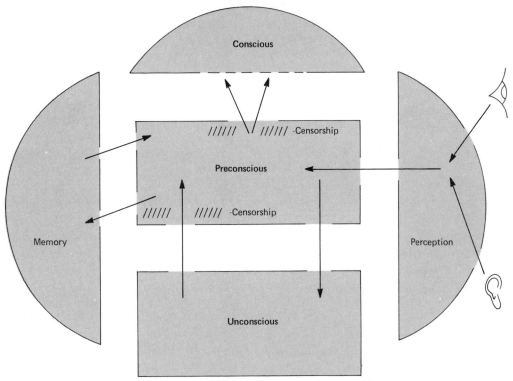

Figure 9.2 Freud's second theory of structure: the conscious (Cs), preconscious (Pcs), and unconscious (Ucs)

that consciousness is fleeting and at one time embraces only a small amount of all that we can become conscious of. Most of it is *pre-conscious*. So there are conscious ideas, preconscious ideas, and unconscious ideas.

Conscious Ideas

Conscious ideas are fleeting, even when they are memories. The notion of $2 \times 2 = 4$ comes into our consciousness from our memory and then fades. Figure 9.2 conveys this separation of memory from consciousness. Because of the qualitative nature of conscious perception (as discussed earlier in connection with Freud's work *Project for a Scientific Psychology*) the processes of perception are also shown as separate from but leading to the

conscious system via the preconscious. The conscious system (Cs) therefore has at least two kinds of contents: perception and memory, that is, present observations and past experiences called again to awareness. The Cs also has feelings of pleasure or pain or of more complex emotions. Freud pointed out that sometimes we make mistakes in consciousness: we are aware of an emotion but we misunderstand it; we give it a wrong label. He emphasized the importance of words in the system Cs. He wrote:

What we could permissibly call the conscious idea of the object can now be split up into the *idea of the word* (verbal idea) and the *idea of the thing* (concrete idea); the latter consists in the cathexis, if not of the direct memory-images of the thing, at least of remoter memory-traces derived from these. It strikes us all at once that now we know what is the difference between a conscious and an unconscious idea. The two are not, as we supposed, different records of the same content situated in different parts of the mind, nor yet different functional states of cathexis in the same part; but the conscious idea comprises the concrete idea plus the verbal idea corresponding to it, whilst the unconscious idea is that of the thing alone (Freud, 1915c/1959, pp. 133-134).

The term *cathexis* means a quantity of energy attached to an idea. It was used by Freud to mean the psychological equivalent of a charge of energy in a neurone. It meant that "a certain amount of psychical energy is attached to an idea or to a group of ideas, to a part of the body, to an object, etc." (Laplanche and Pontalis, 1973, p. 62). For most young people the idea *woman's breast* has a greater emotional charge than the idea *loaf of bread*.

In Freud's model of consciousness two quantities of energy are required, one associated with the visual image (of breast or bread) and one with the words themselves (*breast* or *bread*). The combined energy forces the idea to consciousness.

The Preconscious System

Even though you had not thought of it until now, you can probably recall the place or places you visited last summer. You could probably recite multiplication tables, beginning with $3 \times 3 = 9$; $3 \times 4 = 12$; $3 \times 5 = 15$; and so on. You probably recall who is President of the United States. All of these items of memory are readily available. The entire store of such readily available items Freud called the preconscious. The items sit on the threshold of consciousness and can come into consciousness on demand or on being triggered by an association.

The preconscious system (Pcs) allows for communication between ideas, according to Freud. The ideas influence each other in the Pcs, joining in groups and sets. The Pcs puts a relationship between ideas and time. Ideas have a date of birth, so to speak, when they are in the Pcs. One memory is dated as before another memory. For example, you graduated from high school before coming to college; and you can probably remember the last day of high school as being before the first day of college.

The Pcs sets up censorships between itself and the Cs, and also between itself and the unconscious (see figure 9.2). Its role is somewhat like that of customs officials at a frontier: undesirable ideas are not permitted to enter.

The Pcs is responsible for checking ideas against perceived reality—the process called *reality-testing*. An elementary test, for example, would be touching an object and establishing its solidity, and integrating this with visual memory.

Obviously the Pcs system does a great deal of the work involved in daily mental life. The ideas in the Pcs come partly from perception, partly from memory, and partly from those aspects of the instinctual ideas which are allowed to penetrate from the unconscious.

The Unconscious System

We have no way of directly knowing the characteristics of the unconscious system (Ucs). But its existence is indicated by the many evidences described above: hypnosis, dreams, symptoms, slips of the tongue or pen, or similar accidents in everyday life. In his self-analysis Freud explored his own unconscious. But few people are able to do that to any great extent without the assistance of a trained psychoanalyst. The reason is in the nature of Ucs: it consists of those ideas which are repulsive to our conscious awareness.

The Ucs system does not allow for communication between ideas, Freud says. The ideas do not influence each other. The Ucs consists of ideas representing primitive instincts, which may exist side by side without affecting each other. Love and hate for the same person can exist side by side without mutual contradiction in the Ucs.

Ideas in the Ucs strive to reach consciousness and expression in action. But because of the censorship exerted by the preconscious the primitive wishes of the Ucs often reach consciousness only in a distorted fashion, as in symbols (such as the checkerboard representing masturbation and the sickle symbolizing the boy's wish to castrate his father).

The emotions associated with ideas in the Ucs also become transformed. For example, in the case of loving and hating the same person, the feeling of love may get through to consciousness but the feeling of hate may not. Under these circumstances the person may actually do things that hurt or harm the other individual, but claim innocence and be consciously genuine in feeling upset about the damage done. At other times the two feelings of love and hate become blended in a curious mixture of feelings, such as in devouring passion. This is both a wish to devour the other person and a wish to love them intensely. Sometimes the passions alternate, with madly-in-love switching to madly furious. Such complexity seems strange to the persons involved. It is called *ambivalence*. One of Freud's great contributions to psychology was the recognition that a great many of us carry ambivalent feelings toward those we love.

The unconscious is quite different from the conscious, since it has no logic, no sense of time, and no concept of negation. Without logic, the Ucs does not argue reasonably: it is *irrational*. Without a time record it mixes up old memories with new. The Ucs has no idea of negation: It cannot contain an idea of *not* doing something, or of something not being present, or not being true. If a parent tells a child, "Don't get into any trouble, now," that message goes straight to the unconscious as, "Get into trouble!"

The Ucs is rarely in touch with reality, although some long-term influence upon it can gradually be exerted through the perceptual system. And the ideas in the Ucs are responsive to stimulation of a suitable kind from the outside world (as in a suggestion to indulge an instinctual wish). By and large, however, instincts press toward expression in thought and action regardless of reality. Without logic or reason, without a sense of time and place, and without any concept of "No" or "Don't," the unconscious is ill equipped for its task of mediating gratification for the instincts whose ideational representatives it contains.

Ego, Id, and Superego

The Third Theory of Structure

Transference. In his book *Beyond the Pleasure Principle* (1920/1948), Freud reported new clinical observations he had made of the widespread tendency among patients and others to repeat or dwell upon certain unpleasant experiences. In relationship to the analyst the patients would not merely *remember* fears, sorrows, or feelings of rejection they had experienced in childhood; they would actually *relive* those experiences. Moreover, they would project the counterparts of threats, deprivations, or hostility onto the analyst. In their relationship with the analyst they would have a renewed experience of whatever miseries and hopeless strivings they had suffered in relation to their parents. In the *transference* of childhood feelings to the analyst patients "(revive) unwanted situations and painful emotions . . . with the greatest ingenuity . . . they contrive once more to feel themselves scorned, to oblige the physician to speak severely to them and treat them coldly; they discover appropriate objects for their jealousy . . ." (Freud, 1920/1948, p. 15). They are compelled to repeat.

Repetition Compulsion. Similarly, in normal people with no sign of neurotic conflict one may see evidence of what Freud called the *repetition compulsion.* The same sad experience is repeated time and again in the lives of many normal people. Examples include "the man whose friendships all end in betrayal by his friend; . . . or the lover each of whose love affairs with a woman passes through the same phases . . . or the woman who married three successive husbands each of whom fell ill soon afterwards and had to be nursed by her on their death-beds" (Freud, 1920/1948, p. 16).

Why would people repeat failures and unhappy experiences? Freud traced this kind of repetition to a feature of organic life which seemed to be constantly tending toward its own breakdown. Even as all living things decay and die, so instinctual forces tend toward a reinstatement of what was there before. In particular he postulated a *death instinct,* saying, "the aim of all life is death . . ." (Freud, 1920/1948, p. 32). There is in all of us, he argued, a tendency toward self-destruction; a tendency to seek pain and nihilation. It is manifested in part in the repetition compulsion.

Of course these forces for self-destruction and for repetition must also be assumed to be unconscious. It had previously been assumed that all instinctual striving had positive, pleasurable aims as represented in the Ucs. Now it appeared that there were self-destructive instincts also. The id contains not only erotic but also destructive impulses. The facts of repetition, then, both in the transference and in daily life, provided one impetus for modifications in theory.

Resistance. Another fact encountered frequently in psychoanalytic practice provided another reason for change. This was the phenomenon of *resistance.* The patient is instructed to let associations come freely, to put aside all censorship. Even so, Freud relates (1923a/1967, p. 7), "his associations fail. . . . We then tell him that he is dominated by a resistance; but he is quite unaware of the fact, and . . . does not know what it is or how to describe it." Resistance blocks the treatment he is paying for.

As the word implies, *resistance* is the patient's own unwitting attempt to avoid facing and accepting some difficult truths about himself or herself. It is the patient's way of keeping her psychological eyes tightly closed, of blocking his psychological ears so as not to see or hear unpleasant deeper truths.

Earlier Freud had assumed that the ego was preconscious, often also conscious. Also he assumed that the preconscious ego was responsible for censorship, for the fact that some ideas from the Ucs were not allowed to pass into the Cs. Now the evidence suggested very clearly that resistance was an unconscious process. Freud described his reasoning as follows (1923a/1962, p. 7): "there can be no question but that this resistance emanates from his ego and belongs to it. We have come upon something in the ego itself which is also unconscious . . . which produces powerful effects without itself being conscious and which requires special work before it can be made conscious."

These clinical facts forced Freud to change his theory of structure once again.

The Id and the Ego

In Freud's final theory of structure there are just two major parts, the *id* and the *ego.* An outline of the theory is given in table 9.1. In writing about his revised theory, Freud (1933/1964, pp. 73-75) described the *id* in

Table 9.1
Freud's Third Theory of Structure

| | Principle Structures | |
	Id	**Ego**
Components	Ideas representing instinctual impulses and emotions in the sex instinct and in the death instinct; also repressed ideas associated with the instincts	Ideas representing the self-preservative instincts; ideas from perception representing reality; mental representation of the surface of the body; identifications
Differentiation	Undifferentiated	Ego and superego
Qualities	Unconscious	Unconscious, preconscious, and perceptual conscious

essentially the same way as he had previously described the system Ucs. It is a "seething cauldron" of instinctual forces; its ideas strive for discharge, not bound by logic, time, or negation. The id's ideas are of two kinds: instinctual impulses and ideas which have been repressed by the censorship. Repressed ideas are memories of earlier instinctual excitations which were unacceptable to the ego.

Not all of the instincts have representations in the id. Freud states explicitly (1923a/1962, p. 30) that the self-preservative instincts must be "assigned to the ego." Note also that earlier systems of Ucs, Pcs, and Cs, are now referred to as *qualities*. Although the id is all in the Ucs, the latter extends over a larger domain, including parts of the ego. The id and the ego are viewed as *agencies* of the mind, that is, major divisions of mental activity.

In *The Ego and the Id* (1923a/1962, pp. 7, 15, 16) Freud described the characteristics of the ego and its origin in some detail. The ego is first "a coherent organization of mental processes . . ." with consciousness attached to it. The ego controls the muscular system by which action on the external world is effected.

It is self-monitoring, supervising its own activities. Even although the ego relaxes and "goes to sleep at night . . ." it continues to exercise the censorship which transforms unacceptable latent thoughts into acceptable dream symbols. For this and other reasons it is evident that some part of the ego is in the Ucs, as we saw above. The ego represents "reason and common sense, in contrast to the id, which contains the passions."

Differentiation. Freud proposes that the ego arises from an originally undifferentiated id, or mass of instinctual strivings. It does so as a result of "the direct influence of the external world through the medium of the Pcpt.-Cs (perceptual conscious). . . ." Also the ego is "derived from bodily sensations, chiefly from those springing from the surface of the body" (Freud, 1923a/1962, pp. 15, 16, fn 1). As the child bumps against the reality of chair legs and hard floors its thoughts and feelings contribute to the formation of the ego.

The ego arises, then, from perceptions of the outer world and from the inner world of the person's own body. Freud points out that the body is actually a very special object of perception; for not only do we have *internal* sensations (such as feeling our fingers tingle in hot water after being cold) but also we have *external* sensations of our body (for example, we *see* our fingers or we can *touch* one finger with another). We therefore get a continuing series of double perceptions of our body, perceptions which are *in depth*, you might say, coming as they do from both inner and outer aspects of one and the same object. In fact Freud said that "The ego is first and foremost a bodily ego . . ." (1923a/1962, p. 16).

Moreover, the ego is a representative of the "self-preservative instincts." This becomes especially clear when we consider the role of *pain*, which signals threats to self-preservation. Freud points out that pain plays a special role in the development of our idea of our body, as when we become acutely aware of our ears if one of them is stung by a bee, or of our skull if we crack it on a table's edge. Freud suggested that painful illness also makes us newly aware of our bodily organs, and thus may provide "a model of the way by which in general we arrive at the idea of our body" (Freud, 1923a/1962, p. 16).

In their discussion of Freud's theory of the ego, Laplanche and Pontalis (1973, p. 140) point out that it develops in two ways. First, the ego is differentiated out of the id as a result of the person's perception and awareness of the external world. The ego develops as a set of specialized functions for dealing with that world and for achieving satisfaction of instinctual drives within the context of opportunities and limitations presented by reality. The second path to development of the ego comes from social interaction, especially with the parents. As a result of interaction the child *identifies* with other people, the boy with the father for instance. This means that the child forms stable memories about that other person, looks, and characteristics, etc.

And then the child takes over those same characteristics into his or her own ego.

Oedipus and the Superego. Freud wrote, "the ego is formed to a great extent out of identifications which take the place of abandoned object cathexes by the id. . . ." (1923a/1962, p. 38). This means that the ego takes on characteristics of people whom the person has loved but who for one reason or another can no longer be expected to be objects of love. The change may arise from the death of the loved one, or from some other form of departure, or from the realization that one can no longer hope to achieve the aims of love with that person. One particularly important identification arises when the child realizes that it is impossible to secure the erotic love of the parent of opposite sex. The preceding hope and romantic attachment to that parent is called the *Oedipus Complex* for boys. There is a somewhat similar complex for girls, the female Oedipus complex. The complex typically develops between the ages of three and six years. It is resolved by abandoning the attachment and by identifying with the same-sex parent. One important outcome of this identification is that it begins to take on an autonomous status and to be separated off from the ego. It forms the *superego.*

According to Freud, the superego has "the character given to it by its derivation from the father-complex—namely the capacity to stand apart from the ego and to master it. . . . As the child was once under a compulsion to obey its parents, so the ego submits to the categorical imperative of its super-ego" (1923a/1962, p. 38). Because of its origin in childhood fear the superego remains somewhat childish in its function. However, taking over the image of the huge and angry parent into itself, the superego is also likely to be angry, demanding, and relentless. Its manifestation in normal conscience is found in self-criticism, self-

reproach, and feelings of guilt. Freud theorized that the superego derives energy also from the child's own instinctual aggression, turning it back upon the ego in accusation and punishment.

Qualities of Consciousness and the Unconscious. While the id is fully unconscious, then, the ego is partially conscious and partially unconscious. The superego tends to be mainly unconscious, with manifestations in consciousness at the level of self-reproach and feelings of guilt.

Summary of the Theory of Structure

The theory that Freud left us is a combination of his second and third theories. The fundamental elements of personality are ideas, along with their charges of energy in the form of affect or of impulse. The ideas are mental representations of instincts and their derivatives, or of the objects of drives, or of the means which may provide satisfaction of impulses. The basic elements are organized into three main substructures or agencies, the id, the ego and the superego. The elements are also partitioned into three main divisions, conscious, preconscious, and unconscious. These divisions do not simply intersect with the agencies so that each agency has one of each division. The ego and the superego do have parts in each of the three divisions of consciousness, but the id lies solely in the unconscious. This overall structure is represented in table 9.2.

The conscious part of the ego has ideas of future goals and forces of determination; the unconscious part of the ego has ideas of what is dangerous to the ego and forces which carry out the necessary repressions of undesirable id impulses. The conscious part of the superego feels obliged to carry out certain good deeds or ritual observances, and exerts forces of guilt against the ego to guarantee compliance; the unconscious part of the superego rages against the least thought of transgression and creates the self-hatred which underlies feelings of depression or—in the extreme—suicidal tendencies. The id is filled with ideas of gratifying instinctual wishes such as sexual union or the destruction of enemies. The workings of these various forces and the interrelationships among the several structural parts constitute the subject matter of Freud's theory of dynamics (or cause), which we will study in chapter 10.

Table 9.2
Freud's Final Theory of Structure

Divisions of Consciousness	Agencies		
	Id	Ego	Superego
Conscious		✿	✿
Preconscious		✿	✿
Unconscious	✿	✿	✿

Accomplishments of Freud's Structural Theory

The discovery of the unconscious revolutionized humanity's understanding of its own nature. The power of the sexual instincts was revealed, and the damage done by repression was made plain. In the ensuing years these findings created a movement that has eventually affected our entire western culture. Not only are we now much more open and accepting about sex. Also the everyday languages of the western world, Japan, and other countries now contain the essential terms conscious, unconscious, id, ego, and superego (see Webster's dictionary, 1973). Ordinary people everywhere now learn the meanings of these terms and know how to use them. The structural theory has become a part of humankind's self-awareness.

Freud's theory has had tremendous influence on many other academic disciplines. Cultural anthropology, sociology, political science, history, even literature have been influenced by the constructs of the unconscious, the id, ego, and superego. As we have seen in earlier chapters of this book, many theorists have been influenced by Freud's theory of personality structure: Maslow to some extent, Murray a great deal, Miller and Dollard a great deal. In later chapters we shall see that Jung, Cattell, and Erikson all were strongly influenced by Freud's theory of structure.

The theory of structure in all versions except perhaps the first was influenced by and also influenced the practice of psychoanalytic treatment and related forms of psychotherapy. The methods of free association and dream interpretation continue to be basic in psychoanalysis proper as it is practiced in major cities throughout the world. Every month in the *Monitor*, the newspaper of the American Psychological Association, notices appear of training and employment opportunities in psychoanalytic therapy and research.

Naturally, the technique of treatment as a whole has been developed and refined through the years. By this time there are a number of approaches to psychological treatment, some of which require that the patient have good ego strength to begin with (psychoanalysis on the couch in the classic sense); some of which require more positive and directive efforts from the analyst (supportive psychotherapy).

Almost twenty years have been spent on a research project at the Menninger Clinic in Topeka, Kansas, evaluating these different types of treatment (Kernberg et al., 1972). It was found that indeed patients with higher initial ego strength improve more with strict psychoanalysis. Patients with poor ego strength do better in a form of treatment combining features of supportive psychotherapy with features of psychoanalysis. This important contribution to the literature will improve therapists' ability to predict which kind of treatment will most benefit particular patients.

Critique of Freud's Theory of Personality Structure

One of the earliest critics of Freud's theory was Gordon Allport. His most general criticism was that Freud's observations were based upon neurotics and other pathological cases and therefore generalizations of the associated constructs to normal personality were of doubtful validity. This is particularly true of the unconscious, which Allport describes as "an inclusive abstraction, referring to all the operations fashioning personality without the individual's direct knowledge. . . . Its primary function is to serve as a store-house of the impulses rejected by the Ego." Such rejection, he says, is due to conflict between the impulses and the "ruling tendencies of the

conscious personality." But he adds that although conflict is undoubtedly important in personality development, "it seems that only in exceptional cases is the psychoanalytic emphasis on its *unconscious* operation fully justified. Most conflicts, psychoanalysis to the contrary notwithstanding, are conscious in all *essential* particulars and for that reason another less esoteric portrayal of conflict seems more adequate" (Allport, 1937, p. 184). Thus Allport asserted that for *normal* personalities the unconscious should be given far less importance than Freud gave it, and perhaps it should be considered irrelevant to normal personality, even if it exists among neurotics and other abnormal personalities.

Allport also said that Freud's division of the personality into three parts—id, ego and superego—was basically no different from the divisions that had been made by Plato and other thinkers into parts roughly equivalent to emotional impulses (id), cognitive self-consciousness (ego), and conscience (superego). In Allport's view such a division is entirely arbitrary. Such arbitrariness has recently been emphasized again by Peterfreund and Schwartz (1971) who argue that "explanatory statements based on the concept of the ego are basically tautological. The psychological observables are assigned to an agent whose nature remains unknown and unexplained" (1971, p. 68). They would rewrite the theory without the construct of the ego. For example, instead of saying "the ego has voluntary movement at its command," they would say "the control of voluntary movement is possible."

Freud himself rarely attempted to rebut criticisms since, like Skinner, he preferred to spend his energy on his own productive work. He has been criticized for this attitude, since it seems arrogant. But his opinion was that only close psychoanalytic work could reveal relevant evidence, while general observations or laboratory experiments would typically be unable to make observations at an appropriate level of psychological depth or detail. Moreover, such crucial phenomena as resistance and transference could only occur in the course of treatment. Other psychologists have disagreed with Freud's viewpoint and have taken his hypotheses to laboratory tests anyway.

As to the question of the importance of the unconscious in normal personality, extensive series of experiments on repression and subliminal perception (Dixon, 1971) seem to have yielded quite conclusive evidence for unconscious functions. We shall deal more fully with this and related topics in chapter 10. Kline (1972) has reviewed a number of studies bearing upon the unconscious and also upon the division of the personality into the three main agencies of id, ego, and superego. Such evidence as there is comes from the results of psychological testing. If tests of certain ego-like qualities tend to correlate positively, this correlation would be taken as evidence for the coherence of "ego functions." Likewise if tests revealing the operation of moralistic controls in the personality would group positively together, then this would provide evidence for the coherence of the superego agency. And if the tests for the ego functions do *not* correlate positively with tests for the superego functions, then that result also would be consistent with the structural theory, which emphasizes the separateness of ego and superego functions in the mature adult. Similar considerations apply to tests for id functions. The balance of the evidence, according to Kline (1972), provides some slight support for Freud's theory. Some other evidence is considered in chapter 18 below when portions of Cattell's theory and data are compared with Freud's theory of structure.

In my own view, the criticism that the unconscious is unimportant in normal people rests upon an assumption that we know very much about normal people. In fact, how much do we know? There are a few carefully studied cases, as mentioned in chapter 3, most of them done by Henry Murray and his immediate group or by scholars who have drawn their inspiration from him. Such evidence as there is suggests that normal people are *not* aware of all of their conflicts, not even in the most essential aspects.

Hilgard and Bower appear to reach a similar conclusion. In their latest review of theories of learning they discuss Freud's overall theory and comment as follows:

> The genetic or developmental aspects of psychoanalysis have brought to the fore the need for an adequate *ego psychology*. If we are to understand the learner as he sets his goals and works realistically toward them, or as he is torn by conflicts that prevent his using his abilities, or as he burns himself out in the quest for futile objectives, we need a theory of personality organization incorporated within our general theory of learning (Hilgard & Bower, 1975, p. 371).

In this passage Hilgard and Bower mention several symptoms of unconscious conflict: "torn," "prevent his using his abilities," "burns himself out," "the quest for futile objectives." These authors clearly do not think that the unconscious is unimportant in normal people. Rather an "adequate *ego psychology*" is seen as necessary to understand "the learner" and the processes of normal human learning, as of college students.

Moreover, the criticism that Freud's three-part division of the personality is essentially the same as Plato's division seems to me to be simply incorrect. We have seen that Freud was forced to conclude that some portions of the ego are *un*conscious. This in itself is a sufficient departure from Plato's conception to constitute evidence that Freud's theory was essentially different. As for the idea that we can dispense with the construct of the ego by saying such things as "the control of volun-

tary movement is possible," we cannot. Such a statement hides the presence of a *will* function in the word "voluntary," and hides the ego structure, which would exert the will function, in the words "is possible."

We said in the previous section that psychoanalytic treatment is one of the accomplishments of psychoanalytic theory. But Eysenck (1952a/1966) has pointed out that rates of improvement among neurotic patients (both in hospital and not hospitalized) who do not receive any treatment by psychoanalysts or psychotherapists of any kind tend to be as good as or better than the rates of improvement reported by psychoanalysts. The so-called "spontaneous recovery" rate is about 66 percent in a two-year period, according to Eysenck, based upon a few studies of large numbers of untreated patients. If the theory of psychoanalysis produces a treatment procedure which does no better than spontaneous remission, it is argued, then surely that theory must be inaccurate.

Eysenck's criticism has itself been criticized. For example, Bergin (1971) reviews the results of fourteen studies of spontaneous remission not included in Eysenck's tabulations, and finds that the rate is only thirty percent in these studies, as compared with 66 percent in those employed by Eysenck. Moreover, Bergin questions the method Eysenck used in judging the rate of improvement in studies of psychoanalytic treatment. Bergin's method excludes those patients who dropped out of treatment and considers improvement to be indicated by a final rating of "moderately improved or better." He finds that 450 out of 540 cases in six different studies showed improvement. Thus an overall rate of 83 percent improvement in psychoanalytic treatment must be compared with a rate of only 30 percent improvement in spontaneous remission.

More recently Smith and Glass (1977) have reported on 375 controlled studies of psychotherapy. They find that "the typical therapy client is better off than 75 percent of untreated individuals" (p. 752).

At the latest accounting, then, it seems that Eysenck's challenge to psychoanalytic treatment is not sustained by the empirical evidence. His challenge to psychoanalytic theory, insofar as it rests upon his earlier summary of rates of improvement, also cannot be sustained on the basis of present evidence. It should be noted that the percentages used by Bergin are arbitrary, as were the percentages used by Eysenck. To obtain more definitive results more definitive criteria must be developed so that percentage of improvement can be assessed with greater precision and reliability.

We conclude this critique by briefly examining Freud's theory of structure in light of the criteria developed in chapter 6: accuracy, power, depth, and fruitfulness. No final statement can be made, of course, without a far more detailed presentation of the relevant data than can be given here. Nevertheless, the work of other reviewers can be cited. Dixon (1971) makes it clear that Freud's division into conscious and unconscious systems allows the generation of accurate models regarding the evidence in experiments on subliminal perception. Kline (1972) concludes from the evidence of studies using personality tests that the division into id, ego, and superego structures receives some support. We know from a great deal of other work (see Royce and Buss, 1976) that there are many more major divisions of the individual differences data

than just the three that would be encompassed by Freud's three-part theory. There are divisions of psychomotor skills and of cognitive abilities, for example. But such facts suggest that Freud's theory of structure is not completely exhaustive. As far as it goes, however, it seems to be quite *accurate*. Its range seems quite broad, furthermore; therefore the theory is *powerful*.

If we are to judge by the penetration that many authors have found possible using Freud's theory, we must conclude that it has substantial depth. It is doubtful whether this depth is provided only or mainly by the theory of structure, however, so the criterion of *depth* is perhaps best passed over in this chapter. The most that can be said is that Freud and other psychoanalysts and other clinicians and scholars have found the constructs of the unconscious and of the id and the superego especially helpful in providing them with a deeper understanding of the human personality. In fact, psychoanalysis has often been referred to as *depth psychology*.

The criterion of *fruitfulness* throws interesting light on the three theories of structure described in this chapter. For Freud's neurophysiological theory was actually fruitless, even in his own further work; the second theory had moderate fruitfulness, as evidenced in the researches of others (such as Jung, chapter 12); and the third theory had widespread influence, with applications as far ranging as the analysis of the family, psychosomatic disorders, and patterns of culture.

Freud's Theoretical Model of Consciousness

Freud's model of consciousness holds that there are two representations of an idea; one is in imagery, one is verbal. The energy of the latter is needed to make the idea conscious. There are two cathexes or sources of energy attached to the idea. Freud called this a **hypercathexis.** Consciousness requires hypercathexis, he said. Actually, an additional **clarity of awareness** would satisfy Freud's hypothesis.

In figure 9.5 on page 232 there is a collection of visual objects. Read the following instructions carefully before looking at it for the first time.

> Do two things: first, count "One-two-three-four-five-six," fixing your gaze on each object in turn as you count, and using about one second for each number. Next, turn away your eyes and try to visualize each object in your mind.

How clearly were you able to picture each object in your mind's eye?
On the average, it was:

clear as the original picture	_____
almost as clear as the original	_____
a bit vague in outline	_____
not clear at all	_____
not even a blur	_____

Now turn to the end of this chapter, page 231, for a list of words to be attached to the objects in figure 9.5. Memorize the words.

Once again, count (according to instructions with that list) as you examine each object in the figure for a one-second period. Look away and try to visualize each object, saying the word connected to the idea of the object.

How clearly were you able to picture the objects this time? It should be somewhat clearer than before, if Freud's theory of hypercathexis is right.

A Brief Experiment to Test Freud's Model of Consciousness

Copy the visual objects shown in figure 9.5 (on p. 232), and also those in figure 9.6 (on p. 233) on a separate card or sheet as shown in figure 9.3. Note that in the top part of figure 9.3 the visual object is reproduced twice, once each side of the center dividing line. In the lower part of the figure the object appears in only one half of the picture and its associated words appear in the other half. You may use either the same set of words as before or make up another set, such as **moon** and **circle, star,** and so on.

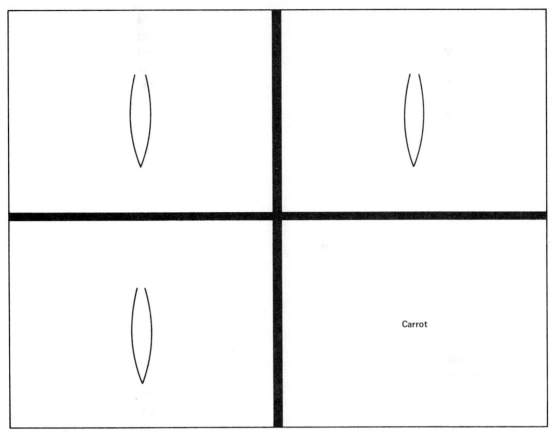

Carrot

Figure 9.3. Examples of study cards for the experiment on consciousness

Now let us assume that greater clarity of consciousness produces a clearer image in memory, and that this additional clarity of the memory image can be carried on to a drawing that the subject will do from memory. If Freud's model of consciousness is correct, then, given these assumptions, it would be expected that adding words to the visual objects should enhance the clarity of the reproductions a subject would give by drawing the pictures from memory. To control the exposure and study time, we present one group with word-picture combinations and a control group with picture-picture combinations. The latter simply give the same picture twice, whereas the former give the picture and its associated words.

You will have at least two subjects, each receiving either the picture-word or the picture-picture combination. Show the subject each card for one second only; pause for one second in between. Tell the subject beforehand: "If you are willing, I will show you some cards and ask you to judge the artistic quality of the drawings as very good, good, moderate, poor, or very poor." If the subject agrees, go ahead and mark down the judgments. Go through all twelve cards. At the end say: "To get another measure of the quality of these drawings I want to see how completely they are remembered. Would you please draw all the pictures you remember. Draw them about the same size as you saw them." Give the subject twelve blank cards with just the center dividing lines. Only one picture of each drawing needs to be reproduced.

Finally it will be necessary to tell how closely each subject's drawings resemble the originals. Match up original and reproduction in each case and have a friend rate the accuracy of reproduction on a five-point scale.

If Freud's theoretical model and our assumptions are correct, then subjects shown the picture-word combinations should make more accurate reproductions. As usual this may not happen with every subject, so try about four subjects in each group and calculate the averages. Also, think about additional controls that might be needed.

The results may not turn out as expected. If so, what could be wrong? If you can rule out errors of procedure, then consider whether the assumptions we made might be wrong. If they seem correct, then perhaps Freud's model of consciousness is incorrect, for at least on this one experiment, with all other sources of error checked, it would appear that the model is inaccurate.

Be sure to debrief the subjects after the experiment.

Summary

Originally a specialist in neurophysiology, Freud built his first theory of personality structure using physiological constructs. He related psychological facts of perception, memory, and consciousness to three systems of neurones, *phi, psi,* and *omega* respectively. The neurones in each system were assumed to have properties which would account for the different psychological facts. The theory proved unable to provide adequate theoretical models of many clinical phenomena, however, and relevant changes would have required the addition of constructs (such as disguised symbols) which would not readily fit existing knowledge of the brain.

Accordingly, Freud's second theory of structure used only psychological constructs. In this theory the personality was thought to be composed of three systems: consciousness, the preconscious, and the unconscious. The ideas and capabilities proposed for each system were unique in several ways, especially concerning memory and relationship to reality. The second theory was later confronted with new clinical facts for which it could not provide adequate theoretical models. New constructs of resistance and transference were developed, and these forced major revisions in the theory.

Freud's third theory of structure was more complex. Upon the three systems of the second theory were superimposed two new major structures, id and ego, with the latter giving rise to a differentiated third part, the superego. Ego and superego appeared in all three systems of conscious, preconscious, and unconscious; the id appeared only in the unconscious system.

Freud's third theory has been criticized as being arbitrary. Nevertheless, empirical evidence suggests that the proposed structural divisions are accurate as far as they go. The profound influence and fruitfulness of Freud's theory of structure is confirmed by the many authors and investigators who have used it in research, therapy, and forming a deeper understanding of human personality. As shown in figure 9.4, however, the theory of structure does not include a complete definition of personality. It includes only the portion that is relevant to itself; other portions are included in other components of Freud's overall theory,

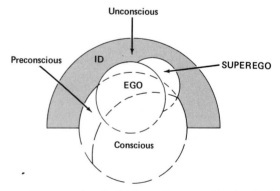

Figure 9.4. Definition of personality implied by Freud's theory of structure

as presented in chapters 10, and 11. The representation in figure 9.4 shows the emphasis upon psychophysical systems in Freud's theory (the id and all unconscious divisions of the personality being located there). It also shows the emphasis upon subjective experience—upon ideas and affects in the preconscious and conscious divisions.

Word List for Visual Objects in Figure 9.5

Clay Pot

Carrot   Flower

Archway

Fallen Tree   Caterpillar

Instructions: Instead of counting "One-two-three-four-five-six," use the words as you examine each object: "carrot, clay pot, flower," and so on.

Figure 9.5. Visual objects for inspection and test of Freud's hypercathexis theory

A Theory of Personality Structure: Freud

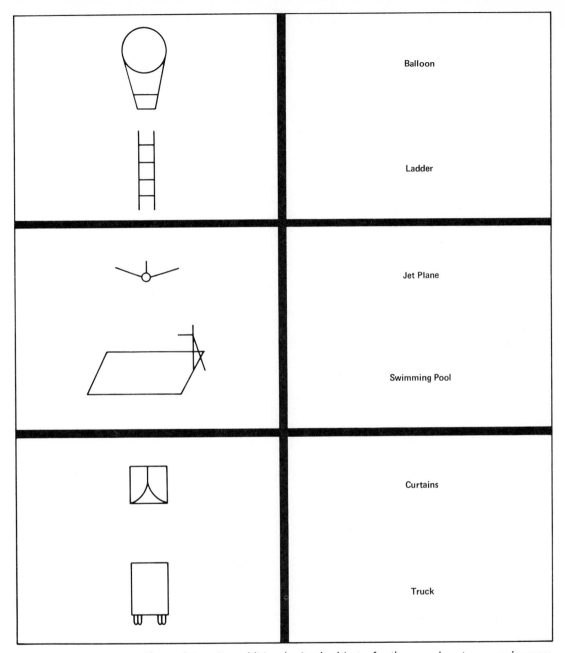

Figure 9.6. Six additional visual objects for the experiment on consciousness

INTRODUCTION

Freud's component theory of cause
Neurophysiological theory
  Energy and feedback loops
  Discharge and cathexis
  Defense
  Ego and inhibition
  Commentary on the early theory
Freud's later theory of dynamics
  Instincts as sources of energy
    Libidinal and aggressive energy
    Source, aim, object, impetus
    Capacity to act vicariously
    Instinctual force
    Forces in conflict
    Fusion of instincts
    Energy and the id
  Emotion as a source of energy
    Instincts and ideas
    Emotions and feelings
    Pleasure and unpleasure
  Anxiety and guilt as sources of energy
    Reality, neurotic, and moral anxiety
    Little Hans, a case of childhood phobia
  Principles of mental functioning
    Pleasure principle
    Reality principle
    Repetition compulsion
  Thought processes
    Primary process
      Displacement
      Condensation
    Secondary process
    Moralistic thought processes
  Ego defenses
    Repression, the dynamic repressed
    Reversal
    Turning round upon the subject
    Projection
    Reaction formation
    Sublimation
Accomplishments of the dynamic theory
  Example of application to dreams
    Importance of dreams
    Dreams as wish-fulfillment
    Condensation in dreams

Manifest and latent content
Symbolism
Representation by the opposite
Dream-work: other processes
Dora's dream and its interpretation
Critique of Freud's theory of cause
  Allport's critique
  Wolpe's critique
  Replies and counter-replies
  Direct evidence for dynamic hypotheses
    Glucksberg and King: experimental repression
    Dixon's work on perception of subliminal stimuli
    Silverman's work: subliminal stimuli trigger drives and reduce them
  Fruitfulness of Freud's theory
  Depth of the theory
Workshop 10.1   Dream symbolism
Summary

10 CHAPTER

A Causal Theory of Personality: Freud

From chapter 8 we recall that a theory of cause is one which hypothesizes either hidden causes or previously unrecognized causes of observed facts and relationships. The theory of personality we shall study in this chapter was the first to attempt to formulate the causes of behavior and experience as truly psychological causes. Many theorists before Freud had proposed causal theories invoking physiological mechanisms or assumed spiritual forces, and indeed Freud himself began with a theory that focused upon nervous mechanisms and quantities of essentially electrical energy. But he abandoned this attempt in favor of purely psychological constructs of mechanisms and energy.

We must remember also from chapter 8 that a theory of structure and a theory of cause are often quite closely interwoven, especially in psychology. Freud's theory of structure hypothesized the existence of three major agencies in the personality: the id, the ego, and the superego. Also he hypothesized that thoughts and wishes can be found in one of three different domains: the conscious, preconscious, or unconscious domains. The agencies are distributed somewhat unevenly among the three domains, so that the id is composed of thoughts and wishes entirely in the unconscious, while the ego is primarily in the preconscious and the conscious, and the superego is mainly unconscious but with important portions in the preconscious and in consciousness. Freud's theory of cause is concerned with the way in which these agencies and domains cause experience and behavior. As we shall see there is an important additional construct, namely that of psychic energy; and the theory of cause seeks to explain how psychic energy is channeled through the various parts of the structure of personality, and how it is transformed on its way to expression in experience, behavior, or even into discharge within the body. We shall study Freud's theoretical models of anxiety and dreams, of instincts, and of affects.

In chapter 9 it was pointed out that Freud worked for fifty-four years in the practice of psychoanalysis and his theories changed as new evidence came in. In this chapter we shall again present his theories in order of development, beginning with the neurophysiological theory.

Neurophysiological Theory

In his *Project for a Scientific Psychology* (1895/1966), Freud postulated the existence of three systems of neurones, *phi, psi* and *omega* for perceptual, nuclear, and conscious processes respectively. Energy, he said, could build up in the nuclear system as a result of feedback loops between that system and the glands involved in emotional response. An emotional reaction would produce energy in the nuclear system, which would then fire some special cells *(neurosecretory cells),* which in turn would deliver additional chemical excitants to the organs involved in emotional reaction, such as the adrenal gland. These organs would react further to these excitants, and would then deliver yet more energy to the nuclear system. In principle there would be no stopping this buildup of excitation in the nuclear system, because of the positive feedback. That is, the more the system responded to input signals, the more input signals would be produced by the response.

We all have had experiences of "getting worked up." The more excited we feel, the faster our heart beats, the more adrenalin is produced, and the more the other glands of emotion secrete their various chemicals. These physiological changes increase the excitement we experience, which then stimulates the glands even more. Sometimes children get "overexcited" in this way and parents have to calm them.

In similar fashion we would all become overexcited all the time if there were no mechanism to calm us down automatically. Freud proposed that a mechanism of defense prevents neural excitation in the nuclear system from building to a danger point. He called this process a *lateral cathexis,* by which he meant a sideways discharge of energy. He conceived of this defense mechanism as being similar to a sluice gate. When a given set of nuclear neurones was reaching the danger point, additional neurones could be linked into the system, thus diverting the excess energy, spreading it through the nuclear system rather than allowing it to flood into the conscious system.

Whenever instinctual needs such as hunger or sex are aroused the excitation flows first to the nuclear system. From the nuclear system energy can be discharged if certain actions are taken (such as reflex sucking for the baby or sexual intercourse for the adult). The experience of satisfaction then consists in the combination of this discharge with the perception of the object (breast or other person) and perception of the muscular movements involved in the action (motor images).

When the instinct is aroused again it will automatically send a charge of energy (*cathexis*) to the memory of the object and to the memory of the motor images. That is, the person will wish to discharge the excitation in the same actions upon the same object. In the conscious system the person experiences pleasure.

In the case of pain a similar rise in level of excitation occurs. Some means of discharge is sought, and a similar connection is established between the object which gave rise to the pain and the pressure toward discharge. In this case the discharge is achieved by avoiding the object. In the conscious system the experience is represented as the opposite of pleasure, or *unpleasure,* as Freud called it.

What special organization of the psi neurones facilitates these connections of memory images for objects and actions with rising levels of either wishful or painful excitation? Freud named this organization the *ego* and stated that its chief function was "influencing the repetition of experiences of pain and of affects" by means of *inhibition* (Freud, 1895/1966, p. 323). This inhibition was effected by the very same mechanism of lateral cathexis. For by so siphoning off excitations the direction of cathectic discharge could be guided away from one path and into another.

In this early theory we see many basic ideas which appeared in Freud's later theory, although of course they came to be formulated in different ways. Tendencies toward discharge in the nuclear system when forced by instinctual pressure, for example, later became the *pleasure principle*. Two ideas, danger due to excessive excitation and defense by means of the lateral cathexes, anticipate the later constructs of *anxiety* and of *ego defense*. We shall take up these ideas in detail below.

The early theory offers a good example of a theory of cause. Hidden entities (neurones, excitations) account for observable phenomena. We have seen perceptual and instinctual excitations converge upon the nuclear system, where, under control of special "ego" neurone sets, learning takes place and results in likes and dislikes or approach and avoidance actions toward particular environmental objects. We have seen these developments occur within the nuclear system first, where the relation to objects is chiefly that of connections with the memory images of previously perceived external objects.

Freud's Later Theory of Dynamics

Table 10.1 sets forth the main ideas in Freud's later theory of personality dynamics. We shall follow this guide in discussing the theory, examining the topics listed in the first column: sources of energy, mental functioning, thought processes, and ego defenses.

Instincts as Sources of Energy

Most scientists accept the existence of instincts in animals or of reflexes and glandular action in human beings. Freud went farther, however, and asserted that instincts provide

Table 10.1
Freud's Theory of Personality Dynamics

Main Dynamic Topics	Three Main Structural Agencies		
	Id	Ego	Superego
Sources of energy for the id, ego, and superego	Libido; energy of the destructive instincts; and impulses connected with repressed ideas	Interest, energy of self-preservative instincts (in his final theory Freud deemphasized the self-preservative instincts); segregated affect, anxiety	Aggressive energy turned against the ego; guilt
Principle of mental functioning	Pleasure principle	Reality principle	Beyond the pleasure principle: repetition compulsion
Thought process	Primary process	Secondary process	Moralistic, imperative
Ego defenses	None	Repression, transformation, discharge channelling	None

the fountain of energy from which springs all higher mental life.

Freud proposed two main groups of instincts (1923a/1962, ch. 4): the sexual and self-preservative instincts and the destructive instincts. Note the plural form of the word *instincts*. He conceived of the sexual instincts as many separate instincts (sucking, elimination, touching, looking, and so on) which ultimately fused into one under the dominance of the genital instinct. The self-preservative instinct comprised those of hunger, thirst, and the like. The destructive instincts included those of hostility toward outer enemies and also the instincts that tend toward self-destruction and death.

Freud often pointed out that the instincts were on the borderland between biological and psychological studies: they are psychophysical systems that have physical and mental sides. On the mental side, he referred to the mental energy associated with sexual instincts as *libido* (meaning pleasure or lust); the mental energy of the self-preservative instincts he called *interest* (Freud, 1917/1963, pp. 350, 351, 411-413, 414, fn. 2). Energies of the destructive instincts appear to be properly called *aggressive energy* (see Freud 1933/1964, p. 105).

Freud analyzed instincts as to their source, aim, object, and impetus. For example, the secretions from sex glands would be a *source* or bodily origin of sexual energy, acting as a stimulus which is internal to the body and which cannot be escaped through flight. The *aim* of an instinct is to eliminate the tension or otherwise remove the condition in the source which gives rise to the stimulus (by achieving a discharge of substances in orgasm, for example). The *object* of an instinct is whatever makes the aim possible (a sexual partner, for instance). In addition, every instinct has an *impetus* or impulse, which is "its motor element, the amount of force, or the measure of demand upon energy, which it represents" (Freud 1915a/1959, p. 65).

Freud states that the early component instincts of sex "have in a high degree the capacity to act vicariously for one another and that they can readily change their objects" (1915a/1959, p. 69). What does this mean? Consider the components of looking and touching. "Capacity to act vicariously" means, for example, that simply looking at another child's sex organs can provide the child with a satisfying alternative to touching them. One part-instinct's behavior can satisfy the aim of another part-instinct. As an example of changing the object, if touching the mother's breast becomes forbidden, then touching some other part of her body (such as cheeks) may come to serve the same aim. This being forbidden, then touching some part of her clothing may satisfy, in which case the clothing becomes the object. Taken to extremes, this vicarious action is the way fetishes are developed; as in the case of a man who, in sexual excitation, can reach a climax only when holding a woman's shoe.

Instinctual force, when dammed up for lack of satisfactory expression, can develop apparently dangerous strength. Aggression turned against the self as in melancholia "rages against the ego with merciless violence, as if it had taken possession of the whole of the sadism available in the person concerned" (Freud, 1923a/1962, p. 43). In Freud's view, then, instinct was a biological powerhouse, a source of mental energy which made itself felt psychologically with the greatest possible urgency. Have you ever been so hungry you would eat almost anything? The group of people who survived a 1973 airplane crash in the Andes did so only because they ate the flesh of their dead companions. Have you ever been in a public place needing desperately to urinate and not been able to find a suitable place? Worse, perhaps, have you gotten to such a place and found it occupied? Such examples help us understand the true meaning of instinctual force or impetus. We feel it impelling us to a very particular kind of behavior.

Strong instincts produce strong conflict. Imagine that certain instinctual pressures are either frightening or abhorrent to the person. The fears would be like wanting to urinate yet not wanting to do it in the middle of a crowded auditorium with everyone looking at you. It would be a state of intense conflict. Freud said that hysterical and obsessional neuroses can be traced in all cases to a "conflict between the claims of sexuality and those of the ego" (1915a/1959, p. 67). Of course, the patient was not aware of this conflict until it was made conscious through psychoanalysis. But would you expect an absence of awareness to make the conflict any less intense? If you succeed in not thinking about it, does that make the pressure of urine in your bladder go away? No. Not thinking about an internal stimulus does not make it go away.

Several instincts may come to have the same object. For example, looking and touching and sucking might all converge upon the breast as object. Similarly, aggressive and sexual impulses converge in the "sadistic component of the sexual instinct . . ." (Freud, 1923a/1962, p. 31). Freud describes this as a *fusion* of the several instincts, and suggests that many behavioral manifestations of instincts are the result of fusions. Ordinary adult sexuality results from the fusion of many part-instincts, according to Freud. For example, loving and biting become fused in a love-bite.

Largely an agency of unconscious ideas and affects, the id draws its energy from instincts and associated emotions and from instinctual ideas which are *repressed*. We shall discuss repression more fully below; for the moment, it means simply that the relevant ideas were so obnoxious to the person's ego that they were not allowed to penetrate to consciousness. Instead they remain unconscious, continuously striving for expression somehow, even in the form of neurotic symptoms, if necessary. The repressed instincts therefore provide a continuous source of energy in the id.

Emotion as a Source of Energy

Instincts are represented in mental life by both ideas and emotions (which are often called *affects* in Freud's writings). "If the instinct did not attach itself to an idea or manifest itself as an affective state, we could know nothing about it," Freud said (1915c/1959, p. 109). He made it clear that the impetus of an instinct cannot become conscious: only an idea representing the instinct can be either conscious or unconscious. Only an idea can be a mental phenomenon. Once the idea representing an instinct is aroused it triggers certain motor and glandular responses in the body: these are the emotions associated with the instinct.

The instinct, then, has its source in some bodily condition (such as secretions of the sex glands or contractions of the stomach). When this source is aroused the relevant idea also is aroused in the id. This idea then triggers another bodily reaction, namely the emotion. (Incidentally this is a very clear example of a physical process leading to a *psychophysical* process: idea triggers bodily reaction.)

Emotions end up being experienced as feelings. That is, the emotion itself is physical process, and the feeling is the consciousness of that emotion. Freud wrote that emotions "correspond to processes of discharge, the final expression of which is perceived as feeling" (1915c/1959, p. 111).

Though feelings come in many different shades, Freud believed that they are basically of two general kinds which he called *pleasure* and *unpleasure*. Feelings of pain, fear, and anxiety would be among those of unpleasure. Feelings of love and happiness and joy would be among those of pleasure.

Freud maintained that the ego gets its energy in part from the self-preservative instincts and in part from the emotions, particularly from anxiety. In his final theory he emphasized mainly segregated emotional energy. As Rapaport has pointed out (1967, p. 439), both the ego and the superego use emotional energies which have somehow been siphoned off from their original instinctual connection and held in reserve. The ego and the superego use these reserve energies from emotional sources when needed to exert control over behavior and experience. Primarily, the ego uses anxiety and the superego uses guilt, a special kind of anxiety about the reactions of one's own conscience to actual or anticipated behaviors.

Anxiety and Guilt as Sources of Energy

Freud became aware of the importance of anxiety quite early in his career. In many cases of acute anxiety he found that the patients engaged in *coitus interruptus* as a method of birth control; sometimes there were other causes of extreme sexual inhibition (1893b/ 1966). It seemed there might be a connection between sexual energy and anxiety. Freud suggested that when sexual expression is blocked the libido is siphoned off and transformed into anxiety. This anxiety is then used by the ego to help maintain the inhibition.

Freud, of course, recognized that anxiety is often related to fear of real dangers. He recognized the prototype of all anxiety reactions in the emotional turmoil of birth. At birth the organism is suddenly deprived of its accustomed sources of sustenance, is subjected to violent pressures and movements, and is pushed out into the world and slapped into yelling and breathing for its life. Birth is an event which must challenge every resource of the organism. It is a situation of enormous change, enormous threat, and enormous mobilization of the body's mechanisms for self-protection. Anxiety is also a mobilization of mechanisms for self-protection, the pulse increases as does the rate of breathing, and other changes occur throughout the body.

Three Kinds of Anxiety. In his final model of anxiety (1923a/1962; 1926/1963) Freud believed that it was chiefly a function of the ego. The ego, he said, faces three opposing forces: the external world, the id, and the superego. From the dangers of the external world the ego has cause for *reality anxiety*. From the id the ego experiences dangers, especially from repressed instincts, leading to *neurotic anxiety*. Neurotic anxiety is based on internal conflict from which there is no escape: no escape from one's own instincts and no escape from one's own abhorrence of them. Finally, the ego also experiences the criticisms of the superego as dangerous: they produce *moral anxiety* or *guilt feelings*. The ego thus is faced with three kinds of anxiety: reality anxiety from the outer world, neurotic anxiety from the conflict with repressed instincts, and moral anxiety from the conflict with the superego.

Freud believed that all normal human beings experience these three kinds of anxiety. But when the total amount of anxiety experienced becomes too great for normal functioning then some kind of psychological disturbance, often neurosis of some kind, results. If the predominant anxiety is neurotic, hysteria or anxiety reactions result. If the predominant anxiety is moral, obsessional neuroses or melancholia develop. In obsessional neurosis the person is preoccupied with particular thoughts or with recurrent impulses, such as the impulse to wash the hands and keep washing them; or the impulse to set every little thing just exactly straight and in its place. In melancholia the person is desperately sorrowful, depressed, possibly preoccupied with the thought of his or her own unworthiness and with thoughts of suicide. In both obsessional neurosis and melancholia the role of guilt is clear: driving the person either to acts of cleansing and expiation or to acts of self-destruction. In both cases the part played by aggressive instincts directed by the superego against the self is also clear.

Freud also commented on the ego's use of anxiety to ward off even greater dangers. Many phobias (intense fears of particular things, like snakes, spiders, high places, or open spaces) serve to protect the ego against a more dangerous cause for anxiety, such as those involving powerful instincts. "The phobia is erected like a frontier fortification against the anxiety," he wrote (1900/1953, p. 581). And again, "animal phobias of children are believed to protect them against still worse fears, such as those associated with libidinal strivings towards parents" (Freud, 1915b/1959, p. 94).

Box 10.1 presents a case of childhood phobia.

Principles of Mental Functioning

We have already seen that the processes of the unconscious press toward discharge regardless of reality. Freud called this overall tendency the *pleasure principle:*

> These processes strive toward gaining pleasure; from any operation which might cause unpleasantness ('pain') mental activity draws back (repression). Our nocturnal dreams, our waking tendency to shut out painful impressions, are remnants of the supremacy of this principle and proofs of its power (Freud, 1911/1959, p. 14).

The pleasure principle is the desire to satisfy every need immediately and to enjoy every pleasure. Presumably in a baby, before the ego and superego are developed, the pleasure-principle is dominant. But it continues to be powerful in adults, Freud says, even though no longer dominant. We can detect the operation of this principle in dreams and in our tendency to avoid looking at or thinking about painful things.

The pleasure principle would tend to produce imaginary gratifications in the absence of a really satisfying object for an instinct, even as starving men may hallucinate the sight or smell of food. The same principle determines that unfulfilled desires lead to discharge in emotional expression (as in a temper tantrum). It is seen also in our tendency even as adults to retain whatever gives us pleasure as long as possible, and to give it up only with difficulty. Even after our thinking processes are well dominated by the need to adapt to reality we reserve a part for *fantasy,* the make-believe of childhood games and of adult daydreaming.

Despite hallucinating, the absence of a real satisfying object for an instinct inevitably leads to frustration, and so the mind had to recognize and cope with reality:

> A new principle of mental functioning was thus introduced; what was conceived of was no longer that which was pleasant, but that which was real, even if it should be unpleasant. This institution of the reality-principle proved a momentous step (Freud, 1911/1959, p. 14).

So far as our instincts are concerned, they strive only for the pleasure of satisfaction: the pleasure principle. But as the ego develops, its task is to take full account of the real world, to evaluate its real potential for providing satisfaction, and, if necessary, to "exert itself to alter" the circumstances out there so that they *would* provide satisfaction. This is the *reality principle*: the tendency to appraise reality accurately and modify it as necessary. We might say that the pleasure principle is *expressive,* while the reality principle is *active.*

Box 10.1
Little Hans: A Case of Childhood Phobia

Freud reported several cases of animal phobia in children, one of which (1909/1959) concerned a five-year-old boy named Hans. He became afraid of going out for walks, and also especially worried around bedtime because he thought a horse would come in his room and bite him. Hans didn't want to go out for walks because he thought a horse might bite him in the street.

The history revealed that a second child had been born to the family not long before. Hans was in the house when the baby was born, and noted that a) his mother's stomach was thinner after than before; b) there was blood in the bed pan after the birth; and c) his father's stork story was unbelievable.

Hans at that time believed that everybody had a penis, including his mother. He had not seen his mother's but he knew where it ought to be and believed that the blood had somehow come out of it. He said that blood did not come out of **his** penis.

Hans was very much interested in his own penis and masturbated regularly. He also had fantasies about examining his mother naked. He struggled with the problem of where babies come from. Presumably this problem was complicated by the fact that his mother had told him his own penis would be cut off if he played with it.

Hans had a close relationship with his mother, spending much time alone with her when father was away, especially when they stayed at a resort. For her part she was very loving and tender toward him. She would take him into her bed sometimes. She also was in the habit of assisting him when he needed to urinate: she undid his buttons and took out his penis.

His relationship with his father was also warm. The two loved each other and played together when possible. But yet his father would not allow Hans to get in bed with his mother when he was around. Also Hans knew that his father was deeply implicated some way in the birth of his sister.

Freud reasoned as follows. Hans had experi-enced sexual excitation in his penis when thinking about his own penis, his mother's penis, and the birth of the baby. Though unclear, these ideas would involve some vague sense of copulating with his mother. But this would entail the threat of his penis being cut off. Sensing also his father's role in the birth, and knowing his father's prohibitions against Hans getting into bed with his mother, Hans attributed this threat to his father. He was also very angry with his father for interfering, for putting barriers between him and his mother. The anger, of course, was in conflict with his love for his father. Thus Hans had a conflict in his attitude toward his mother (erotic striving versus fear of loss) and toward his father (hate versus love). He resolved these conflicts through repression of the erotic ideas about mother and of the hostile ideas about father.

As a consequence he was left consciously feeling anxious for no apparent reason. One day on a walk he told the maid that he wanted to go home, wanted to see his mother for some reason. The reason was that he was, he said, afraid a horse would bite him. He had earlier heard a man tell his child not to put his finger in the horse's mouth in case the horse bit it off. The castration theme is evident. Immediately before the first signs of his phobia, Hans had also seen a horse fall down in the street. There was no doubt from what he said and did (such as playing a game which involved biting his father) that Hans identified the horse with his father (Freud, 1909/1959, p. 266).

We have seen that father was now a dangerous rival, in Hans's mind. Add to that, the repression of Hans's own hostility toward his father was not very successful. It required some additional reinforcement to keep it under repression. This was achieved by **projection**: the hostile wishes were attributed to the father himself, and hence also to the horse. Now the horse was really after Hans! Not only on the street if he dared go out (which he did not, except for great coaxing and protection from his mother), but even breaking through into Hans's bedroom at night! The horse would somehow get in and bite him.

Freud observed self-destructive behaviors —people causing themselves pain—both in psychoanalytic treatment and elsewhere. To explain these facts Freud hypothesized a *death instinct*, "beyond the pleasure-principle." That is, in light of the evidence of *masochism* (inflicting pain on oneself, or having someone else do it); in light of the *resistance* many patients show whenever they make a slight improvement; in light of the *repetitions* of painful childhood experiences in the transference phenomena seen in almost every case of psychoanalytic treatment; in light of these and other evidences Freud concluded that another principle of mental functioning existed: the *repetition compulsion*. In part a manifestation of the death instinct, the repetition compulsion refers to a tendency to repeat painful experiences.

The principles of mental functioning refer to *major* characteristics or directions of the flow of ideas and feelings. They refer to three broad classes of results our thought processes achieve: pleasure, useful change in relation to reality, and repeated pain. In summary, there are three principles:

1. The tendency to achieve pleasurable discharge of tension due to instinctual energy and to avoid pain is the *pleasure principle*.
2. The tendency to appraise and if necessary alter environmental reality so as to maximize instinctual and derivative satisfactions in the real world is the *reality principle*.
3. The tendency to repeat painful experiences is the *repetition-compulsion*.

We should notice that the repetition compulsion is not merely "beyond" the pleasure principle; it is actually opposed to it. It is paradoxical, perhaps, but so is much of actual human experience. People do strive for pleasure or happiness; yet the same people are apt to do the same old things that have brought them pain before.

Thought Processes

Each mental agency consists of thought processes and associated drives and affects having a particular quality. The id is the first agency, out of which all others are differentiated. It is the domain of primitive instincts, each striving for satisfaction as soon as it is aroused (the pleasure principle).

Primary Process Thinking. Freud proposed that thought processes in the id would lead directly to some form of gratification regardless of realistic possibility or logical sequence. Fulfilling a wish by hallucinating the appropriate object would be a typical type of thought in the id, which is unconscious. Freud refers to the id's thoughts as *primary process thinking*, the unrealistic thinking of the unconscious mind. It is not logical or reasonable, it is not sensible or ordered in time or logical sequence. It takes fantasy for fact, just as hallucination is accepted as a goal object for a wish. It is symbolic thinking, often using some concrete visible object to represent the person's wishes or fears. For example, in chapter 9 one of Freud's cases was described in which a boy fantasized a sickle lying on a chessboard; it represented his wish to castrate his father. An example of fear being represented in a concrete object is given in the case of Hans described in box 10.1, where the horse represented Hans's fear of castration by his father.

Primary process thinking is primary in the sense of being the earliest kind of thinking in the child's development. Recall that a baby is dominated by the pleasure principle before the structures of ego and superego are formed. Its thought processes likewise tend to move without logic or reason toward gratification of impulses. Freud says that the primary processes are "residues of a phase of development in which they were the only kind of mental processes" (Freud, 1911/1959, p. 14). This means that the primary processes are ways of thinking which characterized us when we were very, very young, before we learned to keep our thoughts logically ordered and in touch with reality. It is also implied that such thought processes do not simply vanish when we grow up. They continue to characterize thinking in our unconscious mind. They show up in our dreams, in fantasies, in slips of the tongue. They are involved in the production of symptoms. For example, in chapter 9 we mentioned another of Freud's cases in which a young girl complained of pains and a feeling that something was sticking into her body, moving forward and backward and shaking her whole body. The symbolism for sexual intercourse is obvious even though the girl and her mother had no insight into it at all. Here again the unconscious wish was expressed in a concrete, tangible experience.

Primary process, as we have said, is the kind of thinking that goes on in the unconscious mind. It is essentially irrational. This does not mean, however, that it is without purpose. On the contrary, it is intensely goal oriented. Nor is it confined to goals of instinct gratification. Although primary process thinking often does express wish fulfillment for sexual or aggressive aims, we must remember that there are also unconscious portions of the ego, responsible for resistance, for repression, and for the defense mechanisms. In such functions of the ego we find primary process thinking employed in the service of keeping instinctual impulses under cover of various disguises. We shall now consider displacement and condensation, two of the basic forms taken by primary process thinking as it enters into the service of ego defense.

Displacement. Displacement is a process in which one idea is deprived of its energy, or emotional charge, and the charge is transferred to another idea. The result is that the receiving idea seems to be given too much importance. The emotion attached to it is all out of proportion.

Freud reports, for example, on the case of Dora, who developed a hysterical neurosis and was sent to Freud for treatment (1905a/1959, p. 38). When Dora was fourteen a married friend of the family invited her to join himself and his wife at his shop, where they would be able to get a good view of a parade. The man arranged to leave his wife at home and dismiss all the employees, however, so that he and the girl were alone. Closing the shutters on the windows, he suddenly took hold of Dora, pressed her to him, and kissed her on the lips. She felt disgusted, tore herself away, and fled. She never mentioned this episode to anyone else.

Freud thinks it is unlikely that a normal, healthy girl would feel disgust in such a situation. More likely, he says, is a feeling of sexual excitement, especially if it was the first time anyone had kissed her, and particularly if the man were young and good-looking, as Freud knew he was. So how was it that Dora felt only disgust? Freud proposes that Dora actually did have a genital sensation in response to the kiss, but this emotional energy was *displaced*. In her unconscious mind the energy associated with her genital sensation was transferred to her sensations of being kissed. The transfer would go between two ideas of similar body parts, namely from a sensation localized at the entrance to the vaginal canal to a sensation localized at the entrance to the alimentary canal (the mouth and throat). In this way, Freud maintains, Dora's experience would be one of disgust rather than sexual arousal, for the feeling of disgust is localized at the top of the alimentary canal, as many everyday expressions suggest ("Yuch!", "I could throw up," and so on. The earliest form of disgust is seen in the baby's spitting out something it finds unpleasant).

The primary process nature of Dora's thinking in this episode is illustrated by another aspect of her reaction. For some time afterward, even while talking with Freud about this earlier episode, Dora said she could still feel the pressure of the man's body on the upper part of her own. Freud said this continued feeling in the absence of a relevant physical stimulus was a sensory hallucination. In another connection Dora reported that she always tried to avoid walking past any man who was talking eagerly or affectionately with a lady. Freud reasoned that both the hallucinatory sensation and this avoidance of strange couples on the street could be attributed to the same cause. He reconstructed the kissing episode as follows: When the man embraced her she also felt the pressure of his erection, and the idea of this perception was an additional source of sexual stimulation to her and hence an additional source of anxiety. This idea was therefore rapidly repressed, and its affective energy was displaced to the idea of pressure from his upper body on her chest. Freud reasoned also that only a very intense charge of energy could account for so extreme a symptom as a continued sensory hallucination. The idea of mere chest contact probably would have insufficient energy attached. It required the addition of an intense energy, displaced from below, in order to give it the strength of a hallucination. The memory of his erect penis pressing against her would be so dangerous to Dora that its energy was partly removed by displacement upward to the memory of chest contact. And to prevent any recurrence of sexual stimulation from such an event she avoided even strange couples where there was the possibility she might see evidence of a man's erection.

Condensation. Condensation is the second main form of primary process thinking. Freud writes, "By the process of displacement one idea may surrender to another the whole volume of its cathexis; by that of condensation it may appropriate the whole cathexis of sev-

eral other ideas" (Freud, 1915c/1959, p. 119). *Condensation,* then, is a process in which displacements occur from several ideas onto one idea. The receiving idea gathers up the affective charges of several other ideas. The case of Hans provides us with a good example of condensation.

In the case of Little Hans (box 10.1), cathexes of several forbidden instinctual ideas were condensed upon the idea of a horse biting the boy: the idea of sexual movements (big animal with big penis falling down), of masturbation, of rivalry and antagonism toward father, and of threatened castration. It was not forbidden to be afraid of a horse.

In the book *Psychopathology of Everyday Life,* Freud attributed many everyday mistakes to the working of the primary process. Slips of the tongue, forgetting of intentions, silly accidents, and many other similar incidents were seen to be due to condensations based on some underlying conflict (Freud, 1901/1960).

One particularly striking experience that many people have is trying to use their own key to enter a friend's house, thereby expressing an unconscious wish to be "at home" there (p. 163). Another example is forgetting a date with a boyfriend or girlfriend, or being late for it and explaining that you were "tied up with some business." The other person correctly senses the real cause, which is lowered regard or waning attraction (Freud, 1901/1960, p. 156, fn. 1).

Secondary Process. Suppose you are going for a picnic. You choose a spot to head for, noting of course that all concerned will be able to get there relatively easily. You arrange to get the various items of the menu that you plan, and especially see to it that there is enough to go round, and that sufficient plates, cups, and other needed utensils are available. Such thinking is typical of secondary process thinking: planning, judging, and adjusting actions to reality in time and space and social customs and convenience. By contrast, dreaming of a picnic at which you are elected mayor and given the keys to a candy cottage exemplifies the primary process.

Moralistic Thought Processes. We have already seen that the superego can be destructive toward the ego in its criticisms. There is no special process of thought that characterizes the superego in an explicit theoretical way. However, its ideas are taken from the incorporation of parental prohibitions and imperatives. They consist of ideas such as "You ought to . . . ," "You should not have . . . ," "You are bad for saying (doing, thinking, wanting) such things." The ideas are therefore restricted to moralistic, imperative, or condemnatory processes.

Ego Defenses

Ego defenses are mental mechanisms whereby the ego protects itself from unacceptable, anxiety-producing ideas. In his first writings on the "defense-neuropsychoses," Freud (1894/1959) stressed that in many patients of previously good mental health their onset of hysteria, obsessional neurosis, or hallucinatory psychosis appeared to have been precipitated by a chain of three preceding events. First, they had had some thoughts or feelings which they found repulsive. Second, they had determined to forget it, "to 'push the thing out', not to think of it, to suppress it" (Freud, 1894/1959, p. 62). Third, the attempt at conscious suppression did not succeed, but led to the various pathological developments they were complaining of.

Freud offered several examples of this sequence. In one case of obsessional thoughts a young girl constantly had the thought occurring to her that she was responsible for crimes she read about in the newspaper, whether counterfeiting or murder. Anxiously she would worry whether she had in fact committed each crime. In this case the first event proved to have been a feeling of sexual desire which led to masturbation, for which she felt intensely guilty. Second, she determined not to allow such thoughts to enter her head again (nor of course to masturbate again). But her effort to suppress these thoughts was not successful and she continued to masturbate. Eventually the obsession developed that she had committed a dreadful crime, thus completing the sequence of three events (Freud, 1894/1959, pp. 69-70).

In cases of hysteria the attempt at suppression gave way to a withdrawal of cathexis or energy from the offending ideas and the diversion of that energy into some form of bodily expression. Freud called this a process of *conversion.* The associated neurotic disorder is still known as *conversion hysteria* (Kolb, 1968, p. 471). In cases of phobia, of which Little Hans is a good example, the anxiety aroused by the repulsive thought would be split off and become attached to some other ideas.

How does this splitting off of the energy or affect of an idea really accomplish anything that serves the purpose of defense, or the original conscious purpose of putting the idea out of one's mind? Freud suggested that the purpose would be approximately achieved if the idea could be transformed from a strong one into a weak one, because then it would "make practically no demands on the work of association" (1959/1894, p. 63). That is, it would not force itself into associative networks of conscious thought.

Freud continued to assert that the essence of repression was precisely a *"withdrawal of energic cathexis"* (Freud, 1959/1915b, p. 93), and that its chief function was that of *"rejecting and keeping something out of consciousness"* (1959/1915b, p. 86).

But more and more he came to realize that it was precisely the *keeping* out of consciousness that had theoretical importance, as well as clinical consequences. That is, once an idea is repressed it must remain repressed; it must be kept in a state of repression. Thus there is an action and also a state of repression. Freud distinguished between *primal repression,* which is the initial action of denying an instinctual idea access to consciousness; and *repression proper,* which is a continued battery of denials directed toward all the ideas which, by more or less closely associated linkages, can lead to the original repressed idea.

In his later work on the theory of repression Freud came to emphasize the activity of repressed ideas:

> Moreover, it is a mistake to emphasize only the rejection which operates from the side of consciousness upon what is to be repressed. We have to consider just as much the attraction exercised by what was originally repressed upon everything with which it can establish a connection. Probably the tendency to repression would fail of its purpose if these forces did not cooperate, if there were not something previously repressed ready to assimilate that which is rejected from consciousness (Freud, 1915b/1959, p. 87).

This conception of a *dynamic repressed* has two sides. On the one hand it accounts for the spread of motivated forgetting to ideas and impressions that seem only remotely connected with the originally repulsive ideas. On the other hand it touches again upon the active, purposive work of the repressed in searching out and fastening upon peculiarly appropriate connections in the formation of symptoms in neurotic and psychosomatic illness. A good example is the already mentioned case of the young girl who experienced peculiar sensations of something shaking her inside.

Another mode of defense described by Freud was that of *reversal,* which serves to create a defensive transformation of instincts. The impulse to see the parents' naked bodies becomes forbidden and is transformed into an impulse to show one's own naked body to them. This example is the transformation from *scoptophilia,* which is prohibited in children (and also in adults as "peeping Tom's"), into *exhibitionism,* which is not prohibited in children. Notice what is reversed. It goes from "I want to look at them" to "I want them to look at me." Both have "I want"; the first makes ego actively looking at them as object, while the second makes them active in looking at ego as object. In fact the transformation is from an *active* to a *passive* experience (Freud, 1915a/1959, pp. 69-73).

Yet another form of defense is that of *turning round upon the subject* (Freud, 1915a/1959, p. 69). Freud's observations of clinical cases indicated that *masochists* (people who obtain perverted sexual pleasure from being tortured) had somehow turned their own *sadism* (delight in inflicting severe pain) round upon themselves. He pointed out that the masochist's pleasure consisted largely in the very "*act* of torturing when this is being applied to himself" (Freud, 1915/1959, p. 70).

In *projection* there is a kind of *turning round upon the object.* Freud pointed out that differentiation between the inner and outer world, between ego and reality, occurs in the infant as a result of harsh experiences, collisions of the pleasure principle with immovable frustrations. Thereafter pleasure is always associated with ego and pain with the outer world. Whenever an instinctual impulse arises within the person which is unacceptable or repulsive to the ego, that impulse is a source of pain (anxiety) too. One way to defend the ego against this pain is to project the idea of its source, to "[thrust it] forth upon the external world . . ." (Freud, 1915a/1959, p. 78). Instead of recognizing his own hatred toward his father, the son projects this hatred and believes that the father hates him. Extreme developments of projection lay the basis for the *paranoid* personality: hostile suspiciousness toward everyone.

In *reaction formation* the ego's control functions are employed in the service of defense against instinct-related anxiety. In many ways reaction formation is an extreme form of defense and also provides for frequently observed alterations in the ego and in character. It consists of a change in the ego which is specifically directed toward the inhibition of instinctual impulses. The ego takes on those characteristics which are precisely opposite to what would appear if the instinct were satisfied. In place of a forbidden love there appears a persistent hostility toward the other person; in place of a sadistic impulse toward a loved person there appears an excessive and fussy concern (Freud, 1915b/1959, p. 96).

The mechanisms of defense are not mutually exclusive, so that two or more may be employed against any particular instinctual impulse. Repression is of course the central defense and also the one most responsible for subsequent problems in personal adjustment. By contrast *sublimation* (Freud, 1915a/1959, p. 69) has been described as the only truly successful form of defense, since it provides a socially acceptable transformation of the *aim* of the instinct (Freud, 1914a/1959, p. 51). That is, the instinct comes to receive a new form of gratification, one which is not only not forbidden but often even encouraged. Hostility comes to be expressed in the form of fierce competitive spirit in sports (American football provides a prime example). Scoptophilia comes to be included in art appreciation. There is nothing reprehensible about enjoyment of fine sculptures, even if they are of nude bodies. But with such appreciation a little bit of satisfaction in sexual looking can be mixed in hardly noticeable form.

Accomplishments of the Dynamic Theory: Freud's Theoretical Model of Dreams

Freud's theory of cause provided interesting and useful explanations of many psychological phenomena, including slips of the tongue, humor, and many symptoms and other signs of mental disorder. In all cases the basic idea is that some repressed impulse is making itself felt, is being expressed in a disguised form. Since everyone dreams, and most people recall some dreams, the psychological dynamics of dreams have broad interest. Accordingly we shall give a brief presentation of Freud's theoretical model of dreams and then give an example of his work using the model in psychotherapy. The example will be a dream of considerable importance in the life of Dora, whose case was briefly mentioned above.

First we must say something about the general importance of dreams. For thousands of years people have assumed that dreams have supernatural or prophetic significance. Joseph in the Biblical story dreamed that he and his brothers were binding sheaves in a field when his sheaf suddenly stood upright and the sheaves of his brothers gathered round and bowed down to it. When he told the dream to his brothers, they interpreted it to mean that he would gain power over them, a fate which they sought to avoid by arranging for him to be carried off to Egypt in slavery (Genesis 37: 5-9). When in Egypt, Joseph found that he could accurately interpret the prophetic meaning of dreams. Once he even forecast the exact day on which a baker would be unexpectedly hanged. After this episode came to the attention of Pharaoh, Joseph was called upon to give interpretations of dreams concerning the future of Egypt. As a result of these forecasts, which were more accurate than some modern economic forecasts, Joseph was able to recommend programs of conservation and storage which helped Egypt survive a number of natural disasters. The Bible has many other accounts of dreams which have a prophetic function.

Dreams have also been thought to reveal the inner states of a person. In ancient Greece, for instance, Aesculapian priests would instruct a patient to sleep and have a dream. In the morning they asked the patient to tell the dream, and from it they would make a diagnosis of the disorder and prescribe a plan of treatment.

Thus dreams have been seen as media through which supernatural forces communicate with human beings; and they have been seen as ways in which the inner condition of a person can be revealed. They have also been considered as meaningless jumbles of mental activity during sleep, fragments that have no significance at all, not worthy of interpreting along any dimension: "just a dream."

By contrast, Freud suggested that dream materials come from the unconscious and should be especially good examples of primary process thinking. Also, dreams should be governed by the pleasure principle. In short, his theoretical model of dreams stated that every dream is a fulfillment of an unconscious wish. The unconscious wish is the central cause of the dream.

Accordingly, every dream is expected to represent the satisfaction of an instinctual impulse. Freud gives several good examples, including one from his own experience in which eating anchovies at night makes him thirsty and he dreams of drinking lots and lots of water, whereupon he wakes up (Freud, 1900/1953, p. 123). The first hypothesis, then, is that every dream fulfills an unconscious wish.

Second, every dream is likely, upon deeper analysis, to reveal more than one wish which is being satisfied in the dream: that is, every dream contains condensations. In particular a wish from very early childhood often provides the real source of energy for the dream

(Freud, 1900/1953, p. 191). In his famous case of Dora, Freud wrote: "A regularly formed dream stands, as it were, upon two legs, one of which is in contact with the main and current exciting cause, and the other with some momentous occurrence in the years of childhood" (Freud, 1905a/1959, p. 86).

Third, the dream as it appears to the dreamer, or as it is told by the dreamer, consists of a certain set of characters, properties, and plot. These form the *manifest content* of the dream: the obvious, known, conscious contents of the dream. But the psychoanalytic method of association and interpretation reveals *another* set of characters, properties, and plot, this is the *latent content* of the dream. The unconscious wish is part of this latent content, a wish that is unacceptable to the ego.

Departing from all previous approaches to the interpretation of dreams, Freud bases his solution for the meaning of a given dream upon this latent content, not the manifest content. As he stated, a new problem was now posed for scientific research, the problem "of investigating the relations between the manifest content of dreams and the latent dream thoughts, and of tracing out the processes by which the latter have been changed into the former" (Freud, 1900/1953, p. 277). In essence, these processes are displacement and condensation, the primary processes whereby the unacceptable latent wish is transformed into some acceptable disguise in the manifest content.

Whenever the latent thoughts are repulsive to the ego the connection between these thoughts and the manifest content which comes to dream consciousness must be obscured. Distortion occurs so that the real meaning of the dream is disguised even to the dreamer. The energy which is displaced from objectionable ideas runs along channels of association which Freud compared to railway lines and switching points (1905a/1959, pp. 87, 99). The points of origin would be a group of ideas associated with forbidden or dangerous impulses; the points of destination would be acceptable ideas which nevertheless are related to the original ideas by definite chains of association. For example, sexual desire might be symbolized by fire; other symbols might represent other experiences.

Dreams are often filled with strange events and things that are hard to understand. Freud proposed that many of these elements of a dream are actually symbols. He showed that many unconscious ideas are given a symbolic representation in the dream.

Often these very same symbols can be found in myths, tales, and jokes. So in the individual case one has to be very careful that a particular element (such as a dagger) really is standing for something else (like a penis) in that person's mind (Freud, 1900/1953, p. 353). Bearing these cautions in mind, though, Freud mentions a number of frequent connections between symbol and unconscious idea. The King and Queen or the President and First Lady often stand for the parents of the dreamer; long, sharp objects represent the penis; boxes, purses, openings of all kinds stand for the female sex organs; walls or the outside of a house over which the dreamer is climbing seem to repeat the childhood memories of climbing on parents; landscapes, plants, and so forth stand for the human body; small animals represent children—insects, fleas, and so on being undesirable like unwanted younger siblings; flowers stand for sexual reproduction, even as they in fact are responsible for bearing seeds of the plants they adorn (Freud, 1900/1953, pp. 353-357).

Among the many examples provided by Freud, one concerned a young woman's dream of walking down the street with a peculiarly shaped hat on. The middle part was bent up, and the two side pieces hung down, one hang-

ing lower than the other. She walked past some young officers, thinking to herself that there was nothing they could do to her. Freud interpreted the hat as the male genital. At first she denied it and then insisted that actually she had not described the hat in that way. She was silent for a bit. Then she asked why it could be that her husband had one testicle lower than the other (Freud, 1900/1953, pp. 360-361).

Often a given latent thought is so objectionable that it must be *represented by its opposite*: as when a dream of joy in the purity of a lily represents latent thoughts of guilt and disgust with self (Freud, 1900/1953, p. 319).

The work that transforms the latent thoughts into the manifest dream content is called *dream-work*. Through displacement of energy and condensation the paths of association are used like the rails of a railway system. What begins as a boxcar of fury and a tankcar of fear, for instance, may be shunted (displaced) both onto the same-switching-point (condensation) at a station named "Earthquake." Still in need of work, the combined load is now put on a turntable (reversal into the opposite) and emerges as a gentle pastoral scene.

In the psychoanalytic method, the patient tells a dream as he or she recalls it. The analyst asks the patient what comes to mind in association with the dream, what memories seem to be related. If particular parts of the dream are omitted but seem significant the analyst may specifically ask what a specific image could stand for. The analyst may suggest an interpretation to the patient for particular parts of the dream and then for the whole meaning of the dream if possible.

Box 10.2 gives the dream of Dora, one of Freud's patients. We have seen this dream earlier, in chapter 9 and in this chapter. The manifest content of the dream is shown in the left-hand column. Read this column first to

Box 10.2

A Dream Which Recurred Three Nights in a Row: From the Case of Dora, Age about Sixteen

Manifest Content	Dora Remembers Related Events	Freud Interprets Latent Content	
		From Recent Events	**From Childhood Events**
"A house was on fire.	Father said he was afraid of fire in the wooden house they had come to stay in.	Clearly he anticipated fire, so Dora blamed him for putting her in danger. The hostile impulse attached to this idea is forbidden. So the idea of father's endangering her is **reversed into its opposite:** he is saving her.	
"My father was standing beside my bed and woke me up.	H. K., a family friend, and the owner of the house, had made a seductive proposal in the morning. In the afternoon she awoke from her rest to find H. K. standing by her bedside.	In the dream the image of father is **substituted** for that of H. K. as standing by her bedside. It means that she has similar feelings toward both men.	Father standing by her bed to wake her up to urinate. This early event made the specific substitution of father-by-bed for H. K.-by-bed possible.
"I dressed myself quickly.	She obtained a key to lock the room, but then found it missing. She decided to dress quickly in the mornings in case H. K. surprised her.	From previous evidence Freud knew that Dora was sexually attracted to H. K., although she repressed this fact. Dressing quickly to get away from the fire in the manifest dream **represents** energetic avoidance of her own sexual impulses toward H. K.	
	She also decided to leave in a few days when her father was due to leave, rather than stay on alone with H. K. and his wife as originally planned.	This resolution had to be repeated each day until it could be carried out: therefore the dream recurred three nights in a row.	
"Mother wanted to stop and save her jewel-case.	Mother was fond of jewelry, but she and father had a big argument a year ago. She wanted drop-shaped pearl earrings and re-	Dora probably thought to herself that she would happily accept what father wanted to give. Also jewel-case **symbolizes** female genitals, and	Dora's early curiosity and jealousy about sexual relations between mother and father are displaced onto the jewel-case. She early guessed the sig-

Continued

Box 10.2
Continued

Manifest Content	Dora Remembers Related Events	Freud Interprets Latent Content From Recent Events	From Childhood Events
	jected the bracelet he wanted to give her. Also, recently H. K. gave Dora a fine jewel-case.	Dora probably felt she owed H. K. a "return present."	nificance of noises of copulation and knew that ejaculation made the female genitals wet. Energy was probably **displaced** from "wet" to "drops," then to "jewel," and finally to "jewel-case." Thus the jewel-case represented jealous feelings and sexual wetness as well as her present temptation: it was ". . . more than any other a product of **condensation. . . .**"
"But father said: 'I refuse to let myself and my two children be burnt for the sake of your jewel-case.'	In their regular home recently Father had told mother she should not lock a door to the brother's room because "something might happen in the night so that it might be necessary to leave the room."		Father protects his two children from fire. But since the brother was not there with H. K., the reference must be to earlier events. "Something might happen in the night" would be an episode of enuresis. To prevent the children wetting the bed, father had aroused them.
"We hurried downstairs, and as soon as I was outside I woke up."		The meaning for Dora was that she could not rest or sleep (a **reversal** of wake up) until she was outside; that is, had left.	Freud interpreted that Dora and her brother had both been bed-wetters beyond the usual age. Reluctantly, Dora confirmed this.
Main theme:	**Main theme:**	**Main themes:**	**Main theme:**
"Father saves me from a fire."	H. K. threatens sexual assault and "if anything happens it will be Father's fault."	She had strong impulses to yield to H. K., and she fears this temptation, and wishes father would save her.	Father saves her from wetting the bed.

(All quotations from Freud, (1905a/1959, pp. 78-111).

get an impression of the entire dream. The second column in box 10.2 shows the girl's answers to various questions Freud asked concerning her associations to parts of the dream. Each association appears next to the relevant portion of the dream. The third and fourth columns give Freud's interpretations from recent events and childhood events in Dora's life. It is not clear whether all of these interpretations were actually told to Dora, but quite a few were. The third column gives just the interpretations which concerned recent events in Dora's life; the fourth column gives the interpretations which concerned childhood experiences in Dora's life.

This dream shows very well the way in which a dream "stands on two feet," one in the recent past and one in childhood. It also shows many of the main thought processes involved in dream work: reversal into the opposite, substitution, representation, symbols, displacement, and condensation. Each of these instances is bold-faced.

At the foot of the box the main themes are suggested. Thus in the manifest content the main theme is that father saves her from a fire. In the associations the main theme is that father is to blame for putting her in danger. And in the interpretation from recent events the main theme is that she wishes father would save her from her own sexual wishes. The latter is an unconscious wish, since the idea that she does have sexual wishes toward H. K. (the same man who kissed her in the shop) is repressed. Even more heavily repressed is the idea that she once had sexual wishes toward her father, which were connected with both her own bed-wetting and with his custom of waking her up to prevent it.

Dora's dream reveals nicely the workings of repression. Her own feelings and her sexual desire for H. K. were the original target for primal repression. As a result of their con-

nection with this idea, the ideas also of "drops" and "wet" were also repressed. "Drops" was an idea still too closely connected with sexual impulses to permit its appearance even in dream consciousness. The closely associated idea of "jewels" was also barred from dream consciousness; although the idea of "jewel-case" got through. It was both sufficiently far removed in the associative chain, and also sufficiently charged with energy from condensation, that it could form a central (even doubly-mentioned) element in Dora's dream. The entire dream is a fine example of wish fulfillment. Dora unconsciously wishes her father would save her from her sexual impulses. In the dream this wish is fulfilled symbolically, as her father saves her from a fire.

Critique of Freud's Theory of Cause

Once again Allport's voice was among those first raised in serious criticism of Freudian theory. He made two major points about Freud's theory of cause: that the construct of libido was superficial and unfruitful even if accurate, and that it was poor science to generalize from particular facts observed in one or two neurotics to the assertion of general facts about normal people, especially concerning the psychosexual motives behind everything. Allport charged that the construct of libido or Eros "covers every life-serving impulse of the human being. . . . Such a generalized postulate of a dynamic, non-specific libido is nothing other than the harmless hypothesis of a basic Will to Live . . . (Allport, 1937, p. 187). He said that the conception of libido was so broad as to be "psychologically valueless." Allport maintained that Freud had reduced all human motivation, not to the broad conception of libido, but in fact to the very narrow motivation of biological sexuality. He wrote,

A remarkably illogical procedure seems to be responsible for overemphasis on sex by psychoanalysts. . . . Whatever form of behavior or thought is *ever* found in *any* life, to be associated with sex, they seem to assume to be *always* connected with sex in *every* life. This procedure produces such absurdities as interpreting the infant's bad memory . . . as guilt repression (the justification being that neurotic adults are known *sometimes* to dissociate painful sexual memories of guilt from their own consciousness) . . . (Allport, 1937, p. 188).

In Allport's view, Freud's singling out of sex as if it were the most important factor in human life was an emphasis which fails to match the reality of biological motives, which in fact never operate singly: "Sex in normal lives never stands alone, it is tied to all manner of personal images, sanctions, tastes, interests, ambitions, codes, and ideals" (Allport, 1937, p. 188). In this latter aspect of his criticism, then, Allport felt that Freud's theoretical model of human motivation was inaccurate.

Wolpe (1954, 1958) has proposed that the formation of phobias and many other symptoms can be explained as the simple conditioning of anxiety responses to previously neutral stimuli that happened to be present at the time the person was frightened. Treatment should aim to inhibit the anxiety. Wolpe has criticized Freud for having been so preoccupied with his theory that he failed to see the more obvious evidences of simple conditioning in his patients. For example, Wolpe and Rachman (1960) have reassessed the case of Little Hans (box 1) and have pointed out that the most straightforward evidence there suggests that Little Hans developed his phobia of horses right after an event in which he was on the street and saw a big horse fall down. The horse was pulling a bus at the time, and Little Hans was very frightened by what he saw. Moreover, when asked by his father if the

phobic feelings had been present before that incident, Hans replied, "No. I only got it then." His mother confirmed that the anxiety broke out directly after that incident.

Wolpe and Rachman cite other evidence suggesting the presence of a conditioned fear response, evidence such as the spread of the phobia to related items such as other large animals. Their criticism is an example of a change in a model object, as discussed in chapter 8. In other words, given all the facts as known, they assert that Freud was led by his theory to focus upon certain facts and to overlook other facts, so that his model of the case of Little Hans was more suited to his theoretical explanation than an alternative model of that case would be.

They also charge that many of the alleged "facts" in this case (such as Hans's wishes for sexual relations with his mother) are actually unsupportable assumptions. For example, the only hard evidence for Hans's incestuous wishes is given in an incident when his mother was bathing him and he asked her why she didn't put her finger on his penis. She replied, "Because it's not proper." Hans then commented with a laugh, "But it's great fun." Wolpe and Rachman say that this incident provides evidence only of Hans's pleasure in stimulation of the penis, not evidence of incestuous wishes. In particular they argue against the assumption that such wishes would be transformed into anxiety and hence be the cause of the phobia. Such an assumption, they say, is not only not warranted by the real facts of the case; it is also completely unnecessary since the phobia can be explained much more easily as having been caused by conditioned anxiety responses at the time Hans was frightened by the horse falling down.

Psychoanalytic treatment is also criticized by Wolpe, who maintains that the essential ingredient in any cure is the *reciprocal inhibition* of anxiety responses (or other self-defeating responses) by some response which is antagonistic to anxiety. For example, if Hans could have been taught to relax as soon as he saw a horse, the physical relaxation would have been incompatible with the tensing of muscles required for an anxiety response. Wolpe and Rachman (1960) suggest that Hans's eventual recovery from the phobia was due to such reciprocal inhibition, which took place naturally in the course of life, rather than to any specific interpretations or psychoanalytic insights given to Hans by his parents or by Freud. Now broadly known as *behavior therapy*, Wolpe's principles are widely used in the United States and other countries.

It is often claimed that behavior therapy is much shorter than psychoanalytic treatment and more effective. Aronson and Weintraub (1968) point out that behavior therapy succeeds in a short period because it aims only at removing the obvious symptoms. From a study of 126 patients in psychoanalysis they find that "those who drop out early, who are often considered analytic failures, show rapid symptomatic improvement" (Aronson & Weintraub, 1968, p. 378). Thus psychoanalysts consider the removal of symptoms to be superficial; and patients who leave treatment after mere symptom improvement are considered failures in analysis. Aronson and Weintraub say, "It is also true that early symptomatic improvement is not a primary goal of analysis" (1968, p. 378). This means that psychoanalysts are pleased if their patients happen to be relieved of their symptoms early in the course of treatment; but other goals are more important: ability to experience pleasure in ordinary living, for example, or to give and receive tenderness in intimate relationships.

Other critics have found psychoanalytic treatment too long and too indirect. To the charge from psychoanalysts that behavior therapies treat only the symptom and not the cause, the behavior therapists reply that there is no cause, at least no hidden causes of the kind assumed by psychoanalytic theory (for example, hidden wishes for sexual relations with the opposite-sex parent). Eysenck (1971) has labeled such notions as the Oedipus complex "phantasmogoria," fictions of an exaggerated imagination. Freud and others maintain that the evidences for the Oedipus complex and other dynamic processes can be seen directly by the psychoanalyst in the course of treatment, even as resistance and transference can be seen. This does not mean that you can "see" these processes in the same way that you can see a baseball diamond and the players as physical entities. It means noticing and being aware of something more subtle, like seeing a player steal a base. Someone just learning the English language might think you meant that the player stole the base pad and walked off with it; a Martian might see one person running to the next base and another person throwing a ball which arrives over the base seconds after the runner reaches it. But all of those movements are meaningless except in the context of the meaning of the game and its rules for competition. You have to know these meanings before you can appreciate (or even "see") the feat of stealing a base. You must understand the game, you must know what the rules are, and how these determine that particular movements and timing constitute a particular "play" such as stealing a base. You must know the rules even as the players know them.

It should be remarked that Wolpe and Rachman (1960) also require you to know the rules of the game, namely those of the theory of conditioning. In constructing their own *model object* they emphasize facts consistent with their expectation that anxiety responses may be conditioned to previously neutral stimuli. They do not emphasize facts from the original narrative which do not constitute "plays" in the game of conditioning theory, items such as Hans's worry at bedtime that a horse would come in and bite him. Surely his bedroom was not one of the previously neutral stimuli present on the street at the time of the accident to the horse.

Evidence from the Laboratory

Is there any direct evidence for Freud's dynamic hypotheses? Some must remain assumptions because it is difficult to conceive of ways of testing them: for example, the hypothesis of psychic energy. But other hypotheses have been studied with great effectiveness. For example, Glucksberg and King (1967) studied repression and carried out an experiment to determine whether or not ideas connected with dangerous ideas are especially likely to be forgotten. In the first part of their experiment they prepared a number of chains of associated words such as "stem—flower—smell." Then they had subjects learn the *first* word of each chain in a paired-associate task, with a nonsense syllable being the stimulus word in each pair. For example, the subjects had to learn the pair "CEF-stem"; so that whenever the syllable "CEF" was presented they could respond with "stem." In order to make certain words connected with danger, Glucksberg and King then gave the subjects a session in which the *last* word of a chain was presented and followed by either a shock or no shock. For example, the word "smell" would be followed by an electric shock. In the last session subjects were again tested on the paired-associates task. Now if the idea of "stem" is associated with the idea of "flower" which is associated with the idea of "smell"; and if the idea of "smell" has become somewhat dangerous as a result of its being followed by electric shock; and if Freud's model of motivated forgetting is correct, then the subjects should have difficulty recalling the words like "stem" which were paired with nonsense syllables; but they should not have

difficulty with first words in a chain for which the last word had not been followed by shock. The results were in accordance with this expectation.

Ego functions at the unconscious or preconscious level are hypothesized to be the cause of the unusual forgetting observed in instances of repression and also of distortions in perception. Dixon (1971) has reviewed a large number of experiments which offer substantial support for the hypothesis that we respond actively to stimuli of which we are not conscious. In one of his own experiments, Dixon placed subjects so that they saw two different visual fields, one with the left eye and one with the right. In one field the subject saw two spots of light whose brightness he could adjust by turning a knob. The subject was instructed to keep these two lights adjusted so that he could just see the brighter of the two spots and not see the other. In the right field the subject was presented with two kinds of stimuli, emotional words (like "penis") or neutral words (like "rider"). However, these words were presented at levels below awareness; that is, the subject did not know the words were appearing in front of him because they were *subliminal*, below threshold. Dixon reasoned that these words would nevertheless arouse conflicting drives if they referred to emotional matters, and accordingly the perceptual apparatus would be switched into a defensive mode. One way in which defense would operate against the input of threatening information would be to block out such information. In the visual sense modality such blocking out would be accomplished by some reduction in sensitivity. How could a reduction in sensitivity be measured? Precisely by noting how much the subject had to raise the physical brightness of the spot stimuli in order to maintain the one spot just visible. In this experimental arrangement Dixon found that subjects did raise the brightness required to maintain the brighter spot above threshold when they were presented with the emotional words subliminally, but not when the neutral words were presented (Dixon, 1958).

That subliminal stimuli of particular contents (such as aggressive pictures or sexual scenes) have effects upon experience and behavior which are specifically predicted by psychoanalytic theory has recently been shown in a series of experiments by Silverman and others (Silverman, 1972). In these studies it is usually assumed that particular drives are active within the individual, and these drives are "triggered" into momentary intensification by specific stimuli. For example, the psychoanalytic model of the cause of stuttering hypothesizes that this symptom derives from conflicts over impulses connected with anal instincts. Silverman reports that subliminal stimulation of stutterers by "a stimulus designed to trigger anal derivatives intensified their speech disturbance to a statistically significant extent" (Silverman, 1972, p. 309). In another study, female college students were exposed to stimuli triggering ideas related to menstruation which resulted in changes in their attitudes toward men in accordance with predictions (Ellman, 1970).

Silverman (1976) has recently given a review of two series of experiments in different laboratories, in all of which unconscious wishes have been aroused and the effects of this arousal predicted in advance. For example, using tachistoscopes to present stimuli at speeds so great that the subjects were not consciously aware of the stimuli, Silverman and his colleages presented aggressive and neutral stimuli to schizophrenic subjects. It was hypothesized from modern psychoanalytic theory that an important component of schizophrenic pathology arises from conflicts over aggression. Stimulating aggressive impulses subliminally should intensify the conflict mo-

mentarily. This intensification should be revealed by increased irrationality of thought or increased inappropriateness of behavior. The aggressive subliminal stimuli included such things as a picture of a charging lion or of a snarling man holding a dagger, or statements such as *cannibal eats person*. Neutral stimuli (used as experimental controls) included pictures of a bird flying and a man reading a newspaper, or statements such as *people are walking*. Sixteen such experiments were carried out, in Silverman's laboratory and in others, and in each experiment it was found that the aggressive stimuli did intensify disturbances of thought processes and behavior as predicted. By contrast, when control experiments were run in which the aggressive stimuli were presented at slow speeds so that the subjects were consciously aware of the stimuli, the disturbances of thought and behavior did not result. This means that, as would be required by the dynamic theory, the arousal of impulses must be *unconscious* in order for it to have the predicted disturbing effects.

Silverman's work is among the finest examples of experimental method in psychology. The replications of his results are now so numerous and the applications to different kinds of subjects so varied that the generality of the hypotheses tested can hardly be doubted. Moreover he has manipulated the system in both directions. By proper choice of stimuli he has shown that it is possible to *reduce* the disturbances in thought and behavior as well as increase them.

Evaluation of the Theory

These and other indications of the fruitfulness of Freud's theory of cause appear in a very large number of studies which have been guided by psychoanalytic theory. These include such monumental investigations as that carried out by Adorno and colleagues (1950) on the authoritarian personality, or

Fisher (1970) on the experience of the body. One of the most recent studies is that reported by Vaillant (1976) on the character development of college men over a period of thirty years, in which it is found that the pattern of defenses observed during college determines the man's subsequent manner of coping with life crises. For example, men employing projection as a dominant defense were among those most likely to decline in socioeconomic class position over the years.

The study by Vaillant also bears upon the criteria of accuracy and power, for its findings contain some results which show psychoanalytic hypotheses to be accurate (such as that mature personalities are better able to delay gratification of instinctual drives in the service of reality considerations), and also some which show psychoanalytic hypotheses to be inaccurate (such as that sublimation is the most successful defense; the study shows that suppression is the most successful defense among the members of this essentially normal population.) This mixture of results on accuracy has characterized researches studying psychoanalytic hypotheses since the earliest such studies (see Sears, 1943). But more recent reviews (Dixon, 1971; Kline, 1972) suggest that, as experiments have become more sophisticated, so the proportion of confirmations has increased. For example, a direct test of the hypothesis that the latent content of a dream produces primary process characteristics in the manifest content of the dream was carried out by Wiseman and Reyher (1973) through the manipulation of hypnotically inducing dreams about each of ten inkblots. One week later the experimental group responded to the inkblots in the manner of a standard clinical assessment. A control group took the standard assessment without the prior dream induction. As predicted, the level of primary process thinking in the experimental group's responses to the inkblots was sub-

stantially and significantly higher than that of the control group. Thus one more point of accuracy accrues to Freud's theory of cause. Altogether the balance appears to be quite strongly in favor of accuracy. This means that the power of the theory is substantial too, since power is the range of accurate hypotheses and predictions.

Freud's theory of cause has great depth. It penetrates beneath the surface and discloses hidden mechanisms such as instinctual impulses, unconscious conflicts, primary process distortions of thought and behavior, mechanisms of ego defense, and much more. Though it may not give us great joy to recognize that at bottom we are creatures of impulse and irrational thought, that difficulty is felt more when we are thinking about ourselves than when we think about other people. For while we know that there are many fine and good people in the world, people who are creative and who contribute to the welfare of others (such as Maslow's self-actualizing people), yet we also know that there is much madness and destruction in the world. The daily newspapers constantly remind us of savagery in the streets, in the air, on the battlefield; of parents abusing, burning, starving their babies and children; of mad snipers shooting to kill anyone they can get their sights on; of rapists, murderers, and muggers of old ladies and blind invalids. There have been systematic attempts to exterminate persons of particular race or religion, and such massacres are still sometimes reported from one or another part of the world. There are orgies, pornography, abductions, trading in persons for commercial sex. There are schizophrenics, paranoiacs, manic-depressives, and countless other forms of mental misery, including nine million alcoholics, a quarter million drug addicts, and twenty-five thousand completed suicides a year in the United States alone (see Lazarus, 1976, p. 10). Freud's theory offers at least a beginning insight into many of these bewildering events on the human scene: They are partly the result of libidinal and aggressive instincts gone out of control. The ego has developed without sufficient integration of impulses and sublimation of aims. But this takes us to the topic of our next chapter, Freud's theory of personality development, his temporal pattern theory.

Workshop 10.1

Dream Symbolism

Below are two reported dreams. Using your knowledge of primary processes in transforming latent content into the manifest content of a dream, try to arrive at an interpretation of the two dreams. List all the symbols you see, and by each symbol state what you think it might mean.

Dream 1: Dreamer, a Twenty-two-year-old Female College Senior

A kitten with pretty fur jumps up by the window. It has such big eyes. Now a cat with a jewelled collar is stalking something among the flowers around a garden pond. There is a loud "Plop!" as a fish jumps in the pond. Suddenly I feel afraid for some reason. The cat is back in the hotel and slips into a cupboard in an upstairs bathroom to sleep. When it wakes up it can't get out.

Symbols   **Meanings**

_____   _____

_____   _____

_____   _____

_____   _____

_____   _____

_____   _____

_____   _____

Interpretation of Latent Content of Dream 1

_____

_____

_____

_____

_____

Dream 2: Dreamer, a Twenty-one-year-old Male College Junior

I see two kids playing ball in a field. They aim at a net but their hands are moving up and down too fast to shoot straight. One of them shouts about a snake in the field and goes after it with his knife. Then I'm pumping gas into my automobile. It feels strange, like I'm being watched by the station attendant from inside. I speed away but keep wondering if I forgot to pay.

Symbols	Meanings

Interpretation of Latent Content of Dream 2

For those who would like to read more on dreams, two recent references of interest are those by Hall and Van De Castle (1966) and Woods and Greenhouse (1974).

Summary

According to Freud's early theory of cause the nuclear system of neurones received charges of energy from instinctual sources in the body and ordinarily discharged energy through actions. However, feedback loops with the glands could produce excessive excitation in the nuclear system, requiring a defensive process which Freud named a *lateral cathexis,* or siphoning off of energy into surrounding neurones.

In his later theory Freud proposed two main groups of instincts: sex and self-preservative on one hand, and destructive on the other. These provided energy for the three main structures of id, ego, and superego in the form of impulses and emotions. The id strives toward discharge of instinctual energy (pleasure principle), the ego strives to meet reality requirements in seeking satisfaction of instinctual wishes (reality principle) and the superego strives to repeat painful experiences, turning aggression against the self via the repetition compulsion. The ego ultimately controls the discharge channels and thus determines whether energy is discharged in action, in fantasy, or into the body.

The ego is faced with three kinds of anxiety: reality anxiety (from external dangers), neurotic anxiety (from the pressure of the id to discharge unacceptable impulses), and moral anxiety (from the attacks against the ego made by the superego). Excessive neurotic anxiety causes hysterical symptoms and, indirectly, phobias; excessive moral anxiety causes obsessive-compulsive symptoms or melancholia. Among the several mechanisms whereby the ego seeks to defend itself against anxiety, repression is the most important. It consists in keeping thoughts of unacceptable impulses out of consciousness. Other defenses include projection, reaction formation, and sublimation.

Two forms of thought process characterize the id and the ego: primary processes of displacement and condensation characterize the id, and secondary processes of judging and planning occur in the ego. The primary processes are employed in Freud's theoretical model of dreams, which proposes that dreams are fantasy products of one or more unconscious wishes. These wishes constitute the essential latent content of the dream and they are transformed by primary processes into a form that is more acceptable for dream consciousness, appearing there as the manifest content.

Freud's assumptions about mental energy have been challenged, and his model of symptom formation has been criticized as inaccurate. The balance of experimental evidence, however, suggests that more of Freud's hypotheses are accurate than are inaccurate. The extensive use of Freud's theory in guiding studies by other investigators indicates its fruitfulness, and the range of studies in which psychoanalytic hypotheses have been found accurate gives the theory a high rating on the criterion of power. The theory provides great depth of understanding, since it offers insights into many psychological phenomena, ranging from dreams to severe mental disorders, crime, and gross destructiveness.

In figure 10.1 on page 262 we offer an illustration of the definition of personality implicit in the combined theories of structure and cause developed by Freud.

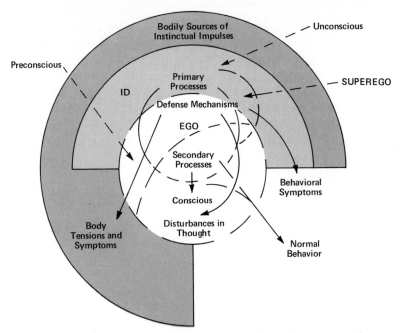

Figure 10.1. The definition of personality implied in Freud's theories of structure and cause

INTRODUCTION

The developmental pattern component theory
  Overview of the theory
Instincts, libido, and erogenous zones
  Aim and object of an instinct
  Erogenous zones and autoerotism
The pattern theory of psychosexual development
  Pregenital and genital organization of the sex
    instinct
  The oral stage and substages
    Incorporative
    Sadistic
  The anal stage and substages
    Expulsive
    Retentive
  The phallic stage and complexes
    Oedipus
    Castration
  The latency stage
  The genital stage
    Forepleasure and end-pleasure
    Object-finding
    Genital organization and mental health
Effect of early psychosexual development on adult
  personality
  Early experiences produce physical symptoms
  Fixation and repression
  Normal development
  Character formation
Particular types of character produced at different
  stages
  Oral character
  Anal character
  Phallic character
    The generation gap
  Genital character
Accomplishments of Freud's pattern theory
  Changed ideas about children
  Influence on scientific research
    Tests of the theory
    Heuristic value
Critique of Freud's theory of developmental pattern
  Allport's critique
  Critique by Bandura and Walters
    On psychodynamic constructs
    On stage theories
    On constructs such as fixation
    Comments on these criticisms
  Critiques by psychoanalytic scholars
    Hartman on ego psychology
    Schafer on the psychology of women
    Accuracy, power, fruitfulness, and depth
Workshop 11 Making inferences from the records
  of conscious experience and behavior
Summary

A Pattern Theory
of Personality: Freud

We come now to the third and last of Freud's major component theories in his overall theory of personality. This is his theory of the developmental pattern of the sex instinct and of its effects upon development in the main structures of ego and superego. This theory is not a complete theory of personality development. For example, Freud did not concern himself with physical growth or with the development of intelligence or other cognitive capacities of the kind that Piaget and others have studied.

From observations made in the course of his clinical practice, Freud found that behind every neurosis was a history of disturbance in sexual development. For example, most neurotics masturbated excessively. In adults, however, overt sexual perversion and neurosis typically were not present in the same individual. An individual patient displayed either neurosis or perversion, but not both.

Freud concluded that one kind of disturbance in sexual development results in perversion in the adult, and another kind of disturbance results in neurosis. The first kind of disturbance was such that it caused an undue importance to be attached to an early and ordinarily passing stage of sexual development, so much so that the person failed to develop beyond that stage. The other kind of disturbance produced the opposite effect, an undue repression (see chapter 10) of sexual instincts.

In 1905 Freud published his *Three Contributions to the Theory of Sex* (1905b/1953, and 1905b/1962), in which he presents his view that there is a natural unfolding of the sex instinct, a pattern of development starting in earliest childhood and proceeding through certain clearly marked stages.

Normally each stage occurs at a particular period in life, and then gives way to the next stage in sequence. A disturbance that overemphasizes and intensifies unduly the component instincts of a particular stage results in a sexual perversion appropriate to that stage. A disturbance that interferes with full expression of component instincts (through repression) leads to neurosis. Lesser disturbances of either kind lead to particular qualities of adult personality.

The several stages proposed in Freud's theory are more properly known as *psychosexual*, rather than simply *sexual*, stages. The important features of each stage are as much or more psychological than physical. Actually, the body and the psychophysical systems portions of personality are involved in the salient characteristics of each stage and in the characteristics of subjective experience and behavior. While the theory is not a total theory of development, then, it certainly is not restricted to some small portion of the personality. The whole personality is involved.

The various stages in Freud's psychosexual pattern theory are each marked by the investment of psychological energy (libido) in a particular organ system of the body. We shall describe this aspect of the theory first. Then we shall consider the theory of pattern itself. Following that we shall take up the discussion of ways in which disturbances of pattern influence adult personality. Finally a small number of researches will be briefly described as illustrative of the very large amount of work that psychologists have done in connection with this part of Freud's theories.

Instincts, Libido, and Erogenous Zones

In chapter 10 we saw that Freud divides instincts into two main classes: those preserving the individual and the species, and those destructive of both. The energy associated with species-preserving instincts (sex instincts broadly conceived) was called *libido*. Freud saw much of human personality as being formed in the service of libidinal satisfactions (pleasures gained from expressing libido). Each instinct has a number of aspects, the most important of which for our purposes are the aim and object. The *aim* is the consummation of discharge or expression of libido which is accompanied by pleasure feelings. The *object* is that through which the discharge is made possible.

Aim and Object of an Instinct

Thumbsucking provides a good example of the aim and the object of an instinct, and Freud uses this example in his discussion.

Thumbsucking is a widespread phenomenon among infants and young children. Freud believes that it offers a prototype for many more clearly sexual processes in the human being. He proposes that many children who become thumbsuckers do so in the following way. While sucking from the mother's breast, or from a substitute, the infant derives pleasure from taking in the milk and also from the sheer rhythmic contact between lips and nipple. The pleasure from sucking is the *aim* of the sucking instinct. Later, feelings of hunger or the external stimuli of something touching the lips produce an irritation in the mouth and lips, whereupon the baby seeks to repeat the earlier pleasure. A child wanting to engage in "sensual sucking searches about his body and chooses some part of it to suck—a part which is afterwards preferred by him from force of habit" (Freud, 1905b/1953, p. 183). Thus the baby's thumb becomes the *object* of the pleasure-sucking instinct.

Erogenous Zones and Autoerotism

Physician and physiologist that he was, Freud drew two general concepts from the example of thumbsucking. First, the lips and mouth are capable of being stimulated in such a way that they produce pleasure of a sensuous kind. Since that sensuous pleasure is ultimately to be employed in specifically sexual ways— erotic kissing, for example—and since it then will be clearly separated from the pleasures of satisfying sheer survival needs,[1] Freud maintains that even in the infant it constitutes

---

1. In 1954 Olds and Milner discovered separate "pleasure centers" in the brain, stimulation of which leads an animal to seek to repeat whatever it was doing when stimulated. Freud's notion of a pleasure-producing mechanism, independent of specific need reductions such as eating, seems to be supported by these findings. Indeed the areas of the brain discovered by Olds and Milner are known as "pleasure-centers."

essentially a sexual pleasure. The parts of the body concerned—the lips and mouth—form an *erogenous zone*: "a part of the skin or mucous membrane in which stimuli of a certain sort evoke a feeling of pleasure possessing a particular quality" (Freud, 1905b/1953, p. 183). While he believes that any part of the skin or mucous membranes can be adapted to produce pleasure through certain kinds of stimulation (such as stroking or rubbing), he also suggests that particular regions are especially suited: mouth, nipples, breast, genitals.

The second general concept drawn from the example of thumbsucking is *autoerotism,* which means erotic pleasure gained from using one's own body or self as the instinctual object. Why would a child suck a thumb? What instinctual aim can be achieved? Certainly not the aim of nutrition. Certainly not the rather clearly sexual pleasure obtained when adults kiss or suck each other's earlobes or toes or fingers in foreplay. Nevertheless, thumbsucking could be an early form of certain adult activities. The pleasure gained in thumbsucking is vaguely related to sexual pleasures in a broad sense. Perhaps *sensuous* pleasures would more accurately describe it.

Freud's conception of sexual instincts is indeed very broad and includes a wide range of sensuous pleasures. All of these are comprehended in his notion of *erotic* pleasure. The fact that a child seeks this pleasure in its own body led Freud to designate such pleasure as *auto*erotic: sensuous pleasure gained from one's own body. The contrast would be pleasure gained from a sexual partner's body: *allo*erotic. With thumbsucking as prototype, Freud points to a variety of other behaviors that are autoerotic, including scratching an itch, urinating when full, masturbation, and erotic fantasy.

When once a child has experienced a pleasure, he or she wants to repeat it. According to Freud, we can all recognize that peculiar "feeling of tension which in itself is rather of a painful character" when we urgently want to repeat a pleasurable sensation. Also we can all recognize a "feeling of itching or sensitiveness" in an erogenous zone. For example, in imagining a romantic kiss, or in thinking about a favorite candy or other food, we find ourselves with that feeling of "itching or sensitiveness" in the lips or mouth. With the favorite food we often salivate as well!

The urge to repeat a pleasurable experience is somehow built into our body, psychophysical systems, and experience. It can be definitely and clearly experienced as a feeling of wishful tension, and a feeling of sensitiveness in the erogenous zone where the gratification would take place. The sexual aim is then achieved by finding an appropriate outer stimulus to remove the feeling of sensitiveness and replace it by a feeling of pleasure. For example, an outer stimulus of scratching can remove the tension-filled feeling of itching. In general, the outer stimulus is something which scratches, rubs, strokes, or otherwise creates friction on the erogenous zone concerned.

Throughout Freud's discussion of these processes he makes it plain that there are structures and processes in the body which interact with our experiences of tension and other feelings. Such events drive the infant to repeat his or her thumbsucking, and similarly they drive other psychosexual experiences and activities. Freud makes the empirical assumption that the initiative lies within the body and within the personality. The environment provides the object of instinctual striving but not its aim. In the case of autoerotic instincts the environment does not even provide the object; the person's own body does.

Since the body's structures and the majority of its processes are endowed at conception and are manifest at birth, Freud emphasizes also the fact that the order of emergence of the various psychosexual stages is determined by biological forces. We now turn to consider the details of his theory of psychosexual stages.

The Pattern Theory of Psychosexual Development

At the outset of his book (1905b/1953) Freud describes the popular view of sexual development in his time. Shortly after puberty, it was believed, some person of the opposite sex suddenly aroused the sexual instinct of the young man or woman. There was no earlier development or preparation.

By contrast, Freud maintained that there was *pregenital organization* of the sexual instinct from earliest childhood. By *genital organization* he meant that, following puberty, genital zones and impulses toward procreation dominate the sexual instincts. He meant that the so-called single sexual instinct is actually a fusion of several partial instincts, each one connected with one of the erogenous zones. The genital organization entailed a dominance of genital instinctual aims over the aims of all the partial instincts, which would be simply

the achievement of local pleasure in the organs of erogenous zones.

Analysis of case histories led Freud to the view that certain clear phases exist in pregenital organization of sexual instincts. In each phase one of the partial instincts is dominant in the sense that its pleasure aims are those through which libido (general sexual energy) is chiefly expressed.

The popular conception is illustrated in figure 11.1; Freud's theory is illustrated in figure 11.2. Comparison of the two figures provides a very sharp contrast.

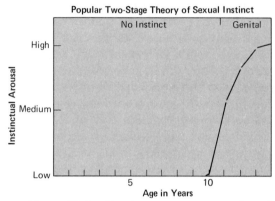

Figure 11.1. Popular two-stage conception of development of sexual instinct in Freud's time

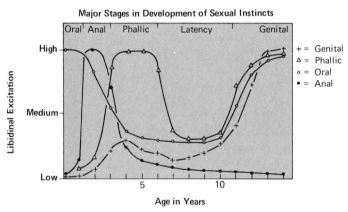

Figure 11.2. Freud's psychosexual development theory, showing levels of libidinal excitation for major stages in development of sexual instincts by age

The Oral Stage

From birth to about one year of age the child's instincts are focused upon the aim of getting nourishment. The achievement of sexual aims is not yet separated from the satisfaction of hunger during the earliest period. Both the hunger and the sexual aim are achieved through *incorporation* of the object, that is, by eating or otherwise taking it into one's own body. The emergence of thumbsucking (in those many infants that do engage in thumbsucking) reveals the separation of the sexual and hunger aims, however.

Since this first stage involves the mouth, lips, throat, and other parts of the upper alimentary canal, with main emphasis upon the mouth and upon sucking, Freud called it the *oral stage*. Sensuous pleasure as well as hunger satisfaction is obtained through the mouth.

The oral stage has been divided into two main parts: before and after the initial eruption of teeth. Prior to this momentous event the child's pleasures involve only incorporation. Afterwards biting becomes a pleasurable, and indeed a preferred, activity. The two substages are called respectively *oral-incorporative* and *oral-sadistic*. The second substage lasts usually from about six months to one year.

To say that the first year of life is an oral stage within psychosexual development is simply to say that sensuous pleasures are derived mainly through the mouth. Pleasurable removal of mouth irritations by sucking or biting constitutes the essential sexual aim of this phase. As shown in figure 11.2, this type of libidinal excitation is high and dominant during the first year of life, and then gradually gives way to excitations associated with elimination.

The Anal Stage

The infant naturally eliminates waste products from the body just as soon as the first intake of food is processed. Freud suggested that elimination can come to have sexual significance for a variety of reasons. First there is close physical proximity of sexual and eliminatory organs. Second, urination takes place through the penis or vulva. Third, excitation of the mucous membranes in eliminatory organs can be reduced through manipulation, hence pleasurable feelings arise when such excitation is reduced by passing excretory fluids or matter. Fourth, the social requirements of privacy in sexual matters also attend elimination. Fifth, the young child's curiosity about parents' and other people's eliminatory functions inevitably gets confused with curiosity about their sexual functions.

Moreover, from the age of about one year the parents turn special interest upon the organs of elimination in efforts to toilet train the child. Many parents are concerned in our culture not merely to teach the techniques and necessities of sphincter control (control of letting go urine or feces through contracting muscles). They also want the child to pass feces in order to maintain health. Because of the salience of the anus in toilet training, Freud called this entire phase the *anal stage*.

This stage also has two substages. In the first the child derives pleasure mainly from the expulsion of feces, and it is therefore called *anal-expulsive*. In the second half of this stage the child derives pleasure more from retaining the feces. In some instances this seems to derive from the pleasure of holding on as such; in others it seems to come from the more intense feelings of expulsion that can subsequently be experienced. At any rate, this second substage was called *anal-retentive*.

As figure 11.2 implies, the anal stage lasts from about one year of age to about three. During this period, libidinal excitations and pleasures from the mouth and lips have not abruptly vanished. They have declined from a position of dominance, however, and the pregenital organization is now lead by the partial instincts associated with elimination. This in turn will give way to dominance by instincts associated with the phallus.

The Phallic Stage

From about age three there begins in the child's life an awareness of physical differences between himself or herself and persons of the opposite sex. Children are concerned to find out where babies come from. They also discover the specially sensitive zones in their own sex organs (clitoris or glans penis in girls and boys respectively). Irritations in these zones lead to scratching or rubbing, with resultant pleasure, so that repetition of the act is sought even as repetition of thumbsucking was sought.

In their concern to identify their own nature, Freud said, children are interested in other people's sex organs and also in those of animals and even inanimate objects. They may actively search animals and other things to find out if they have equipment similar to their own. He wrote (1923b/1959, p. 246):

> This part of the body, so easily excitable and changeable, and so rich in sensation, occupies the boy's interest to a high degree. . . . He wants to see the same thing in other people to compare it with his own. . . . The driving force . . . expresses itself in childhood essentially as an impulsion to inquire into things—as sexual curiosity. Many of those deeds of exhibitionism and aggression which children commit . . . prove on analysis to be experiments undertaken in the search for sexual knowledge.

In finding that some people do not have a penis like his own, the little boy is at first prone to disbelieve it, later liable to believe that the person had one but that it has been taken away. Hence develops the possibility that his own might be removed, and this then becomes a fate to be feared. Freud proposed that the little boy first turns his libido upon his mother and feels jealous of his father, his powerful rival. This conflict (known as the *Oedipus complex*) is resolved in part through feelings of anxiety lest, in retaliation, his father would actually castrate him (Freud, 1924/1959). (These fears of retaliation are called the *castration complex*. See box 10.1.) The little girl's first love object is, correspondingly, her father. But she is similarly anxious about what seems to be her existing state of castration. From lack of satisfaction for her striving toward her father she too turns away. The boy turns toward an identification with his father; the girl turns toward an identification with her mother. Thus normally by the age of six both have passed beyond the first stage of erotic attachment to a person of the opposite sex. For both of them, however, the stage is one of preoccupation with the phallus, the presence or the absence of the male genital. Therefore Freud named this stage the *phallic* stage of psychosexual development. The case of Little Hans presented in box 10.1 of the previous chapter gives some examples of the many complications that can arise during this stage of development.

The Latency Stage

As figure 11.2 shows, the phallic stage lasts from about age three to about five or six. The Oedipus complex is a culmination of this stage, and with its passing there passes also the entire period of infantile sexuality. Freud said humans have two different periods in their sexual development: the infantile period, ending around age six, and the adult period, beginning around the age of eleven at puberty. He remarked that this feature of sexual development is not found in "man's animal kin" and that it seems to be especially connected with the human tendency toward neurosis. The intervening period of five years or so he referred to as the *latency* stage.

The latency stage is characterized by the

widespread repression of all sexual instincts, according to Freud. Were it not for the biologically determined resurgence of chemical stimulation at puberty the latency stage would presumably continue indefinitely.

The Genital Stage

How does adult sexuality finally emerge? Freud's hypothesis was that the chemical and anatomical changes of puberty provided for an integration and redirection of all the partial sexual instincts developed during the infantile period. These partial instincts came to play the important role of providing *forepleasure* (during the foreplay of sexual relations). Pleasurable in themselves, kissing, touching, looking at the loved one, all these tend to arouse the more specific tension of genital impulses. For the male these are aimed at discharging "sexual products," and in the female they are aimed at receiving these sexual products, through appropriate glandular discharges in the vagina. Puberty is accompanied by the definite signs of development of external genitalia and also of the internal machinery for reproduction. Freud distinguished the forepleasure from the *end-pleasure* associated with these discharges in orgasm.

Whereas in the infantile period the phallus and the clitoris had been the leading zones for males and females respectively, during pubescence the leading zone of the girl must be the vagina. The excitability of the clitoris must be transferred by a kind of spreading of effect. In cases where early masturbation has produced a fixation upon the clitoris such transfer is likely not to take place, in which case the person becomes frigid. In both men and women similar fates may befall during any part of the foreplay. The related infantile instinct may have become fixated so that the forepleasure itself is prevented from giving way to a combining buildup of pleasure and tension culminating in intercourse. Freud

said that this is "the mechanism of many perversions, which consist in a lingering over the preparatory acts of the sexual process" (Freud, 1905b/1953, p. 211).

Freud also pointed out that adult sexuality is directed toward another person; it requires *object-finding*, whereas infantile sexuality was autoerotic. Thus he called the adolescent period the *genital* stage in psychosexual development. This means that the psychosexual organization is normally under dominance of genital organs and that the dominant aim of discharging or receiving sexual products requires another person as object. In an important sense the child's attachment to the opposite-sex parent during the oedipal period provides precursors for later object selection. Even those who successfully negotiate the oedipal conflict are nevertheless influenced in adulthood by early object choices. Freud believed that many young men first fall in love with an older, mature woman, who essentially reawakens in them the feelings they had for their mother. Girls would love an older man who reminds them of their father.

A man, especially, looks for someone who can represent his picture of his mother, as it has dominated his mind from his earliest childhood; and accordingly, if his mother is still alive, she may well resent this new version of herself and meet her with hostility. In view of the importance of a child's relations to his parents in determining his later choice of a sexual object, it can easily be understood that any disturbance of those relations will produce the gravest effects upon his adult sexual life. Jealousy in a lover is never without an infantile root or at least an infantile reinforcement. If there are quarrels between the parents or if their marriage is unhappy, the ground will be prepared in their children for the severest predisposition to a disturbance of sexual development. . . . (Freud, 1950b/1953, p. 228; also 1905b/1962, p. 94).

It will be recalled that Freud had found sexual disturbance to be at the root of every neurosis, guilt over masturbation to be at the root of every neurotic suffering related to being conscience-stricken. The integration of infantile sexual instincts under a successfully dominant genital organization was therefore viewed as the sine qua non for adult mental health. Deviations and disturbances leading to failure of this integration could only result in suffering and sickness. Thus Freud also proposed a theory of priority, which was overlaid upon his theory of pattern. In the theory of priority it would be claimed that successful genital organization should be the goal of every human being if they wish to be healthy adults. We turn now to consider some of the consequences of fixation and repression at earlier stages of the developmental sequence.

Effect of Early Psychosexual Development on Adult Personality

The title of this section reflects the basic hypothesis that Freud formulated concerning the relationship between early childhood experiences and later personality or character as an adult. It is a causal hypothesis, and it remains a cornerstone of modern clinical practice in psychoanalysis, where it would be formulated as follows: *The causes of present neurotic disturbances or of present character traits are to be found in the person's experiences as an infant and child.*

Many students have expressed the view that this hypothesis is quite implausible. How could events of so long ago be affecting a person's experience and behavior now? Perhaps the best answer is that it matters little how long ago the events occurred, but it matters very much whether they left any lasting effects. Box 11.1 describes some pronounced effects that were left by experiences in the first year of life.

It is possible that diseases or injuries in early life so affect the body that it bears the marks throughout life. Muscular damage at an early age quite often remains in the form of underdevelopment or special weakness. The person may strive to compensate for this deficiency in some way, such as body-building exercise or the creation of other forms of strength.

Whether Freud's hypothesis is correct in general or not, it cannot be dismissed simply by ridiculing the possibility of long-ago events affecting behavior now. Box 11.1 shows clearly enough that relevant events took place in the patient's first year of life. Nothing had been able to cure the eye disease. But toward the end of treatment, after the breakthroughs in deep hypnosis like that illustrated in box 11.1, the patient's vision returned to normal and the disease symptoms disappeared. The example of early muscle damage is clear enough. Such illustrations should suffice to create a broader acceptance of the possibility that early experiences in psychosexual development contribute to later personality and character.

Fixation and Repression. The two basic processes which, according to Freud, transform particular events in early childhood into more permanent characteristics of personality are *fixation* and *repression*. These processes do their work by strengthening tendencies to express libido in one of the early partial instinct forms (fixation) or by blocking expression of libido in one of those forms (repression).

Fixation and repression can arise at any stage of psychosexual development. Each stage has intricate characteristic features, potentials, and dangers. As the personality wrestles with these complexities on each succeeding day of life, far-reaching changes occur in the ego. The personality is changed even as it grows, some-

Harold has a disease involving uncontrollable rapid eye movements, with less than 20 percent normal vision. He cannot stand glaring lights. When he was a child other children called him Squinty and he still gets very angry if anyone looks at or makes remarks about his eyes. Currently he is serving a long sentence for criminal assault, and is undergoing hypnoanalysis. In the thirty-third hour of treatment deep hypnosis uncovers material from the first year of his life. "L" is the analyst.

L: "Now you are even younger. . . . You are sitting in your high chair. . . . Are your eyes open? Look carefully. Are your eyes open or are they blinking?"

"The sun is coming in. They are blinking. . . . Everything—is—coming up from the —floor. It makes my eyes blink. . . . It hurts me. There. It comes up. I hit it with the spoon. . . . Everything is so bright. It is early in the morning. The sun is shining in. . . ."

L: "Now listen to me, Harold. I am going to ask you a question. Listen carefully. Why did you first start to blink your eyes? What made you blink your eyes the first time? Now you are very small, very small. This is very long ago, when you were in the cradle."

"I am in the cradle, right next to my father's bed. I see him. I see—I can see—it—way up. My mother—I see my father on top of her. . . . I—it is early in the morning—not very dark—not light—and—I'm in—the cradle.

My mother's nightgown is—up—over her hips, and—she—is on her back. My father is on her—and they—Oooo—the. . . . He gets off her—and I—see—his—I see my—mother. The light is coming in."

Harold was extremely agitated throughout this period. He moaned continually and tossed himself about. His breath came fast and his whispered words came from between dry lips.

"The shades on the windows are drawn, I can see plain—the covers are off. . . Mother is—she's hollering. Get off—her. Don't be so rough. . . ."

L: "Now, Harold, listen. You saw your mother and father having intercourse when you were a little baby. How old were you then?"

"I am about a—year old."

L: "And until then your eyes were wide open? That experience was something you wanted to forget?"

"O yes—yes."

L: "Is that the secret you are hiding? Is that why your eyes are closed?"

"I—My mother tells me—it's from the—measles. I don't know. . . . The sun—the sun is too—bright." (Lindner, 1944, pp. 193-194).

As a result of the treatment Harold's eyes returned to normal vision and the blinking stopped.

---

times fatefully for the rest of life. Take the boy who for one reason or another is left without resolution of his oedipal feelings of rivalry toward his father. He is apt to go through life wanting to fight all the older men and other symbols of authority in the world. Eric Berne, originator of the currently popular Transactional Analysis, has recently put it this way:

"What do you say after you say Hello?" The Oedipal drama and the Oedipal life, for example, both hinge entirely on this question. Whenever Oedipus meets an older man, he first says Hello, the next thing he has to say, driven by his script, is: "Wanna fight?" (Berne, 1972, p. 38).

Another way to describe Oedipus is to say that

fixation occurred during the phallic stage of his psychosexual development.

Whether a person will develop a normal genital sexuality or not depends upon the course of early development and of later experiences. Normally the person will pass through a series of stages in which first one and then another of the erogenous zones is for a time the focal point of libidinal energy. It is as though each is then primed for integration in adult sexuality. But two other main outcomes can occur. In the first the libido becomes fixated, or attached to a particular zone, so that when adulthood arrives the individual can experience sexual pleasure only through that zone and its associated partial instinct expression. Such are those who gain sexual pleasure from beating or being beaten (anal sadism or masochism), or from looking (phallic stage fixation on seeing the parents engaged in intercourse). On the other hand, in the psychoneuroses the partial instincts have come under too much repression during the course of development. When sexual impulses return with urgency in the puberty stage the repressions must be exerted with greater effort, and the libido then follows channels of symptom-formation. Thus there are two extremes: overactive fixation on partial instincts and overrepression of partial instincts. The first leads to perversion in adult life, the second to. neurosis.

Although particular traumatic events may produce a fixation, it is most commonly attributable to one of three main types of parental treatment, according to Fenichel (1945, p. 65): excessive gratification of instinctual impulses at the given stage, excessive frustration, or excessive alternation between the two.

Freud suggested that normal development would show the progressive incorporation of earlier partial instinctual impulses in an appropriate subordination to later, broader, more outwardly oriented aims. But he seemed to believe that only with luck could the parents avoid producing fixations or repressions in their children. For almost all of the ministrations parents must perform, Freud says, can arouse sexual excitement: warm baths; rhythmic shaking of the body such as rocking; muscular activity in contact with the parent's skin, as in playing or struggling through mock contest; any intense emotional or physical experience such as an excited game or spanking on the buttocks. The mother especially is likely to rock and pat and bathe and kiss the baby.

Even as they look after their baby, then, parents cannot help but stimulate erogenous zones: the mouth, the anus, the skin, the external genitals, the eyes, the nose and so on. In the course of normal development each of these zones comes under integrative controls. The controls include shame, disgust, moral stricture and the controls of the ego. The latter adapt the person to external limiting factors such as "limitation of freedom, inaccessibility of a normal sexual object, the dangers of the normal sexual act, etc. . . ." (Freud, 1905b/1953, p. 170). The integrative objective of the controls is that of putting all partial instincts at the service of the genital and procreative instinct, which is the mature form of libidinal impulse.

The interplay of fixations and controls contributes to character formation in normal personality development. Freud suggested (1913/1959, p. 129) that, in character formation: "either repression is not at work at all or it easily attains its aim, which is to replace the repressed impulses by reaction-formations and sublimations." We see that the same instincts are involved; the same mechanisms of defense are employed; the same general structure and dynamics of personality are assumed; but the results of development for normal persons are particular types of character rather than particular forms of neurosis.

Particular Types of Character Produced at Different Stages

Oral Character

Fixations tend to arise as a result of excessive gratification of the partial impulse. The child may continue to suck things or may revert to sucking whenever stress arises. As adults, such children "will become epicures in kissing, will be inclined to perverse kissing, or . . . will have a powerful motive for drinking and smoking" (Freud, 1905b/1953, p. 182). Fixations may also be due to excessive frustration of oral needs, however, or to combinations or alternations of excessive gratification and excessive frustration (Fenichel, 1945, p. 405).

Fenichel summarizes the many character traits associated with events during the oral stage (1945, pp. 488 ff). Pronounced satisfaction of oral needs tends to result in a self-assured personality, with an optimistic outlook on life. The infant came to expect that its needs would be met, that it would receive whatever it cried out for; and (provided nothing in subsequent experiences seriously contradicted this expectation) such a general feeling of assurance then persists in the individual's attitude toward the world. This would be a normal, positive kind of outcome.

If the infant is unduly deprived of oral satisfactions, however, quite the opposite general character is likely to result: a gloomy, doubting, somewhat depressed personality, with a pessimistic view of life.

Within the bounds of "normal" development, some degree of fixation may occur, in which case the person is apt to demand that others take care of him or her. They may complain a great deal if others fail to deliver constant supplies of gratification. One man cited by Fenichel had first lived with his grandmother and been given much oral satisfaction. Then he was taken to live with his father who was very stern and ungenerous. The man later lived on money received from his father, having no job himself. His life was a prolonged bitter complaint that his father did not give him enough. As Fenichel describes it, the man's dominant motive in life was to get reimbursement from his father for having deprived him of his early oral gratification.

In many cases oral character types appear as dependent people, always wanting others to do things for them. Sometimes they almost physically latch onto the person they expect to feed them. As Fenichel says, they "affix themselves by 'suction'". Other character types, formed from fixations in the second half of the oral stage, the oral-biting stage, tend to be very sarcastic, often with a "biting" wit.

Anal Character

During the anal stage of development from about one to three years sensuous pleasure may be obtained from the passing of urine and fecal matter. But bowel and bladder training are typically begun during this time in most societies. Children are "put on the pot" and told to do their business. Freud proposed that a struggle between child and mother at this point could revolve around the child's rights over his or her own bodily waste materials. Freud wrote "it represents a 'donation,' the disposal of which expresses the pliability while the retention of it can express the spite of the little being toward his environment."

Fixations at this period are apt to produce what Freud called the *anal character* (1908/1959): "*orderly, parsimonious*, and *obstinate*. . . . 'Orderly' comprises both bodily cleanliness and reliability and conscientiousness in the performance of petty duties. . . . 'Parsimony' may be exaggerated up to the point of avarice; and obstinacy may amount to defiance, with which irascibility and vindictiveness may easily be associated."

Fenichel's account of the anal character

(1945, pp. 278 ff.) stresses that most of the traits arise from the resistance the child puts up against the training, from obedience to parents' demands, or from compromises between these two conflicting tendencies. Resistance or rebellion continues in the character trait of obstinacy, the refusal to be budged from a position one has taken. Parsimony or stinginess carries on the habit of retention: the person becomes what is known as a tightwad.

The foregoing qualities are developed primarily as a result of fixations on the *retentive* phase of elimination, the holding in. Other characters are formed from fixation on the *expulsive* phase (letting go). These persons tend to be messy, leaving litter wherever they go, including around the house. Sometimes even the character of a benefactor, or philanthropist can be traced in part to fixations on the expulsive phase of elimination. In this case the person continues in adult life to spread his or her wealth around.

Phallic Character

Freud early remarked that adults who had suffered from enuresis (bed-wetting) were often found to have "an intense, 'burning' ambition" (Freud, 1908/1959, p. 50). Enuresis was considered to have sexual significance, particularly because the passage of urine and the passage of sexual fluids proceeds through the same bodily channels. This close physical connection between the phallus (or vulva) as channel for urine and as the means of genital union apparently leads to similarities in the character types associated with each function.

According to Fenichel (1945, pp. 69, 139, 492), the ambition often found in persons who had been enuretic or otherwise given to sexual excitation through the urethra stems largely from a reaction formation to shame. They strive to overcome or disprove their shame. The shame itself apparently comes from being shamed by parents for having wet the bed or otherwise lost control of the urethral sphincter. Fenichel describes the phallic character as one whose behavior is "reckless, resolute, and self-assured—traits, however, that have a reactive character; they reflect a fixation at the phallic level, with overvaluation of the penis and confusion of the penis with the entire body. . . ." (Fenichel, 1945, p. 495). This overvaluation is itself a reaction formation against castration anxiety: such persons throw their aggression at anything or anyone symbolizing the threat of castration, including women.

The phallic stage is especially complicated because it encompasses an intense interest in sex organs and a special attachment to the opposite-sex parent. The child suddenly becomes part of a dimly realized but nevertheless potent triad, in which love for the opposite-sex parent is embroiled in rivalry with the same-sex parent. Castration fears arise in connection with anticipated retaliation for fantasized accomplishment in winning the loved parent for oneself to the exclusion of the other parent. The physical focus of this competition is the genital organ. Freud says that fixations at this level of development are likely to make it difficult for the child later to solve the problems of adolescence. Masturbation occurs first in infancy, then is likely to have a resurgence in the phallic period, and another resurgence in puberty, often providing the basis for much neurotic guilt. But fixated attachments to the parents can have the serious consequence of making it difficult or impossible for the adolescent to break away from parental authority and from sexualized attachment to the parents. Girls who remain attached to their parents "make cold wives and remain sexually anaesthetic" (Freud, 1905b/1953, p. 227). Box 11.2 gives Freud's reasoning on why it is in general very important that such attachments be abandoned.

The Genital Character

Fenichel states that the genital character represents full sexual maturity, with the ability to attain orgasm. This ability "puts an end to the damming up of instinctual energies, with its unfortunate effects on the person's behavior. It also makes for the full development of love (and hate), that is, the overcoming of ambivalence . . . the end of reaction formations and an increase in the ability to sublimate" (Fenichel, 1945, p. 496).

The genital character, then, is the psychoanalysts' conception of a psychologically healthy person. Fenichel stresses the contrast with neurotic characters, in whom pregenital impulses remain sexualized and interfere with interpersonal relationships. In normal people such pregenital impulses are partly expressed in sex play under the primacy of genital instincts, but mostly they are sublimated, and therefore at the service of the ego for rational purposes. Freud emphasizes that the healthy adult is characterized by the capacity for work and for love, for creative or productive effort and for genital intercourse with an attractive and appropriate member of the opposite sex. These are his criteria for healthy personality development.

Accomplishments of Freud's Pattern Theory of Psychosexual Development

Before Freud proposed his theories of psychosexual development most people thought that children were sexless but that adolescents were stimulated into sexual arousal by members of the opposite sex. The pattern theory caused a great uproar because people thought Freud was accusing children of depravity. He did on one occasion say that children are "polymorphous perverts." By that he meant that they show all the forms of perversion, like thumbsucking, voyeurism, interest in feces and urine, and so on. But of course they show such interests in the infantile sexual form of partial instincts.

Freud's views changed the world's ideas about children. The possibility that children might be *caused* to be depraved by improper parental treatment became rather widely understood. The idea that parents' handling of their children's sexual interests could have long-range influence on their character development provoked a revolution in authoritative recommendations to parents (see Wolfenstein, 1963). In 1914 mothers were told they should battle the child's sinful nature and eradicate it. Masturbation, for example, was to be stopped by mechanical restraints if necessary. By 1945 mothers were told that handling of genitals was quite natural in babies, but that mothers should be sure to provide the baby with plenty of other interesting things to do. Extremes of overindulgence or deprivation were increasingly seen to be harmful.

In the world of science Freud's view had two different effects of a positive nature. First, many psychologists were stimulated to test the hypotheses of the pattern theory in formal research. For example, Goldman-Eisler (1951) found some relation between early weaning (deprivation of oral satisfactions) and later tendencies toward pessimism. The influence of oral fantasies on adult memory was demonstrated in a study by Spence and Gordon (1967). Some subjects were made to feel rejected by indication that peers did not want them as friends. According to psychoanalytic theory such rejection should make people feel hungry. In fact, subjects who were rejected later reported more hunger than nonrejected subjects. Half of both groups were exposed to a subliminal stimulus word "milk," just before being shown thirty words which included some that were related to infantile experiences (such as "suck"). The rejected subjects who were

then exposed to the subliminal stimulus recalled an even greater proportion of infantile words than those not so exposed or those not rejected.

As a final recent example of research on the oral character, Masling and colleagues (1974) demonstrated in two separate studies that males with higher oral imagery were better able to predict the responses of other males, thus confirming the psychoanalytic hypothesis that persons with oral character are more dependent on others and therefore pay more attention to the cues others emit.

Many of these studies have shown the expected associations between oral character and other aspects of behavior; some have suggested a connection with events in the first year of life. But most of the research on such connections has not been conclusive. Similarly with studies of the anal character, the existence and power of traits has been established. The traits of orderliness, parsimony, and obstinacy do vary together as would be predicted (Kline, 1972). But it has not been established that the development of such traits is related to particular kinds of events during childhood.

On the question whether the different stages of psychosexual development do come in the sequence Freud proposed, a number of studies suggest that they do. The pattern was tested in regard to anxiety by Friedman (1952) and the hypothesis received some confirmation. Several hundred children of different ages were asked to complete some fables like this one: A monkey had a bushy tail that was fun to play with; one day he woke up to find something was very different. What had happened? Children who completed the story without removing the tail took twice as long to respond; they were judged to be anxious about castration. The percentage of such children rose to a high point among six year olds, declined substantially through the latency period, and rose again sharply at age eleven to twelve.

Since Erikson's theory of psychosocial development is explicitly linked to Freud's theory of psychosexual development throughout the period of childhood, tests of Erikson's theory often also provide evidence for Freud's theory. Thus Ciaccio's work (1971), demonstrating that the various stages do rise to dominance in the order hypothesized (see chapter 14), owes indirect support to Freud's theory.

A second way in which Freud's pattern theory has influenced scientific research is in the new lines of study it has suggested. Recall that most of Freud's direct observations were made on adults in treatment. Direct observational studies of children were quite rare before 1900. Although child psychologists from other schools of thought contributed to the development of observational methods, those who worked from the Freudian viewpoint brought special hypotheses to their investigations. Among the outstanding researches by psychoanalysts may be mentioned those of Spitz (1965) on the development of the image of the mother and also of anxiety responses during the first year of life; and of Brody and Axelrad (1970) on the development of the ego in infants as related to mother-infant interaction. The work of Robertson (1958, 1962) should also be mentioned. He studied and made films of the effects of separating very young children from their mothers, especially when the children had to go into hospital. As would be expected from psychoanalytic theory, the separations caused marked emotional disturbance in the children. As a result of his work, hospital practices throughout England were changed to reduce separation time and even eliminate it where possible.

Most psychoanalytic researchers acknowledge that the ratio of theory to established fact is very high. At the Hampstead Child-Therapy Clinic in London, England, where Anna Freud and other psychoanalysts practice child therapy, the Well-Baby Research Group has for several years been constructing a schedule of factors to be ascertained through observation of children and their parents attending the clinic. The schedule, called a *Baby Profile,* has only recently been completed (W. E. Freud, 1972).

The purpose of the profile is to convey "a global, overall picture of an infant's personality from the impression of one or more observers . . ." (p. 173). As a student using the microscope must be instructed as to what will be seen, so direction must be provided as to what to look for when the unaided eye and brain are directed toward the vast complexity of a baby's behavior. The profile gives this direction for observation from the psychoanalytic point of view.

The first part of the profile treats the environment: parents, family background, birth, current management of the baby in feeding, cleanliness, contact, fostering of pleasure or unpleasure, and so on. The mother is given special consideration in her role as an auxiliary ego (support, guidance), with regard to both her manifest behavior and her latent attitudes.

In the second part of the profile various aspects of developmental trends are evaluated through current description at the time of observation and notation of changes since previous observation. Topics studied include body needs and functions such as sleep patterns, conditions of feeding, characteristics of feeding process, rooting behaviors, signs of pleasure and unpleasure during feeding, response to interruptions, and interaction of mother and child during feeding; elimination, movement, skin contact, and other needs also receive study. Drive development is observed through focus upon oral excitation, pleasure sucking, use of mouth for exploration and making sounds; signs of pleasure or unpleasure in the anal and phallic zones are also studied; precursory signs of anaclitic object relatedness (loving someone who feeds or protects you) and also further steps of proper love are recorded. Aggression as undirected, directed toward the child's own body, or directed toward the outer world is described in detail as to the behaviors and the circumstances in which they arise. Rates of buildup and recovery after discharge of aggressive energy are recorded. Affective states, forerunners of fixation (special sensitivities) or of later tendencies to regression, and general characteristics having probable significance for the future development of the baby (such as level of tolerance for frustration of needs) are given special attention.

Each of the points in the profile has theoretical significance, and it is expected that the gradual accumulation of observations on a longitudinal basis (repeated observations on the same child over a period of several years) will permit the discovery of answers to many theoretical as well as empirical questions. As one example, the Hampstead workers expect to be able to answer the question: "When, how, and why are quantities of aggression, which should find an outlet toward the object world, deflected and directed toward the body . . . ?" (W. E. Freud, 1972, p. 176). Their results will be awaited with great interest.

As even the brief description of the *Baby Profile* given above suggests, this schedule for observation is soundly based upon Freudian theories of psychosexual development. The schedule is almost a concise summary of the theory. Any student who is seriously interested in advancing psychoanalytic psychology would do well to consult the schedule and possibly seek to use it in supervised and controlled observational studies.

Critique of Freud's Theory of Developmental Pattern

As with other aspects of Freud's theories, Allport was among the first to direct cogent criticisms at the theory of developmental pattern. Allport thought it was inaccurate to assume that sex is the most important single factor in personality development, stating that *"sex would be the most important single factor if there were any single factors, which there are not.* Biological motives never operate singly" (Allport, 1937, p. 187). Closely related to this criticism was Allport's view that Freud's emphasis upon the role of sublimation in development was exaggerated. We saw above that, as Fenichel relates, the ideal "normal" character is genital, and is characterized preeminently by the person's ability to sublimate pregenital sexual impulses. As Allport read Freud's views, sublimation—

> is the device above all others that normal personalities employ to render their anti-social impulses acceptable. If this were the case, sublimation would be the most important genetic mechanism in the study of normal personality, but . . . the maturing of normal personality is a far more complex process than simply redirecting the aim of originally unallowable wishes (Allport, 1937, p. 185).

Further, Allport questions a major assumption of Freud's theory, that children prefer the parent of the opposite sex. Psychological studies, he relates, have failed to find any significant evidence for this tendency.

Bandura and Walters (1963) have argued that all psychodynamic constructs such as "unconscious psychic forces," "cathexes," or "complexes" are superfluous, since they are hypothetical conditions or states having only a tenuous relationship to the social stimuli that precede them or even to the behavioral 'symptoms' or 'symbols' that they supposedly explain" (Bandura and Walters, 1963, p. 30).

Especially critical of stage theories of development such as Freud's, they state that there is little agreement among such theories concerning the number and nature of the stages. They criticize Freud's and other stage theories for emphasizing a "relatively prefixed sequence of stages which are more or less discontinuous," when it would be more reasonable to expect "a good deal of intraindividual continuity in behavior at successive age periods" (Bandura and Walters, 1963, p. 24). This continuity would be based upon the likelihood that familial, subcultural, and biological factors influencing an individual's social training will remain relatively constant throughout childhood. Bandura and Walters also charge stage theorists with obscuring the facts of individual differences at the same age level even among children from similar social and cultural backgrounds. In fact, they state, such children often display marked differences in social behaviors as a result of different social training received in their particular family or group. Finally, they assert, stage theorists have been very vague about the conditions leading to changes in behavior from one stage to another:

> In some of these theories it is assumed that age-specific behavior emerges spontaneously as the result of some usually unspecified biological or maturational process. In others it seems to be assumed that the maturational level of the organism forces from socializing agents patterns of child-training behavior that are relatively universal, thereby predetermining the sequence of developmental changes (Bandura and Walters, 1963, p. 25).

They thus imply that Freud and other stage theorists have made a number of empirical assumptions which are probably untenable.

Bandura and Walters are equally critical of such constructs as "fixation." They cite Fenichel's statement that fixation results from excessive gratification or from excessive deprivation or frustration of impulses at a particular stage in the developmental pattern. Bandura and Walters note that the proposed explanation for fixation as a result of excessive gratification is consistent with an explanation in terms of learning theory: habits that have received much gratification through intermittent reinforcement will be maintained over a long period and be relatively likely to govern responses to relevant stimuli. But the same theory would suggest that frustration does not strengthen a habit; indeed it would lead to extinction of the unrewarded response. Bandura and Walters therefore propose that cases of fixation which have been described as originating in excessive frustration are probably in error. In fact, they have been given intermittent reinforcement but "emphasis is shifted to the nonreward trials . . ." (Bandura and Walters, 1963, p. 23).

It should be noted that Bandura and Walters refer to social behavioral responses and are attempting to discover the relevant antecedent environmental stimuli and the relevant contingencies of environmental reinforcement. Though they occasionally write elsewhere of "internal stimuli," such concepts would seem to be basically alien to a point of view which rejects all constructs pertaining to hidden forces. They do not address matters of experience as opposed to behavior; nor do they strictly address the body as part of personality (their remarks about "biological factors" notwithstanding). Above all, they explicitly reject concepts associated with psychophysical structures and processes. In their criticisms of Freud's theory for using precisely the kinds of constructs which they themselves reject out of hand, are they really doing anything more than repeating their basic methodological assumptions concerning which parts of the total picture of personality should be looked at and which should not? It becomes quite obvious in their remarks about "stages" that they are concerned with stages in "social behavioral responses," whereas Freud was concerned with stages in physical and psychological development; involving the bodily organs and neural and chemical processes; involving experience of many kinds but especially fantasy; and involving long-run effects of early fixations, effects which have their influence through the mediation of relatively enduring psychophysical structures and processes. Indeed Freud proposed (1905b/1953, p. 226 fn.) that certain fantasies appear to arise in the minds of almost all young adolescents: fantasies of spying upon parental coitus, of early seduction by loved ones, of the threat of castration, and of being in the mother's womb. If the existence of such fantasies is considered to be a fact (and why not, for they presumably share the stuff that dreams are made of and dreams are nowadays a widely accepted subject matter for research), then a competing social learning model of psychosexual stages must account for the fantasies of relevant stages as well as the attendant social behavioral responses. The term "fantasy" does not appear in the index of the book by Bandura and Walters. It is hard to see how fantasy could be properly included in the meaning of "social behavioral responses." So it seems that Bandura and Walters do not address the same set of facts that Freud was dealing with.

Within the ranks of psychoanalytic scholars there has been increasing criticism of Freud's theory in recent years. This trend was begun by Hartman (1958) and is now known as the movement toward *ego psychology*. It is also a movement *away* from id psychology, away from a predominant interest in the id and its instinctual and unconscious forces. Ego psychology aims rather to increase psychoanalytic understanding of ego functioning in relation to cultural, biological, and developmental factors. Although ego psychology is moving away from Freud's emphases it in no way rejects his basic theories of structure, cause, and pattern.

In some respects there have been definite critical rejections of Freud's thinking, however. One of these concerns the psychology of women. For example, Schafer writes that Freud's ideas about women, though rich in clinical insight, were "flawed by the influence of traditional patriarchal and evolutionary values" (Schafer, 1974, p. 483). These values clouded Freud's vision and marred his usual investigative curiosity. Hence he stopped thinking about problems of women's development as soon as he had reached an insight that seemed satisfactory from a patriarchal point of view. For example, he believed that a girl assumes she is anatomically identical to boys prior to that eventful occasion on which she first sees a penis and realizes she is lacking a penis. As a result, Freud said, the girl develops *penis envy*, wishing she had one too. But Schafer points out that this is much too simplistic a view and fails to reflect Freud's usual care in following through the various developmental phases and crises that lead up to a particularly eventful experience. Why was it so important to the girl that there be no differences between herself and boys? If the realization of difference is so eventful and formative in her personality development, surely that fact in itself indicates that the girl was "already heavily invested in and worried about genital comparison and intactness" (Schafer, 1974, p. 475).

The various researches quoted earlier provide evidence of the usual mixture of results so far as support for psychoanalytic hypotheses is concerned. For example, it appears that the evidence for the existence of character types is quite strong, but evidence on the relationship between these types and specific childhood conditions suggests that the psychoanalytic hypotheses are inaccurate. The central propositions of Freud's theory of pattern hold that psychosexual organization develops in discriminable stages, and although there seem to be correspondences between the proposed pattern and what may be observed in everyday situations (such as babies sucking, or four year olds masturbating) nevertheless there seems to be no direct tests or confirmations of the changing *cathexes*. Apart from the evidence of psychoanalytic work with children and adults, which is guided by psychoanalytic theory, there appear to have been no longitudinal studies which answer the question whether a child's experience of sensuous or erotic pleasure begins with the mouth, then shifts to the anus and urethra, then shifts to the sex organs, then vanishes during latency. Thus not only is there a mixture of accuracy and inaccuracy with respect to the theory of pattern, but also there is a great need for more research, difficult though it may be.

While the power of the pattern theory is restricted by the present paucity of research, its fruitfulness is great, as manifested in the extensive studies of child development referred to above. Its fruitfulness also can be seen in the formulation of related theories, as by Erikson (see chapter 14).

There can be little doubt about the depth of Freud's theory of pattern. It offers profound insights into childhood and also into adult character. The depth of these insights may perhaps be measured by the profound impact the theory has had on child-rearing practices in the western world.

Workshop 11

Making Inferences from the Records of Conscious Experience and Behavior

Especially in the psychoanalysis of children it has become accepted practice to make use of observations of surface experiences and behaviors for the purpose of inferring to probable constellations of unconscious impulses and defenses (Anna Freud, 1965). For example, a child who has fantasies of being beaten probably is fixated at the sadomasochistic anal stage; a little girl who is always loving and uncomplaining has probably repressed the greedy and hostile impulses that one would ordinarily find as part of the child's total experience and behavior. Using your knowledge of fixations and defenses in the course of psychosexual development, make some relevant inferences from the following portions of the record, using the model of the first example:

Portion of the Record	Possible Mechanism	Inference
A five-year-old boy shows complete indifference to matters about where babies come from or why girls are different from boys.	Repression	The oedipal conflict has been settled by repression rather severely
A six-year-old boy always gets very anxious and concerned when his father goes out at night or when he is not home by the usual time.	(Hint: reaction formation)	_____ _____ _____ _____

Portion of the Record	Possible Mechanism	Inference
A ten-year-old boy is always orderly, punctual, and clean.	_____	_____ _____ _____
An eight-year-old girl is greedy, clinging, demanding of constant demonstration of love.	_____	_____ _____ _____
A six-year-old girl refuses most food and is afraid of being poisoned.	_____	_____ _____ _____
A nine-year-old boy is filled with a burning ambition to be a race-car driver. He is very active, energetic, impulsive.	_____	_____ _____ _____
A five-year-old girl has a fantasy that her tummy is filled with eels.	_____	_____ _____ _____
A six-year-old boy is a very tough and noisy kid, always ready for a fight, always getting into trouble.	(Hint: overcompensation)	_____ _____ _____
A four-year-old girl is crazy about horses and spends as much time as she can on her rocking horse.	_____	_____ _____ _____
A five-year-old boy has a fantasy that a big horse will come through the wall of his bedroom and attack him.	_____	_____ _____ _____ _____

Portion of the Record	Possible Mechanism	Inference
A twelve-year-old girl loves horses and spends a lot of time grooming her horse.	_____	_____
		_____
		_____
A nine-year-old girl sides with her mother and is very cool toward her father.	_____	_____
		_____
		_____

Summary

Freud's theory of developmental pattern proposes that psychosexual development proceeds through a number of relatively discrete stages. Each stage is marked by the focusing of sensuous pleasure upon a particular organ system of the body, called an *erogenous zone*. A characteristic feeling of tension or sensitiveness is projected into that zone and it can be pleasurably relieved only by some physical stimulation such as sucking or rubbing.

The oral stage occupies the first year of life, when either sucking or biting remove mouth irritations. Before teething, the pleasure produced by sucking and taking things into the mouth predominates; after teething the pleasure of biting predominates. The next two years see the anal stage, in which the focus of tension is shifted to the organs of elimination. In the first part of the anal stage the pleasure of expelling wastes is dominant, and in the later part the pleasure of retention dominates. From age three to six sensuous and erotic pleasure centers upon the sex organs: the phallic stage. Many children masturbate and are curious about the sex organs of others and have fantasies related to parental intercourse. The child's sexual feelings become attached to the parent of the opposite sex in the Oedipus and Electra complexes, and these years are crucial in laying down early models for the person's later choice of adult love objects. After the latency phase, when repression covers over the sexual instincts, puberty brings the chemical and anatomical changes which produce a resurgence of sexual interest. In this final, genital, stage all of the earlier part-instincts are brought together under the dominance of genital and procreative sex with a partner.

In the course of psychosexual development traumatic conditions or other forms of excessive influence may bring about *fixations* so that the child's erotic satisfaction remains fixed to an early erogenous zone, resulting in adult preference for one of the pregenital forms of erotic satisfaction such as sadomasochism (anal stage) or voyeurism (phallic stage). Alternatively the outcome of traumatic early influences may be neurosis through the effects of repression. Within the boundaries of more normal influence, what happens during early psychosexual development has consequences for character formation. For example, if a child is exposed to severe conditions during toilet training, and if the child handles this problem with the defense of reaction formation, then he or she will develop character traits of orderliness, cleanliness, thrift, punctuality, and so on: the anal character.

Freud's pattern theory has made substantial accomplishments, and even though there is a mixture of inaccuracy with accuracy among its hypotheses, it has proved very fruitful in stimulating and guiding research. It has led to recent emphasis upon child psychoanalysis and upon direct observation of infant and child. While the power of Freud's pattern theory is still largely unknown, its depth is substantiated both by its comprehensiveness in terms of our definition of personality and by its contributions of insight through specification of mechanisms involved in neurosis, perversion, and character formation. The illustration of Freud's theories of structure and cause given in figure 10.1 would provide identically for illustrating his theory of pattern in terms of the components of our definition of personality given in chapter 2.

We have now completed presentation of Freud's theories, and in the process it has been possible to show that a theory of structure of personality deals with the parts of personality considered as long-term enduring structures: The total structure is made up of part structures. We have seen that a theory of cause in personality refers to hidden causes (like unconscious conflict) or unrecognized causes (like the effects of infantile sexual experiences and behaviors upon adult character). Finally we have examined Freud's theory of developmental pattern—the ordering over time of distinctive stages in dominance of different zones of the body in interest, sensitivity, and sensuous or erotic pleasure. We noted that Freud proposed a theory of priority, overlaid upon the theory of pattern.

In the next chapter we shall consider three component theories developed by Carl Jung, one-time close associate of Freud; and following that it will be interesting to compare the theories of these two outstanding scientists.

INTRODUCTION

Introduction to Jung's life and work
  Jung's life and professional career
  Work with Bleuler and Janet
  Influence of Freud
  Visions and dreams
  Travels
Jung's theory of structure
  Consciousness
    Four mental functions: sensation, thinking,
      feeling, intuition
    Volitional processes
    Instinctual processes
    Directed and undirected processes
  Personal unconscious
    Impressions of low intensity
    Repression
  Collective unconscious
    Myths
    Archetypes
    Instincts
Jung's theory of types: a pattern theory
  A classification pattern theory
  Extravert and introvert
    Meanings of extraversion and introversion
    Origins of extraversion and introversion
    Characteristic attitudes and behaviors
    Compensation in the unconscious
  The eight types
    Thinking types
    Feeling types
    Sensation types
    Intuition types
Jung's theory of cause
  Complexes
    Word associations reveal complexes
  Energy
    Libido as psychic energy
    Physical energy
    Psychic energy and spirit
    The archetype of God
    Symbols of energy
  Repression
    Source in conflict
    Role of projection
  Archetypes

    As dispositions
    Autonomy of archetypes
    As forms and trends
  Archetypes and personality functions
    Persona
    Shadow
    Animus/anima
    Self: mandala as archetypal form of the self
  Summary of three component theories
  Accomplishments of Jung's theory
  Psychotherapy
    Needs different at different ages
    Role of spiritual needs
    Procedures
  Dream analysis: theoretical model
    Competition with Freud's model of dreams
  The unconscious and modern society
Critique of Jung's theories
  Criticism that the theories are confused
  Criticisms that the theories are unscientific
  Empirical studies of Jung's constructs and
    hypotheses
  Accuracy, power, fruitfulness, and depth
Workshop 12 Constructing a questionnaire to
  assess Jung's eight types
Summary

12

Carl Jung's Theories: Structure, Cause, and Pattern

One of the giant intellects of our age, Carl Jung is perhaps most widely known for his typological pattern theory concerning extraverts and introverts; but as we shall see in this chapter his overall theory of personality went deeply into both structure and cause.

Jung was born in a little town on Lake Constance in Switzerland in 1875. As told in his autobiography (Jung, 1965), his early childhood was filled with experiences of both the beauty and the danger of natural phenomena (the sunlight on yellow leaves and the threatening roar of waterfalls). He often sat alone outside the house, playing with sand. His father was a pastor, as were eight uncles; and many of his earliest memories deal with their black robes and shining shoes and lamentations over the dead. At a very early age he had dreams containing symbols of profound meaning, and he believed that an intelligence far beyond his own was shedding light to him upon dark matters of reality which all of us must ultimately confront. Thus he was launched on his lifetime career of studying the unconscious, the occult, the riches and the recesses of inner experience; but he wanted to study these things as a scientist, objectively.

Jung aimed to become a physician and a psychiatrist. At the age of twenty-five he obtained a position in the Burghölzli Mental Hospital in Zurich. He studied and worked under the direction of Eugen Bleuler, the famous Swiss psychiatrist who first described the psychosis of schizophrenia. Two years later Jung went to Paris to study under the outstanding French psychiatrist, Pierre Janet. Jung had read Freud's works and had been active in disseminating psychoanalytic theories; nevertheless he did not adopt all of Freud's ideas, as became plain when Jung's book, *The Psychology of Dementia Praecox* (Jung, 1907/1960), was published. In a letter to him, Freud made some critical remarks, to which Jung responded in part by acknowledging his own limited experience and talent and in part by pointing to the fact that he was working with uneducated patients suffering from insanity (McGuire, 1974, pp. 11-16). Freud worked mostly with patients who suffered from neurosis but were not insane. The two men continued to correspond and first met in Vienna later in the year 1907. Jung became closely allied with Freud and in 1909 traveled with him to Clark University (Worcester, Massachusetts) where Freud lectured on psychoanalysis and Jung reported on his experiments with word-association and reaction times. (These will be discussed more fully below.) In 1911 Jung was made the first President of the International Psychoanalytical Association.

After his work with Janet, Jung returned to the University of Zurich, where he received an appointment as lecturer in psychiatry and as senior physician in the psychiatric clinic there. He held this appointment from 1905 to 1909. During this time he continued to devote himself to his research into the unconscious and specialized in studying symbols that had been of importance in myths and dreams throughout the ages. One outcome of this study was his work on symbols of personal change, as in birth, conversion or rebirth, and death, which was published first in 1911 (Jung, 1967). There his differences with Freud on matters of basic importance to psychoanalytic theory became plain (the details are discussed in chapter 13) and it heralded the end of his association with psychoanalysis and his friendship with Freud.

In 1912 Jung was again invited to America, this time to lecture at Fordham University in New York City. In 1914 the British Medical Association invited him to lecture on the role of the unconscious in psychopathology. It was timely, since Jung had been delving deeply into his own unconscious since Christmas of 1912. In private practice in Switzerland, he spent lunch hours and some evenings building houses and castles out of stones he gathered from the lakeshore, doing whatever occurred to him in an effort to let his own unconscious fantasies emerge and give him whatever messages they carried. In the autumn of 1913, while traveling alone, he suddenly experienced a vivid vision of a flood over Europe, turning the cities to rubble and carrying the bodies of citizens like flotsam on its surface. Suddenly the flood turned into a sea of blood. He was sickened and puzzled

and felt ashamed. But two weeks later the same vision returned. He asked himself if it meant a revolution, but concluded that it did not; rather it seemed to him that he was on the brink of a psychosis.

In the spring of 1914 Jung had a dream that it was midsummer and a cold wave came over Europe and froze everything to ice; all trees, shrubs, and grass were killed by frost and there were no people. But in the third of these dreams there was one tree left with leaves on it, and these had been transformed into grapes filled with healing juices. He "plucked the grapes and gave them to a large, waiting crowd" (Jung, 1965, p. 176).

War broke out August 1, 1914; its widespread destruction made the dreams and visions clairvoyant. For Jung it meant that he "had to try to understand what had happened and to what extent my own experience coincided with that of mankind in general." His first task, it seemed, was to penetrate the depths of his own unconscious mind, so he began by writing down all the fantasies that had occurred while he was building the houses and castles out of rocks from the lakeshore.

Jung entered military service in 1914 but took up his researches again as soon as possible. In the 1920s he traveled extensively, learning about myths and rituals among different tribal peoples, including the Pueblo Indians of the American southwest. In 1930 he was vice-president of the German Medical Association for Psychotherapy, and in 1933 president of the International Medical Association for Psychotherapy. He continued to lecture widely, at the Federal Institute of Technology in Zurich, the Institute of Medical Psychology in London, and Yale University, for the Terry Lectures. In 1932 he was awarded the Literary Prize of the City of Zurich. In 1935 he was nominated Titular Professor in the Federal Institute of Technology, Zurich; and in 1944 he was appointed Professor of Medical Psychology at Basel University, where he had taken his early training in medicine. In 1945 he was awarded an honorary doctorate from Geneva University.

Looking now at his personal life, Jung married Emma Rauschenbach in 1903 and they had five children. In addition to the family home in Zurich, they had a country place in Bollingen on the shores of the lake. Much of this place was built by Jung himself, and it was kept as rustic as possible, without electric light or power, telephone or running water. He enjoyed gardening, carving wood and stone, and painting. The family spent many enjoyable hours swimming, sailing, and hiking at Bollingen. Jung cooked the meals when they had guests.

Jung's home in Zurich was filled with treasures he had collected on his travels, including engravings, etchings, paintings, sculptures, and ancient manuscripts. But for all the evidence of riches in his outward activities and in his collection of art, Jung said that they were insignificant by comparison with the train of his inner experiences. These, he said, constituted the essence of his autobiography. He died in 1961, at age eighty-six. It was reported that at the time of his death an unusual storm sprang up on the lake and lightning struck and split his favorite tree.

As we present Jung's theory of personality we shall cover each section on structure, pattern, and cause separately. Then we shall attempt to gain an appreciation of the accomplishments of this theory in its application to a number of problems in psychology.

Jung's Theory of Structure

Jung proposed that personality has a structure of three tiers or levels: conscious, personal unconscious, and collective unconscious.

Consciousness

In his paper on *The Structure of the Psyche* (1927/1971) Jung wrote about his theory of personality structure, and he said of consciousness that it "seems to stream into us from outside in the form of *sense-perceptions.*" Thus one of the characteristics of consciousness is *sensation,* a construct denoting that mental function which registers or notes the basic material of experience. It is a perceptual function, operating upon both the information derived from the external world and also the information from within our bodies, such as sense of position, movement, pain, and so on. In Jung's considered opinion only four different functions or modes of consciousness can be distinguished: *sensation, thinking, feeling,* and *intuition.* These traditional terms nevertheless have specific theoretical meaning for Jung. *Thinking* discriminates one perceptual object from another and compares and contrasts them on one or more dimensions. For example, we contrast the redness of fire with the redness of a robe. We note that a mouse is smaller than a rat, a gerbil is smaller than a prairie dog. *Feeling* is the function of consciousness which evaluates objects and events: they may be pleasant or unpleasant, desirable or undesirable, and so on. *Intuition* is a "perception of the possibilities inherent in a situation." We are not ordinarily aware of how we get an intuition: It springs into consciousness, or else it is consciousness springing beyond the sensory information given. Much intuition seems to occur without sensory evidence in the usual way, as when, having lost something, we get a hunch as to where it might be. Or sometimes we feel observed and, turning our heads, we meet a stranger's smile. We might summarize the four functions as follows: We sense the *existence* of something, we think what it *means,* we feel our *liking or disliking* of it, and we intuit its *possible implications*.[1]

We must pause to emphasize one fact about Jung's construct of the mental functions. They are not structures in themselves; they are simply ways in which consciousness of objects, events, and relations occurs. They therefore are important characteristics of consciousness, which is one of three structural layers in the personality: conscious, personal unconscious, and collective unconscious.

Two other major characteristics of consciousness are volitional and instinctual processes. Volitional processes are "defined as directed impulses, based upon apperception, which are at the disposal of so-called free will" (1927/1971, p. 27).

Jung means that we have experiences of wishing or consciously intending to do something and that we experience the wish as originating in our own conscious ego. We decide for ourselves that we will go to the movies tonight; take Spanish next semester; work toward a certificate in first aid; or make a strong New Year's resolution to quit smoking, cut down on liquor, and save energy by limiting automobile use. We are aware of our own origination of these plans and wishes. Courts of law likewise recognize the existence of actions which are "premeditated," or carried out after having been consciously planned and intended so that they are undoubtedly the full responsibility of the person concerned.

By contrast, there are what Jung calls the "instinctual processes," originating in the body or in the unconscious. They are impulses which have a compelling quality, impulses which force themselves upon our consciousness, impulses that may lead to actions for which we

disclaim responsibility. For example, from the body might come an impulse to throw up the last meal, and although we are fully conscious of it we certainly do not originate the impulse in the same way that we consciously initiate a volitional process. We are merely spectators of something happening from within our body. Again we sometimes feel compelled to do something which we know is contrary to our best interests and which, in terms of conscious deliberation, we really do not wish to do. Quite often such events happen in family arguments when one person feels compelled to blurt out charges, accusations, or abuse, deeply wounding the other's feelings. Again we are sort of spellbound, watching these attacks spew out of us at the other person, knowing it will lead to no good, but caught in a flow of impulses that has a will of its own. We are not consciously initiating such attacks, but rather we find it happening to and through us. Often we are unable to retract and feel obliged then even in our conscious will to support what has happened, to bolster it with justification, to say they deserved it, to deceive ourselves into thinking that the attack was something we consciously willed and initiated. Only later perhaps do we gain enough strength to admit that we were wrong. "I was not myself; I'm sorry it happened; I was beside myself with anger." Not "in control of myself with anger," but "beside myself"—a bystander, part of the helpless audience. Such is the effect in consciousness of an instinctual process arising from the unconscious.

Finally, Jung said, there seem to be both *directed* and *undirected* processes in consciousness. Directed processes are those we would describe as "paying attention"; undirected processes are those of reverie, daydreaming, fantasy, and the like. Directed processes are accompanied by a definite feeling of tension in the monitoring required. We have

---

1. I am indebted to Anne De Vore for having given a critical reading to chapters 12 and 13 and for making valuable suggestions at this and numerous other points in these two chapters.

to be careful, pay attention, be alert, watch it closely.

A major feature of consciousness is its center: the *ego*. Jung describes the ego as the subject of all conscious acts. It rests, he says (1951/1971, pp. 140-141), on a bodily and on a mental basis. The bodily basis is the continuous flow of perceptions of our own body—its positions, movements, functions, and so on. These form a background of stimulation and sometimes also a foreground, as when we become aware of a pain in the stomach. Thus the ego is placed in the context of both conscious and unconscious (subliminal) processes, so far as its bodily sources are concerned.

The mental basis of the ego is the entire realm of conscious events; it is the "point of reference" of conscious processes, grounded on the bodily perceptions. It is as though one could say: "I see, hear, feel, think, guess, want, certain objects. I am also the bodily entity from which all perceptions of the interior of a body keep coming in. Yet I am more directly just that point at which all these perceptions are received; and I am also the point to which all perceptions of the outer world are referred. My ego is this continuity of reception from inside the body and perception of things outside the body."

Another crucial aspect of the ego is that it has a subjective "feeling of freedom," that we call our free will. It is first and foremost an associate of consciousness. "Losing consciousness" is the same as losing free will: we are no longer "in control." If things happen to us or cause us to behave in strange ways we say that "something came over" us. We are aware of such forces in ourselves. They are not part of consciousness. Sometimes we can learn to infer their origin in unconscious processes, in the unconscious part of our minds. Jung makes an important distinction between two major sections of the unconscious, which

he calls the *personal unconscious* and the *collective unconscious*.

The Personal Unconscious

The personal unconscious contains two kinds of contents. The first are all the impressions and thoughts that had insufficient strength to come into consciousness. As an example of this kind, we may recall becoming aware of an itch on the ear or the back of the neck. Or we may recall gradually realizing that the telephone is ringing. In each of these cases the impression eventually makes it to consciousness, perhaps by its very persistence. But how many itches have not gained sufficient strength to reach awareness? How many phones have rung unheard?

Next, we have all had an intention to say or do something and then forgotten this intention. We have all known someone's name and then forgotten it. These facts exist in the unconscious, as well we realize when eventually we do recall them. Jung says that some of them have simply lost their intensity; others have been *repressed*, which means that consciousness was actively withdrawn from them.

Can the various mental functions take place in the personal unconscious? Jung believes they can. The unconscious receives sense impressions; indeed the importance of itches, phones, and other stimuli of which we belatedly become conscious lies in the fact that they have made some impression on the mind even though we were not consciouly aware of them before. Feeling, thinking, and intuiting also proceed in the personal unconscious, as do initiations of volitional movements. For example, Jung quotes a case (1927/1971, p. 27)in which a patient was deaf as a result of hysteria. That is, the patient could not ordinarily hear things, but this deficit was not due to physical damage to the ear; it was a psychological disturbance. This patient enjoyed singing, and one day the doctor was playing a piano accompaniment to the patient's song. On the second verse the doctor changed key. Immediately the patient also changed key, but without any conscious recognition. So the unconscious must have noticed the change of key and responded accordingly.

Jung also cites many instances of people who have solved puzzles in their sleep. The unconscious mind keeps working, and must do so in a way that resembles thinking. Indeed Jung believes that all the activities that go on in consciousness also go on in the personal unconscious. He writes (1927/1971, p. 29): "Over and over again I have seen how thoughts that were not thought and feelings that were not felt by day afterwards appeared in dreams, and in this way reached consciousness indirectly." So these thoughts and feelings must have had some intermediate existence in an unconscious state.

The Collective Unconscious

Jung contrasts the personal unconscious with the collective unconscious, which, he says, is the real basis of the human mind. Even as the body contains vestiges and forms reminiscent of earlier stages of evolution, so does the mind. This part of the mind would have adapted throughout the eons of time to the changing environmental circumstances the human being would encounter. "The collective unconscious . . . appears to consist of mythological motifs or primordial images, for which reason the myths of all nations are its real exponents" (1927/1971, p. 39).

The myth of the death and rebirth of the hero, for example, seems to be a "sort of psychic parallel to regular physical occurrences." These occurrences are the rising of the sun each day and its travel from east to west, where it sets only to rise again next morning. One version of the myth holds that a godly hero mounts the sun as a chariot in the morning and travels across the sky, only to be devoured by the Great Mother Earth in the eve-

ning. Somehow he travels in a dragon's belly through the sea. In the morning, after battling the "serpent of night," the hero is born again, once more to mount the chariot. Jung asks, "why does the psyche not register the actual process, instead of mere fantasies about the physical process?" (1927/1971, p. 40).

His answer is that what remains as an image in the mind is precisely the fantasies that are aroused by the physical processes, rather than a photographic rendering of the physical process. It is not the storm that is remembered but the fear and awe the storm inspires, along with imagery of "threatening" clouds, "fierce" thunder, and "forked" lightning. From time immemorial it seems that people have believed in the power of the gods to express wrath and inflict punishment through storms. Fear and guilt are aroused by these natural events, and beliefs in supernatural powers rise up to "make sense" of such happenings. Emotions and fantasies mingle then with more or less chaotic impressions of the colors and sounds and forces of the storm. Such is the stuff that myths are made of; and such is the sort of material that constitutes the collective unconscious.

Regularities appear in the human body also, and many of these are emotionally charged. Hence components of the collective unconscious can arise in respect to food and sex, male and female, wisdom and cruelty, birth and death.

The collective unconscious is collective only in the sense that it is inherited by every human being regardless of race, creed, color, or origin. It is given in the same way that the brain is given. It is made up of predispositions or tendencies or models or forms out of which images and emotions can arise spontaneously or in response to appropriate environmental situations. Jung calls these forms *archetypes;* they are the source of the symbols and motifs the unconscious normally tends to express (Jung, 1964, p. 64).

The archetypes give rise to experiences in dreams and other aspects of mental functioning which are completely new, so far as the person is concerned. They are not matters that have been repressed. They are absolutely new mental contents, of the kind that accompany most truly creative works of art or scientific insight. Jung tells us that the French mathematician Poincaré obtained insights in the form of sudden visualization of things he had never seen before.

Jung recounts the story of one professor who burst into his office to report a strange vision; he thought perhaps he was going insane. After hearing the man's description of the vision Jung reached for an ancient text showing medieval woodcuts. One of them matched exactly the vision this professor had experienced (Jung, 1964, p. 69). Although the image was completely new and indeed shocking to the professor, the symbolic forms he had seen in a vision had been seen before by others in visions of their own, hundreds of years before.

Jung states that the collective unconscious contains both instincts and archetypes. The former are seen more in actions; the latter more in experience. He defined *instincts* (1919/1971, p. 54) as modes of behavior that are typical for a species. Likewise the archetypes are typical modes of perceiving. As an example of the relation between instinct and archetype, Jung cites the yucca moth. This moth somehow recognizes the one night on which yucca flowers will open; it takes pollen from one flower and makes it into a pellet, which it stuffs into the pistil of another flower after laying eggs there. This happens only once in the moth's lifetime.

How does the yucca moth recognize the time and the plant and flower? It would be sufficient if it somehow was looking for an open flower of a certain shape, color, and so on. Of course it would have to know when

it found it. Jung proposes that the moth is born with an appropriate image, a *primordial image,* which is another name for archetype. That is, the moth inherits a specific capacity or disposition to form an image against which it can compare actual sensory inputs and "know" when it has found a match to the inner image among the myriad stimulus patterns coming from the environment.

Once the flower has been found the moth goes into its complicated routine of taking pollen, kneading it into a pellet, going to the second flower, cutting open the pistil, laying eggs, and stuffing the pellet into the opening of the second flower's pistil. All of these instinctive activities are triggered by the matching of an archetypal image with the environmental stimulus pattern.

The Archetypes also play an important role in Jung's theory of cause, and we shall return to discuss them further in that connection later in this chapter.

Jung's Theory of Types: A Pattern Theory

Recall from chapter 8 that the two most common forms of pattern theory are the temporal pattern theory, in which an order of events over time is proposed, and the classification pattern theory, in which one or more classes are described, each with a distinguishing pattern or constellation of characteristics. Some classifications are organized in a hierarchy such as the divisions, orders, families, genera (plural of genus) and species of flowering plants. Jung's theory of pattern is of the classification variety, a theory of types of personality.

Jung's theory is quite well known, especially as regards the contrast between *extraverts* and *introverts,* which will be described in detail below. Jung did not seek to label people simply as being of one type or the other, however (Jung, 1921/1971, p. xiv.)

That is, a person may be predominantly extraverted and yet have some signs of being introverted. Jung thought of each type as a set of characteristics associated with an underlying mechanism, one mechanism for introversion and one for extraversion (Jung, 1921/1971, p. 285). Although every person has both mechanisms, one becomes more fully developed in the conscious mind while the other remains undeveloped and unconscious. Jung places a person in a particular type according to characteristic pattern of conscious mental functions.

Actually this association with the mental functions is an integral part of Jung's theory of pattern. No one is simply introverted or extraverted, but is one or the other with respect to one of the four mental functions. Only one of these becomes fully developed in consciousness, be it thinking, feeling, sensing or intuiting. So the material that is actually available to an investigator who wishes to determine a person's type consists of evidence for predominant mental function in consciousness together with the particular attitude of mind in which that function operates, namely introverted or extraverted (Jung, 1923/1971, p. 519). According to Jung, functions that are not fully developed remain more less unconscious in operation, and appear only in quite undifferentiated form in the conscious mind. A brilliant thinker, for example, with poor feeling function, may have difficulty deciding what she likes. One with poor sensation function may wander down a street without noticing flowers, houses, or people. One with poor intuitive function may be plagued by premonitions of disease.

It will be convenient for our present purposes of exposition to begin with a discussion of extraverts and introverts without specific reference to the four functions, and then to go on with a description of the eight complete types, such as extraverted thinking, introverted thinking, extraverted feeling, introverted feeling, and so on.

Extravert and Introvert

The pair of contrasted types—extravert and introvert—based upon a person's attitude of mind was Jung's best known contribution to psychology. Although we think of an extravert in everyday life as a jolly, outgoing person and of an introvert as quiet and withdrawn, these characteristics are merely the visible surface manifestations of deeper and more pervasive aspects of personality. In part, *extraversion* means the preference for consciousness to be preoccupied with sense perceptions coming from the external world; *introversion* means preoccupation with perceptions from within.

If a person is predominantly reaching out toward stimuli in the environment, then the person has the *extra* (outward) *verted* (turned) mode of adaptation. If the person stays within and conserves and consolidates energy, then they are *intro* (inward) *verted*. The introverted type sends as little life energy as possible into the environment; environmental stimuli are denied the right to absorb one's interest and energy.

Jung says that the difference between an extravert and an introvert can often be seen in early infancy, and certainly during early childhood. This is true in cases of clear personality types, anyway. People do have degrees of introversion and extraversion. In fact Jung seems to indicate that a perfectly healthy adult would adapt in both ways, depending upon their suitability to the environment. But most people tend to have one attitude predominating in their makeup. That is, most people are either more extraverted or more introverted, and some are quite clearly one and not the other. Jung prefers to speak of the *attitude* of extraversion or of introversion, since this term conveys the idea of the subject's relation to the object; of the person's view of or interest in the things and people of the environment.

Jung suggested that there are physiological bases for the difference, although at the time of his writing these facts were not known. (Compare the work done by Eysenck on this subject, chapter 17.) Jung acknowledges, however, that the family may have an influence, especially if the parents are dominating. Moreover he also notes that the culture can insist upon one mode of adaptation rather than the other. American culture, for example, seems to insist on the extraverted attitude, and extraverted behaviors are given preference: one should be outgoing, jolly, friendly, sociable, active, responding with enthusiasm to the latest craze or fad. The success of advertising seems to depend upon this encouragement of persons to be guided by external stimuli.

However, Jung claims that if a child's natural bent is overridden by parental or cultural training the child becomes a good candidate for neurosis in adulthood. Extraversion and introversion seem to be randomly distributed, he notes: they are likely to occur equally in any social class, in men and women alike. This suggests that since there is a social preference for the extraverted type, large numbers of naturally introverted persons are forced to put on the appearance of extraversion in order to gain acceptance. All will be subject to strain, and many may become neurotic largely as a result of this strain. Conceivably such processes account for many persons who are mentally ill, although an appropriate research study has not yet been carried out to investigate this hypothesis.

Jung says the extravert's attention and interest are directed toward the environment—people as well as things. The extravert's behaviors are largely determined by such environmental factors, and his or her actions are "recognizably related to external conditions" (1921/1971, p. 334). The extravert is permanently fascinated by objective events. The moral code of an extravert is taken over unquestioningly from the social environment; if the social mores change so does the extravert's moral stance. The extravert fits in well regardless. Pouring all energy into objects and actions, the extravert often becomes oblivious to personal, subjective needs, even those of the body. Such persons can do great damage to their nervous systems through overwork.

By contrast, the introvert is oriented by subjective factors and interposes a subjective consideration between every environmental stimulus and her or his behavior in regard to it. Often this barrier makes the action less suited to the situation, and certainly does not result in the "expected" reaction. The introvert is more interested in "what this person or event means to me" than in "what does this person want or this situation demand?"

All of the above descriptions refer to the conscious part of personality, but there are also effects in the unconscious. In general, Jung says that the effects in the unconscious are *compensatory*. All of life involves both an object and a subject. Every perception involves something perceived (the object) and the perceiver (the subject). No knowing takes place without a knower. The subjective side of experience is just as much a fundamental aspect of existence as is the objective side. It is a given fact of mental life. The fact that people agree in their perceptions of basic entities like heat and cold, wet and dry, solid and soft may obscure for us a ready awareness of the fact of subjectivity. It comes out with sudden and sharp impact when someone sees things in a different way than usual. A hypnotized person may wince with pain when touched lightly with a piece of india rubber if he or she believes it to be a burning cigarette. I have seen novices in the Buddhist faith walk unperturbed across forty feet of smoldering coals. Every dentist knows that some persons have extra "sensitivity" to pain and so they give them shots for the slightest drilling. So the subjective factor is as much a fact as the objective. Many things in the culture are even acknowledged to be predominantly subjective, as preferences for musical styles among mature individualists. This is reflected in such aphorisms as "Beauty is in the eye of the beholder."

No less does the objective exist—the sticks and stones and other people of this world. They exist regardless of the amount of attention or interest a particular person accords them. So both the extreme extravert and the extreme introvert must be blind on one side, at least in consciousness. But their unconscious will compensate, says Jung. The more extraverted a person is in consciousness, the more introverted in the unconscious; and vice versa.

The effects of the compensation become apparent in extreme cases. For example, a man became a printer and gradually worked his way up till he owned a prosperous business, but he was completely absorbed in it and had no other interests. In compensation his unconscious roused up memories of childhood when he enjoyed drawing and painting. Rather than develop this as a hobby he turned it into his business and began putting childish drawings on his printed products. His business collapsed as a result. In this case the introverted tendencies of childhood memories rose up in revolt within him, demanding representation in his life from which he had consciously excluded every subjective factor in favor of "the business."

Eight Personality Types

As we saw earlier, Jung postulated eight basic personality types, that is, the introverted and extraverted varieties of persons predominantly adopting each of the four mental functions: thinking, feeling, sensation, and intuition. We shall examine the eight types in pairs, taking the two thinking types—extraverted and introverted—first.

Thinking Types. The conscious life of some people is governed mainly by thinking. Whatever they do is based upon thought.

In the *extraverted thinking type,* courses of action are pursued according to intellectual considerations of either objective facts or generally agreed-upon ideas. Some form of objective reality is given prime importance in this person's life, so that all good and all beautiful and all other valued and valuable aspects of living are determined by this objective framework. Such a person may easily take up arms for some social cause and become a reformer or public prosecutor or chief of police.

Within the intellectual formula there is no room for deviation based upon feelings or fantasy. "Irrational phenomena such as religious experiences, passions, and suchlike are often repressed to the point of complete unconsciousness" (Jung, 1921/1971, p. 348). The repressed trends of introversion can sometimes break forth in strange behavior in the extraverted thinking type. If they are especially altruistic people generally, an unaccountable bit of selfishness can suddenly rise up. Those who become "guardians of public morals" find themselves in situations which cast sudden severe doubt upon their own morality. Such cases can be found often in the daily newspaper.

The *introverted thinking type* is also concerned mainly with ideas, but the ideas spring from the subjective domain. This person is little related to objects, whether persons, things, or causes. He or she is more concerned with purely philosophical implications. Even in a direct exchange with another person the introverted thinking type gives the impression of being detached, cold, arbitrary. This person is pleased with his or her own ideas and wants them to be respected; but that should happen somehow without publicizing them or "pushing" them. Ideas should be put out simply, and then they should be appreciated by the force of their own intrinsic compelling worth. The introverted thinker does not feel it necessary to advertise them or repeat them or make necessary arrangements so that more people can understand them. The person tends to be silent and withdrawn, often awkward in social behavior. Such people make very poor teachers because they are unable to understand their students; they think solely about the material and not about how to present it.

Feeling Types. Jung groups feeling with thinking because both are in some sense "rational" processes (such as comparing and evaluating). He makes no mention of the person's sex in connection with thinking types, but of both feeling types he says that the most fully developed examples are to be found chiefly among women.

The *extraverted feeling type* is well adjusted to her environment, since her feelings tend to be harmonized with objective criteria. She does well in society. Even her love life is so conditioned and she tends to love and marry a man who would be considered "suitable" by family and friends. Her love is not the less genuine; it is merely "shrewd," based upon sound judgment (like other forms of feeling function, judgment is an evaluation). She makes a good wife and mother as long as her husband and children remain "conventional."

This person represses thinking functions, since thinking interferes with clear feeling. Everything that could disturb her acceptance of objective values is simply not thought. Since life is filled with situations which are complex in their effects on feeling, the only way

this person can adjust to such inner realities is to have them dissociated from her ego: their effects "come over" her in unaccountable "moods." The more these unconscious reactions threaten to upset the conventional patterns of evaluation, the more gushing and extravagant the person becomes.

In the *introverted feeling type* we find a melancholy depth of personality and motive. You never know what their true motives are. Outwardly such people seem quiet and easy, without ostentation; yet their relationships with others remain superficial, for the most part. However, they have a tendency to develop deep and obscure passions, sometimes expressed in secret religious devotion or poetic expressions. Also they have a way of relating to others which appears to be silently dominating. Especially toward men they are likely to undercut the other person's enthusiasms and emotional expressions with a slightly superior intimation that it is degenerate to express oneself on such matters. "It gives a woman of this type a mysterious power that may prove terribly fascinating to the extraverted man, for it touches his unconscious" (Jung, 1921/1971, p. 390).

Sensation Types. By contrast with thinking and feeling, the functions of sensation and intuition are called *irrational*, which means simply that they do not involve logical or evaluative propositions.

The *extraverted sensation type* is most commonly a man, according to Jung. In this person realism is carried to an extreme. His life consists of rushing around from one experience of concrete things to another. Life is to be lived to the full, this person thinks; and that means eating, drinking, and good times. He is a good host and people like him. He is good company and makes lively entertainment. He loves a woman primarily for her physical attractiveness.

In such people intuition functions are the most heavily repressed. If they are repressed too much and begin to reassert themselves, an irrational suspiciousness emerges.

The *introverted sensation type* places great emphasis upon the subjective side of sensations. That is, these people are guided by what happens to them as a result of stimulation. If you interact with such a person, for example, he or she acknowledges what you have said and then immediately reacts with a subjective (and often unrelated) development. "The Cardinals won last night," you say. This type is liable to reply, "Somehow I don't get the same thrill out of ball games anymore as I once used to;" or "It really turns me on when the Orioles come from behind." Just what these expressions really convey is difficult to understand; indeed the introverted sensation type is not easily understood, even by himself or herself.

Intuition Types. The *extraverted intuition type* is highly dependent upon external situations, but in an unusual way, always on the lookout for new and interesting possibilities. Stable conditions are not what this type thrives on. If this person develops a vision of some new program everything else becomes subordinate to the achievement of that goal; it controls his or her moral judgment. But as soon as the new program is established this person becomes bored with it and moves on to something else new and interesting. Such people are often found in entrepreneurial positions, as speculators, or as politicians who can move from one great cause to another. Valuable to society since they initiate change, they promote new enterprises and champion minorities "with a future." Somehow they inspire others and set things in motion.

Introverted intuition type tend to be seers, artists, dreamers. At the extreme such people become cranks with a vision. They seem remote from reality and often do not do more with their vision than proclaim it. But if their attitude goes to extremes, if the world of sensation is denied completely, then it reasserts itself in the unconscious, and the intuitive type is the one who represses sensation the most. Sensation will then be unconsciously restored by the compensatory power of the unconscious. For the introverted intuitive type it is extraverted sensation that is unconsciously expressed. In extremes, such people are crudely dependent upon sensation, in symptoms of sickness and hypersensitivity of the sense organs, and also in strangely compulsive ties to particular objects or to persons. In less extreme forms they are found to be slow in all matters requiring attention to external sensory details. One of Jung's close associates, Marie-Louise von Franz (1971, p. 8) gives the example of an intuitive introvert having trouble with official forms, such as tax forms. The more the details must be accurate the slower and more difficult the task is for such people. She relates a trip to a store with an introverted intuitive woman who wanted a blouse. But choosing which blouse to buy took the woman ages—"an eternity—until the whole shop is mad!"

Jung's Theory of Cause

Complexes

The theory of cause developed by Jung has five basic constructs which will be examined below. These are: *energy, libido, repression, archetypes,* and *symbols.* The basic underlying notions can perhaps best be seen in the work he did early in his career on the topic of word association. For here he came upon some clear psychological events which suggested to him the existence of relatively autonomous centers of energy attached to a set of related ideas. It was as though there existed in the unconscious a *complex* of ideas highly charged with emotion. A complex consists of ideas which are related either by having similar meaning or by reference to a common situation or event that is filled with conflict for the person concerned. Evidence of the complex was seen in several features of the individual's responses to a word-association test (Jung, 1909/1973).

Jung used a standard list of words selected to cover typical conflicts. The list included one hundred words (such as *water, dead, to dance, angry, yellow, lead pencil, to marry, wild, anxiety, mouth,* and others). The subject was instructed to listen to each word as given by the examiner, and to respond as quickly as possible by giving the first association word that came to mind. For example, a subject might respond as follows: *water—*wet; *dead—*duck; *to dance—*to sing; *angry—*man. . . . For normal subjects Jung reports that most reactions are given within three seconds, timed by stopwatch from the moment when the accented syllable of the stimulus word is given.

Subjects vary in their average reaction time, and because of the occasionally very long reaction times (and some complete failures to react). Jung recommends that a subject's average time be estimated by the median value, that time which exactly divides the subject's reaction times in two so that 50 percent are longer and 50 percent shorter. From extensive studies with normal subjects, men and women, educated and uneducated, Jung concludes that the median value for a subject is most likely to lie between 1.3 and 2.2 seconds (Jung, 1905b/1973, p. 227).

One sign of a complex is an unduly long reaction time relative to the subject's median time. For example, one normal subject had twelve reactions longer than five seconds. These included seven reactions to words suggesting an erotic complex: *wedding, to kiss, to love, male nurse, dream, ripe, to bless* (Jung, 1904, 1973, p. 111). Failure to respond at all is similarly a *complex indicator,* the technical term Jung gave to signs indicating the presence of a complex. Another indicator is given when the subject responds by repeating the stimulus word (as if trying to make its meaning sink in). Reasoning from Freud's hypothesis of repression, Jung proposed that subjects would be especially likely to forget the response they gave to words which stimulated a complex. Accordingly he added a second run through the stimulus words, allowing the subject time to recall his or her previous responses. When the recall failed it was taken as another complex indicator. For instance one patient appeared to have a complex surrounding the idea that he might commit suicide by drowning himself. He failed to recall, among others, his responses to numerous stimuli touching this complex, such as: *water—*to drown; *ship—*crew; *to swim—*not; *to threaten* —me; and so on (Jung, 1905a/1973, pp. 275-278).

To summarize, Jung maintains that the presentation of a word stimulus arouses imagery and emotional reactions related to the scene or situation referred to by the word, and so the subject's response to that situation is effectively reproduced by the word stimulus. If the related memories and images are charged with disturbing emotional energy then the subject's adaptive response is impeded in some way, either by undue delay, by complete failure to comply with the simple instructions, or by a clouding of consciousness so that the person repeats the stimulus word, fumbling for its meaning. When several disturbed responses appear connected in meaning Jung proposes that an underlying complex is responsible for the energy used in effecting the disturbance.

Energy

Energy is one of five main constructs in Jung's theory of cause. Jung takes two views of energy, one physical and one psychological. In the physical sense energy as found in life forms is exactly the same as energy found in electromechanical and nuclear phenomena. In the psychological sense energy is the basis of psychic power, or *libido*. Jung writes of energy in the biological or physical sense that it comes from the sun: "The sun is the father-god from whom all living things draw life; he is the fructifier and creator, the source of energy for our world" (1911/1967, p. 121).

This formulation makes it sound as though Jung takes a purely ecologic or ecosystem view of energy. He does not. Although he asserts time and again that our physiological life is based upon solar energy, he states even more often that it has a psychic side, as revealed in the inward perceptions of mystics, for example. In such views the source of energy becomes personified and is felt to be located within the person, an ultimate Self. Jung quotes the description of Rudra (a wind- or storm-god) in the Hindu Upanishads: "There is one Rudra only. . . . He is the one God who created heaven and earth. . . . A mighty Lord is . . . that Person, no bigger than a thumb, the inner Self, seated forever in the heart of man, is revealed by the heart, the thought, the mind." (quoted in Jung, 1911/1967, p. 122).

The psychological side of energy also seems to be stored up, quite like stored energy in coal or oil, so that it does not depend upon momentary supplies of sunshine. For Jung writes: "psychic energy . . . the life of the psyche is the life of mankind. Welling up from the depths of the unconscious, its springs gush forth from the root of the whole human race, since the individual is, biologically speaking, only a twig broken off from the mother and transplanted" (1911/1967, p. 202). Somehow this energy accumulates through generations and is passed on in the shape of "ideas, forms, and forces which grip and mould the soul. These . . . are the archetypal contents of the (collective) unconscious, the archaic heritage of humanity, the legacy left behind by all differentiation and development and bestowed upon all men like sunlight and air" (1911/1967, p. 177-178).

Now in this latter form the energy seems to be spiritual. Jung often calls it *numinous,* which means supernatural, mysterious, wonderful, awesome, divine. It is the kind of energy we all know more clearly as a feeling of being energetic or exuberant or potent. It seems to me that it is the kind of energy that is meant when we speak about "high morale" in an athletic team or in a business group. It is something that goes beyond the energy of food and oxygen. It often appears in the form of spiritual revival or renewal, a freshening of mind and hope and outlook. It is the kind of energy that a person of purpose has and a person in neurotic conflict and depression does not have.

Jung examines the question of a spiritual life, of God. He does not ask whether God exists, nor does he try to prove it. He simply observes that all people at all times have formed an idea of God: as light, as fire, as the sun, as love, as omnipotent. "Psychologically, God is the name for a complex of ideas grouped round a powerful feeling; the feeling-tone . . . [and] represents an emotional tension which can be formulated in terms of energy" (1911/1967, p. 85). Some people, Jung says, will attribute the idea of God to the environmental fact of the sun, preferring an explanation of these phenomena which makes the environment causal. Others believe rather that the inner psychic dispositions provide observations of the sun with a feeling of numinous power. Thus the second belief holds that psychic experience is spontaneous, welling up from within. Jung's own view is that "the psychoenergic phenomenon not only takes precedence, but explains far more than the hypothesis of the causal primacy of the environment" (1911/1967, p. 86).

Jung believes that there is an archetype of God, a primordial image which can harness the person's psychic energy around a particular image of God. Using psychic energy in this way leads to the release of additional stored energy. For now the person can gain morale from the recognition that God is within. Such beliefs are part of many religions, according to Jung, who quotes Seneca: "God is near you. . . . He is within you." Jung suggests that it means a great deal to carry a god around in yourself, for it can be a guarantee of happiness, of power, a strengthening of the individual against the weakness and insecurities of personal life. The seeds of spiritual energy, it seems are within the person, and—possibly—through the medium of belief in God this energy may be released and provide additional sources of strength.

Libido

Jung uses the term *libido* to mean "psychic energy in the widest sense" (1911/1967, p. 64). It certainly includes sexual interests, but it refers more generally to all instincts, all appetites, compulsions, wants, wishes, pleasures, and longings: "the concept of libido in psychology has functionally the same significance as the concept of energy in physics . . ." (1911/1967, p. 131).

Libido is directed outwards, normally, in the form of interests in things and people, in the form of love and creativity. It is compared to "a steady stream pouring its waters into the world of reality . . ." (1911/1967, p. 173).

The libido both serves the ego and presents the ego with demands for expression. Jung says that [the libido] "stands in part at the disposal of the ego, and in part confronts the ego autonomously, sometimes influencing it so powerfully that it is either put in a position of unwilling constraint, or else discovers in the libido itself a new and unexpected source of strength" (1911/1967, pp. 64, 65).

Evidence suggests that libido is symbolized in one of four different ways. First it may be symbolized *by analogy,* as when it is compared with the sun or with fire. Then it may be symbolized *by its objects,* as when nudists and other sun worshippers revere and love the sun because of its health-giving properties. Third, it may be symbolized *by the instruments used to express it,* as for example in the phallus (symbol of male genital) or an analogue (such as a snake or pole). The fourth way of symbolizing the libido is *by comparing its activity with the symbol,* as for example "Libido is fertile like the bull, dangerous like a lion (because of the fury of its passion . . ." (1911/1967, p. 97).

Jung's book on the *Symbols of Transformation* from which we have been quoting is actually about the symbols used by human beings throughout time to represent the libido and transformations in libido. Such transformations occur at major points of change in our lives, as in the transition from childhood to adolescence, or from school to work, from single to married state, and so on. They also occur in transformations that are due to conflicts and repression.

Repression

A good example of repression is given by Jung (1911/1967, p. 58). A young lady watched a ship's officer singing on the bridge and felt not a little romantic about it. Later she produced a poem about God making sound throughout the universe, but the ship's officer was not mentioned. That provides an example of repression. Jung says that this term "repression" best denotes a voluntary act of putting something out of our minds. Nervous persons, he says, can manage to hide such voluntary decisions from themselves, as the young lady apparently did.

Repression is "an illegitimate way of evading the conflict, for it means pretending to oneself that it does not exist . . ." (1911/1967, p. 59). It also has bad consequences, for it leads to "regressive reactivation of an earlier relationship or type of relatedness, in this case the reactivation of the father-image." Jung says that repression leads to a regression of libido and reawakens or "constellates" unconscious contents, first from the personal unconscious (the person's own father-image, for instance), and then from the collective unconscious. For if the regression goes back beyond the period of childhood, "then archetypal images appear, no longer connected with individual's memories, but belonging to the stock of *inherited possibilities of representation* that are born anew in every individual" (1911/1967, p. 181).

In the case of the young lady and her poem, the regression goes first back to the childhood father-image, and then on back to such an "inherited possibility of representation," namely, God as the Father of All Things, including sound. The image of the all-powerful deity, Creator of the universe, is an archetypal image, an inherited possibility of representation. Notice that the image is *projected* into the environment. Jung says that unconscious contents are always projected, in the sense of being "discovered" out there in external objects, or believed to exist outside of our own psyche. He writes: "A repressed conflict and its affective tone must reappear *somewhere*" (1911/1967, p. 59). This projection makes it reappear outside the individual psyche, and such projection is unconscious, Jung says. It happens automatically as a consequence of the repression.

Archetypes

We have already described the essential features of *archetypes*: they are inherited dispositions to form images of a certain kind. In studying the dreams of a black American male, Jung found the image of Ixion (a king in Greek mythology) stretched out and bound by hands and feet to the sun-wheel. This man had had no previous exposure to mythology. Many similar instances lead Jung to conclude that archetypes are not related to particular racial heredity but are universally human. They are not strictly inherited ideas, but are rather *dispositions* to produce the same or similar ideas (1911/1967, p. 102).

Archetypes are said to have a numinous or spiritual power capable of forcefully confronting the person's ego. Jung wrote, "All archetypal contents have a certain autonomy since they appear spontaneously and can often exercise an overwhelming compulsion" (1911/1967, p. 178).

In the dreams of patients and even in their symptoms one sometimes finds motifs that are incomprehensible in terms of the patient's life experiences. In one case a fairly healthy military officer developed pains around the heart, a lump in his throat, and piercing pains in the left heel. It turned out that the girl he loved had run off with another man. He had tried to ignore his emotion, but the "broken heart" made itself felt anyway, and the tears that he choked back returned as a choking lump. Although these two symptoms were cleared up, the heel continued to hurt and resisted explanation. Then the officer had a dream in which a snake bit him on the heel. This dream made the symptom understandable in terms of the motif in Genesis and in ancient Egyptian mythology of woman damaging man through snake bite. The officer was not aware of this theme, which rose up from the collective unconscious into the dream, even as it had risen up into the strange symptom (Jung, 1927/1971, p. 33).

Countless examples of such matching have provided evidence that the archetypes exist as archaic motifs, ever ready to form a representation or symbolization of some complex experience. They may rise up to represent a complex event that has already happened, as in the officer's case. They may rise up to represent a complicated change of personality that is about to take place. They may rise up to warn the person of an impending event, as in the case of a young girl whose dreams clearly foreshadowed her impending death (Jung, 1964, pp. 70-71).

The archetypes are forms that seek expression. They are instinctive *trends,* Jung said (1964, p. 69): "instincts are physiological urges, and are perceived by the senses. But at the same time, they also manifest themselves in fantasies and often reveal their presence only by symbolic images . . . the archetypes. They are without known origin; and they reproduce themselves in any time or in any part of the world—even where transmission by direct descent or "cross-fertilization" through migration must be ruled out."

Archetypes and Personality Functions

Energy flows into particular forms and structures, according to archetypes. The archetypes include a number of widely recognized "numinous" figures such as God, the wise old man, the Great Mother Earth, and so on. They also include representations of important parts of the personality, notably the *persona,* the *shadow,* the *self,* the *animus,* and the *anima.*

The *persona* is a mask the individual consciously adopts in interaction with society. It is the social personality. It is, Jung says, a compromise "between individual and society as to what a man should appear to be. He takes a name, earns a title, exercises a function, he is this or that" (Jung, 1928/1966, p. 158). Jung makes it clear that even this semblance of individual personality is actually prearranged as an archetypal form of the collective unconscious, for all men since earliest times have had to adapt to society's demands in one way or another.

The *shadow* is made up of aspects of ourselves that have been repressed. It is "the 'negative' side of the personality, the sum of all those unpleasant qualities we like to hide . . ." (Jung, 1917/1966, p. 66, fn. 5). It corresponds more or less to the personal unconscious. The shadow corresponds to baser emotions, more primitive features of our personality. Though it has mainly a "dark" side of potentials for evil, the shadow also contains those potentials for good which for some reason we have tried to hide from ourselves. As Hillman says (1974, p. 80), the shadow can "carry any incompatible aspect—one's unlived sexuality or primitivity and one's unlived potential achievements and cultural sensitivity."

The human being has a bisexual origin and the personality contains aspects of both male and female. In the woman the masculine side is referred to as *animus;* the feminine side in the man is called the *anima.* Jung states that no experience would be possible without built-in subjective capacity for such experience. So also with experiences of the other sex; each human being has appropriate "innate psychic structures." Jung says, "Thus the whole nature of man presupposes woman, both physically and spiritually. His system is tuned in to woman from the start, just as it is prepared for a quite definite world where there is water, light, air, salt, carbohydrates, etc. The form of the world into which he is born is already inborn in him as a virtual image. . . . An inherited collective image of woman exists in a man's unconscious, with the help of which he apprehends the nature of woman" (Jung, 1928/1966, p. 190). This inborn image of woman also contributes to femininity in a man's soul. Similarly, the woman has an inborn image of man.

Society requires a given persona, however; notably a masculine persona for men and a feminine persona for women. What happens to the animus and anima? They become suspect. Jung (1964, p. 29 ff.) quotes one patient who dreamed of a drunken and disorderly woman as being his wife. In fact his wife was quite different. Jung interpreted the dream as meaning that the patient's female side was in a disorderly state; in other words, the patient was behaving in some ways like a disorderly female.

We have left consideration of the *self* till last, because it is the archetype of unity, the goal of all psychological development. Whereas the ego is essentially on its own, the center of the person's own separate individual consciousness, the self shares deeply in the collective unconscious. The self is not alone, but is aware of the basic similarity with other selves. It feels kinship with all mankind and with all spiritual as well as biological forms of life. When the archetype of the self becomes active within the person it is located partway between conscious and the unconscious, with the person accepting and even enjoying the energies and images of the collective unconscious. When an individual can abandon the precarious hold on reality that the ego has, locked as it is in a world only of conscious contents, and when the person can rest upon and draw strength from the energies of the unconscious, then the center of his or her being is shifted from ego to self, from consciousness to a point midway between consciousness and the collective unconscious.

There are numerous archetypal images of the self, all in the general form of a *mandala*. Mandalas are typically round forms enclosed by a square, often with towers or figures at the corners. Figure 12.1 shows the typical mandala self and one man's personal image of unity in the shape of a clock surrounded by a circle. It also portrays archetypal images as reaching up through consciousness, gathering up many ideas into complexes, each complex charged with energy associated with a particular archetype.

The image shown in figure 12.1 comes from another of Jung's patients (1938). This man's dreams and drawings gradually converged on this image of a clock set in a horizontal circle with four figures equally spaced around the circle's rim. In this instance it took Jung a long time to find another version of the image. Finally, in the writings of a thirteenth-century monk, he found a passage describing his patient's vision exactly. The clock was a "world clock" and the figures were forms of God: the Trinity plus one other. What could the other be? It was Mary the Virgin Mother. The entire symbol reflected the man's struggles with religion, which he had rejected as incompatible with his scientific creed. It pointed the way toward integration: an acceptance of both science (the world clock, with exact measurements) and religion encircling but not interfering with science (the forms of the Trinity and also Mary the Mother of Jesus, the four worshipped in the Catholic faith).

Many archetypal images appear in the form of symbols such as the mandala symbols. Jung said that symbols are "images of contents which for the most part transcend consciousness . . ." (1911/1967, p. 77). A symbol is "an indefinite expression with many meanings, pointing to something not easily defined, and therefore not fully known. . . . The same creative force which is symbolized by Tom Thumb . . . can also be represented by the phallus or by . . . *creative dwarfs* [who] toil away in secret . . . and the *key* [which] unlocks the mysterious forbidden door behind

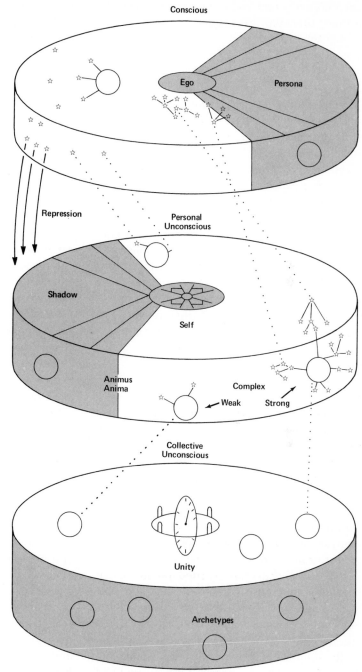

Figure 12.1. Some of the main dynamics of personality according to Jung's theory. From Cartwright, D. S., **Introduction to Personality,** Chicago: Rand McNally, 1974, p. 135. Reprinted by permission of the publisher.

which some wonderful thing awaits discovery" (Jung, 1911/1967, p. 124).

Summary

We have now completed our presentation of three main component theories in Jung's overall theory of personality. Perhaps they may be summarized as follows. We are born with instincts and archetypes. The archetypes reach up to control the development of our personality, including persona, ego, shadow, and other aspects. The archetypes control the emergence of consciousness and, in interaction with a given culture (which specifies broadly the contents of the persona), they also control the formation of the personal unconscious. The archetypes of course are principal forms of activity in the collective unconscious. They therefore are directly responsible for the formation of the personality structure and also provide the forms through which psychic energy flows through the personality.

Accomplishments of Jung's Theory

Impact on Psychotherapy

Jung's theories have had a marked impact upon psychotherapy. The body of techniques he developed is known as *analytical psychotherapy*, and is now practiced by Jungian analysts all over the world. In addition to the C. G. Jung Institute, which was founded in Zurich in 1948, there are training institutes for Jungian analysis in most countries of Western Europe, Brazil, and the United States. Their training may be carried on in one of the three main institutes (New York, Los Angeles, and San Francisco), or in one of the several Regional Training Divisions, in which the academic curriculum is pursued at a locally suitable university and the trainee undergoes a training analysis with a qualified Jungian analyst. As of 1973 about 400 qualified analysts were members of the International Association for Analytical Psychology (Whitmont and Kaufmann, 1973).

Jung conceived of the process of psychotherapy as bringing the individual into closer contact with the unconscious, both personal and collective, and enabling the person to draw upon the great resources of the unconscious in guiding and developing the total personality and its expression in living. He believed that the demands of life are different for people over forty than they are for younger people, and that the process of therapy would be quite different. The young must strive to make concrete adaptations to the society and the economy, must establish themselves somehow and create the necessary base for raising a family. Their lives are properly filled with materialistic ambition and the strivings for reputation that motivate exceptional effort. But for older people such similar strivings cannot be realistically maintained. Older people, having themselves developed their extraverted capacities to the full in building a position for themselves in the social world, must now turn to proper development of their introverted side. They must turn inward and direct their attention to the accomplishment of spiritual goals. They must seek to become centered anew in the archetype of the self. These concepts are readily revealed in Jung's actual practice. For example, the patient whose image was described above as a unification of his consciously valued career as a scientist with his previously unconscious striving for spiritual peace was a patient in the middle years of life. What was unconscious was precisely the struggle for spiritual experience. By contrast, Jung reports the dream of a young man in which he saw his father drunkenly careening down the street in an automobile and then crashing into a wall. The young man had an excellent relationship with his father, admired him, and knew very well that his father actually was a very safe driver and most unlikely to get drunk. Jung assumed simply that the young man's unconscious had a good reason for producing this dream, and since it clearly depreciated his father, then its compensatory purpose would probably be to suggest that his relationship with his father was *too* good. By depreciating the father, the dream warns that the son is living a "provisional life," guaranteed by the father's greatness and thereby hindering the son's realization of his own potentials for accomplishment and growth (Jung, 1933, pp. 19-20). Neurosis for a younger person is marked by shrinking back from the demands to expand and conquer material and social rewards for oneself (Jung 1933, p. 58), and simply basking in the father's light is one way of avoiding the demand for personal expansion. For an older person neurosis is similarly marked by the attempt to continue youthful expansion or preoccupation beyond its due season.

A variety of procedures may be found in Jungian analysis, and Jung himself employed a great many techniques that seemed suitable for a given patient, including drawing, dream work, and active imagination, a technique derived from his studies of his own fantasies. Whitmont and Kaufmann (1973) suggest four main phases in a Jungian analysis. First, through an investigation of the patient's current life situation and personal history, the analyst attempts to understand as fully as possible the nature of the patient's present conscious personality. Second, through questions about the meanings of various features of experience, the analyst begins to teach the patient to look into hidden feelings and unspoken assumptions. The third phase goes more directly to working upon the products of the unconscious through fantasies, dreams, or other expressive media. As this "encounter with the unconscious" continues, the person inevitably goes into the fourth stage, realizing that the ego is not in charge of everything; power-

ful forces at work within the unconscious, the archetypes, are autonomous in operation and often independent in origin of anything in the individual's personal history or learning.

A Model for Dream Analysis

Dream analysis is central in Jungian psychotherapy. Jung's approach to actual work with dreams was extremely practical, ready to lay theoretical preconceptions aside at all times. Yet his theoretical model of dreams guided the practical work. His general view of the dream as a psychic phenomenon (his model object of the dream) was that it was a solid existing fact in the psychic life of the dreamer, with as much importance for the self-regulation of the psychic system as the level of sugar in the urine has for the self-regulation of the body (Jung, 1933, p. 5). Jung's theoretical model of the dream drew upon the constructs of the conscious and the unconscious parts of personality structure, upon the causal constructs of the archetypes and upon the hypotheses of repression, and also upon what Jung regarded as the *law of compensation*. The psyche is a self-regulating system which maintains relative equilibrium; every process which goes to extreme immediately elicits a compensatory process. He likens compensation in the psyche to metabolism in the body. In particular, too little in the conscious mind results in too much in the unconscious (Jung, 1933, p. 17). We have seen this law at work in Jung's theory of extraversion-introversion above. In the context of dreams, the law states that the dream conveys to the person's consciousness the current compensatory state of the unconscious. Thus dreams reveal whatever subjective state is denied consciously.

Dreams do more than that, however. Since the causes of neurosis are in the unconscious, dreams can reveal the causes. In addition they often offer a forecast of how the neurosis or the recovery will progress, and sometimes offer suggestions for treatment. For example, the dream of the young man who was too devoted to his father suggested that he give active conscious consideration to the contrasts between himself and his father, and thereby develop a fuller realization of his own separate identity.

Jung's theoretical model of dreams, then, holds that they are unconditionally meaningful, even if we consciously find them confusing and obscure. Their language is that of image, myth, and symbolic representation; hence they are to be considered as texts which we must translate. Sometimes their meaning is readily understood, and sometimes it takes prolonged study. Jung rejects the Freudian idea that dreams are the manifest form of a latent unconscious striving; he rejects the distinction between manifest and latent content of dreams. He also rejects the idea that free association to the dream elements will lead to the ultimate sources of the dreams. Rather, such associations lead *away* from the dream and wind inevitably down to whatever complexes the individual has, points which would be reached anyway starting from anywhere. By contrast, since the contents of the dream are symbolic, and since a symbol is a representation of that which is obscure and difficult to describe, Jung seeks to *establish the context* for every image in a dream. If a woman dreams of an oak table, she is not to be asked to associate to it willy-nilly, associating it, for example, with her wrought-iron garden table, and then to a table of contents of a book, and so on and on. Rather, she would be asked directly to describe this oak table and give its history in a way that would make it completely understandable to someone who did not previously know what an oak table was.

After the context is established, interpretation can begin. If the meaning is not already clear, the first question asked by the analyst takes account of the law of compensation: What aspect of consciousness does the dream compensate? (The answer requires a very good understanding of the patient's present conscious state, of course, which would be the very first stage in therapy as described above.) Again the case of the young man devoted to his father offers an illustration: What would a dream depreciating his father be compensating for? Precisely for overvaluation of the father at the expense of his own identity development.

The vague notion of "conscious contact with the unconscious" is made very specific in the course of dream work with an individual patient. Interpretations of the dream images as symbols with archetypal meaning are conveyed to the patient for consideration. The discussion between patient and therapist provides a training for internal discussion: The patient must ultimately work for assimilation on a continuing basis for the rest of life. *Assimilation* is the penetration of consciousness by meanings from the unconscious and vice versa. It goes both ways: There must be continuing dialogue. The patient is instructed in the technique of establishing the context of each dream image on his or her own and of writing down the dreams and context. Later in treatment the therapist encourages the patient to formulate interpretations and seek the guidance of suggestions for change contained in the dream. Ideally, the goal of being in contact with the unconscious is achieved by a continuing exercise of assimilative experience, drawing upon the contents of the unconscious as presented especially in dreams.

We have concentrated in this section upon the accomplishments of Jung's theory in psychotherapy and dream analysis, partly because of the great importance in our time of concrete efforts toward the amelioration of mental suffering, and partly because it allows for a very concrete demonstration of those accomplishments. Jung's model of dreams is in fact a major competitor with Freud's model, and the two models often arrive at exactly opposite interpretations of a given dream, as Whitmont and Kaufmann (1973, pp. 91-92) emphasize. For example, in one dream cited by a Freudian analyst, a woman patient dreamed first that she was being photographed in the nude, in different positions; second, that a man was holding a curved yardstick with sexually suggestive writing on it; and a red monster was biting the man with sharp teeth, and the man rang a bell for help, but no one except the patient heard it and she didnt care. The Freudian's interpretation suggested that the dreamer was resisting recognition of her disgust with her own sex organs (her own femininity). The Jungian interpretation would suggest that the dreamer was resisting recognition of her own masculine side (the animus archetype, represented by the man in the dream). As Jung said, the second of two dreams is usually more specific.

The Unconscious and Modern Society

The importance of the model of dreams lies not only in scientific struggle between giant theoreticians, about which we shall learn more in the next chapter. It lies also in the implications for the nature of the unconscious: and that means for the nature of each human being as an individual and for the human race as a whole.

Many believe that humanity will not survive if progress in self-understanding fails to catch up with progress in understanding the forces of the atom, and Jung also believed that, as he made clear in the body of his work on *Modern Man in Search of a Soul* (1933). He believed that modern society places too much emphasis upon the conscious mind and knows too little of the unconscious. Jung grappled with the problems faced by individuals who have rejected the irrational from their conscious lives, people who deny the existence of a spiritual side in human nature, and who thereby attempt to depreciate and diminish the unconscious and its manifestations in religion and art on one side and in mental disorder and war on the other. In Jung's view the Freudians had contributed to the problem by emphasizing the primitive, bestial, destructive nature of the unconscious. By contrast, Jung held that the unconscious becomes dangerous only when repressed, a condition which is helped along by depreciation, ridicule, and refusal to acknowledge its existence.

Jung notes that he is not the first to point to the existence and power of the unconscious; he acknowledges the contribution of Freud and Janet, and, beyond them by the great German philosophers Kant and Leibniz, writing respectively one hundred and fifty and two hundred and fifty years ago. The point of citing this history is to dramatize the fact that human beings do not easily accept the idea that they have an unconscious mind which has autonomous power; they do not easily accept the general proposition, and consequently human progress in understanding the detailed working of the unconscious has advanced very little in two and a half centuries. For it was Jung's opinion to the end that his own attempts to penetrate the depths of the unconscious had succeeded only a little, and that the realm of the yet unknown was infinite.

Critique of Jung's Theories

Jung's theories have been criticized primarily for two reasons. First, it is claimed they are confused and unclear in meaning; second, they are called unscientific.

The construct of a *collective unconscious* is certainly open to several different interpretations, and Jung did not state one formal definition for this construct which he was willing to retain basically unchanged. The idea that the collective unconscious resides in every individual's brain as a set of potentials for experience was an early formulation of the construct; in later years, as he developed his search of ancient myths as the carriers of archetypal motifs, he emphasized also the differences between the mythologies of different cultures and different eras. It was due to the fact of these differences that he had to positively *search* for the themes that could be shown to be common between Hindu, Greek, Persian, Chinese, and other mythologies. As Progoff (1973, p. 145) has written, Jung maintained that "the archetypes are psychic patterns present in all mankind as a species, but . . . they are carried through time and reach individual personality only via the symbolism of myths and unconsciously held beliefs transmitted within national cultures." It is thus not clear whether the archetypes (as prime structural components of collective unconscious) are transmitted through genetic means ("as a species") or cultural means ("only via the symbolism of myths"). Perhaps both means of transmission are intended, but if so, then neither can be the "only" means of transmission. Or perhaps the pattern is transmitted genetically and the content culturally; if so, it is not clearly spelled out, and that has led to confusion.

Another source of confusion among scientists has been the proliferation of constructs. Eysenck (1970, p. 15), for instance, has pointed out that Jung's construct of extraversion is actually a complex of several constructs, "involving four 'functions' arranged in contrasting pairs, all of which can be extraverted or introverted, and which compensate each other in a complex manner. . . ."

Jung was frequently charged with being unscientific, especially in connection with his work on religion, alchemy, astrology and other "mystical" matters. For example, Eysenck says of Jung: "by allowing his mystical notions to overshadow the empirical, observational data he has done his best to remove the concept of personality type from the realm of scientific discourse" (Eysenck, 1970, p. 15).

Jung's reply to the charge of mysticism was always in essence as follows: If an important aspect of human psychology is mysticism, then it is a legitimate subject for scientific psychological study. Indeed he maintained that religious striving and imagery are at the core of human personality and therefore cannot be avoided by an unbiased observer. We shall encounter this issue again in chapter 13 when we examine the criticisms leveled at Jung by Freud.

As with so many of Freud's constructs, those of Jung are slowly being given operational meaning by other researchers. Two well-developed and reliable questionnaire measures of Jung's type constructs are now available (Gray & Wheelwright, 1946; Myers, 1962). In one series of careful studies (Stricker & Ross, 1964a, 1964b), the scores from the Myers instrument have been found reliable and stable and to have good validity (see Appendix B for a brief discussion of statistics, reliability and validity). However, the scores do not seem to be precise measures of the variables in Jung's theory: extraversion, introversion, sensation-intuition, and thinking-feeling. For example, the measure of extraversion is based upon degree of talkativeness and similar reported characteristics, and it is suggested that other determinants of talkativeness may be more influential than extraversion in affecting the scores obtained. Moreover, it was found that the scores fail to reveal two modes in the distribution, one for extraverts and one for introverts. Rather, the scores are spread evenly about the midpoint of the scale. It suggests that extraversion is a continuous variable rather than a sharply split characteristic. People may fall anywhere along the continuum from extreme extravert to extreme introvert, with most being only slightly extraverted or slightly introverted.

Katherine Bradway (1964) has shown that a sample of twenty-eight Jungian analysts classified themselves as predominantly introverted-intuitive types and were also so classified by the Myers and by the Gray-Wheelwright tests.

Shapiro and Alexander (1975) note that many psychologists have attempted to measure the extraversion-introversion variable, but that the many different measures proposed have had little in common. They explore fully Jung's various definitions of the constructs and conclude that an approach from the phenomenological viewpoint is likely to be most fruitful. This viewpoint refers to the experience of the subject. Thus introversion would be studied as it feels or is experienced by an introvert. Shapiro and Alexander develop procedures to find measurable aspects of experience with respect to which extraverts differ from introverts. They first divide a sample of persons into extraverts and introverts on the basis of a clinical interview, and then examine the responses of the two groups to the *Thematic Apperception Test* (TAT; see chapter 3 for a description of the instrument). Their results, while meager, are quite interesting. First, they find that introverts assume there is a greater psychological distance between people. For example, they do not introduce another person into their stories told to TAT cards showing just one person. Moreover, when there are several persons in a group whose unity or shared interests could be emphasized, introverts do not make such emphasis; rather they emphasize the differences between the individuals. For example, suppose three students were roommates and two left for spring vacation. J. B., the remaining student, wakes up the next morning and thinks about the others. Which of the following thoughts do you suppose J. B. has?

1. Gee, there's little in common between us all.
2. How different Bob and Jack are from each other.
3. What a close-knit group we've become.
4. How similar we all are.

According to the results obtained by Shapiro and Alexander, if J. B. were an introvert his or her thoughts would more likely be 1 or 2 than 3 or 4; and vice versa if J. B. were an extravert.

Shapiro and Alexander also find that introverts are more likely to explore themselves and seek self-development as an end in its own right. They do not have an external goal in mind for such development, such as getting rich.

These several researches provide new data for the model object and generally support Jung's constructs of personality type, even though the expected clean split between extraverts and introverts has not been demonstrated. However, even this expectation may have been erroneously devised. As Stephenson wrote (1953, p. 185): "There can be no doubt that the conception of types as extremes of normal distributions in no way represented what the Jungs, Sprangers, and Kretschmers had in mind. . . ." A careful reading of Jung's work on types indicates that he did not intend for extraversion—introversion to be measured without reference to the mental functions. A person's type is given by special development of one of the eight combinations of extravert or introvert with thinking, feeling, sensing, or intuiting. By scoring without regard to the mental function, questionnaire measures of extraversion—introversion have failed to measure exactly what Jung had in mind.

It may be charged once again that Jung's theory (or his writings about it) are too confused. His own reply to this charge was that, if reality is complicated in fact, then you must respect this complexity. A scientific description of a confused part of reality will probably be confusing. But to impose upon it a clarity that is not there is unscientific.

Evaluation of the Theory

Whether the confusion resides chiefly in Jung's writings, or whether it resides in the fact that he deals with matters which are inherently very difficult for us to understand at this stage of human progress, it is obvious that the confusion or difficulty will also make it hard for anyone to test the theory or to evaluate its accuracy. The psychological test results mentioned above bear strictly upon the typological pattern theory only, and so far as they go it seems that the theory is partially accurate. But most of Jung's theory has not been tested experimentally, and it is not clear what if any observations could provide confirmation or disconfirmation. And yet it is apparent that particular hypotheses can be formulated, as in the interpretation of particular dreams. For example, Jung was once called in to contribute to differential diagnosis. The patient's symptoms were suspected by one physician to be beginning atrophy of the muscles and by another to be hysteria. Jung's interpretation of the dreams was that they conveyed a converging message of destruction of the physical basis of life, and hence that the diagnosis of organic disease was the most probable. Events proved later that this was the case. Thus a particular diagnosis and prediction was made which could have been either accurate or inaccurate.

On the basis of his theory Jung would say that persons with the greatest self-confidence, or people who are skilled and accurate observers, or those who are the most capable of unbiased reporting, would be precisely the ones to have developed their conscious side at the expense of the unconscious. Hence they should be particularly likely to experience visions of unidentified flying objects, which, he claims (1959), are projections of the archetype of wholeness (circular or cylindrical) and reflect the collective anxiety of mankind concerning the effects of overpopulation and other threats of destruction for life on this planet. In part the objects are seen as potential saviors ready to take some of us off to the safety of another, distant, civilization. If this application of the theory is correct, then appropriate study of the population of persons reporting UFOs should reveal very few cranks, many conscious tricksters, and many eminently reliable persons such as pilots, navigators, ship's captains, engineers, radar operators, and so on. In this matter as in many others Jung's theories lead to predictions which are subject to confirmation or testing. Little has been done, however, so at present we really do not know how accurate the theories are. Hence we can say little about their power.

The fruitfulness of Jung's theories is not easy to evaluate for similar reasons. Nevertheless it can be said that the spread of Jungian thought and treatment practices across the world betokens an important evidence of fruitfulness. There are also professional journals devoted to Jung's theories and applications of them in clinical practice and in the understanding of art and history and religion. These include the journal *Spring* and the *Journal of Analytical Psychology*. Similar objectives are pursued by C. G. Jung Societies, one of which is very active in Colorado, U.S.A. It is also possible to trace the influence of Jung's thought in the work of several other theorists: Assagioli, for example, employs the construct of the collective unconscious in his theory of personality (Assagioli, 1965, p. 19). In sum it seems that Jung's theory of personality has been and continues to be fruitful. Since the publication of his *Collected Works* (1953-1973) an increasing interest in Jung's theories has been developing among psychologists, and it seems likely that their fruitfulness will continue to increase and be directed into more conventional forms of scientific research activity.

It seems to me that Jung's theory has depth, for he offers explanations of psychopathology, of dreams, visions, myths, and even UFOs in terms of the psychic mechanisms of archetypal image formation, repression, projection, and compensation. Also, his theory of pattern, the theory of psychological types, appears to me to provide enormous potential for understanding of the differences between persons and of the relationships between persons. People of different types typically have a hard time understanding each other, so that interpersonal conflicts (arguments, quarrels, or differences of opinion) can often be understood very well in terms of differences in type among the people concerned.[2]

Finally it seems to me that one of the most important messages in Jung's theory is that our individual destinies are controlled primarily by the archetypes within us. If that is so, then the least we should do is try to become acquainted with these potent influences upon our lives, seeking perhaps to establish a conscious cooperation with them in place of unwitting opposition.

---

2. I am deeply appreciative of an opportunity to participate in a series of seminars given by Dr. Hilda Binzwanger of the Jung Institute in Zurich. These seminars were held at the University of Colorado in Boulder in the summer of 1976. Dr. Binzwanger made clear to me for the first time just how important the type constructs are in the practice of Jungian psychology. She showed how necessary it is to understand the types when we attempt to comprehend almost any concrete events in human psychology. Leaving home for the first time to go to college, for example, is a totally different experience for an extraverted intuitive type than it is for an introverted feeling type. The former hardly notices the actual change in surroundings but responds consciously to the vast new possibilities opened up by the move. The introverted feeling type, however, will likely be melancholy, silent, closed off from the new surroundings. And yet those new surroundings will have deep impact upon this person, for the thinking function is at a premium in the university environment; it is precisely this function which is inferior and hence relatively undeveloped in feeling types. The introverted feeling types will have trouble with examinations because they cannot muster their thoughts when necessary. They are easily led by propaganda (Von Franz, 1971, pp. 66-67), since they are quick to judge but slow to grasp the lack of logic in propaganda. Accordingly, such people will respond readily to any suggestion that their difficulties are perpetrated upon them by external forces, and depending upon other features of their particular personality, they may either drop out or join the group making the propaganda.

Workshop 12

Constructing a Questionnaire to Assess Jung's Eight Types

In this workshop you are invited to begin construction of a questionnaire which would allow the identification of Jung's eight types among ordinary adults of the western world. You can complete the construction as far as getting all the items and responding to them yourself; for full completion statistical studies would still be needed. But these cannot be carried out until the first and most creative part is accomplished, the part you can do here.

Go back to the section on the typological pattern theory and consider each type in turn. Your task is to make up items so that the subject's response indicates whether he or she probably belongs to that type or not. You might aim for four to six items per type, but even three would be a good start. If you wish to spend more time you should consult Jung's book **Psychological Types** (1921/1971). It is best to keep the items as short and clear as possible and to make them with response alternatives that are the same throughout. Here are some examples, with a possible scoring key in parentheses.

General Instructions

Please answer the following questions about yourself. There are no right or wrong answers, only answers that are mainly true for you. All answers are completely confidential. If you have any questions please ask the administrator.

Practice: Would you like to be a lion tamer in a circus? **Yes** ___ **Maybe** ___ **No** ___

If you have no further questions please go ahead at your own pace.

1. When you undertake to do something, do you try to get all the facts about it first?

Yes ___ **Sometimes** ___ **No** ___
(Score 2 for Yes, 1 for Sometimes on extraverted thinking types.)

2. Do you judge a show or sports event mainly in terms of whether it turns you on?

Yes ___ **Sometimes** ___ **No** ___
(Score 2 for Yes, 1 for Sometimes on introverted sensation type.)

3. Do you become absorbed in fighting for a good cause?

Yes ___ **Rarely** ___ **No** ___
(Score 2 for Yes, 1 for Rarely on extraverted intuition.)

4. Do you find that your eyes or hearing are more sensitive than most people's?

Yes ___ **Sometimes** ___ **No** ___
(Score 2 for Yes, 1 for Sometimes on introverted intuition.)

5. Do you have a knack for liking things that other people consider to be just right?

Yes ___ **Some** ___ **No** ___
(Score 2 for Yes, 1 for Some on extraverted feeling type.)

6. Do you tend to keep your motives pretty much to yourself?

Yes ___ **Sometimes** ___ **No** ___
(Score 2 for Yes, 1 for Sometimes on introverted feeling type.)

7. Can you be content with your own thoughts?

Yes ___ **Rarely** ___ **No** ___
(Score 2 for Yes, 1 for Rarely on introverted thinking type.)

8. Do you live life to the full, with good food, drink, and parties?

Yes ___ **Somewhat** ___ **No** ___
(Score 2 for Yes, 1 for Somewhat on extraverted sensation type.)

When you have written about two more items per type, making three total, add up the scores for your own answers to the three items. Your score for each type would range between 0 and 6. You could plot a profile as follows:

Type Scale	Raw Score	Profile						
		0	1	2	3	4	5	6
Extraverted:								
Thinking	2			*				
Feeling	3				*			
Sensing	0	*						
Intuiting	1		*					
Introverted:								
Thinking	3				*			
Feeling	6							*
Sensing	2			*				
Intuiting	2			*				

In the example there is one outstanding score: introverted feeling. The interpretation might be that this person is primarily of that type. You might wish to add up all four scores for the introverted types and compare with all four scores of the extraverted types. In this example, addition shows the person to be slightly introverted overall. We must remember that Jung would not have made such additions, however.

Summary

In Jung's theory, personality has a structure of three tiers, consisting of the conscious, personal unconscious, and collective unconscious. The conscious has four modes or functions: sensation, thinking, feeling, and intuiting. Its processes may be either volitional or instinctive, and either directed or undirected. At the center of consciousness is the ego, a structure which serves as our central receiving point for perceptions from the outer world and also for sensations from our inner body. The ego has a subjective feeling of freedom, of free will.

The personal unconscious consists of impressions and thoughts which lack sufficient intensity to become conscious, and also of thoughts from which consciousness has been withdrawn, repressed thoughts. The four mental functions of sensation, thinking, feeling, and intuition characterize the personal unconscious as well as the conscious.

The collective unconscious consists of mythological themes, instincts, and archetypes. It is collective in the sense that all human beings inherit the potentials or predispositions to form the relevant images and emotions.

Jung's theory of typological pattern distinguishes between two main attitudes: extraversion and introversion. An extravert's consciousness tends to be preoccupied with the external world, an introvert's with the inner world. The extravert reaches out to people and things and is strongly influenced by outside stimuli; the introvert gives as little energy as possible to the environment. Within each attitude any one of the four mental functions may predominate, making a total of eight types who have characteristically different modes of consciousness, social relations, and work preferences.

In Jung's theory of cause the psychophysical energy is derived ultimately from the sun and is manifested in the psyche in the form of libido, which covers all kinds of psychological energy such as instincts, wishes, interests, and so on.

The collective unconscious contains representational forms for a variety of structures in the psyche, the archetypes. Among others these tend to produce a persona, or public personality which is conscious but which cannot accept every one of the person's natural instincts or personal characteristics. Thoughts about these matters are repressed into the personal unconscious, forming the structures of the shadow (the dark side of the personality) and the animus (for a woman, her masculine side) or anima (for a man, his feminine side). The archetypes also produce symbols in visions and dreams, thus bringing messages from the unconscious to the dreamer's consciousness. These messages may reveal that the unconscious is compensating for some excess or deficit in the conscious part of the personality, or may warn of dangerous trends in the person's conscious life. Since it is collective, the collective unconscious may also convey to an individual person something of the anxieties or other major psychic condition prevailing in a nation or in mankind at a given time.

Jung's theory of personality has been criticized for being confused, but his own view is that the subject matter he deals with is inherently confusing. His influence is gradually increasing around the world, where several hundred Jungian analysts now practice the kind of psychotherapy he developed. His theory appears to be fruitful in this sense of practical application but not in laboratory research so far. What little is known of its accuracy indicates some degree of accuracy. The power of the theory is not known. It seems to be a theory which offers considerable depth

of understanding. Figure 12.2 illustrates the definition of personality implied in Jung's theory.

In the next chapter we shall examine the competing models of the unconscious which Freud and Jung proposed. It will be seen that Jung's construct of the collective unconscious led him to offer entirely different theoretical models of dreams and other phenomena explained by Freud in terms of an entirely personal unconscious.

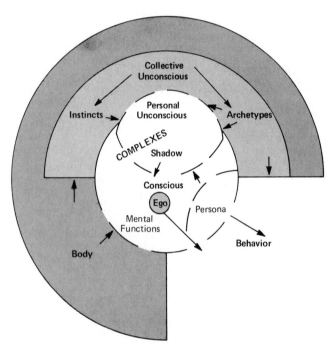

Figure 12.2. Definition of personality implied in Jung's theory

INTRODUCTION

Competing theories
  Different types of theory have different bases
    of competition
  Relationship between Freud and Jung
Two theories of structure
  Freud's theory of structure
    The unconscious
  Jung's theory of structure
    Personal unconscious
    Collective unconscious
  Comparisons
Two theories of cause
  Freud's theory of cause
    Libido
    Sexual attachments and conflicts
  Jung's theory of cause
    Solar and psychic energy
    Archetypes and repression
    Life-sustaining power of the collective
      unconscious
What Freud said about Jung's theory
  Disconnects facts from the impulse-life
  Substitutes abstractions and mythology
  Avoids the true childhood origins of neurosis
What Jung said about Freud's theory
  Empirical assumptions in error
  Narrow and one-sided
  Error of opposing death instinct to love instinct
  Based on logic but not on psychologic
  Overemphasizes the pathological
  Rejects the spiritual
    Example of Freud's treatment of religious
      experience
  Overemphasizes sex
Two competing theories
  Some disagreements as to facts
  Some agreements on facts and competition in
    theory of structure
    Phenomena of transference in psychotherapy
    Phenomena of resistance in psychotherapy
  Competition in theories of cause
  Is the unconscious helpful or only harmful?
Workshop 13 Designing a crucial experiment
Summary and conclusion

13

Comparing Two Models of the Unconscious: Freud and Jung

In chapter 8 we saw that truly competing theories must not differ on the relevant statements of fact. Nor may they disagree on the total set of laws from which each may draw a subset in order to provide an explanation. Their difference should preferably lie in some rather definite hypothesis. This hypothesis will be of a different kind, depending upon the type of theory that is being considered. If the two competing theories are theories of cause, for example, then the hypothesis in question must be one referring to a hidden cause (proposing the existence of some entity, such as a previously unsuspected galactic gas) or a causal relationship (proposing that some already known entity actually has causal influences which previously had not been suspected).

In the case of a theory of structure, the competition must refer to the nature of the finer grain or of the component parts of the entities or processes under consideration. Alternatively, not differing on the nature of these parts, the two competing theories may differ with respect to the ways in which the parts come together or interact in order to yield the whole entity or process under study. The latter hypotheses refer to the laws of com-

position, the rules whereby the parts form the whole. An example would be a theory of how atoms are linked together in the formation of piece of tangible matter.

Theories of other kinds will have other kinds of bases for their competition. Two theories of pattern might differ with respect to the sheer order of events, or which sets of traits go together in a personality type. Two theories of priority might differ as to the importance of one life goal over others.

In the present chapter we shall concentrate on two types of theory dealing with the unconscious: theories of structure and of cause. As we noted in chapter 8 theorists very often combine different types of theory in their overall theory of personality. If there is a component theory of structure there is usually also a component theory of cause, although the reverse is not true (Maslow, for example has a theory of cause but not of structure, see chapter 1). The reason for this seems to be that there is little point in proposing component parts of the personality without also suggesting what aspects of experience and behavior these parts are causally related to.

In this chapter we shall compare the theories of Freud and Jung. I have selected the topic of the unconscious as the focus of this comparison since it is central to the theories of each man, and also because it became the focus of their expressed differences in viewpoint. Freud and Jung were at one time close collaborators, but eventually they parted ways and became critical of each other's theories.

This much is often reported of the relationship between Freud and Jung. Today a great deal more is known because of the publication of the letters between these two men (McGuire, 1974), and also from Jung's reflections on their relationship (1965). For our present purposes we need little more than directly pertinent context. Jung read Freud's *Interpretation of Dreams* when it first appeared (1900/1953) and was much impressed. A much younger man than Freud, he saw immediately the possibilities of Freud's theory of unconscious processes for the study of personality. In 1907 Jung published his study of schizophrenia and used Freudian theory, but even then he had his private doubts about the role of the sexual instincts. He met Freud for the first time in that year. About that meeting Jung writes, "We met at one o'clock in the afternoon and talked virtually without a pause for thirteen hours. Freud was the first man of real importance I had encountered; in my experience up to that time, no one else could compare with him" (Jung, 1965, p. 149).

Jung reports that Freud's remarks about the sexual theory impressed him, but were insufficient to remove his doubts. Jung could not decide to what extent Freud's emphasis upon the sexual libido was based upon factual observations, or to what extent this emphasis "was connected with subjective prejudices. . . ." He reports that on many occasions during their conversation he tried to tell Freud about his reservations, "but each time he would attribute them to my lack of experience. Freud was right; in those days I had not enough experience to support my objections" (Jung, 1965, p. 149).

What ultimately came to be the basis of their disagreements was actually expressed quite fully, however, in that very first meeting. Jung writes, "Wherever, in a person or in a work of art, an expression of spirituality (in the intellectual, not the supernatural sense) came to light, he suspected it, and insinuated that it was repressed sexuality. Anything that could not be directly interpreted as sexuality he referred to as 'psychosexuality.' I protested that this hypothesis, carried to its logical conclusion, would lead to an annihilating judgment upon culture. Culture would then appear as a mere farce, the morbid consequence of repressed sexuality. 'Yes,' he assented, 'so it is, and that is just a curse of fate against which we are powerless to contend.' I was by no means disposed to agree, or to let it go at that, but still I did not feel competent to argue it out with him" (Jung, 1965, pp. 149-150).

Five years later, after their friendship had been consolidated by joint effort in the creation of a scientific society (The International Psycho-analytical Association), of which Jung was made the first president, Freud and Jung frequently wrote letters to each other, mainly about society business and matters of psychoanalytic interest, but adding newsy pieces of information and telling about family events. In one letter (McGuire, 1974, p. 491) Jung reaffirms his devotion to Freud and psychoanalysis. Nevertheless, he quotes a line from Nietzsche to the effect that a pupil should not remain only a pupil if he is to do justice to his teacher. When Jung's book *Symbols of Transformation* was published he and his wife sent copies first to Freud. It contained some views which were sharply in contradiction to those of Freud and made the difference quite explicit. In the same year Jung traveled in America and lectured at Fordham University. He gave nine lectures on psychoanalytic theory to a class of about ninety psychiatrists and neurologists. In writing to Freud about his trip Jung said, "Naturally I also made room for those of my views which deviate in places from the hitherto existing conception particularly in regard to libido theory. I found that my version of (psychoanalysis) won over many people who until now had been put off by the problem of sexuality in neurosis (McGuire, 1974, p. 515).

Freud's view of such "winning-over" was expressed fully two years later in his paper "On the History of the Psychoanalytic Movement (1914b/1959, p. 348): "In 1912 Jung boasted, in a letter from America, that his modifications of psycho-analysis had overcome the resistances of many people who had hitherto refused to have anything to do with it. I replied that that was nothing to boast of; the more he sacrificed of the hard-won truths of psychoanalysis the quicker would he see resistances vanishing. This modification . . . was again nothing else but a theoretical suppression of the sexual factor."

By 1914 the friendship between the two men was at an end. In 1913, following some deterioration in their personal relationship, Jung resigned the editorship of the *Annual of Psychoanalytic and Psychopathological Studies*. On April 20, 1914, Jung sent Freud a letter in which he also resigned his position in the International Psycho-analytical Association. In that letter he wrote, "The latest developments have convinced me that my views are in such sharp contrast to the views of the majority of the members of the Association that I can no longer consider myself a suitable personality to be president. I therefore tender my resignation. . . ." (McGuire, 1974, p. 551).

What was this "sharp contrast" of views which could divide such a powerful friendship? Freud and Jung each thought his own view was closer to the truth of human personality; both were very much concerned to find out what that truth was.

Central to each man's theory was a conception of the unconscious. We shall first review their theories with respect to the unconscious as a structural part of personality, and then as a set of causal processes.

Two Theories of Structure

Freud's Theory of Structure

Freud's theory (chapter 9) held that the personality consisted of a conscious, preconscious, and unconscious part. All items in the preconscious may come into consciousness more or less on demand, even as we ordinarily have no difficulty recalling what we had for lunch today should there be a necessity to do so. Within the preconscious, ideas may communicate with and influence each other, and they are ordered in time. These ideas come in part from perception, in part from memory, and in part from such aspects of instinctual ideas as are allowed to penetrate.

In Freud's construct of the unconscious a major role is given to ideas which are prevented from coming to consciousness by reason of their being repulsive. These ideas represent primitive instincts, existing side by side with each other but without mutual influence. Conflicting ideas of love and hate can exist there simultaneously. No rules of logic relate the ideas in the unconscious to each other, and these ideas are unrelated to time. No notion of negation exists among these ideas.

Ideas in the unconscious include not only those originating as representations of instinctual impulses. They also include the repressed ideas—such representations as have already been barred from access to consciousness. They include repressed memories of prior instinctual striving that was alien to the person.

In terms of Freud's final structural theory, the unconscious contains ideas representing the id and also those which have been repressed by the ego on its own account or at the requirement of the superego.

Within the final theory also, parts of the ego are themselves in the unconscious: those parts which are responsible for resistance and indeed for the mechanisms of defense, especially the primary mechanism of repression. Further, most of the superego, that body of incorporated prohibitions and commands, lies within the realm of the unconscious.

Jung's Theory of Structure

Jung's theory of personality structure held that there is a conscious part, a part called the personal unconscious, and a part called the collective unconscious. The personal unconscious consists of all those ideas (thoughts, impressions) that had insufficient strength to come into consciousness; there are also ideas which came into consciousness at one time but have since been "forgotten." Among the latter some are repressed in the sense of having been almost purposefully denied further access to consciousness.

The collective unconscious consists of the most basic mental possibilities of the human race, as developed through the ages, in response to repeated forms of experience. It is collective in the sense of being the same for all persons: all inherit alike the potentials or the dispositions to develop certain kinds of images and certain differentiated structures in the personality. All develop an ego, a persona (the public presentation of self), a shadow (the hidden, seamy side, repressed into the personal unconscious), and so on. All have a potential to form an image of a mother and of a father; of a rising and setting sun; of God; and so on. These potentials come to fruition in the individual life clothed in the particular forms that individual's life experiences provide.

According to Jung the collective unconscious contains both instincts and archetypes. The instincts move to action, and the archetypes mold the forms of experience. The instincts are the potentials for behavior; and the archetypes are the potentials for experience.

Comparisons

We must recall a few more details about the theories of Freud and Jung before making comparisons. First, Freud said that there was a perceptual conscious which seemed to be part of the conscious domain, but he also said that ideas in consciousness were fleeting. He gave little attention to consciousness and indeed thought that it was overrated by most people, who seem to believe their conscious thoughts mainly determine what they do. By contrast Jung paid great attention to consciousness and elaborated the four mental functions: thinking, feeling, sensing, and intuiting. These functions characterize consciousness, according to Jung, although they also are found in the personal unconscious.

Freud placed no structures exclusively in consciousness. Consciousness as a domain of the mind according to the second structural theory (chapter 9) intersected with a portion of the ego and a portion of the superego (third structural theory). The ego and superego structures were mainly located in the preconscious domain.

Recall that Jung felt that repression was primarily conscious activity; the shadow, holding the repressed ideas, was somewhat accessible to the conscious mind. That very accessibility gives the shadow its ominous characteristic in consciousness.

These various facts about the two theories mean that they cannot be simply aligned, conscious to conscious, preconscious to personal unconscious, and unconscious to collective unconscious. There is a rather complex overlapping, which I have attempted to represent in table 13.1.

In table 13.1 we see that major parts in Freud's theory bear an uneven relationship to major parts in Jung's theory. Jung's conscious includes all of Freud's conscious and some of Freud's preconscious. The rest of Freud's preconscious characteristics (that the ideas can become conscious) are included in Jung's construct of a personal unconscious. Some of Freud's conceptions of the unconscious are also included in Jung's construct of the personal unconscious, namely the repressed ideas and affects, which constitute part of the shadow in Jung's theory. Whereas Freud believed that the ego had parts in each of the three structures of conscious, preconscious, and unconscious, Jung held that the ego was entirely within the conscious part of the personality, indeed in its very center. For Freud the instincts were placed in the unconscious, but for

Table 13.1
Comparison of Freud's and Jung's Theories of Personality Structure*

Freud	Jung
Conscious Perceptual conscious Fleeting ideas	**Conscious** Sensations, intuitions Thinking, feeling Functions such as thinking Structures such as persona
Preconscious Ego structure Ideas are related to each other, to logic and to time	Ego structure Thinking and feeling involve relations
	Repression is more or less a conscious act
	Personal unconscious
Ideas can become conscious	Weak impressions and ideas temporarily forgotten can come into consciousness
Unconscious Repressed ideas not available to consciousness Ideas representing individual's instincts (id)	Repressed ideas are actually available to consciousness in most normal people
Portion of ego structure that effects repression	Some individual instinct ideas repressed in shadow (see above: repression is a conscious act)
	Collective unconscious
Most of superego controls	Instincts and archetypes include spirit, wisdom
Displacements and condensations produce symbols	Archetypes produce symbols and images Instincts

*Similar, related, or specially contrasting points in each theory are placed on the same horizontal line wherever possible.

Jung they were located along with the archetypes of the collective unconscious.

Here lies the essence of the argument between Jung and Freud. For Freud believed that all the unconscious originated in the individual person, but it was Jung's firm belief that the collective unconscious was impersonal and objective and given by heredity. Freud believed that all so-called spiritual experiences, including ideas of God and all religious rites, were derivatives of personal unconscious conflicts. He believed that the powerful idea of an omnipotent God was derived from infantile fears of an all-powerful human father. Jung believed that such attribution of omnipotence to the father was due to the investment of the human father-image by the numinous forces of the God-archetype. The causal sequence was exactly reversed for the two men.

But this discussion takes us into considerations of causes, and we shall now examine the two theories of cause.

Two Theories of Cause

Freud's Theory of Cause

Freud proposed (chapter 10) that two main groups of instincts provide energy for all mental life: the sexual and self-preservative instincts in one group and the destructive instincts in the other group. The energy of the sex instincts he called *libido*. Along with aggressive energy, anxiety, and other emotional sources of energy, the libido plays a fundamental role in Freud's theory of cause. Libido constantly seeks expression according to the pleasure principle. When blocked it nevertheless seeks expression somehow, either through hallucinations or through other features of the primary process of thought: displacement and condensation. The blocking itself is typically initiated by repression, unconscious withdrawal of energy from an idea

so that it can not enter consciousness. Many other particular forms of ego defense, such as projection and reversal, aid repression in keeping certain libidinal ideas out of consciousness. The only truly successful form of defense, according to Freud, is sublimation, a channeling of the libido into culturally acceptable forms of expression.

In Freud's theory, an important part of the motivation for blocking libidinal impulses arises first from fear of castration, and subsequently (after superego formation) from guilt, which is conceived as aggression against the ego in the service of moral prohibitions. The superego itself is derived from incorporation of these prohibitions as given first by the father and augmented by the child's own fears of retaliation for incest wishes.

Thus for Freud the entire drama of causation in personality is rooted in the child's earliest sexual attachments and conflicts in relation to the parents: the male and female Oedipus complexes, along with the castration complex (see chapter 11 and also box 10.1 and related text). Blocking of these libidinous impulses (due to the incest taboo and fear of retaliation) leads to their reappearance in all manner of disguises, including dreams, fantasies and neurotic symptoms. Further elaborations of defense include transformations of the ego in reaction formation and the formation of various characteristics associated with defense (such as suspiciousness due to projection of hostility). Fixations of component partial instincts (chapter 11) also lead to particular character constellations (such as the anal character, with its traits of orderliness, stinginess, and so on).

Jung's Theory of Cause

Jung maintained that our physiological life is based upon solar energy and that personality functions are based upon a parallel psychic energy. This general psychological energy he called *libido*. This energy infuses all instincts and is manifested through forms laid down in the brain, the archetypes, which are potentials or dispositions for particular kinds of experience. Archetypes are in the collective unconscious. The archetypes seek expression in consciousness even as the instincts with which they are associated seek expression in behavior. The archetypes also control the flow of energy into the development of personality components such as the ego, persona, shadow, and self. The archetypes are often expressed in the form of symbols, appearing in dreams, fantasies, drawings and other modes of representation to consciousness.

In Jung's theory repression plays an important role in providing the actual contents of the shadow in the personal unconscious. It also plays an important role in connection with transformations of libido. For if a particular conflict (for example, between sexual interest and fear) is repressed, then it produces a regression of libido. This means that some earlier relationship or relatedness is reactivated in memory and the libido flows into this constellation. For example, the regression might go back to the child's relationship with a parent, and thereby reactivate the father-image as with one young woman discussed in chapter 12. Rather than recognize her feelings for the ship's officer (who actually stimulated them), this woman thought reverently of her father. But if for some reason the regression goes farther back (beyond childhood through infancy and back into even prenatal experience), archetypal images are then reactivated. The archetypal image might be of God the Father of All Things, for example, and the young woman would feel reverently toward God.

Jung therefore considers the collective unconscious, powered by general libido, to be the origin and matrix of all mental life. The roots of consciousness are in the archetypes, according to Jung. The energy of libido tends toward expression, reaching out for suitable forms in the environment, even as baby birds strain their necks and open their mouths toward the form of a parent bird with worm in mouth.

Obviously such a notion of the unconscious endows it with life-sustaining power. Devore has pointed out (1976) that Jungian psychotherapy aims to enrich the individual's life by allowing the unconscious to enter more and more into awareness and to be expressed in creative living. It is a recognition of the limitless sources of energy and ideas that the individual may continue to utilize throughout life. By contrast, Freud's construct of the unconscious held that it was to be cleaned out and overcome as a result of psychoanalytic treatment: "Psycho-analysis is an instrument to enable the ego to achieve a progressive conquest of the id" (Freud, 1923a/1962, p. 46).

What Freud Said about Jung's Theory

At first Freud could not understand the changes Jung had made in the theory of libido: "The nature of the change . . . is not quite clear to me and I know nothing of its motivation" (McGuire, 1974, p. 510). Even after reading the original published version of *Symbols of Transformation* Freud was still unable to understand it very well and wrote that it "has not clarified your innovations for me as I might have wished" (McGuire, 1974, p. 518).

By 1914, however, Freud had understood Jung's views sufficiently to describe their error. After commenting that psychoanalysis was first a theory of neurosis, Freud pointed out that it began with three facts: resistance, transference, and amnesia. Resistance is the patient's stopping free associations and in other ways hindering analytic progress. Transference is the reliving of childhood cathexes and conflicts in relation to the analyst. Amnesia refers specifically to the gaps in a patient's memory for his or her own life experiences (compare Freud, 1904/1959, p. 267). These three statements of fact were explained, Freud said, by the "theories of repression, the sexual propelling forces in neurosis, and the unconscious" (Freud, 1914b/1959, p. 338).

Freud said that "Jung's modification . . . disconnects the phenomena from their relation with impulse-life" (Freud, 1914b/1959, p. 350). He accused Jung and his Swiss colleagues of finding no new facts, making no new observations, but rather of making simply a new interpretation. As a result, he said, "the things they see look different to them now from what they did before" (Freud, 1914b/1959, p. 351).

There was, however, a new contribution which provided the basis for their new interpretation, Freud admitted, and this was their tracing of "the way in which the material of sexual ideas belonging to the family-complexes and the incestuous object-choice is made use of in representing the highest ethical and religious interests of man . . ." (Freud, 1914b/1959, p. 351). He pointed out that this contribution amounted to a detailed description of a process of sublimation, with the forces of erotic instincts being sublimated into strivings whose nature can no longer be described as erotic, but must rather be admitted to be highly acceptable to the culture.

However, they could not leave it at that, Freud continues. They could not bear to foresee the storm of opposition that would come from other Swiss compatriots, as "the world would have risen in indignation and protested that they were sexualizing ethics and religion!" (Freud, 1914b/1959, p. 352). And so they pulled a switch. The nature of the switch was best described first as a parable, Freud said. Suppose someone boasted of having been born of noble parents who lived far away. But then it was proved to him that his real parents were simple people living quite nearby. The only way out is to say that they were really of noble descent but that they had fallen on hard times. So one "keeps face."

So Freud thought that Jung and his colleagues believed first that their ethical and religious ideas came from God. But then through exposure to psychoanalytic work and facts they saw that actually religious and ethical ideas are sublimations of childhood sexual fantasies and conflicts: "the descent of the ideas . . . from the family and Oedipus complex appeared undeniable" (Freud, 1914b/1959, p. 353). Thus it was proved to them that their parents actually lived nearby, simple, poor people with no special claim to noble descent at all. So what did Jung and his colleagues do? They invented the story that the real parents (Oedipus complex and so forth) were actually of higher descent (had a higher meaning). This higher meaning (locked in the archetypes of God, of wisdom, of the birth of the hero) alone made it possible for such fantasies and complex components to reappear in abstract ethical thought and religious mystical experience.

Freud said that Jung had substituted "an abstract term" for sexual libido: that was Jung's psychic energy concept, "of which one may safely say that it remains mystifying and incomprehensible to fools and wise alike" (Freud, 1914b/1959, p. 353). Freud noted that Jung had reinterpreted the Oedipus complex as something merely "symbolic," in which the mother means simply the unattainable and the father means the "inner father" from whom all must become free in the course of growing up to independent adulthood. "In the place of a conflict between erotic trends obnoxious to the ego and the self-maintenance tendency of the ego there appears the conflict between the life-task and 'psychic inertia' . . ." (Freud, 1914b/1959, pp. 353-354).

Freud charged that Jung's work on mythology and other aspects of historical and cultural materials was diversionary. He said that investigation of any individual person has shown and will always show that the sexual complexes in their original sense are active in him. For this reason the investigation of individuals has been neglected (by Jung) and replaced by conclusions arrived at from points arising from study of the race" (Freud, 1914b/1959, p. 354).

Freud also charged that Jung's innovations in therapeutic method were likewise motivated to avoid recognition of true childhood origins of the complexes. He said that if you deal with the patient's early childhood you almost inevitably discover the original, undisguised meaning of these misinterpreted complexes; consequently in therapy the precaution of dwelling as little as possible on this past history has been developed, and the main emphasis is laid on reverting to the current conflict . . ." (Freud, 1914b/1959, pp. 354-355).

Freud repudiated such theoretical and practical developments publicly at a meeting of psychoanalysts in Munich in 1913, and wrote about the "total incompatibility of this new movement with psycho-analysis . . ." in his 1914 paper (p. 356).

What Jung Said about Freud's Theory

Jung wrote a great deal more about Freud's theory than Freud wrote about Jung's. Jung thought that Freud's empirical assumptions were in error. He took particular exception to the assumption that all instinctual energy came from the sex instinct (an assumption Freud made until he realized the importance of the destructive instincts). Later on, after Freud had introduced his construct of the death instinct and associated aggressive energies, Jung wrote that Freud did this only after their friendship had broken up. Jung's position was stated as follows: "Elsewhere Freud remarks that in respect of the destructive instinct he lacks 'a term analogous to libido.' Since the so-called destructive instinct is also a phenomenon of energy, it seems to me simpler to define libido as an inclusive term for . . . sheer psychic energy" (Jung, 1917/1966, p. 53)

Jung charges that Freud's theory is narrow and one-sided, and that even when Freud develops a second source of energy in his theory (the destructive instinct) he does so in a narrow and prejudiced way. All the evidence, both from a great array of other thinkers and from the experiences of everyday life and of the history of culture, point to the existence of many different instincts and many different forces in opposition or tension, says Jung.

Jung points out that different authorities emphasize different instincts as being the most important. When they emphasize just two instincts, these instincts are usually placed in opposition, in recognition of the fact that all energy flows only along gradients set up between opposites, just like positive and negative poles for electricity.

Jung of course maintains that when one of a pair of opposing instincts is in consciousness the other is repressed into the shadow, the personal unconscious. "But the repressed content must be made conscious so as to produce a tension of opposites, without which no forward movement is possible. The conscious mind is on top, the shadow underneath, and just as high always longs for low and hot for cold, so all consciousness, perhaps without being aware of it, seeks its unconscious opposite. . . . Life is born only of the spark of opposites" (Jung, 1917/1966, pp. 53-54).

In Jung's opinion, Freud made a grave error in placing the death instinct in opposition to the love instinct or Eros. He said that

Freud was motivated by psychological prejudice and by the considerations of intellectual logic (rather than psychological rules). "For, in the first place, Eros is not equivalent to life; but for anyone who thinks it is, the opposite of Eros will naturally appear to be death. And in the second place, we all feel that the opposite of our own highest principle must be purely destructive, deadly, and evil" (Jung, 1917/1966, p. 54).

Jung makes two more points. In the first place there are naturally occurring opposites which one should recognize and accept instead of postulating artificial pairs of opposites. Love's natural opposite is the will to power, according to Jung; the instinct to love someone is opposed by the instinct to dominate. This natural opposition is not recognized by Freud, who makes up an artificial opposition between the love instinct and a death instinct. In the second place, natural pairs of opposites follow the principle that when one is in consciousness the other is repressed, and Freud fails to recognize this natural principle too. In short, Jung feels that Freud's theory is out of touch with the very nature it attempts to explain. It is based on logic but not on psychologic.

Jung criticizes Freud for being narrow. He says that there are many different pairs of opposites in human personality, not just the one pair posited by Freud. He believes also that there are many instincts, not just the two Freud proposed. Jung says that Freud's narrowness is especially evident in his treatment of spiritual forces. He charges that Freud has insufficient humility before the facts. Jung grants that sex instincts or power drives are propelling forces in our lives. But he insists that such instincts are constantly meeting opposition from something within us. He believes that it is the spirit (Jung, 1929/1961, pp. 336-337).

Jung reproaches Freud for overempha-

sizing the pathological features of human personality, for basing his theory of the normal upon his observations of the sick. He says that a convincing example of this tendency may be found in Freud's book *The Future of an Illusion* (1927/1961), where Freud wrote at length on the bases of civilization and religion, asserting that religious doctrines are illusions; religious beliefs are based upon childhood feelings of helplessness. Jung held that Freud was simply unable to understand religious experiences. Box 13.1 gives an instance of Freud's treatment of religious experience, and reveals the central role of the Oedipus complex in Freud's thought.

Jung acknowledged that there was "a marked disturbance today in the psychic sphere of sex" (Jung, 1929/1961, p. 338). But he felt that Freud's overemphasis on sex was similar to the overemphasis we all put on a toothache: We can think only of that, and nothing else. Civilization is caught in it, Jung said, and so is Freudian theory.

It points no way that leads beyond the inexorable cycle of biological events. In despair we would have to cry out with St. Paul: "Wretched man that I am, who will deliver me from the body of this death?" And the spiritual man in us comes forward, shaking his head, and says in Faust's words: "Thou art conscious only of the single urge," namely of the fleshly bond leading back to father and mother or forward to the children that have sprung from our flesh —"incest" with the past and "incest" with the future, the original sin of perpetuation of the "family romance" (Jung, 1929/1961, pp. 338-339).

Jung says that Freud would never learn that God is his father. That cannot be learned by intellectual and scientific analysis, for it demands faith. Jung's own view holds that the "fleshly bond leading back to father and mother" can be loosened only through "that opposite urge of life, the spirit. . . . It is the

Box 13.1

Freud's Analysis of One Man's Religious Experience

Freud (1928) reports that an interviewer had written about his lack of religious faith, and that this had come to the attention of an American physician. The physician wrote to Freud and told him of his own religious conversion and begged Freud to seek the truth of God for himself. The physician's letter stated in part:

> I am writing to tell you of an experience that I had in the year I graduated. . . . One afternoon while I was passing through the dissecting-room my attention was attracted to a sweet-faced dear old woman who was being carried to a dissecting-table. This sweet-faced woman made such an impression on me that a thought flashed up in my mind, "There is no God: if there were a God he would not have allowed this dear old woman to be brought into the dissecting-room."
>
> When I got home that afternoon the feeling I had at the sight in the dissecting-room had determined me to discontinue going to church. The doctrines of Christianity had before this been the subject of doubts in my mind.
>
> While I was meditating on this matter a voice spoke to my soul that "I should consider the step I was about to take." My spirit replied to this inner voice by saying, "If I knew of a certainty that Christianity was truth and the Bible was the Word of God, then I would accept it."
>
> In the course of the next few days God made it clear to my soul that the Bible was his Word. . . . Since then God has revealed himself to me by many infallible proofs.

Freud responded politely to the letter. In his paper he analyzed the experience. Why would the physician's indignation against God break out on this particular occasion? Surely the physician knew of such dissections before. Freud then described what probably must have happened.

The sight of a woman's dead body, naked or on the point of being stripped, reminded the young man of his mother. It roused in him a longing for his mother which sprang from his Oedipus complex, and this was immediately completed by a feeling of indignation against his father. His ideas of "father" and "God" had not yet become widely separated; so that his desire to destroy his father could become conscious as doubt in the existence of God and could seek to justify itself in the eyes of reason as indignation about the ill-treatment of a mother-object. It is of course typical for a child to regard what his father does to his mother in sexual intercourse as ill-treatment. The new impulse, which was displaced into the sphere of religion, was only a repetition of the Oedipus situation and consequently soon met with a similar fate. It succumbed to a powerful opposing current. During the actual conflict the level of displacement was not maintained: there is no mention of arguments in justification of God, nor are we told what the infallible signs were by which God proved his existence to the doubter. The conflict seems to have been unfolded in the form of an hallucinatory psychosis: inner voices were heard which uttered warnings against resistance to God. But the outcome of the struggle was displayed once again in the sphere of religion and it was of a kind predetermined by the fate of the Oedipus complex: complete submission to the will of God the Father. The young man became a believer and accepted everything he had been taught since his childhood about God and Jesus Christ. . . .

The point which our present observation throws into relief is the manner in which the conversion was attached to a particular determining event, which caused the subject's scepticism to flare up for a last time before being finally extinguished (Freud, 1928/1959, pp. 243-246, passim).

only way in which we can break the spell that binds us to the cycle of biological events" (Jung, 1929/1961, p. 339).

Jung notes that he is accused of mysticism on account of his views, but that it is simply a fact that people have always spontaneously developed religions, have always had religious feelings.

> "Whoever cannot see this aspect of the human psyche is blind, and whoever chooses to explain it away, or to "enlighten" it away, has no sense of reality" (Jung, 1929/1961, p. 339).

There can be no doubt that Jung thinks Freud's theory is blind and lacking in a sense of reality. He says that, like Nicodemus, Freud thinks the only way to be born again is to enter your mother's womb a second time (Jung, 1929/1961, p. 340).

Two Competing Theories

In order to determine whether two theoretical models are in competition we must be sure that they refer to the same facts. Some instances of disagreement between Freud and Jung appear to be disagreement as to the facts. For example, Freud said that transference in psychotherapy is the rearousal of early cathexes upon parents but now attached to the therapist. Jung describes the transference in the same way that Freud did. He says that the patient transfers the memory-image of his or her father to the therapist with excessive amounts of feeling, and it cannot easily be corrected (Jung, 1933, p. 38). But, in contrast to Freud's view that all transference phenomena are essentially the same, Jung maintained that some patients do not develop a transference attachment to the physician, but rather to the images of their father and mother as such. Thus there is a disagreement about facts here, namely, whether the transference has only the therapist as an object or whether images can also be the objects in some pa-

tients. But in regard only to those instances where they do agree about the facts, namely about transference to the therapist, then the two theorists formulate strictly competing theoretical models of the transference. For Freud maintains that the transference arises from incestuous fantasies, but Jung maintains that it arises from the archetype of rebirth, from a desire to be born again. It has a figurative psychological meaning—the desire to have a new and healthy personality—and also a spiritual meaning, but to understand both meanings one must have regard for both empirical and symbolic truth, Jung says (1911/1967, p. 226). Since the patient comes to the therapist precisely for assistance in getting rid of symptoms and developing a healthier personality there is little wonder that the therapist plays a prominent role in the patient's feeling and fantasy life, whether it be regarded as a transference of incestuous longings or of expectations for spiritual midwifery. There seems to be no way at present to decide between the two theoretical models.

Some of the differences between Freud and Jung in terms of particular theoretical models can be attributed directly to differences in their theories of structure. For example, Freud and Jung agree on the facts of resistance in therapy; but they explain it differently. For Freud, resistance is a manifestation of the ego in its unconscious part; for Jung, resistance is more likely to be a manifestation of the ego or the persona, both in the conscious domain of personality (1933, p. 36).

Other points of competition stem from the two theories of cause. For example, Freud's model of religious experience holds that it arises from sublimation of the sex instinct; Jung's model states that it is a direct expression of the spiritual instinct, or religious archetype. "The church," said Jung (1917/1966, p.

105), "is simply the latest, and specifically Western, form of an instinctive striving that is probably as old as mankind itself . . . the institution or rite of initiation into manhood." As another example, Freud's model of dreams held that they were disguised wish-fulfillments, and that the manifest content is produced by primary process distortion out of the latent content materials. By contrast, Jung's theoretical model of dreams held that a dream is a direct message to the conscious of the dreamer from the unconscious, and that it is written in the only language the unconscious speaks, namely the language of archetypal symbols. These symbols bring the essential message, even though there may be elements of imagery from the day's waking experience involved in the dream. A fuller discussion of this competition between the two theoretical models was given in chapter 7.

A final important difference is that Jung's theory goes beyond causal influence and points to the frequently purposive, guiding, helpful role of the unconscious if only its messages will be heeded by the conscious ego; whereas in Freud's theory the unconscious is the source only of unacceptable impulses and conflicts.

Workshop 13

Designing a Crucial Experiment

Many studies have attempted to test Freud's hypotheses about the source of religious feelings and ideas in our early experiences with parents. A useful collection is presented by Brown (1973). But none have been directed toward the problem of discriminating between a Freudian and a Jungian interpretation of religious experience.

We might argue that the contrast between Freud's model and Jung's model can be reduced to the following question:

Does the tendency toward spiritual rebirth (archetypes of the hero and of rebirth) provide the original source of energy for the Oedipus and Electra complexes, or do the latter provide the original energy for the tendency toward spiritual rebirth?

Of course, our research might show that neither is true. Also we might find that we are unable to answer the question in an objective way. Again, we might find that we need to rephrase the question.

How would you rephrase the question to make it more testable?

_____

_____

_____

_____

After thinking about this matter myself, I wondered if it would be possible to arouse ideas and feelings about spiritual rebirth and then see if they lead to special sensitivity toward or interest in oedipal materials; and, again, whether it would be possible to arouse oedipal ideas and feelings and see if they lead to interest in spiritual rebirth. We know that it is possible to arouse particular categories (Wickens, 1970) and also particular feeling tendencies such as aggression (Turner & Layton, 1976). The latter technique consists of having subjects do paired-associate learning with words that are evocative of the particular feeling.

The operational form of the question would then be something like this: Does arousal of ideas and feelings about spiritual rebirth produce a mood in which persons find material relevant to oedipal themes most fitting; or does arousal of oedipal ideas and feelings produce a mood in which persons find material relevant to spiritual rebirth most fitting?

Of course, we can see immediately here that the answer could be one, or the other, or both, or neither. Is there a better way of phrasing it? There probably is. But perhaps we should wait until we have some materials and a design before considering a rephrasing of the question.

Consider the following design. Subjects are randomly allocated to one of two groups, A and B. Group A subjects first learn a series of paired-associates which are intended to arouse feelings and ideas of spiritual rebirth; then they are asked to indicate which of two words most or best fits their current mood, and in each pair of words presented one is considered to be relevant to oedipal themes, the other is considered to be neutral. Group B subjects first do a paired-associate learning task with materials intended to arouse feelings and ideas related to oedipal themes; then they are asked to indicate which of two words most or best fits their current mood, and in each pair of words presented one is considered to be relevant to the theme of spiritual rebirth, the other is considered to be neutral.

First Problem

Does the design allow us to answer the question? _____

_____

_____

It seems to me that, with additional controls and measures, it does allow us to answer the restricted or operational form of the question. It would be necessary to control the length of lists for paired-associate learning and the number of trials. It would be highly desirable to have an independent sample of judges evaluate whether the selected words do in fact tend to arouse ideas and feelings related to themes of spiritual rebirth or oedipal complexes respectively. It would be essential to have independent judges rate the degree to which the "mood-fitting" words do in fact fit the mood they are supposed to. It would be essential to have judges rate the extent to which the "nonmood-fitting" words are in fact "neutral." Perhaps the best that can be achieved here is that these "neutral words" would be rated as best fitted to other moods than the target mood, and that each would be best fitted to its own different mood. All this will take a lot of work and perhaps should be relegated to effort after an initial pilot study has determined whether the procedures work at all. For instance, with actual subjects, does the paired-associate task actually induce the expected ideas and feelings? Perhaps a depth interview would give answers to this question.

Second Problem

Can suitable materials be devised? The answer to this question can probably be given best by trying to devise the materials. My efforts resulted in the following lists:

Materials for Group A Paired-associates			Materials for Group B Paired-associates		
HERO	—	SPRING	BULL	—	NIGHT
SUNRISE	—	CROWN	KING	—	FEAST
BUTTERFLY	—	EAGER	PURSE	—	SERPENT
RENEW	—	LIGHT	SHEET	—	GOAT
SPIRIT	—	HOPE	UPSTAIRS	—	SEED
CHANGE	—	YOUTH	QUEEN	—	TOWER
LIFE	—	GOD	BED	—	BAG
NEW	—	SKY	SWORD	—	ROOM
FRESH	—	PRAYER	ANIMAL	—	CASTLE
ENLIVEN	—	ARISE	SECRET	—	VELVET

Which Word of a Pair Best Fits Your Mood?

BULL	or	FULL	HERO	or	RITUAL
WING	or	KING	SUNSET	or	SUNRISE
PURSE	or	VERSE	BUTTERFLY	or	CABBAGE
SAIL	or	SHEET	CASHEW	or	RENEW
UPSTAIRS	or	BASEMENT	SPIRIT	or	FERRET
GRASS	or	QUEEN	RANGE	or	CHANGE
BED	or	CHAIR	LIFE	or	LOUNGE
SOAP	or	SWORD	CREW	or	NEW
ANIMAL	or	VEGETABLE	FRESH	or	MESH
PLASTIC	or	SECRET	FOLLOW	or	ENLIVEN

In the mood-fit lists the neutral words are alternately in second and in first place. The score would be number of expected mood-fit words actually selected. The chance expectancy would of course be five mood-fitting words and five neutral words. The predictions would be as follows: If Jung is right, then group A should select mood-fitting words on the average more than would be expected by chance: Say, between seven and eight mood-fit words; and group B would select on average just about the number of mood-fit words expected by chance, namely five. If Freud is right, then group B should select more mood-fit words than chance on the average, and group A should select only the chance expectancy number of mood-fit words on the average. If both are right, both groups would select more mood-fit words than chance expectancy; if neither is right, both groups should select about the chance number of mood-fit words.

Third Problem

Can we really draw the conclusions implied in the previous paragraph, that, for instance, the results with group A more than chance and group B equal to chance lend support for Freud's position? Is there perhaps an inherent bias in one of the lists for preference of mood-fit words? What if subjects prefer **less** than the chance number of mood-fit words? What control groups might we need to be quite sure of our conclusions?

_____

_____

_____

Summary and Conclusion

We may summarize the differences between the two theories quite briefly, Freud says all the unconscious is individual and personal; Jung says there is such an unconscious but in addition there is an impersonal, objective, collective unconscious which does not arise from the personal history and repressions of the individual. As to the causes of personality, Freud sees the fundamental energy as that of sexual libido (and later also of aggressive energy from the destructive instinct). But Jung holds that not all facts can be explained (or explained away) by appeal to a sexual libido and its various forms of transformation. Many facts require the assumption of primordial images and of spiritual forces in the collective unconscious.

These differences lead to quite different theoretical models for particular sets of phenomena, which constitute the meeting points for competition between the two theories. These points include the nature of religious feelings and ideas, the significance of dreams, and the phenomena of treatment, such as transference. One of the most practically important consequences of the differences between the two theories is that Jung relies upon the growth forces of the unconscious to promote and maintain psychological health during analytic treatment, and such reliance determines many of the specific techniques of treatment employed. Thus Jung encourages an alliance with the unconscious, whereas Freud encourages its conquest.

In chapters 9 through 11 we examined Freud's theory with respect to the criteria of accuracy, power, fruitfulness, and depth. We found it to have a mixture of accuracy and inaccuracy, with the balance in favor of accuracy. In chapter 12 our consideration of Jung's theory led to the conclusion that its accuracy (and hence its power also) is largely unknown. Both theories were considered to be quite fruitful, although the stimulation of laboratory research has been much greater from Freud's theory than from Jung's. The two theories appear to be equal in depth of understanding provided.

When we concentrate on the constructs of the unconscious as found in Jung's and Freud's theories we find definite disagreements. In these particulars, as in others, we can begin to see points at which the conflicting theoretical models can be brought into quite precise competition. Is it our task at this stage to say whether we judge the one theory better than the other? Must we conclude that the prize should go only to one theory? Since it is not a matter of nominating a candidate for president in the next seventy-two hours, I personally prefer to remain uncommitted. Both theories of the unconscious are enlightening to me. The way ahead seems richest if we retain both theories in honor and allow them to guide us in attempts to design crucial experiments.

As we move on now to consider the theories developed by other scientists, we shall frequently notice that their work has profited from knowledge of the theories developed by Freud and Jung. This is particularly true of Erikson, whose pattern theory is presented in the following chapter.

INTRODUCTION

Introduction to Erikson's life and work
  Erikson's life and professional career
  Work with Anna Freud and Henry Murray
  The study of the ego
  Social milieu and ego identity
Erikson's eight stages of psychosocial development
  Oral stage: trust versus mistrust
    Organism, ego processes, and milieu
      The mode of taking in; the modality of getting
      The sense of trust or mistrust
  Anal stage: autonomy versus doubt
    The modes of retention and elimination
    The modalities of holding and letting go
    The battle for autonomy
    The sense of autonomy or of doubt
  Phallic stage: initiative versus guilt
    Modes of intrusion and of inclusion
    The modality of making it
    The sense of initiative or of guilt
  Latency stage: industry versus inferiority
    Sublimations of sexual and aggressive
      impulses
    The extending horizons of childhood
    Skills
    The mode of putting together and the modality
      of producing
    The sense of industry or of inferiority
  Genital stage: identity versus identity confusion
    Psychosocial identity
    Identity elements: identifications, given
      characteristics and abilities, the sense of
      trust, autonomy, and so on
    Psychosocial moratorium
      Reworking the elements of identity
      Special requirements for creative people
    The sense of identity or of identity confusion
  Later genital stage: intimacy versus isolation
  Generativity versus stagnation
  Integrity versus disgust and despair
Accomplishments of Erikson's theory of
  developmental pattern
  A development of Freud's psychoanalytic theory
  Contributions to ego psychology
  Contributions to general developmental
    psychology

Empirical studies of the stage theory
New subdiscipline of psychohistory
Case example: Erikson's study of Martin Luther
Critique of Erikson's theory
  Criticisms associated with psychoanalytic theory
  Distinctions between Freud's and Erikson's theory
    of pattern
  Medical and psychosocial descriptions of sickness
  Psychosexual and psychosexual descriptions of
    personality development
  Causal components in Erikson's theory of pattern
  Accuracy, power, fruitfulness, and depth
Workshop 14 Measuring a construct: the sense of
  initiative
Summary

14

Erikson's Pattern Theory of Personality Development

Erik H. Erikson was born in 1902 and studied psychoanalysis at the Vienna Psychoanalytic Institute, under the guidance of Anna Freud, August Aichhorn, and others. He specialized in child analysis. In 1933 he joined a team of workers at Harvard University under the leadership of Henry Murray, whose work we studied in chapter 3. Murray's project aimed to explore personality in every possible way through the use of interviews, questionnaires, miniature situations, and other psychological assessment devices. Erikson used a "dramatic productions test" in which subjects had to make a dramatic scene out of a group of toys (Erikson, 1937). The themes of the drama so created were then interpreted as reflecting features of the subject's personality.

While at Harvard Erikson met a number of influential anthropologists, including Gregory Bateson, Ruth Benedict, Alfred Kroeber, and Margaret Mead. Their influence shows especially in his first major book on *Childhood and Society* (1950/1963), and continues to be seen in much of his later work (compare Erikson, 1962, 1969, 1974). Erikson has created a unique specialty within developmental psychology, one which blends psychoanalytic clinical observation with sensitive in-terpretation of social and cultural forces as these work upon and are transformed by the developing individual personality. He refers to this specialty as *psychohistory*, which he describes as "the study of individual and collective life with the combined methods of psychoanalysis and history" (Erikson, 1974, p. 13).

Using his psychohistorical method, Erikson wrote a biography of the great Indian religious leader Mahatma Ghandi (1969), for which he received the National Book Award and the Pulitzer Prize in 1970. In 1974 he received the Mental Health Research Achievement Award for his contributions to psychology, psychiatry, and psychoanalysis.

For many years Erikson was professor at Harvard University. Yet he remained primarily a psychoanalyst, both in the practice of that profession with child and adolescent patients, and also as a training analyst. For over ten years he worked at the Austen Riggs Center in Massachusetts. In his Foreword to the first edition of *Childhood and Society* (1950/ 1963, pp. 15-16), he wrote:

Psychoanalysis today is implementing the study of the ego, a concept denoting man's capacity to unify his experience and his action in an adaptive manner. It is shifting its emphasis from the concentrated study of the conditions which blunt and distort the individual ego to the study of the ego's roots in social organization. This we try to understand not in order to offer a rash cure to a rashly diagnosed society, but in order first to complete the blueprint of our theory. In this sense, this is a psychoanalytic book on the relation of the ego to society.

In 1956 Erikson was invited to give a lecture at the University of Frankfurt on the occasion of celebrating the one-hundredth birthday of Sigmund Freud. Erikson recalls that, as a young artist and tutor to a family who were friends of the Freud family, he had known the venerable "first psychoanalyst" as a man on outings with children and dogs in the mountains and elsewhere. Later, when Erikson became a psychoanalyst he came to know Freud more deeply through his writings. Freud, he said, made a creative "step in scientific conscience . . . [which] implies a fundamentally new *ethical orientation of adult man's relationship to childhood*: to his own childhood, now behind and within him; to his own child before him; and to every man's children around him" (Erikson, 1964, p. 44).

Before Freud's discoveries concerning the sexual character of much infantile experience it was widely held that people were asexual beings until the time of puberty. After these discoveries it was long held that the nature and course of infantile sexual development was laid down by factors of biological constitution. Freud himself believed that accidental experiences of various kinds could modify the outcome of this developmental sequence, and also that certain normally expectable stimulus conditions in the environment (such as the sight of the genitals of a child of opposite sex) would typically contribute to the awakening of successive stages. Erikson accepted these basic notions. Nevertheless he came to

place even greater emphasis upon these "accidental" and "normally expectable" outer factors in the child's immediate environment. Where Freud focused primarily upon the biological organism and its individual experiences of pleasure and pain, Erikson came to realize the importance of social and cultural patterns in determining what outer factors are "normal" and hence what would be considered by the parents as "abnormal." Erikson shifted emphasis away from the biological and constitutional source of sexual development, and directed attention more to the social determinants. In addition, he elaborated the theory of psychosexual development with respect to the ego, showing especially how the outer factors of the total social milieu contribute to formation of *identity*, that is, of the ego as an individual in society.

In chapter 8 we pointed out that theories change by modification in their models. In the same way a theory may be developed further by changes in models. In particular we noticed instances in which a theoretical model changes in response to factual changes in the model object. The difference between Freud's theory of temporal (developmental) pattern and Erikson's is based upon major *additions* to the model object that Freud worked with. Erikson has added the sociocultural facts surrounding a child's psychosexual development. He has stressed the importance of the society in which an adult personality will eventually participate, so that development of identity is considered in terms of both the constitutional capabilities of the individual and the social opportunities of the environment. These opportunities intersect with the developing personality in two ways. First, they affect the kinds of educational offerings available to a child; second, they provide available employment opportunities, marriage forms, and other features of social position which contribute to an individual identity. Since these are realities with which the individual must cope they inevitably influence the course and content of ego development, since (in psychoanalytic theory) the agency responsible for adaptation to reality is the ego (see chapter 10). But in order for a theoretical model to encompass such sociocultural aspects of ego development the related model object must include reference to sociocultural facts.

It is well to realize that Erikson has not abandoned psychoanalytic (Freudian) theory. On the contrary he has taken precisely the original model object of individual developmental stages and added sociocultural facts to the constitutional and family behavioral facts with which Freud worked. In addition, Erikson has extended the age range of developmental observations. Freud effectively stopped his model object of developmental facts with the attainment of genital sexuality, presumably somewhere between fourteen and twenty-two years of age in the majority of people. But Erikson has added to the model object in this direction also, taking his observations over the entire span of life. Where Freud discerned five stages up to young adult age, Erikson discerns eight stages altogether, going up to old age.

Erikson's Eight Stages of Psychosocial Development

We shall consider Erikson's theory of developmental pattern in accordance with the proposed sequence of stages. In the first five stages it will be possible to make direct comparisons with Freud's theory of pattern and so each stage will be introduced by both its Freudian label (for example, *oral stage*) and its parallel label in Erikson's theory (for example, *trust versus mistrust*).

Oral Stage: Trust versus Mistrust

Erikson pays attention to three main aspects of personality. The *organism* is the physical aspect, the actual physical body with all of its anatomy and physiological functions. The *ego-processes* are the various experiences of the person: feelings, impressions, and so on. The *milieu* is the surrounding environment, especially the social and cultural features of that environment. This means not only the general state of the nation, its forms of government, and so on. It includes the immediate social situation of the person: the family, the neighborhood and the neighbors, the school, club, or military unit.

During the oral stage of development the organism's mouth is the bodily *zone* upon which attention is focused. The zone is simply the bodily part or system with respect to which the major interactions between organism and milieu take place.

Freud spoke of *incorporation* as the aim of the child at this first stage of life, beginning right after birth. The baby's main efforts are directed at the goal of *taking in* sustenance. Erikson calls this a *mode*: a way of relating to the environment, a relationship of taking in nourishing substances. This mode is not confined to the mouth; the infant "takes in" its visual environment with the eyes too. The skin and all other sense organs are "hungry for proper stimulation" (Erikson, 1963, p. 74). Thus in Erikson's theory the mouth serves as a prototype for a broader orientation in life.

As coordination and awareness develop, the child encounters the artifacts and training techniques of the culture. These provide "the basic modalities of human existence . . ." (Erikson, 1963, p. 75). *Modalities* are ways of participating in the culture. Incorporation as an organismic mode becomes the cultural modality of *getting*, accepting what is given.

Erikson divides the oral period into two

parts (following Karl Abraham, 1927). The second period begins with eruption of teeth. This brings "pleasure in biting *on* hard things, in biting *through* things, and in biting pieces *off* things." Incorporation is still the main mode, but the modality becomes that of *taking* by grasping and holding on. The period is fateful for the child because it may coincide with weaning and other indications of separation from mother and is often accompanied by the pain of the teeth coming through. Erikson believes that "good" and "evil" enter the child's world at this point. If breast feeding is continued, the child must also learn now to suck without biting, on pain of the mother's withdrawing. The baby is liable to fits of anger, even rage, at the pain from the teeth within and at the frustrations imposed by mother. If the first oral stage was paradise, the second is apt to be paradise lost. It is likely that the infant feels somehow responsible for this fate, since the crucial cause of the catastrophe seems to be within the self: Evil pains or anger or biting tendencies apparently result in eviction from paradise.

Depending upon the success with which the culture (and the immediate family) provides for substitute satisfactions or otherwise eases the transition into the oral-biting stage, the child will be left with an incipient sense of *trust* or of *mistrust,* which "remain the autogenic source of both primal hope and of doom throughout life" (Erikson, 1963, p. 80). That is, the child's achievement of a sense of trust or failure to achieve it can color his or her general attitudes and expectations for the rest of life. This failure has serious consequences. Filled with mistrust in the beginning of life the person expects to be badly treated by the world from then on. This very likely interferes with satisfactory resolution to later developmental crises, for example, in the stage of *autonomy versus doubt* to be discussed below. The child who ends the first year of life filled

with mistrust will have little motivation for making those commitments to his family which result in autonomy. Rather such a child will most likely become filled with self-doubt and resentment, and will enter the rest of life with an embattled attitude toward social authority. The attitude may be one of continual fighting, in which the child turns into a rebel (compare the rebel in box 11.1). Or the attitude may be one of defeat, in which case the person always feels beaten before any game begins, and life is a source of constant feelings of shame and unworthiness.

As summarized by Fenichel (1945) numerous psychoanalysts had proposed that an especially satisfying period of nursing leads to the person's having a generally optimistic character throughout life. Erikson prefers the concept of trust, which means trust in oneself and also trust in the providence of nature, at first the providence of mother. He proposes (1968, p. 106) that "the glory of childhood also survives in adult life. Trust, then, becomes the capacity for *faith,* a vital need for which man must find some institutional confirmation." That institution most commonly is religion, although a poltical ideology may serve a similar purpose.

We must note Erikson's usage of the term *sense* (of trust). By this he means three things: 1) a part of conscious experience, something we may determine for ourselves by introspection; 2) something which shows in our behavior, as others may plainly see; and 3) an unconscious state determinable by psychological testing or by psychoanalytic interpretation.

Anal Stage: Autonomy versus Doubt

Freud had described the anal stage as that during which the child's erotic interests are concentrated upon the organs of elimination. Excitation of these organs in the form of itching or irritation is a kind of pregenital sexual stimulation. The tension could be reduced by scratching or rubbing. If tension was built up by retaining feces in the body, elimination would reduce tension and therefore be pleasurable.

Erikson has put more stress on the importance of *retention* and *elimination* as modes of relating organism and milieu. The corresponding social modalities of *holding on* versus *letting go* are of great importance in those aspects of social life that concern property and other matters that can be used in exchanges or as gifts.

In the case of Peter, age four, whose stomach had become bloated by holding in feces, Erikson found that the boy was afraid to let go. The reasons were quite complicated. As Erikson describes it (1963, pp. 55-58). First, Peter had been very fond of his nursemaid but she had left, preferring to tend small babies. Somehow Peter got the idea that she would like him better, and might come back, if he were a baby. Failing that, at least he could have a baby inside himself (his stools). Second, he had heard (and feared) that his mother had to have a strap to keep him from falling out of her when she was pregnant with him, and that she had to be cut open in order for him to be born because he was too big for her. So now he was afraid to let go of his stools partly because that would be letting go of the nurse and partly because that would endanger both his mother and himself.

Motivations for retention can obviously be very complex. Erikson proposes that the mode of retention is commonly used in a struggle for control between mother and child, and that an important conflict revolves around the child's willingness to comply with societal regulations. This willingness is tested not only in bowel training, but also in more general relationships with the environment. For at this point the muscular system is becoming much stronger and the child is now able to reach out and grab, throw, or push away things. The force of muscular development at this age is noticed everywhere in the child's body, not only in the anal sphincters. Freud had suggested that the muscular development coincided with development of cruelty, the urge to crush and destroy things; hence he had called this stage the *anal-sadistic* stage.

But Erikson argues that "This whole stage . . . becomes a battle for autonomy" (Erikson, 1963, p. 82). Indeed, the focus upon the anus and upon bowel training can be seen as concrete representation of an entire range of psychosocial tasks confronting the child during this stage. In all of these there is the issue of control and the opportunity for struggle between parent and child. In all of them there is a chance for a good solution which retains the autonomy and dignity of the child, or for a bad solution which results in depreciation of the child or the fostering of rebellious resentments.

The growing awareness of the difference between "I" and "you," between "mine" and "yours" accentuates the essentially interpersonal nature of the struggle. Whose will shall prevail? Whose bowel movements are these? Who shall control them? These are the crucial issues. Erikson says that the child must be helped to resolve these issues by firmness and protection. Somehow the child must develop *self-control* in the way of doing what society requires by willing compliance—by consent of the ego.

The relation between stages can be made clear in this connection. Erikson says that a satisfactory resolution of the problem at the anal stage depends upon what happened at the oral stage: "To develop autonomy a firmly developed and convincingly continued state of early trust is necessary" (Erikson, 1963, p. 85). That state must not be "jeopardized by this sudden wish to have a choice, to appropriate demandingly and to eliminate stubbornly." The alternative outcome is doubt and shame. Erikson writes: "His environment must back him up in his wish to 'stand on his own two feet' lest he be overcome by that sense of having exposed himself prematurely and foolishly which we call shame, or that secondary mistrust, that looking back which we call doubt" (Erikson, 1963, p. 85).

Clearly resolutions at one stage affect resolution at later stages. If trust emerges from the oral stage, then autonomy is more likely to result from the anal stage. If the oral stage yields only mistrust, the anal stage will probably yield shame and doubt. As we shall see later, the two stages and their resulting senses of trust versus mistrust and of autonomy versus shame and doubt have quite distinct implications for identity development during adolescence. They also have different implications for the social institutions people have evolved to satisfy the associated needs. Whereas trust needs religion, autonomy needs the institutions of law and order. Erikson writes: "A sense of rightful dignity and lawful independence on the part of adults around him gives to the child of good will the confident expectation that the kind of autonomy fostered in childhood will not lead to undue doubt or shame in later life" (Erikson, 1963, p. 254.) The sense of autonomy in the child becomes the sense of justice in the adult.

Phallic Stage: Initiative versus Guilt

Between the third and fifth years of life, Freud observed, the child becomes preoccupied with the external genitals. Both boys and girls become very curious about the origins of babies and they vaguely relate their theories of birth to the genital organs. Boys are fascinated by the comparison of their own penises with those of other boys and more especially with those of their fathers or older brothers. Girls develop a fascination for male genitals also, according to Freud, largely because of the absence of such an organ in their own bodies. Thus for both boys and girls this stage of development may be called the *phallic* stage, meaning the stage during which children of both sexes are especially interested in the male organ or phallus.

Erikson pays attention also to the mode of relationship between organism and milieu during the phallic stage. Boys and girls have different modes, he says. For the boy, the dominant mode is that of *intrusion*. Erikson describes it as (1963, pp. 87-90): "the intrusion into other bodies by physical attack; the intrusion into other people's ears and minds by aggressive talking; the intrusion into space by vigorous locomotion; the intrusion into the unknown by consuming curiosity." Intrusion goes along with activity and imagination.

For girls, too, there is an intrusive mode; the mode of *inclusion*, however, is much more dominant. She learns that she must offer receptivity to the male's physical intrusion and she has growing awareness of the fact that she, like her mother, has spaces inside of herself for the accommodation of a baby. Some doubts are still occasioned by the lack of a penis, however, and the possibility of her becoming a mother is not yet made clear by the development of breasts. She is apt to develop a pattern of playing with doll babies and become more demanding, teasing, and dependent.

The social modality associated with this stage is that of *making it*, which means "head-on attack, enjoyment of competition, insistence on goal, pleasure of conquest . . . in the girl it sooner or later changes to making it by teasing and provoking or by milder forms of 'snaring'—i.e. by making herself attractive and endearing" (Erikson, 1963, p. 90).

During the phallic stage a nuclear conflict arises between a sense of *initiative* and a sense of *guilt*. Both sexes develop components of the ability to select goals and to pursue them, although " 'oedipal' wishes (. . . the boy's assurance that he will marry his mother and make her proud of him and . . . the girl's that she will marry her father and take much better care of him) lead to vague fantasies bordering on murder and rape. The consequence is a deep sense of guilt . . ." (Erikson, 1963, p. 90).

For Erikson it is precisely this sense of guilt which "helps to drive the whole weight of initiative and the power of curiosity toward desirable ideals and immediate practical goals. . . ." Whereas Freud had argued that castration anxiety brought the oedipal feelings to an end simply, Erikson proposes that the guilt which underlies the anxiety drives the individual into productive activities, thus initiating the next stage of development.

Latency Stage: Industry versus Inferiority

Erikson accepted Freud's notion that conscience was developed in response to castration anxiety and as a means of reinforcing the prohibitions against erotic striving toward the parent of the opposite sex. The child's internalizing of these prohibitions leads to the development of the *superego,* that powerful part of the ego which brings libidinal impulses under strict control. In Freud's view the latency stage is not merely a time during which impulses have subsided; it is also a time during which repressive controls have been brought to bear upon those impulses. Only the upsurge of sexual excitation at puberty will prove sufficient to break the domination of the superego over libidinal impulses.

This period has positive and unique consequences for the developing personality, Erikson argues. The sexual and aggressive initiative of the phallic period now becomes sublimated—diverted into positively constructive and socially acceptable channels of activity. These activities involve learning to use tools and other aspects of the culture's technology. Instead of "making" people the child now learns to make things. A normally successful experience here produces in the child a *sense of industry*: "He can become an eager and absorbed unit of a productive situation. . . . His ego boundaries include his tools and skills: the work principle . . . teaches him the pleasure of work completion by steady attention and persevering diligence" (Erikson, 1963, p. 259).

The child's horizons are further extended during this age period. Children of other families in the neighborhood and school become more frequently encountered. Erikson points out that during this stage the child first develops an idea of the division of labor and of the associated notions of making things together with other people and of cooperating.

Comparisons with the skills and knowledge of other children are also frequent at this age, both in school and in the neighborhood. Erikson writes (1963, p. 260), "The child's danger, at this stage, lies in a sense of inadequacy and inferiority. If he despairs of his tools and skills or of his status among his tool partners, he may be discouraged from identification with them and with a section of the tool world." Such discouragement can lead to psychological regression to an earlier stage, such as that of oedipal rivalry, and also to a foreboding of personal uselessness in later life.

Thus the nuclear conflict of this stage is that of *industry* versus *inferiority.* Though Erikson does not say as much, it is evident that the mode of this era is that of *putting together,* and the zone is the combination of eyes, hands, and brain. The social modality, Erikson says, is that of *producing* things.

Freud said very little about the role of the latency stage in contributing to personality, but Erikson's views are quite definite in this matter. The general sense of industry or inferiority will follow the person perhaps for his or her entire life. The particular skills learned are preparation for particular adult roles.

In his study of the Sioux culture, for example, Erikson noted that boys' games of catching a wild rabbit on foot with bare hands only, or of roping stumps of trees, were explicit preparation for becoming a hunter or a cowboy. Indeed the acquisition of these skills and their later adult versions (such as roping a steer) "assure the development of the hunter or cowboy identity" (Erikson, 1963, p. 143).

Here we can see the impact of the social milieu upon identity formation. The occupational role components of personal identity must be given initially by the prescriptions and opportunities that society provides. One cannot become a stenographer in a society where no one gives dictation.

In addition to offering the possible occupational goals, society prepares the child to participate through training in the elementary skills that will be required, whether roping stumps or writing the letters of the alphabet.

Genital Stage: Identity versus Identity Confusion

Identity Elements. According to Freud's view, during adolescence the several impulses toward securing the separate, pregenital pleasures of the erogenous zones (mouth, muscular exertion, skin, phallus) are brought together under the dominance of genital pleasure. Pregenital pleasures become subservient to the genital aim in adult sexual relations. Erikson, accepting these insights, goes beyond them. He points to each of the infantile sexual stages as providing certain components which will be integrated into *psychosocial identity.* From the oral stage comes the modality of getting and taking, and also the sense of trust or mistrust. From the anal stage comes the modality of holding on and letting go, and also the sense of autonomy or of doubt. From the phallic stage comes the modality of making it, and also the sense of initiative or of guilt. From the latency stage comes the modality of producing things, and also the sense of industry or of inferiority. Each of these now becomes an *identity element.*

Identity elements are all those things that go to make up a person's psychosocial identity.

> The sense of ego identity . . . is the accrued confidence that the inner sameness and continuity prepared in the past are matched by the sameness and continuity of one's meaning for others. . . . [Ego identity is] more than the sum of the childhood identifications. It is the accrued experience of the ego's ability to integrate all identifications with the vicissitudes of the libido, with the aptitudes developed out of endowment, and with the opportunities offered in social roles" (Erikson, 1963, p. 261).

We shall define identity later on, after considering its many components.

Identifications, in Erikson's view, are inner images of the ego construed as being similar to or the same as the image of some outer person. Erikson describes a little boy who had been very well behaved while living with his mother and aunt. Then his father became a war hero and came home to visit. Shortly after that the boy's behavior became difficult. He began to play rough games, swooping dangerously downhill on a bicycle and racing through groups of other children, making strange noises which could only be interpreted as an airplane on a bombing mission. Erikson writes,

> To my little neighbor the role of bombardier may have suggested a possible synthesis of the various elements that comprise a budding identity: his temperament (vigorous); his maturational stage (phallic-urethral-locomotor); his social stage (oedipal) . . .; his capacities (mus-

cular, mechanical); his father's temperament (a great soldier rather than a successful civilian); and a current historical prototype (aggressive hero) (Erikson, 1963, pp. 239-240).

Thus identity can be a synthesis of many elements, including identifications of the ego with characteristics of other people (the boy's father's temperament and status, for example). The elements can also be those of the person's own given characteristics and abilities, as when someone vigorous and strong delights in that feature of self and includes it as an important element of identity: "I am a vigorous and strong person."

Another major class of elements of identity comes as a result of unresolved conflicts from earlier stages of psychosocial development. Erikson (1968, pp. 114 ff.) proposes a characteristic phrase of self-description that emerges from each stage, especially from the sense of trust, autonomy, initiative, and industry. From the sense of trust versus mistrust comes an identity element which may be phrased as, "I am what hope I have and give." From the sense of autonomy versus doubt comes the element, "I am what I can will freely." From the sense of initiative versus guilt comes an element of identity resting in the imagination and focusing upon the future: "I am what I can imagine I will be." From the latency stage comes the element, "I am what I can learn to make work."

Psychosocial Moratorium. In adolescence each of these identity elements must be brought together in a satisfying whole if sound ego identity is to be achieved. The synthesis sometimes is not easy, particularly if difficulties in the earlier stages have left the person with impediments, or if the right kind of career opportunity simply is not available. Sometimes, particularly for creative people, the synthesizing of identity requires a pro-

longed period of time out. Erikson calls this period a *psychosocial moratorium.* The young person needs to experiment freely with different roles and thereby hopes to find some niche in society that is uniquely suitable. Some people leave school for a year or so, travel, or find an interim job.

During the moratorium each previously established element of identity must be reworked. The sense of trust becomes a sense of faith; the search for trust becomes a search for people and ideals to believe in. As it enters into identity formation it might be expressed as follows: "I am what I believe in." Without trust the person believes in nothing.

The sense of autonomy continues and is transformed into a sense of the right to choose freely among the duties and services that persons must perform. In the home, for instance, someone has to do the chores and the errands. The adolescent and young adult seeks to establish with honor those chores which he or she will be committed to perform. This element might be phrased subjectively as follows: "I am what services I freely choose to render." Without autonomy the person doubts the worth of his or her possible services.

The sense of initiative is transformed into an appreciation of future possibilities for oneself. It becomes ambition, a search for the better life or fuller personal development. It is a striving, seeking for persons who offer inspiration and imaginative possibilities for one's future. Subjectively, this element could be expressed as: "I am what goals I am reaching for." Without initiative the person does not strive for distant goals.

The sense of industry developed during the latency stage provides the basis of searching for and selecting the "right" occupation. We might say: "I am what my occupation is." For this element to form a solid component of identity, it is particularly necessary that the person feel especially suited to the occupation, as if he or she were uniquely qualified. Without industry the person feels inferior; without a job a person feels unnecessary to society.

Erikson points out that different people will take different amounts of time to achieve identity. In part the present state of the culture or the economy plays a role. However, people who have had more of the negative consequences in their early stages of development (mistrust, doubt, guilt, inferiority), or people who have had unduly complicated experiences (mistrust in one segment of living, trust in another, for example) will take longer.

People who are very creative may require an exceptionally long moratorium. It is just that much harder for them to find an appropriate niche. One reason for this is that a creative person is one who can bring something new to the society and culture. Hence there is no ready-made and well-defined niche in which the person can fit. A new one must be fashioned. Erikson believes that many creative people do not achieve identity until their later twenties. Martin Luther was such a person; later in this chapter we shall examine Erikson's account of Luther's life and identity development.

Until a sense of identity is formed people in this stage experience a sense of *identity confusion,* characterized by much uncertainty and worry about who they are, how they fit, and where they are going in life.

How then shall identity be defined? The *sense* of identity, like all senses in Erikson's theory, has at least a threefold status: conscious awareness, manifestation in behavior, and presence in the unconscious. What is this awareness, this manifestation, and this presence about? It is about a very complex set of *images* and *potentials for images.* A potential for an image is perhaps best thought of as a memory. For example, there is a potential for a certain image in the reader's mind right now, a potential which can be brought to activity by my suggesting that the reader think of a recent vacation. It may have been in the woods, on a lake, in the mountains, by the sea, or just lazing around at home. The sights and sounds can come back to the inner ear and the inward eye, presenting themselves as images with more or less vividness. Or again the reader might think of this morning and imagine waking up, taking a shower, cleaning teeth, the taste of toothpaste, the smell of soap. . . . In each case, before the actual image becomes active it exists as a potential image, presumably in memory. Identity is a complicated set of such potential images. (I am not sure that Erikson would agree entirely with this statement, but that is the way I think about it. He would agree with the next remarks, because they refer to the content of the images and follow his own statements about it.)

Identity is a composite image of the person's own body, abilities, needs, and character traits. Some of the traits have been taken over from other people whose nature and role the person once imagined and then took to be himself or herself (childhood identifications). The identity is also partly composed of images of the person's actual and possible roles in society, along with images of other people's confirming attitudes and behaviors toward the individual in these roles. These role images include reference to the person as citizen, worker, spouse, member of particular ethnic, social, or political groups, and so on over the entire range of the individual's participation in his or her society and culture.

Later Genital Stage:
Intimacy versus Isolation
The primary developmental task of the young adult, according to Erikson, is to achieve intimacy with another person. Although Freud (1905b) discussed the trans-

formation that takes place with puberty and adolescence, he did not clearly separate those changes from the ones which lead to full genital expression. As Erikson (1968, pp. 136-137) has pointed out, psychoanalysis has always emphasized that genitality is the core of developmental maturity, yet goes far beyond mere orgasm. It means love, generosity, and intimacy.

Erikson believes that much of sexual motivation during adolescence is essentially "of the self-seeking, identity-hungry kind; each partner is really trying only to reach himself. Or it remains a kind of genital combat, in which each tries to defeat the other" (Erikson, 1968, p. 137). He believes that a full sense of *intimacy,* of love and mutuality, can be achieved only by persons who have resolved their identity crisis. The inability to risk such intimacy characterizes the alternative pole of this psychosocial crisis, namely a sense of *isolation.*

Generativity versus Stagnation

Hitherto the stages of psychosocial development have been linked in parallel with stages and periods in psychosexual development, as previously formulated by Freud. Freud's theory did not go beyond the genital stage, however. In the next stage delineated in Erikson's theory the basic conflict is between *generativity* and *stagnation. Generativity,* says Erikson, is "primarily the concern for establishing and guiding the next generation" (1968, p. 138). Thus parents have special responsibilities in this stage, but others do too: teachers and preachers and city managers, for example. Generativity involves a whole-hearted participation in planning with others for the benefit of children and youth. Such losing of oneself "leads to a gradual expansion of ego-interests and to a libidinal investment in that which is being generated. Where such enrichment fails altogether regression to an obsessive need

for pseudointimacy takes place, often with a pervading *sense of stagnation,* boredom, and interpersonal impoverishment" (Erikson, 1968, p. 138). A person in such condition seeks to be pampered, treating oneself as one's own child. Such people may unconsciously seek sickness and invalidism, thus guaranteeing that others will look after them.

Stagnation is not the only, or even the worst alternative outcome of this period. Erikson points out that this period brings us full cycle. As individuals we have progressed through most of the psychosocial stages, with outcomes made better or worse by the social environments we encountered. Now we reach the point at which it is our turn to *be* a social environment for members of the next generation. The outcomes of their psychosocial crises are now in our hands. By our behaviors as parents and teachers we can create the conditions for trust instead of mistrust, for autonomy instead of doubt and shame, for initiative instead of guilt, for industry instead of inferiority.

Integrity versus Disgust and Despair

The final stage of life brings yet another psychosocial crisis. Erikson says (1968, p. 139) that the "fruit of the seven stages" gradually becomes ripe in an aging person who has accomplished something, taken care of some people, and adapted to the many successes and failures of living. This fruit is a sense of *integrity,* an assured acceptance of one's life as it has been, of its significance in terms of one's own ego strengths, and of its kinship to the lives of other men and women throughout history. This is the age of wisdom.

The contrasted state at this period is *despair* of ever reaching one's own goals in life. Sometimes this is hidden under a veneer of disgust with the modern world or with particular people in it.

Accomplishments of Erikson's Theory of Developmental Pattern

Erikson's theory is in essence a further development of Freud's psychoanalytic theory. As Erikson himself stated, psychoanalysis has turned increasingly to the study of the ego, and the ego may be conceived as a construct which, in part, refers to the human person's ability to integrate experience and behavior in a way that both satisfies instinctual needs and adapts to the limitations and realistic opportunities of the environment. These limitations and opportunities are perhaps most keenly felt in the contacts between child and parents, between ego and society. Erikson set himself the task of studying more deeply the roots of the ego in society and culture, not forgetting its origins in biological and psychosexual maturation, but focusing the microscope of psychoanalytic study upon the interaction between childhood and society. One measure of the success of Erikson's work is the opinion of his peers, and there can be do doubt of their high estimation of his contributions to the psychoanalytic theory of the ego. For instance, R. W. White writes (1975, p. 11) that Erikson has made *the* "outstanding contribution to ego psychology."

Erikson's theory has had a major influence on general developmental psychology as well as upon psychoanalytic ego psychology. In their recent text, *Development Through Life,* for example, Newman and Newman (1975) make Erikson's theory the framework and principal basis of their presentation. Research studies on Erikson's theory are on the increase, as reported in psychology journals. As one example, Ciaccio (1971) used five pictures to which children aged five to eleven were asked to tell stories. The stories were then analyzed according to the psychosocial stage of development that was reached in them; the prevailing stage of the child was thereby estimated. Plotting each child's stage against actual age, Ciaccio found that the stages of psychosocial development do progress as Erikson has stated. Moreover, few children had reached the stage of identity by the age of eleven. One unexpected finding was that the conflicts over autonomy versus doubt were still very important among the five-year-olds, being reflected in nearly half their responses. Even among the oldest group, these conflicts represented about 15 percent of the total. It appears that this second psychosocial crisis is apt to be prolonged far beyond .the toilet-training period.

A number of studies of college students have been made. What should be their identity status, for example? Through a special interviewing technique, Waterman and colleagues (1974) have shown that less than 25 percent of freshmen have achieved identity status. But about 45 percent of seniors have achieved identity status. However, more than 30 percent of each group continues in a state of identity confusion.

Does identity achievement yield the kind of inner strength that Erikson proposes? Toder and Marcia (1973) examined this question by putting students who had achieved identity status into a situation where they were in conflict. Confederate subjects were told to make an incorrect judgment on a perceptual task. Then came the target subject's turn: would he conform to the judgments of his peers? Or would he give the answer that seemed best indicated by his perception? It is known from other studies that subjects often conform to erroneous judgments under such circumstances. It was predicted that students who had achieved their identity status would be less likely to conform to peer pressure. This was found to be true.

Erikson's theory has also introduced a new subdiscipline within psychology, namely *psychohistory,* a psychological approach to the study of history. While psychoanalytic and other theories had been applied to historical events and sequences before, it was Erikson's idea of studying the evolution of personality in a great man in history that sparked a new subdiscipline that already is engaging more than a dozen scientists (Lifton, 1974; especially p. 27). Erikson's first publication using the new approach was *Young Man Luther* (1962), in which he studied the struggle for identity of this intense, creative genius, who matured to become a powerful religious reformer.

As a young adult Martin Luther's psychosocial moratorium was spent in a monastery. His identity as a reformer, not finally synthesized until the age of thirty-one, led to his becoming the father of the Protestant Reformation.

During the first stage of life Luther experienced both comfort and danger. The home was secure, but both parents were strict. His father had outbursts of violent temper. For little Martin the outcome was a mixture of trust and mistrust, with mistrust prevailing.

In the second stage, in which the child's autonomy is established or questioned, Luther was exposed to frequent whippings from both parents. Once he was whipped until the blood ran because he had stolen a nut. As a result he developed a sense not of autonomy but of forced compliance. Yet underneath there was rebellion and stubbornness.

Martin's energy, coupled with the thrust of rebellion, brought about extremes of both initiative and guilt during the third stage of life. The underlying guilt, strongly felt, paved the way for a fiercely stern conscience; moreover, it conditioned the very nature of the initiative he felt. It was initiative that he sensed could be expressed only in the context of obedient service. Thus to some extent autonomy was restored in the guise of energetic and even self-initiated compliance.

It is during the third stage of life that the fateful Oedipus complex is formed. Erikson believes that Martin Luther probably experienced this conflict with great intensity. His father whipped him so badly one time that he fled from him and became "sadly resentful toward him." As Martin later recalled it, his father worked on him subsequently, until "he gradually got me accustomed to him again." Erikson suggests that Martin was unable to really hate his father even in the worst of his feelings toward him. And, on the other side, his father could neither let the boy come close nor let him go. The result of this complex relationship with his father strongly influenced the resolution of the Oedipus complex for Martin, namely in the formation of a "precocious, sensitive, intense conscience" (Erikson, 1962, p. 73).

Martin's native energy, buoyed by rebellion, moderated by a demanding conscience, and empowered with a brilliant mind, led him to develop outstanding skills during the latency period. These included voice training for singing and an extensive vocabulary in Latin and German, as well as a powerful memory. Thus he had a sense of industry solidly established at the end of this period.

With more mistrust than trust, a very conditional autonomy, strong initiative driven partly by guilt, and a sound sense of industry, the elements in Martin's identity were chaotic enough to render him in a state of identity confusion. He was guided to enter a monastery, despite his father's protestations. There, Erikson believes, Martin Luther found the boundaries that he needed for his psychosocial moratorium. There he could wrestle with the complexities of his identity. This period lasted from age twenty-two to age thirty-one.

In the early part of this period Luther believed that God's justice is ultimate and wrathful; and that it is based upon what we do in this life. In part this belief reflected the convictions he developed in the first two stages of psychosocial development: a mixture of trust and mistrust, with the latter predominant, and a sense of forced compliance on pain of dire punishment.

Largely through the nurturant guidance of his superior, Staupitz, Luther learned the meaning of unmixed love and trust; but this took several years. When he was thirty, Luther studied the Book of Psalms intensively, in preparation for a series of lectures. A plea from Psalm 31, "and deliver me in Thy righteousness," had always seemed fearful to him, for he interpreted it as meaning deliverance through harsh judgment and punishment. Working on a related portion of the Bible, Luther read Paul's words in Romans, 1:17, "For therein is the righteousness of God revealed from faith to faith: as it is written, The just shall live by faith."

By faith. Not by punishment. . . .

The idea had a revolutionary impact on Luther. He came to see at last that there was a universe of difference between his earthly father and his Heavenly Father. His earthly father had in fact deserved the mixture of trust and mistrust that Martin had felt for him. But this was not true of God. Erikson writes (1962, p. 201), "The power of these words lay in a new perception of the space-time of life and eternity. Luther saw that God's justice is not consigned to a future day of judgment based on our record on earth when He will have the 'last word.' Instead, this justice is in us, in the here and now; for, if we will only perceive it, God has given us faith to live by, and we can perceive it by understanding the Word which is Christ."

Thus the resolution of trust was accompanied by the resolution of autonomy in Martin Luther's sense of identity. Surely compliance would continue, now no longer forced by fear of punishment, but rather given willingly from a sense of the dignity and justice within him, freely to choose a life of service to a loving Father.

Martin's skills with words made him a first-rate lecturer and preacher. He was promoted often within the hierarchy of his monastic order. He lectured at the University of Wittenberg. Elements of autonomy, initiative, and brilliant industry were now combined with clear and unshakable faith. There emerged a man of erect posture and inspiring voice, the Martin Luther of history: an identity long in the making but, once made, never to be forgotten.

Critique of Erikson's Theory

Most criticisms leveled at Freud's theory of pattern can also be leveled at Erikson's theory, since the latter includes and goes beyond the former. They may be found in chapter 11. One criticism that has been brought specifically against Erikson's theory, however, is that it fails to go far enough in breaking away from Freud's construct of the id as a biologically given substratum of personality. Guntrip (1973) charges that Erikson provides us with a theory which is internally inconsistent because he accepts "the idea of infantile organic drives that are later woven into culturally determined adult motive-patterns. . . ," and this idea is unsatisfactory because it assumes that personality is developed later "on the foundation of purely biological drives at the beginning. . . ." The reason this empirical assumption is unsatisfactory, says Guntrip, is that "There cannot be any time when a human being is all soma [body] and no psyche [mind]. Psyche and soma are there together from the most primitive or early stage to the latest and most developed" (Guntrip, 1973, p. 83). It is not clear how Erikson would answer this criticism. My own thought about it is that it is not really a criticism but an assertion of an alternative empirical assumption. Since neither Erikson's nor Guntrip's assumptions have actually been tested neither can be dismissed. Neither, however, seems to have any readily testable consequences, so perhaps the "unsatisfactory" assumption actually makes little difference to the theory.

As we come to apply the several criteria of evaluation of a theory discussed in chapter 6 it will be necessary first to examine the extent to which Erikson's theory makes a unique contribution. We have to distinguish his theory from Freud's.

It is not necessary here to recapitulate in detail Freud's theory of psychosexual development. It is given in chapter 11. Rather, our purpose is to examine the aspects of personality each theory describes. Are they the same? Are the two theories in competition?

Table 14.1 sets out the main stages according to Freud and Erikson. In the list of stages proposed by Erikson I have omitted his thoughts on the psychosexual components, since these are largely refinements of Freud's

statements. Also omitted are Erikson's contributions concerning the *modes* and *modalities*. In fact table 14.1 is merely schematic and serves the main purpose of aligning the proposed stages of each theorist with respect to time.

Note that in the outline of Erikson's theory in table 14.1 the stage titles, Trust versus Mistrust, and so on, refer to *sense*. The child develops a sense of trust, a sense of autonomy. Each sense has three aspects to it: a conscious experience, a way of behaving which others may describe as "trusting," and an unconscious state of affairs which may be discovered by psychoanalysis or by diagnostic testing. Thus it refers to a portion of *experience*, a portion of *behavior*, and some feature of the *psychophysical systems*. It seems unlikely that Erikson treats the psychophysical systems alone as causal. Rather the succession of stages designated by a sense of trust or a sense of autonomy refers to stages in the *record* of experience and behavior. Freud's contrasting

Table 14.1   ·

Freud and Erikson's Theories of Developmental Pattern in Personality

Approximate Age	Freud's Theory	Erikson's Theory
Birth to 1 year	Oral	Trust versus Mistrust
1 to 2 years	Anal	Autonomy versus Doubt, Shame
3 to 5 years	Phallic, Oedipal	Initiative versus Guilt
6 to 10 years	Latency	Industry versus Inferiority
11 to 21 years	Genital	Identity versus Role confusion
22 to 35 years		Intimacy versus Isolation
36 to 65 years		Generativity versus Stagnation
65 and over		Integrity versus Despair

emphasis upon the *body* and *psychophysical systems* is shown in the titles of his stages, which refer to the organ primarily involved.

Notice that Erikson's and Freud's theories are not in competition. Freud's stages describe organizations of sexuality; Erikson's stages describe organizations of social relatedness surrounding ego. The connection between the two theories is given first by the fact that Erikson explicitly accepts the essential framework of Freud's psychosexual theory and builds upon it, and second by the continuities of formal quality between psychosexual organization and psychosocial organization. Thus psychosexual *incorporation* is aligned temporally and in form-quality with psychosocial *getting*. In the phallic stage, when males are concerned with penetrating and females with being penetrated, psychosexual *intrusion* and *inclusion* respectively are aligned with appropriate forms of psychosocial *making it*.

There is a similar form-quality continuity between the modalities and the senses. For example, the *getting* modality of the oral stage has its psychosocial expression in *trust* (or mistrust) of the supplier. Similarly the phallic stage modality of *making it* has its expression in a sense of *initiative*, willingness, and energy to venture into new enterprises or other people's territory.

In making our comparison of the two theories we may profit from analogy with a familiar circumstance and its two sides. Almost everyone has been sick at some time. We get sick, feeling unwell, collapse in bed, take medicines, see a doctor, perhaps go into a hospital, get nursed back to health, and then, still a bit weak, we stumble back into rehabilitation, gradually regaining strength and returning to normal. Now an organ description of our sickness could focus upon the infection of lungs and stomach, the congestion and pains, the gradual easing of these conditions, and the final clearing of both organs. Such a descrip-

tion would be analogous to Freud's account of psychosexual stages. Alternatively we could describe the sickness in terms of the patient's feelings and relation to other people. The patient would complain and seek relief. With trust in those around, the patient would get some home remedies. With trust in the physician the patient would get some prescriptions. With the patient's initiative temporarily out of action, the physician would do the necessary work of getting the arrangements made for the patient to enter a hospital, where nurses would take over the patient's nourishment, routines of elimination, and so on. The patient would have to give up some autonomy. As the patient feels better and begins to talk about going home and going back to work, a sense of industry, autonomy, initiative, and identity gradually return. On the one hand the patient's lungs and stomach are returning to an uninfected and otherwise medically normal state; the lessening of experienced pain accompanies these physiological changes. On the other hand the patient's feelings of impairment and helplessness are giving way to returning autonomy and eagerness to go back to work.

The medical description of sickness and recovery is true in its own right, and the psychosocial description of sickness and recovery is true in its own right. There are undoubted continuities between the two; but they do not offer alternative theoretical models of the same facts. So they cannot be competing theories. Nor are they in any useful way really *complementary*: the one does not help the other from a theoretical point of view. The theory of germs and antibodies does its job very well without a discussion of the patient's feelings of helplessness. Likewise the theory of psychosocial relations does its job very well without a discussion of biophysical concomitants.

Similarly Freud and Erikson deal with related but different sets of facts. In terms of the components of a definition of personality, Freud's theory of pattern focuses upon the body (erogenous zones) and psychophysical systems (cathexes); Erikson's theory of pattern focuses upon the record (of experience and behavior), upon a different aspect of psychophysical systems (the unconscious part of the sense of trust, autonomy, and so on), and upon the social environment. Erikson of course deals with the body (as in his reference to the mouth as prototype for the mode of incorporation). But here Erikson is simply using Freud's theory, which he accepts. His own distinctive emphases do not dwell upon the body. The model object he works from includes the body and other features of the model object Freud worked from, but it goes beyond Freud's, and Erikson's focus is on the sociocultural aspects as discussed earlier in the chapter.

Nevertheless Erikson has been criticized for his suggestion that the anatomy of female children determines their preference for an inclusion mode rather than an intrusion mode during the stage of initiative versus guilt. This seems to imply that anatomy controls destiny to some—probably very small—extent.

We may ask whether there is any causal component in Erikson's theory. There certainly seems to be, since the early resolutions of stages are apt to affect later stages, even as the earliest stages have outcomes that constitute components for the later identity formation. It is not clear that these kinds of influences are thought to be strictly causal, however; rather they seem to exert a kind of sequential constraint. A sense of early trust, for example, makes it easier to develop a sense of identity through faith when the time comes. We must notice also that the texture of relationships holds between this early sense and that later sense, that is, between different portions of the record. This means that one portion of experience has consequences for a later part in the experiential record; one portion of the behavioral record has consequences for a later portion of the behavioral record. Erikson also makes it clear that the prevailing culture and social order have causal impact upon the content and timing of the stages, through influence upon experience and behavior in the first place and upon the psychophysical structures as a result. Thus his theory proposes a pattern of development in the record which on one hand runs parallel to Freud's proposed pattern of development in the body and psychophysical systems with respect to sexuality, and on the other hand runs in causal nexus with the temporal patterns of social and cultural history.

Evaluation of the Theory

We may now consider the first criterion for evaluating Erikson's theory, *accuracy*. The research of Ciaccio, Marcia, Toder, Waterman, and others, which was reported in the previous section, shows that Erikson's theory of pattern is accurate regarding the order of stages, although the unexpected prolongation of autonomy-versus-doubt conflicts indicates that an early stage is not necessarily resolved when a later stage rises to dominance. This observation leads us to question whether the proposed temporal alignments between psychosexual and psychosocial stages are accurate; for certainly the anal stage (with which autonomy-versus-doubt is aligned) does not persist unresolved beyond age five.

Obviously, much is unknown at present concerning the accuracy of Erikson's theory. This is true also of the parts of the theory relating earlier portions of the record to later ones; for example, we just do not know whether an early sense of trust becomes an adolescent search for faith. Nor do we know whether sociocultural influences work upon the stages of psychosocial development in the manner proposed by the theory. A large body of cultural anthropological data exists from which suitable tests might be devised, but so far they have not been. We have the actual observational evidence used by Erikson himself in his seminal work, which is suggestive of accuracy but cannot be taken as final. It is one man's judgment of very complex matters; for example, a child's acquisition of a sense of trust or mistrust depends upon the success of the culture and the parents in providing substitute satisfactions for oral incorporation when the child moves into the oral-biting stage. We must regard Erikson's views on sociocultural causes as viable hypotheses still in need of confirmation and testing.

Altogether it seems reasonable to conclude that little is known at present of the accuracy of Erikson's theory. The little evidence that is available suggests that the theory is mainly accurate, though in need of further specific elaboration such as exactly how long the nuclear conflicts (e.g., autonomy versus doubt) can be prolonged. The limited evidence for accuracy means that there is little evidence on the criterion of power also.

Erikson's theory has been *fruitful,* however, both in guiding research (such as on the identity status of college students), in producing a new subdiscipline of psychohistory, and also in providing a new systematic orientation for the study of personality development. Many psychologists find Erikson's theory appealing and stimulating.

How much *depth of understanding* does Erikson's theory provide? In my own experience it is helpful to many students, especially those in the state of identity confusion. Recognition that the condition has a name somehow eases its burden for them. They are apt to look with greater interest into their immediate environment and life experience for cues as to the elements of their still unformed identity. Sometimes they are able to see their way toward an active cooperation with the process of searching out elements of their identity. For example, one student decided that it would be very desirable to spend a year or so doing a variety of jobs in order to find out something about his real preferences and competencies in work. Another decided to take a battery of personality and interest tests in order to gain some guidance in what would be a suitable major.

I find Erikson's theory helpful for my own developmental stage, generativity versus stagnation. Simply to realize the possibility of stagnation (for me that calls up the image of a man in sweaty undershirt slumped before a TV tube) is enough of a repulsive stimulus to encourage me in the direction of maintaining active interests in scientific and educational work. My own experience also suggests that the crisis of identity may not always be resolved once and for all. Identity confusion may recur in different form later in life, triggered either by changing professional roles, job conditions, social circumstances, or philosophical or religious persuasions. I believe that such crises in later life are not uncommon, at least according to reports of men and women making major career changes in middle age.

Measuring a Construct: The Sense of Initiative

Erikson's central construct is **a sense of**—of trust, autonomy, initiative, industry, identity, generativity, or integrity. This construct has three aspects: experience, behavior, and unconscious state. Erikson seems to say that a particular sense is equally present in all aspects, and that the conscious experience may be determined by introspection, the behavioral aspect may be assessed by observation, and the unconscious state may be gauged by means of psychological testing, such as the Thematic Apperception Test.

We may question whether all aspects will actually reveal the same thing. In Jung's theory, for example, we would expect **compensation** to produce opposite tendencies in the conscious and unconscious parts of the personality. The evidence from psychological testing would lead us to expect that variables having the same content (such as trust) but measured from different viewpoints (such as self-report, behavior rating, and diagnostic evaluation) frequently have a chance relationship only. Often they are not highly correlated. Granted that we are attempting to design a measure of Erikson's construct, however, we should have to expect initially that the three approaches to measuring the three aspects of **a sense of initiative** would yield data that are positively correlated. Obviously just one approach (such as self-report through questionnaire) would not be adequate to an assessment of the construct since Erikson states explicitly that the **sense of** has three aspects. Our task then, would be to design or select instruments capable of providing valid measurements of each aspect of the sense of initiative. In this workshop we shall simply begin by making a list of possible items or categories out of which the instruments would be constructed. We might begin by going back to the section on the phallic stage and considering various possible items there. Here are some beginning possibilities. Your task is to assemble a much larger initial list and then refine it for pilot assessment studies.

Experience, Introspection: Questionnaire	Behavior, Observation: Rating Scale	Unconscious, Interpreting: Pictures like TAT
Are you interested in how things work, their inner mechanisms?	Does the person take things apart to see how they work?	Picture of a boy with a toy train partly in pieces.
Would you like to be a private detective?	Does the person usually know what's going on in his neighbors' lives?	Picture of someone in the garden and two people talking at the back door of the next house.
When you speak to someone confidentially, do you like to say it directly into their ear?	Does this person tend to "button-hole" people when talking to them?	Picture of two people talking. Does the hero tend to start the conversation?
When you have a job to do, do you usually want to make a head-on attack at it?	Does this person tend to attack a problem or job head-on?	Picture of two engineers looking at a blueprint of a bridge. Does the hero attack the problem head-on?

Can you think of any problems with these items? What about the respondent's possible unwillingness to disclose true feelings in a questionnaire? What about the effects of repression on overt behavior and on stories? Are any items particularly affected by such matters? What can be done about it?

You could start again going through the section on the phallic stage, making up new items as appropriate. Try to get at least four more items for each aspect of the construct.

Summary

Erikson's theory of developmental pattern proposes eight stages, the first five of which are temporally aligned with the Freudian stages of oral, anal, phallic, latency, and genital development. For Erikson, these stages are conceived as periods during which particular psychosocial conflicts arise and must be resolved. Resolution yields a particular attitude or sense in the individual. For example, successful resolution of the incorporative conflicts in the oral stage yields a sense of trust in the child, trust in other people as suppliers of needs and trust in self as worthy of having needs satisfied. The sense of trust (like all other such senses) has aspects in conscious experience, in behavior, and in an unconscious state which may be tapped by psychological testing or psychoanalysis.

The eight stages in Erikson's theory are as follows: trust versus mistrust, autonomy versus doubt or shame, initiative versus guilt, industry versus inferiority, identity versus identity confusion, intimacy versus isolation, generativity versus stagnation, and integrity versus despair.

Whether a child emerges from the oral stage with a sense of trust or a sense of mistrust depends heavily upon how well the parents (or the culture) provide for the preferred resolution to take place. Thus the sociocultural environment affects the outcomes at particular stages. Also the outcome at an earlier stage affects the outcomes of later stages. There are thus causal connections between portions of the record (experience and behavior) as well as causal connections between the environment and individual.

Erikson's theory has been quite fruitful, and what evidence there is suggests that the theory is accurate. The amount of evidence is small however. This means that we are at present largely unable to properly estimate the theory's accuracy and hence unable to estimate its power. The theory provides helpful understanding for many college students, especially those caught in the stage of identity confusion.

Figure 14.1 illustrates the definition of personality implicit in Erikson's theory.

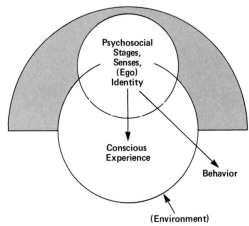

Figure 14.1. Definition of personality implicit in Erikson's theory

In the next chapter we shall turn to a different type of theory. Cattell's functional theory is based upon psychological measurement data. It will be interesting to notice, among other things, how influential the theories of Freud and Jung have been in Cattell's own theoretical developments and how he has put many of their important constructs to good use in a mathematically sophisticated context.

INTRODUCTION

Basic assumptions
  Behavior is a function of the strength of
    underlying traits
  Certain source traits characterize most people
  Dynamic traits motivate certain behaviors
Introduction to Cattell's life and work
  Life and professional career
  Influences of Spearman and Thorndike
  Focus on objective measures of personality
The concept of a personality trait
  A trait describes a disposition
  Traits can be isolated and measured
Cattell's approach and procedures
  Factor analysis and the scientific method
  Isolating source traits: correlation and factor
    analysis
  How factor analysis works
  Oblique rotation, parallel projections
Assumptions about traits and their measurements
  Three divisions of traits: ability, temperament,
    motivation
  Media of observation: ratings, questionnaires,
    objective tests
Cattell's theory of personality structure: temperament
  Source traits reflecting **Exvia:** A, F, H, Q2
    Affectia
    Surgency
    Parmia
    Self-sufficiency
  Organization of source traits in strata
  Implications of the correlation methods
  Source traits reflecting **Anxiety:** C, L, O, Q4
    Ego strength
    Protension
    Guilt proneness
    Ergic tension
  Source traits reflecting **Cortertia:** I and M
    Premsia
    Autia
  Source traits reflecting **Inner control:** G and Q3
    Superego strength
    Self-sentiment
  Interaction of source traits

Cattell's theory of personality structure: motivation
  Some principles of motivation measurement
    applied in device construction
  Tentative set of items for an information test
    of one of Cattell's ergs
  Interrelation of temperament and motivation
Theory and models of cause
  The dynamic calculus
  Conflict
  Situational causes
Accomplishments of Cattell's theory
  Diagnostic application
  Personnel selection
  Marital evaluation
  Structured learning
  Assessment for particular age groups
Critique of Cattell's theory
  Bias in measurement and factor analysis
  Orthogonal versus oblique factors
  Evaluation of the theory
Workshop 15 Comparing Cattell's second-order
    temperament factor with Jung's types
Summary
Test Key

15 CHAPTER

Cattell's Functional Theory of Personality Structure and Causal Dynamics

In this chapter we shall deal with a modern theory of function, the personality theory developed by Raymond B. Cattell.[1] The most basic empirical assumption of this theory is that a person's behavior in a given situation is a function of the individual's underlying personality traits and also of the extent to which each trait is triggered into action by that situation (Cattell, 1950, p. 628). If this assumption is correct, it should be possible to discover what those underlying personality traits are and also to discover the circumstances under which they are triggered for a particular individual. For example, it might be found that proneness to anxiety is one of the most important underlying traits, and that different individuals vary in how prone they are to becoming anxious. One person might rarely become anxious, even under quite stressful circumstances; another might get anxious several times a day, or whenever an upcoming task looks the least bit difficult.

Cattell also makes a methodological assumption that those traits of personality truly important for scientific study are the ones that are found to characterize many people. For instance, proneness to anxiety is something that many people seem to have; tranquilizers and other methods of calming anxiety are widely used. At the same time, many other people never need a tranquilizer since they remain relatively calm under most normal circumstances. In the middle are the majority of persons who become anxious now and then, whenever life stresses begin to pile up on them. So proneness to anxiety would be an underlying trait of importance for scientists to study since it is so widespread, with many people having high proneness, many people having very low proneness, and the majority having some small degree of proneness to anxiety. By contrast, consider a trait like superciliousness. The great majority of persons are simply not supercilious; occasionally we encounter someone who is, however, and this might be an outstanding characteristic of that person. We might even remark, "Oh, So-and-So is so supercilious!" But we would rarely describe someone in these words: "Oh, So-and So is so *un*supercilious!" Since almost everybody is not supercilious, the only useful feature about it is to describe the few who are. So superciliousness as a trait would not be

---

1. I am grateful to Professor Cattell for reading and commenting on an early draft of this chapter.

nearly as important for scientific purposes as anxiety proneness is.

Cattell's purpose, then, has been to determine just what are the main underlying personality traits. In the body of the chapter we shall examine exactly how he goes about this task and what results he has achieved so far in more than forty years of research. After briefly describing his life and work we shall consider Cattell's theories of structure and cause. His theory of structure centers upon the important underlying traits of personality, the *source traits* as he calls them. The theory proposes how many there are, the inner nature of each one, and, the organization that exists among the various source traits. His theory of cause proposes that situations trigger the source traits into activity in particular ways, and that there are also certain kinds of source traits (which he calls *dynamic traits*) which play an especially important role in motivating behavior.

Introduction to Cattell's Life and Work

Cattell was born in England in 1905 and graduated with a B.Sc. in chemistry and physics at the University of London when he was nineteen. Having begun his career in the so-called "hard" sciences, he then turned to psychology because it seemed both interesting and greatly in need of hard mathematical development. He did his doctoral studies under Professor Charles Spearman at University College, London. Spearman is famous for his work on the nature of intelligence and for inventing some statistical tools to study intelligence. Spearman offered Cattell precisely the kind of tough-minded image of scientific psychology that Cattell was seeking. Cattell received his Ph.D. in psychology in 1929, and was awarded a D.Sc. some years later.

After completing his doctoral work with Spearman, Cattell obtained a teaching position at what is now the University of Exeter, England. Subsequently he was appointed Director of the Psychological Clinic at Leicester from 1932 to 1937. In these years he gained a great deal of practical experience in the application of psychology to clinical problems among children and adults. Deeply concerned with England's social problems during these years, he published a number of books on social progress, national intelligence, and the religious quest. In a lighter vein, he also wrote a book about his favorite sport, sailing.

E. L. Thorndike, at Teachers' College, Columbia University, read Cattell's work on intelligence and invited him to become a Research Associate at Columbia. Cattell accepted, and since 1938 he has lived in the United States, holding teaching positions at Clark University and at Harvard. In 1944 he was named Research Professor at the University of Illinois, where he still directs the Laboratory for Personality and Group Analysis.

In the years at Illinois, Cattell has concentrated first upon the research needed to establish the main source traits of personality. His laboratory became renowned throughout the world for its accomplishments in isolating these source traits and in providing psychological tests to measure them. Students from countless foreign countries came to Cattell's laboratory to study for one or several years. Versions of Cattell's tests have been translated into more than a dozen different languages, and in each language the tests are used extensively for research and for practical applications such as clinical diagnosis or personnel selection. In order to handle the demand for these tests Cattell established the Institute for Personality and Ability Testing in Champaign, Illinois.

Recently Cattell established an Institute for Research on Morale and Adjustment in Boulder, Colorado. Subsequently he taught for a number of years at the University of Hawaii, all the while maintaining his research programs at the University of Illinois.

A man of boundless energy and fertile intellect, Cattell has by no means been limited to research strictly concerned with personality. He has also done extensive work in social psychology and behavior genetics, and he has made a great many important contributions to research methods, especially in the development of mathematical and statistical techniques. In one brief chapter it is impossible to give a full account of his theory and research, and so it will be necessary to take a very selective approach and concentrate on the main portions of his work on personality, emphasizing such topics as anxiety, control, and the organization of source traits in the structure of personality. Before going to the substance of Cattell's theories, however, we must spend a little time in further discussion of the concept of *traits,* and then on some essential statistical methods.

The Concept of a Personality Trait

The concept of *trait* in psychology refers to a relatively enduring disposition to respond to certain sorts of situations in certain sorts of ways. For example, an *irritable* person is one who responds with scowls, grunts, sarcasm, glares, and angry tossing of head or shrugging of shoulders. But these kinds of behaviors are not apparent under all circumstances. They appear only in response to certain kinds of situations, such as interruptions while reading, telephone calls, requests for charity, dates who are late, ambiguous questions on an examination, and so forth. It is assumed that no two people respond in exactly the same way, and that no two people respond to exactly the same set of triggering situations. It is assumed that people respond to one or more situations of a given type (frustrating, distracting, disturbing, delaying, interfering, boring, challenging, and so on), and that they do so with varying degrees of intensity. For example, to one and the same experimental disturbance (such as snatching away some tools and materials before the person can finish an assigned interesting task), one subject reacts with great anger, another is mildly annoyed, another is undisturbed. One subject may feel indignant, another may think it funny. One subject may flush with anger, another may go pale under the threat to self-esteem. These examples reflect behavioral, experimental, and bodily reactions to the disturbance. If they are actually characteristic of the subject in the sense that he or she is likely to have similar reactions to other disturbing situations of the same kind, then those reactions would indicate the presence of a personality trait, a particular kind of psychophysical system as described in chapter 2.

As our example suggests, there may be many different reactions to the same disturbing stimulus: anger, amusement, feeling of threat, and so on. Also any one kind of reaction, such as anger, might occur with different intensity. For example, one person might be truly angered while another is merely annoyed. To add to the complexity, the same person who responds with amusement to the experimental disturbance may respond with fury when frustrated by a lover; the one who responds with annoyance to the experimental disturbance may respond with feelings of hurt and rejection when frustrated in love. Before we can usefully apply the concept of a trait we need evidence that a person responds in a similar way and with similar intensity to a variety of situations. For example, to determine whether a person has a trait of easily feeling hurt and rejected, we might assess the person's reaction to several likely situations. These could include telling the subject that most people had shown a much better performance in attempting to solve some difficult puzzles, that the subject had done so poorly in a group situation that he or she would not be selected for the previously announced wilderness excursion, and finally that the subject need not show up for the second half of these tests since the experimenters had enough data already. If the subject showed about the same degree of hurt feelings in response to each of these situations it would be sensible to conclude that he or she is quite high on the trait of proneness to feeling hurt and rejected.

It is obvious that the experimental situations described above are callous and possibly dangerous. Psychologists would do such research only after very careful evaluation of the risk balanced against the worth of the results. And yet people do encounter such effectively barbaric treatment in everyday life, and while many have developed an ability to ride on through such rough-and-tumble treatment, others remain sensitive to brusque treatment and depreciating situations. Since this is so in everyday life it becomes possible to make an assessment simply by asking for a report on how an individual typically responds to such situations, asking first about one sort of situation and then another. This report can be obtained from other people who know the individual well, or else the individual may be asked to respond to a series of questions. These methods will be discussed more fully below.

We have suggested that a trait of some importance in the personality can be confidently determined only by finding qualitatively and quantitatively similar responses to a variety of situations. Each of these responses would then be an indicator of the trait in question. But how shall we choose among the thousands of possible traits? Which shall we attempt to measure? Countless words and phrases in the English language refer to human traits: lean, hungry-looking, eager,

spoiled, awkward, charming, easy-going, intense, grim, tough, bubbly, excitable, serious, stern, affable, steady, popular, reliable, trustworthy, irritable, sociable, and so on and on. Cattell's approach to this problem is very practical, even though it involves some fairly hard work with statistics. We discuss his approach in the next section.

Cattell's Approach and Procedures

Cattell's approach to the problem of determining which of the thousands of traits to measure has been carefully described in a number of his publications. We shall follow one of the earlier ones, a chapter entitled "The Place of Factor Analysis in Scientific Method" (Cattell, 1952, pp. 3-23).

Factor Analysis and Scientific Method

Cattell compares the thousands of traits that could be measured to the appearances of a strange coastline. Personality researchers are like the crew of a ship in a fog, he says. "It is easy to seize on some arbitrary, transient point of visibility and still easier to convince ourselves that it proves the existence of structures created by our own imaginations . . ." (Cattell, 1952, p. 16). Even as the crew of the ship really needs radar to distinguish between what is real and what is unreal in the impressions looming out of the fog, so personality researchers need the statistical method of factor analysis "to avoid the trivial and the unreal, for it gives us—however roughly at first—the shape of the real structures hidden in the swirling multiplicity of variables" (Cattell, 1952, p. 16).

Cattell points out that many researchers in the past have selected one or a few traits for measurement and have studied the effects of various environmental circumstances on these traits. He gives the example of a hypothetical study in which the investigator seeks to test a hypothesis concerning the role of brain metabolism in schizophrenia and especially the effects of social isolation in producing disorders in brain metabolism. The researcher may select his schizophrenic subjects "by the variable of being or not being diagnosed as such by a group of four psychiatrists or by falling below a certain ratio of 'adaptive' to 'verbal' intelligence test performance, or by talking to imaginary voices and so on" (Cattell, 1952, p. 9).

Then the researcher might select red blood count as the measure of possible disturbance in brain metabolism. But these choices could just as well be wrong, Cattell says. These variables might be very poor indicators of schizophrenia or of disorder in brain metabolism. They might be quite "misleading indicators of the condition, concept, or whole they are supposed to represent" (Cattell, 1952, p. 9).

Like the ship's crew in the fog, researchers can so easily settle on one or another dim appearance and suppose it is a major cliff, rock, or promontory of the strange coastline. How can a real structure be determined? When something appears dark from many sides, when the roars of smashing waves can be heard all around the dark appearance, when the plumblines show increasing shallowness of water, when the oars of a scouting rowboat strike against solid matter, these signs indicate the presence of a massive rock structure of some kind. The signs "go together." They "add up." Dark appearances alone can be misleading, but with all the other clues considered, the evidence is clear. Cattell proposes that we need comparable procedures in personality research. We need a way of determining when the indicators are adding up so that the presence of a real structure can be inferred. The method of factor analysis allows us to do precisely that.

Isolating Source Traits

The method begins with the knowledge of individual differences, the knowledge that people differ from each other in a great variety of measurable traits. Cattell proposes that this multitude of traits can be reduced to a smaller number of really important underlying structures. The thousands of traits are simply surface indicators of the real underlying sources of variation among individuals. Cattell calls these real underlying sources of variation *source traits*. Whereas the surface traits can be fairly easily seen and measured in all their profusion, we do not know how many source traits there may be nor what their nature might be. In order to find the answers to these questions Cattell employed the methods of *correlation* and *factor analysis*. *Correlation* tells us the extent to which two surface traits vary together across individuals. *Factor analysis* uses all the correlations among a large number of traits in order to tell how many factors there are—how many underlying sources of influence produce the correlations.

A method for calculating a correlation coefficient is given in Appendix C. For the present it is enough to say that a coefficient of correlation is a statistical value showing how much two trait measures vary together. Consider five people you know who differ in how generally *happy* they are. You might use the following scale to rate each one:

Sad		Happy
Rarely smiles, seems sad, serious most of the time.	In between extremes	Smiles often, is cheerful, happy most of the time.
Rating 1	2 3	4 5

If the person rarely smiles and seems sad or serious most of the time you would give that person a rating of 1. If the person is happy and cheerful most of the time you would rate that person a 5. If the person seems to be sad or serious a lot of the time, but with occasional periods of happiness, you would rate that person a 2. Someone who is predominantly happy and cheerful but occasionally falls into periods of sadness or seriousness would be rated 4, and a rating of 3 would indicate a person who is cheerful and happy about half the time and either serious or sad about half the time.

Now rate those same five persons again, this time on *talkativeness*. Use the following scale:

Silent		Talkative
Rarely says a word to anybody.	In between extremes	Talks almost all the time, talks to everybody

Rating	1	2	3	4	5

Let us suppose the people's names are as follows, along with their ratings on the two traits:

Trait	Pierre	Michelle	Ron	Orlando	Beth
Happy	2	3	3	4	5
Talkative	2	3	3	4	5

This would be a perfect correlation. The values for *happiness* vary across the five individuals, going from 2 for Pierre to 5 for Beth; and the values for *talkativeness* vary across the individuals in *exactly the same way*. We would express this result in a correlation coefficient of $+1.0$.

Now suppose the names and ratings were as follows:

Trait	Pierre	Michelle	Ron	Orlando	Beth
Happy	2	3	3	4	5
Talkative	5	4	3	3	2

This time the values for *talkativeness* vary across individuals in *exactly the opposite way*. Where Beth has the highest value on *happi-

ness*, for example, she has the lowest value on *talkativeness*. We would express this result in a correlation coefficient of -1.00 (minus 1.0).

Correlation coefficients can take any value between -1.0 and $+1.0$. For example, the following sets of ratings would give the various coefficients indicated:

Trait	Pierre	Michelle	Ron	Orlando	Beth	Correlation coefficient
Happy	2	3	3	4	5	
Talkative	4	2	5	3	3	$-.35$
Happy	2	3	3	4	5	
Talkative	4	2	3	5	3	$+.04$
Happy	2	3	3	4	5	
Talkative	3	2	4	5	3	$+.23$
Happy	2	3	3	4	5	
Talkative	3	2	3	4	5	$+.80$

We have now seen the two extreme values of the correlation coefficient: $+1.0$ when the ratings are exactly the same for *happy* and for *talkative* across the five people, -1.0 when the rating numbers for *happy* are exactly reversed for *talkative*. We have also seen several instances in between. The coefficient is $-.35$ when there is some tendency for higher rating numbers on *talkative* to be associated with lower rating numbers on *happy*. The coefficient goes to $+.04$ (almost zero) when there is no discernible relationship between the numbers given for *happy* and those for *talkative*. It increases slightly to $+.23$ when there is a slight tendency for higher numbers on *happy* to be given to the same persons who receive higher numbers on *talkative*. The coefficient is $+.80$ when there is a strong tendency for higher numbers on *happy* to be given to the same persons who receive higher numbers on *talkative*.

What do these correlation coefficients

mean about the relationship between the two traits? When the coefficient is high and positive (like +.80) it means the traits are very closely related. They might be two aspects of the same thing (like happiness and joy), or two things which influence each other (such as being friendly and having many friends). Or they may be distinct traits which nevertheless are both similarly influenced by a third factor. An example would be height and weight, which are correlated about +.6 in the general population. Quite likely the activity of growth hormones determines that any given person will be both taller and heavier than another person. The common underlying factor influencing the two traits of height and weight would be the glandular secretion of certain hormones.

To summarize, people differ in surface traits, one being stronger and another weaker in each trait, and with all degrees in between. These real variations among people are reflected in variations of the numbers assigned to the people by rating or some other procedure of measurement. When the numbers assigned for two traits tend to vary together we find a positive correlation coefficient. The larger the coefficient, the stronger is the tendency for those two traits to vary together.

How Factor Analysis Works

Factor analysis works with a large number of traits. Each trait is measured on each person in the study, and usually there are many people in the sample, say a hundred or more. Imagine that we have asked trained raters to rate one hundred students on five-point scales (similar to the ones for *happiness* and *talkativeness*) as illustrated in the right-hand column on page 366. For purposes of demonstration we will limit ourselves to just these seven traits. Now are there really seven different major structures here? Or are there

Ratings

1	2	3	4	5
		In between extremes		
Rough				Gentle
Independent		"		Dependent
Practical		"		Imaginative
Difficult		"		Easygoing
Cold		"		Warm
Suspicious		"		Trustful
Cautious		"		Impulsive

fewer? To find out we must first calculate the correlation between each trait and every other trait. This will give us a table of correlation coefficients as in table 15.1.

Notice in table 15.1 that each trait is represented along the rows and also down the columns. For example, going down the first column, under *Gentle,* we find first of all the value 1.0. This means that the ratings on *Gentle* are perfectly correlated with themselves (the *Gentle* in the first row). Next we find the value .4. This means that ratings for *Gentle* are correlated +.4 with ratings for *Dependent.* And so on down the column and down the other columns.

To determine how many factors underlie the correlations in table 15.1 we employ a mathematical procedure. First of all we find that factor which can produce the greatest possible amount of the correlational values in the table. The factor is represented by one number (varying between −1.0 and +1.0) for each of the traits. These numbers are called "factor loadings." Table 15.2 shows the loadings for the first factor, Factor I in the first column of the upper part of the table. The loadings are .4, .4, .5, .8, .9, .8, and .9. We shall not present the details of how these loadings are obtained; suffice to see how they "produce" correlational values. Notice in table

Table 15.1

Hypothetical Correlations Among Seven Traits Rated on One Hundred Students

	Gentle	Dependent	Imaginative	Easygoing	Warm	Trustful	Impulsive
Gentle	1.0	.5	.4	.3	.3	.3	.3
Dependent	.5	1.0	.6	.2	.1	.2	.2
Imaginative	.4	.6	1.0	.4	.3	.4	.3
Easygoing	.3	.2	.4	1.0	.8	.7	.8
Warm	.3	.1	.3	.8	1.0	.8	.9
Trustful	.3	.2	.4	.7	.8	1.0	.7
Impulsive	.3	.2	.3	.8	.9	.7	1.0

15.2 that the loadings are repeated across the top row. The amount of correlational value produced by the factor loadings for any two traits is equal to the loading of the first trait multiplied by the loading of the second trait. The amount of correlation between *Gentle* and *Imaginative* produced by Factor I is $.4 \times .5 = .20$. The amount of correlation produced by Factor I between *Warm* and *Trustful* is $.9 \times .8 = .72$.

Now look back a moment to table 15.1, where the original correlation coefficients are found. There we see that the original correlation between *Warm* and *Trustful* was $+.80$. Now we find that the amount of correlation between these two traits that is produced by Factor I is .72, almost all of the original. By contrast, the original correlation between *Gentle* and *Imaginative* was $+.4$, but the amount produced by Factor I is only .20, about half of the original.

We can easily see how much is left in each correlation after the amount due to Factor I is removed. We do this simply by subtracting the values produced by Factor I from the orig-

inal correlation values. The results are shown in the lower half of table 15.2. There we see for the remaining correlation between *Gentle* and *Imaginative* the value of .20 $(.40 - .20 = .20)$; for the remaining correlation between *Warm* and *Trustful* we have the value .08 $(.80 - .72 = .08)$.

Now that we have all these remaining values, the amounts of correlation left after the first factor has been removed, we can ask whether there is another factor producing the remaining amounts of correlation. Accordingly, we find that factor which can produce the greatest possible amount of the remaining correlational values. The loadings for this second factor, Factor II, are shown in the first column of the upper part of table 15.3.

Once again we calculate the amounts of correlation produced by Factor II, and these values are shown in the body of the upper part of table 15.3. In the lower part once again we have the values of correlation remaining after having subtracted the amounts produced by Factor II. Some of the "self-correlations" remaining are quite large (compare

Table 15.2

Loadings of Traits on Factor I, Correlation Coefficients Produced by Factor I, and Table of Remaining Coefficients

Table of Correlation Coefficients Produced by Factor I

		Gentle	Dependent	Imaginative	Easygoing	Warm	Trustful	Impulsive
Factor I loadings		.4	.4	.5	.8	.9	.8	.9
Gentle	.4	.16	.16	.20	.32	.36	.32	.36
Dependent	.4	.16	.16	.20	.32	.36	.32	.36
Imaginative	.5	.20	.20	.25	.40	.45	.40	.45
Easygoing	.8	.32	.32	.40	.64	.72	.64	.72
Warm	.9	.36	.36	.45	.72	.81	.72	.81
Trustful	.8	.32	.32	.40	.64	.72	.64	.72
Impulsive	.9	.36	.36	.45	.72	.81	.72	.81

Table of Correlation Coefficients Remaining After Subtracting Correlations due to Factor I

	Gentle	Dependent	Imaginative	Easygoing	Warm	Trustful	Impulsive
Gentle	.84	.34	.20	−.02	−.06	−.02	−.06
Dependent	.34	.84	.40	−.12	−.26	−.12	−.16
Imaginative	.20	.40	.75	.00	−.15	.00	−.15
Easygoing	−.02	−.12	.00	.36	.08	.06	.08
Warm	−.06	−.26	−.15	.08	.19	.08	.09
Trustful	−.02	−.12	.00	.06	.08	.36	−.02
Impulsive	−.06	−.16	−.15	.08	.09	−.02	.19

.68 for the remaining self-correlation of *Gentle;* .39 for *Imaginative,* .35 for both *Easygoing* and *Trustful*). But these values are not important now, for as we look at the remaining correlation values between different traits we find that all of them are very small. The highest absolute value is −.08 for *Dependent* and *Imaginative*. The rest are all .06 or smaller. We conclude that just two factors are at work in producing the correlations between these seven traits, for after we have removed the influence of two factors hardly any correlation remains between the traits.

Having found two factors—two major un-

Table 15.3

Loadings of Traits on Factor II, Correlation Coefficients Produced
by Factor II, and Remaining Coefficients

Table of Correlation Coefficients Produced by Factor II

		Gentle	Dependent	Imaginative	Easygoing	Warm	Trustful	Impulsive
Factor II loadings		.4	.8	.6	−.1	−.3	−.1	−.2
Gentle	.4	.16	.32	.24	−.04	−.12	−.04	−.08
Dependent	.8	.32	.64	.48	−.08	−.24	−.08	−.16
Imaginative	.6	.24	.48	.36	−.06	−.18	−.06	−.12
Easygoing	−.1	−.04	−.08	−.06	.01	.03	.01	.02
Warm	−.3	−.12	−.24	−.18	.03	.09	.03	.06
Trustful	−.1	−.04	−.08	−.06	.01	.03	.01	.02
Impulsive	−.2	−.08	−.16	−.12	.02	.06	.02	.04

Table of Correlation Coefficients Remaining After Subtracting Correlations Due to Factor II

	Gentle	Dependent	Imaginative	Easygoing	Warm	Trustful	Impulsive
Gentle	.68	.02	−.04	.02	.06	.02	.02
Dependent	.02	.20	−.08	−.04	−.02	−.04	.00
Imaginative	−.04	−.08	.39	.06	.03	.06	−.03
Easygoing	.02	−.04	.06	.35	.05	.05	.06
Warm	.06	−.02	.03	.05	.10	.05	.03
Trustful	.02	−.04	.06	.05	.05	.35	−.04
Impulsive	.02	.00	−.03	.06	.03	−.04	.15

derlying structures responsible for the correlations among the traits—we must next try to determine the nature of these structures. The method of finding the factor loadings was first developed by Karl Pearson (1901), and we shall refer to it as Pearson's method. Spearman (1904) used related procedures in his first factor analysis of psychological test data. It is still a widely used method, and many researchers use it also to determine the *nature* of the underlying structures. Cattell does not. Following Thurstone (1947), Cattell seeks the clearest possible view of those structures, a view which may be found by first represent-

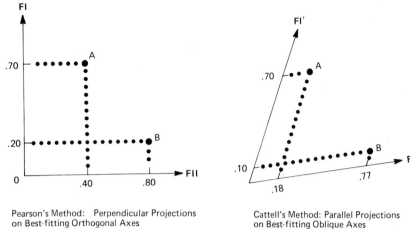

Pearson's Method: Perpendicular Projections
on Best-fitting Orthogonal Axes

Cattell's Method: Parallel Projections
on Best-fitting Oblique Axes

Figure 15.1. Comparison of Pearson's and Cattell's methods of finding factors

ing traits as points and the factors as two lines at right angles to each other. This is shown in figure 15.1 for just two traits, A and B, left part of the figure.

Oblique Rotation, Parallel Projections

Notice that the loadings of A are represented as perpendicular projections onto the two lines, one for Factor I (FI) and one for Factor II (FII); these loadings are +.7 and +.4 respectively. This is Pearson's method. Cattell begins with Pearson's method but goes on to *rotate* the lines representing the factors so that they go nearer to points representing the traits, nearer to the data points. In doing that the lines are almost always going to depart from a right-angle relationship. They become *oblique* (either acute-angled or obtuse-angled). Notice that the projections are then made not perpendicular but *parallel*. That is, the projection of trait A on the new line for FII' is made to go parallel to the line for the new FI'. Similarly the projection from A onto the line for FI' is made parallel to the FII' line. These projections result in a clearer picture of the relations between A and the two

new factors. Instead of .7 and .4 (a good portion of influence from both) we have .7 and .18 (a predominance of influence from the structure indicated by FI'. The picture for trait B is also made clearer. Previously we would have had to say that FI reflects a structure which influences both traits A and B, though A a little bit more; FII also reflects a structure which influences both traits. That hardly helps to distinguish one structure from another. In Cattell's method, however, we see that the FI' structure is mainly associated with trait A and the FII' structure is mainly concerned with trait B.

Now we will apply the methods to our two factors from seven traits. Figure 15.2 shows the graphic representation of the seven traits as points and the two factors as lines. We may compare the factor loadings in tables 15.2 and 15.3 with the perpendicular projections implied in figure 15.2. Indeed each point was placed so that its projections exactly represent its loadings. Thus *Imaginative* has a point placed so that its perpendicular projection on Factor I is +.5 and its projection on Factor II is +.6; *warm* has projections of +.9 and −.3. Figure 15.3 gives the graphic representa-

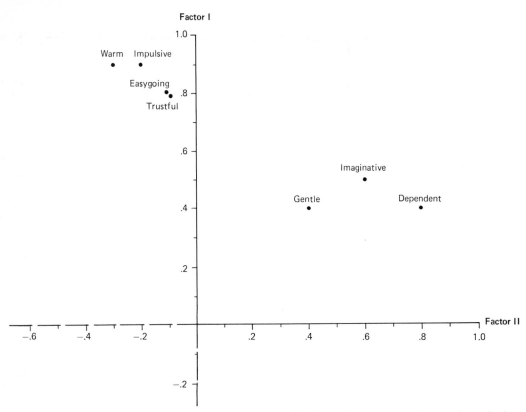

Figure 15.2. Graphic representation of factor loadings of traits, using Pearson's method

tion of the seven traits and their loadings in terms of oblique axes and parallel projections, according to Cattell's method. Notice that the axes have been moved away from their original positions (which are shown in dotted lines). Each line has been moved so that it goes right through a cluster of data points. Instead of being an arbitrary factor, the line going through *Warm, Impulsive, Easygoing,* and *Trustful* now represents a major underlying source of influence, a *source trait* that produces the correlations among those traits by influencing each of them in a similar way. Yet its degree of influence varies. It influences *Warm* and *Implusive* more than *Easygoing* and *Trustful,* and this difference is captured in the parallel projections. The values

of the parallel projections are shown in table 15.4.

As may be seen in table 15.4, the source trait influences *Warm* and *Impulsive* in the amount of .97 and .91 respectively; it influences *Easygoing* and *Trustful* in the amount of .76 each. While slightly negative in its influence on *Imaginative,* this source trait mostly does not influence *Gentle* and *Dependent* at all (considering values of −.10 to +.10 essentially equal to zero). Considering both what it does influence and what it does not influence, it seems reasonable to conclude that this source trait has to do with a general quality of *personal warmth,* a kind of inner freedom and glow which shows forth in the person's relationships with other people and in the easy

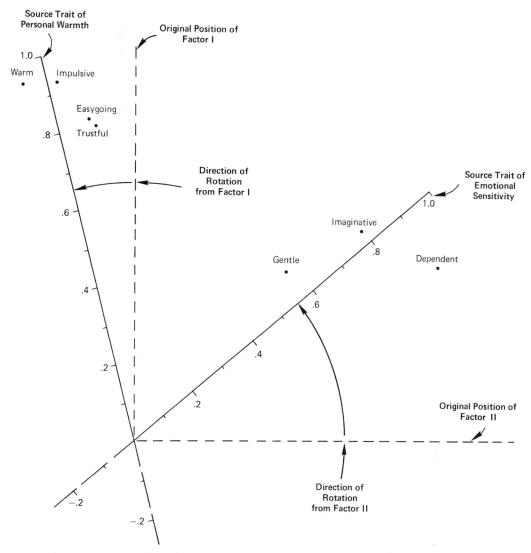

Figure 15.3. Graphic representation of oblique rotation to source trait positions: Cattell's method

expression of impulses within those relationships. You might predict that a person high on this source trait of personal warmth would rather freely express his or her feelings to other people, and that these feelings would be generally benevolent.

The second source trait in figure 15.3 is reflected by the line going through *Gentle,* *Imaginative,* and *Dependent.* Quite possibly it is a kind of *emotional sensitivity* which causes the person to shudder at harshness, whether in his or her own behavior (*Gentle*) or from others (*Dependent*). The sensitivity also produces new nuances of feeling tone, perhaps, so that the person's *Imaginative* trait carries with it a delicate and tender quality. Notice that

Table 15.4

Loadings of Original Trait Measures on
Source Traits of Personal Warmth
and Emotional Sensitivity

| Trait measures | Source traits | |
	Personal warmth	Emotional sensitivity
Gentle	.09	.52
Dependent	.04	.95
Imaginative	−.17	.76
Easygoing	.76	.09
Warm	.97	−.08
Trustful	.76	.10
Impulsive	.91	.02

the other four traits are not at all influenced by this second source trait. This means that the sensitivity does not directly affect the person's ease and warmth of feelings and expression. Possibly it has more to do with emotional reaction to certain kinds of stimuli such as pain, and one might hypothesize that its essence lies in a tendency for certain nuclei in the midbrain to be overreactive.

Cattell's method, then, aims to give a clearer picture of the hidden structures, the source traits. It starts with Pearson's method, but uses that method only to determine the number of source traits. It then goes farther, and by oblique rotation and parallel projections it seeks to identify the source traits. In order to determine the nature of a source trait attention is paid both to the surface traits which it does directly influence and also to those traits which it clearly does not influence directly.

Many researchers still prefer to use Pearson's method, although more and more are turning to Cattell's method. In chapter 17 we shall study Eysenck's theory of personality, in which Pearson's method has played a major role. Eysenck maintains that Pearson's method makes fewer assumptions and yields factors which are statistically more reliable than Cattell's source traits. The final evidence is not in, but we shall see how important these issues are when we discuss Eysenck's criticisms of Cattell's theory and Cattell's criticisms of Eysenck's theory.

Earlier in this chapter we commented on several of Cattell's assumptions. But several more need to be discussed as we proceed with a description of Cattell's approach and theory.

Assumptions about Traits and Their Measurement

Three Divisions of Traits

Cattell makes the empirical assumption that there are three kinds of traits: ability, temperament, and motivation. *Ability* traits refer to our capacities to solve problems, remember information, move quickly, and so on. In all of these there are external criteria by which the ability can be measured: so many problems solved per hour, so much information remembered out of a one-hundred-page book, so many seconds to move twenty-five pegs from one box to another, and so on. People differ widely in these abilities, but often these differences are not thought to reflect "personality" in the narrower sense of motivational patterns or social and emotional characteristics.

Temperament characteristics, in Cattell's analysis, refer to both those features of personality which are inherited and those features which are affected by the training and other influences of the social institutions around us. Temperament refers to ways of behaving, whether with calmness or fuss, eagerly or reluctantly, guiltily or gaily, and so on.

Motivational characteristics are those that are responsive to variations in incentives or in drive states. Impulses, needs, and interests are motivational characteristics. In this chapter we shall concern ourselves primarily with what Cattell calls temperament and motivation. These important aspects of personality have been the main topics of his research.

Media of Observation

Cattell specifies three main ways to obtain psychological measurements: ratings, questionnaires, objective tests. These three *media of observation* differ in important ways.

With *ratings,* for example, it is necessary to have raters who know each subject well enough to give reliable ratings. We saw an example of ratings above, in rating *Happiness* and *Talkativeness.*

Most people are familiar with *questionnaires,* but perhaps not with the scoring techniques. Suppose we ask three questions aimed at assessing how *hard-headed* people are. For each item we ask the respondent to check one of three alternative answers. For example:

1. Do you usually know what you want and go after it?
   (a) True
   (b) In between
   (c) False

2. If you have made up your mind can another person change it?
   (a) Very easily
   (b) In between
   (c) Only with great difficulty

3. Which musical instrument do you prefer to listen to?
   (a) Xylophone
   (b) Clarinet
   (c) Harp

We might score these items using the values 0, 1, and 2, with 0 being given to the least *hard-headed* alternative, 2 to the most *hard-headed,* and 1 to the in-between response. Then item 1 would have response *a* scored 2; response *b* scored 1; response *c* scored 0. Item 2 would be scored differently, response *a* being scored 0. Item 3 would be scored like item 1.

So much for scoring the *items.* How would we score the entire questionnaire to get a measure of *hard-headedness?* Simply add the scores obtained by a particular person on each item. Suppose someone answered *True* to item 1, *In between* to item 2, and *Clarinet* to item 3. These answers would receive scores of 2, 1, and 1 respectively, so the person's total score would be 4. This is actually the way scoring is done on Cattell's 16PF questionnaire, which we shall discuss below.

The third medium of observation, according to Cattell, consists of *objective tests,* which he defines as miniature situations in which the subject cannot easily tell what trait is actually being assessed. Such tests are difficult to fake and do not depend upon the subject's memory (as questionnaires do). An example is a maze in which the lines of the maze are grooves in a piece of wood; the subject must trace the maze with a finger while blindfolded. The measure being taken by the experimenter could be the total distance explored by the subject in a fixed time interval. That measure might be a good indicator of the subject's general personality trait of assertiveness.

Cattell's researches have been directed at mapping the major source traits of personality as found in each of these three media of observation. It might be expected that the same source traits would be discovered through each medium. As we shall see this is true to a certain extent, although there are important differences between the media. For example, raters cannot really get at the details of a subject's inner experience unless the subject expresses it into a tape recorder constantly for the several weeks or months needed for raters to obtain sufficient knowledge of the subject. So the subject will have access to all the information about his or her inner experience, and will draw on that information in responding to a questionnaire. But the rater will not have that same information in making the ratings. So there are bound to be some differences in the results from ratings and from questionnaires; similar considerations lead us to expect some differences in the results from objective tests.

We turn now to Cattell's results and his substantive theory of personality.

Cattell's Theory of Personality Structure: Temperament

Cattell's results suggest that temperament can be characterized by a person's total scores on thirty-five primary source traits. From correlations among the primaries, further factor analysis suggests the existence of fifteen second-order factors. Thus the person's score pattern on thirty-five primaries partly reflects the influence of these fifteen second-order source traits. The research also suggests five third-order factors.

The thirty-five primaries consist of twenty-three normal traits such as assertiveness or radicalism, and twelve traits chiefly known from their manifestations in psychological disorder, such as depression or paranoia. Looking back at table 15.4, the reader could imagine a much larger factor matrix in which there were 120 different measures of personality traits and 35 source traits, giving a table with 120 rows and 35 columns!

In order to present a clear picture of these results we shall concentrate here on just twelve primaries grouped according to four second-order source traits: extraversion, anxiety, alertness, and inner control. These are the most important source traits measured by Cattell's well-known Sixteen Personality Factor Questionnaire (16PF) (Cattell et al., 1970). The twelve primary source traits are briefly defined in table 15.5.

The definitions offered in table 15.5 are very similar to those offered by Cattell and his co-workers in several places (Cattell et al., 1970; Cattell, 1973, pp. 52-53; IPAT, 1972, p. 7). Over the years the letter designations (A, F, and so on) have remained the same, providing a continuous identity for the source trait. But precise definitions have changed somewhat as new evidence has accumulated and new items have been found to measure the traits better. The technical names shown in table 15.5 are intended to provide brief suggestive titles for the scientific hypotheses regarding the factors; the everyday descriptions are meant to give an idea of how a person scoring high or low on each factor would appear to others.

We will consider the twelve factors in four groups, reflecting those second-order traits Cattell has labeled *Exvia, Anxiety, Cortertia,* and *Control.*

Source Traits Reflecting Exvia: A, F, H, Q2

Source trait A (*Affectia* or warmth) is a very broadly influential structure concerned with the range and intensity of emotional experience and expression. (Refer to table 15.5 as we discuss these traits.) Eugen Bleuler, the Swiss psychiatrist (Jung's superior at the Burgholzli hospital; see chapter 12), first described a related variable, which he called cycloid-schizoid, which forms a dimension along which the major psychoses can be differentiated. The psychotic personality can be cycloid (manic-depressive psychosis) or schizoid (schizophrenia). In our context the trait is not associated with psychological disorders; its range is over the normal population, from *Affectia*

Table 15.5

Twelve Primary Source Traits Among Those Measured by the 16PF

Description of Low-scoring Person	Technical Name for Low Score	Letter	Technical Name for High Score	Description of High-scoring Person
Cool, reserved, detached	Sizia	A	Affectia	Warm, outgoing, easy in manner
Serious, prudent, glum	Desurgency	F	Surgency	Enthusiastic, impulsive, happy
Restrained socially, shy	Threctia	H	Parmia	Socially adventurous, uninhibited
Likes to join groups	Group adherence	Q2	Self-sufficiency	Resourceful, self-sufficient
Emotionally unstable, immature	Ego weakness	C	High ego strength	Emotionally stable, reality-oriented
Trusting, without jealousy	Alaxia	L	Protension	Suspicious, opinionated
Confident, self-assured	Untroubled adequacy	O	Guilt proneness	Worrying, depressed, apprehensive
Peaceful, relaxed	Low ergic tension	Q4	Ergic tension	Frustrated, tense
Tough-minded, hard-headed	Harria	I	Premsia	Tender-minded, sensitive
Careful, practical, conventional	Praxernia	M	Autia	Bohemian, imaginative, self-preoccupied
Evades rules, expedient	Weak superego	G	Superego strength	Persevering, conscientious
Undisciplined, careless	Low integration	Q3	Self-sentiment strength	Will power, controlled, disciplined

(high emotionality) to *Sizia* (a low, flat feeling tone). It is implied, however, that if mental disorder appeared, the affectic person would become manic-depressive; the sizic person would tend toward schizophrenia.

Cattell reports that studies of behavioral genetics concerned with this source trait suggest that individual differences on this trait are substantially influenced by heredity (see Appendix D for a discussion of the methods involved). Identical (one-egg) twins are found to be much more similar than fraternal (two-egg) twins on measures of source trait A. As a rough estimate, 50 percent of variation among people on *Affectia* seems to be due to the genes.

Cattell hypothesizes that this genetic component is carried by certain areas of the brain (the hypothalamus; Cattell, 1973, chapter 5). The affectic person has brain functions which allow for easy emotional expression; the sizic person does not. The other 50 percent of determination seems to be due to how the person's environment has encouraged the expression of emotions (producing high *Affectia*) versus how much it has punished such expression (producing low *Affectia*).

Among occupational groups, *Affectia* is

high in people who become business executives or social workers. Cattell suggests that Franklin D. Roosevelt was a good example of someone who is high in *Affectia.*

Source trait F (*Surgency* or enthusiasm) also seems to have some genetic determination—(about 60 percent), according to researches on identical and fraternal twins and other degrees of kinship. Cattell theorizes that this genetic component determines the person's response to punishment; that is, if the nervous system and other relevant organs are such that the effects of punishment are dissipated quickly, the person becomes high in *Surgency.* If the effects of punishment are felt for a long time, however, the person becomes *desurgent,* or low in the source trait of *Surgency.* The environmental influences on *Surgency,* seem to be due to economic and social conditions in the person's life. The individual who has an easy life of getting the "breaks" is more likely to become high in *Surgency.*

Among occupational groups, football players have the highest scores on *Surgency,* with swimmers and other athletes scoring very high. Traveling salespeople are also very high on this source trait.

Source trait H (*Parmia* or adventurousness) is believed to reflect the balance among the two main parts of the individual's autonomic nervous system, the parasympathetic and the sympathetic. If the former is dominant, the individual is relatively immune to upset by threatening events (*Parmia* is Cattell's contraction of parasympathetic immunity). The opposite pole, *Threctia,* stands for threat reactivity; that is, the sympathetic part of the autonomic nervous system is dominant and the person is very easily upset by threatening stimuli. This source trait has about 40 percent of its variation genetically determined. Environmental contributions seems to involve parental affection. High expression of affection is associated with *Parmia* and strict dis-

cipline coupled with maternal overprotection is associated with *Threctia.* In occupations, garage mechanics as a group show high *Parmia.* Persons who attempt suicide show extreme *Threctia.*

Source trait Q2 represents the extremes of *Self-sufficiency* versus Group adherence. It has been found that individuals high in *Self-sufficiency* are likely to have been only children or else to have been the oldest in a larger family, so that they had no brothers or sisters of their own age in the home. Research also suggests that people high in *Self-sufficiency* had parents who were happily married. It is possible that the highly self-sufficient person was often left alone as a child, probably occupied with her or his own toys and other interests, and yet without being made to feel "alone" or "neglected." The child would have a constant assurance that mother and father are there, close by. That assurance would give the child freedom to be self-reliant in a world that is basically secure. As examples of outstanding personalities who are high in *Self-sufficiency,* Cattell suggests Bob Hope and Louis Pasteur.

Organization of Source Traits in Strata

The source traits A, F, H, and Q2 were discovered as separate factors which could be rotated to appropriate oblique positions according to Cattell's method of factor analysis. This means that they can be correlated with each other. In fact A, F, and H are all positively correlated among themselves; Q2 is negatively correlated with each of the other three. Because it is possible to find correlations among the source traits it is also possible to find new factors and new source traits at a second level. If A, F, H, and Q2 are source traits in the primary stratum, or first level, of personality then a single source trait found at a higher level to be influencing all four of the primaries would be a source trait in the second stratum of personality.

Recall that there are thirty-five primary traits, fifteen second-stratum traits and five third-stratum traits. A stratum is a layer in the personality, a layer in the hierarchy. Such a hierarchy can be thought of as a hierarchy of control similar to a business organization with workers and clerks at the first layer, foremen and supervisors at the second level, and management at the third level. So the primary source traits are considered to be in the first stratum of personality; groupings of these primaries then show up at the level of the second stratum.

The source traits of *Affectia, Surgency,* and so on are intercorrelated in such a way that they yield a single second-order source trait Cattell interprets as extraversion (see chapter 12) and labels *Exvia.* Table 15.6 gives the latest results on the loadings for *Exvia* and for the three other groupings of primaries shown in table 15.5.

Table 15.6
Loadings of First-Stratum Source Traits on Second-Stratum Source Traits[*]

| | | Second-Stratum Source Traits | | |
| | I | II | III | IV |
First-Stratum Source Traits	Exvia	Anxiety	Cortertia	Control
Affectia	.58	.01	−.25	−.01
Surgency	.51	−.03	.01	−.27
Parmia	.50	−.38	−.14	.00
Self-sufficiency	−.65	−.01	−.04	.01
Ego strength	.07	−.66	.10	.05
Protension	.05	.54	.06	.04
Guilt proneness	−.02	.78	−.06	.03
Ergic tension	.00	.80	−.05	−.02
Premsia	.07	.00	−.73	.02
Autia	.12	.03	−.47	−.08
Superego strength	.06	−.03	.01	.67
Self-sentiment strength	−.05	−.43	.01	.47

[*]The values here are averages in each cell taken over fourteen studies. Individual studies can be found, for example, in Cattell et al., 1970, p. 121 or Cattell, 1972, p. 178. The particular values for this table were taken from those given by Cattell in a larger table (covering sixteen primaries and eight second-order factors) in Cattell, 1973, p. 116).

Implications of the Correlation Methods

The patterns shown in table 15.6 result from averaging fourteen different studies. Very similar patterns are obtained in the English version of the 16PF taken by British, American, and New Zealander subjects; and in the respective foreign-language versions of the 16PF for Japanese, German, Brazilian, and Venezuelan subjects (Cattell, 1973, Table 52, pp. 337-339). All of these patterns approximate the one shown in table 15.6.

These results are exceptional in several ways. They are exceptional in the clear pattern of loadings. Note that every column of the table has several high values, and many values close to zero, but few in between. The results are also exceptional in that, complex as they are, they nevertheless can be replicated time and again in different countries throughout the world. The appearance of this same pattern in so many different situations suggests strongly that the source traits are real structures, basic influences on the human personality that can be found anywhere on earth.

Returning briefly to *Exvia*, the second-stratum source trait associated with *Affectia, Surgency, Parmia* and *Self-sufficiency,* Cattell states that it must be understood as essentially the same dimension that Jung (chapter 12) called extraversion. Like all second-stratum source traits it is not to be identified with the four main primaries themselves. Rather it is a higher-order unitary influence which controls these four and also has other influences and connections within the personality. Cattell theorizes that the central characteristic of extraversion is somewhat different from what Jung had in mind. In Cattell's view (1973, p. 183) the central feature is what he calls *lower susceptibility to social inhibition.* The more extroverted person is less responsive to punishments from social forms of restraint or deterrence. Due to their lesser degree of autonomic reactivity, and also due to a history with less social punishment, extraverts tend to respond less strongly to the inhibitory stimuli emitted by the environment. As a result the extravert is more willing to take risks, makes more rapid social judgments, is more optimistic and less concerned about following rules and less worried over any mistakes he or she makes. Because of the measurement basis upon which this construct of extraversion rests, and because of the differences provided by new data and new components of theory, Cattell prefers to call this second-stratum source trait *Exvia* versus *Invia* rather than extraversion-introversion.

Source Traits Reflecting Anxiety: C, L, O, and Q4

Source trait C (*Ego strength* or emotional maturity) according to Cattell (1973, p. 160), "is clearly the reality behind Freud's concept of ego structure strength." All clinical associations since the discovery of the trait in 1947 support this conclusion. Furthermore, a low C score, representing ego weakness, is found in virtually all types of psychopathology (Cattell, Eber, and Tatsuoka, 1970). Cattell theorizes that this source trait is a structure of controls which develops in response to the organism's needs to control impulses, especially impulses that come to arouse anxiety as soon as they are felt. Successful experience with reduction of anxiety through exertion of ego controls leads to increasing strength of the control system. Cattell suggests that Washington, Bismarck, and Lenin all provide eminent illustrations of high ego strength.

Source trait L (*Protension* or suspiciousness) is interpreted as a tendency to use projection as a mechanism of defense. Its surface character of suspiciousness and jealousy reveals the inner tendency to project tensions outward, especially hostile impulse tensions. Special studies have shown a positive correlation between this source trait and the tendency to use projection as a defense mechanism. Neurotics tend to be very high on this source trait, especially if they suffer primarily from an anxiety reaction.

Source trait O is *Guilt proneness* or worrying. A high score is interpreted as denoting a general state of loneliness and inadequacy. Discipline of the child through physical punishment is found in the home background data of persons high in this trait. They are characteristically moody, melancholy, and depressed in feelings. The trait is high in clinical groups such as alcoholics, neurotics, and schizophrenics. Among occupations effective administrators are typically low on *Guilt proneness.*

Source trait Q4 is *Ergic tension* or frustration, the presence of which reflects the level of undischarged drive tension that has accumulated in the individual as a result of frustrations and deprivations. Unhappy love affairs, deaths of loved ones, and doing poorly in school are events that raise the level of Q4. It is therefore interpreted as *Ergic tension,* *ergic* meaning instinctual or associated with drive energy. Alcoholics tend to be very high in *Ergic tension.*

These four primaries are grouped together in the second-stratum source trait of *Anxiety.* As table 15.6 shows, this source trait also influences *Parmia* and *Self-sentiment* to some extent (−.38 and −.43 respectively). Its essence, however, arises from high drive combined with low expression of drive energies, leading to accumulated tension. This failure to obtain adequate release of drive energies is in part due to ego weakness (low C); for the ego is strong when it controls drive energies only so much as is necessary to achieve their satisfactory expression. Failure to express drives adequately may also be partly due to the sense of inadequacy involved in *Guilt proneness,* since the expectation that one cannot achieve one's goals is an important deterrent to an attempt to do so. The association of *Protension* with the second-stratum source trait *Anxiety* appears to be more a consequence than a cause. That is, if anxiety is high, the tendency to use defense mechanisms to preserve the ego is likely to be greater.

Source Traits Reflecting Cortertia: I and M

Source trait I (*Premsia* or sensitivity) is a contraction of protected emotional sensitivity. Its opposite pole, *Harria,* stands for hard reactions to tough realities. This source trait reminds us of the distinction made by William James—tough-minded as opposed to tender-minded. Although some evidence shows that overprotective homes which shield their children tend to produce highly *premsic* individuals, there is also evidence that this trait is highly heritable, roughly 60 percent of its variation being due to genetic determination. Eleanor Roosevelt was probably high in *Premsia,* Cattell suggests.

Source trait M (*Autia* or unconventionality) reflects a somewhat *aut*istic approach to life, a tendency to rely more on subjective fantasies than on outer realities. The substantial genetic component (40 percent), is interpreted as a propensity to have images and ideas of greater intensity than usual, relative to the intensity of sensory stimuli. People high on this trait tend to be negligent of conventional requirements regarding dress, sex life, and other personal habits. Its opposite pole, *Praxernia,* denotes a practical concern with the things of reality. As might be expected, artists and art students tend to be very high on *Autia.*

These two primaries along with *Affectia* (see table 15.6) yield evidence for the second-stratum source trait of *Cortertia,* or cortical alertness, versus *Pathemia,* or reacting to everything in a highly emotional manner. Cattell hypothesizes that *Cortertia* reflects a dominance in brain function by the cerebral cortex (thus producing cortical alertness to the environment) as opposed to dominance by the hypothalamus, the part of the brain which appears responsible for emotional activity. The person with low *Cortertia* tends to be dreamy, sentimental, sensitive, sad and deep in feeling, while the person high in *Cortertia* tends to be alert and realistic, and to keep feelings well under control.

Source Traits Reflecting Inner Control: G and Q3

Source trait G (*Superego strength* or conscience) seems to carry all the signs of strength in the superego as described by psychoanalytic theory: persistence, conscientiousness, and so on. Students high on this trait are more likely to be married, to be members of a church, to work long hours and need less sleep, to drink less alcohol, and to stay through to graduation. It is significant that persons with high scores on this trait received fewer criticisms from their parents, suggesting that they identified earlier or more strongly with parental standards. Also significant is the fact that those high on this trait are more likely to have seen a parent or other loved one die. In psychoanalytic theory this would result most probably in incorporation of the lost love object and a strengthening of the introjected moral code. A quite unexpected feature of the findings on G is that it has moderate heritability (40 percent) which suggests a previously unsuspected genetic component to superego development. It might be that some people are born with a greater tendency to experience disgust or other reactions which can lead to developing a stronger superego. Cattell suggests that many outstanding personalities display high *Superego strength;* he cites Florence Nightingale and Abraham Lincoln as excellent examples.

Source trait Q3 (*Self-sentiment* strength or control) reflects the clarity of an individual's self-concept and the degree to which the individual adheres to that concept in actual behavior. It is therefore another form of control, one which is focused upon the image others have of the person as well as upon the self-image.

It has been found that research scientists tend to be quite high on *Self-sentiment* strength. Persons who have been diagnosed as sociopathic are likely to be low on this source trait.

Together with low F, the source traits G and Q3 are grouped in a second-stratum source trait labeled *Strength of inner controls.* Cattell hypothesizes that this source trait is produced mainly by the kind of upbringing the child encounters. Someone who is high on this second-stratum source trait presumably had parents who successfully inculcated strong moral values in their child.

Interaction of Source Traits in a Person

An individual can have a high degree of any source trait. For example, a person might be high on *Affectia,* high on *Ego strength,* and low on *Autia.* Such an individual would be warm and calm, and would tend to be rather conventional in dress and manners. Because of the influence of the second-stratum source trait of *Exvia,* someone who is high on *Affectia* is likely to be higher than average on *Surgency* and *Parmia,* as well as lower than average on *Self-sufficiency.* This individual would not only be warm but also quite enthusiastic and adventurous, and would prefer to spend time with friends rather than alone.

We recall that Cattell sees temperament as only one phase of the personality, a phase or aspect having to do with *how* the person goes through life. For example, someone might prefer to spend time with friends largely because the friends can serve the person's main goal of social advancement. Temperament tells us nothing about the person's actual goals in life. But study of the motivational aspect of personality does tell us precisely about the person's goals. We turn to this part of Cattell's theory now.

Cattell's Theory of Personality Structure: Motivation

The second modality division of traits in personality is motivation. Each motivational source trait is to be discovered in a variety of objective tests which, on the surface, assess an individual's attitudes. In Cattell's theory, the construct of *attitude* is expressed subjectively as, "I want (so and so much) to do a particular thing with such and such."

The strength of an attitude (the "so and so much" part of the expression) is assessed by any of sixty-eight different types of ob-

jective testing device as illustrated in box 15.1, which shows the range of ingenuity employed by Cattell and his associates in measuring motivation strength.

Objective tests include all kinds of perceptual measures, indications for preferences, and a variety of learning and memory tasks as box 15.1 shows. In the area of motivation Cattell reasons that many perceptions and activities reveal motive strength. For example, how much you remember of the sexy, romantic parts of a novel, as compared with the workaday parts or the parts about what people ate, would be one indication of your interest in love and sex. All of our lives have limits of time and energy. The more we put into one activity the less we put into others. If our drives and interests govern our time allocation, then we reveal our drives through the amount of information we acquire in one area rather than another. Your degree of drive to

---

Box 15.1
Some Principles of Motivation Measurement Applied in Device Construction

With increase in interest in a course of action expect increase in:

1. Preferences: Readiness to admit preference for course of action.
2. Autism: Misperception. Distorted perception of objects, noises, etc., in accordance with interest (e.g., Bruner coin perception study).
3. Autism: Misbelief. Distorted belief that facts favor course of action. . . .

31. Perceptual closure. Ability to see incomplete drawings as complete when material is related to interest.
32. Selective perception. Ease of finding interest-related material imbedded in complex field.
33. Sensory acuity. Tendency to sense lights as brighter, sounds as louder, etc., when interest is aroused. . . .

51. Learning. Speed learning interest-related material.
52. Motor skills. Apt performance to affect interest.
53. Information. Knowledge affecting and related to course of action. . . .

61. Memory for rewards. Immediate recall of rewards associated with interest.
62. Reminiscence. . . . Increased recall over short intervals of interest-related material.
63. Reminiscence. . . . Increased recall over long intervals of interest-related material. . . .
68. Reflex inhibition. Difficulty in evoking certain reflexes when interest aroused (Horn, 1966, pp. 617-618).

---

be with other people (gregariousness), for instance, might be assessed through your knowledge of social events, clubs, sporting events, and the like. Your level of drive for self-gratification (narcissism) might be estimated through your knowledge of different kinds of wines, luxury beds, massage techniques, bath soaps, and perfumes. If your knowledge of these things outweighed your knowledge of social events and so on, you would be relatively higher on narcissism than on gregariousness. Box 15.2 illustrates an information test.

Using data gathered with devices of this kind Cattell has applied factor analytic methods to discover the structure of motivation traits in human personality. Each item reveals how much the person wants to do a particular thing with a particular companion or object. Correlations among these items and subsequent factor analysis reveals the motivation source traits or *ergs*. *Erg* means unit of energy. Cattell and his co-workers (Cattell et al., 1964) have published the *Motivation Analysis Test,* which uses objective devices to measure the following ergs: *fear, sex, assertion, aggression,* and *narcissism.* It also measures a number of *sentiments,* which means the gathering of various ergs upon a single attitude object, person, or institution. This organization is illustrated in figure 15.4. Through the four attitudes in the middle of the figure the three ergs—sex, self-assertion, and fear—all converge upon the sentiment to

---

Box 15.2

Tentative Set of Items for an Information Test of One of Cattell's Ergs

1. Which of the following is not a disease?
   A. Multiple sclerosis
   B. Simple fibrilla
   C. Phthisis
2. During the past few years, what has been the approximate annual number of deaths from vehicle accidents on the highways of the United States?
   A. 20,000
   B. 40,000
   C. 60,000
3. The largest number of fires is caused by . . .
   A. Smoking and matches
   B. Children and matches
   C. Defective wiring
4. What are the chances of being robbed if you live in a city like Chicago?
   A. Eight per thousand
   B. Four per thousand
   C. Two per thousand
5. What is the average life expectancy for a male in the United States?
   A. 67
   B. 71
   C. 74

6. Among persons twenty-five years and older in the United States several million have had one year of college or more. Of those persons, what percentage failed to complete college?
   A. 50%
   B. 80%
   C. 65%
7. In order to avoid respiratory disorder due to air pollution, which of the following cities should be avoided?
   A. Santa Fe (N.M.)
   B. Providence (R.I.)
   C. Nashville (Tenn.)
8. Which of the following causes the greatest number of deaths in the United States?
   A. Diabetes
   B. Influenza and pneumonia
   C. Cirrhosis of the liver

Scores on these items would be compared with scores on other sets of items measuring gregariousness, assertiveness, sex, and so on. Turn to page 396 for answer key.

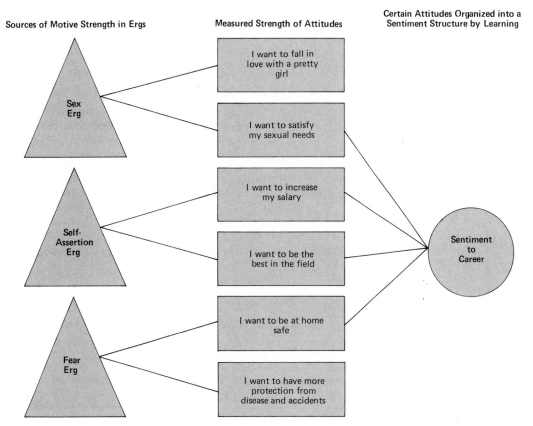

Sources of Motive Strength in Ergs

Measured Strength of Attitudes

Certain Attitudes Organized into a Sentiment Structure by Learning

Sex Erg

Self-Assertion Erg

Fear Erg

I want to fall in love with a pretty girl

I want to satisfy my sexual needs

I want to increase my salary

I want to be the best in the field

I want to be at home safe

I want to have more protection from disease and accidents

Sentiment to Career

Figure 15.4. Cattell's theory of the organization of attitudes, ergs and sentiments. Via the middle four attitudes the three ergs all converge upon, and provide energy for the sentiment to career. The top and the bottom attitudes would perhaps join other attitudes to converge upon some other sentiment object.

career (at right). The top and bottom attitudes would perhaps join other attitudes to converge upon some other sentiment object.

The *Motivation Analysis Test* includes measures of five sentiments, namely those for one's *career*, *sweetheart* or *spouse*, *parents*, one's own *superego*, and for one's *self*. Cattell and his associates have also found five other ergs not measured in the published test: *Appeal* (the drive to be dependent and seek help), *Construction, Exploration* (or curiosity), *Protectiveness*, and *Gregariousness* (Horn, 1966; Sweney, 1967).

In Cattell's theory the ten ergs account for all or most of the emotionally charged sources of drive energy in the human personality. The sentiments are more related to the particular cultural setting in which an individual is raised, since sentiments more often reflect the objects or institutions available in the culture to which the ergs can become attached. Thus the subjects involved in table 15.7, which follows, could sensibly develop a sentiment toward the U.S. Air Force since all were Air Force personnel. Seventh-grade children in Bangladesh could hardly be expected to develop a sentiment to the U.S. Air Force, but would likely have a strongly developed sentiment toward their country.

Interrelation of Temperament and Motivation

How do the structures of temperament and of motivation relate to each other? It may be expected that certain strengths of drive may affect certain styles or manners of behaving. More generally it would be expected that certain structures in the temperament source traits (such as inner controls) would be accompanied by certain strengths of ergic pressure or of sentiment formation. This indeed is found to be the case, as table 15.7 shows.

It is apparent in table 15.7 that many interesting and theoretically useful relationships exist between measures of temperament structure and measures of motivation structure. For example, *Exvia* is positively related to both *Assertiveness* and *Gregariousness* ergs and also to sentiment to the Air Force and the Self. The *Fear* erg is definitely different from the *Anxiety* source trait in temperament structure —even slightly negatively related. This result

Table 15.7

Relationships Between Second-Stratum Temperament Structure and Motivation Structure[*]

Second-stratum temperament source traits measured by 16PF	Motivation Source Traits, Each Measured by Six Different Devices								
	Ergs						Sentiments		
	Fear	Sex	Assertion	Narcissism	Exploration	Gregariousness	Air Force	Religion	Self
Exvia			22			34	19		19
Anxiety	−17	24					−28		−22
Cortertia				30	−20				
Strength of inner controls	26	−34		−43			20	29	27

[*]All correlations are significant at better than the .01 level of probability except the coefficient between *Fear* and *Anxiety*, which is significant at better than the .02 level. Values having a lesser degree of significance are omitted throughout. Decimals are also omitted throughout. All correlation coefficients are calculated from the data provided by Cattell and Child, 1975, p. 55, using the general equation for the correlation between a composite C (the second-stratum trait) and a single outside measure (i). C is made of components c, and it is assumed all components and the outside measure are in standard-score form with variance equal to unity.

$$r_{Ci} = \frac{\text{Sum Covariances } ci}{\sqrt{\text{Variance } C} \cdot \sqrt{\text{Variance } i}}$$

The original sample size was $N = 199$ (see Cattell, 1957). Values for the intercorrelations of primary traits of the 16PF (Cattell, Eber, and Tatsuoka, 1970) were employed in calculating the variances of composites.

is consistent with a number of theoretical models of anxiety which suggest that it is quite different from fear (for example, Freud's model of realistic, moralistic, and neurotic anxiety). The relation of *Fear* to *Strength of inner controls* in table 15.7 suggests that fear plays a part in development of strong inner controls. The negative relationships between *Sex* and *Narcissism* ergs on the one hand and *Strength of inner controls* on the other provide a good example of the essentially *functional* nature of many relationships in Cattell's work. Although the coefficients obtained are statistically significant, it is not possible to specify the direction of causality in most instances. In the present case it could be that strong inner controls weaken sex drives, or it could be that strong sex drives weaken inner controls. Either way would be compatible with psychoanalytic theory of the role of the superego in compelling renunciation of libidinal strivings. But for all we know the causal texture of this relationship as revealed in table 15.7 may be such that both the *Sex* erg and the *Strength of inner controls* source trait are both modified by some third source of causal influence.

We turn now to consider in more detail Cattell's theory of cause, which he usually refers to as the *dynamic calculus*.

Theory of Cause

Although Cattell's theory of function is of primary importance, it is nevertheless viewed as an avenue to causal analysis. For example, source traits of temperament are thought to be causally prior to the particular behaviors which may be predicted from them. The chain of causation is more complex than that, however; genetic influences join various environmental forces such as "good upbringing" in the causal molding of source traits. We might characterize Cattell's view of the causal chain as follows:

Genetic influence   Environmental molding

Source trait structure

Present behaviors

The Dynamic Calculus

It seems that past influences (such as genetic influence) must operate in the present, and they do so as a result of their structural products, in this case the source traits. The source traits carry the resultant of all earlier causal influences; they continue to operate in the present as causal contributors to the behavioral record.

In the sense of providing energy and direction for present behaviors, however, it seems that the motivation source traits are more important in Cattell's theory. The overall model of their effects is conceptualized under the term *dynamic calculus,* where *dynamic* refers to motivation source traits and their functions in energizing and guiding behavior, and *calculus* refers to the potential for measuring these forces and calculating degrees of confluence or conflict among them. The latest complete statement of this part of Cattell's theory is contained in a recent book by Cattell and Child (1975), whose discussion of conflict will be followed here.

Model of Conflict

The most evident sign of an existing ergic tension is given when any one such force comes into conflict with another, as whether to lash out at an opponent in anger or to hold one's peace in better judgment. Such conflict is momentary and is to be distinguished from what Cattell and Child call *stabilized conflict* (1975, p. 89), because when a course of action is chosen and settled down to, it is usually a compromise in which various demands have flowed together (confluence) in a course aiming to satisfy them all as much as possible. In fact, however, it commonly increases the satisfaction of some at the cost of reducing the satisfaction of others. The conflict between various ergs thus becomes accepted as a relatively permanent state of affairs. . . .

The measurement of stabilized conflict is thus made possible by consideration of the *reductions* in satisfaction associated with particular courses of action. For example, consider someone who married a person who is overbearing but who nevertheless is sexually attractive and very nurturant. In such a case, the *Sex* erg would be well satisfied, as would the *Narcissism* erg; the *Assertiveness* erg would receive much reduced satisfaction because of the spouse's overbearing ways. Being married (m) would be associated with some degree (b) of satisfaction for the *Sex* erg (E_1) and for the *Narcissism* erg (E_2), but with relative lack of satisfaction ($-b$) for *Assertiveness* (E_3), yielding

$$m = b_1E_1 + b_2E_2 - b_3E_3$$

The amount of conflict in marriage would be expressed as the size of the negative weight, $-b_3$. You might envision the person saying "I enjoy our sex life (b_1E_1) and he/she gives me lots of goodies and lets me sleep late (b_2E_2), so I put up with feeling downtrodden by his/her overbearing ways ($-b_3E_3$)."

If there are several negative weights, they can simply be totaled. For example, the marriage might interfere with the person's wish to travel and find out about other countries, producing a negative weight on the *Exploratory* erg ($-b_4E_4$). Then the total amount of conflict in the marriage would be expressed as the sum (Σ) of the negative weights:

$$\overset{i}{\Sigma} -b_i = \Sigma \,(-b_3, -b_4)$$

Cattell and Child (1975, p. 94) point out that such indices of conflict can be worked out for a representative sample of the situations (s) in the person's total life, including marriage, friends, clubs, recreation, occupation, and so on. Then the total conflict (C_t) in a person's present personality would be expressed as

$$C_t = \overset{s}{\Sigma} \,(\overset{i}{\Sigma} - b_{is})$$

Conversely, assuming that personality integration (I) is the extent to which the individual has managed to achieve satisfaction of all ergs and has minimized conflict, then we have a measure of personality integration as the complement of conflict: $I = (1 - C_t)$

Model of Situational Causes

The situation also serves as a causal influence in Cattell's overall theory, because a trait is seen as closely connected with situations which arouse or trigger its action in a person. The method of questionnaire research relies upon the empirical assumption that persons can remember the many situations they have encountered and recall their own reactions in the situations. The memory does not have to be photographic, but simply accurate enough to provide a reasonably good recording of the person's usual behaviors. Thus situations are immediately involved in the assessment of traits by questionnaire. Each item implies a series of situations, for example: Do you ever get to feeling sentimental? Answer: Sometimes. Those "sometimes" refer to unnamed situations. As you travel on vacation, do you like to take guided tours, or do you prefer to go around on your own? The situations are explicit here: on traveling vacations. Do you usually have difficulty going to sleep at night? The situations are obvious.

As a respondent replies to fifteen items designed to measure *Premsia*, for example, the several items evoke memories of relevant behavioral reactions in relevant situations. Thus the person's score reflects behavioral dispositions in relation to a large range of situations. To gather such information by the method of ratings would take thousands of dollars and long-suffering teams of observers.

Cattell proposes (1966, 1973) a distinction between two kinds of situations. The *focal stimulus* is the one immediately occupying your attention, like an examination sheet on your desk. The other situation is the more general, or *ambient situation*. For example, you might be taking the examination on your own in a closed room, or you might be in a large auditorium with three hundred other students. The difference in noise and oxygen alone would be immense.

Theoretical analysis of situational triggers may begin with the notion that people differ in how much their usual level of a trait (say, surgency) is turned on (excited, or triggered) by a particular situation. For example, some people rise to defend themselves at the slightest challenge to their dignity; others let it pass.

Cattell represents the effects of both focal and ambient stimuli in his theoretical treatment (1970). We recall that, according to his basic empirical assumption, all traits are involved in all situations and behaviors; however, some traits are more heavily aroused than others. For the sake of simple description let us represent *all* the traits involved in a particular action and situation by referring only to one ergic trait, say E_1. It might be *Assertiveness.*

A young woman's general level of *Assertiveness,* let us say, is quite high. In making purchases, in dealing with employees, and in most other situations this person's high level of *Assertiveness* is apparent. However, when she is in any kind of evidently competitive situation her *Assertiveness* is triggered even

more. That competitive situation is an effective *ambient situation* which raises the excitation level in her *Assertiveness* erg. But if in the course of a contest she finds herself behind, that *focal stimulus* constitutes an additional spur to her ergic tension for *Assertiveness,* so that she puts forth an extraordinary amount of effort to catch up and win.

The effects of the ambient situation and of the focal stimulus can be represented as amounts of additional excitation to the ergic tension. Let the additional amount be represented as a change in the state (S) of the individual produced by (weighted by $= b$) either the ambient (a) or the focal (f) stimulus. Then the person's behavior in a given complex situation (ambient plus focal) will be given by two things: First the extent to which the person's ergs (E_1) are triggered; and second by the individual's proneness to a change in state with respect to E_1 (S_{e1}) when in such a situation. Letting B_{af} represent the person's behavior in that complex situation, we have:

$$B_{af} = b_{a_1 \cdot f_1} E_1 + b_{a_s \cdot f_s} S_{e1}$$

Thus the effects of the situation are conceptualized as a multidimensional change in state, effected by "a multidimensionally represented situation" (Cattell, 1970, p. 4; also see especially pp. 14-20.)

Accomplishments of Cattell's Theory

Cattell's theory of personality has already accomplished a great deal in fields where psychological tests are required: diagnosis, vocational guidance, personnel selection, evaluation of treatment programs, and so on. The diagnostic capabilities of the 16PF are illustrated in figure 15.5 by the profiles of two groups of attempted suicides, males and females. Figure 15.5 shows that the two groups have closely similar profiles. Notice that in the

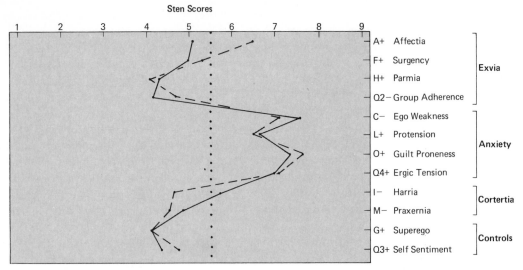

Sten Scores

A+	Affectia
F+	Surgency
H+	Parmia
Q2−	Group Adherence
C−	Ego Weakness
L+	Protension
O+	Guilt Proneness
Q4+	Ergic Tension
I−	Harria
M−	Praxernia
G+	Superego
Q3+	Self Sentiment

Exvia

Anxiety

Cortertia

Controls

Figure 15.5. Mean profiles on 16 PF for 50 female (—) and 50 male (- -) attempted suicides in Britain. Adapted from Cattell, Eber, and Tatsuoka (1970). Total adult population averages shown for comparison in dotted line (. . .).

scores employed here (standard scores) a value of 5.5 would be the mean of the general adult population for both males and females separately. The profiles seen in figure 15.5 are very sharp departures from the average. Notice that the primary source traits are grouped according to the main second-stratum grouping, and that *Self-sufficiency* is represented by its opposite pole, *Group adherence*, so that it will go in the same direction on the graph as do the first three primaries in *Exvia*. Similarly, source trait C is represented by its negative pole, *Ego weakness*, to make it go in the same direction as the other source traits in the *Anxiety* group. Also, source traits I and M are drafted in the negative pole directions of *Harria* and *Praxernia*, which are the right directions for *Cortertia*.

It may be seen that the departures from average are as follows: the attempted suicide subjects are low on *Exvia* (more introverted), high on *Anxiety*, close to average on *Cortertia*, and low on *Strength of inner controls*.

Examples from personnel selection are the

two professions shown in figure 15.6, airline hostesses and airline pilots. Notice the very great similarity of profiles. The pilots seem to have slightly more *Cortertia* and the hostesses slightly more *Exvia*, but the overall profile shapes are extremely close. Notice the content of the profiles: high on *Exvia*, low on *Anxiety*, high on *Cortertia*, and higher still on *Strength of inner controls*. These characteristics give one a feeling of security and confidence when traveling by air. The profiles are almost exactly opposite to those of the attempted suicides represented in figure 15.5. Obviously, someone with a personality profile like that of the attempted suicides would never be accepted for training as an airline hostess or pilot.

Use of the *Motivation Analysis Test* in studying marital satisfactions has yielded some interesting results (Barton et al., 1972). For example, couples are more likely to have frequent disagreements when the husband has a weak *Self-sentiment* and the wife has a stronger sentiment toward her spouse. This

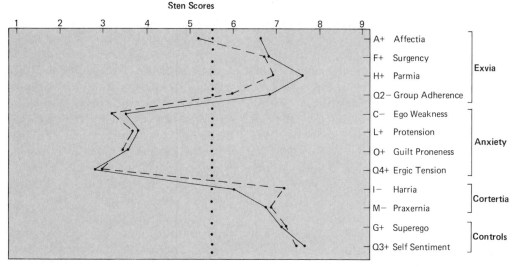

Sten Scores

		Exvia
A+	Affectia	
F+	Surgency	
H+	Parmia	
Q2−	Group Adherence	

		Anxiety
C−	Ego Weakness	
L+	Protension	
O+	Guilt Proneness	
Q4+	Ergic Tension	

		Cortertia
I−	Harria	
M−	Praxernia	

		Controls
G+	Superego	
Q3+	Self Sentiment	

Figure 15.6. Mean profiles on 16 PF for 139 airline hostesses (—) and 360 airline pilots (- -). Adapted from Cattell, Eber, and Tatsuoka (1970). Total adult population average shown for comparison in dotted line (. . .).

suggests that she puts a greater investment of her ergic needs into him than he has personal strength to deliver. Husbands with a high degree of *Assertiveness* erg are also likely to provoke disagreements with their wives over child-rearing. This suggests that they try to have their own way in a matter that by custom falls into the prerogatives of the wife. It appears that marital counseling would be greatly assisted by assessment of the present motivation structure of husband and wife in terms of ergs and sentiments.

In the process of *structured learning* described by Cattell (1973), the ergs and sentiments become rearranged in connection with a course of action. For example, during a semester in which no apparent improvement in grades occurs, students might nevertheless learn to attach more career significance to the materials they are studying. At the same time they may find that their *Sex* or *Assertiveness* ergs begin to gain more satisfaction from studies (reducing conflict). Results substan-

tiating such expectations have been obtained by Cattell and Hendricks (1972).

One of the most difficult tasks faced by scientists doing research on the development of personality arises from the fact that younger children cannot respond to items suitable for older ones. For instance, a highly successful adult questionnaire may be impossible to use with children because of the vocabulary level. Also, many aspects of adult interaction are quite improbable or have different meaning for children. Consider an item of this kind: "I stay away from public meetings unless I absolutely have to go." Answering True to such an item would score positively for *Surgency* if the respondent were an adult. It would be meaningless for a five-year-old child. If a ten-year-old answered True to this item it would likely mean no more than the child's reluctance to be dragged to something dull by his parents.

Accordingly, years of research have gone into the development of different forms of

Cattell's questionnaire for different age groups. The *High School Personality Questionnaire* (*HSPQ*) (Cattell and Cattell, 1969) is for ages eleven to eighteen. The *Children's Personality Questionnaire* (CPQ) (Porter and Cattell, 1960) is for ages eight to twelve. The *Early School Personality Questionnaire* (ESPQ) (IPAT, 1972) is for ages six to eight. The *Pre-School Personality Questionnaire* (IPAT, 1972) is for ages four to six.

Source traits A, C, F, I, O, and Q4 have been replicated at all age levels studied, and G and H have been found all the way down to the ESPQ level (six to eight), but were not found at the preschool ages (four to six). This would be expected from psychoanalytic theory, which holds that the superego is developed largely from conflict resolution and identifications beginning about the age of five. Source trait Q3 has been found only as far down as the CPQ (eight to twelve years). This suggests that *Self-sentiment* does not form as a definite pattern until about that time. *Self-sufficiency* does not emerge as a factor until the twelve-year-old level, and both *Protension* and *Autia* have not been found so far at any younger ages (Cattell, 1973, p. 84).

Making available such a wide range of tests for all ages is one of the several outstanding accomplishments of Cattell's research and that of his colleagues. This research has been guided at all times by his theory of source traits and the dynamic calculus, and thus the theory can also be given credit for these accomplishments.

Critique of Cattell's Theory

Many of the most severe criticisms of Cattell's theory have been directed precisely to its basis in measurement and factor analysis. Some have argued that it is not a theory at all because it simply enumerates lists of empirically discovered source traits. But such a criticism can hardly stand up to confrontation with the complex theorizing that Cattell has actually put into his interpretations of these source traits. Thus his analysis of *Exvia* and *Anxiety* as we have examined them would surely have to be called *theoretical models* of extraversion and anxiety, since they seek to explain the operation of numerous genetic, training, and interactional (feedback loop) sources of causal influence in producing high and low levels of relevant behaviors and experiences. A related criticism is that the source traits Cattell discovers are merely averages of the measurable parts of common traits, and therefore cannot truly represent any individual personality. Allport (1937) was the first to make such a criticism of common traits. But Cattell would argue that science must start somewhere, and that its concern is with the general and not with the unique in the first instance. Having determined what source traits are truly general in the population, then measurements can be obtained for individuals. For example, an airline might use the 16PF (measuring general source traits) to test an applicant for employment as a pilot.

Controversies have raged between Cattell and several other scientists engaged in factor analytic research. These controversies have centered upon such matters as that relating to the difference between orthogonal and oblique factors, which we discussed at the beginning of the chapter. Guilford (1975), for example, has stated that although factors may be correlated obliquely we have no way of determining the correlations with any reliability; hence it is preferable to stick with orthogonal solutions. Guilford also criticizes Cattell's work for results which "are not well replicated outside his own laboratory." Guilford cites the work of Sells and colleagues (1971) who factored 300 Cattell items and found only eleven source traits, some of which replicated Cattell's (A, F, G, H, Q1, and Q4), and others which did not. Their factor C1, for example, had items mostly from C, O, and Q4 (Sells et al., p. 183). Howarth and Browne (1971), using a subset of items from Sells's study, replicated his factors rather than Cattell's. What does Cattell say about results of this kind? He says (1974) that these and similar studies have failed to use appropriate techniques for determining the number of factors and that accordingly they have confused second-stratum source traits with first-stratum source traits. For example, Sells's first-stratum source trait C1 actually matches Cattell's second-stratum source trait *Anxiety*. If Cattell's results have not been well replicated by other investigators, he says, it is because they have not employed the same methods of assembling items into parcels for initial factoring, nor have they employed the same standards in estimating the correct number of factors to be extracted, nor have they pursued the problem of rotating the original axes toward ever greater clarity "until a plateau is reached unimprovable by further shifts" (Cattell, 1974, p. 110). It is obvious that this controversy is based as much upon technical details as it is upon issues of fact. Until other investigators do use precisely the same methods of analysis that Cattell does it will remain an open question whether their results using his items do or do not replicate his results.

Evaluation of the Theory

Turning to our usual criteria for evaluating theories, it appears that Cattell's theory is very *accurate*, largely because the constructs are heavily dependent upon measurement data in the first place. However, some aspects of his theory go far beyond available data; for example, his hypotheses concerning the involvement of brain functions in *Affectia* and other source traits. In my judgment we do not know enough about the brain at this time to say whether such hypotheses are accurate or not.

Does Cattell's theory have *power*? In one sense it does; that is, in its ability to account accurately for individual differences in behavior in a large variety of situations. In another sense its power is *limited* to accounts of individual differences. Where the theory goes beyond that kind of account, as in suggesting physiological explanations for these individual differences, then it is proposing hypotheses for which there is currently no way of estimating its accuracy and hence no way of estimating its power. We conclude that it has power in the limited realm of accounting accurately for individual differences.

Cattell's theory has been very *fruitful* in guiding and stimulating work by other scientists interested in the multivariate approach, and his testing instruments have been widely used throughout the world in a variety of research and applied settings (such as personnel selection and clinical diagnosis). Nevertheless it has been pointed out that his theory has not so far influenced the mainstream of academic psychology: learning, perception, cognitive psychology, experimental approaches to personality, and so on. Perhaps this failure has been due to Cattell's own concentrated emphasis upon the assessment of individual differences, for experiments in mainstream psychology are often less concerned with individual differences among subjects than with systematic group differences associated with different experimental treatments. In these experiments, individual differences are often considered as part of "error variance." Cattell's work on such topics as structured learning does not seem to have progressed far enough yet to have had an impact on mainstream psychology.

Some critics find Cattell's theory of personality to have little *depth*. They assert that constructs which are derived directly from psychological test measurements lack a convincing degree of penetrating thought or manipulative precision. Hence they would be considered shallow, being little more than descriptive of the component test data.

Some critics indeed have asserted that factor analysis only gets out what the factor analyst puts in. This is an inaccurate criticism based upon misunderstanding of the procedure. If you "put in" twenty test measures you do not "get out" twenty test measures; you might get out four factors, each with five tests highly loaded. There are 15,504 ways of taking five things from twenty things, and your factor results have used only four of those ways. There are 15,500 alternative ways left, ways in which the results *could* have turned out but did not. Had you predicted which tests would go together in the factors, the probability of your prediction being correct by chance is exactly .000258, or less than three in 10,000. Cattell has of course replicated his factor patterns many times; other scientists have also replicated his patterns when using the same procedures. Thus they are receiving information about a highly organized structure that is being repeatedly detected by the use of their tests. This structure is not at all the same thing as the set of twenty (or sixteen or thirty-two or whatever) tests they start with.

Nevertheless, the interpretation of a factor must necessarily draw upon the evidence of the tests which do load highly upon it, and upon the negative evidence of tests which do not load highly upon it. Because of this it appears to many that the factor constructs amount to little more than whatever constructs could be derived from the individual tests. Hence the depth of insight into mechanisms provided by Cattell's theory appears to be slight. When Cattell departs quite drastically from the given test data (as when he interprets a set of questionnaire responses as indicating "parasympathetic immunity" or *Parmia*), then critics think his theory is far-fetched, little more than guessing. But it is in fact a deep hypothesis, and whether critics like it or not, Cattell's theory is actually capable of providing substantial insight into mechanisms, and therefore is much deeper than it appears.

Workshop 15

Comparing Cattell's Second-order Temperament Factors with Jung's Types

As we proceed in the book we shall more and more frequently attempt to draw parallels between the constructs of different theories. Sometimes these comparisons will involve competing theoretical models when the facts involved are the same. When dealing with a theory's constructs, however, we do not have a particular set of facts given. We have only the descriptions of the constructs and their role in the theory. To some extent we have to make intuitive leaps in order to discern similarities. In this workshop we shall try to make some comparisons between Cattell's factor-defined constructs of temperament and Jung's clinically based constructs of typology.

We can begin with extraversion versus introversion, because Cattell has indicated that his second-stratum source trait **Exvia** essentially refers to the same construct that Jung had in mind. Cattell's second-stratum source trait Exvia embraces four first-stratum source traits, which can be thought of as main components or aspects of the overall construct of Exvia. If Jung and Cattell are thinking of the same construct, then presumably it will be possible to isolate those same four components in Jung's ideas about extraversion. Go back to the section in chapter 12 on Jung's theory of types for the details on his construct; consider also the descriptions of source traits A, F, H, and Q2 in the present chapter. After the first few examples, continue as suggested.

Cattell's First-Stratum Source Traits Entering the Exvia Grouping	Comparable Ideas in Jung's Construct of Extraversion
A. Warm	Interested in people
Outgoing	Attention directed toward environment
Easy emotional expression	Extraverted feeling type is easy in emotional expression.
F. Enthusiastic	_____
Happy	_____
Impulsive	_____
H. Adventurous	_____
Uninhibited	_____
Q2. (Low pole) Group dependent	_____
Not self-reliant	_____
	(Note: Compare extraverted thinking and feeling types on this one.)

Are there other points of similarity between Jung's and Cattell's constructs of extraversion?

_____

_____

_____

_____

_____

What do you think of the possibility that the distinction between thinking types and feeling types is comparable to the second-stratum source trait **Cortertia?**

_____

_____

_____

_____

_____

_____

Summary

Cattell's theory of personality is functional, and its basic equation states that behavior is a function of source traits as triggered by situations. The source traits are underlying unitary influences, revealed both in psychological test responses and in life behaviors. These traits are assumed to be organized into strata, with source traits at higher strata having more general influence than lower strata traits. Four main second-stratum source traits discovered so far are *Exvia, Anxiety, Cortertia,* and *Strength of inner controls.* Each of these influences several first-stratum source traits. For example, *Anxiety* is related to first-stratum source traits of *Ego strength, Protension, Guilt proneness,* and *Ergic tension.* These source traits are traits of temperament, of the way people do things. Cattell has also explored traits of motivation (needs, interests, motives), where he finds ten basic source traits called *ergs,* including *Fear, Sex, Aggression, Assertion,* and others. The ergs are also found to coalesce upon particular cultural or social objects (such as religion, career, or family), and when these arrangements are found in the data they are interpreted as *sentiments.*

Cattell's theory and the many measuring instruments he has devised for each major trait have found applications in a great variety of fields of psychology: personnel selection, clinical diagnosis, program evaluation, and others. His work on conflict and personality integration is becoming increasingly important for the clinical understanding of pathological and normal persons. His new constructs in structured learning promise to be of considerable interest to mainstream psychologists and scientists in education.

The theory appears to be very accurate but limited in its accuracy to the understanding of individual differences. Hence its power is limited also. It has been very fruitful among scientists adopting a multivariate approach, and is deeper than it appears. Figure 15.7 illustrates the definition of personality implied in Cattell's theory.

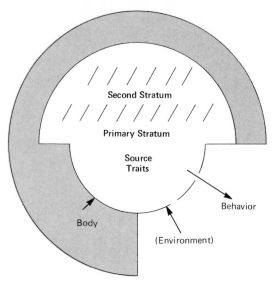

Figure 15.7. Definition of personality implicit in Cattell's theory

Key to Information Test on Page 384

The correct scores are as follows:

1. B
2. C
3. A
4. A
5. A
6. C
7. B
8. B

The erg which is intended to be measured here is the fear or security erg.

INTRODUCTION

Theoretical models of the self
  Twenty-one different constructs: A confusing
    state of affairs
  Removing redundancies
Two models: Jung and Cattell
  Jung's model
    Ego
    Self
  Cattell's model
    Ego strength and superego strength
    Self-sentiment
      Development of the self-sentiment
      Does the self-sentiment integrate the id,
        ego, and superego?
      The self-sentiment in different strata of the
        personality
  Comparison of the two models
    Jung's self and Cattell's self-sentiment:
      different
    Cattell's social self and Jung's persona: similar
    Removing more redundancies
Erikson's model: identity
  The sense of ego-identity
  Differentiation from ego and superego
  Identity as a higher-order organization of
    images, ideas, and feelings
  Identity integrates the ego, superego, and
    ego ideal
  Comparison with Cattell's model
    Erikson's identity and Cattell's self-sentiment
    Differences between the two constructs
    Possible reconciliation of the differences
    Ambivalent roles of identity and of the
      self-sentiment
    Identity and the self-sentiment sufficiently
      similar
    Removing more redundancies
Maslow's model:
  The self that is actualized in self-actualization
  How the real self is found
  Comparison with Erikson's model
    Identity in the context of society
    The self in spite of society
    Erikson's identity and Maslow's self: different

Comparison with Jung's model
  Jung's self and Maslow's self: similar
Rogers's model: the self-concept
  The self-concept and the ideal self
  Comparison with Maslow's model
    Similarities
    An important difference: Maslow's self-
      actualization is Rogers's actualization of the
      organism, not Rogers's self-actualization
  Comparison with Erikson's model
    The self-concept and identity: different
Several constructs related to self
  The ideal self and the ego ideal
    Similarities and differences in various theories
    Removing further redundancies
  The superego
    Conditions of worth (Rogers) and the superego
      (Freud): different
  Erikson's construct of "I"
    Distinction between "I" and identity
    The meaning of "I": center of awareness
      and felt assurance
    Comparison of the "I" and the self: different
Conclusion: three models
  Cattell-Erikson model
  Jung-Maslow model
  Rogers's model
Workshop 16 Comparing Erikson's "I" and Jung's
  ego constructs
Summary

Ego, Self, Identity:
Five Competing Models?

In chapter 1 it was suggested that theoretical models of personality not only are important for scientific work, but also can be useful for everyday understanding of ourselves and other people. The case of compensation was mentioned, as was the difference between extraverts and introverts. One of the most pervasive constructs we have encountered so far in this book refers to the individual's own self: the *ego,* the *self,* the *superego,* the *self-ideal,* the *self-sentiment, self-actualization, self-concept, identity,* and so on. Do all of these refer to some particular model of the self that is accurate and useful?

Table 16.1 outlines the several constructs, and also includes some that have not been referred to before in this book but will be referred to in the present chapter. In the table Cattell's constructs are listed both in terms of his theoretical work *apart* from the personality traits or factors (for example, the construct of *ego* is taken over by Cattell from Freud's theory) and also in terms of the related source trait (such as *Ego strength*). These tied constructs, joined by "and," are meant to be considered together. That being so, how many different constructs referring to the self can be found in table 16.1? It looks as though there are at least six, one for each column. But that assumes that all entries in a given column mean the same thing, which we know is not the case. For example, Jung's construct of the ego is different from Freud's construct of the ego (compare chapter 13). Jung's *ego* is in the center of consciousness and is all in the conscious portion of personality. It therefore might have been similar (or identical) to Freud's early conception of the ego in his first and second structural theories (see chapter 9). But in the third structural theory Freud found it necessary to conceptualize the ego as having portions in all three domains of consciousness, the preconscious, and the unconscious. So the final construct of *ego* in Freud's theory differs from Jung's construct of *ego.*

There are at least two different constructs in the first column, despite the identical language. Are there perhaps two different constructs in each column except the fifth, *identity?* If so then we have perhaps a total of eleven different constructs dealing with different aspects of the self. It is no wonder that Donald Fiske, voicing the collective despair of our science, can say, "neither investigators nor theorists have much consensus on any-

Table 16.1
Constructs Dealing with Ego, Self, Identity, and Related Matters

THEORIST	CONSTRUCT					
	Ego	Self	Ideal	Superego	Identity	Other
Maslow		The self that is actualized in self-actualization				
Rogers		Self-concept or Self-structure	Ideal self	Conditions of worth (?)		
Freud	Ego		Ego ideal	Superego		
Jung	Ego	Self				Persona
Erikson	Ego		Ego ideal	Superego	Identity	I
Cattell	Ego and Ego strength (Factor C)	Self-sentiment and Self-sentiment control (Q3)	Ideal self-sentiment	Superego sentiment and Superego strength (G)		Physical self Social self

thing" (Fiske, 1974, p. 1). Altogether in table 16.1 we see twenty-one entries. Could there be twenty-one different constructs?

Of course the different columns in table 16.1 might *not* refer to different constructs even though they have different words in their headings. Is *ego* different from *self*? Is *ideal* different from *superego*? We know that within one theory (for example, Jung's) the two words that seem similar (such as *ego* and *self*) actually refer to quite different constructs. But perhaps two different words used by two different theorists might actually refer to the same construct. For instance, perhaps the construct of *identity* as used by Erikson, actually is the same construct Cattell calls *self-sentiment*. Perhaps Jung's construct of the *persona* means something essentially similar to Rogers's construct of the *conditions of worth*. If we examine all these pairs of constructs carefully, perhaps we shall find that there are not actually eleven different constructs there. Per-

haps we can arrive at the idea that at most three different constructs are needed to produce a theoretical model having to do with ego, self, or identity.

We know already that Maslow uses only one construct; Rogers, Freud, and Jung have three; Erikson and Cattell have five or more. We know also that Cattell and Erikson have taken over Freud's three constructs of *ego*, *ego ideal*, and *superego* and added to them in their own theoretical work. Is it possible for Maslow to say everything with one construct that others need five or more to accomplish? Or perhaps they are not accomplishing the same goals at all?

Table 16.1 reflects an unusually confusing state of affairs in psychology. In this chapter we shall try to sort out some of the tangles, but we cannot hope to succeed completely. Our aim, however, will be to reduce the twenty-one constructs in table 16.1 to a much smaller set that is more usable in the construction of an integrated theory and model dealing with ego, self, and identity. We begin with elimination of Freud's three constructs because these are represented in the theories of Erikson and Cattell. We further remove the redundant information on *ego, ego ideal* and *superego,* constructs which Cattell and Erikson share. As a result we have table 16.2, which is already simpler than table 16.1. Table 16.2 has only sixteen different entries.

Throughout the remainder of this chapter I shall compare and contrast theoretical models dealing with ego, self, or identity. Some theorists use only one construct, as we noted above; others use five. Do they nevertheless result in similar or identical models or do they not? If not, are there *any* correspondences? Some psychologists believe it is unprofitable to look for similarity of constructs between theorists as different as Rogers and Jung or Cattell and Freud. To insist that the constructs are different because they come from totally different theories, and to do so without even looking at what evidence there might be to support or refute a claim of similarity, is to guarantee that the science of personality study will remain in the dreadful condition that Fiske describes.

An alternative approach is to roll up our sleeves and try to find out whether perhaps some of the differences are more apparent than real. And if they are real we will then need

Table 16.2

Constructs Dealing with Ego, Self, Identity, and Related Matters:
Obvious Redundancies Removed

THEORIST	CONSTRUCT					
	Ego	Self	Ideal	Superego	Identity	Other
Maslow		The self that is actualized in self-actualization				
Rogers		Self-concept or Self-structure	Ideal self	Conditions of worth (?)		
Jung	Ego	Self				Persona
Erikson			Ego ideal		Identity	I
	Ego and Ego strength (C)			Superego and Superego sentiment and Superego strength (G)		
Cattell		Self-sentiment and Self-sentiment control (Q3)	Ideal self-sentiment			Physical self / Social self

Ego, Self, Identity: Five Competing Models? 401

to figure out a way of either joining them into a single coherent body of constructs or else formulating new constructs which rise above the differences and make them irrelevant. Anyway, the bias of this chapter will be to find some similarities between apparently different constructs. If the chapter is successful we shall find at the end that we need less than the five models shown in the rows of table 16.1.

Two Models of the Self: Jung and Cattell

If ever a pair of technical terms sounded as if they mean the same thing, surely the pair *ego* and *self* do. And yet Jung uses them both, and Cattell has a closely related pair of constructs (see table 16.2). I shall begin the comparisons with Jung's model.

Jung's Model

Jung conceived of the ego as the center point of reference for consciousness. It is grounded on bodily perceptions, the receiving station for all sensations and feelings in consciousness. It also has a unique quality of felt freedom to choose, the experience we have of our "free will."

The self is quite different from the ego. It "comprises the totality of the psyche altogether, i.e., conscious *and* unconscious" (Jung, 1955/1972, p. 5). The self is a center of being that is in contact with the collective unconscious, and hence is an awareness of continuity between the individual human being and the entire human race, past and primitive as well as present and modern. Jung discovered the self in 1918, when he was commandant of a camp for prisoners of war. Each morning he sketched a small circular drawing, which he later called a *mandala,* a certain kind of symbol of self. The drawing seemed to correspond to his inner state, and through the drawings he was able to observe the changes in his personality from day to day.

For example, one day Jung received a letter from a lady he knew in which she stressed the artistic quality of his productions. This letter irritated him, since it seemed to him to suggest that he was drawing for the purpose of satisfying his pride. The suggestion left him wondering just how natural and spontaneous these drawings really were. He writes "Out of this irritation and disharmony within myself there proceeded, the following day, a changed mandala: part of the periphery had burst open and the symmetry was destroyed" (Jung, 1965, p. 195).

Jung continues: "Only gradually did I discover what the mandala really is: . . . the self, the wholeness of the personality, which if all goes well is harmonious, but which cannot tolerate self-deceptions. My mandalas were cryptograms concerning the state of the self which were presented to me anew each day. In them I saw the self—that is, my whole being—actively at work" (Jung, 1965, pp. 195-196).

Jung asked himself where all these mandalas were leading. He recognized that the goal he had set for himself—from his ego— was to continue his researches on myths. Now he realized that that was not to be; that he had to give up his position of dominance in the ego. The self was changing toward its own goal.

I began to understand that the goal of psychic development is the self. There is no linear evolution; there is only circumambulation of the self. Uniform development exists, at most, only at the beginning; later everything points toward the center. This insight gave me stability, and gradually my inner peace returned. I knew that in finding the mandala as an expression of the self I had attained what was for me the ultimate. Perhaps someone else knows more, but not I (Jung, 1965, pp. 196-197).

What was this strange process he describes? It was represented in the mandala drawings as the fact "that everything, all the paths I had been following, all the steps I had taken, were leading back to a single point —namely the mid-point. It became increasingly plain to me that the mandala is the center. . . . It is the path to the center, to individuation" (Jung, 1965, p. 196).

About seven years later Jung painted a mandala (shown as figure 6 in Jung, 1955/1972) which had a golden castle at the center point and seemed to have overall a Chinese cast of form and color. Jung could not understand the Chinese aspect. But strangely, he received a letter with a manuscript from an ancient Chinese text sent by a friend in Frankfurt. The manuscript, which dealt with a text in alchemy and was entitled *The Secret of the Golden Flower,* described "the yellow castle, the germ of the immortal body." This was the first inkling Jung had that the development of his own thought was not completely without precedent in this world. "I became aware of an affinity," he wrote, "I could establish ties with something and someone" (Jung, 1965, p. 197).

About the same time he had a dream of being in Liverpool with some Swiss friends. It was dark and rainy. Reaching the city center at the top of the hill he found it was a square with the various parts of the city radiating outward. Everything around was dark and foggy. But in the middle of the square was a pool; in the middle of that an island, ablaze in sunlight. In the middle of the island stood a single magnolia tree with reddish blossoms. The tree both stood in the light and seemed to be the source of the light. His companions did not see the tree; they only commented on the weather and the darkness.

The picture of the city is itself a mandala, of course, with the circular city neighborhoods radiating out from the central square, and with a round pool in the center of the square. Liverpool is the pool of the liver; the liver is the seat of life, that which produces living. Jung felt that the dream revealed the goal of his life, everything being directed toward the center.

> Through this dream I understood that the self is the principle and archetype of orientation and meaning . . . here the meaning had been made clear. When I parted from Freud, I knew that I was plunging into the unknown. Beyond Freud, after all, I knew nothing; but I had taken the step into darkness. When that happens, and then such a dream comes, one feels it as an act of grace. It has taken me virtually forty-five years to distill within the vessel of my scientific work the things I experienced and wrote down at that time (Jung, 1965, p. 199).

The self is the "principle and archetype of orientation and meaning." One of Jung's patients showed this principle at work dramatically in the first three of a long series of mandala drawings (1955/1972, pp. 6-70). A fifty-five-year-old spinster felt stuck in her development, and perhaps sensing the unconscious tie to her mother that still bound her, she visited the old country (Denmark) before going to Zurich. Her first drawing showed sky and sea and large rocks. Out of one of these rocks emerged the upper half of a woman's body. As Jung interpreted it the sky was the conscious part of the personality; the rocks the unconscious. She was stuck in the unconscious. In the second drawing there is no person, only a circular shape with a red nucleus. Lightning has struck the rocks, and is shown curled around the circle, as if wrenching it out of the rocks. Jung interprets the lightning as the power to liberate her, a sudden change wrought in therapy. The third drawing shows the circle, this time with a red band on the periphery, bluish in the center. This sphere is bound around the middle by silver strands, and the whole sphere seems to be gliding through an airy space, with much light around. There is now a golden serpent hovering above the sphere. She explained that the silver band keeps the sphere in balance.

About this third picture Jung writes,

> The patient felt the moment of painting this picture as the "climax" of her life and also described it as such. . . . The sphere blasted from the rock in Picture 2 has now, in the brighter atmosphere, floated up to heaven. The nocturnal darkness of the earth has vanished. The increase of light indicates conscious realization: the liberation has become a fact that is integrated into consciousness. The patient has understood that the floating sphere symbolizes the "true personality" (Jung, 1934/1969, p. 307).

To summarize, the ego is the center of the consciousness and the seat of felt personal free will. But the self is the center of all the personality, unconscious as well as conscious. As the self develops within the person it embraces more and more of the directions of the personality as these are given by unconscious determinants, by unconscious will, we might say. The total state of the personality is the total state of the self. It may be represented in mandala forms either in dreams or in drawings, the latter moved chiefly by unconscious urgings rather than conscious deliberations. The patient distinguished between her "reason" and "the eyes." Her reason may want to draw something, but "the eyes" would not like it, would force it to become something else more suitable to their own intention. If satisfying only the reason, the ego, the conscious intention, the picture would "not look right." This self, this total state of the personality, can change. The principle of orientation and meaning of human life can change. The condition of disharmony can change and can be-

come one of harmony. The reverse is also true. Such changes are reflected in the momentary state of the self and in the momentary forms of the self's archetypal images, the mandalas.

Later in this chapter we shall consider another related construct in Jung's theory, the *persona*. First we will explore what similarities there might be between Cattell's model and Jung's.

Cattell's Model

Cattell's model includes constructs of *ego strength* and *superego strength,* and uses also the original clinical constructs developed by Freud (see Cattell, 1950; Cattell, 1957; Cattell & Scheier, 1961; Cattell, 1973). Cattell also uses constructs of *self-sentiment, ideal-self-sentiment,* and *superego sentiment* (see especially Cattell & Horn, 1963).

In Cattell's theory a sentiment for an object arises when a person develops numerous attitudes toward that object, attitudes which represent different instinctual or other sources of drive. Cattell calls all of these drive sources *ergs* (see chapter 15). A sentiment toward one's career, for example, may represent the union of the self-assertive erg (for getting ahead), the parental-assertive erg (to be supporting one's family), and even the sex erg (to provide the means for more sexual satisfaction). It might also be energized in part by the gregarious erg (if the job requires dealing with people, for instance).

But how can a sentiment develop toward the self? Cattell states that two main facts of life in society provide that the self becomes a means to the satisfaction of almost all ergs. First, every satisfaction of drive A is made through some part of the physical body, either in its work, in its physical relations of closeness or love for others, or in its service as a final consumer of food and other goods. The same is true for drive B and any other drive. Thus all drives or ergs come to be satisfied through the physical body, and thereby the body itself becomes an important mediating object for every drive satisfaction.

Second, "the continuation of the social self in good standing is almost as important for the maintenance of *all* ergic satisfactions as is the continued existence of the physical self. (There have been phases in history, e.g., the French Revolution or the Russian Revolution, where loss of the social self is quickly followed by loss of the physical self. . . .)" (Cattell, 1950, p. 654).

The development of a self-sentiment will obviously take time, probably longer than the development of ego and superego. Cattell wrote in 1950 (p. 657), "in clinical research there should be indications of the gradual emergence in the growing individual of a fourth structure—the self-sentiment—less obvious than id, ego, and superego, developing out of the ego and integrating it more and more with the superego, at least with its conscious manifestations."

When Cattell wrote these statements there was no clear evidence of the existence of source traits for all of these structures, id, ego, superego, and self-sentiment. Twenty-seven years later, in 1977, however, there are ample grounds for certainty concerning the source traits of Ego strength (C), Superego strength (G), Self-sentiment (Q3), and Ergic-tension (Q4). A full discussion of these source traits is given in chapter 15.

Does the self-sentiment emerge gradually, as Cattell predicted? It would seem so. Factor Q3 does not appear until the eight- to twelve-year-old level of testing with child versions of the 16PF.

Does it appear that the self-sentiment emerges as a major controlling force, integrating all ergic expression and binding especially the ego and the superego in one harmonious unity? This is more difficult to say. Let us consider the correlational evidence.

At the level of primary factors (Cattell, Eber, & Tatsuoka, 1970, pp. 113 ff.), Factor Q3, Self-sentiment, is correlated roughly $+.50$ with Factor C, Ego strength, among adult college students; it is also correlated roughly $+.55$ with Factor G, Superego strength. But C and G are correlated together only $+.20$. This suggests that the self-sentiment does indeed have more in common with the ego and with the superego than these two have in common with each other. Moreover, Q3 has a strong negative correlation with Ergic tension, Factor Q4. This correlation is roughly $-.54$, averaging for males and females. This is entirely in accordance with the theoretical expectation, since a stronger self-sentiment should be stronger in securing all-around harmonious gratification of instincts, hence less undischarged tension.

These data offer no evidence concerning the origin of the self-sentiment. That is, we cannot say whether indeed it "developed out of the ego." Nor can we say whether it really is "integrating the ego with the superego" in all that such a proposition means. We can only say that the correlational evidence is consistent with that prediction. It would also be consistent with the hypothesis that the self-sentiment serves to integrate id pressures as well as ego and superego, a higher-order agency somehow monitoring the functions of all three other agencies. But if this were truly so, then we would expect it to play a central role in bringing these three other agencies together at the second-order level of analysis. Does it do this? It appears not.

In the second-order results (as discussed in chapter 15 we saw that Ego strength and Ergic tension were closely related in the second-stratum source trait of Anxiety. That is, within the anxiety factor, ego weakness and more undischarged tension are involved. This suggests that even among adults the most potent factor in mediating harmonious discharge of instinctual energies is the strength of the ego, not of the self-sentiment.

In the complete picture of the second-order factor pattern both the primaries of self-sentiment control and of ego strength are negatively related to the second-order anxiety pattern. That means the stronger the self-sentiment the less anxiety in the second stratum of the personality. The self-sentiment primary has its highest loading on the second-order control factor, however, averaging $+.59$. Factor G, superego strength, averages $+.82$ on that control factor. Elsewhere at the second order level the superego primary is quite unrelated to the others. Its loading on anxiety is a mere $-.02$ for females and $+.01$ for males; both values are essentially zero.

It appears that, whatever else is happening, the superego is *not* being integrated with the ego at the second-order level, either through the self-sentiment or by any other means. But the self-sentiment plays two roles at the second order, being integrated with the superego and also being associated with lesser anxiety.

The third-order factors present another story. There we find that the anxiety factor *and* the control factor come together to load positively on self-criticism, a factor in the third stratum of personality. As we saw in chapter 15 this result is entirely in accord with psychoanalytic theory. It does not seem to fit Cattell's early hypothesis concerning the harmonizing influence of the self-sentiment, however. For the self-sentiment is positively loaded on the control factor at the second order, along with positive superego strength. And then at the third order this control factor is positively loaded on self-criticism along with positive anxiety.

Thus it appears that the self-sentiment plays an ambivalent role in the personality. On one hand it is connected with lesser anxiety at the second stratum; on the other it is connected with greater anxiety at the third stratum.

The total picture of the self-sentiment presented by the data so far, then, is that it is an independent agency in the primary stratum of the personality, which is nevertheless related positively to both ego and superego and negatively to id pressure. Then at the second stratum, the self-sentiment joins positively with the superego to form the control factor, and negatively with id pressure to form the anxiety factor, playing two roles in this stratum. Then at the third stratum these two roles are somehow brought together since both the anxiety factor and the control factor are positively related in the third-order factor of self-criticism. Perhaps, following the spirit of Cattell's early theorizing, this self-criticizing role of the self-sentiment stems precisely from its mediating function with respect to all of the ergs. The person increasingly realizes the necessity for caution in maintaining the physical and social basis for sustained gratifications; and increasingly realizes that failure in either of these bases means failure of gratifications. Put in a different way, the more integrated the person becomes under the one guiding sentiment toward self, the more at risk the person places all gratifications; for they all depend on the maintenance of the body in good physical order and good social standing. Threats to either of these components are rapidly converted into threats to integration as a whole and to all ergic satisfactions.

Comparison of Two Models

Both Jung and Cattell refer to a self as well as an ego. Since Cattell's ego construct is well aligned with Freud's notion of the ego, and since Jung's construct of the ego differs from Freud's, therefore Jung also differs from Cattell in regard to the ego. Jung believes the ego to be in the center of consciousness;

Freud believes it to be in all three domains of the personality: conscious, preconscious, and unconscious. For Freud the ego remains the supreme agency of guidance, control, and defense; for Jung the ego is always a less effective agency than we are apt to believe. Eventually, in Jung's view, we are all forced to move the center of our being to the self.

For Cattell also the ego is a strong integrative agency; his main factorial variable of the ego is its strength, factor C. But Cattell, like Jung, introduces an agency of the self, namely the self-sentiment, which is indicated by the emergence of a separate factor, Q3. Like Jung's construct of the self, Cattell's self-sentiment plays an integrative role. In Cattell's theory, however, the self-sentiment integrates id, ego, and superego. By contrast, in Jung's theory the self integrates the conscious and the unconscious. It might be thought that these two aspects are pretty much the same. But Cattell explicitly states that the integration of the self-sentiment with the superego proceeds with regard to the conscious aspects of the superego only.

There is no real equivalent for a superego in Jung's theory, although within the collective unconscious are numinous forces as well as animal instincts. These numinous or spiritual tendencies are inherited just as the animal instincts are. They enter into conflict with the instinctual forces in much the same way that the superego combats instinctual forces in Freud's theory. But they are equally part of the collective unconscious, and therefore cannot be taken as equivalent to the conscious part of the superego. So it seems quite clear that Cattell's self-sentiment is not the same as Jung's self.

If they are not the same even though the word *self* is used in both constructs, then how are they related? Do they refer to totally different components of psychophysical structure? Are the relevant facts the same? Is it possible the relevant facts are different? Is it possible that each theorist uses a different verbal label to refer to the facts considered under the term *self* by the other theorist?

In Jung's overall theory we find also the *persona,* a construct which refers to the public personality, the mask. Is there perhaps some similarity between the persona concept and self-sentiment?

Recall that the self-sentiment develops out of the ego and integrates it with the conscious aspects of the superego, according to Cattell's early theory. Also, the self-sentiment refers to a social self and a physical self. The social self is one that can become endangered by unfortunate turns of history. Surely this would have to be roughly equivalent to Jung's construct of the persona.

Let us think for a moment in terms of the person's imagery. The construct of persona can be conceived as referring to the image of self presented to the world. It might be more or less accurate. It might even be a false image. Now think also of the social self as an image. What would this be but an image of the self as appearing to the world? Perhaps we can equate the constructs of persona and social self as referring to a person's imagery of self as presented to other people.

In light of these considerations it seems plausible that the social self part of Cattell's self-sentiment construct refers to a set of facts closely similar to the set referred to by Jung's construct of persona. But what about the physical self part of the self-sentiment? There seems to be no explicit counterpart in Jung's theory. On the other hand, the self-sentiment primary factor is a unitary factor, which suggests that the physical and social self components may be so well integrated together that they function as virtually one whole. If that is so, then is it possible that Jung's construct of the persona actually includes ideas about the *physical* self as presented to or appearing to other people? There is no such indication in Jung's writings. The persona is a "false self." Jung says that the persona is built up from experiences of our effect on other people and of their effect on us. The persona is thus a "general idea of . . . how one *appears* to oneself and the world, but not what one *is*" (Jung, 1921/1971, p. 218). This has neither a physical self component nor an integrative function of the kind that Cattell attributes to the self-sentiment.

So the persona certainly cannot be equated completely with the self-sentiment. But at least it seems to refer to some portion of the facts addressed by Cattell. These facts probably have to do with the front people put on, their public image, the Ms. and Mr. Jones at the office. Jung assumes that it is merely a front—"that which in reality one is not." Cattell assumes that it is part of a more active, integrative unit, the self-sentiment. Among other things, the self-sentiment maintains a social presence, an image of the self adapted to social expectations.

The *self* of Jung and the *self-sentiment* of Cattell have nothing in common. But the *persona* in Jung's theory is a construct which is essentially the same as *social self* part of Cattell's construct of the self-sentiment. Therefore we can link up at least persona and social self in table 16.2. Since it is evident that the social self and the physical self are encompassed in Cattell's construct of the self-sentiment, these might well be pooled. The result can be seen in table 16.3.

Erikson's Model: Identity

Erikson accepts Freud's theory of the ego, superego, and id, but goes farther in describing the development of *identity*. We saw in chapter 14 that identity is a three-dimensional *sense*: in consciousness, in behavior, and in the unconscious. Erikson writes,

The sense of ego identity . . . is the accrued confidence that the inner sameness and continuity prepared in the past are matched by the sameness and continuity of one's meaning for others . . . [ego identity is] more than the sum of the childhood identifications. It is the accrued experience of the ego's ability to integrate all identifications with the vicissitudes of the libido, with the aptitudes developed out of endowment, and with the opportunities offered in social roles (Erikson, 1963, p. 261).

All of these components of identity (identifications, skills, defenses) are apprehended in the context of the social environment. There are both social opportunities for the individual's roles and social appraisals of the individual's performance of those roles. He or she is known as a good friend, a good player, a trustworthy worker, and so on. The continuity of identity rests as much in the individual's assurance that other people will continue to see and recognize that identity as it does in the individual's own self-consciousness.

Recall that the sense of identity, in Erikson's theory, is slowly fashioned. It comes into being much later than the ego and superego. It is constructed out of the residues from early crises: the sense of trust or mistrust, of autonomy or doubt, of initiative or guilt, of industry or inferiority. Each of these must be transformed from childhood meanings into adult meanings. Each must become a viable and enduring principle of personal relatedness to society. Society provides institutions for such relatedness: religion for the individual's search for faith (derived from trust); law and order and justice for the individual's search for just service and mutual responsibility (derived from autonomy); politics for the individual's striving for a better world for himself and others (derived from initiative); and the job market for a person's occupational identity (derived from the sense of industry).

The sense of identity is a higher-order or-

Table 16.3
Constructs Dealing with Ego, Self, Identity, and Related Matters: Further Redundancies Removed

THEORIST	CONSTRUCT					
	Ego	Self	Ideal	Superego	Identity	Other
Maslow		The self that is actualized in self-actualization				
Rogers		Self-concept or Self-structure	Ideal self	(Conditions of worth ?)		
Jung ———	Ego	Persona or social self **part of** self-sentiment and Self-sentiment control (Q3)				Self
Cattell	Ego strength (C) and Ego		Ideal self-sentiment	Superego strength (G) and Superego sentiment and Superego		
Erikson			Ego ideal		Identity — I	

ganization of images, ideas, and feelings about the individual's place in the world of society. It is above and beyond the ego itself; it is above even the superego. Erikson writes,

> The child internalizes into the super-ego most of all the prohibitions . . . which are perceived and accepted with the limited cognitive means of early childhood and are preserved with a primitive sado-masochism inherent in man's inborn proclivities for "turning upon himself" not only the moralistic ag-

gression of his elders but also his own inexpressible rage. . . . Yet without a further development of truly *ethical* strivings, that is, an absorption of his moralism into the shared affirmation of values, as first envisaged in youth, man could never build the social structures which define his adult privileges and obligations (Erikson, 1975, pp. 101-102).

Such affirmation of shared values, he adds, is part of the identity formation process:

the individual's capacity to relate to an ever expanding life space of people and institutions, on the one hand, and, on the other, the readiness of these people and institutions to make him part of an ongoing cultural concern. All this, in fact, prepares and determines the nature of the identity crisis, the solution of which firmly assigns a new and subsidiary place to the superego (Erikson, 1975, p. 102).

Identity thus goes beyond the ego, beyond the superego, beyond even the ego ideal (ethical strivings). It integrates all of these, putting them all in subsidiary position within a higher organization of personality. This higher organization includes the individual's value system, his or her participation in the values of the culture. It includes the individual's relationships to the people and institutions of society. It represents in part the individual's place in that society, all in complex imagery as discussed in chapter 14.

Comparison with Cattell's Model

Since Cattell and Erikson both accept Freud's model of ego, ego ideal, and superego they already have much in common. Is there any construct in Cattell's theory that provides a reasonable match to Erikson's construct of *identity*? Possibly the *self-sentiment* does. Like identity, the self-sentiment provides higher-order integration over ego, superego, and id. Like identity, the self-sentiment integrates also the *social self*, the image of the person in society. There is in addition a *physical self* conceived as part of the object toward which the self-sentiment develops. Is there a counterpart in Erikson's construct of identity? None is obvious. On the other hand, the assurance of inner sameness and continuity of meaning for others would seem to require an image of continuity in the body, the physical housing for inner sameness and the physical basis of continuous meaning for others.

Also, the construct of the ego in Freud's theory included an image of the body, a *body ego*. At that lower level of organization, then, as well as at a higher level in integration of the individual with society, Erikson's conception of identity must include a physical self even if only implicitly.

There are several differences between the construct of identity and of self-sentiment, however. First, the integrating role of the self-sentiment is supposed to affect only conscious portions of the superego. Identity covers conscious, behavioral, and unconscious components and is thus more inclusive. Second, the self-sentiment plays different roles at different strata of the personality, according to Cattell's results; no comparable differentiation into strata appears in Erikson's theory. Third, Erikson's construct of identity includes integration of the ego ideal; no comparable integration of the ideal self is referred to in Cattell's theory.

In the interest of pursuing all possible leads to similarity of constructs, however, we might try to reconcile the foregoing differences. For instance, if the construct of identity is more inclusive with respect to conscious, behavioral, and unconscious domains, then perhaps the construct of the self-sentiment is simply a part of the construct of identity. If the construct of the self-sentiment plays different roles in different strata of the personality, possibly the construct of identity also plays different roles of comparable nature even though not "located" in different strata. For example, in Cattell's results we find evidence for the self-sentiment contributing to reduced anxiety at the second stratum but to increased anxiety at the third stratum. At the second stratum the self-sentiment is organized with the ego in reducing anxiety; in the third stratum it is organized with the superego in raising anxiety. Could such relationships be found for identity? It is conceivable. For identity, Erikson says, "is the accrued experience of the ego's ability to integrate all identifications with the vicissitudes of the libido. . . ." This means that identity is allied with the ego in holding down anxiety that would arise from libidinal pressures (id pressures), allowing for the second-stratum role of anxiety reduction. Also, the child has internalized the prohibitions of elders into the superego, and these are preserved and given power not only by "the moralistic aggression of his elders but also [by] his own inexpressible rage" turned upon himself. If identity embraces the superego, then, it must share something of the latter's effects in *producing* anxiety. Recall (chapter 10) that Freud proposed a model of anxiety in which three kinds of anxiety can be distinguished: realistic (some real external threat), neurotic (instinctual impulses are a source of threat), and moralistic (the superego is a source of threat to the ego). If the identity of the child gradually "absorbs" the moralism into a "shared affirmation of values" it must meanwhile share in the production of moralistic anxiety.

Thus what we called the ambivalent roles of the self-sentiment in reducing anxiety at the second stratum and raising anxiety at the third stratum can be seen to have a close match in the roles of identity. For in alliance with the ego a stronger sense of identity will serve to reduce neurotic anxiety, but in alliance with the superego a stronger sense of identity will serve to increase moralistic anxiety. There thus seems to be a correspondence between anxiety as found at two different strata (Cattell's theory) and anxiety of two different kinds, neurotic and moralistic (Erikson's theory).

As to the third difference between the construct of identity and the construct of self-sentiment, namely that the former also integrates the ego ideal, there is no obvious reason why such a possibility should not be included in Cattell's theory. Accordingly I propose that

Erikson's construct of identity and Cattell's contruct of self-sentiment be considered sufficiently similar to warrant pooling. Since Erikson's construct appears to be the more inclusive, it seems proper to merge Cattell's concept into Erikson's. This means also that Jung's construct of the persona would be seen as redundant with a part of Erikson's identity construct. The results are shown in table 16.4.

Maslow's Model

In chapter 1 we studied Maslow's theory of personality, especially his constructs of needs and self-actualization. The need for self-actualization is the need for a person to be "doing what *he*, individually, is fitted for. A musician must make music, an artist must paint, a poet must write, if he is to be ultimately at peace with himself. What a man *can* be he *must* be. He must be true to his own nature. This need we call self-actualization" (Maslow, 1970, p. 46).

Self-actualization refers to the transformation of potential character traits, abilities, or talents into real ones. This means that the self is in some sense a set of potentials. Maslow has written:

Self-actualization is a matter of degree, of little accessions accumulated one by one. . . . People selected as self-actualizing subjects go about it in these little ways: They listen to their own voices; they take responsibility; they are honest; and they work hard. They find out who they are and what they are, not only in terms of their mission in life, but also in terms of the way their feet hurt when they wear such and such a pair of shoes and whether they do or do not like eggplant or stay up all night if they drink too much beer. All this is what the real self means. They find their own biological natures, their congenital natures, which are irreversible or difficult to change (Maslow, 1971, p. 50).

Table 16.4

Constructs Dealing with Ego, Self, Identity, and Related Matters: One Column Eliminated

THEORIST	CONSTRUCT				
	Ego	Self-Identity	Ideal	Superego	Other
Maslow		The self that is actualized in self-actualization			
Rogers		Self-concept or Self-structure	Ideal self	(Conditions of worth ?)	
Jung	Ego	Persona or social self part of self-sentiment and			Self
Cattell	Ego strength (C) and Ego	Self-sentiment control (Q3) included in identity	Ideal self sentiment	Superego strength (G) and Superego sentiment and Superego	
Erikson			Ego ideal		I

Here we have a clear view of the horizons both near and distant encompassed by Maslow's concept of the self. The "real self" means both small bodily facts (such as hurting feet or the effects of beer) and ultimate personal destiny (such as mission in life). It means everything in between these frontiers: inner voices (which may mean simply inclinations or urgings as well as occasional "voices"), continuous food preferences, and other features of our interaction and appraisals of everyday living circumstance.

Steps to the Real Self

How do we find this real self? The nine points Maslow gives were mentioned briefly in chapter 1 but bear repeating here somewhat more fully.

1. *Throw yourself into some enterprise.* Become wholly involved and absorbed in it, "go at it 'whole-hog.'" Maslow says the key word is "selflessly." It means that your attention is concentrated so much in the ongoing experience that you forget about yourself. Do it more often. Start small if necessary.

2. *Choose growth, movement, helpfulness, honesty, work.* You can get up or stay in bed. You can do some exercises or not. You can eat nourishing food for breakfast or not. You can work or not. You can help or not. You can be honest with yourself and others or you can deceive. Choose growth.

3. *Close your eyes and really find out if you like it.* If it's wine or liquor or a new food or candy or cigarettes or whatever, taste it first, close your eyes and see how you really feel about it inside. Then only can you know for sure whether you like it or not. Then only can you avoid the phoniness of liking something because your host or your mother or your friend or the label says it is great, really "in," good for you, or served to the Queen of Tartcrosia.

4. *When in doubt take responsibility, be honest.* It means calling something by its real name, not pussyfooting, not bluffing, not playing games. It means dropping the pose. If your persona is granite and your heart is breaking inside, cry. If you know the answer, say so. Don't get it wrong just to be "one of the bunch." If you are strong in a knowledge or belief, be it; if weak, let it be.

5. *Express your own real view of things.* All the first four steps help you do this. They help you know what your destiny is, who your mate in life will be, what is constitutionally right for you. If you look at a painting in a gallery and it puzzles you, say so. Don't be noncommittal, saying, "Very interesting." Maslow says there are too many constraints on our likes and dislikes, from art critics down to the street corner gang. They expect us to think the same way they do, to agree with them. But we must learn to make honest statements expressing what we really feel.

6. *Work hard at doing well whatever you want to do.* Study to become smarter. Do the finger exercises on the piano. Someone said genius is 5 percent brains and 95 percent sweat. Put out effort, says Maslow. The way to actualize your self, your potentials, is bring them into being and into better and better real manifestation. It takes work, daily exercise; you have to look after them, nurture them, encourage them, do everything to help them grow.

7. *Look for joy.* Joy and ecstasy, moments of what Maslow calls "peak experience," typically come to us suddenly. They take us by surprise. All people have such experiences, but many brush them aside as "mystical nonsense." Some people try to live in their lab coats all the time. But self-actualization as a process needs these moments of ecstasy. We must be ready to hear the beauty in music as well as the sounds, ready to see the glory in a sunset as well as the color.

8. *Lift the veil.* As we find out more of who we are, what we like, what our mission is in life, and in other ways open up ourselves to our own gaze, so we find some unpleasant things. They may be unpleasant memories, or wishes, or fears, ways we torment ourselves or tear down others. Ordinarily these are kept under repression. "If the psychoanalytic literature has taught us nothing else, it has taught us that repression is not a good way of solving problems" (Maslow, 1971, p. 49). We must lift the veil on these things too.

9. *Lift the veil on eternity, the holy, the symbolic.* Maslow says our generations have rejected values and the holiness of persons. "Our kids have desacralized sex, for example. Sex is nothing; it is a natural thing, and they have made it so natural that it has lost its poetic qualities in many instances, which means it has lost practically everything. Self-actualization means

giving up this defense mechanism and learning or being taught to resacralize" (Maslow, 1971, p. 49). Maslow sees this desacralizing as a defense mechanism against the feeling of being swindled—by parents, by life, and by cultural values. We must try to recover the sense of "the sacred, the eternal, the symbolic." A medical student at a dissection sees only a concrete brain, a thing. But he could see a marvelous creation. We see a man or woman on the street. But we can see them as persons walking upon the earth, part of a happening under the sun or stars; real in a span of time connected to the future and to the past. For yesterdays and tomorrows ultimately reach out to eternity. Maslow says this will probably be seen as "corny" or "square"; logical positivists will say it is "meaningless." But it is essential for *self-actualization*, he says. Those who mock will stay in their ruts.

Comparison with Erikson's Model

How does Erikson's construct of identity match with Maslow's idea of the self? They are obviously similar in many ways, yet their differences are evident too. For identity rests upon outcomes of crises in psychosocial development and identifications, and upon the fit with social opportunities presented by our time and culture. It is a "sense" of identity, an important stress being placed upon identity *in the context of society.* That seems to go against Maslow's view of the self, which is given before birth and which must be actualized *despite societal pressures to the contrary.*

Part of the difference here can be traced to the component types of theory with which each theorist is working. Erikson's overall theory contains components of structural, causal, and pattern type. Maslow's is primarily a theory of priority. That was his original goal: to find out how people can become better, how to

bring out the good, how to help mankind reach upward to higher levels of human development. Maslow says that self-actualization has priority; it is the first thing we must attend to as soon as food, security, friendships, and respect have been achieved. We *should* strive for self-actualization. Maslow sees that social constraints of many kinds block fulfillment of this goal, and therefore he is more likely to emphasize the hindrance factor of society. Erikson sees the need to delineate the role of the social environment in its entirety, hindering (creating mistrust, doubt, guilt, and inferiority) but also helpful (creating trust, autonomy, initiative, industry) and facilitative (providing the educational, employment, political, and social opportunities within which the many aspects of identity may be established).

Another part of the difference between the two models can be traced to the underlying notions of how the self came to be what it is. Although Erikson includes certain elements of biological potential as contributing to the formation of identity, these elements do not play the major role. On the contrary, the identifications and integrations of inner agencies with the social context make up the major origins of identity. For Erikson, the story of identity formation is essentially a psychosocial story. For Maslow, however, the self that is actualized in self-actualization is given as a set of biological potentials at birth. Thus the construct of identity in Erikson's model and the construct of self in Maslow's model are not similar.

Comparison with Jung's Model

If Maslow's model differs from Erikson's then it also differs from Cattell's. But possibly a similarity exists between Maslow's model and Jung's. Indeed Jung's construct of the self does seem to match Maslow's construct of the self that is actualized in self-actualization. Both encompass daily matters and higher aspirations; both recognize the mission in life (Jung's orientation and meaning) as somehow inherent in the individual before birth. Both acknowledge the force of inborn constitution. Both stress the presence of animal instincts and spiritual striving as given unconsciously, matters to which we must turn our attention. We must listen to our inner voices. Both see the persona as something which probably does not fit the individual and which one must outgrow.

Jung spoke of *individuation* as the process whereby the self emerges as the goal of psychic development. It seems that individuation and self-actualization are one and the same. Maslow's conception of the self that is actualized in self-actualization seems to be essentially the same as Jung's construct of the self.

Rogers's Model: The Self-Concept

In no other theory is the notion of the self so explicitly formulated as it is in Rogers's theory,

> [The words] Self, Concept of self, Self-structure . . . refer to the organized, consistent, conceptual gestalt composed of perceptions of the characteristics of the 'I' or 'me' and the perceptions of the relationships of the 'I' or 'me' to others and to various aspects of life, together with the values attached to these perceptions. It is a gestalt which is available to awareness though not necessarily in awareness. It is a fluid and changing gestalt, a process, but at any given moment it is a specific entity which is at least partially definable in operational terms by means of Q sort . . . (Rogers, 1959, p. 200).

The organized self-concept, according to Rogers, is formed out of individual *self-experiences*, events "in the phenomenal field discriminated . . . as 'self,' 'me,' 'I,' or related thereto." There is also an *ideal self*, which is the self an individual would most like to have, and which in other respects is similar to the self-concept.

In summary, Rogers's self is an organization of perceptions and concepts and values pertaining to the "I" or the "me." It is entirely available to awareness.

Comparison with Maslow's Model

As we recall from chapter 5, Rogers states the importance of being open to experience; the more open people are to their experience the more fully functioning they become, and the less vulnerable. It is quite clear that Rogers believes we *ought* to be more open to our experience, even as Maslow believes we *ought* to become more self-actualized, so Rogers's overall theory contains a theory of priority, as does Maslow's.

Like Maslow, Rogers stresses the impediments that society places in the path of individual development to full functioning. The demands of significant others create conditions of worth that cause failures in awareness and symbolization; as a result people are not as open to experience as they ought to be; their self-concepts become distorted and misrepresent the reality of their experience. Particular self-experiences are denied to awareness or distorted in awareness, so that the total self-concept gestalt includes not only perceptions but misperceptions, not only concepts but some inaccurate concepts.

It has often been said that the two men have similar views, and in fact Maslow states, "Carl Rogers's findings . . . and those of his students add up to the corroboration of the whole syndrome [found in self-actualizing people]" (Maslow, 1971, p. 42). We must respect Maslow's statement and accept the notion that these two theorists have much in common. Yet Maslow has no construct of a specific set of self-relevant symbols in awareness such as Rogers's construct of the self-concept. For Maslow, self-actualization is simply the actualization of biologically given potentials, not of cognitive symbols. So far we would have to say that Maslow refers to the reality of facts about the physical and social self and especially to the potentials waiting to be actualized. Rogers, by contrast, refers to the individual's awareness of those facts or to his distorted awareness of those facts. As Maslow recommends that one be honest, to find out who one really is, Rogers recommends becoming open to all experience.

With full functioning the chief priority, openness to experience is the characteristic that should be encouraged. As a result, the self-concept will come to represent the entire set of real self-experiences with complete accuracy.

It can be seen immediately that the self-concept is "the goal of all psychic development," or at least the perfectly accurate self-concept is such a goal.

The self-concept in Rogers's model may be more or less congruent with the totality of self-experiences but, Rogers says, "If self and experience are incongruent, then the general tendency to actualize the organism may work at cross purposes with the subsystem of that motive, the tendency to actualize the self" (Rogers, 1959, p. 197). Thus, for Rogers, self-actualization is the actualization of potentials in the symbolized, aware self-concept, as contrasted with potentials in the organism. Yet it is precisely such potentials in the organism (biological potentials) which Maslow has in mind when speaking about self-actualization.

It becomes clear that, although Maslow found corroboration of the syndrome of self-actualizing people in the findings of Carl Rogers and his students, that corroboration is not matched by similarity in the two theories. The findings in question presumably refer to changes in personality taking place among successful cases in client-centered therapy.

These changes would be in directions that both Maslow and Rogers would deem good. Both would say that the changes are in the direction of self-actualization, but they would actually mean very different things. Rogers would mean change toward actualization of potentials inherent in the self-concept and its associated ideal self, potentials of which the clients were aware. But Maslow would mean change toward actualization of potentials inherent in the biological givens of each client.

Comparison with Erikson's Model

If Rogers's model is different from Maslow's, then it is also different from Jung's model, which shares a construct of self essentially identical with Maslow's. Can Rogers's model be similar to Erikson's?

Compare Rogers's idea of the self-concept with Erikson's idea of identity. Erikson envisages more dimensions of personality than does Rogers, for the sense of identity is present in consciousness, in the unconscious, and in the behavior as seen by others. Nevertheless the sense of identity as experienced in awareness or consciousness may be closely similar to Rogers's idea of the self-concept. In other words it seems likely that Rogers's self-concept is similar to a part of Erikson's notion of identity. Both emphasize cognitive and emotional components; both emphasize physical and social characteristics; both emphasize relationships of self to others and to other aspects of life (such as the cultural norms and opportunities).

Erikson's construct of identity plays an important integrative role in the personality, going beyond the ego and superego, integrating the ego ideal also. Of course Rogers's construct of the self-concept cannot play a similar role since no structural constructs like the ego and superego exist in Rogers's theory. Nevertheless the self-concept is of central importance in guiding the personality as a whole. It plays an executive role just as much as the sense of identity does. But it does so in such a different way that the "executive" similarity is hardly sufficient to justify concluding that the two constructs are really similar. This seems to be the case even when we take into account the similarities mentioned in the previous paragraph. Despite similarities, then, the overall model proposed by Rogers seems to be so different from that proposed by Erikson that we must conclude that the self-concept and identity are different constructs.

Several Constructs Related to Self

The Ideal Self and the Ego Ideal

So far we have not commented extensively on the constructs of an ideal. It was suggested earlier that Cattell's ideal self sentiment would very likely be integrated along with the self-sentiment, even as the ego ideal is integrated with identity. It seems reasonable to place the ideal self sentiment and the ego ideal in one construct, and this is reflected in table 16.5, along with the pooling of the self from Maslow's theory and the self from Jung's theory.

Table 16.5

Constructs Dealing with Ego, Self, Identity, and Related Matters: Further Condensation

THEORIST	Ego	Self-Concept Identity	Ideal	Superego	Other
Rogers		Self-concept or Self-structure	Ideal self	(Conditions of worth ?)	
Maslow					Self
Jung	Ego	Persona or social self part of — — — — — — — — self-sentiment and Self-sentiment control (Q3) included in identity			
Cattell			Ideal self-sentiment or Ego ideal	Superego strength (G) and Superego sentiment and Superego	I
Erikson	Ego strength (C) and Ego				

Arguments like those applied to consideration of Rogers's construct of the self-concept apply equally to his construct of the ideal self. Indeed the ideal self is a kind of mirror of the entire self, representing the ideally desirable characteristics of all the self. This is quite different from the ego ideal in Freud's or Erikson's theory. So the ideal self in Rogers's theory must remain a separate construct.

The Superego

Rogers's construct of *conditions of worth* refers to conditions under which the individual initially is deserving of positive regard from significant others. Later these become conditions for positive self-regard. There is some similarity to the notion that internalized prohibitions threaten the ego, which is central to Freud's construct of the superego. Conditions of worth, however, are not powered by aggression turned against the self, and several other features are quite different. It seems best to leave conditions of worth separate from the superego construct.

Erikson's Construct of "I"

Erikson writes (1975, p. 107) that Freud's theory did not provide "a comprehensive model of human consciousness." In his studies of religious men like Luther and Ghandi Erikson describes their struggles for complete self-awareness, in which the conscious "I" confronts fundamental problems of existence. Such awareness of the conscious "I," he says, first appears during adolescence, when identity is being fashioned. Is it not that period, he asks, when "the 'I' can first really perceive itself as an existential phenomenon? It does so, as it finds itself both involved and estranged in peculiar states which transcend the identity crisis as defined in psychosocial terms, because such states reflect not only the fear of otherness and the anxiety of selfhood but also the dread of an individual existence bounded by death" (Erikson, 1975, p. 108).

This passage makes plain the distinction between the "I" and the sense of identity. The "I" is involved in states which "transcend the identity crisis as defined in psychosocial terms." What then is the "I"? Erikson writes:

But "I" is nothing less than the verbal assurance according to which I feel that I am the center of awareness in a universe of experience in which I have a coherent identity, and that I am in possession of my wits and able to say what I see and think. No quantifiable aspect of this experience can do justice to its subjective halo, for it means nothing less than that I am alive, that I *am* life. The counterplayer of the "I" therefore can be, strictly speaking, only the deity who has lent this halo to a mortal and is Himself endowed with an eternal numinousness certified by all "I"s who acknowledge this gift (1968, p. 220).

The "I," then, is a center of awareness and felt self-assurance; it is a subjective "halo" or surrounding light of personal knowledge. Lest there be any doubt concerning its spiritual nature, Erikson continues:

. . . only a multitude held together by a common faith shares to that extent a common "I," wherefore "brothers and sisters in God" can appoint each other true "You"s in mutual compassion and joint veneration. The Hindu greeting of looking into another's eyes—hands raised close to the face with palms joined—and saying "I recognize the God in you" expresses the heart of the matter. But then so does a lover by his mere glance recognize the numinosity in the face of the beloved, while feeling, in turn, that his very life depends on being so recognized (1968, p. 220).

Comparison of the "I" and the Self

Like the construct of the *self* in Jung's theory, Erikson's construct of "I" carries an aura of spirituality and an image of relatedness to God. However the "I" is not in any way a "goal of psychic development," nor an expression of the total psyche. It appears moreover to be entirely conscious, whereas the self is only halfway between conscious and collective unconscious even when individuation has proceeded a long way toward completion. So although they are evidently related in some way, the "I" and the self do not seem to be essentially similar constructs.

Conclusion

Table 16.5 seems to be as far as we can go in eliminating redundancies among constructs dealing with ego, self, identity, and related matters. There are ten different constructs in table 16.5, as compared with twenty-one entries in table 16.1.

Are there five different models represented in table 16.5? I believe there are not. With the exception of the "I," the models of Cattell and of Erikson employ closely related constructs. Indeed, these constructs are essentially the same, with the further exception that Erikson's construct of identity includes and goes beyond the self-sentiment. Jung's model includes the single construct in Maslow's model, namely the self that is actualized in self-actualization. Rogers's model is different from the others. So we see only *three* different models are represented in table 16.5.

Are these three different models also com-peting models? It would seem that they are in competition, since presumably each is addressing the totality of facts encompassed by notions of ego, self, identity, and related matters. This is speculation, of course, because we would really need to spell out the exact model object studied in each case. Doubtless there would be differences in many particulars. For example, perhaps Cattell has never taken into consideration the meeting and greeting of two persons who say to each other, "I see the God within you." In the overall set of facts considered, however, it seems quite likely that each model is addressing a number of facts in common with every other model. Such facts would include the person's reference to his or her own body, to capabilities, to social image and presence, to participation in the social context, to personal destiny, and so on.

It is obvious that more detailed analysis needs to be done. It seems likely, however, that such detailed analysis can progress faster with only three models and ten constructs than it could with five models and twenty-one constructs.

From a practical point of view, it seems that a person wishing to understand the matters of ego, self, identity, and so on, could select either the Rogers, or the Jung-Maslow, or the Erikson-Cattell model and get a firm grasp on the relevant concepts.

Comparing Erikson's "I" and Jung's Ego Constructs

We did not make a direct comparison of the construct of "I" formulated by Erikson and the construct of **ego** formulated by Jung. It would be interesting to make this comparison.

Some essential similarities (if any): _____

_____

_____

_____

Some basic differences (if any): _____

_____

_____

_____

Conclusion from the comparison: _____

_____

_____

_____

_____

Summary

The constructs pertaining to ego, self, identity, and related matters from five different theories were examined in order to find similarities wherever possible. The twenty-one original constructs were reduced to ten by a process of eliminating redundancies and pooling constructs where the one seemed to be a part of the other.

It was found that only three distinct models need to be considered: the Rogers's model, a Jung-Maslow model, and a Cattell-Erikson model (which includes Freud's model).

In the next chapter we shall consider a theory of personality in which there is *no* model of self-reference, namely Eysenck's theory. Eysenck's theory will raise for us the question: Do we really need *any* model of ego, self, identity, and related matters? I think that a thorough answer to this question will take a lot of work. In the meantime perhaps each reader can think about it and arrive at his or her own tentative conclusion.

INTRODUCTION

Introduction to Eysenck's life and work
  Eysenck's life and professional career
  Studies of psychiatric casualties
  Factor analysis
  Two powerful dimensions: extraversion and
    neuroticism
Eysenck's approach and method
  Science does not have to deal with all the
    complexity
  Free-wheeling theories are useless
  There are no firmly established facts relevant
    to scientific personality theories in psychiatry
  The meaning of established facts: quantitative
    data, properly analyzed and replicated
  Behavior a function of body's structures and
    processes
Eysenck's theory of structure
  Dimensions of personality
  Measurement through the Eysenck Personality
    Inventory
  The meaning of neuroticism and extraversion
Eysenck's theory of cause
  Biological model of neuroticism
    Emotions, the brain, and autonomic nervous
      system
    Neuroticism and hypothalamic excitability
    Neuroticism and Spence's construct of **drive**
    Drive and the Yerkes-Dodson Law
    Prediction from the model
  Biological model of extraversion
    Excitatory and inhibitory potentials in the
      cerebral cortex
    Theoretical model of extraversion-introversion:
      role of reactive inhibition
    Predictions from the model
  Genetic origins of personality
    Studies of identical and fraternal twins
    Genetics of psychoticism: sequences of
      hypotheses and tests
Accomplishments of Eysenck's theory
  Extensive applications
    Behavior therapy
    Drugs and personality

Critique of Eysenck's theory
  Critique of assumptions behind genetic
    analyses
  Critique of explanations using brain functions
  Critique of use of conditioning principles
  Accuracy, power, fruitfulness, and depth of
    the theory
  Critique of Eysenck's position on scientific
    theories
Workshop 17 Studying extraversion with lemon
  test
Summary

17

Eysenck's Functional Theory of Personality Structure and Causal Dynamics

H. J. Eysenck was born in Berlin in 1916. At the age of eighteen he went to London and studied psychology at the University of London. Charles Spearman had established a tradition of mathematical approaches to psychology there. Professor J. C. Fluegel, the well-known psychoanalyst, was Senior Lecturer. Eysenck followed Spearman's tradition of mathematical sophistication tempered by an awareness of urgent social needs to which psychology could be applied. From J. C. Fluegel, who was also an experimental psychologist as well as a practicing psychoanalyst, Eysenck derived an appreciation for the importance of manipulative experiment aimed at the resolution of critical issues concerning the analysis of human behavior. Eysenck was not at all impressed with psychoanalytic theory itself, however, and in fact has become one of its most outspoken critics.

Eysenck obtained his Ph.D. in 1940. England was at war; and emergency hospitals had been established outside the city to prepare for the saturation bombing London later was subjected to. Eysenck was appointed to one of these emergency hospitals at Mill Hill, to which several thousand enlisted men and women were sent with a wide variety of symptoms. The majority, however, appeared to suffer from symptoms of anxiety, depression, hysteria, and hypochondria (overconcern with health, along with some imaginary health problems). The precipitating causes of breakdown appeared to be roughly the same in most cases: hardship of army life and discipline; being separated from home; and being confronted with demands to perform tasks for which they were not well suited in physique, intelligence, or temperament. Everyone had to cooperate in the war effort, to "pass the ammunition," but some found it too heavy, some could not learn the necessary habits, and some found it personally repulsive. The stress engendered in persons having these reactions was sufficient to produce disability of a mental and emotional nature.

What underlying personality would react in such a way to wartime conditions? These people were not confronted for the most part by the actual dangers of war, such as bullets, mines, and bombs. Rather the abnormal living conditions, and deprivations from accustomed sources of security were sufficiently stressful to cause problems. As a group they showed little strength of will power, little real purpose in life, and much worry and moodiness, along with a glum but hysterically excitable outlook on life (Eysenck, 1947, pp. 2-3).[1]

In the attempt to understand this very large problem of incapacitated people, a systematic psychological research study was begun under Eysenck's direction. As a first pass, psychiatrists who interviewed all admissions were asked to rate them on thirty-nine traits such as history of civilian unemployment, history of mental abnormality in the family, membership in groups, hypochondria, muscle tone, anxiety, headaches, and so on.

Following Pearson's method of factor analysis (see chapter 15), Eysenck studied intercorrelations among thirty-nine traits for seven hundred patients. Patients suffering from epilepsy or other diseases involving physical disorders were omitted from the sample, so that characteristics of a purely personality origin could be examined. The general factor appeared to be one of neurotic tendency or neuroticism (N) and the first bipolar factor appeared to be a dimension which contrasted anxiety and depression at one end with hysteria at the other end. Thus the first factor measured the severity of neurotic disorder regardless of the kind of disorder; the second factor measured something related to the kind of symptoms displayed by the patient.

Eysenck named the hysterical end of the second dimension *hysteria* and the opposite pole *dysthymia*. In defining dysthymia, he wrote that it refers to a collection of symptoms which often go together: anxiety, reactive depression, and obsessional tendencies (1947, p. 37).

A review of the literature showed agreement that dysthymia corresponded with Jung's concept of introversion (see chapter 12) since both displayed characteristics of being more subjective, engaging in more cerebral than behavioral activity, and having more self-control. The picture of extraversion seemed correspondingly related to that of hysteria: more objective, more behavioral than cerebral activity, and less self-controlled. While recognizing that the sample was composed entirely of neurotic subjects, Eysenck concluded that the second factor represented the dimension of extraversion-introversion within a neurotic population; he felt it probably would hold up as a dimension when studied among normal subjects. Subsequent research proved that it did. Moreover it was shown that the two dimensions of neuroticism (N) and extraversion-introversion (E) were sufficient to characterize a substantial proportion of the individual differences among normal and abnormal populations alike.

The two dimensions of E and N thus provided Eysenck with a powerful and economical basis for classifying personality. What exactly was the nature of these dimensions? Were they created by differences in upbringing? By differences in inherited constitution? How did they function? What mechanisms in the nervous system mediate differences in N and E? Are there any other major dimensions of closely similar breadth and importance? Such questions arose early in Eysenck's career as a research scientist. He has pursued them vigorously ever since.

He was made Reader in Psychology in the University of London and Director of the Psychological Laboratory of the Institute of Psychiatry, Maudsley Hospital, University of London. When a department of psychology and a professional chair were established in the Institute in 1955 Eysenck was named the first occupant of this chair, a position he still holds.

---

1. I am grateful to Professor Eysenck for reading and commenting on an early draft of this chapter.

Eysenck's Approach and Method

Eysenck's theory has been criticized as too limited, too poor in concepts to really deal with the richness of human personality. Eysenck rejects this criticism as unscientific. Science does not have to deal with all the complexity. It does not need the usual collection of un-substantiated (but "rich") concepts that Freud and others have devised. What science needs is facts, he says. In his inaugural address (1955) Eysenck described his approach to science and the direction his research would take in the ensuing years. He compared psychology with physiology, the latter being the science upon which the practice of medicine must rest. In a similar way psychiatry, which aims to cure psychological diseases and disorders, must look to psychology for its scientific support. Eysenck quotes extensively from Emil Kraepelin, the eminent German psychiatrist who introduced principles of systematic classification based upon clinical observation and psychological experiment. Kraepelin deplored the tendency among psychiatrists of his day to engage in free-wheeling theories based upon fanciful ideas. "In our psychiatric case conferences we constantly find a superabundance of individualistic brilliance, an undisciplined arbitrariness which finds sufficient room for its games only because as yet the slow advance of real science has not narrowed down the possibilities sufficiently" (quoted in Eysenck, 1955, p. 4).

Kraepelin ridiculed these free-wheeling theories in psychiatry. By contrast, he said, no self-respecting specialist in medicine would propound a new theory of physiology "which did not base itself on facts laboriously acquired and tested in the laboratory. . . ." If there are no such facts in psychiatry at present, then someone must get them before the theories are spun. Eysenck proposed that the psychologist should be that someone. As physiology is the pure science undergirding medicine, so should psychology be for psychiatry. The psychologist should conduct basic ". . . experiments in an endeavor to build up more far-reaching hypotheses and theories, and trying to link up general psychological knowledge with the specific problems of the psychiatric clinic . . ." (1955, p. 4). He contrasted this view of the psychologist with a view then prevalent in the training of clinical psychologists in America. There the intention was to produce a clinical psychologist who assisted psychiatrists by doing diagnostic testing and sometimes by doing psychotherapy under psychiatric supervision. Such principles, Eysenck said, make three assumptions: 1) that psychiatric theory is well developed and supported by facts; 2) that applications of this theory in psychotherapy and related treatments have been proven to be valuable; and 3) that diagnostic testing through projective techniques (like the TAT) is actually useful.

What shall we make of these assumptions? Surely Freud's theory (chapters 9-11), Jung's theory (chapter 12), and Rogers's theory (chapter 5) are well supported by factual observations and essentially correct? Surely the application of psychoanalysis, Jungian analysis, or client-centered therapy are of proven value? Surely the projective techniques do get at underlying personality dynamics?

Many psychologists and psychiatrists, not to mention most intelligent lay observers, are likely to answer such questions immediately, one way or the other. They assume the assumptions are correct or they assume the assumptions are incorrect. Eysenck's first approach to such questions is to examine the relevant scientific literature. On this basis, he concludes that the available evidence fails to prove any special efficacy of psychoanalysis or psychotherapy, and also fails to show that projective techniques have any special value as diagnostic tools. The three empirical assumptions made by America's clinical psychologists are not supported by the facts.

Eysenck's famous challenge to clinical psychology in America (1952a) produced a long series of attempted rebuttals and experiments aimed at showing that psychotherapy does have special effectiveness.

What about the first assumption, that psychiatric theory is well advanced; is it basically correct? Of this assumption Eysenck wrote:

> The truth surely is that no such general theory or theories exist at present, or indeed could exist at the present stage of our knowledge. Scientific theories are generalizations from firmly established empirical facts which make possible the prediction of new and hitherto unknown facts; where there are few, if any, firmly established facts we cannot, in the nature of the case, have theories of that kind (1955, p. 5).

Eysenck's challenge is serious. Is it true that no such general theories exist at present, or indeed could exist at the present stage of our knowledge? The theories concerned include all or most of those represented in this book. Eysenck seems to be saying that they cannot exist because there are insufficient "firmly established facts" from which to generalize. Let us ask two questions about Eysenck's statements. First, is he correct in asserting that the only theories which are scientific are theories which generalize from firmly established facts? Second, what does Eysenck mean by a *firmly established fact*? We shall take up the first question in the critique section of the chapter, below. For the present, let us see what Eysenck means by an established fact by examining the illustrative example he gave at the time of his inaugural address (1955, pp. 7-16).

For fifty years prior to 1955 there were two views of the relationships among major types of psychological disorder, neuroses and psychoses. In the classical view neuroses and psychoses were qualitatively different, but in the Freudian view they were qualitatively similar although quantitatively different: psychoses were simply more severe disturbances of the same general kind as neuroses. In the Freudian theory, then, neuroses would come midway between normality and psychosis on a single dimension of severity of illness. But in the classical theory that would not be the case. No resolution of this fundamental problem had been achieved: psychiatrists and others could believe whichever they preferred or according to whichever authority they respected most. While sheer psychiatric observation of patients had produced the opposing viewpoints it seemed powerless to make a decision between the two. Neither view could be considered "a firmly established fact" nor was it simply a theory based upon such facts; the facts, whatever they are, are presumably not susceptible to either theoretical interpretation with equal cogency. Can psychology contribute a solution? Can it establish the facts once and for all? Eysenck set out to show that it can.

First, a study of the symptoms and case histories of one thousand patients in the Maudsley Hospital had produced a matrix of correlations among forty different items. Factor analysis revealed that the items fell into two distinct clusters. The first showed the presence and previous history of anxiety, neurotic traits in childhood, lifelong symptoms of hysteria, and so on. Such traits were clearly recognizable as the pattern of neuroticism (N). The second cluster contained items referring to delusions, hallucinations, impairment of thinking, disturbances of mood, and family history of psychosis. There seemed little doubt that this cluster referred to psychosis (P). Moreover, two orthogonal factors yielded a very good fit (see chapter 15) to the data of the two clusters of traits, showing that the clusters are independent of each other. This means that a person can become more and more psychotic without becoming in the least neurotic, and vice versa. Severity of illness with respect to neurosis is quite different from and independent of severity of illness with respect to psychosis. This statistical result is consistent with the classical theory but inconsistent with the Freudian view of these disorders.

Since one study of ratings is apt to be too subjective, Eysenck reports on two quite different studies bearing upon the same problem. In the first, twenty subjects from each of three groups, normal, neurotic and psychotic, were given four psychological tests. In one test the subject's visual acuity was measured in almost exactly the same way that all of us have our eyes tested once in a while. In another test a form of tachistoscope was used. Subjects looked with one eye through a hole in which a shutter would open for brief periods ranging upward from .01 second. Through the hole they could see a definitely recognizable but not familiar object placed against a white screen. One object was a small statue (head and shoulders), for example. The shutter was opened for successively longer periods until the subject correctly identified the object. Subject groups were equated for age, sex, and intelligence.

A *weighted, composite* score was produced by multiplying each test score by a certain constant, and adding the results for all four tests. The constants were chosen so that the resulting composite score would show the largest possible differences between the groups. Such a combination is known as a *canonical variate*. After everything is accounted for by the first canonical variate there may or may not be sufficient score variation in the data to produce a second combination— a second canonical variate, orthogonal to the first. The appearance of a significant *second* canonical variate would support classical theory; its absence would support Freudian the-ory. In fact, two canonical variates were obtained, supporting the classical theory.

The utility of the second dimension can be illustrated in the following way. If you have only one score series, running from 0 through 10, say, then the best way to discriminate between groups is to take cutting points. For three groups we would need two cutting points, say C1 at 2.4, C2 at 3.6. That divides the score range into three parts. In Eysenck's data (1955, p. 13) the best cutting points on the first variate would yield these frequencies for each group.

	Up to C1	C1 to C2	C2 and above
Normals	16	4	0
Neurotics	3	10	7
Psychotics	0	6	14

This procedure is diagrammed in figure 17.1, part A. If a subject has a score between C1 and C2 what would you say is that subject's most likely diagnostic group? On the evidence there are 4 chances out of 20 that the subject is normal, 10 chances that the subject is neurotic, and 6 chances that the subject is psychotic. The decision is not very clear.

A single score is like a single line, extending in one direction only. Now if we add a second score, which extends in a direction at right angles to the first, then we have not a line but an area, not just one edge of the field, but the whole field. If in a football game all you knew about the position of the players was their distance from the goal line you would not be able to tell whether they were in center or on either wing. To know exactly where the players are you have to know their positions in both directions—how far they are from their own goal line and from the center to the left or right wing. In the same way we use the second variate to help us place our test subjects more exactly. Instead of cutting *points* we now have cutting *lines* drawn

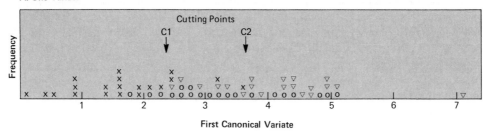

A. One Variate

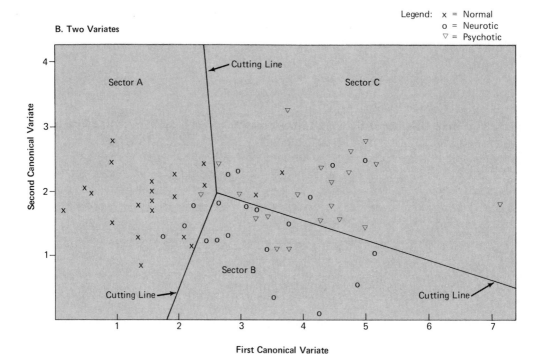

B. Two Variates

Legend: x = Normal
         o = Neurotic
         ▽ = Psychotic

Source: Modified from diagram given by Eysenck (1955, p. 13)

Figure 17.1. Classifying subjects using only one canonical variate (A), and using two canonical variates (B)

through the total area, giving us three sectors altogether:

	Sector A	Sector B	Sector C
Normals	18	0	2
Neurotics	3	12	5
Psychotics	1	4	15

This procedure is diagrammed in figure 17.1, part B.

We can do the same thing as before with the central sector. Here is a subject whose score on the first variate and his score on the second variate make him fall in Sector B. The decision as to his diagnostic group is somewhat clearer now. On the evidence, there is no chance that the subject is normal; there are 12 chances out of 16 that the subject is neurotic, and 4 chances that the subject is psychotic.

In order to make a direct comparison with the single variate situation, look at the diagonal cells, the largest ones in each set: they are 16, 10, and 14 with one variable; they are 18, 12, and 15 with two variables. Taking into account the numbers in the columns of each table, there is clear improvement of discrimination when we add the second variate. Again, that means that the classical theory is more correct; the Freudian theory is inconsistent with the data.

A replication of this result was obtained in a much larger experiment, carried out by Sybil Eysenck (1955), using six objective tests and more than 220 subjects.

With two replications of controlled experiments, each providing results consistent with previous factor analytic work and all supporting the classical theory as opposed to the Freudian theory, we gained some firmly established facts and a decision on one problematic issue that had plagued psychiatry for fifty years. The theory of continuity from normal, through neurotic, to psychotic must be rejected; the theory of qualitative differences between neurotics and psychotics must be provisionally accepted. The existence, moreover, of two dimensions, one for severity of neurosis and one for severity of psychosis, seems to be an established fact. Upon such facts further theory can be developed.

At the front of the book containing Eysenck's inaugural address (1955) is a quotation from Sir Francis Galton, which states that a branch of knowledge can assume the "status and dignity of a science" only when the phenomena in question have been "submitted to measurement and number." Throughout the remainder of this chapter we shall see how this dictum has constantly guided Eysenck's

work. We shall consider his theory of structure and his theory of cause. We shall examine some of his theoretical models which invoke functions of the brain, of the autonomic nervous system, and of heredity. In these models behavior is seen as a function of the body's structure and processes. Behavior as a function of the environment is explained through conditioning and learning, and certain other areas of general experimental psychology. Finally we shall consider the accomplishments of Eysenck's theory. These have ranged across psychotherapy, behavior therapy, crime, education, and drugs.

Eysenck's Theory of Structure

As we have seen already, Eysenck's first analysis of psychiatric ratings led to the conclusion that two dimensions of personality could be found among the 700 enlisted men studied. These dimensions were interpreted as neuroticism (N) and extraversion (E). In later work (Eysenck, 1952b; also studies reported above from 1955), in samples of more severely disabled patients, it was found that two dimensions again were required to account for the variations among individuals: N, as before, with a new dimension, psychoticism (P). Putting these results together we have a three-dimensional view of the structure of human personality.

Actually we should add one more dimension: intelligence. Eysenck accepts the dimension of general intelligence as established by Charles Spearman (1927). Thus his complete view of personality structure holds to a four-dimensional representation. Although he has done most of his own work in the establishment of N and E, in recent years time has also been spent on the study of P. For the purposes of analyzing most normal populations, however, the psychoticism dimension is not much in evidence. There is very little variation on this dimension among a normal population. We shall return to P briefly in a later section on genetics. For the present we shall concentrate (as Eysenck has done for twenty years) on the dimensions of N and E.

Through a long series of trial sets of items a brief questionnaire has been developed which measures N and E. Known as the Eysenck Personality Inventory or EPI (Eysenck & Eysenck, 1968), this instrument has just fifty-seven items, each answered by checking Yes or No. Some of the items look similar to the following questions:

1. Do you find that you often cannot concentrate when you want to?
2. Do you have periods of great energy and other periods of feeling sluggish?
3. Do you sometimes get specially depressed without obvious reason?
4. Do you daydream a lot?
5. Do you like to be at really lively parties?
6. Do you like to have lots of friends?
7. Are you generally slow and cautious in your actions?
8. Do you make new friends only when someone else takes the initiative?

A hypothetical factor plot for these items is shown in figure 17.2. Yes answers to the first four would score 1 point for neuroticism; Yes answers to 5 and 6 would score one point each for extraversion, while yes answers to 7 and 8 would score one point each for introversion. Notice the symptoms of mental distraction and of emotional instability in the neuroticism items. One main manifestation of extraversion is sociability (items 5 and 6) and another is impulsiveness (shown here as lack of impulsiveness, indicating introversion, in items 7 and 8). There has been debate whether these two components are separable dimensions of sociability and of impulsiveness, but evidence seems conclusive that they are not separable components but two highly correlated (.5) aspects or manifestations of extraversion. Surprisingly, correlations with the

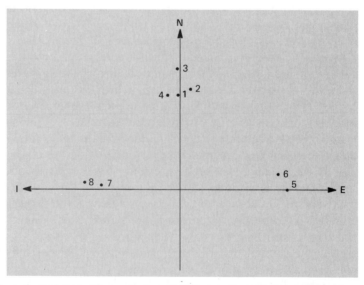

Figure 17.2. Plot of hypothetical factorial results for eight items: four for **Neuroticism**, four for Extraversion-Introversion

Lemon Test of extraversion (Corcoran, 1964) show sociability items and impulsiveness items, as well as some energy and activity items, almost equally correlated (Eysenck & Eysenck, 1969, pp. 141-154).

In the Lemon Test, four drops of lemon juice are applied to the subjects' tongue and the amount of saliva produced is compared with the amount produced without lemon juice. The smaller the difference, the more extraverted. This measure correlates highly (.71) with scores on E from EPI. Introverts produce substantially more saliva to the lemon juice.

The EPI, in earlier or final form, has been given to over 40,000 subjects in England, the United States and other countries (in translations where necessary). It has high reliabilities (over .8 for both N and E), and essentially zero correlation between the scores of E and N. Extensive evidence of validity has been found. Much of this can be illustrated by the comparison of occupational classes and abnormal groups, as in figure 17.3.

Figure 17.3 presents in graphic form the positions of various groups in the two-dimensional space of N and E. Note that the three abnormal groups are all substantially higher than the four normal groups. Note that the abnormal groups range from higher extraversion for hysteria to lower extraversion for the anxiety and obsessional neuroses, confirming the very first findings on the Mill Hill Emergency Hospital sample over twenty years earlier. Note that salespeople exceed other classes in extraversion, as would be expected.

Neuroticism is defined briefly as a general tendency to respond excessively with emotion and to be liable to neurotic disturbances such as anxiety reactions under stress. *Extraversion* is defined briefly as the general tendency to be sociable, outgoing, and given to impulsive thought and action. The structure of personality is made up of these two ingredients, ac-

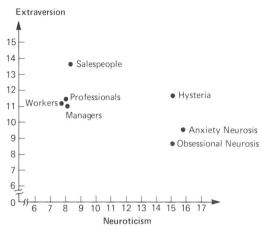

Figure 17.3. Positions of various groups with respect to their means on N and E of the Eysenck Personality Inventory. Each group is composed of both men and women, and the group mean ages vary between 30 (hysteria) and 44 (managers). Basic data from Eysenck and Eysenck, 1968, by permission.

cording to Eysenck. That is, every person has a certain amount of N and a certain amount of E. These amounts are measurable, as for instance through use of the EPI.

Some readers may think this is too simple an account of the structure of personality. We must recall from chapter 6 however that simplicity (as opposed to complexity) is not one of the useful criteria for evaluating theories. Accuracy is much more useful since it means that generalizations are likely to be true. For example, it might appear fantastic that the Lemon Test should measure extraversion so well. Who would have guessed it? The author of the test (Corcoran, 1964) reasoned that salivation would be more responsive among introverts. Such reasoning requires a theory that goes beyond the notions of low sociability, low impulsiveness, and so forth. One might say these are descriptive characteristics of behavior. Readiness to salivate is not an overtly apparent characteristic, but is more obviously connected with physiological functions. Nevertheless, both outgoing characteristics and salivation characteristics can be explained by reference to the same mechanisms in the nervous system. We shall now turn to the theories of cause Eysenck has formulated in his attempt to elucidate such mechanisms.

Eysenck's Theory of Cause

Eysenck's theory of cause holds that either some body function related to one or more specific organ systems is responsible for observed behavioral phenomena or that related psychophysical systems are responsible. Eysenck's position regarding scientific validity requires, however, that such hypothesized systems be established in experimental laboratory work in general or physiological psychology. From this basis specific theoretical models are designed.

Biological Model of Neuroticism

It has long been realized that emotions have bodily components, as when we flush with anger, go cold with fear, or feel our hearts leap with joy. These physiological manifestations of emotion are connected to working of the autonomic nervous system. Recently it has been shown that part of the middle brain is closely connected with emotions also: the so-called *limbic structures* (Maclean, 1970). One particular part of these structures, known as the *hypothalamus,* appears to control emotions through its control over the pathways to the autonomic nervous system. But the hypothalamus itself is stimulated by a variety of inputs, coming from sense organs (as when a young man sees an attractive girl) and from various other parts of the brain. According to Eysenck (1967, pp. 234-238), experiments indicate that damage to different parts of the hypothalamus produces abnormal functioning in one or other of the two divisions of the autonomic nervous system, the sympathetic

and the parasympathetic. Depending upon the nature of this abnormality the person experiences different emotional states. Thus there appears to be a direct connection as follows: hypothalamus → autonomic nervous system → emotions.

It has also been shown that excessive stimulation of the hypothalamus produces so much discharge into the cerebral cortex (as well as into the autonomic nervous system) that the person's attention and conscious discriminations are seriously affected.

Certainly the picture of neuroticism we have seen above would lead one to suspect that subjects with high N have a considerable amount of uncontrolled (and mainly negative) emotions. Eysenck proposes a causal connection between functioning characteristics of the hypothalamus and the level of neuroticism as measured by the EPI. Specifically he suggests that a higher level of N is associated with a lower threshold for excitation of the hypothalamus. That means that the more neurotic person is one whose hypothalamus is more easily stimulated to excessive discharge.

This theory has a large number of immediate implications. A higher discharge from hypothalamic centers would mean more emotionality and more general level of *drive* in the sense intended by Spence (1956). The notion that excessive discharge from the hypothalamus interferes with cortical functioning corresponds to the so-called Yerkes-Dodson Law, which states that performance will improve with increasing levels of drive up to an optimum point, but that further increases in drive lower the level of performance. What this law implies is that there can be excessive levels of drive, such that perceptual and cognitive coordination functions are impaired.

If this entire causal theory is correct, then people with different levels of neuroticism should have different patterns of performance, especially as shown in tasks of differing complexity. In more complex tasks it will be easier for interference with cortical functions to take effect. Figure 17.4 illustrates these general relationships. Results consistent with these expectations have been achieved in a number of studies. Jensen (1962) found that the error rate for high N subjects increased sharply when stimuli for paired-associate learning tasks were presented at twice the usual rate. Presenting the pairs of words to be remembered at twice the usual speed would make the task more complex. Low N subjects did not have more errors under the faster presentation. As seen in figure 17.4 this arrangement would cause the performance of the high N group to decrease sharply as the task is changed from easy to difficult. By contrast the low N group (shown as Stable in figure 17.4) should have hardly any difference in performance as the task changes from easy to difficult. If anything their performance might improve somewhat. This was found to be the case in Jensen's study.

Another study (Doerr and Hokanson, 1965) divided children into high and low emotionality on the basis of heart rate. Here again

it would be predicted that high N subjects (those with fast-heart-rate) would lose efficiency if their level of emotionality were increased by frustration, but low-heart-rate subjects should increase efficiency of performance under frustration. The situation is illustrated in figure 17.4. Whatever resting level of drive, emotionality, or neuroticism each subject has before frustration will be increased by the effects of the frustration. In figure 17.4 the high-heart-rate group is represented as N (more neuroticism) and the low-heart-rate group is represented as S (stable). The results were in accordance with these expectations.

Not all experiments suggested by this theory have had consistent results. Eysenck states (1967, p. 49): "Most of the studies are positive . . . but there are always other studies which give negative results or which are at best inconclusive." This means that the theory generates models which are only partly accurate. Additional factors, as yet unidentified, must be working to mask the main influences under certain conditions. The task of establishing the nature of these other influences and the conditions under which they

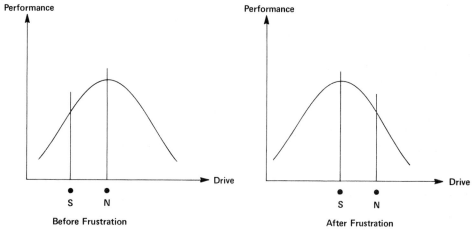

Figure 17.4. Theoretical implications of raising drive level for low emotionality (S = stable) and high emotionality (N = neurotic) subjects

exert a masking effect must be determined by future theoretical work and experiment.

Biological Model of Extraversion

Eysenck's causal model of extraversion-introversion holds that it reflects the balance between excitatory potentials and inhibitory potentials in the cerebral cortex. Eysenck first advanced this theory in 1957, and in 1967 added that the reticular formation (part of the lower brain) is also implicated in a feedback loop with the cerebral cortex. However, as he points out (1967, p. 75), it is possible to consider the concepts of excitation and inhibition in a nonphysiological way, namely as part of a formal psychological theory such as that of Hull (1943). Eysenck's statement of the theory is predicated upon the well-known fact that the cerebral cortex exerts inhibitory controls over lower brain centers. Many people know what happens when a little alcohol gets into our cerebral cortex: We loosen up and become either much gayer or more depressed, more aggressive or more fearful, depending upon our individual dispositions. At all events, lowering of the alertness levels of our cerebral cortex interferes with its usual inhibitions over our lower (emotional) brain centers. So when the cerebral cortex is excited, it exerts controls over the lower brain centers thereby inhibiting them. But when the cerebral cortex is inhibited, it no longer exerts controls over the lower centers, thus letting them get excited.

With that topsy-turvy fact in mind, we can now state Eysenck's theoretical model of extraversion-introversion. The more extraverted subject is one in whom "excitatory potential is generated slowly and in whom excitatory potentials so generated are relatively weak . . . [and] in whom reactive inhibition is developed quickly, and in whom strong reactive inhibitions are generated, and in whom reactive inhibition is dissipated slowly . . ." (Eysenck, 1967, p. 79).

We must pause for one more clarification. *Reactive inhibition* is a kind of inhibition first described by Hull (1943), but broadened somewhat by Eysenck to mean a tendency for any mental activity to produce a condition in the organism which is opposed to continuation of that activity. That state is the inhibition; it is *reactive* in the sense of reacting to the activity. In a very broad analogy, you know how you can get bored with some task like scanning the sky for a comet that is supposed to come into view but doesn't. Here the scanning activity would produce its own reactive inhibition, its own resulting state or condition which is opposed to the continuance of that scanning activity. Some people get bored more easily than others—reactive inhibition is generated more quickly and more strongly and lasts longer in them. They are the extraverts.

Perhaps the reader can form an intuitive understanding of the model. Someone who can sit brooding over his or her own thoughts for a long period of time must not be generating much reactive inhibition; that person must be introverted. Someone who can hardly sit still most of the time and needs crowds of animated friends around to provide new stimulation is the kind of person in whom thinking or paying attention builds up reactive inhibitions quickly and strongly. Because the inhibition inhibits continuance of that particular activity one turns to another activity; that also quickly arouses its own great quantity of inhibition so they have to go to the next mental activity as soon as possible, and so on. These are the extraverts.

In sum, the theory holds that extraverts have an excitation/inhibition balance in favor of inhibition; introverts have an excitation/inhibition balance in favor of excitation. It is obvious that such a general theory, locked into vast sectors of learning theory and other aspects of general experimental psychology, is able to generate extensive predictions.

One of the predictions was that made by Corcoran (1964), as mentioned earlier in connection with the Lemon Test. He reasoned that if introverts have a greater balance in favor of excitation, their state of arousal should be higher; the outputs from glandular organs should be greater when given a constant amount of stimulation. In two separate samples of subjects Corcoran showed that administration of four drops of lemon juice to the tongue produced twice as much saliva in introverts as in extraverts.

Reasoning that introverts would differ from extraverts in activities where performance is highly dependent upon inhibition, Eysenck (1971) has made a number of highly specific predictions concerning the rate of classical conditioning. He notes that both the work of Pavlov and more recent neurophysiological evidence suggest that inhibition accumulates during unreinforced trials, that is, those trials in which the conditioned stimulus is presented but the unconditioned stimulus does not follow. Recall Pavlov's classic experiments in pairing a tone (the conditioned stimulus or CS) with a burst of meat powder (the unconditioned stimulus or UCS), given very shortly after the tone sounds. After a number of trials the sound of the tone alone is sufficient to make the dog salivate. Now if the UCS is presented on every trial (100 percent reinforcement) very little inhibition will build up; but if reinforcement is given only 50 percent of the time then substantial amounts of inhibition will build up. So Eysenck's first prediction is that, since introverts get rid of inhibition fast and extraverts retain inhibition longer, when 50 percent reinforcement is given (so that inhibition has a chance to build up), the extraverts will not condition as well as the introverts.

Second, weak UCS are liable to generate inhibition also, because of the rapid adaptation that can occur to weak stimuli. Hence, when the UCS is weak introverts should condition better than extraverts.

Third, experimental and physiological evidence suggests that the higher excitation levels of introverts would enable them to react faster when the interval between CS and UCS is shorter than the optimal length of .5 seconds.

Eysenck reports an elaborate experiment carried out in the Maudsley Laboratory by A. Levey, in which these precise conditions of theory were tested out. Each condition was set up in the most favorable way for introverts (50 percent reinforcement, weak UCS, and short intervals between CS and UCS); and also in a way most favorable to extraverts (100 percent reinforcement, strong UCS, and longer intervals). The task was eyelid blink conditioning, in which the UCS is a puff of air onto the eye. Eight groups of subjects were given forty-eight trials each, and the curves of acquisition of the conditioned response were plotted separately for subjects scoring high and low on the Extraversion scale of the EPI.

The results were very clear. In every condition theoretically expected to favor the introverts they did in fact condition faster and reach a higher frequency of conditioned responses. In those conditions not expected to favor the introverts either little difference appeared between the two groups or the extraverts conditioned better.

Among the eight groups studied, one group received the conditions favorable to introverts in all three respects: 50 percent reinforcement, weak UCS, and short intervals; one other group received the conditions unfavorable to introverts in all three respects: 100 percent reinforcement, strong UCS (stronger puff), and long interval (.8 secs). Comparison of these two groups should produce the most dramatic differentiation between high and low E subjects, of course. Indeed it did. For the group with conditions all favorable to introverts, these subjects reach 46 percent conditioned responses by the thirtieth trial; by that same trial the extravert subjects have shown no evidence of conditioning at all! In contrast, under the conditions all unfavorable to introverts, these subjects have achieved far less percentage of conditioned responses than the extravert subjects (Eysenck, 1971, p. 507).

These results, then, are closely in accord with theoretical expectations. Eysenck points out that many studies which have failed to obtain the expected difference in conditioning rate between introverts and extraverts are studies in which the precise conditions have not been met. The study by Levey shows exactly what happens when conditions are met for the superiority of introvert conditioning and what happens when they are not met. The data presented for the two groups with all three conditions favorable to introverts or all unfavorable reveal another' interesting fact. The introvert subjects actually tend to condition at about the same rate in both groups. But the extravert subjects are very different: In the one group they show no conditioning by the thirtieth trial, but in the other group they show close to 80 percent conditioning by the thirtieth trial. This seems to make it clear that the crucial difference between introverts and extraverts with respect to conditioning lies in the inhibition component. For, as the reader will recall, the theory states that extraverts have a balance of excitation/inhibition in favor of inhibition. When you allow their inhibitory potentials to accumulate they fail to condition even after thirty trials; when you arrange it so that their inhibitory potentials have no chance to accumulate they show 80 percent conditioning after thirty trials, almost twice the rate attained by introverts.

Researchers continue to amass evidence concerning the inhibitory potentials of extraverts and their effects upon performance under a variety of conditions. In one of the latest of such researches, for example, Brebner and Cooper (1974) showed that extraverts missed more signals and had slower reaction times to low rate but regular signals. This suggests that extraverts would be less helpful as technicians monitoring heart beats during major surgery, or in similar circumstances.

Genetic Origins of Personality

What causes one person to have a low threshold of response in the hypothalamus and another a high threshold? Why does one individual have balance in favor of excitatory potentials, another a balance in favor of inhibitory potentials? Two broad possibilities suggested in the past are: 1) either the traits are inherited and the individual was born that way, or 2) environmental influences produced the pertinent characteristics.

Eysenck (1967, pp. 187 ff.) has reviewed a large number of relevant studies conducted during the past forty years. On balance these studies tend to support the first hypothesis; they indicate the likelihood that neuroticism, extraversion, and psychoticism (the tendency to become ill with a disorder such as schizophrenia) are all inherited to a good extent.

The logic of genetic studies rests upon the known amounts of genetic relatedness to be found in different pairs of persons. For example, unrelated persons presumably have no genetic relatedness. Such pairs would be found by picking one person at random from the population, and then picking another person to be paired with the first, but picking this second person also by a random process. At the other extreme we would find two persons who were born from a single egg, *identical* twins. If we measure all the subjects on E and find that the identical twins are more similar to each other than the unrelated pairs, then we have initial evidence that the trait of E is heritable to some extent. That is, since identical twins have far more similarity of genetic endowment than unrelated pairs of persons, then if we find that identicals also have far more similarity in some characteristic such as E, it is reasonable to suppose that the similarity is due to the genetic source. (See also Appendix D.)

It is possible that environments are more similar for identical twins than for unrelated persons, so it is customary to compare identical twins with *fraternal* twins, twins not born from the same egg. Presumably there is much more similarity in environments for fraternal twins reared in the same home than for unrelated persons reared separately.

But it might be argued that identical twins look so much alike that their parents treat them more similarly than they would a pair of fraternal twins. So it would perhaps be best to study both fraternal and identical twins *reared apart,* that is, placed separately in foster homes. This kind of study has been carried out also. Evidence from all sources suggests strongly that E, N, and P have genetic origins to a large extent.

The methods of modern biometrical genetics have most recently been applied to N, E, and P by Eysenck and his associate Lindon Eaves, a geneticist at the University of Birmingham (Eaves & Eysenck, 1975; Eaves & Eysenck, 1976a, b). Their paper on the genetics of psychoticism is especially instructive for the tight sequence of theoretical models it provides. Using a twenty-five-item scale measuring P, they received returns from several hundred identical and fraternal twins. Among the identical pairs some were male and some were female; among the fraternal pairs some were both male, some were both female, and some had one member of each sex in the pair. That provides a total of five different kinds of pairs:

male identical twins, female identicals, male fraternal twins, female fraternals, and both-sex fraternals. From these questionnaire data and knowledge of the type of twin involved, Eaves and Eysenck try to determine whether genetic effects are as strong as or stronger than environmental effects in producing psychoticism as measured by their twenty-five-item scale.

We shall describe just three models, increasing in complexity, beginning with Model 1:

Suppose, for example, all the individual differences in P were due to environmental influences which were quite specific to individuals, and shared with no one else, not even with members of the same family. We could equate the phenotypic variation observed for P* in a given population simply to a parameter, E_1, say, and write:

$$\sigma^2_p = E_1$$

A simple test of this model is, of course, provided by observation of individuals reared in the same family. If all our variation were due to quite unique individual experiences we would expect individuals in the same family to be no more and no less alike than families of individuals produced artificially by grouping our test scores at random (Eaves & Eysenck, 1976b, p. 10).

Model 1 implies that there is the same quantity of variation within families as between families. Since all of the influential environmental impacts are specific to individuals, under Model 1, this means that parents do not exert an influence over their children which makes one family different from another. So the variation between twins coming from different families will not have any increment from parental or other sources of influence which affect all children in a family equally. The only thing making children of different families different from each other is the very same thing that makes children within any one family different from each other: the environmental influences specific to individuals, E_1.

Is it true then that the variation between families is no greater than the variation within families? It is not, as the data show. In each of the five groups of twins the variation between families is at least 25 percent greater than the variation within families. In fact among male identicals the between-family variation is about 1.38 times as large (Eaves & Eysenck, 1976b, table 3).

Our hypothesis predicted that the two types of variation would be the same. In fact they were substantially different. Therefore the hypothesis was wrong. In this way Eaves and Eysenck prove that Model 1 cannot be supported.

The next model, Model 2, assumes that, in addition to the influences specific to individuals, E_1, there are in fact environmental influences exerted by parents and other forces within a family, and these influences would be commonly felt by all children in the family. This means that there would be differences between families, so that twins coming from different families would vary as a result of these environmental forces (E_2) as well as the E_1 influences. But, since we are supposing that only environmental influences affect variation in psychoticism, P, this means that the variations between identical twin families will be the same as the variation between fraternal twin families. Is it? The answer is no. Among males, for instance, the variation between families of identical twins is 3.6 times that between fraternal twin families. So we must reject Model 2. The quantities $E_1 + E_2$ do not account for all the variation in P scores.

What are we left with? Assuming that fathers and mothers have mated on an essentially random basis (at least regarding gene similarities), Eaves and Eysenck go on to spe-cify Model 3, which allows a genetic component to contribute greater similarity between the two members of an identical twin pair than that between the two members of a fraternal twin pair. That is, the variation within fraternal families should be larger than that within identical families, because fraternal twins have only 50 percent of their genes in common, whereas identical twins have 100 percent in common. For Model 3, the variation in P scores is assumed to be due to $E_1 + E_2$ *and* G_1 which is degree of genetic difference. The results obtained by Eaves and Eysenck show that genetic effects are about twice as influential as environmental effects in accounting for psychoticism, thus supporting Model 3.

Accomplishments of Eysenck's Theory

The accomplishments of Eysenck's theory have been so widespread that it would be difficult to find an area of psychology not influenced at least to some degree by his work. Applications have included education, social attitudes, political psychology, criminology, clinical diagnosis, and behavior therapy. He has done research on topics of suggestibility, figural after-effects, reminiscence, practice effects, problem-solving, drive, conditioning, verbal learning, and anxiety. He has worked on problems of urgent social concern such as smoking and health, the effects of psychotherapy, the measurement of intelligence, and the effects of drugs on behavior. Eysenck's theory has changed the course of clinical psychology in England, Canada, the United States, and other countries; although part of this influence must be attributed to his penetrating attacks on psychoanalysis and psychotherapy, along with his prescriptions for proper experimental design in research on therapy. Also his work on behavior therapy (Eysenck, 1960; Eysenck & Rachman, 1965) and his launching of a new journal, *Behavior Research and Therapy,* have been potent influences on clinical psychology.

Eysenck's theory has stimulated the work of many other scientists (compare Franks, 1963; Gray, 1973), and has provoked controversy with many others whose own theories are in one way or another challenged by Eysenck's position. For example, in the next chapter we shall examine briefly the long-standing difference between Cattell and Eysenck concerning the proper number of factors to extract in factor analytic research on personality.

Application to Drug Study. As an example of Eysenck's accomplishments in various fields of applied psychology I have selected a series of studies on drugs and personality.

We have seen that genetic sources of influence contribute substantially to individual differences in N, E, and P. We have seen that sound biological theories have been advanced for the brain functions underlying differences in these traits. Eysenck proceeds to the hypothesis that drugs having known stimulant (uppers) or depressant (downers) effects will have predictable consequences with respect to N, E, and P.

For example, Eysenck states (1967, p. 265) that "the prediction would be that stimulant drugs lead to greater arousal and hence to more introverted behavior, while depressant drugs lead to greater inhibition and hence to more extraverted behavior."

Eysenck cites a study by Franks and Trouton (1958) in which eyelid conditioning is carried out under a stimulant drug (Dexedrine) and a depressant drug (Amytal). As would be expected from the theory, the Dexedrine group perform much like introverts under conditions favorable to introverts (see above), conditioning fast and reaching a frequency of conditioned responses roughly

three times greater than the Amytal group. The latter performed much like extraverts. (However it may be questioned whether this is true "conditioning," for reasons to be discussed in the critique section.)

In another approach to this topic, Eysenck argues as follows (1967, p. 265): "introverts, being in a comparatively high state of cortical arousal, would require less stimulant drug than extraverts to reach a specified state of excitation, but would require more of a depressant drug to reach a specified state of inhibition."

This prediction means that people will respond differently to a given amount of a given drug. How they will respond depends on their level of extraversion. If they are high E people they can take more of an excitant drug such as Dexedrine before getting excited; but it will take relatively little depressant drug such as Amytal to make them sedated. If they are low E people (introverts) then a very little Dexedrine will give them a high; while it will take more Amytal to sedate them. Thus Eysenck's general theory generates a specific theoretical model of drug effects. If it is correct, it will obviously be important for anyone who is invited to take drugs to know beforehand whether she or he has a high or low E score.

Is the model correct? Eysenck's view (1967, p. 314) is that some evidence supports the model, but other evidence suggests that the precise conditions may be more complicated than the model implies as presently stated. Nevertheless a number of very careful studies have provided evidence which does seem entirely consistent with Eysenck's theory. For example, Shagass and Kerenyi (1971) measured the sedation threshold by objective changes in the electroencephalographic (EEG) recordings taken from patients' scalps. It was shown that greater amounts of Sodium Amytal were required to produce sedation in introverts. Laverty (1971) also injected Sodium Amytal and found a higher sedation threshold among introverts, as would be predicted from Eysenck's theory. Moreover, Laverty administered a test of extraversion before and after the injections. He found that the extraversion scores did increase after the Amytal (but not after injection with an inert substance called a placebo). Thus as required by theory, it takes more depressant drug to produce sedation in introverts; and giving a depressant drug makes people more extraverted!

Critique of Eysenck's Theory

There are many aspects to Eysenck's theory and accordingly many different kinds of critiques must be considered. The question of whether Eysenck is correct in extracting only two (or at most three) factors from personality questionnaire data must be left for chapter 18. There we shall consider the arguments raised by Cattell, who maintains that such a small number of factors is contrary to the demands of the data. The emphasis that Eysenck places upon genetic and neurological sources of causal influence upon behavior means that his own theory of personality must be judged in part on the adequacy of those bodies of science. In the case of behavioral genetics there is far more uncertainty surrounding inferences to genetic determinants of human behavior than there is when the organism is infrahuman. Thus one reviewer of the manuscript for this book commented on the assumption made by Eaves and Eysenck (see above) that fathers and mothers have mated on an essentially random basis. The reviewer commented that people are known to mate on a nonrandom basis with respect to certain characteristics such as intelligence. That is, males of higher intelligence have usually married females of higher intelligence; those with lower intelligence mate with others of lower intelli-

gence. Therefore the assumption of random mating is implausible and the derivations based upon that assumption are implausible. Although genetics is a well-developed science, its application to human behavior has yet far to go before it can offer anything like a sound set of established generalizations upon which to base theory.

Another example comes from Eysenck's reliance upon principles of neuroanatomy and neurophysiology. Although the invocation of brain mechanisms in the explanation of neuroticism and extraversion brings those matters into testable condition it does not actually guarantee testing. In fact, quite different and competing theories of the underlying brain functions can be generated (compare Gray, 1973), and tests of the alternatives may prove exceptionally difficult. Not enough is really known yet about brain functions to assume that translation of a psychological hypothesis into neurophysiological terms will straighten out the pathway to proof.

A final example may be drawn from Eysenck's usage of the principles of conditioning in some of his theoretical models. In brief his theory postulates that strong conditioning is responsible for neurotic symptoms and that weak conditioning is responsible for delinquent and criminal behavior. This theory has the immense advantage of tying such esoteric matters back into general psychology, and thereby permits application of the armamentarium of experimental conditioning techniques in the treatment of neurotic disorders and in penal correctional systems. Strong conditioned responses can be weakened and weak conditioned responses can be strengthened. But it seems that Eysenck's employment of conditioning principles assumes that they are established for humans when in fact there is serious doubt about this. One very able analyst has recently reviewed the literature on conditioning and concludes that "There is no evidence for operant or classical conditioning in adult humans" (Brewer, 1975). All the apparent evidence is illusory, he says: Subjects appear to be conditioned but in fact they are not; they are simply "developing conscious hypotheses and expectations about the experiment, and . . . these produce the resulting 'conditioning.' " Brewer concludes his review of the evidence with the statement that the entire system of stimulus-response psychology was built on a foundation of sand. Whatever strengths Eysenck's theory has derived from his reliance upon stimulus-response theory and conditioning theory must purchase for him all the attendant weakness as well. The most important of these is inaccuracy when applied to human beings.

Evaluation of the Theory

This does not mean that all of Eysenck's theory is inaccurate, of course. In much of the physiological part of his theorizing we probably do not know at this time whether it is accurate or not. His models of neurosis as drive appear to be quite accurate so far as the experimental evidence goes; and other models employing formal psychological constructs (such as inhibition, without the physiological meaning) appear to have substantial accuracy. The essentially descriptive constructs of neuroticism and extraversion as measured by the EPI are highly accurate, of course, since they are so closely tied to sound measurement procedures.

The mixture of accuracy, inaccuracy, and unknown accuracy which characterizes Eysenck's theory is not uncommon among theories of personality. But the sheer extent of work which has been done (by Eysenck and his associates and by other scientists working on aspects of his theory) has earned the theory the right to a very high score on power, which is the number of accurate applications. The extent of fruitfulness of this theory has

already been suggested in the section on its accomplishments: It it highly fruitful.

Now we come to our final criterion, depth of understanding. On one hand the theory is deep in providing insight into physiological and neurological mechanisms and also into some psychological mechanisms, but the insight it provides into "conditioning" mechanisms is probably spurious. Here the criterion of accuracy has a bearing on the criterion of depth. We can be clear about depth when accuracy is established or unknown; what do we do when it is known that explanations are inaccurate? I believe we should simply ignore those parts of Eysenck's theory which rest upon conditioning in humans. The remaining psychological and neurophysiological models offer a good deal of scientific insight, but hardly any everyday or clinical insight. Eysenck's constructs do not appeal to someone trying to understand oneself or a friend. His constructs are not intended to do that, as our discussion of his method and approach at the beginning of this chapter clearly shows.

This brings us finally back to Eysenck's challenge to theories of personality (those that lie back of psychiatric theory). These theories include almost all that are presented in this book, especially Freud, Jung, and Rogers. Eysenck claims that no scientific theories exist at present because "scientific theories are generalizations from firmly established empirical facts," and there are insufficient such facts in existence. We may agree that such generalization is one sound part of many scientific theories. But is it a completely necessary and sufficient condition? When we consider the several component theories in one overall theory, we find they may be any one of six varieties: structure, cause, function, pattern, system, or priority (see chapter 8). A theory of structure, for example, proposes a set of basic elements combined in certain ways to make up the whole of whatever is observed. This kind of theory uses certain known facts and puzzles, and then offers a *new* hypothesis; it makes a leap in proposing a new structure, but the leap itself is not a generalization from established facts. If it were it would not be a leap. A causal theory may propose hidden causes, which also are obviously not generalizations from known facts. A causal theory may also propose a causal relation between two already known facts, the relation having previously been unrecognized. Perhaps this is the kind of theory Eysenck has in mind, but it surely is not the only kind of theory which deserves the name "scientific." While a pattern theory (of classification or temporal order)

must also have some facts to work with, the essence of the theory is not itself a simple generalization from facts but rather a proposal for new relationships among sets of facts.

In short, while we must accept the proposition that scientific theories can be generalizations from established facts, they are obviously not limited to that. It seems to me that Eysenck's challenge cannot be supported, because there can be component scientific theories which are not generalizations from established empirical facts. In addition, laboratory work is not the only route to facts, although Eysenck erroneously implies that it is. But that's another issue.

Workshop 17

Studying Extraversion with the Lemon Test

You might like to try the Lemon Test on yourself. No doubt there are many ways to set it up, but here is a way that requires only household equipment. Take a Q-tip or other double-tipped cotton swab, a 12-inch length of thread or dental floss, a bottle of reconstituted lemon juice, a teaspoon, and a watch or clock with a second hand. The thread or floss should be tied firmly to the center of the swab, adjusted so that when you hold it up the swab hangs perfectly horizontal. Place a small amount of juice in the teaspoon and practice pouring a drop at a time into the palm of your other hand, until you can get exactly four drops. Set the juice well aside for now to avoid smelling it; but make sure there is enough for four drops in the spoon.

Procedure. Swallow three times, then immediately put one end of the cotton swab into your mouth letting it rest against the tip of your tongue just behind the front teeth, with lips closed around it. Count thirty seconds (count one minute if you do not have a second hand). Remove swab. Put four drops of lemon juice into your hand and lick it up. Immediately place the **other end** of the swab in the same position in your mouth. Count thirty seconds and remove (or one minute if you did that before).

Expected results. After the first end of the swab has been in your mouth it will have absorbed saliva and will no longer hang horizontally. Intake of lemon juice will affect your saliva production. After the second end of the swab has been in your mouth the swab should hang closer to horizontal if you are an extravert, but should swing over sharply and hang down in the other direction if you are an introvert, because you will produce more saliva.

Daily variation in extraversion-introversion could be studied by repeating the Lemon Test each day for a week. Before doing that you might wish to refine the method to get an exact measurement of how much the swab departs from horizontal. How could you do that?

Is there some aspect of your daily living that you believe results in a greater or lesser degree of extraversion or introversion in your personality for a period of time? Perhaps it is Monday morning that turns you in on yourself a bit more. Perhaps it is a weekly (bridge game) that turns you outward a bit more. If so you should find it reflected in the Lemon Test, and you could check this out by establishing a baseline measure of several days in a row (say Tuesday through Saturday) and then obtaining a critical measure on Monday morning (or after the bridge game). Once again you should think through the matter of measurement very carefully and be sure to record the results each time.

Description of your materials and procedure, including especially any innovations or refinements:

_____

_____

_____

_____

_____

Results:

DAY	1	2	3	4	5	6	7
TIME	____	____	____	____	____	____	____
ANGLE*	____	____	____	____	____	____	____

*Angle may be recorded by drawing with lemon juice end of swab to the right:

_____ or may be recorded in degrees or some other way.

Summary

Eysenck's theory of personality structure holds that there are three main traits or dimensions of personality: extraversion-introversion, neuroticism, and psychoticism. The first two have been explored most, and may be assessed reliably by the Eysenck Personality Inventory (EPI). Eysenck's theory of cause holds that behavioral phenomena are caused by characteristic brain functions or other neurophysiological functions, or alternatively by psychophysical systems, the constructs of which have been established in the laboratories of general or physiological psychology. Thus his theoretical model for the causation of high degrees of neuroticism holds that the hypothalamus is likely to discharge excessive stimulation into the cerebral cortex and into the autonomic nervous system in such cases. Alternatively, high neuroticism may be due to excessive drive level (a psychophysical systems construct). His theoretical model of extraversion-introversion holds that extraverts are characterized by a balance of excitation versus inhibition of the cortex in favor of inhibition; the balance is exactly the opposite for introverts.

These theoretical models have been very

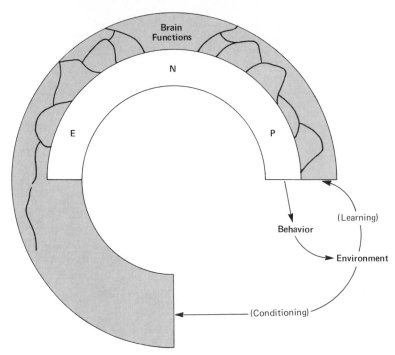

Figure 17.5.   Definition of personality implicit in Eysenck's theory

fruitful and have produced a large number of accurate hypotheses, so that the theory has great power. That part of the theory which appeals to principles of conditioning, however, should be ignored because the evidence for conditioning in human beings is extremely questionable. The theory has provided much insight to scientists but not to the general public or to clinicians. Of course it is not in-

tended to provide insight into everyday experiences and interactions. Figure 17.5 illustrates the implicit definition of personality in Eysenck's theory.

In the next chapter we shall have the opportunity of comparing certain aspects of Eysenck's theory with Jung's theory and with Cattell's theory.

INTRODUCTION

Comments on comparing theories
Freud and Cattell: Two theories of structure
   Factor C: Ego strength
      A measure of output efficiency of the ego
   Factor G: Superego strength
      Some divergences between psychoanalytic
        theory and factor analytic results
      Possible resolutions in the theory of strata
   Factor Q4: Ergic tension
      A measure of damming of the libido and
        other instinctual sources of energy
   Conceptions of structure
      The agencies of ego, superego, and id
      The factor analytic description of differences
        between individuals in the influences of
        these agencies
Jung and Eysenck
   Jung's theory of types
      Extraversion and introversion mechanisms
      The four mental functions
   Concepts of extraversion-introversion compared:
      different but nonetheless comparable
   Patterns of characteristics compared
   Behavior characteristics compared: divergences
      are not real, only apparent
   Two theories of cause compared: are not in
      competition
   Methodological assumptions compared: deep
      differences found
Cattell and Eysenck
   Two theories of structure and cause
   The problem of number of factors
      Rotational technique and order of factoring
   The problem of reliability and factor
      intercorrelation
Workshop 18   Comparison: Freud and Eysenck
Summary

18

Comparing Four Theories: Freud, Cattell, Jung, and Eysenck

When we compare two theories or theoretical models we learn whether they are perhaps the same despite different terminology; whether they are in real competition; or whether, despite possible appearances to the contrary, they are unrelated. In this chapter we shall compare Freud's theory of structure with Cattell's theory of structure, Jung's theory of typological pattern with Eysenck's theory of structure and cause regarding extraversion-introversion, and finally Cattell's theory of structure with Eysenck's theory of structure.

Freud and Cattell

Freud's final theory of structure held that there were two main agencies of personality: the ego and the id. The ego becomes differentiated so that a third main agency also is active within the personality: the superego.

Cutting across these agencies are the three qualitative layers of the consciousness, the preconscious and the unconscious. The ego is mainly conscious and preconscious; the superego is mainly unconscious; and the id is totally unconscious.

The id consists of primitive instincts of sexuality and aggression, along with repressed derivatives of earlier sexual and aggressive strivings. The ego consists of the structures necessary to adapt the organism's behavior to reality demands so that satisfaction of instinctual needs can be met somehow; it also consists of the apparatus of ego-defense mechanisms necessary to keep both instinctual impulses and anxiety under control. Another way of comprehending the ego is to focus upon its composition from identification elements. In part the ego contains the images of other people with whom the person has identified. Such identifications are especially important in the development of the superego, which consists in essence of identifications with the prohibitions and commands of parental authorities.

Thus the id is composed of instinctual impulses in one form or another; the ego is composed of behavior guidance devices, ego defense mechanisms, and identifications; and the superego is composed of internalized moral controls, powered in part by aggression turned against the self. Freud's theory of structure posits the existence of these several agencies operating in various domains of consciousness, the preconscious, and the unconscious, as detailed in chapters 9 and 10.

Cattell's theory, as presented in chapter 15, does not make a complete break with Freud's constructs[1] but it does make a complete break in methodology. Cattell believes that modern methods of factor analysis allow us to see a more differentiated structure of personality than could be discovered through Freud's clinical method. Specifically, large samples of respondents answer large numbers of questionnaire items or react to the stimulus situations of objective tests, and the resulting measures are correlated and then further analyzed to determine the underlying factors which account for the pattern of obtained correlations. Cattell's method brings objective measurement support and further development to those of Freud's constructs which are robust enough to appear in the search procedures of factor analysis. Thus the constructs of ego and superego do receive confirmation. Freud's hypothesis of two main instincts (sex and aggression) is supported only insofar as these have indeed appeared as ergs in Cattell's analysis of motivation structure. But there are evidently more than just two main sources of drive, for Cattell's research shows at least ten ergs. Also there is evidence for more separate constructs than just ego and superego. For apart from intelligence, research on the 16PF shows that there are at least fifteen factors in questionnaire responses, factors such as Surgency (enthusiasm), Radicalism, and so on. Among these are factor C, Ego Strength, factor G, Superego Strength, and factor Q4, Ergic Tension, all of which have special relationship with Freudian constructs.

Factor C: Ego Strength

Cattell writes (1973, p. 160), "[The factor C] pattern in questionnaire items and observer ratings is clearly the reality behind Freud's concept of ego structure strength." He adds, "This dynamic control structure grows from reward by experience of successful control over impulse, particularly by the reduction of the indecision component in anxiety. . . . This trait represents a high ratio of successful expression to drive tension level (hence its negative relation to Q4 in the second-order anxiety factor . . .)" (Cattell, 1973, p. 161).

Cattell stresses that, in accordance with psychoanalytic theory, factor C is low in almost all forms of psychological disorder, including neurotic and psychotic disorders. Such disorder of course would be judged to be a symptom formation, the last resort in an uneven struggle between a weak ego and a strong id or strong superego. Much experimental work has now related source traits to criteria in daily life. For instance it is found that factor C is higher in group participants and in married as compared with unmarried persons; it is further found that factor C is higher in those married people who get more satisfaction from sex. Thus the strength of the ego as measured by factor C is reflected in freedom from disabling psychological symptoms, and in greater ability to secure satisfactions of instinctual needs through social and sexual activities. It suggests that the defense functions of the ego are stronger, since they have not crumbled and been replaced by symptoms. It suggests that the control functions of the ego are intact, since satisfactions are obtained in the real world. It suggests that adequate identification with the same-sex parent has taken place so that the person can successfully engage in marriage.

Altogether the C factor appears aptly characterized as a measure of ego strength. It should be noted, however, that the strength of the ego is not the only feature of the ego

---

1. I am grateful to Professor Cattell for reading and commenting on an early draft of this chapter.

in Freud's theory. For example, the ego is predominantly conscious and preconscious, but nevertheless has some unconscious parts involved especially in repression and other defenses. These aspects of the ego structure, along with the details of identifications and of changes in the ego due to reaction formations and other adaptations are unmentioned in the analysis of factor C. It is as though factor C has captured what is perhaps the most salient *output* characteristic of the ego in terms of its overall contribution to personality: the efficiency with which it performs its chief functions.

Clearly an automobile may be characterized by its *efficiency* in terms of braking distance at fifty miles per hour, its speed on a flat runway after sixty seconds of full acceleration, and so on. Such facts would depend upon engine power, weight of auto, type of suspension, shocks, wheels, tires, and so on. But it would take much further study of these component parts, including their initial description, in order to arrive at a full account of the nature of the automobile. The discovery of a factor for ego strength which is consistent as far as it goes with Freud's theory of the ego is at best a beginning and a challenge to develop further psychometric techniques to isolate and measure aspects of the ego in detail.

Factor G, Superego Strength

It seems that factor G is a measure of the strength of the superego as Freud conceptualized that agency. Cattell (1976) writes that "it behaves indubitably as the superego should, and evidence shows that no other of the twenty or so demonstrated factors do so." In accordance with psychoanalytic theory it is found that factor G is higher in people who have been given more responsibilities, higher in those who have suffered a death in the family, higher in people who reject loose morals, higher in people who are active in church, and so on.

Cattell notes one outstanding difference from psychoanalytic theory about the superego insofar as empirical results with factor G are concerned. It is found in both adult samples and among children that this factor is *negatively* correlated with the second-order anxiety factor and indeed is negatively correlated with factors L, O, and Q4, which are positive primaries in the anxiety factor (Cattell, Eber & Tatsuoka, 1970, pp. 113, 114). He points out that this result is contrary to psychoanalytic theory, which states that a strong superego produces anxiety (guilt) through its demands for instinctual renunciation and through the aggression turned against the self.

Cattell considers this theoretical inconsistency at some length (1973, p. 166) and suggests that the difference lies in the samples of subjects: Freud studied neurotic patients primarily, while Cattell's results have been obtained on people in the normal range for whom the functioning of inner controls does not lead to neurosis as it does in individuals with ego weakness. In normal persons a strong superego is helpful in keeping anxiety at a minimum, perhaps because it lowers the likelihood that the person will get into trouble. But at the upper levels of severity of superego, in cases of severe anxiety neurosis for example, the correlation between strength of superego and anxiety may be positive. This is the essential new fact and interpretation that arises from results with measurements of factor G.

A reviewer of this manuscript pointed out Freud's speculation that women have weaker superegos than men do (Freud, 1925/1961, pp. 257-258). The data on factor G show that in fact the opposite is true; women have a small but statistically significant superiority over men (Cattell et al., 1971, p. 70).

In the overall theory of personality developed by Cattell the source traits are organized into a hierarchic structure, with source traits in higher layers or *strata* exerting broad influence over source traits at lower strata. The higher the stratum the fewer the source traits and the broader the influence exerted by each. Factor G, however, reaches up and joins the second-stratum factor of anxiety in being influenced by a third-stratum source trait tentatively labeled self-criticism (Cattell et al., 1970, p. 124). This fact suggests that Freud's hypothesis might be correct at a higher level of organization than is revealed by the primary source traits or the second-order source traits. This would suggest that a two-process theory of the relationship between moral anxiety and strong superego should be explored. The results of the third-order factor analyses indicate that when anxiety and superego strength are both high, then intelligence and cortertia (cortical or mental alertness) both tend to be low. Putting it another way, if the superego is strong and also the functional intelligence and alertness are impaired, then conditions are ripe to produce substantial increments in anxiety. Precisely such conditions would have brought patients to Freud's treatment.

Factor Q4, Ergic Tension

Cattell states that factor Q4 reflects "the amount of undischarged instinctual energy" (1973, p. 177). Many kinds of frustrations and deprivations are associated with increases in this factor, including low status in jobs and groups, deaths of loved ones, and so on. Exposure to high stimulation, such as working in a supermarket, appears to raise this factor. Frequent job changes also raise the factor, probably because of the high stimulation associated with changes, or perhaps because of the frustrations that lead to change. It also seems that participation in some special activities such as church work tends to decrease ergic tension.

Is factor Q4 related to Freud's concept of the id? Cattell believes it is partly related, since the id is the agency of all instinctual drives according to Freud. It would seem reasonable, however, to expect the strength of the id to vary quite substantially according to heredity. That is not found to be the case for factor Q4: Its coefficient of heritability is only .10, very small indeed.

What then can be the relationship between factor Q4 and the id? Cattell suggests that "ergic tension is not related to high natural drive, that is, to id energy *per se,* but that it constitutes the difference between energy endowment plus stimulation minus discharge" (Cattell, 1973, p. 178). We can represent this as endowment (E) + stimulation (S) minus discharge $(D) = E + S - D$. Thus the variations between persons would result as much from increases or decreases in stimulation and discharge as they would from endowment, or resting level of instinctual energy. Steady stimulation (as from taunts or sexy advertisements) would tend to build up ergic tension. Steady opportunities for discharge (as in competitive sports and stable marriage) would tend to reduce ergic tension.

Factor Q4 is therefore best conceived as Cattell suggests: the amount of *undischarged* instinctual energy. He stresses that this factor must also be partly a *state* as well as a trait. A person might have a relatively stable set of stimulations and opportunities for discharge, thereby creating a trait; the person might nevertheless be subject to occasional increases in level of stimulation or decreases in opportunities for discharge. Therefore it would be expected that this factor would show systematic changes over time, that is, from one occasion to another. Different people would be exposed to different changes in life circumstances, and so their factor Q4 score would go up or down accordingly. Such a result has been found empirically (Cattell & Bartlett, 1971).

Freud would have called such a build-up of ergic tension a "damming of the libido." But in accordance with his later theory he would have had to include aggressive energy in the total pool of energy in the id. Cattell feels that the ergic tension involved in factor Q4 may stem from any and *all* instincts, including the sexual and destructive instincts, but not restricted to them. He therefore says that factor Q4 is only partly related to Freud's concept of the id.

In addition, of course, we would have to note that factor Q4 is another measure of output. It involves not only the id but also the ego, for it is the ego which is responsible for securing satisfactory discharge of libidinal and aggressive energy. It would be expected that a strong ego would secure greater satisfaction, and therefore there should be a negative correlation between factor C, ego strength, and factor Q4, ergic tension. This is invariably found to be true. On large samples of both males and females, for example, Cattell, Eber, and Tatsuoka (1970, p. 114) report correlations of $-.27$ for males and $-.50$ for females.

Since stimulation can be prolonged by inner reverberations (brooding, grumbling, dwelling on hurt feelings or unsatisfied longings) we would expect Q4, ergic tension, to be greater with more suspiciousness (factor L), more proneness to guilt (factor 0), and more sensitivity (factor I). These expectations are all supported by results of correlational analysis (Cattell, Eber, & Tatsuoka, 1970, p. 114).

Conceptions of Structure

Despite the very interesting convergences between Freud's theory and Cattell's there is an important difference of basic conceptualization. For Freud the notion of structure refers to *agencies and qualities*: to ego, id, and superego and to conscious, preconscious, and unconscious qualities or realms. Cattell's notion of structure refers to the factor-analytic structure found in a set of correlations. Thus Freud's conception of structure refers to the parts of an individual personality, or of any individual personality: anyone at all will be said to have an ego, an id, and a superego, with consciousness extending over most of the ego, some of the superego, and none of the id.

But Cattell's concepts of factors are meaningful initially only in terms of the differences between individuals. That is, no individual person would be said to have a factor C or a factor G or a factor Q4. All one can say about an individual person is that he or she has a certain score on a measure of each factor. Typically that score reflects a degree of strength—of ego or of superego or of undischarged ergic tension. Factor C is not a construct of an agency; it is a construct referring to the strength of an agency. Similarly, factor G is not a construct of an agency but a construct referring to the strength of an agency. Factor Q4 reveals the difference even more sharply. It is not a construct of the id; it is a construct of the strength of id pressures which remain undischarged by ego action. It therefore draws upon the working of at least two agencies, the id and the ego.

Cattell's factor constructs do not distinguish between qualities of consciousness in the questionnaire data we have been considering (although related distinctions are made in his work on motivation). Perhaps this is not necessary when dealing with output notions such as strength and so on. Nevertheless it points up the fact that there is a difference of perspective between the two theorists, Freud looking at the absolute nature of deep structure, Cattell looking at the functional influences of such structure in output variables.

Despite these differences, there is evidence for a substantial degree of convergence between the two theories of structure. Cattell has discovered three factors (among others) which rather clearly reflect the influences of the ego, the superego, and the id as Freud conceived these agencies.

Jung and Eysenck

Jung's Theory of Types

After extensive discussion of previous formulations about types, Jung described (1921/1971, p. 330): "those reserved, inscrutable, rather shy people" so different from "the open, sociable, jovial, or at least friendly and approachable characters who are on good terms with everybody, or quarrel with everybody, but always relate to them in some way and in turn are affected by them." Jung believed that everyone can recognize these patterns of traits once they have been pointed out. He called them introverted and extraverted respectively.

Jung described these two opposing pictures as attitude types. From the point of view of his causal theory he maintained that the essential difference between them was that of a direction of libido. In the extraverted person libido reaches out to environmental stimuli and is expended on actions toward those environmental facts and events. In the introverted type the energy is held within the person. Accordingly the extravert is attentive to and interested in things and persons in the environment; the introvert is attentive to and interested in subjective matters, events within the self. The extravert is concerned with what another person wants or what a situation demands. The introvert asks, What does this person or event mean to me?

As described in chapter 12, Jung proposed that extraverted and introverted attitudes are expressed through the four mental functions of thinking, feeling, sensing, and intuiting. In all of these functions the extraverted type is more concerned with action in the world: courses of action based on objective evidence (thinking type); actions in accordance with conventionally accepted values (feeling type); actions serving to emphasize sensory satisfactions of eating, carousing, and so on (sensing type); and actions bringing about change and offering exciting new possibilities and programs (the intuiting type). By contrast the introvert in all function types is more interested in his or her own ideas than in actions: Ideas of philosophy involved in actions and events (thinking type), deeply hidden feelings (feeling type), ideas of the impact of sensory events upon themselves (sensing type), and visionary ideas without implementing action (intuiting type).

Jung proposed that these types are seen first in the conscious domain of the individual. But for every degree of extraversion in consciousness there is a degree of introversion in the unconscious, he said, thereby compensating for one-sidedness in the personality.

Jung maintained that the visible degree of extraversion or introversion could be seen in early infancy in many instances, and he suggested that there were physiological bases of the mechanisms of extraversion and of introversion, though it was impossible in his time to speculate upon their nature. Such influences were not the whole story, however; he felt that family and cultural pressures could constrain a person to be more extraverted or more introverted. He believed that all persons possessed the necessary mechanisms for both extraversion and introversion, and that the balance of the two created the degree of extraversion or of introversion that characterized a particular person. He noted that these patterns did not appear to be associated with social class position nor with being male or female (although there were some associations between sex and function types, with women being more frequent among feeling types, men among sensing types).

Two Concepts of
Extraversion-Introversion

Eysenck's theory of extraversion-introversion is presented in chapter 17. He notes that there have been many similarities in type theories from the time of Galen, a second-century Greek physician. Galen proposed that there were four main types of personality: Sanguine, melancholic, choleric, and phlegmatic. Each comprised a particular pattern of traits; for example, the phlegmatic person is slow and apathetic, the sanguine person is enthusiastic. For each type he also proposed a causal theory, holding that the type was produced by a predominance of one or another "humor" or fluid in the body: Blood for the sanguine, black bile for the melancholic, yellow bile for the choleric, and phlegm for the phlegmatic. Following through the works of Kant, Wundt and other writers, Eysenck shows that the characteristics of extraverts are like those of the choleric and sanguine types, sociable and impulsive, while those of introverts are like those of melancholic and phlegmatic types, serious and controlled. One main predecessor classified the two types as changeable (extravert) and unchangeable (introvert) (Eysenck & Eysenck, 1969, pp. 3-18).

Eysenck reports that the terms *extraversion* and *introversion* had been in use for several hundred years in Europe before Jung's selection of them to capture the main essence of the type patterns he described. Moreover, Eysenck believes that Jung's contribution was mainly negative, in that the relatively clearcut descriptive patterns were made too complicated by the addition of Jung's distinctions among the thinking, feeling, sensing, and intuiting types. Jung's discussion of compensa-

tion in unconscious processes also clouds the issues, according to Eysenck. He states that his own use of extravert and introvert is taken much more from the early work from Galen to Wundt, and reflects more the conception of changeable as opposed to unchangeable types that Wundt introduced. Eysenck writes, "When in the rest of this book the terms *extraversion* and *introversion* are used it should always be borne in mind that they do not refer to the conceptions introduced by Jung . . ." (Eysenck & Eysenck, 1969, p. 21).

It is perfectly clear that Eysenck has not sought to carry on Jung's theory or even to test it.[2] Indeed he doubts that the theory is strictly attributable to Jung. He rejects much of Jung's theoretical elaboration of functions or the unconscious, stating that "by allowing his mystical notions to overshadow the empirical, observational data [Jung] has done his best to remove the concept of personality type from the realm of scientific discourse" (Eysenck, 1970, p. 15).

Patterns of Characteristics

We are left with two clear notions: first, that it is possible to propose patterns of co-present traits which Jung labeled as extravert and introvert and which Wundt labeled as changeable and unchangeable; second, that some causal explanation for these patterns can be offered. Eysenck does not contradict the behavioral parts of Jung's patterns of the extraverted and introverted types, but he does reject the elaboration into thinking, feeling, sensing, and intuiting types, and into conscious and unconscious domains. Eysenck rejects also the causal theory that Jung put forward, namely the theory that extraversion is caused by outwardly directed libido and introversion

---

2. I am grateful to Professor Eysenck for reading and commenting upon an early draft of this chapter.

by inwardly directed libido. Also Eysenck focuses on the dimension between the two poles, the continuum. For his part Jung focused on the patterns at the two ends of the continuum.

Despite the differences in methodology and contextual theory, we may treat these two theories of extraversion-introversion in a strictly comparative light. Does the pattern discovered by Eysenck through factor analytic work match or differ from the pattern described by Jung from clinical observation? To make this comparison we have to focus solely upon the matters of observation upon which they agree. We must consider only the patterns of extraversion and of introversion, omitting discussion of mental functions and conscious and unconscious domains.

If there is agreement on these patterns, then we can ask also whether Jung and Eysenck have the same or different theories of the causes of these patterns.

There is a little matter of slippage that must be cleared up. In Eysenck's factor analytic approach to the questions of extraversion-introversion he is primarily concerned with structure: How many factors are required to account for the observed correlations among test or rating items? And what is the nature of each factor? But in the course of establishing a factor it is inevitable that the investigator will rest upon the correlations among a certain set of items. This means that his inference for a given factor depends upon the empirical observation of a pattern, that is, a pattern of descriptive items grouped according to their correlations among themselves and according to whether they mark the extravert pole or the introvert pole of the dimension.

Behavior Characteristics

As we saw in chapter 17, Eysenck discovered a factor in psychiatric ratings and in questionnaire responses that appeared to be best described as extraversion-introversion. It had such items as liking to be at lively parties, liking to have lots of friends, liking to move around fast, and doing things on impulse a lot. These items appear to be summarized as sociability and impulsiveness in the main, with the more extraverted person showing more of both.

Certainly the sociability component matches Jung's description of the extravert as more sociable, although he emphasized that the sociability was not necessarily of a friendly nature. The impulsiveness component is somewhat more questionable, since, although Jung felt that extraverts pour their energy into action, not all of them do so impulsively. For example, the thinking and feeling types gauge their courses of action rather carefully, the one on the basis of intellectual considerations, the other on the basis of conventional values. Indeed, only the intuitive type seems to have some degree of impulsiveness, at least as Jung described the varieties of extraverted people.

We recall that introverts do put a block between the object and themselves, a hesitation between any stimulus and their response. Meanwhile they evaluate its meaning to them. This results in a certain social awkwardness among introverts. Hence we might say that in Jung's theory introverts are more hesitant, whereas in Eysenck's theory extraverts are more impulsive.[3]

Eysenck and Eysenck (1969, p. 152) have shown that there is no statistical difference between impulsiveness and sociability items in their validity for measuring extraversion-introversion. They took the criterion of an item's correlation with the Lemon Test as a pure measure of the factor. Then they plotted such correlations against the factor loadings

---

3. I am grateful to Dr. Gideon Weisz, who clarified for me this odd relationship between hesitancy of introverts and the apparently higher impulsiveness of extraverts.

of the items on extraversion-introversion. The correlation between the array of correlations with the Lemon Test and the array of factor loadings was +.97; the plot leaves no doubt that impulsiveness items and sociability items are about equal.

It therefore seems possible to disregard the divergence between Jung's and Eysenck's patterns for extraversion and introversion: The difference lies in the presence of a substantial impulsiveness component in Eysenck's pattern. But his results suggest that there is actually no essential difference between items of the impulsiveness kind and items of the sociability kind, at least so far as their loadings on the extraversion-introversion factor are concerned. Since it seems reasonable to align the sociability characteristics in Jung's description of the extravert pattern with those found in Eysenck's pattern, it is perhaps equally reasonable to align the preference-for-action part of Jung's description with the impulsiveness part of Eysenck's.

We conclude that the divergence between the two pattern theories is more apparent than real, so far as the behavioral component of the record is concerned.

Two Theories of Cause Compared

What of the two theories of cause? Jung's theory is that psychic energy flows outward in extraverts and is retained inward among introverts. Eysenck's theory is that the excitation-inhibition balance in the cortex is higher among introverts, or alternatively that the degree of cortical arousal due to activity of the reticular formation is greater among introverts. Are these competing theories? It is not immediately clear whether they are or not.

Both Jung (for example, see Jung 1921/1971, p. 333) and Eysenck point to the influence of genetic factors in creating a more extraverted or a more introverted constitution, Eysenck on the basis of recent good research

evidence (see chapter 17). Jung believed that there were physiological mechanisms underlying extraversion and introversion, though he had no inkling of what these might be at the time he formulated his theory. Eysenck has proposed quite precisely what these physiological mechanisms might be and has been able to derive experimental predictions based upon the theory, many of which have received support from empirical studies (Eysenck, 1967). No such predictions were made by Jung, nor has anyone else attempted to make predictions from his theory.

We are reminded however that Jung theorized first that all energy is derived from solar energy, whether it be physical energies of the body or psychic energies of the personality. He believed that psychic energies are real in their own right but that they have counterparts in physical energies. For Jung, neither is causally prior, and so it seems likely that he would accept Eysenck's hypothesis of greater balance in favor of excitation of the cortex among introverts. Such relative arousal would be a consequence of libido being directed more toward the self than toward the environment. Subjectively it would appear as greater interest in and intensity of inner feelings, sensations, thoughts, and meanings. It would seem, then, that Eysenck's model of introversion-extraversion is compatible with Jung's model; the two are not in competition.

The converse is not true, however; while Eysenck's model may be compatible with Jung's, Jung's total model is not compatible with Eysenck's. The reason appears to be that Jung's theory includes explicit reference to the record of experience in personality and Eysenck's does not. Eysenck maintains, as we recall, that Jung's theory is filled with "mystical notions [which] . . . overshadow the empirical, observational data . . ." (Eysenck, 1970, p. 15). We recall that the entire construct of extraversion in Jung's theory begins with characteristics of consciousness and of compensatory characteristics in the unconscious. The entire set of types rests upon the constructs of functions: thinking, feeling, sensation, and intuition. Of course Eysenck rejects this elaboration of the typology, for it depends upon different functions of conscious experience, and if you reject conscious experience as a whole then you cannot accept constructs referring to its differentiated functions.

Methodological Assumptions

There are obviously some deep differences between Jung and Eysenck with respect to the meaning of "empirical, observational data." Jung argued that the contents of dreams, visions, or fantasies are empirical and observable; that religious strivings are empirical facts characterizing humanity; that many seemingly inexplicable occurrences such as worldwide reports of unidentified flying objects are nonetheless proper topics for scientific study. Jung also believed that his *own* fantasies and visions and dreams and the functions of his own consciousness were empirical data to be recorded and studied systematically. Jung apparently made a methodological assumption that subjective experience is part of nature, part of the proper topics for psychology to study. Eysenck disagrees; he apparently makes the methodological assumption that subjective experience is not part of nature and/or not part of the proper topics for psychology to study. This means that, once we leave the field of observable behavior in describing the patterns of extraversion and introversion, we enter a situation in which the two theorists no longer agree on the model object: Eysenck thinks it has only behavioral features, and Jung thinks it has both behavioral and experiential features. The experiential features are thus the immediate source of difference between them as to the facts to be

explained. Personally I agree with Jung on this matter; and I believe that carefully designed experiments will be able to show that the subjective experience components of Jung's typology have measurable consequences even for behavioral outcomes.

Cattell and Eysenck

The theories of structure formulated by Cattell and Eysenck both put behavior as the dependent variable and both seek underlying (factor) causes. They differ in certain presuppositions and in the final picture of the structure. Eysenck, as we have seen, proposes a structure of two main factors, neuroticism and extraversion, with possibly a third factor, psychoticism, when abnormal populations are under study. By contrast Cattell proposes fifteen factors outside of intelligence. However, Cattell also argues for a stratified model of personality, with the fifteen primary stratum source traits organized into at most eight second-stratum source traits, and these into five third-stratum traits, and so on.

Discrepancies in Procedure

Considering just extraversion-introversion, Eysenck finds one factor; Cattell finds at least four. How can this be if both scientists are employing the same method, factor analysis? The answer is that factor analysis is a *kind* of method: It covers a large range of alternative procedures, not just one procedure. In chapter 15 we examined the difference between Pearson's method and Cattell's method, the former resting with initial extraction of orthogonal factors, the latter rotating to oblique simple structure. Cattell claims to be using more sophisticated techniques, including objective procedures for determining the number of factors (compare Cattell, 1966). Eysenck follows Pearson's method and selects only the first two or three factors for interpretation since the later factors account for too little variance and cannot be measured with any reasonable degree of reliability, in his judgment. Cattell claims, however, that Eysenck's single factor of extraversion confuses second-stratum with first-stratum sources of influence. Obviously these are technical differences, but in this instance such differences have great importance for theory. As we saw in chapter 17, the question of the unitary nature of extraversion has been raised by critics such as Carrigan (1960), and Eysenck has offered experimental demonstrations that his factor is unitary. But Guilford's recent review of the issue (1975) states of this factor that one "is forced to conclude that it is not a factor at all, but a kind of "shotgun" wedding of R (Restraint versus Impulsiveness) and S (Sociable versus Seclusive)." In Guilford's theory R and S are first-order factors; and in his model of hierarchic structure of personality extraversion-introversion is a second-order factor embracing R (but not S) and also T, which is Thoughtful versus Unreflective. It must be noted that Guilford's methods of factor analysis are again different: While extracting more factors than Eysenck he retains an orthogonal structure in rotation.

Guilford's critique of Cattell's factors is no less trenchant. He points out that Cattell's factors have not all been replicated in laboratories of other scientists such as Sells and colleagues (1971) or Howarth and Browne (1971). Also French (1973), in reviewing the literature, has concluded that only four of Cattell's factors have been established through replication: factors C, D, F, and Q3. Factor F, of course, is one of the four main first-stratum factors in the second-stratum factor of extraversion, according to Cattell. To all such criticisms Cattell has correctly replied that the other investigators do not analyze the data in the same way that he does, relying as they do on different methods for deter-

mining the number of factors and on shortcut rotation techniques which do not achieve maximum simple structure (Cattell, 1975). When proper techniques are used, Cattell reports replications of his factors are found in ten different populations (Cattell, 1975, 1976; Cattell and Nichols, 1972; Gorsuch and Cattell, 1967).

What can be concluded from this series of claims and counterclaims? There is the problem of the number of factors; there is the question of rotational technique; and there is the issue of level or order or stratum of personality. Is extraversion one first-order factor? Or is it two or four first-order factors? If the latter, it must be at the second-order. But we have seen that different investigators can arrive at first-order factors which other investigators believe are second-order factors. So it would seem that there has to be some way to decide *independently of the factor analysis* whether a factor is at the first or second order. Simply extracting one set of factors, rotating them to oblique position, and then correlating and extracting a second set of factors obviously is not adequate to provide a clear definition of what factor is at which order.

It must be emphasized that the differences between Cattell and Eysenck are *empirical* differences first, and theoretical second. This means that there can be resolution of the differences by providing for third parties to carry out investigations on agreed-upon populations using agreed-upon test items and analytic methods. It has not been done so far; no interlaboratory contracts have been signed. However, we may not walk away feeling justified in dismissing the whole matter as too controversial to be given serious scientific attention. These issues, unlike so many controversies between Freud, Jung, and other clinical theorists, can be settled *straightaway* by application of known empirical methods to carefully gathered bodies of data.

The Problem of Reliability

Eysenck's criticisms of Cattell have also addressed the question of factor reliability and factor intercorrelation. On the matter of reliability Eysenck notes (1972, p. 266) that varying estimates have been given and that there are different ways of interpreting reliability, including the reliability of correlation between two parallel forms of the same test. Eysenck quotes the parallel-form reliabilities given by Cattell and colleagues (1970, p. 33): The range is from .21 for factor N to .71 for factor H, with a median of .51. These are indeed lower than one would wish if one were convinced that such correlations represented the most important aspect of reliability. But Cattell tends to emphasize *stability*, the ability of the test to order individuals in a similar manner upon a repeated administration of the same test at a later date. Stability coefficients for Cattell's 16PF scales range from .58 (factor B) to .83 (factor H) (Cattell et al., 1970, p. 30), with a median of .78. These values are within the normally acceptable range of stability coefficients.

The truly critical part of Eysenck's argument states that the reliabilities of the individual factor scales are so low and the intercorrelations among those primary factor scales are so high that the several primaries grouped together into a single second-order factor should really be considered to be just one factor. This would reduce the number of factors in Cattell's set to a number closer to Eysenck's. But Cattell counters (1972) that the true number of factors, as estimated by several widely accepted criteria, is shown to be actually more than sixteen in the data of the 16PF on sample after sample. He shows that the low reliabilities referred to by Eysenck are *intentional*, because thereby he is able to obtain higher validity of factor measurement (paradoxically, it seems; but the details are described by Ghiselli, 1964, p. 184).

As for the high correlations among primaries for a given second-order group, Eysenck deals chiefly with the anxiety and exvia groups (1972, p. 267), of which anxiety has the most highly intercorrelated primaries (for factors C-, L, O, and Q4, the median intercorrelation is .61). Compared with a parallel-form median reliability of .51, these intercorrelations are very high, as Eysenck shows. Compared with a stability coefficient median of .78 they are still high, but not enough to conclude that they are measuring the same thing and add no unique information over and above the anxiety second-order factor as a whole.

Still we must think about such high correlations between oblique primary factors. Even if the reliabilities were perfect (1.00) these correlations averaging .61 would be quite high. Would that mean that perhaps after all they should be pooled into one factor measure? It would not for two reasons. First, the evidence states that the four factors exist separately in the data, as part of the more than sixteen factors indicated by the tests for number of factors. Second, high correlation between two variables does not mean that they are the same variable. For instance, height and weight tend to be correlated +.50 in the general population.

If the primary factors are truly different variables despite being correlated on the average +.61, then there must be some way to show that each contributes unique information which is not contained in the measurement of the second-order factor Anxiety. Eysenck has so far specifically challenged Cattell by claiming that the reliability evidence indicates the primaries do not provide unique information. Cattell has countered that the reliability evidence used by Eysenck is inappropriate. In my judgment Cattell is correct in his counterclaim. But then what *is* the appropriate evidence on reliability? Is it the stability coefficient data cited above? If so, then the unique information contributed by each primary would be proportional to the difference between the stability coefficient (average .78) and the square of the correlation between the primary and the Anxiety second-order factor (this probably averages between .30 and .45, but one needs special matrices, the so-called *structure* matrices in the primary factor system, in order to make an exact calculation). It is obvious that we are unable to answer our questions here. But so far as a guess is possible, it seems to me the primary factors in the anxiety second-order group do contribute some unique information, possibly less than Cattell would estimate, and more than Eysenck would estimate. The most important direction to take, it would seem, would be to discover techniques for demonstrating the unique information contributed by primaries in an experiment that does not involve factor analytic methods and does not rely upon estimates of reliability. For the present, and pending such more definitive evidence, it appears that Cattell's view is correct: Apart from general intelligence, the structure of personality has at least fifteen primary factors.

Workshop 18

Comparison: Freud and Eysenck

In chapter 13 we compared certain aspects of the theories of Freud and Jung. In the present chapter we have compared Freud and Cattell, Jung and Eysenck, and Cattell and Eysenck, regarding selected portions of their theories. In chapter 15 we briefly examined a comparison of Cattell's second-order factor Exvia with Jung's construct of extraversion, and further comparisons were made in workshop 15. Thus all possible pairs of the four theorists have so far entered into some comparative analysis with the exception of Freud and Eysenck. What could be compared between them? Several possibilities exist, and you are invited to take one and do a brief comparison:

1. Freud's early neurophysiological theory with Eysenck's neurophysiological theory (chapters 9 and 10 and chapter 17).
2. Freud's constructs of excitation and inhibition with Eysenck's constructs of excitation and inhibition (chapters 10 and 17).
3. Freud's distinction between hysteria, anxiety reaction, and obsessional neurosis in terms of type of anxiety with Eysenck's distinction between these disorders in terms of hysteria versus dysthymia (beginning of chapter 17 and also figure 17.3; (see chapter 10 for Freud's view).

Freud and Eysenck: Comparison with Respect to _____

_____

_____

_____

_____

_____

Summary

There is substantial convergence between the theories of structure proposed by Freud and Cattell. Certain of Cattell's factors appear to measure various output characteristics of the id, ego, and superego agencies.

Jung and Eysenck are in agreement on the behavioral part of the patterns shown by extraverts and introverts, and it seems likely that Jung would accept Eysenck's physiological theory of cause for these patterns. However, Eysenck does not accept Jung's theory of cause in terms of psychic energy. Outside of the behavioral parts of the pattern the two theorists disagree in their formulation of the model object, for Jung includes the record of subjective experience in the patterns and Eysenck does not.

Cattell and Eysenck have competing theories as to the number of factors in the (factorial) structure of personality, and it seems at present that Cattell's theory of fifteen or more factors (over and above intelligence) is more accurate than Eysenck's theory of two or three.

In the following chapters we shall study some quite different approaches to personality than any we have studied so far. Nevertheless it will be possible to see many points of comparison which will provide an emerging sense of continuity. We shall see, for example, that the emphasis upon the environment found in Murray's and Erikson's theories is a major part of Lewin's theory of personality as described in the next chapter.

INTRODUCTION

Introduction to Lewin's life and work
  Lewin's life and professional career
  Role of gestalt psychology
  Behavior is a function of both the person and
    the environment
Life space
  Experienced space and behavioral environment
  Development of life space
  Goals and life space
  Action wholes
  Levels of reality and unreality
    Role of barriers
  Child's level of reality as affected by adult
    leadership style
The psychological environment
  The field
  Individual characteristics and the momentary
    situation
  Valences and needs
  Driving and restraining forces
  Regions of the life space
  Kinds of conflict
  Field of forces
The person
  Needs, regions, and boundaries
  Permeability of boundaries
  Differentiation of structure
  Quasi-needs
  Tests of hypotheses
Accomplishments of Lewin's theory
  Action research and group dynamics
  Viability of assumptions and particular constructs
  Success and failure
  Level of aspiration
    Laboratory studies
    Field studies
    Factors affecting level of aspiration
    Level of aspiration among students
Critique of Lewin's theory
  Critique of Lewin's mathematical formulations
  Commentary on the critique
  Representation of a psychological whole
    Mackinnon's theoretical model of anxiety
    Social wholes
    Accuracy, power, fruitfulness and depth

Workshop 19 Some fields of force: conflict and
  detour
Summary

19

Lewin's Functional Theory of Personality Structure and Dynamics

Kurt Lewin was born in Germany in 1890, was wounded in World War I, and during his convalescence published a paper on how the landscape looks to a soldier in war. He describes it as having a definite directionality: it is dense and impenetrable all along the front line but open and free in the other direction. Everything in the soldier's world is changed by this basic fact. Close to the front, for instance, only pieces of cover or ground of special tactical advantage are of interest. Weapons, shells, and bullets, along with explosions and thumping sounds of war, are the "natural" landscape. Getting straw to sleep on or bread to eat from a farmhouse under these conditions becomes "unnatural."

Young people in love know well the meaning of this change in landscape. There is something quite different about the street where the loved one lives. The world is polarized into places close to and places far from the loved one.

These observations laid the foundation for Lewin's contributions to psychology. Shortly after demobilization he joined the University of Berlin as a teacher, sharing the excitement of the new school of gestalt psychology. Max Wertheimer, Kurt Koffka, and Wolfgang Kohler were revolutionizing psychology. They rejected the prevailing idea that the foundations of mental life were elementary particles, elementary ideas which somehow become associated together to form perceptions and memories. In contrast, they proposed that experience is made up of wholes—*Gestalten*, in the German. The whole is more than the sum of its parts; indeed the shape of the whole gives to the part whatever significance it has.

As an illustration of this view consider figure 19.1. There are two pieces of pie, A and B. Which piece is bigger? You may determine the answer by measuring from point to point within each part using a ruler. A and B are the same size. Their positions in the whole figure influence their apparent size, however, so B *looks* bigger.

If you consider the upper curve in B you can see that it is longer than the lower curve in A. That relationship between the lower curve of A and the upper curve of B is influential in affecting the appearance not only of the upper curve of B but also of the entire piece. There is also an apparent perspective difference. The enclosing V lines are farther away from piece A than from piece B, also making B look bigger than A.

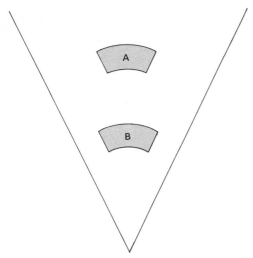

Figure 19.1. An illustration of the gestalt psychology view. Which of the two pieces of pie is bigger, A or B?

Lewin felt that, in addition to such forces in the perceptual field itself, the person's needs and emotions would also affect the appearance of the environment. The soldier's awareness of the line of battle influences his "war landscape" in part because of fear, for example.

Over the years Lewin developed his ideas somewhat independently of the other gestalt theorists. They were more interested in perception and thought. He was more interested in needs and emotions.

When Hitler came to power in Germany Lewin moved to the United States. He taught at Cornell, Iowa and Michigan universities, and at Massachusetts Institute of Technology. His passionate interest in both psychology and democracy led him to work on many projects of an applied nature. He invented *action research*, in which psychology is applied to social problems and contributes to social change. He founded the Research Center for Group Dynamics at M.I.T., thereby instituting the entire subspeciality of group dynamics in social

psychology. He was partly responsible for the creation of sensitivity training, in which business people develop better understanding of the needs and feelings of others through communication with individuals in groups. Marrow (1969) gives a lively biography of Lewin.

In this chapter we will focus upon Lewin's theory of personality. Lewin was also renowned as an experimental psychologist, and personality experiments carried out in his laboratory are widely known and emulated. He introduced many constructs (such as level of aspiration) which have provided fertile fields for other psychologists to study. In the course of this chapter we shall briefly describe a number of his experiments and several of these constructs. We shall also briefly examine the accomplishments of Lewin's theory, especially on the subject of level of aspiration.

Lewin's most important general equation was

$$B = f\ (PE)$$

where B stands for behavior, P for the person, and E for the environment as experienced or perceived. The equation states that behavior is a function of both the person and the environment. Going out to buy a new swim suit is a function of the person's wish to go swimming and of the advertised availability of stunning new swimsuits in the department store. The person and the perceived environment make up the *life space*.

Life Space

The life space is composed of the environment as perceived and also the person perceiving it. This entire space is an *experienced* space, though not everything in it need be clearly perceived. For example, a young child might sense the tension of a nearby adult and be affected by it. That tension would be part of the momentary life space for the child.

Part of the life space is similar to the "behavioral environment" described by Koffka (1935). This basic concept of gestalt psychology refers to the fact that what we perceive and what is actually there can be quite different. One favorite example is the New Yorker, driving on an Arizona highway at night who thought he was going to hit a boulder. It actually was tumbleweed, as his traveling companion, a local, well knew. The distinction between the geographical and the perceived environment is essentially the same as the distinction made by Henry Murray between *alpha* and *beta press* (see chapter 3).

Figure 19.1 provides one opportunity to note the distinction between what is there and the way it appears. Figure 19.2 gives another. What do you think these pictures represent? Figure 19.2A is a chipmunk standing up—or is it? Figure 19.2B is a baseball player with cap down over his eyes—or is it a hand holding a kite string? Actually, the baseball player's head and cap are the same curved line as the chipmunk's tail, in a different position. For that matter, there is really nothing there at all except some line doodles. What you see depends in part on what you want or think you will see.

As Lewin pointed out, if you want to mail a letter you will see the first mailbox, but you may pass up sixteen mailboxes without seeing any if you do not wish to mail a letter.

Life space is both the environment one is aware of and oneself in that environment. To understand any piece of behavior we must understand the concrete situation as it is lived by a person at the moment, and we must understand the nature of that person at that time.

Lewin described how the life space of a child develops (1935, pp. 172-179). The world

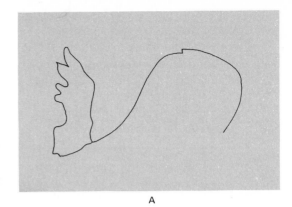

A

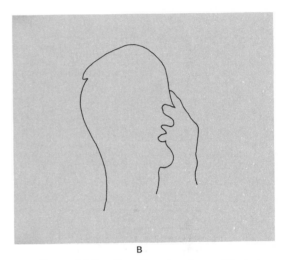

B

Figure 19.2. Two line drawings with various possible interpretations

of the very young child is small in space and in time. The crib and the nursery may be all there is, spatially. Moreover the child lives in a very small duration around the present. The past and the future have little meaning, extending perhaps a few minutes in either direction. So the infant lives very much in the present.

Extension of the child's life space must proceed spatially and temporally. Spatial extension will gradually include other rooms and other people and objects. Temporal extension will develop to include yesterday and tomorrow, last week and next week, and so on.

Extension of the life space into the future does not occur independently of particular forms of experience, according to Lewin. Specifically, the *goals* for the child's behavior, those ends toward which the child strives, become increasingly remote from the present. Extension of the life space takes place through a greater number and greater breadth of *perceptual* wholes: rattle, bed, nursery, bathroom-corridor-nursery, bedroom-corridor-kitchen, plus the living room suddenly adds up to a whole place called "home," next to another place, called "Auntie May's home." Extension also proceeds through *action wholes:* the initiation of a wish or intention, followed by efforts to achieve the goal, followed by its accomplishment. Beginning with a wish to suck, followed by sucking, action wholes develop with increasing time spans between initiation and accomplishment. For example, quite early the child is told, "Today you must look especially nice because Auntie May is coming to see you"; later, "Are you getting ready for Christmas?"; later still, "I'm sewing this dress for the school play next month." Much later still the statement might be, "We have the first drawings of the spacecraft that will carry six families to Alpha 34 in 2010 A.D."

Far out in the future may be far out in imagination too. Something quite distant in the future may easily seem unreal. Yet, a *level of unreality* can be present in the life space right now. Right now we can imagine a pink elephant flying through the window. Right now we can imagine riding a white horse at breakneck speed across the sands. In the very young child the *level of reality* is barely separated from that of unreality. Such separation is an important part of educating the child and depends upon two main conditions, according to Lewin.

The first condition for separating reality from unreality is that the child encounters the *will of another person,* both as a barrier to what the child wishes and as a source of power leading the child to do certain things regardless of its own wishes. The second condition is the presence of objective barriers to the satisfaction of a child's wishes. The *barrier* is something that puts an impassable boundary between the child and the goal.

Lewin points out that objectivity cannot develop unless the child is free to seek satisfaction in goals determined by its own wishes. The realization of reality depends upon the child's *own* needs being thwarted by a barrier. If the child is continually under constraints to act or not act in a certain way there is no opportunity for the child to express its own needs, nor for those needs to encounter barriers. In regard to both social goals and physical goals it is important that the child be allowed to encounter difficulties in attaining its own goals, but not difficulties so overwhelming that the child gives up.

Giving up is likely accompanied by a flight into unreality. In one case quoted by Lewin, a little boy was locked in his room to await punishment. In these circumstances he had to give up any attempt to escape. His fantasy brought to mind the possibility that he was not really his father's son, but a waif. He would confront his father with this fact and assure him that he would now leave since it was not right for him to impose on this man any more. At the thought of parting he burst into tears. Then he remembered the real situation of being in the room and waiting for punishment.

Our life space contains a level of reality and a level of unreality. Actually it is a continuum, with some layers in between which are more or less unreal—remote possibilities, for instance. When we dream or daydream we move into a deeper level of unreality. When we are facing squarely a task before us, such as how to fix two pieces of wood together exactly at a ninety-degree angle, we are definitely functioning in the level of reality. Lewin says that reality and unreality make another dimension in our life space.

To give a child a full-bodied life space we must therefore enable him or her to separate reality from unreality, and we must also allow room for the development of those middle zones, such as fantasy or artistic expression. Lewin notes that the separation appears to occur earlier for working class children, perhaps because they are more likely to encounter barriers. He also points out that a strictly authoritarian home will produce a child who early learns to separate reality from unreality. But such early and arbitrary separation can conceal great weakness. First, the child may seek hidden substitute satisfactions; second, if the authoritative structure collapses (because of a parent's death, for example) the child's whole level of reality collapses in consequence, for it has been built up in complete dependence on the authority.

Lewin made these statements in 1931, in Germany. Ten years later two associates of Lewin conducted a study which provided some evidence consistent with the theoretical expectations (Lippitt & White, 1943). In this study four groups, of five boys each, met after school for eighteen weeks. Every six weeks the leader of the group was changed—in fact, the same four leaders rotated from one group to the next. Each leader had been trained to behave in one of three ways: autocratic, democratic, or laissez-faire. For example, the autocratic leader gave orders 50 percent of the time whereas the other two gave orders only 5 percent or less. The democratic leader guided the group toward its own decisions and policy making; the autocratic leader made all policy decisions; the laissez-faire leader participated minimally.

These children were already in school.

They met only once a week with the leader. The clubs were supposed to be recreational. Nevertheless it was expected that there would be differences in the atmosphere of the clubs and in the behaviors of the boys as a result of the different leadership climates.

Observation of the interactions in the groups did in fact reveal different behaviors. The number of "dependent" remarks made to the leader average fourteen to sixteen in the autocratic climate, and only four to six in the laissez-faire or democratic climate. This highly significant difference suggests that the source of "reality" resided heavily in the leader under the autocratic conditions; much less so in the other conditions. Typical dependent remarks included, "Shall I paint the bottom of this or not?" or "Is this OK?" Such remarks amount to saying, "You know what reality is or should be. Please tell me." In sum, the more autocratic the leadership, the less independent were the subjects.

Further it was found that the continued physical presence of the autocratic leader was important. In addition to having fun, the boys engaged in painting, carpentry, and other kinds of hobby work. Such work would certainly be construed as presenting tasks at the level of reality. When the autocratic leader was present in the room the boys in that group were absorbed in such work 74 percent of the time; when he left the room that percentage dropped to 29 percent. By contrast, in the democratic climate the work involvement occurred 50 percent of the time when the leader was present, and 46 percent of the time when he was out of the room.

If we may equate "functioning at the level of reality" with "involvement in hobby work," then the autocratic leadership produced a greater percentage of reality-level functioning while the leader was present. When he left, however, the reality-level structure of the boys' life space disintegrated.

The Psychological Environment

Lewin called the environment-as-experienced *the psychological environment*. This was the *field* within which all behavior is determined, a field of forces. Lewin maintained that each science is basically different in the concepts it must develop; he did not try to apply the concepts of physical science literally to biology or to psychology. As sciences develop, he maintained, they become more distinct. And yet there may be formal, especially mathematical, similarities. Thus, for example, he did not envision a field of psychological forces that was the same as a field of physical forces, such as magnetic forces. The forces themselves would have to be purely psychological pressures or barriers. Yet formal similarity lay in the sense that a union of forces converging on a point from different directions would have a resultant force in some new but inevitable direction.

In physical science, Lewin pointed out, no amount of statistical work, taking the averages of falling bodies such as sticks, stones, leaves, and other things, could lead to the discovery of laws of falling bodies. Only by developing and analyzing pure cases can such laws be discovered. Similarly, environmental forces and their laws of operation can be discovered in psychology only by taking very simple total situations that are concrete and individual. Conceptualizing this concrete situation with great clarity, we are then able to formulate a penetrating analysis of it and generate propositions about it which can be tested experimentally. These tests rest upon systematic variation of the crucial conditions. An example is the variation of leadership climates in the experiment described above.

Lewin said that the actual behavior of a child always depends on two factors: his or her individual characteristics and the momentary situation in the psychological environment. That is, it depends on both the person and the environment. In order to study the environmental forces we must have similar individuals or the same individual under different conditions. The boys in each club of the Lippitt and White study were equated as far as possible for personality.

Valences, Forces, and the Life Space

The same physical environment has different properties for different individuals, and even for the same individual at different times. A wood block in a toy box may be now an artillery piece, and half an hour later a steamship. If you are hungry the smell of someone else's cabbage cooking is pleasant; half an hour later, when you have had a good meal, the same smell may be repulsive.

This dependence between the momentary state of the person and the structure of the psychological environment is of fundamental importance, says Lewin (1935, p. 76); it becomes especially clear in relation to the person's needs. The objects in a child's life space are not neutral. They have an effect on the child's behavior. A piece of candy is for eating, a ball for throwing, a doll for caring (or sometimes for tearing). Objects attract and repel the child, according to the child's needs, even as the neighbor's cabbage may attract or repel. Lewin insists that these qualities of objects are not like stimuli in the usual stimulus-response sense. Rather they are like a command, request, or invitation. A recent term in experimental psychology is a "demand characteristic" of the experiment, something which more or less constrains the subject to behave in a certain way. Lewin called such characteristics of objects in the natural life space *valences*.

Valences are most important in the psychological environment. Their nature, strength, and distribution are crucial characteristics of the environment. The particular valence of an object is usually related to a need of the person, in the sense of being a means to satisfaction of the need or a hindrance, or otherwise related either to satisfaction or dissatisfaction.

Corresponding to each valence in the psychological environment there exists a force in the life space which is a) *applied* to the person, b) *in a direction* toward a positive valence or away from a negative valence, c) with a particular *degree of strength*. Figure 19.3 illustrates the forces applied to a child who is confronted with two positive valences, two goals. It might be a choice between a candy and a toy. It might be a choice between going to the 300 on Saturday or going to a movie. The choices, on either side of the diagram, are both shown as having positive valences: + valence Z and + valence M. The forces are shown impinging on the child (C) at the center.

Despite the infinite range of valences, it is possible to place them into two general groups, positive and negative. Positive valences attract the person: negative valences repel. Two general kinds of forces may also be discerned. Those which correspond to valences, positive or negative, are *driving* forces. Those which correspond to barriers are *restraining* forces. A playpen or a child's harness provide good examples of the barriers and also of the restraining forces associated with them.

The entire life space may be divided into different *regions,* areas characterized by different valences and other force characteristics. For example, the child in a playpen is within a region bounded by the round or square barrier of the playpen wall. Beyond this barrier lies the region of the rest of the room, possibly with attractive objects in it. Within the playpen the restraining forces of the barrier can be felt at all points. One can readily imagine the child inside the barrier looking out, feeling the restraint inside and longing for the freedom outside. The life space of the child can be visualized as similar to the space of figure 19.4.

Three Types of Conflict

Lewin described three basic kinds of conflict. The first, represented in figure 19.3, is like a child's conflict between going to the zoo or going to a movie. This is an approach-approach conflict, a conflict between two approach tendencies. To be a real conflict the two choices must be equally desirable.

The second kind of conflict is represented by a child wanting to climb a tree but being afraid. This approach-avoidance conflict has both a positive and a negative valence. The forces drive the child both to approach the task and to avoid it.

The third basic type of conflict may be represented by a child's being faced with a threat of punishment if he or she does not do a certain task; the task is also very unpleasant to the child. This conflict between

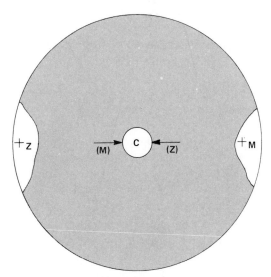

Figure 19.3. Life space of a child having to make a choice. Forces of two relatively equal positive valences are shown by arrows.

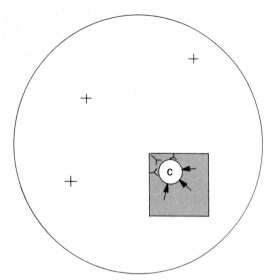

Figure 19.4. Life space of a child in playpen. The barrier emits restraining forces (⟶<) felt especially in the direction away from an attractive object. Each attractive object exerts a driving force (⟶) in its own direction.

two avoidance tendencies is labeled avoidance-avoidance conflict.

Fields of Forces

The third type of conflict is particularly instructive as to the total field of force exerted by objects and persons in the life space. A *field of force* refers to the actual force that would be exerted at each point of the life space if the person were at that point.

Important differences arise depending upon the kind of valence an object possesses. A positive valence creates a *converging* field, a field in which the force at all points is directed inward toward the valence. A negative valence produces a field in which forces at all points lead away from the valence.

These assumptions permit some explicit predictions about behavior in conflict situations. In the third type of conflict, for example, each negative valence will emit a field of force so that the interaction of the two tends to

result in a force driving the individual out of the field entirely. This is represented in figure 19.5, which illustrates our earlier example. The child feels the force of the negative valence P (punishment) and the negative valence T (task). The child will be driven out of the field by the resultant force (R). This means the child will do something else in order to escape from this field of conflicting forces.

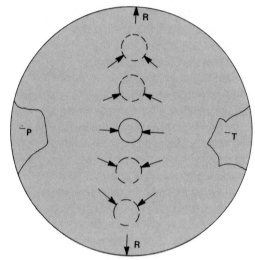

Figure 19.5. The total field of forces in an avoidance-avoidance conflict situation

Lewin points out that the field forces resulting from avoidance-avoidance conflict mean that a child will always attempt to break out of such a situation. Hence, if the threat of punishment is to be effective there must be a strong barrier so that escape is impossible. By contrast, no barrier is needed for the other two kinds of conflict, because both tend to produce a resulting force which is directed at a stable point. In an approach-approach conflict situation the point is midway between the two positive goals. In an approach-avoidance conflict situation the point is somewhere near the goal but still separated from it by the driving forces of the negative valence. Lewin gives an example (from an actual film of behavior) in which a child is rooted to a spot on a beach, facing the toy swan he wants, but faced by the water, of which he is afraid.

The film also provides a good instance of the responsiveness of behavior to changes in the total field of forces. For as the waves recede, the point of immobility due to conflict recedes also. So the child moves forward. Then as the waves come in again, the point of immobility also comes in, and the child moves backward.

The Person

As the child develops greater and greater interest in the environment so the structure of his inner person increases in complexity. New skills are acquired, new goals are sought, new friends are made. New places are discovered with new excitements: the basement, the attic, the alley. In relation to each of these new regions of the psychological environment there arise regions of memory and interest in the child's person.

Needs, Regions, and Boundaries

Between regions in the psychological environment there are boundaries or barriers. Similarly, boundaries separate regions in the person. What goes on in one region may have greater or lesser influence on what happens in another region. Successes in alley or backyard games, for instance, may give one child more confidence at school; for another child there may be no carryover.

In environmental regions there are objects and persons and their associated valences. These valences are correlated with needs of the person. The momentary state of the life space is a function of the objects and their valences, but these valences are a function of the needs of the person.

Driving forces associated with valences are also associated with needs. The person's need states are therefore crucial in influencing the momentary state of tension in the person, for tension consists of forces in opposition. Whenever a need arises and is unsatisfied a state of tension exists.

If a need is active in one region but cannot be satisfied there, it often happens that the person manages to relieve the tension through substitute satisfaction. The child prevented from going to a party may settle for going to a movie and be satisfied. A child frustrated in the attempt to make a model plane may be satisfied with success at making a model train.

If the satisfaction of one need can serve to reduce the tension in another, unsatisfied, need, then the boundaries between the regions of the two needs must be relatively *permeable*. That is, the boundary must be such that tension from one region can be discharged through the neighboring region.

The more different interests and needs a person has the more *differentiated* is that person's structure. There are more regions, with more intricate connections between regions. The newborn is undifferentiated but rapidly develops interests beyond sucking. As more and more interests develop the structure of the person becomes more and more differentiated.

Personality structure may vary both in differentiation and in permeability of boundaries. Different extremes are illustrated in figure 19.6, which also shows the outer boundary between person and environment. A second boundary separates the perceptual-motor region from the regions of the inner person.

Many experiments have investigated the implications of Lewin's theory of personality. For example, it was reasoned that children who were interrupted in particular drawing tasks would later return to finish their draw-

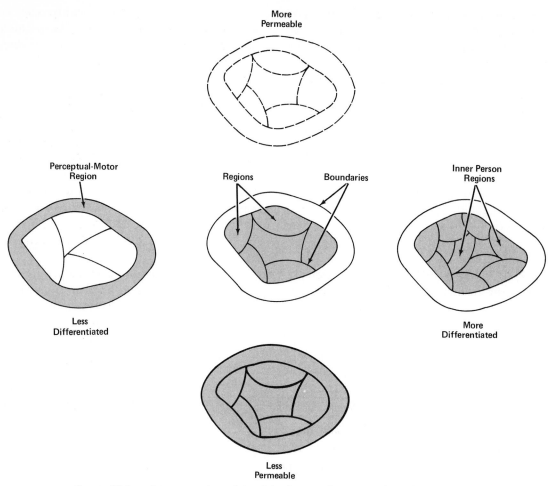

More
Permeable

Perceptual-Motor
Region

Regions   Boundaries

Inner Person
Regions

Less
Differentiated

More
Differentiated

Less
Permeable

Figure 19.6. Representation of Lewin's theory of regions, boundaries, differentiation, and permeability. Drawings modeled on and expanded from Lewin (1935, pp. 207-210).

ings if given the opportunity. It was found that 80 percent of normal children and 100 percent of mentally retarded children did return to complete their drawings, entirely on their own volition. These findings show that an incomplete task is associated with a state of tension, with a driving force toward completion. Lewin interprets such a drive toward completion as indicating the child's *intention* or *purpose* or *wish* or *desire* to finish the job. Such psychological phenomena are familiar to everyone. Lewin reasoned that they are just

like physical needs such as hunger. They are associated with tension states until satisfied, which means that the aim of the intention must be accomplished or the goal of the desire or wish must be obtained. Lewin called such phenomena *quasi-needs*.

To test the hypothesis that substitute tasks can reduce the tension in a neighboring region, several of Lewin's students did experiments in which substitute tasks were given to children whose first task had been interrupted. It was found that fewer children returned to complete the unfinished task under these conditions. As compared with 80 percent who returned to their unfinished task after a period of relative inactivity, only 33 percent returned after successfully completing a substitute task. It was found also that more similar tasks make better substitutes.

Interesting studies were carried out to examine parts of the theory dealing with the boundaries between regions. In one study mentally retarded children were compared with normal children, because it was reasoned that the former have a personality structure characterized by greater rigidity. In theoretical terms this means that the boundaries between regions should be *less* permeable among the retarded. If this is true, one would expect substitute tasks to have less influence on them.

Results were in accordance with expectations. It was found that giving retarded children a substitute task made almost no difference in their tendency to return to the previously unfinished task. Actually 94 percent went back spontaneously to complete the unfinished task, as compared with 33 percent of the normal children.

Lewin's theoretical model of mental retardation states that the boundaries are less permeable in the retarded; therefore, when tension is reduced in one region no effect will be felt on the tension level in a neighboring region. The results of several experiments with normal and retarded subjects provide support for this model.

Accomplishments of Lewin's Theory

It has often been remarked that Lewin was a truly great experimentalist and that his innovative ideas have inspired other investigators to this day (see Heider, 1959, for example). Lewin invented many constructs and research procedures (like *action research* or *group dynamics*) which have entered into the standard conceptual equipment of behavioral and social science. It is also often remarked that somehow Lewin managed to design brilliant experiments which were actually unrelated to his formal theory in the sense of logical deduction from the theory's empirical assumptions and hypotheses. Somehow the theory was developed in such a way that it was untestable; Lewin did experiments, nonetheless, with the result that theory and experiment remained unconnected. On the contemporary scene, despite the prevalence of Lewin's constructs and methods in psychological research, his theory is rarely if ever invoked. How can this paradox be explained? Why are Lewin's constructs and methods so much in use but not his theory? Deutsch (1968, p. 478) comments:

> It cannot be said that field theory as a specific psychological theory has much current vitality. None of the grand theories in psychology is any longer much in vogue. Nor can it be said that Lewin's specific theoretical constructs, his structural and dynamic concepts, are central to research now being carried on in social psychology. His impact is reflected instead in his general orientation to psychology, which has left its impress on his colleagues and students. He believed that psychological events must be explained in psychological terms; that central processes in the life space (distal perception, cognition, motivation, goal-directed behavior) rather than peripheral processes of sensory input and muscular action are the proper focus of investigation; that psychological events must be studied in their interrelations with one another; that the individual must be studied in his interrelations with the group; . . . and that a good theory is valuable for social action as well as for social science.

Deutsch seems to say that it is only Lewin's methodological assumptions which remain influential today, but I believe some of his constructs and models persist too.

Lewin's theory of tension systems generated a theoretical model of success and failure as felt experiences. When do we experience a feeling of sucess? Ferdinand Hoppe carried out experiments under Lewin's direction which showed that a feeling of success is experienced when a) the results of some activity are believed to be due to one's own ability, rather than luck or something else, and b) those results meet or exceed the level of performance to which the person aspires. An experience of failure also requires that the results be attributed to one's own ability and performance, the level of that performance falling below what the person aspired to.

Both successes and failures are only experienced in a narrow range of difficulty, however. That is, poor performances on tasks considered far too difficult for a person do not result in feelings of failure; good performances on tasks considered far too easy for a person do not result in feelings of success. A child does not experience failure for inability to do adult jobs such as typing a letter. An adult does not experience success for accomplishing a child's task well, such as tying one's own shoe laces.

Setting a goal for our performance is very similar to forming an intention or having a wish. If the goal is achieved, Lewin said, then the tension associated with this quasi-need would be discharged. If the goal is not achieved the tension would remain at a high level. If the achievement of the goal in a given task is important for our general self-esteem, then the level of tension is increased by the fact that the need to achieve the particular goal is imbedded in our more general need to maintain our self-esteem.

The setting of a goal for our next attempt at a particular task is a common experience, and has even been glorified by some proverbs like "If at first you don't succeed, try, try, try again." In sporting activities it is common to try to meet some standard, such as swimming one length of the pool without a rest, then two lengths, then five lengths, then a quarter mile, and so on. If we manage to get a spare in bowling, then we try for two, or maybe we go for a strike. After bowling an 80, we aim for 100; after bowling 100 we aim for 150; and so on.

According to Lewin (1951, p. 287), the *level of aspiration* is the degree of difficulty of the goal selected for the next action. If you have just bowled a line at 130, you might set 150 as your next goal. That would be your level of aspiration at that moment. The level of aspiration is a momentary frame of reference against which the related performance results are evaluated. If you make 150 or better you feel you have succeeded. Actually, most people seem to experience a distinct feeling of pleasure if they make a good score (for them) in bowling. It is especially satisfying to take aim at a lone pin left standing after the first ball and hit it.

A person's level of aspiration is affected by many factors, the first of which is the person's own estimate of his or her ability on this particular task. Success in one performance leads to a higher level of aspiration for the next performance; failure has the opposite effect, as many experiments have shown. Considering different degrees of success, it has been shown that stronger success in performance is associated with even greater probability of a raised level of aspiration. A worse failure is likewise followed by a greater probability of a lower level of aspiration.

Both of these well-established results in experimental studies have been replicated in research on everyday life (Child & Whiting, 1949). College students were asked to describe three incidents in their lives, one involving complete frustration, one in which frustration was followed by success, and one in which they simply achieved their goal. After each description the students were asked to indicate whether it raised or lowered their level of aspiration (which was carefully explained to them).

In one incident of frustration a student had wanted to maintain an 80 average in order to get into medical school. Despite studying hard he got a 65 in zoology. In another incident a student wanted very much to go to Bermuda on vacation but knew that financial circumstances at home were not too good. Nevertheless he first asked his mother and she thought it was a good idea; then (with some anxiety) he asked his father. To his joy his father agreed to the trip and provided the money.

Our knowledge of factors affecting the level of aspiration would lead us to expect that the student who got a 65 in zoology would lower his level of aspiration. Having tried for an 80 and gotten a 65 in the zoology course, he might aim for only a 70 in his next natural science course. The student who was successful in his effort to go to Bermuda would be expected to raise his level of aspiration. Perhaps next time he would try for Acapulco or Paris.

As Lewin points out, many factors can affect the level of aspiration. For example, other people may place new demands or expectations upon us. In many cases, he suggests, a child's aspiration level may be forced up beyond his natural ability by the expectations of parents or older siblings. Since the child's ability will not allow such a high level of aspiration actually to be achieved, failures will be persistent and the child will probably develop a feeling of inferiority.

Another factor is the person's degree of experience with a particular kind of task. Through experience people come to know just about what to expect of themselves. Under these circumstances a fluctuation up or down from the usual level of performance is more

likely to be attributed to momentary luck or other factors not bearing upon the self's responsibility for the performance level.

Yet another factor is the effect of successes and failures in other fields of endeavor, since it has been found experimentally that success in one activity is likely to raise the level of aspiration in another activity if there is sufficient similarity or connection between the two. Clearly such a finding requires relatively permeable boundaries between the two regions associated with these activities. But, for example, if the student who obtained a 65 in zoology had received a 95 in anatomy it might have served to balance out the effects so that his level of aspiration for the next course in natural science would have remained at 80 instead of being lowered.

All of these findings make it possible for a student to track his or her own level of aspiration for grades. Some students aim for an A or 100; others for a B or 80; others will aim for a passing grade only. In their first semester as freshmen these aims must be based upon their knowledge of their ability as demonstrated in high school; perhaps on the last grades they received in high school; possibly on what they believe is expected of them as members of their family or of their group of friends.

After the first hourly quiz or midterm examination in a particular course, their level of performance might be higher than, lower than, or equal to their expectations. If it is higher, what should this do to their level of aspiration? If it is lower, what should happen to their level of aspiration?

We would expect from theory that a series of failure experiences would lead the student to escape from the field: that would mean dropping out of school, perhaps, or getting sick. We would expect a series of success experiences to raise the student's confidence and enthusiasm as well as the level of aspiration.

We would expect also, from Lewin's theory, that these experiences of success or failure would be tied as much to the individual student's expectations as to the actual grades received.

Critique of Lewin's Theory of Function

We have said very little about Lewin's mathematical formulations, for which he was both famous and heartily criticized. He introduced concepts of mathematical topology (Lewin, 1936) in order to provide formal treatment of his constructs of psychological space, and regions, paths, and boundaries within that space. Let us examine an example. Lewin (1951, pp. 321-322) undertook a mathematical representation of boundary forces (bf) differentiation (dif), and their relation to the unity (uni) of a whole (W). The whole is composed of a number of cells (c). The independence of two cells (c_1, c_2) is defined in terms of the extent to which change in one cell effects change in a neighboring cell: the more the spread of effect, the less the independence of the two cells. If the change is a change in tension, then the "degree of independence can be correlated to the strength of forces on the boundary of one cell which will not affect the state of another cell." Lewin drew a diagram similar to figure 19.7A, which may be viewed as an enlarged detail from one of the diagrams in figure 19.6. In the upper section is represented a state of equilibrium in which the forces at the boundary of cells c_1 and c_2 are equal and opposite. Figure 19.7B shows another state of affairs, namely one in which bf_{c_2} is smaller than bf_{c_1}. This means that there is no longer equilibrium and the states of the cells are likely to change. Change will occur, said Lewin, when the resultant boundary force (bf^*) reaches some critical value:

$$bf^*_{c_2, c_1} = \left| bf_{c_1, c_2} \right| - \left| bf_{c_2, c_1} \right|$$

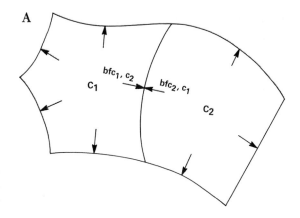

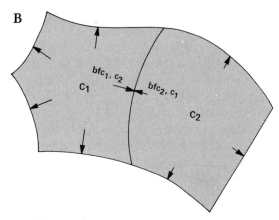

Figure 19.7. Lewin's constructs of equilibrium and disequilibrium in neighboring cells

The critical value (e) will be greater when there is a greater degree of independence (*indep*) between the cells. This greater degree of independence would be related to the *strength* of the boundary. As an analogy from mechanics, the independence of the air pressure inside a spacecraft with respect to the air pressure outside the craft is related to the strength of the materials in the hull. If the hull is thin and weak it would take but a small difference in air pressure to make the craft explode (if the inner pressure were higher than the outer) or to cave in (if the outer pressure were higher than the inner).

Lewin then expressed the independence of adjacent cells as follows:

$$indep \ (c_1, c_2) \ = \ bf^{\circ \ max}_{c_1, c_2} \ \text{for which } ch \ (c_2) < \xi$$

Here $ch(c_2)$ means a change in cell c_2; the total expression says that independence is equal to the maximum value e can take before the degree of change equals or exceeds some constant ξ.

Lewin also defined the diameter (dia) of a whole in terms of the maximum distance (d^{max}) that can be found between any two cells (c_i, c_j) within that whole:

$$dia \ (W) = d^{max}_{c_i, c_j}$$

Now the dependence of two cells is defined as the reciprocal of the independence:

$$dep \ (c_1, c_2) = 1.0/indep \ (c_1, c_2)$$

If independence corresponds to strength of boundary and degree of resultant boundary force (bf°) needed to make a change of state, then dependence corresponds to the *smallness* of the bf°. Thus Lewin is able to reach out for a psychological constant of profound importance in proposing the following expression for the degree of unity (uni) of a given natural whole:

$$uni \ (W) = F \ \left(\frac{dep \ (c_i, c_j)}{dia \ (W)} \right) \ = constant$$

I have gone to some length to provide the reader with an example of Lewin's thinking and his use of mathematical symbols and derivations so that the target of much criticism can be clear. Estes (1954) charged that Lewin failed to make clear the empirical facts to which his theoretical constructs referred, so that it is impossible actually to test the theory. What does *life space* or *boundary* really mean? What does *differentiation* of the person, or *unity* of the whole person really mean?

London (1944) criticized Lewin for having used some but not all of the constructs and relationships in topology and physics, and therefore giving them an incorrect interpretation (for example, *tension* and *force* mean quite different things in physics and in Lewin's theory). Hall and Lindzey (1970, p. 253) criticize Lewin's attempt to make "a mathematical model of behavior from which specific predictions can be made, when in fact no such predictions can be formulated. . . . Lewin's so-called mathematical model has no utility whatsoever in generating testable propositions. Whatever mathematical manipulations Lewin indulged in, he performed after the observations had been made."

Our first inclination might be to agree with these criticisms. Surely the mathematical formulations described above are obscure in reference. However, they do not appear to have been made *after* any observations had been collected. Indeed, Lewin's point of departure was in the main imaginative, in the way that persons in "think tanks" (such as the Brookings Institute) try to imagine certain scenarios as alternative possible realities for the future and then deduce the consequences for survival of the nation. He wrote, for example,

> Suppose it is necessary, for some reason or other, to keep parts within a whole (e.g., an organism) independent of each other. The number of such independent parts depends on the difference in tension (the strength of the resultant boundary forces) relative to which the cells should be independent and the position of the regions in tension. How the degree of differentiation of a given whole decreases with increasing forces depends on the strength and the position of the boundaries of the natural cells within the whole. However, it is always possible to determine a strength of a resultant boundary force relative to which a natural whole is to be regarded as undifferentiated, and a certain strength relative to which the whole cannot be treated as a natural whole (Lewin, 1951, p. 323).

These complicated remarks are made just prior to his formulation of the degree of unity of a whole, as presented above. They do not refer to any particular set of observations already collected; they refer to some possible observations and manipulations that might be necessary "to keep parts within a whole . . . independent of each other" while at the same time not making the parts so independent that they no longer form a whole at all.

Actually the meaning of Lewin's statements about wholes appears to be even more abstract than the contemplation of future possible scenarios to be faced by a nation. For these are at least particular scenarios being envisaged. Lewin's intent seems to be to think about *any* psychological or social whole whatsoever, not merely a limited set of particular possible wholes. His conception appears in no way to be based upon statistical averages of factual observations about particular empirical wholes. It is rather a conception of the "pure case," even as Galileo conceived of the pure case of any freely falling body whatsoever.

When might it be useful to represent a psychological whole in terms of degree of unity? One example is provided by MacKinnon (1944) in his application of Lewin's topological methods to anxiety. MacKinnon proposes a theoretical model of anxiety in which anxious people are unable to make good connection between their level of unreality and their level of reality. In anxious people these levels have a smaller degree of mutual dependence, less interaction. In the psychological present, and increasingly in the psychological future, the anxious person's life space therefore has less unity. There are two levels of unreality, one positive with hope, one negative with fear. The more anxious person is more affected by both of these levels of unreality, but cannot incorporate reality knowledge to lessen the intensity of unrealistic hopes any more than unrealistic fears. Even if the person makes a realistic appraisal of the future, that somehow does not affect his or her hopes and fears because the levels of reality and unreality are so completely independent.

The model provides an explanation for the so-called *catastrophic* anxiety often found. In this reaction anxious patients do not know what to expect, and feel that their world is breaking down (MacKinnon, 1944, fn. 10). The lowered unity of the life space in the present, and the increasingly lower unity of the life space in near and distant futures would also allow the prediction that anxious patients will feel that *they* are going to pieces, or that they are going insane, a characteristic of anxious patients that Raimy (1975, pp. 105-106) observes frequently.

Also for social wholes there might often be occasion to conceptualize the unity of such wholes and to adjust both dependence and diameter accordingly in order to retain their integrity. For example, in an army at war, the separate parts must not be kept too close together because they would present too attractive a target; nor must they become so independent of each other that all communication breaks down. The more spread out they are (diameter of whole larger), the more dependent upon each other the parts must be made if the unity of the whole is to be maintained.

It seems that Lewin's topological constructs are sufficiently abstract that they provide great flexibility in application to particulars (as Estes noted, 1954, p. 332).

Evaluation of the Theory

We close this critique with considerations of our usual criteria for evaluating a theory. How *accurate* is Lewin's theory? It seems that a large number of experiments by Lewin and his associates had results in accord with expectations. If we accept the position of some critics that the mathematical model Lewin constructed could not make any formal predictions, then the evidence of accurate experiments is not evidence for accuracy of the theory. My own thought about it is that the essential theory consists of the constructs, empirical assumptions, and hypotheses. As long as these sensibly led to specific predictions (as in the substitution experiments, for example), then the accuracy of the predictions is evidence for the accuracy of the theory.

As we saw in the section on accomplishments Lewin's methodological assumptions have had substantial influence on other scientists to this day. But these are *pre*theoretical and so should not count for the *fruitfulness* of the theory. A limited number of Lewin's constructs (such as level of aspiration) have continued to be used by theorists and researchers (as we shall see particularly in the next chapter, on Rotter's theory). But these again do not seem to qualify for fruitfulness of the theory as a whole. It seems that the theory must be judged to have had very limited fruitfulness. Perhaps that can be linked to the fact that strictly Lewinian experiments have almost ceased to be carried out since Lewin himself moved on to social problems in World War II. Hence the power of the theory is limited to the areas that he and his associates studied before that.

What about *depth*? Let us first consider the components of personality in the theorist's implicit definition. The three main terms in Lewin's own statement of the central function are behavior (B), person (P), and perceived environment (E). There can be no doubt from the constructs of *levels of reality,* *time perspective, valence,* and others, that Lewin meant *experience* of the environment. Nor can there be doubt but that he saw the geographic environment as contributing to the psychological environment. What did he mean by *person?* It seems that he meant two things: first, an awareness of the self in the life space; second, the underlying psychophysical systems associated with needs, differentiated regions, permeable boundaries, and other features of the structure of the person. Therefore Lewin's implicit definition of personality covers behavior, experience (of self and environment), and psychophysical systems, but not the body.

On the degree to which Lewin's theory provides penetrating insights into mechanisms it seems to me that it has great depth, but that much has been obscured by the unfamiliarity of his mathematical notation on one hand, and by the inexactitude of reference on the other. By the latter I mean that his use of words like person or environment can be taken to mean physical entities like the body or the geographical environment, and many people will at first so construe these terms. But whereas he did distinguish the geographical from the psychological environment he did not distinguish the anatomical from the experiential person. Had he done so a more accurate appraisal of his theory could be made, for it seems that he focused primarily on the nature of experience (experience of the environment and of the self), on the psychophysical structure of the person and its effects on experience, and on the effects of experience on behavior.

Some Fields of Force: Conflict and Detour

Conflict

The field of force surrounding a positive valence is convergent. Therefore in a type 1 conflict (approach-approach) between two positive valences each will emit a converging field of forces. Draw a diagram similar to that of figure 19.5 showing the field of forces and the resultant force in the situation of a type 1 conflict:

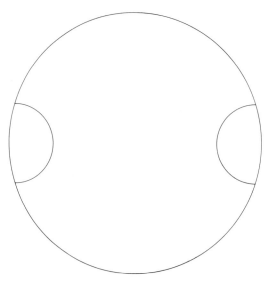

Detour

When a child encounters a barrier it may be possible to go around it, to make a **detour** to the goal. Lewin says (1935, p. 82) that the detour task is more difficult for a child if the barrier makes it necessary for the child to begin the detour by moving in a direction **opposite** the force of the attractive object. Try this simple experiment. A cat or dog or mouse would do if a young child is not available or willing. Choose a desirable object (candy, dog bone, piece of fish, whatever is suitable for your subject). Build a simple barrier having the shape shown in figure 19.8. Then try several different positions as shown in the figure. In each case the absolute linear distance between subject and goal at the start must be the same. Also, in every case the absolute distance the subject must travel from start to goal must be the same, regardless of directions. Finally then, the only difference between situations is whether and to what extent the subject must begin the detour by going in a direction opposed to the force emitted by the goal. Note that in all cases it is necessary to have a side barrier to prevent the subject from taking alternative routes. This can be a wall.

Try three measures. First take the time lapse between subject being placed at the starting point and the subject actually setting off on the detour journey and continuing to the goal. If the subject starts off and then retraces steps, that does not count for this measure; the time lapse extends until the subject starts off and proceeds on that trip without retracing. A second measure is number of retracings. A third measure is total time taken from being placed at the starting position to arriving at the goal.

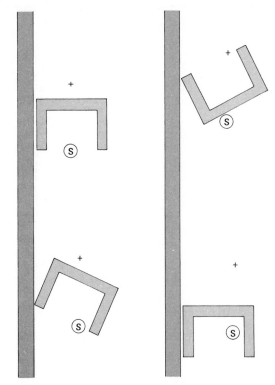

Figure 19.8. Four detour problems with different initial directions and movement required

---

Summary

In Lewin's theory the basic functional equation states that behavior is a function of the person and the experienced environment. *Life space* is a central term. The life space is space as experienced and includes both environment and person. It is the way the environment seems to a person and the way the person seems to himself or herself. Objects and other persons in the life space have positive and negative attractions called valences. A valence exerts a driving force on the person. The space is divided into regions which are espe-

cially clear when there is a barrier between two regions. The regions may also contain valences of similar or opposing sign. An object or task with positive valence creates a converging field of force throughout the life space; a negative valence creates a diverging field of force. A field of force is force that would be exerted on the person at any point in the field if the person were at that point. A life space contains past, present, and future references as well as levels of reality and unreality.

The person is also differentiated into regions representing needs in tension.

Lewin adapted the formal system of mathematical topology to represent many constructs in his theory, and was criticized for this because there seemed to be little relation between the formal system and his experiments. But he was widely recognized as an outstanding experimentalist. His theory seems to be accurate as far as it goes, but it has little power. Also it has not been fruitful (although his methodological assumptions have inspired many other scientists, and some of his constructs, such as level of aspiration, have continued to be useful). The theory has moderate to great depth. Its implicit definition of personality is illustrated in figure 19.9. In the next chapter we study Rotter's theory, which is a direct descendant of Lewin's.

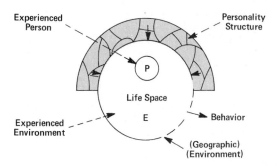

Figure 19.9. Definition of personality implicit in Lewin's theory

INTRODUCTION

Workshop 20   Using Rotter's theory
Summary

Introduction to Rotter's life and work
  Rotter's life and professional career
    Influence of Lewin and Adler
  A classical learning theory
  Also a field theory
    Emphasis on personally meaningful
      environment
Basic constructs
  Behavior potential
  Expectancy
    Subjective estimates
    Generalized expectancies
  Reinforcement value
    Reinforcement-reinforcement sequences
  The functional theory
Complex constructs
  Needs
    Recognition
    Dominance
    Independence
    Protection-dependency
    Love and affection
    Physical comfort
  Need potential
  Freedom of movement
  Need value
Accomplishments of Rotter's theory
  Psychological adjustment
  Internal versus external control (I-E)
    Measurement of I-E
    Predictive power of I-E
    Extensive studies of associations with I-E
    Inner structure of I-E
  Problem behavior
    Work of Jessor and associates: loss of
      virginity and personality traits
Critique of Rotter's theory of function
    Criticism by Bandura and Walters: the theory
      cannot account for occurrence of a novel
      response
    Commentary on the criticism
    Contrasts between Rotter's theory and Lewin's
      theory
      No topological constructs in Rotter's theory
      Externalized meanings in Rotter's theory
    Accuracy, power, fruitfulness, and depth

20

Rotter's Social Learning Theory of Personality Functions

Julian B. Rotter was born in 1916 and is currently Professor of Psychology at the University of Connecticut. For many years he taught at The Ohio State University. He was early interested in both learning theory and the study of personality and clinical psychology. Both Lewin and Adler provided some of the most important influences on his thinking. He carried out extensive studies on one of Lewin's constructs, *level of aspiration,* and developed a controlled procedure for measuring it. As we shall see, this and many others of Lewin's constructs play an important part in Rotter's theory of personality.

The basic features of this theory were put forward in 1954 (Rotter, 1954). Since that time the theory has won increasing acceptance on the part of many psychologists working in clinical, personality, and social psychology. Many further developments have taken place. Countless experiments have been completed. New tests and measurements of the theory's constructs have been developed. Applications have been made to counseling and psychotherapy, to adolescent development, to cross-cultural studies, and other topics.

In many ways Rotter's theory is a classical learning theory. It invokes the famous *law of*

effect, which states that behaviors yielding satisfying results will tend to be repeated; those yielding unsatisfactory results will not. In its most essential features, however, the theory is a *field* theory. It emphasizes the environment in guiding behavior, but stresses that it is the *personally meaningful environment* which is of primary interest for the student of personality. Those aspects of the environment that the individual experiences as significant for satisfaction of needs are the ones that are meaningful and that have influence on the person's behavior.

Lewin argued that the past is significant only as it is now effective in the person's memory and experience. Similarly, Rotter believes that the past is important in influencing present experience, and this range of influence is what is meant by *learning.* In Lewin's view the future is important as it has a continuing effect on experience and behavior. In Rotter's view the future is important in affecting present behavior through the person's expectations.

The future was seen by Lewin as implicit in all truly human behavior. Lewin considered such phenomena as intentions, purposes, wishes, and will. These aspects of experience reflect our thrust forward into the world. They are not mere bodily needs, like food or oxygen, which must be filled in order for the organism to survive. Rather, intentions and similar experiences are pointing toward some future state of affairs in our relations with the environment of people or things. Lewin proposed that those objects of our intentions have particular values of attractiveness or undesirability which he called *valences*. Corresponding to the valences in the psychological environment were drive forces and tensions in the person. Our personal forces driving toward valued goals in the environment constitute the essence of human action, according to Lewin (1935). In the same manner Rotter has placed the utmost emphasis upon human striving toward valued future goals.

One of Lewin's methodological assumptions was that we should always try to form a clear idea of a concrete behavioral situation whenever we attempt to analyze any psychological problem. This implied taking full account of the precise situation confronting a person. It implied taking care to spell out the momentary state of the psychological environment, and also the momentary state of the person. Neglect of either would lead to a useless exercise, in Lewin's opinion.

Rotter's theory is no less explicit about the role of the momentary state of the environment and of the person. However, this entire complex of events and conditions is summarized in the concept of a *situation*. Every proposition about personality and behavior made in Rotter's theory either carries with it an actual statement specifying what situation is intended or makes it clear that the situation is implicitly referred to.

Basic Constructs

We turn first to a detailed consideration of basic constructs. There are just three basic constructs in Rotter's social learning theory: behavior potential, expectancy, and reinforcement value.

Behavior Potential

Following the latest formulation of this theory by Rotter (Rotter & Hochreich, 1975), *behavior potential* (*BP*) is the likelihood that a particular behavior will occur in a given situation where a particular reinforcement may be obtained. The behavior in question is that of an individual. "Situation" may also refer to a class or type of situations (such as competitive examinations in general). Behavior means any overt movement, or verbal expression, or cognitive or emotional reaction. It therefore refers to a very wide class of responses and is a flexible concept.

Note that *BP* is specific both for the particular behavior and for the related reinforcement. This means that Rotter holds it necessary to say what goal the behavior is connected to before it is possible to say how likely that behavior is to occur.

Expectancy

Expectancy (*E*) is the individual's subjective estimate of the probability that his or her particular behavior in a specific situation will lead to a given reinforcement. In other words, the expectancy refers to the probability that one thing (the behavior) will lead to another (the reward or reinforcement). It should be emphasized, however, that expectancy does *not* refer to the connections between environmental events on their own. It does not apply, for instance, to a person's belief that a new Middle East crisis will lead to a new oil embargo. In social learning theory as formulated by Rotter, expectancy refers only to the connection between one's own behavior and the consequences of that behavior in terms of reinforcement.

Rotter and Hochreich point out that expectancies are based on previous experience. Someone who has consistently received C grades is apt to expect another C in the next course. Someone who has always done well in mathematics probably expects a B or better in Calculus II. It is important also that the expectancies are *subjective* estimates of probability, not necessarily true estimates of probability based upon all objective facts obtainable in reality. They reflect the way the person feels about the matter.

Rotter and Hochreich also state that an expectancy may be quite broad or quite narrow. A narrow expectancy would refer to the consequences of behavior in one restricted situation. For example, the expectancy that you would score better than 180 at bowling tonight would be quite narrow, relating just to tonight's game. By contrast, if you had an expectancy of doing exceptionally well in most ball games (including baseball, softball, football, and tennis, as well as bowling) that would be a broad expectancy. The breadth of an expectancy refers to the range of situations and behaviors in which it holds. The broader the range, the more *generalized* the expectancy is said to be.

Some very generalized expectancies are of central importance in the individual personality. These include the expectancy that, in general, one's own efforts will bring the consequences one desires (called expectancy for *internal control*). This contrasts with the general expectancy that what happens in relation to one's own behaviors is mainly dependent on external forces such as fate or the power of other people (called expectancy for *external control*).

Generalized expectancies such as internal versus external control (*I-E*) are not closely tied to particular situations, but relate rather to broad groups of situations which are in some way similar. They therefore characterize the person in a stable way. For example, the person takes his or her own level of *I-E* into all situations which in some way invoke a question of responsibility for outcomes of action. Presumably a substantial portion of living is of this kind, so that *I-E* is a pervasive characteristic of the person.

Reinforcement Value

Reinforcement value (*RV*) is the "degree of preference for any reinforcement to occur if the possibilities of their occurring were all equal" (Rotter & Hochreich, 1975, p. 97).

Sometimes at a fair one finds shooting games or balancing contests in which a variety of prizes can be won. For scoring three bullseyes you can choose either a teddy bear or a box of candy. One person might prefer the teddy bear and therefore it would have a higher *RV* than the candy for that person. Another might choose the candy. People differ in the *RVs* they hold for different objects and action.

An example given by Rotter and Hochreich is the social situation of a party. People go to a party for many different reasons: some to find a new romantic interest, some to find new business prospects, some to get intellectual stimulation, some to get high, some to dance, and so on.

Many of these goals at a party can of course be combined, or at least sought simultaneously: finding a new boyfriend and dancing, for instance. But many are incompatible, such as dancing and getting intellectual stimulation. It is among such mutually incompatible goals that choices must be made: the more time dancing the less time being intellectual, for example. When choices must be made the essential relative importance of different reinforcements becomes clear. One person will dance most of the time and get intellectual stimulation some of the time; another will reverse the order. Here the reinforcement values of each possible goal relative to the other goals becomes evident.

Rotter and Hochreich suggest that there is some consistency in the value hierarchies people place on different reinforcements. That is, Jill *usually* prefers to spend more time dancing when she goes to parties; while Jack mostly prefers to get high and leave the talking and dancing to politicians and athletes. Here again there is a basis for stability in the individual, a characteristic set of preferences that the person takes along to party situations in general.

Another way in which reinforcements may be related to each other lies in their consequences over time. For example, Maria may work hard at school because high grades have a strong reinforcement value for her. But in addition she expects that the high grades will then enable her to enter the college of her choice. Going to this college will allow her to enter advanced training in physics. With a Ph.D. in physics she will be able to work on solar energy research. In working hard at school now, she is working for each of these goals. All the reinforcements consequent upon earlier goals are also connected to the first link in the chain, which is working for good grades in school. Therefore the reinforcement value of good grades is increased to some extent by its participation in all these later reinforcement values.

Rotter calls these chained sets of goals and subgoals *reinforcement-reinforcement sequences*. He argues that people form expectations about these sequences, and it is these expectations which allow for such future chains of reinforcements to influence a given person's behavior right now. They *look forward* to the later rewards which depend upon attainment of the earlier ones.

To distinguish these kinds of expectations from those which relate the probability of reinforcement to one's own behaviors, he labels them as expectancies with a superscript: E^2.

This makes sense since the later goals are also dependent upon one's behavior, even though there is the added complication that the behavior must first actually achieve the first goal, and *then,* through further behaviors, it can lead to getting the next goal, and so on.

The Functional Theory

Now that we have examined the three basic constructs in social learning theory we are ready to study the way in which these constructs are put together in the explanation and prediction of behavior, which are the principal aims of Rotter's theory (unlike the primary aim of understanding personality, which motivated Freud and others).

Briefly, within the context of a particular situation (S_1), a person's behavior potential for behavior x in connection with reinforcement y is a function of his or her relevant expectancy and reinforcement value.

In algebraic terms:

$$BP_{x,\,y} = f\ (E_x \rightarrow_y \ \& \ RV_y),\ (BP,\ E,\ RV,\ \text{in}\ S_1)$$

This expression means that the *BP* of x for y equals some function (f) of both the E that x will result in y and the *RV* for y; and that *BP*, *E*, and *RV* are all relevant to S_1. That is, the *BP* is a *BP* for that S_1 only; likewise the E and the *RV* are for that S_1 only. The $\&$ means that E and *RV* affect each other.

How can these constructs be applied to a single situation only? What does it mean to say they are connected with or related to or relevant to a particular situation, S_1? It means precisely that most things in life are situation-bound.

Consider for example that you might be a good dancer so long as you have a suitable partner. People might say to you, "Say! You're really something!" You really enjoy dancing, and one of the reinforcements you get is such admiration. You get recognition for your superior dancing. But of course that is true only at parties or in informal gatherings of suitable kind. For suppose you were at a funeral for someone you love deeply. Not only would it be difficult to dance, but you might not appreciate such favorable comments under the circumstances. That would mean that the *RV* for applause would be very low on such an occasion. Sympathy might be more to the point; or a sharing of sorrow. Nor would you really expect anyone to applaud you for dancing at the funeral.

With the *E* low and the *RV* low, what is the implication for *BP*? It must be low too. You probably would not dance for admiration at a funeral.

The situation conditions behavior potential as a result of conditioning both expectancy and reinforcement value.

Complex Constructs

The constructs of behavior potential, expectancy, and reinforcement value refer to a single situation or relatively narrow class of situations. They are useful for prediction in particular events or in the laboratory. In daily life, however, we typically deal with broader categories of situations and behaviors. For example, we are interested in whether a new acquaintance likes sports; is an aggressive, dependent, or acquisitive sort of person; or whether we should invite him or her to join our club.

Rotter defines a *need* as a "group of behaviors which are related in the sense that they lead to the same or similar reinforcements." These groups are determined through empirical research. To date, at least six have been established. These are (Rotter & Hochreich, 1975, pp. 101-102):

1. *Recognition*: the need to be given recognition or respect for being good at sports, academic work, in some technical or professional skill, or even simply in social status.

2. *Dominance*: the need to influence other people and have power over them.
3. *Independence*: The need to be autonomous in decision-making and to be self-reliant.
4. *Protection-dependency*: the need to be protected against harm or frustration and to be assisted in attaining goals.
5. *Love and affection*: the need to be loved, liked, regarded well by other people, and to have them interested in us or concerned for our well-being.
6. *Physical comfort*: the need to be comfortable and free of pain, and also the need for bodily pleasure.

How are these needs related to reinforcement value and expectancy?

Since a need is a group of behaviors related through the reinforcements they produce it is therefore a complex of behavior potentials, expectancies, and reinforcement values. A group of behavior potentials is called a *need potential*. A group of expectancies is called *freedom of movement*. A group of reinforcement values is called *need value*.

Need Potential

The construct of *need potential* (*NP*) means the behavior potentials of a need-related group of behaviors. For example, James' need potential for recognition is made up of the behavior potentials James has for training hard to win a trophy in sports, for working hard to get good grades in academic work, and campaigning to get a high position in student government. All of these behaviors can lead to recognition through their particular reinforcements: trophy, good grades, high position.

Freedom of Movement

The construct of *freedom of movement* (*FM*) means the expectancies a person has with respect to a need-related group of behaviors. That is, it means the average expectancy for that group of behaviors.

According to social learning theory we learn to respond with behaviors which have provided the greatest satisfaction in particular situations. For example, James found that only by training hard could he win in competitive sports; he also found that he had to study consistently in order to get high grades in school; in addition he learned that he had to campaign actively in order to be elected to class office in school. More generally, he learned that directed efforts of his own could secure him these desired goals. For each goal he developed a high expectancy. His level of E for training hard was high, his level of E for studying hard was high, and his level of E for campaigning actively was high. Writing E_t for expectancy level on training, E_s for expectancy level on studying, and E_c for expectancy level on campaigning, we would find James' freedom of movement for recognition:

$$FM_r = [E_t + E_s + E_c] \cdot 1/3$$

We would add up the three scores for level of expectancy and divide by 3 to get James' score on freedom of movement for recognition.

One wonders why this construct is not called *need expectancy* or something like that, more or less parallel to *need potential*. Regardless, Rotter uses the term *freedom of movement* for this construct. The term itself was used quite often by Lewin, and he seemed to mean two things. First, he spoke of the person's freedom of movement in the life space. In space without barriers the person is free to do as he pleases. Locomotion may take place toward any goal available in the space, and that means not only spatial locomotion but psychological motion toward a goal of any kind. Sitting and practicing a piece on the piano, for instance, would be such a locomotion toward the goal of accomplished playing. Freedom of movement that day might mean

practicing or not; writing a letter or not; cooking eggs for breakfast or not; going for a walk or not. Freedom of movement means the freedom to do what you want within the naturally occurring limitations of the physical situation.

In the second sense employed by Lewin, the freedom of movement referred more explicitly to a literal freedom in space. For example, a child's freedom of movement might be restricted by locking the child in a room (Lewin, 1935, p. 128).

Thus in Lewin's sense, *freedom of movement* meant the absence of physical, social, or psychological barriers or constraints. Now consider what it means to the individual if there are barriers or constraints. It means that his or her own behaviors are not likely to achieve the desired reinforcements. Behaviors are blocked from reinforcements. What does this mean in Rotter's theoretical terms? It means precisely that the individual's expectancies are low.

When a person encounters barriers of one kind or another in respect of an entire group of behaviors related to a given type of reinforcement (such as recognition or affection), that person has low expectancies for each of them. Hence the person's freedom of movement is low. There is no way his or her own efforts can result in movement toward desired reinforcements.

Need Value

Need value (NV) refers to the average relative preference for one group of reinforcements over another. It is therefore an average of reinforcement values taken over a number of similar reinforcing circumstances.

Let us consider the party situation again. Mary Jane prefers to get high, but not to the complete exclusion of dancing. However, she is not at all interested in finding business contacts. Using h for high, d for dancing, and b for business contacts, we would write:

$$RV_h > RV_d > RV_b$$

Suppose we know also that Mary Jane turned down a job offer making $800.00 a month as a sales representative for a big company, but accepted an offer of $450.00 a month as a resident sports counselor at a resort, with special emphasis on tennis and exercise. On her free time there she spends more hours swimming, relaxing in the sauna, and getting a massage than she does arranging for extra hours of tutoring for extra money.

We could represent these facts as follows:

$$RV_t > RV_s \quad \textit{(tennis and sales)}$$
$$RV_m > RV_x \quad \textit{(massage and extras)}$$

When we look at all three situations now (party, job, time off) we find that there are commonalities between certain reinforcements from different situations. We find that highs and massages involve bodily comfort; dancing and tennis involve physical activity; and business contacts, sales, and extras earned through special tutoring all involve getting ahead financially.

If we add up the equations so that reinforcements of the same type are put together, we conclude that Mary Jane has a higher need value for bodily comfort (bc) and physical activity (pa) than she does for recognition (r) through financial success.

Parallel to our expression for freedom of movement, we could write:

$$NV_{bc} = [RV_h + RV_m] \cdot 1/2$$
$$NV_{pa} = [RV_d + RV_t] \cdot 1/2$$
$$NV_r = [RV_b + RV_s + RV_x] \cdot 1/3$$

We could conclude that, for Mary Jane,

$$NV_{bc} > NV_{pa} > NV_r$$

Is there any advantage to formulating the NV levels? There certainly is, because we can now predict to new situations in which similar reinforcements are available. Although the person has not yet encountered those situations, we may predict their levels of expectancy and reinforcement value because these *generalize* or spread over to situations involving similar reinforcements.

Accomplishments of Rotter's Theory

Rotter's theory has accomplished a great deal already, and we select only a few illustrative topics here: psychological adjustment, I-E, and problem behavior.

Psychological Adjustment

Rotter and Hochreich (1975, p. 102) point out that one pattern of complex potentials has special importance for personality adjustment. It is the pattern of high need value and low freedom of movement. The person wants a certain kind of reinforcement very badly but feels unable to secure that reinforcement by his or her own efforts.

For example, a young man may very much want to receive love and affection from a girl but feel completely unable to make the necessary moves. For one reason or another in his history he expects to fail in any attempt he makes to become friends with a girl or to date her. Following Lewin's suggestion that the life space contains a level of unreality as well as a level of reality, Rotter states that the young man with such a personality pattern may resort to *irreal* or fantasy behaviors in the attempt to achieve his goals. He might spend a great deal of time daydreaming about lovely girls beseeching him to return their ardent passion for him.

The young man might also seek to avoid the pain of failure by avoiding situations in which such failures might be experienced. He pretends that he dislikes dances, parties, and other situations where he might meet a girl.

Or he may convince himself that he has no need for affection from girls. Rotter and Hochreich state that in social learning theory all of the defenses and symptoms of psychopathology or mental illness are considered to be avoidance or irreal behaviors.

How would such a person be helped by a clinician using social learning theory? The problem arises from a discrepancy between the person's level of need value and his freedom of movement. So the clinician would attempt to help the person reduce this discrepancy by increasing his freedom of movement.

In some cases, such as need value for dominance, it might be possible to reduce the discrepancy by reducing the need value as well as by increasing freedom of movement.

Internal-External Control

We have seen that a person's feeling of being able to secure a particular reinforcement through his or her own efforts is called *expectancy*. Josephine's expectancy for good grades might be high; for winning at track, medium; for being nominated outstanding senior girl, quite high. We have seen that these expectancies influence each other and average out to a more generalized expectancy that the person can obtain a particular *kind* of reinforcement. Josephine would have a pretty high expectancy that she could obtain recognition through her own behaviors. We would say that she has high *freedom of movement* for recognition. She can get recognition in the amounts she desires through a wide array of different behaviors and situations.

Having high freedom of movement for recognition, will Josephine also have high freedom of movement for affection? For dominance? For independence? We cannot say without further information. But even as high expectancy can generalize to high freedom of movement for an entire class of reinforcements, so high freedom of movement for one or a few classes of reinforcements can generalize to all or most classes. Persons can come to believe that, in general, the reinforcements they receive are consequent upon their own behavior. Alternatively they can learn to believe that reinforcements happen to them independently of their own efforts. In the latter case they might believe either that other people control all their reinforcements or that it is a matter of luck.

Obviously there is a continuum of belief. We have cited the two extremes. At one extreme the person believes that all of the rewards and punishments he or she gets in life are strictly the results of the individual's own behaviors, skills, knowledge, stupidity, or ignorance. At the other extreme the person believes that whatever the quality of his or her own performances something out there is really responsible for the rewards and punishments dealt out. In between there is an entire range of beliefs. We might believe that most rewards are contingent upon our own behavior but some are controlled by external forces. We might believe that most rewards are controlled by external forces but that sometimes effort on our part can affect the outcome. We might believe that most things in life come to us as a result partly of our own efforts and partly of factors over which we have no control.

This continuum has been called the variable of *belief in internal versus external control of reinforcement*. Various attempts have been made to measure this variable as a stable characteristic of personality. The most widely used measure is the I-E Scale (internal-external control scale) described by Rotter (1966). This measure contains twenty-three items of the following kind:

Choose the one statement in each pair which best fits what you personally believe to be the case in life:

Pair 1. A. When I plan for something it nearly always happens that way.

B. Planning ahead is not much use because so many things happen that upset your plans.

Pair 2. A. People who study and try hard usually get to be a success.

B. Getting ahead in life is mainly a matter of luck.

Pair 3. A. Any American citizen can make his voice felt in government.

B. The world is controlled by a few rich and powerful people, so that most people cannot influence it one way or the other.

In these items, which are similar to those of the original test, the choice of alternative A in each pair reflects a belief in internal control—in the ability of the person to control outcomes or reinforcements; B alternatives reflect a belief in external control. In the actual I-E Scale the external control choices are scored, and a high score on the I-E Scale reflects a high degree of belief in the external control of reinforcements. The test has been found to be quite reliable and to be independent of intellectual ability. This means that belief in internal or external control is not correlated with intelligence or other measures of general ability.

Since there are twenty-three items in the I-E Scale the maximum possible score would be 23, with one point for each external choice. On a national stratified sample of high-school youth the mean score was found to be 8.50. A group of Peace Corps trainees received 5.94, the lowest mean score reported by Rotter (1966). A group of eighteen-year old males from the Boston area received 10, the highest mean score reported.

Does the I-E Scale predict ordinary behavioral and experiential phenomena? Rotter's (1966) summary of evidence suggests that it does. Patients with greater degrees of belief in internal control were found to know more about their own sickness and to have questioned doctors and nurses more in search of relevant information. Reformatory inmates with higher internal control (lower I-E scores) remembered more facts about how the reformatory was run and about the legal and economic conditions they would be facing when they got out. Black students with higher internal control scores were more ready to commit themselves to activist participation in the civil rights movement; in an independent study it was found that subjects who already were engaged in civil rights activity had higher internal control than those who were not. In Sweden it was found that workers with union membership, more activity in the unions, and greater knowledge of political matters also had higher internal control than those who were not members or were less active or had less knowledge.

The I-E Scale has been widely used by other investigators. Lefcourt (1972) for example reports on many studies relating I-E to anxiety or depression. In almost all cases the more external subject is also more anxious or depressed. It is not clear why this should be so, since the more external person should also be less likely to take failures personally. Lefcourt and colleagues (1974) suggest that even though the internal control subject believes in personal responsibility for life outcomes, he or she somehow manages to keep such experiences at a distance, often through the use of humor. These authors used a word association test in which subjects listened as the experimenter read out the list of words. Only subject and experimenter were present in the room; however, the subject's facial expressions were videotaped and all verbal responses were recorded. It was found, as expected, that the more internal subjects used more humor throughout the experiment. This included both social humor directed toward the experimenter and other kinds of humor elicited by some of the test materials that had double meanings (such as *bust* or *pet*).

Phares and Lamiell (1975) note that many studies have been done which show that those higher on internal control have greater mastery tendencies, greater resistance to influence from other people, and greater likelihood of achievement striving. All these are general personality characteristics of the more internal person. How do such people treat others? Do they think others are or should be internal too? Phares and Lamiell presented case his-

tories of people in trouble (exconvict, welfare recipient, and war veteran); subjects were asked to rate these in terms of the help and sympathy each person deserved. Subjects who were more internal gave ratings which showed that they thought people in trouble were less deserving of help and sympathy.

It is clear that internal versus external control is a powerful and pervasive characteristic of personality. Figure 20.1 illustrates how internal control is built up from generalization of freedom of movement, which is built from generalization of expectancies.

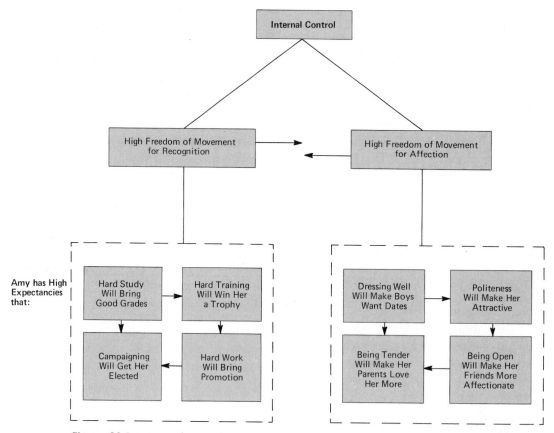

Figure 20.1. Internal control is built up from freedom of movement in several domains. Freedom of movement is built up from expectancies in particular situations. Arrows indicate generalization.

Problem Behavior

At the University of Colorado Richard Jessor and his associates have for several years pursued a program of research into problem behavior. This includes drinking and alcoholism, drug use, delinquency, and other deviant behaviors. The theory has incorporated Rotter's social learning theory and has added to it in numerous ways. For example, in addition to expectancies and reinforcement or need values, Jessor and his colleagues invoke concepts of controls by society and controls within the individual. They measure the person's environment as perceived, especially focusing upon the person's perceptions of how his or her friends or parents respond to various matters.

One major study, published in 1968 (Jessor et al., 1968), showed that drinking (beer, wine, and liquor) is influenced by the discrepancy between a person's need values for recognition and his or her freedom of movement for getting recognition reinforcements. It showed that societal pressures were important also.

In the latest series of researches, Jessor and his colleagues have asked how problem behaviors develop in youth. They have studied high school and college students over a four-year period, searching for those factors in the person and in the environment which are likely to produce various types of problem behavior. Problem behavior is viewed as behavior that goes against prevailing norms or social expectations for a person of a given age. During middle or late adolescence it becomes increasingly more acceptable for young people to do those things that characterize adult behavior in a given society.

One of the recent studies focused upon the question of when young people make the transition from virginity to nonvirginity (Jessor & Jessor, 1975). All subjects were asked in each year of the study whether they had

ever had sexual intercourse with a person of the opposite sex. Those who replied no were classified as virgins; those who replied yes were classified as nonvirgins. Thus it was possible to study the transition from virginity to nonvirginity by noting whether a person's classification changed from one year to the next.

Need values were assessed by having students rate how important it was to them to secure various goals or reinforcements in the domains of academic achievement, personal independence, and love and affection from peers. For example, they would be asked to rate how much they liked to have friends with them on holidays or to be thought of as a best friend by many of their peers. Answers indicating they would like these things very much would be scored as indicating a high need value for affection from peers.

Freedom of movement was scored from similar ratings. Subjects would be asked to rate how strongly they expect to have friends want to be with them on holidays, or how strongly they expect several of their peers to consider them as a best friend. Thus the expectancies for getting affection reinforcements in various situations with friends would be added up to produce a measure of freedom of movement for affection with peers.

Among the virgins in year three of the high-school study some became nonvirgins during the fourth year of the study, having their first experience of sexual intercourse during that year. How did those who made the transition from virginity to nonvirginity compare with those who did not? Were there personality differences between the two groups even in year three, *before* some made the transition and others did not?

The results showed that males and females had quite different patterns. Males who became nonvirgins during that year had higher need value for affection and higher need value for independence than those who remained virgins. Moreover they had higher freedom of movement for both affection and independence. Recall that the affection has to do with love and affection from peers (friends) in *nonsexual* aspects of relationship. We conclude that becoming a nonvirgin can be predicted among young males who especially prize the love and affection of their friends and who also value highly their own independence, especially from family and conventional restraints.

By contrast, females who became nonvirgins during the succeeding year were *lower* on need value for affection and lower on need value for achievement than those who remained virgins. Thus the pattern of motivation and freedom of movement that differentiates male nonvirgins from male virgins differs from the pattern that distinguishes female nonvirgins from virgins. These differences hold *before* the transition to nonvirginity.

One feature of the results was shared by males and females. For both it was found that those who became nonvirgins had lower freedom of movement for achievement in academics. Jessor and Jessor show that there is strong evidence against the hypothesis that having sexual intercourse is a way of gaining status among these students. Therefore it is unlikely that becoming a nonvirgin is used as compensation for lower expectancy with regard to academic achievement. Indeed, although the result by itself is similar for males and females, it should be coupled with the results for need value of academic achievement. There was a tendency for male nonvirgins to be *higher* than male virgins on this need value, while female nonvirgins were significantly *lower* than female virgins. This suggests that, whatever the precise dynamics are, they differ for males and females.

As Jessor and Jessor state, within the total patterns of results obtained in their study (which included measures of perceived environment, controls, and other variables), the results on personality give once again clear evidence of the theoretical power of social learning theory.

Critique of Rotter's Theory of Function

Perhaps the most damaging criticism of Rotter's theory of function is that advanced by Bandura and Walters, who write (1963, p. 2), "Rotter's account of the learning process presupposes the existence of a hierarchy of responses that tend to occur in different situations with varying degrees of probability; it is therefore quite inadequate for explaining the occurrence of a response that has not yet been learned." In other words, Rotter's theory cannot account for the occurrence of a novel response.

It may be that this criticism fails to take account of the principles of generalization and interaction between expectancies. Consider the following statement of Tolman's theory of purposive behavior, which is very similar to Rotter's theory of personality. Tolman distinguishes between two kinds of expectancy: 1) *means-end readiness*, which is an acquired dispositional structure; 2) when activated by the arousal of a drive, means-end readiness emerges as an *expectancy*. Tolman writes (1959, p. 105):

These dispositions or readinesses can be thought of as dispositional sets for certain types of stimulus $\rightarrow$ response $\rightarrow$ stimulus sequences or for certain types of stimulus $\rightarrow$ stimulus sequences. In other words, when an *instance* of an s_1 [a stimulus of sort 1] is presented, there tends to be released an expectancy . . . that an instance of the kind of performance symbolized by r_1 will lead to an instance of s_2. . . . [Symbolically]

$$[(s_1 r_1 \rightarrow s_f) \cdot (s_f r_f \rightarrow s_m) \cdot (s_1 \bar{r}_1 \rightarrow s_{\bar{f}}) \cdot (s_{\bar{f}} \rightarrow s_{\bar{m}})]$$

This stands for the fact that the animal has acquired a disposition or set to the effect that an s_1 *type* of stimulus, when manipulated by an r_1 *type* of response, will lead to a food stimulus of *type* s_f; and that he has also acquired a set to the effect that food stimuli of the *type* s_f, when manipulated by the eating *type* of response r_1, will lead to mouth, stomach, and nutritional goal stimuli of *type* s_m; and that he has a set to the effect that not performing an r_1 (i.e. $\bar{r_1}$) will lead to, or leave him in the presence of, nonfood stimuli of type s_f . . . [and so on].

Note the similarity between Tolman's construct of *means-end readiness* and Rotter's construct of *expectancy*. Tolman's construct of *expectancy* is implied by but not included in Rotter's construct of *expectancy*, which is entirely dispositional in meaning: It serves to determine behavior *potential* rather than the actual occurrence of a behavior only. We have the view in Tolman's theory of a set of readinesses which are not manifested except when activated. For the rat, these readinesses "remain present in him (or, if you prefer, in his nervous system) *whether or not he is hungry at the moment* and *whether or not any instances of the type of stimuli and responses in question are present at the moment*" (Tolman, 1959, pp. 105-106). Tolman also notes that the separate items in a total set of means-end readinesses (such as described above in the formula) can exist and function independently of the others. For example, an animal can learn that eating certain food leads to certain taste stimuli without having first learned that going down a certain alley leads to the presence of those food stimuli. The separate readinesses are separate and can recombine. Moreover they can *telescope,* so that the animal learns to take shortcuts. For example, the lengthy sequence above might telescope as follows:

$$(s_1 r_1 \rightarrow s_m) \cdot (s_1 \bar{r_1} \rightarrow s_{\bar{m}})$$

We should note further that Tolman emphasizes that the readinesses are concerned with a *type* of s_1, a *type* of r_1, and a *type* of s_2. Within the type there may be significant variations. The possibility for *generalization* is obviously present. No wonder then that these separate, chainable, telescopable *types* of means-end readinesses "combine and interact . . . the experiments on insight, reasoning, and short-cutting suggest that readinesses can be added and multiplied as well as telescoped. And when so added or multiplied, they may lead to new responses, never before exhibited" (Tolman, 1959, p. 106). Tolman's suggestion is thus a direct answer to the criticism of Rotter's theory that it cannot account for the occurrence of novel responses.

One may wonder why it is that Rotter's theory has been so widely accepted and continues to be so fruitful, when Lewin's theory on which Rotter's is based has fallen into disuse. Does Rotter's theory have any particular constructs that account for the difference? Certainly the construct of internal versus external control has been very important in recent research and theory in personality and social psychology. It seems to be conceptually related to Lewin's construct of *power,* however (see chapter 19). Other relationships are numerous, as table 20.1 suggests.

Two things become clear in the comparisons of table 20.1. First, Lewin's topological formulation (field, force, regions, tension systems, boundaries, permeability) does not find a comparable set of constructs in Rotter's theory. Second, related constructs are apt to be given a more externalized meaning in Rotter's system, and hence are often accompanied by readier operational definitions. An example is Rotter's construct of *need,* which is defined as a group of behaviors related by leading to similar reinforcements, contrasted with Lewin's *need* or *quasi-need* which was a "sort of reservoir of energy" (Lewin, 1935, p. 50).

Table 20.1

Comparisons of Some Constructs in Lewin's and Rotter's Theories

Rotter's Theory	Lewin's Theory
Behavior potential	Behavior
Expectancy (that behavior will lead to reinforcement)	Hope of success and fear of failure; level of aspiration
Reinforcement value	Valence
Need potential	?
Freedom of movement	Freedom of movement
Need	Need, Quasi-need
Reinforcement-reinforcement sequences	Imbedded needs
Meaningful environment or psychological situation	Psychological environment
Real and irreal behavior	Levels of reality and unreality
Internal-external control	Power
	Force Permeability
	Field Tension system
	Barrier Person
	Region Life space
	Boundary Whole

Because it is possible to point to behaviors and reinforcements while it is not possible to point to a sort of reservoir of energy, it is also possible to *measure* needs and need potentials and need values in Rotter's approach. Thus Rotter's theory, although having much in common conceptually with Lewin's theory, nevertheless is more serviceable to scientists because its constructs have been formulated in ways more amenable to measurement.

Evaluation of the Theory

As we come to evaluate Rotter's theory on our usual criteria, we realize that we have already said much that needs to be said. The research evidence amply indicates the theory's *accuracy,* and the large amount of research in diverse fields testifies at once to the *power* of the theory and to its *fruitfulness.* Before considering the theory's depth, let us examine its implicit definition of personality, in terms of the concepts developed in chapter 2. There is no reference to the body. Psychophysical structures are implied by stable needs, expectancies, and characteristics. The reference to experience is not as explicit in Rotter's theory as it is in Lewin's, but it is clear in at least two major contexts: in the meaning of *behavior* (which includes overt behaviors, verbal behaviors, and *cognitive* "reactions") and in the "subjective" probability aspect of *expectancy.*

This lack of precision in distinguishing between behavior and experience may account for some of the confusion that some readers feel about Rotter's theory (myself included). The puzzle seems to rest on the fact that the basic constructs of the theory sound very precise and objective, and they are. The more complex constructs of the theory seem precise also, phrased simply as complications of the more basic constructs, even as *freedom of movement* is defined as being merely a collection of *expectancies* with respect to a need-related group of behaviors. But somehow these more complex constructs take on a greater flexibility of interpretation than seems consistent with their presumed objectivity. Thus a clinician, seeking to increase a client's freedom of movement, using Rotter's theory, is presumably addressing himself or herself to helping the client *feel* more confident, *think* more positively, use the *irreal* "behaviors" more constructively. But what are irreal behaviors? They are *fantasies,* and indeed all of these things such as feelings, thoughts, and fantasies are very subjective matters, part of what we have called subjective experience. These puzzles actually can be traced back to the basic construct of behavior (and behavior potential), however; right there Rotter does not distinguish between behavior and experience but includes them both under the term *behavior.*

Returning to the criterion of *depth,* insight into mechanisms, my own judgment is that the theory is not very deep. I believe this is by design, for Rotter has apparently aimed to externalize and measure rather than penetrate into mechanisms. He has won accuracy, power, and fruitfulness at the expense of depth. Perhaps the ability to measure behavioral constructs has also been purchased at the cost of insightful representation of subjective experience and unconscious dynamics. In this respect Miller and Dollard (chapter 7) do very much better.

Workshop 20

Using Rotter's Theory

A good clinical psychologist, upon receiving a copy of a new psychological test, will always check it out first by a simple validation procedure: the psychologist takes the test just like any subject or patient would. Then the results can be compared with what the psychologist believes to be the real facts of his or her personality.

We can do a similar thing with almost any personality theory and check what we might call its **experiential validity** against our own self-understanding. One way to approach it in the case of Rotter's theory is to take the list of needs so far discovered and estimate our own need value and freedom of movement on each. The list of needs is given earlier in the chapter. Relevant expectancies may be set out as in figure 20.1. Fill in suitable events for yourself opposite b, c, and d below.

Rate your estimates on a scale of 1 to 5 in the following way:

Very high = 5; High = 4; Medium = 3; Low = 2; Very Low = 1.

Needs	Reinforcement values		Expectancies	
	For me, **this event** would have **this value**		For me, that event would result from **my behavior** with this **level of probability**	
1. Recognition	a. Good grades	_____ (1, 2, 3, 4 or 5)	Working hard	_____ (1, 2, 3, 4 or 5)
	b. _____ (fill in)	_____	_____	_____
	c. _____	_____	_____	_____
	d. _____	_____	_____	_____
		Sum= _____		Sum= _____
2. Dominance	a. Winning an argument		_____	_____
	b. _____	_____	_____	_____

Needs	Reinforcement values		Expectancies	
	For me, **this event** would have **this value**		For me, that event would result from **my behavior** with this **level of probability**	
	c. _____ _____		_____ _____	
	d. _____ _____		_____ _____	
	Sum=_____		Sum=_____	
3. Independence	a. Paying my own tuition		_____ _____	
	b. _____ _____		_____ _____	
	c. _____ _____		_____ _____	
	d. _____ _____		_____ _____	
	Sum= _____		Sum=_____	
4. Protection	a. Getting a medical check-up		_____ _____	
	b. _____ _____		_____ _____	
	c. _____ _____		_____ _____	
	d. _____ _____		_____ _____	
	Sum= _____		Sum= _____	
5. Affection	a. A new romance _____		_____ _____	
	b. _____ _____		_____ _____	
	c. _____ _____		_____ _____	
	d. _____ _____		_____ _____	
	Sum= _____		Sum= _____	
6. Comfort	a. Getting a waterbed		_____ _____	
	b. _____ _____		_____ _____	
	c. _____ _____		_____ _____	
	d. _____ _____		_____ _____	
	Sum= _____		Sum= _____	

Divide every sum by 4 to get an average. Plot the average reinforcement values to get a profile of your need values over the six needs. Sum the six probability averages (which are freedom of movement scores) and divide by 6 to get your estimate of internal-external control.

Summary

Rotter's theory has two main equations. The simplest states that *behavior potential* is a function of *expectancy* and *reinforcement value*. The second refers to a complex collection of behavior potentials, all related to the same or similar reinforcements. These behavior potentials are called a *need potential*. A collection of need-related expectancies is called *freedom of movement* with respect to the given need. The related collection of reinforcement values is called *need value*. The second equation, then, states that need potential is a function of freedom of movement and need value with respect to the given need. A need itself is a group of behaviors leading to similar reinforcements. Rotter and his associates have so far empirically determined the existence of six main needs: recognition, dominance, independence, protection, affection, and physical comfort.

Freedom of movement with respect to a given need means the subjective probability a person feels with respect to how likely his or her own behaviors are to produce the satisfactions (reinforcements) desired. Adding up the freedom of movement of an individual across all six needs provides an estimate of overall freedom of movement, which is called internal-external control. The more internal person believes that, in general, outcomes are dependent upon one's own efforts. The more external person believes that, in general, outcomes are dependent on luck, fate, other people, powerful authorities, and so on.

The theory has had outstanding accomplishments in social, clinical, and personality psychology. It seems to be quite accurate, powerful, and fruitful, but has only slight depth. It is much like Lewin's theory, except that his topological constructs have been omitted and the other constructs have been given a more externalized meaning more amenable to measurement. Figure 20.2 illus-

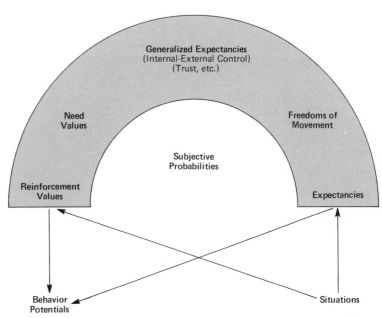

Figure 20.2. Definition of personality implicit in Rotter's theory

trates the implicit definition of personality in Rotter's theory.

In the next chapter we will study the theory of social behavior developed by Bandura and Walters, a theory which is related to Rotter's in name but, as we shall see, is much closer in concept to Skinner's, and is in competition with the theory developed by Miller and Dollard.

INTRODUCTION

A social learning theory born in competition with
other social learning theories
Introduction to the life and work of Bandura and
Walters
Bandura
Walters
Main purpose and methodological assumptions
Account for human learning in social contexts
Methodological assumptions
Imitative learning occurs without response or
reward
Psychodynamic constructs to be avoided
Important variables in antecedent events
Examples of assumptions in various critiques
of other theories
Critique of Miller's and Dollard's model of
displacement
Critique of psychodynamic disease constructs
Critique of body constructs
Critique of trait constructs
More productive approach through selection
of variables of child behavior and of parent
behavior
Principles of learning
Observational learning
Classical and instrumental conditioning
Extinction, schedules, generalization,
discrimination
Procedures which teach children to inhibit
responses
Punishment may produce conditioned emotional
responses in both actor and observer
Details of observational learning
Technical meaning of observational learning
Acquisition and performance
An experimental demonstration
Effects of consequences to the model
Four effects of observational learning
Vicarious reinforcement
Characteristics of the models
Symbolic models
Coding and higher mental processes
Accomplishments of the theory
Behavior modification
Treatment through social imitation
A case of systematic desensitization
Critique of the social learning theory developed by
Bandura and Walters
An integrative summary of modern learning
theory applications
Compatible with theories emphasizing cognitive
processes
Compatible with classical conditioning
Compatible with operant conditioning
Is social learning theory a theory, an application
of other theories, an approach, a conceptual
framework, or what?
Is it a single set of principles? No.
Is it a set of principles characterized by their
social nature? No.
Does it exclude internal processes as causal
links? No.
Are its principles capable of explaining
laboratory findings? Most are not.
Accuracy, power, fruitfulness, and depth
Are the theoretical models of imitation offered
by Miller and Dollard on one hand and by
Bandura and Walters on the other actually
in competition with each other? No; they deal
with different sets of facts.
Workshop 21 Matched-dependent and
observational learning
Summary

21

A Competing Social Learning Theory of Personality: Bandura and Walters

Like Miller and Dollard (chapter 7) and like Rotter (chapter 20), Bandura and Walters offer a social learning theory of personality. Unlike these other social learning theorists, however, Bandura and Walters believe that the data of personality can be better formulated by applying the principles of learning, especially by applying those principles in a strictly social context. To understand their approach to personality, then, we shall have to understand how they conceptualize learning. As we shall see, the theory developed by Bandura and Walters was born in competition, created in the center of disagreements with the theories of Miller and Dollard, Rotter, and others. As might be expected, because it is somewhat later in development, it reflects the maturity of psychological science to date.

Albert Bandura was born in 1925 and was trained in clinical psychology at the University of Iowa, where he received his Ph.D. in 1952. In 1953 Bandura joined the faculty of psychology at Stanford University where he is currently professor of psychology. His work has been devoted almost entirely to the development of adequate principles of learning for use in clinical psychology under the very general heading of *behavior modification*. His first two books were written in collaboration with Richard Walters on social learning and his later work has continued to address topics of the same kind, for example, *Principles of Behavior Modification,* 1969. Bandura served as President of the American Psychological Association for the year 1974-75.

Richard Walters was born in Wales and studied philosophy at Oxford University. He taught philosophy at Auckland University College in New Zealand for a few years before deciding to do graduate work in psychology. He obtained a Ph.D. in psychology at Stanford University where he studied under Bandura, with whom he subsequently did collaborative work. Walters became professor of psychology at Waterloo University, Ontario, in 1963. There he pursued a vigorous program of research in social learning until his untimely death in 1968.

Main Purpose and Methodological Assumptions

In their collaborative work Bandura and Walters have two main aims: first, to develop the most effective possible account of human learning in social contexts; second, to develop scientifically sound procedures for the modification of undesirable social behavior. Toward this aim they make the methodological assumption that principles of learning may be taken from a wide variety of theories, including those of Hull and Skinner (see chapter 4). They also assume that laboratory-based theoretical principles can be applied with equal scientific confidence to situations of importance in the everyday world, as for example in their work on aggression (Bandura & Walters, *Adolescent Aggression,* 1959) and on personality development, deviancy, and behavior modification (Bandura and Walters, *Social Learning and Personality Development,* 1963).

Briefly, the principles of learning adopted by Bandura and Walters include those of Miller and Dollard (drive, cue, response, reward, conditioning, extinction, spontaneous recovery, generalization, discrimination) and of other learning theorists. Their main purpose, however is to apply these theories to a comprehensive account of human learning in ordinary social life. For this purpose they find the existing theories inadequate because they neglect the social variables of parental influence. Parents exert such influence through direct training and also by providing, largely without knowing it, examples of behavior which children observe and learn without actually emitting matched responses and receiving rewards.

Methodological Assumptions

Many of the methodological assumptions in social learning theory as formulated by Bandura and Walters are couched in terms of polarized views of other theories as contrasted with their own theory. Miller and Dollard, they say, proposed an inadequate theory which requires response and reward to be present for imitative learning to take place; Bandura and Walters, on the other hand, recognize the importance of imitative learning without re-

sponse and in the absence of reward. Many theorists of learning (including Miller and Dollard) have attempted to take the psychodynamic constructs of psychoanalysis and translate them into the constructs of learning theory. But Bandura and Walters believe that whatever processes these psychodynamic constructs (such as *displacement*) refer to may be best conceived as *mediating events*—if indeed they are to be allowed in the theory at all. They themselves explicitly attempt to avoid psychodynamic constructs, since they believe that such constructs do not help in the goal of achieving behavior modification: "they cannot be directly manipulated and consequently are of little importance in implementing programs for modifying behavior" (Bandura & Walters, 1963, p. 31). Moreover, they believe that use of such concepts makes the user focus upon underlying psychological causes and conditions in the person, and that this focus diverts attention away from more important variables such as the direct training behaviors parents have emitted toward their children. They emphasize that it is important to look for such antecedent events in attempting to understand a child's behavior patterns, and that detailed descriptions of the child's behaviors must be related as dependent variables to the antecedent events so observed.

For example, they note that the model of displacement formulated by Miller and Dollard has been used to understand results concerning highly aggressive boys whose parents have been found to punish aggression severely in the home (Bandura & Walters, 1959). Such findings appear to confirm the theoretical model that tendencies to express aggressive responses will be displaced away from the original target when those responses have been punished if emitted toward that target. But other findings show that those same parents also *encourage* aggression outside; therefore "the apparently displaced aggression may be primarily an outcome of discrimination training" (Bandura & Walters, 1963, p. 18). In other words, instead of seeing the aggression as displaced, Bandura and Walters believe it results from parental encouragement.

As another example, Bandura and Walters argue that the psychodynamic model of inner psychological causes is part of a more general "medical model" or "disease model." They write about this more fully as follows:

> The psychodynamic "disease" model thus leads one to seek determinants of deviant behavior in terms of relatively autonomous internal agents and processes in the form of "unconscious psychic forces," "damned-up energies," "cathexes," "counter-cathexes," "defenses," "complexes," and other hypothetical conditions or states having only a tenuous relationship to the social stimuli that precede them or even to the behavioral "symptoms" or "symbols" that they supposedly explain. In contrast, our social learning theory, instead of regarding internal processes as primary links in causal sequences that generate deviant patterns of response, treats such processes as mediating events, the nature of, and modifications in which, must be inferred from the conjunction of certain manipulable stimulus conditions and observable response sequences (Bandura & Walters, 1963, pp. 30-31).

While they acknowledge that some genetic and other influences associated with the body may have indirect consequences for an individual's development (for example, by being too small in a society that prizes large stature), Bandura and Walters feel that "even when genetically determined attributes remain relatively constant, social-learning variables may produce marked differences in patterns of social behavior" (Bandura & Walters, 1963, pp. 28-29). They therefore set such constructs aside, saying that "there is more to be gained by studying the role of undoubtedly important social-learning variables in personality development than by seeking to establish relation-ships between constitutional factors and personality characteristics" (Bandura & Walters, 1963, p. 29).

Bandura and Walters believe that theories employing trait constructs (such as those of Cattell or Eysenck; see chapters 15 and 17) are based upon erroneous assumptions and have had a bad influence because they arise from "observations of highly deviant individuals" and utilize "categories borrowed from descriptive psychiatry" (Bandura & Walters, 1963, p. 37). Such categories, they believe, are not useful because they are based upon "diverse responses exhibited by different groups of patients, most of whom do not fall precisely into any available category . . ." (Bandura & Walters, 1963, p. 37). To sum up their views on this matter of trait theories and personality tests they state that "the existence of such trait theories and related measuring devices has, in general, had the effect of encouraging imprecise, descriptive research and so of hampering progress in the discovery of the antecedent-consequent relationships that regulate social behavior" (Bandura & Walters, 1963, p. 37).

Moving to the opposite side of this polarity, they continue with the contrasting features of social learning theory by quoting from an earlier book (Bandura & Walters, 1959, p. 362) in which they state: "A more productive and less confusing approach to the understanding of behavior disorders is to examine carefully the process by which socialization of behavior is achieved and to select dimensions or variables of child behavior that appear to be of importance for the socialization process." Similarly, they recommend selection of variables of the behavior of parents and others who wield socialization influence. These may then be studied through appropriate assessments in field research or through appropriate manipulation in experimental research. Bandura and Walters believe that both kinds of research are necessary to make sure that what is studied in the laboratory is as closely relevant to real life as possible and also that what is discovered in field studies is put into the crucible of carefully controlled experiment.

In searching for relationships between parental behaviors and child behaviors Bandura and Walters recognize that causal relations may be difficult to disentangle. For example, aggressive fathers encourage aggressiveness in their sons and also place heavy demands on their wives. As a result the wives may give less time to the children; it might be concluded that deprivation of maternal attention produced aggressiveness in sons. The only way to tease out such causal intricacies is to do very carefully controlled field studies of contrasting groups or to manipulate the variables independently. But Bandura and Walters recognize also that it is extremely difficult to do manipulative experiments on human beings, especially when the variables are concerned with punishment, deprivation, and the like. Here it is often necessary to use animal subjects and extrapolate to human beings as best one can. In other instances it is possible to simulate situations sufficiently closely so that the operation of one or two crucial variables can be examined. They give the following example:

> . . . if the experimenter is interested in the socialization process and wishes to test a hypothesis concerning the effect of family interactions, his grounds for extrapolation will be firmer if he experimentally creates an analogue of the nuclear family, in which male and female adults serve as the mother and father figures, than if he simply observes the child's responses to mother and father dolls. In the former case, he can systematically vary the behavior of the experimental "parents" and observe the effects upon his child subjects (Bandura & Walters, 1963, p. 42).

Bandura and Walters have thus provided a clear picture of what they believe should and should not be done. They also make clear the purpose of these actions and avoidances; they aim to "provide data for an adequate science of social learning" (Bandura & Walters, 1963, p. 42). Although much of their system is reminiscent of Skinner's theory (see chapter 4), Bandura and Walters insist that Skinner's system cannot adequately account for much social learning, precisely because it does not allow for observational learning. Let us turn now to consider what principles of learning Bandura and Walters do accept from previous theorists, and what new principles they contribute.

Principles of Learning

We have already said briefly that Bandura and Walters accept most of the concepts and principles used by Miller and Dollard (even though they may not accept some of the specific theoretical models Miller and Dollard developed, such as displacement, for example.) But Bandura and Walters are quite explicit about the deficiencies in the system proposed by Miller and Dollard. They point out that Miller and Dollard conceived of imitation, for example, as one form of *instrumental conditioning*, in which responses are learned if they lead to reward. In imitation, or specifically in the form Miller and Dollard called *matched-dependent* behavior, the matching response is supposed to be learned only if it is actually made by the imitator and rewarded.

Indeed, in the commentary upon the case of Bobby and his brother in chapter 7, Miller and Dollard made it explicit that Bobby's learning of the imitative response would have been impossible without his having the drive, impossible without his perceiving the cue of his brother's running, impossible if he had not been able to respond by running himself, and impossible if he had not been rewarded for making that response. This formulation, however, is directly contradicted by the findings that subjects can learn by observing a leader's or model's behavior without actually making a matching response and without receiving a reward. That is, they learn simply by observing the behavior of the other person. Additionally, subjects' learning of behavior from a model is influenced by the consequences to the model. That is, whether the model is rewarded or punished for the behavior affects the learning of the observer. The process whereby this influence is exerted on the observer is called *vicarious reinforcement*. For example, a young boy who sees an older boy get money by stealing learns that stealing brings rewards. Therefore the principles of learning formulated by Hull and by Skinner must be revised and extended to take account of purely observational learning.

Bandura and Walters continue with a brief summary of principles they feel should be retained in the revised version. These include both *classical* and *instrumental conditioning* (Type S and Type R in chapter 4), *extinction, schedules, generalization,* and *discrimination* (see chapters 4 and 7). Much of social training, they note, requires that certain responses be eliminated or at least suppressed. For example, behaviors not fitting local customs must be inhibited. Again, children see adults engaging in a variety of permitted behaviors which are prohibited for children (such as smoking or drinking liquor), and so observational learning of these behaviors must be augmented by procedures designed to counteract the tendency of children to perform such responses themselves. Such procedures would teach a child to *inhibit* those responses.

Three ways to teach inhibition are: *nonreward*, withholding a previously given reward (now known as *frustrative nonreward,*

after Amsel, 1958), and *punishment*. Nonreward is simply ignoring all responses other than those which are socially approved. Punishment is the delivery of aversive stimuli, such as pain. In experimental studies of conditioning with painful stimuli it has been shown that a neutral cue can acquire the ability to elicit an avoidance or other response that was previously elicited only by the original painful stimulus, and it has been shown that such conditioned avoidance responses are very resistant to extinction; that is, when the previously neutral stimulus has been conditioned by repeated pairing with the painful stimulus, then subsequent presentations of the previously neutral stimulus *without* the painful stimulus present will continue to elicit avoidance responses for a long time (Solomon, Kamin, & Wynne, 1953). Following Neal Miller's demonstration that fear may be acquired as a drive and serve as reinforcement (through drive reduction) for the learning of new responses (Miller, 1948a), Bandura and Walters accept the principle that punishment may produce conditioned emotional responses (as well as avoidance responses) which serve to motivate further learning. For example, they write, "Conditioned emotional responses may, in fact, be elicited simply by the presence of an adult who has been the agent of punishment; in such cases, the external cue may result in response inhibition without the child's making any preparatory neuromuscular or postural adjustments associated with the commission of the act" (Bandura & Walters, 1963, p. 13). They note also that punishment administered to one person may give rise to conditioned emotional reactions in observers (the deterrence effect). This brings us to the topic of observational learning, which is so central to the approach developed by Bandura and Walters that it will occupy the bulk of our attention in the remaining pages of this chapter. Observational learning is the specifically new contribution Bandura and Walters bring to learning theory.

How Observational Learning Works

It might be wondered how any organism could learn (or even survive) if it could not observe something in its environment. Surely Miller and Dollard must have known that Bobby and other children observe the behaviors they copy from models. Surely Skinner must have known that a rat in an experimental box observes the lever and the food dish. What then can be new about observational learning?

The answer is that all other theorists have taken observation for granted and have assumed simply that it means no more than that a stimulus or cue has some effect on the organism (or, in Skinner's case, is met with a discriminative response in the organism's behavior). Thus, if a pigeon is trained to peck at a green disc but not at a pink disc, then the pigeon has made a discrimination the results of which (or even the only evidence of which) may be seen in the fact that the pigeon pecks when the disc is green and does not peck when the disc is pink. It is not supposed that the pigeon "knows" which is which, or has any sort of figural representation of green and pink discs in its head. One could not get the pigeon to behave in a green disc way.

But in the kind of observation Bandura and Walters have in mind one could get the organism to behave in the observed way. Observational learning, as they understand it, is restricted to observation of the behaviors of imitable other human beings. It therefore goes beyond the observation as mere registration of physical stimuli. The other human being might be green or pink, but that fact is not what observational learning is about; it is about the behavior pattern of that other human being. Of course the person responds to his or her environment and feels cold when

the temperature drops or startles to a sudden loud noise. Of course the person sees when the light turns from red to green. Such observations are part of the implicit assumptions of all learning theories, and they might be called the *background function* of observation. But the observations of special interest to Bandura and Walters are focused; they spotlight the behaviors of models which the person can learn *and* imitate. The difference is of considerable importance.

Acquisition and Performance. Skinner and many other theorists have paid little attention to the possible difference between *learning* in the sense of acquiring a new response pattern and *behaving* or actually performing that new behavior. Bandura and Walters name these two aspects *acquisition* and *performance* of responses. In the case of imitative responses, they suggest that acquisition "results primarily from the contiguity of sensory events, whereas response consequences to the model or to the observer have a major influence only on the performance of imitatively learned responses" (Bandura & Walters, 1963, p. 57). They suggest that we learn or acquire many forms of behavior without at the time actually behaving in those ways. Thus it is proposed that we may learn many patterns of behavior by observation of parents and other models, but we may perform only those patterns which receive special consequences in reinforcement either to the model or to ourselves. Also, if the consequences are punishing, then it may be that our performance of the learned patterns is even less likely. This would be due to the inhibition or avoidance responses reinforced vicariously by punishment. That means that we have added those behaviors (or avoidances) to our repertoire of *potential* ways of acting, but we have not actually performed those behaviors. As an example, many people now can imitate the movements of an astronaut in outer space, simply from having observed astronauts and cosmonauts on television. We have acquired those patterns of slow, floating somersaults and ponderous reaching. But few people actually perform such behaviors, for obvious reasons.

Bandura and Walters typically do not remain content with an example or illustration from daily life. Principles like the distinction between acquisition and performance must be given experimental demonstration if possible. Figure 21.1 shows the results of one such demonstration, taken from an experiment by Bandura (1962b) and reported by Bandura and Walters (1963, pp. 57-58). In the experiment children watched a film of a model who made four different novel aggressive responses to a large inflatable plastic doll: sitting on it and punching it, hitting with a mallet, tossing in the air, and kicking it. Three different conditions were established: the model was re-warded with food for attacking the doll; the model was punished for attacking the doll; and no consequence occurred to the model. Would these conditions affect the children's subsequent behavior toward the doll? After watching the model the children were taken to another room and allowed to play with a similar doll. Of the children who had watched in the reward and no-consequence conditions, boys imitated three or more of the model's different kinds of aggression; girls imitated two of those kinds of aggression. The number of imitated responses was substantially smaller if the model had been punished. Subsequently, each child was told he or she would receive a prize for reproducing as many of the model's responses as they could. Under these conditions the differences between reward and punishment groups were eliminated. In fact almost all children performed all four of the model's novel responses. As can be seen in figure 21.1, all groups made substantially

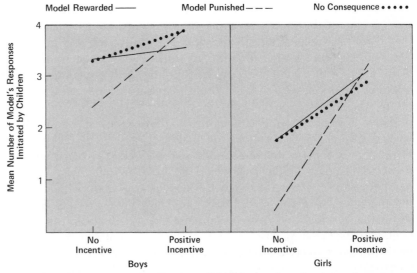

Figure 21.1. Results of experiment by Bandura (1962b) showing simple performance of imitated responses (no incentive condition) and acquisition of the responses as revealed by performance under positive incentives. Adapted from basic data given by Bandura and Walters, 1963, p. 58.

more imitative responses when there was some incentive to do so. Consider the most dramatic increase, for example: The girls who had seen the model punished for aggression made on the average less than one half of one imitative response, which means that less than half of them performed as much as one whole imitative response, and the others performed no imitative responses at all. But when offered an incentive for reproducing those responses of the model, they were able to reproduce on the average 3.3 responses, which means that most of them performed all four. The difference between acquisition and performance, then, seems well established.

Four Effects of Observational Learning. Bandura and Walters describe four effects of observational learning, which they name *modeling effects, inhibitory effects, disinhibitory effects,* and *eliciting effects.* Modeling effects are shown in the observer's acquisition of response patterns which previously were not in his or her repertoire. The other three effects all refer to performance rather than acquisition. In an inhibitory effect, observation of the model strengthens already existing inhibitions in the observer; in a disinhibitory effect observation of the model weakens existing inhibitions in the observer. An eliciting effect occurs when observation of a behavior that the observer has previously learned elicits the performance of that behavior by the observer. Coughing during the intermission of a concert and clapping at the end would be examples of such effects, although the coughing might be the result of disinhibition. The distinction is not always easy, as Bandura and Walters note (1963, p. 60).

Modeling effects are of great interest in understanding the behavioral differences between cultures and also between families within a culture. In a restaurant you might see all members of a family eating in a sim-

ilar way, for example. But such instances do not prove modelling effects. To do this one must find distinctly novel responses and present them via models and see whether the observers of these models imitate the novel responses. One study, for which results are summarized in figure 21.1, showed that children of both sexes tended to imitate at least some novel aggressive responses portrayed by a filmed adult (no incentive condition). This general result has been replicated in several experiments. For example, Bandura, Ross, and Ross (1963) had one group of children observe filmed models, had another group observe live models, and had another group observe cartoon models. A control group was not exposed to aggressive models. All of the models exhibited the same four novel aggressive responses described earlier as well as verbal responses such as, "Sock him!" Afterwards, subjects were mildly frustrated by being first invited to play with some very nice toys and then being told that they could no longer play with them. They were then led next door where various other toys were present, including a somewhat smaller inflatable doll, a mallet, dart guns, tether ball, and so on. Their behaviors were rated every five seconds for twenty minutes by judges who watched from behind one-way mirrors; verbal imitative and non-imitative responses were scored as well as nonverbal responses.

The children ranged between three years and five-and-one-half years of age. All were enrolled in Stanford University Nursery School. Figure 21.2 summarizes some of the main results from this experiment. Since results from the filmed human models were essentially similar to those for the live human models, figure 21.2 omits the results for the filmed models. On each side of figure 21.2 there are two main contrasts to be examined: first, the differences between groups exposed to different treatment conditions; and second,

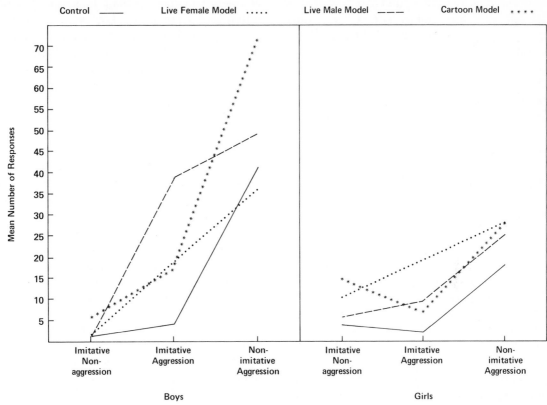

Figure 21.2. Graphs of results of modelling experiment, based upon data given by Bandura, Ross, and Ross (1963)

the differences within groups in types of behaviors. The four groups shown for boys, for example, are the three exposure-to-model groups and the control group. The three exposure groups are: those who saw a female model, those who saw a male model, and those who saw the cartoon model. (The cartoon model was actually the female model dressed up as a cat and named *Herman the Cat.*) The same three exposure groups and control group are shown for girls. Three types of behaviors are scored: imitative non-aggressive behaviors (actually, just sitting on the doll without punching it), imitative aggressive behaviors (verbal and nonverbal), and non-imitative aggressive behaviors. Each child was scored

for each type of behavior, and the means for each group on each type of behavior are represented in figure 21.2.

As may be seen, the control groups exhibit almost no imitative behavior of either non-aggressive or aggressive type. This is true for both boys and girls. However they do show non-imitative aggressive responses, with means of 40.4 for boys and 17.8 for girls. Presumably these means reflect either a normal baseline of aggressive behaviors for nursery-school children, or the effects of the mild frustration, or both. They serve as baseline for the exposure groups also. All exposure groups have higher means than the controls for both non-aggressive imitative behaviors and for aggressive imitative behaviors, and the pooled data for all exposure groups versus all control groups show the differences to be statistically significant ($p < .05$ for non-aggressive; $p < .001$ for aggressive). It may be concluded that exposure to live, film, and cartoon models of novel aggressive or non-aggressive responses causes subsequent imitation of those responses. These results constitute a demonstration of modelling effects.

Bandura and Walters report several studies demonstrating inhibitory, disinhibitory, and eliciting effects also. For example, Walters Bowen and Parke (1963) showed male subjects a film of nude males and females. A spot of light indicated to the subjects where a previous "subject" had been looking, thus providing each real subject with an imagined model and the evidence of where that model's gaze had been fixed. For half of the subjects the model's gaze had been fixed on breasts and genitals most of the time; for the other half the model's gaze had been fixed on the background of the pictures most of the time. Each subject's eye movements were subsequently recorded as he saw slides from a parallel set of photographs of nudes and seminudes. Subjects exposed to models who gazed at points of sexual interest themselves spent more time looking at nude bodies rather than at background aspects of the slides. This result was statistically significant and demonstrates a disinhibitory effect.

Vicarious Reinforcement. The principle of vicarious reinforcement holds that rewards and punishments administered to models will affect the probability of performance of imitative responses by observers. The experiment reported above, with results shown in figure 21.1, illustrates the principle very well since those children who saw the model punished were less likely to make imitative performances under the no-incentive condition. It is of interest in those results, however, that no differences were found between the model-rewarded and the no-consequences groups under the no-incentive condition. That is, for novel aggressive responses, punishment of the model lowered the probability of observer imitative response, but reward of the model did not raise the probability of imitative response. In other experiments, however, it has been found that the group exposed to a punished model did not differ from a control group in performance of imitative aggressive responses; while subjects who saw a model rewarded for aggression made significantly more imitative aggressive responses (Bandura & Walters, 1963, p. 82.) However, in this latter study the aggressive model was interacting with another adult and the nature of the aggression was different. It appears that the precise effects of positive or negative vicarious reinforcement are highly dependent upon the exact nature of the responses of the model.

Many other kinds of behaviors have been modeled in experiments. For example, Walters, Leat, and Mezei (1963) forbade children to play with some attractive toys and then showed them a film in which a child violated the prohibition and played with those very toys. In one group, the model was subsequently rewarded by his mother; in the other group the mother scolded the child. Subsequently the subjects in each group were left in the room with the toys for fifteen minutes. Would they resist temptation? Those who had seen a child rewarded for not resisting temptation were more likely to violate the prohibition themselves; those who had seen a child scolded were less likely to violate the prohibition. A control group who saw no model showed intermediate tendencies to violate.

These many studies leave little doubt that reinforcement consequences to models strongly affect the probability of performance of imitative responses among observers.

Characteristics of the Models. A number of characteristics of the model have been shown to be influential in affecting the degree of observational learning or performance. In general more prestigious models wield greater influence, as do more attractive models. One repeated finding is that males are more likely to perform imitative responses when the model is male; and females are more likely to perform imitative responses when the model is female. Relevant results can be found in figure 21.2, where boys perform sharply more imitative aggression responses to a live male model than they do to a live female model; and vice versa for girls.

Symbolic Models. Bandura and Walters (1963, p. 49) argue that models may be presented in a variety of ways, including television, pictures, and written or verbal instructions. They would include the filmed models as symbolic models. The experiment in which male subjects saw only the spots on a film indicating where previous subjects had focused their gaze were thereby exposed to a symbolic model. The notion that written and verbal instructions provide symbolic models greatly expands the realm of potential sources of modeling influence. Bandura and Walters note that the instruction manuals that come with our new household appliances, power tools, and other gadgets constitute symbolic models. Similarly the characters in novels act as symbolic models for our behavior and attitudes.

Interest in the role of symbolic models has led Bandura and his associates to consider symbolic and other coding processes in human cognition. How can a verbal instruction provide sufficient evidence for the subject to "imitate" the unseen but described model responses? Bandura (1971) proposes that sensory conditioning accounts for the ability of words to arouse images of the de-

scribed behaviors, in much the same way that mention of someone's name is able to bring to mind a memory image of that person's face. Another important process is *symbolic coding*, in which symbols are made to stand for certain movements. For example, Bandura and Jeffrey (1973) showed that subjects learn the movements of a model better when they attach numbers to each movement than when they simply imagine. In this instance moves to the left and downward were to be coded as 1, 3, or 5; moves to the right were to be coded 2, 4, or 6; larger numbers indicate greater distance covered by the movement. Jeffrey (1976) has recently demonstrated that symbolic encoding and rehearsal of modeled activities are superior to purely motor rehearsal in observational learning. In this study the models constructed three-dimensional forms out of wooden rods and joints (presumably not unlike Tinkertoys). In the symbolic rehearsal condition the subjects closed their eyes and imagined themselves practicing the construction activities they had seen. These behaviors are evidently in the same class as those referred to by Miller and Dollard as *higher mental processes* (see chapter 7).

Accomplishments of the Theory

Among Bandura and Walters's principal aims is the important one of being able to offer effective procedures for modification of undesirable behavior. Such procedures must surely be reckoned among the accomplishments of the theory.

The term *behavior modification* covers all possible systematic and intentional changes of behavior by means of the application of any principle from among those established by laboratory experiments on learning. However, it tends to be restricted to particular behavioral problems as presented by clients, rather than addressed to total reorganization of the personality (which would be the aim in psychoanalytic or client-centered therapy, for example).

In the sense described, the notion of behavior modification is not new. For example, J. B. Watson, the first proponent of a radical behaviorist view in America, showed that a one-year-old child who was not afraid of furry animals could be made afraid of them by a simple conditioning procedure in which a metal bar was struck with a hammer whenever the child touched the animal. Since the sound of the hammer elicited a fear reaction it served as an unconditioned fear stimulus. Pairing it with the furry animal eventually made the animal a conditioned fear stimulus. In other words the child's behavior had been modified from being unafraid of furry animals to being afraid of them (Watson & Raynor, 1920). Watson named this effect a *conditioned emotional reaction*.

Bandura and Walters (1963, pp. 224 ff.) provide a quite extensive list of procedures designed to effect behavior modification, with several examples of such change induced by *extinction* (changing an undesirable behavior by withdrawing the reinforcer), *counterconditioning* (classical conditioning, to fear-arousing stimuli, of responses which are incompatible with fear responses), *aversive conditioning* (conditioning aversion, avoidance, or withdrawal reactions to problematic approach situations, as for example in making a patient nauseated at the sight of fetish objects such as ladies' handbags), *operant conditioning with positive reinforcement* (see chapter 4), *discrimination learning* (accomplished by labeling and higher mental processes, according to Dollard and Miller), and *social imitation*.

The possibilities of treatment through social imitation have been extensively explored by Bandura and his associates. For example, adults with intense fear of snakes have been provided with a program of behavior modification involving symbolic modeling and vicarious extinction. Subjects were shown a graduated series of pictures in which children and adults modeled increasingly frightening behaviors with a king snake, including looking at it through glass, reaching into the vivarium for it, and holding it up with both hands and closely examining it (Bandura, Blanchard, & Ritter, 1969). Another group of subjects were taught to relax deeply while viewing the scenes and (at their own pace) to go back to the beginning and start over whenever a particular scene evoked anxiety; this would be counterconditioning in a procedure known as *systematic desensitization*. A third group was provided with a live therapist, who actively handled the snake and invited the subjects to participate in touching and handling the snake. This latter condition was named *live modeling with participation*. It was found that all three techniques substantially reduced patient fears of snakes as revealed both in actual behaviors toward a test snake and in measures of attitudes toward snakes. The results showed that live modeling with participation was most effective, symbolic modeling next, and systematic desensitization somewhat less effective. A control group receiving no special treatment procedures failed to show any improvement in fear responses.

In many ways the graduated presentation of stimulus situations in live or symbolic modeling is essentially the same as the delivery of stimuli in a hierarchy of anxiety-producing potency that has been used in systematic desensitization. These procedures were incorporated in a systematic set of principles for behavior therapy (or modification) formulated by Joseph Wolpe (1954). He proposed that the essential component of all successful techniques was *reciprocal inhibition*, that is, "if a response incompatible with anxiety can be made to occur in the presence of anxiety-evoking stimuli it will weaken the bond between these stimuli and the anxiety responses . . ." (Wolpe, 1954, p. 3). In systematic desensitization with relaxation as the incompatible response, the hierarchy of stimuli consists of a list of anxiety-arousing stimuli, with the most disturbing items at the top of the list and the least disturbing items at the bottom. The patient will begin with the least disturbing items. With or without hypnosis the patient is then asked to imagine the scene referred to by the item at the same time as he or she is given instructions to relax thoroughly. At first the patient can only go through per-

haps the one least disturbing item without becoming tense and anxious. But within ten to thirty sessions, each using two to four items in the hierarchy, the patient can go all the way to the top of the hierarchy and still be relaxed. Box 21.1 presents one of the cases treated by Wolpe in this way.

Critique of the Social Learning Theory Developed by Bandura and Walters

In a recent appraisal of social learning theory as developed by Bandura and his associates, Hilgard and Bower (1975, p. 605) have written that it offers "the best integrative sum-

---

Box 21.1
A Case of Systematic Desensitization Therapy

"A 23-year-old divorced tram driver entered the consulting room in a state of acute anxiety. Eight hours before a woman had walked into his slowly moving tram. She had been 'knocked out and her head was bleeding.' Although a doctor had told him that the woman's injury was not serious, he had become increasingly shaky and had developed severe epigastric pain. He had recovered from previous accidents in an hour or two, but in these no human injury had been involved.

"The significance of the statement **no human injury was involved** is that when the patient was 13 his father had died after an accident and since then he had had a fear of human blood. Even the tiny bead of blood that might appear on his face during shaving gave him an uncomfortable feeling. He was quite indifferent to animal blood— had seen oxen killed and had himself cut the throats of fowls. It was clear that his grossly excessive reaction to the present accident was due to his phobia for human blood, and to overcome this phobia was the central aim of therapy.

"The first five interviews, which occurred over six days, were confined to obtaining of the patient's personality and background and to overcoming his immediate disturbed state by intense, hypnotically induced relaxation. At the fifth in-

terview he reported feeling very well. He was told to drive a tram again for a short distance, which he did later that day without any ill effect.

"At the sixth interview various situations involving human blood were arranged in ascending order of their disturbing effect. From this time onward, at each interview, while the patient was in a state of hypnotic relaxation, he was made to 'visualize' blood situations. The feeblest was a slightly blood-tinged bandage lying in a basket. When this failed to disturb his relaxation, he was presented with a tiny drop of blood on his own face while shaving. In this way, with the presentation of two or three images at each session, it was possible gradually to work up to a stage at which the patient could visualize a casualty ward full of carnage and not be disturbed by it.

"The significance of this method for real-life situations was revealed in this case in a most dramatic way. Two days before his last interview the patient saw a man knocked over by a motorcycle. The victim was seriously injured and was bleeding profusely. The patient was absolutely unaffected by the blood and, when the ambulance arrived, helped to load the victim on to it" (Wolpe, 1954, pp. 18-19).

---

mary of what modern learning theory has to contribute to solutions of practical problems." They believe that social learning theory also is compatible with information-processing theories, modern theories of language behavior, imagery, problem solving and other fields of cognitive psychology. They conclude that it is a "consensus" theoretical framework. These remarks suggest that social learning theory is first a repository of practical applications of modern learning theory; second, it is compatible equally with learning theories which emphasize response modification and those which emphasize central or higher mental processes. This conclusion appears to be one that Bandura and his associates would agree with. For example, Bandura writes (1974, p. 865): "Social learning includes within its framework both the processes internal to the organism as well as performance-related determinants." He emphasizes the importance of cognitive processes such as information acquisition, storage and retrieval. Bandura and Walters (1963, p. 49) discussed the importance of *symbolic models* (including written and oral instruction, pictorial representations, and so on), and their research on such symbolic modeling has clearly invoked information-processing constructs such as verbal or imaginal *encoding*.

On the other hand, social learning also encompasses the constructs of Pavlovian conditioning, as in Bandura's discussions of the use of aversive conditioning in the treatment of alcoholism through nauseating drugs (Bandura, 1969, p. 541). Similarly, Mischel's analysis of a pilot's fainting spells at high altitude is based upon classical conditioning theory, since it is known that the pilot was injured during a bombing raid. Mischel writes (1976, p. 87), "if Brack's injury occurred at about 10,000 feet, then any altitude cues present at that time might have become conditioned stimuli capable of eliciting a traumatic reaction (such as fainting)." Mischel offers this explanation, as he says, from the point of view of social behavior theory.

Symbolic modeling, live modeling, classical conditioning, and several other parts of modern learning theory are incorporated in the social learning or social behavior theory developed by Bandura and his associates. Bandura and Walters (1963, pp. 4 ff.) are explicit in their acceptance of the general theory formulated by Skinner, especially the principles of scheduling reinforcements. They write, for example (Bandura & Walters, 1963, p. 7), "In social situations, then, reinforcements are usually dispensed on a combined schedule, with both the number of unreinforced responses and the time-intervals between reinforcements continually changing."

The role of vicarious reinforcement in modeling is another important principle. Although they showed that the subject can learn by observing a model without actually making a response or receiving a reinforcement, they also showed that the model's responses and reinforcements were influential in affecting the acquisition of novel response patterns and the performance of those patterns by the observer. Thus Bandura and Walters accept not only the principles of reinforcement learning proposed by Skinner but also a kind of remote operation of those principles, an operation of the principles of stimulus, response, and reinforcement not when these are happening in connection with the observer's organism but when they are happening to the model's organism only. This latter set of remote operations is made possible by the symbolic processes of the observer. Thus social learning theory covers a very broad span of different types and theories of learning and performance.

But we may ask whether social learning theory is really a theory. Hilgard and Bower describe it as a summary of practical applications of other theories, or as a "consensus" theoretical framework. Bandura and Walters (1963, pp. 1 ff.) refer to it as a "socio-behavioristic approach" or as an "application of learning theory." Bandura (1974, p. 865) also refers to social learning as a "framework." Elsewhere (Bandura, 1969, p. v) he speaks of it as both a "conceptual framework of social learning" and also (implicitly) as a psychological theory, whose worth "must be judged by how well it explains laboratory findings but also by the efficacy of the behavioral modification procedures that it produces." Obviously there is some doubt whether social learning is a framework for other theories (of learning) or whether it is a theory itself. Often the term *social learning* seems to refer mainly to learning by human beings in a social context. Indeed it was for their treatment of imitation in *nonsocial* terms that Miller and Dollard were criticized by Bandura and Walters, who strove rather to emphasize *social* factors such as parental influence in reinforcing and shaping the children's behaviors. Bandura and Walters aimed to demonstrate (1963, p. 32) that "a single set of social-learning principles can account for the development of both prosocial and deviant behavior and for modifications of behavior toward greater conformity or greater deviation."

It is of interest to ask what is meant by a "single" set of principles when we find that it covers all theories of learning, including classical conditioning in totally nonsocial settings, with nonsocial stimuli such as altitude cues becoming conditioned stimuli for such apparently quite nonsocial responses as fainting. And one may ask whether aversive conditioning treatment using emetic drugs to modify behavior is also claimed to be based upon social factors. Even the rehearsal of symbolic or imaginal motor movements or sequences of numbers by a silent and unmoving subject appears to be quite nonsocial. So

we see that at both the physiological level of conditioning and at the level of learning through higher mental processes, the principles of social learning do not appear to be members of a single set characterized by their "social" nature.

Whether it is a theory or a framework, the set of principles of social learning developed by Bandura and his associates has changed in essential ways over the past fifteen years. For example, they originally aimed to exclude treatment of "internal processes as primary links in causal sequences that generate . . . patterns of response" (Bandura & Walters, 1963, p. 30). But such internal processes *are* proposed as primary links in causal sequences in recent studies. For example, *rehearsal* and *symbolic coding* are internal processes which are hypothesized to be primary links in causal sequences involving symbolic and live modeling (compare Bandura & Jeffrey, 1973; Jeffrey, 1976). Internal processes are tacitly assumed in the hypothesis that the observation of models can produce acquisition of new patterns of behavior. Since the subject does not respond and is not reinforced, what could possibly be accounting for the acquisition except internal processes? A good example of Bandura's own acceptance of internal processes is given in his citation of the case of a gang member whose silent ruminations about his reputation and about the invitations of others to join a fight lead him to decide to do so (Bandura, 1969, pp. 6-7). The whole acceptance of silent ruminations, of imagery, and other cognitive and problem-solving constructs is also an acceptance of constructs dealing with internal processes. Indeed Bandura has recently recanted his sociobehavioristic position, saying (Bandura, 1974, p. 867), "Behaviorists generally emphasize environmental sources of control, whereas humanists tend to restrict their interest to personal control. Social learning encompasses both aspects of the bidirectional influence." Coupled with the previously quoted statement (Bandura, 1974, p. 865) that social learning includes "processes internal to the organism as well as performance-related determinants," these various admissions and experimental constructs and behavior modification procedures (particularly modeling and desensitization), lead to the conclusion that the single set of social learning principles developed by Bandura did not succeed in excluding "internal processes as primary links in causal sequences that generate deviant (or other) patterns of response."

It might be that the "single" set of principles is determined largely by the intention that all principles included in the framework must be, as Bandura proposes, capable of explaining laboratory findings and also capable of producing effective procedures for behavior modification. If that is so, then it appears that most of the principles in social learning should not be there, for while they may be somehow associated with effective procedures (compare the efficacy of Wolpe's treatment of the tram driver in box 21.1), it seems that most of the principles drawn from "modern learning theory" are open to serious doubt. We find deep controversy among the learning theorists themselves. For instance, in their penetrating critique of procedures for behavior modification based on learning theory, Breger and McGaugh (1965) have pointed out that "the very core of 'modern learning theory' . . . has been seriously questioned or abandoned in favor of alternative conceptualizations."

If social learning theory offers an "integrative summary of what modern learning theory has to contribute" that characteristic of social learning theory turns out to be a liability rather than asset. Moreover it has been shown (see Brewer, 1975; and a summary in chapter 4) that the principles of conditioning (classical and operant) are probably not applicable to adult humans, so that procedures of behavior modification based on such principles must at present have a questionable rationale. Also, the results of such procedures must be attributed at present to unknown sources of curative influence. Since adults are now known to simulate the expected results of conditioning if they are aware of what is expected and if they wish to comply with the experimenter's expectations (Brewer, 1975), it seems reasonable to suppose that similar events are taking place when such "conditioning" is attempted with therapeutic intent.

Evaluation of the Theory

Insofar as social learning theory rests upon conditioning principles, it is probably inaccurate with respect to adult human personality. In its principles of observational learning, however, it appears to be accurate. We must note that these principles have become essentially cognitive in recent years. If eventually they are extended to language (as surely they must be when dealing with symbolic modeling), then any claim that such behaviors are built up purely from social learning will have to meet the criticisms levelled by Chomsky against Skinner's related claim (see Chomsky, 1959; and discussion in chapter 4 of this book).

Our overall evaluation of the theory of social learning advanced by Bandura and Walters must conclude that it has a *mixture of accuracy and inaccuracy*. Since many of the applications of the theory have rested upon conditioning principles, the *power* of the theory is at best moderate, because power reflects the extent of accurate applications.

The theory has nevertheless been extremely *fruitful* in stimulating research in diverse fields, both by the original theorists themselves and by their associates and other scientists right up to the present day. Since the experimental bases of behavior modification resting upon conditioning principles are now in question for adult humans, it may be expected that vigorous research will be addressed to the question of what exactly is producing beneficial changes in those instances of behavior modification treatments which are successful. This too would be evidence of the fruitfulness of the theory advanced by Bandura and Walters.

The criterion of *depth* seems to require that the theory be at least free of evidence suggesting its inaccuracy. Much of the theory developed by Bandura and Walters is not free of such evidence, however, so considerations of depth must be restricted to those portions of the theory which involve observational learning. Here the insights provided are substantial, especially in regard to the characteristics of models and the consequences to models as these influence the individual's acquisition and performance of new behavior patterns.

As was pointed out earlier, Bandura and Walters developed their theory in the course of disagreeing with other theorists. They were especially opposed to the model advanced by Miller and Dollard (chapter 7) to account for imitative learning. Did Bandura and Walters succeed in producing a theoretical model which competes with the Miller and Dollard model?

Miller and Dollard made it clear they thought response by the subject and reinforcement of that response were necessary for imitative learning to take place. Bandura and Walters denied this, and proposed instead that observational learning, meaning acquisition of a response pattern, could take place without either a response by the subject or reinforcement of that response. It appears that we have an instance of direct competition between theories in their models of a narrow range of phenomena.

However, we recall that Miller and Dollard distinguished *same* behavior, *copying,* and *matched-dependent* behavior. In the first there was no question of reinforcement; in the second the reinforcement rested upon the subject's noting similarities and differences between his or her own behavior and that of the model; in the third the subject was rewarded for imitating the behavior of a leader who could discriminate cues that were not available to the follower.

Which of these forms of same behavior match the usual paradigm of observational learning as studied by Bandura and Walters? In that paradigm observers watch novel behaviors by a model (novel in general or novel for themselves, as handling a snake would be for someone with snake phobia). Afterwards the observers are given an opportunity to perform that behavior (or are asked to perform it for an incentive). It is not simply *same* behavior; it is not *copying,* since no special reinforcement attaches to the observer's adequacy of matching the model; it is not *matched-dependent,* since the test session does not include the leader (model) and anyway the leader had no special access to cues which were unavailable to the follower (observer). So it must be some other kind of imitation that Bandura and Walters have in mind. They *seem* to be offering a competing theory but in fact they are not; they have staked out a related but different set of facts to be explained. The confirmation of their theoretical model with respect to those facts in no way challenges the theoretical model formulated by Miller and Dollard for a different set of facts.

Matched-dependent and Observational Learning

It may be possible to see just how much the matched-dependent learning situation envisaged by Miller and Dollard differs from the observational learning situation envisaged by Bandura and Walters if we put them both into the same experimental arrangement. We could begin with figure 7.2 which illustrates Miller and Dollard's design for matched-dependent learning. How might we modify that experimental design in order to study observational learning as well as matched-dependent learning?

_____

_____

_____

One idea might be to have a group of children who simply watch the leader during the training session without themselves either responding or receiving a reinforcement (candy). But then we would wonder how to produce a suitable test session. We would presumably need a novel response for the observer to witness. What might be a suitable novel response in the situation shown in figure 7.2? Or how might we change that situation so that a novel response is required of the leader and the follower (and later the observer)?

_____

_____

_____

Using the idea developed by Bandura and Walters, we might simply replace one of the chairs with an inflated clown doll and require the leaders and followers to punch the doll's nose before getting their reward from the box (punching the nose could be made to trigger a release mechanism which deposits a piece of candy in a box held by the doll).

Miller and Dollard also had a group of children who were trained **not** to imitate. Should we include this part of the experiment?

_____

_____

It would provide a sharp contrast to do so. For, suppose our groups are the Followers, the Independents (trained not to imitate), and the Observers. All groups watch the leader. But only the Followers and Independents actually respond and receive reinforcement. In the test session we could have a different room with a chair and box (Chair), a clown doll and box (Doll), a toy kitchen stove (Stove), and a toy chest of drawers (Chest). The leader could go first, and would be told by the experimenter to reach inside the stove. Then the child subject could go, being told to do whatever he or she wishes. How will the three groups behave?

_____

_____

_____

My expectation is that all of the Followers would reach into the stove, for they have been rewarded for doing what the leader does. The Independents would do anything except reaching into the stove, for they have been rewarded for doing what the leader does not do. Half the Observers would go to the Chair and half to the Doll, for these are the behaviors they have acquired from watching the leader in the training session.

Does it seem possible that Miller and Dollard have considered how people learn to imitate another **person?** And that Bandura and Walters have considered how people learn to imitate a new **behavior?** How could we really pin this down by modifying our experimental design further?

Summary

Bandura and Walters offer an approach or framework which is sociobehavioristic and which embraces virtually all forms of learning theory. They require that an acceptable principle be able to generate explanations for experimental results and also useful procedures for effective behavior modification. They emphasize the importance of strictly social factors in learning and personality development, factors like parental reinforcements of child behavior. They also have placed a heavy emphasis upon what is perhaps the most distinctive feature of their viewpoint, which is *observational learning* and the study of characteristics of *social models* as they influence such learning. Bandura and Walters distinguish between *acquisition* of a new behavior and *performance* of that behavior. Acquisition means that the observer learns the pattern of the behavior without actually doing it; performance means actually emitting the behavior. The acquisition is relatively independent of reinforcements either to the model or the observer. But performance by the observer is affected strongly by the reinforcements (positive or negative) received by the model; they call this effect on the observer *vicarious reinforcement*.

Bandura and Walters have apparently changed their theory from early declarations that internal causes are not to be hypothesized, and have now reached a position in which such totally internal processes as symbolic encoding and symbolic rehearsal are hypothesized to be causally effective in human learning.

Portions of the theory appear to be accurate, especially the sections on observational learning and modeling. These portions also provide the main sources of depth in the theory. The theory has been very fruitful and will probably continue to be fruitful, especially in stimulating renewed research into the real principles involved in successful behavior modification.

Bandura and Walters reject the theoretical model of imitative behavior advanced by Miller and Dollard, asserting that in fact it is not necessary for the imitator to respond and receive reinforcement. It seems that Bandura and Walters offer a competing theoretical model of imitative behavior, because they claim that observational learning produces imitative behavior without prior response and reinforcement. On careful analysis it appears, however, that the two theoretical models are not in competition since they deal with different sets of facts. To characterize these sets of facts briefly, one might say that Miller and Dollard offer a model of how one person learns to imitate another *person*; Bandura and Walters offer a model of how one person learns new patterns of *behavior*.

Figure 21.3 offers an illustration of the definition of personality implicit in the theory of social learning developed by Bandura and Walters. It is a sparse definition. However, Bandura and Walters explicitly reject matters having to do with the body and with psychophysical dispositions, leaving subjective experience and behavior as the main components of their definition. These components do not receive treatment in terms of the record in this theory.

This is the last chapter of the book to present a particular theory of personality. In the final chapter we shall try to take stock of what we have learned and think about plans for future theoretical work in personality science.

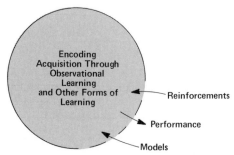

Figure 21.3. Definition of personality implicit in the theory developed by Bandura and Walters

INTRODUCTION

Components in the definition of personality
  The body
    Theorists' use of the body
    Evaluation of uses of the body
  Psychophysical systems
    Theorists' use of psychophysical system
      constructs
    Are psychophysical system constructs
      necessary?
  Experience
    Theorists' uses of experience
    The unconscious and unaware experience:
      unresolved problems
    Evaluation of the uses of experience
      components
  Behavior
    Theorists' uses of behavior
    Evaluation of uses of behavior
  Summary recommendation
    All components are necessary
    Causal network between components should
      be given more attention
    Behavior should be given less attention as
      the dependent variable component
    More attention should be given the body
Types of theories
  Theories of cause
    Instances of hypothesized causal relations
      between variables from body, psychophysical
      systems, experience, and behavior
  Theories of function
  Theories of structure
    Kinds of facts requiring a structural theory
  Theories of pattern
  Theories of priority
  Theories of system
  Summary on types of theory
    Each type may be found among theories of
      personality
    The types fall into two sets:
    Set A: structure, cause, pattern
    Set B: function, system, priority
    Theories of set B may always include or be
      superimposed on theories of set A, but
      not vice versa

Methods
  Theory development
    Three guidelines
      Practice formulating and using theoretical
        models
      Test models through explicit predictions
      Think directly about model objects
  Model objects
    Distinction of model object from theoretical
      model
    Two approaches to formulating model objects
      Common language
        Behaviorism seeks this goal
      Experimental procedures
    Limitations of the two approaches
    Experiments should be linked to major theories
      Coordination of model objects and
        theoretical models
    Written descriptive statements placed in the
      public domain: a third approach
  Confrontation experiments
    Nature of confrontation experiments
    Value of confrontation experiments
Some thoughts for the future
  The appearance of human conditioning
  Implications for the model object
  Implications for theoretical models
  Implications for theory and method
  All theories of personality are now suspect

22

Looking Back and Thinking Ahead

In this chapter we will look back over the work of the previous chapters and also try to indicate some directions that would be profitable for future work in personality theory.

First we will examine each of the four components in our definition of personality as given in chapter 2, seeking in each case to clarify commonalities and differences among several theories with respect to the constructs they propose which appear to involve that component directly. We will consider in turn the components of body, psychophysical systems, experience, and behavior. The treatment will be brief because more detailed study would simply duplicate what is already there in relevant chapters. This will be an overview, but also it will provide an opportunity to evaluate the worth of our formulations in chapter 2 and make recommendations for further work on definitional problems.

Next we will survey the different types of theory: structure, cause, function, pattern, priority, and system. Over and above consideration of each in terms of examples, we will try to decide whether the list should be changed or whether it should be reorganized in some way.

Next we will review some issues of method

in personality theory and research, and try to discern some fruitful paths of further work. In this section we will return to the abstract analysis of changes in theories which was developed in chapter 8. It will be argued that this analysis can be put to practical use in developing a set of guidelines and methods for further theoretical and empirical research in personality.

In the fourth and final section of the chapter I shall present some thoughts about new directions in personality theory.

Components in the Definition of Personality

The Body

Theorists' Use of the Body. The theories we have studied are divided on their views of the part played by the body in personality. Freud, Jung, Cattell, Eysenck, and Maslow all give the body a major role. Both Freud and Jung felt that the body supplied the source of instincts. Freud placed the body in a central role in personality development with respect to psychosexual stages focused upon different erogenous zones, although he believed that the irritations of these zones were in some way produced centrally and then projected onto the particular zone. Jung, however, emphasized the body's direct production of stimuli as the source of experienced sensations. Thus for both theorists the body was indirectly connected with experience through psychophysical systems and also directly connected with experience through sensations. Freud also emphasized that the ego was guardian over the access of impulses to motility and could block action of the skeletal musculature; he also maintained that, in the event of the ego's effectively barring access to an impulse, the impulse could sometimes nevertheless find expression through discharge into the interior of the body (glands, smooth muscle, and so on). Freud held the latter possibility to be at the root of psychosomatic disorders and conversion symptoms in hysteria.

Although we evaluated the theories of Murray and Erikson as not referring explicitly to the body, it must be borne in mind that both theorists accept Freud's theory as basic; their own theories are developed on top of Freud's. Maslow's theory differs in most important respects from Freud's, and yet he too places the body in a source role with respect to personality, namely, in the biological potentials that constitute the self which is to be actualized. Also he emphasizes the physiological needs which have prime prepotency over all other needs. If they are not satisfied no other needs can be activated. Indeed, Maslow says that all the other classes of needs in his theory (including even the need for self-actualization and related spiritual strivings) are *instinctoid,* meaning that they are part of biological inheritance.

Cattell's constructs of the *ergs* of motivation refer to bodily sources. More frequently, though, Cattell uses the body as a source of independent variables which influence measurable dependent variables of behavior. Thus

Cattell's theory incorporates the body in this way, often referring to genetic sources but also to brain and autonomic nervous system as providing independent variables. Such variables are sometimes referred to as *biological determinants,* which means that they are important contributors to causal processes affecting whatever is reflected in the dependent variable. Eysenck also uses the body as a source of biological determinants of behavioral variation in extraversion, neuroticism, and so on. In Eysenck's work such biological determinants are mainly genetic or neural or glandular in nature.

It is worth observing that Maslow's use of the body seems to be basically different from Freud's, Cattell's, and Eysenck's. His idea of biological potentials conveys neither the energic implications that Freud intended nor the causal determinant implications of Cattell and Eysenck. While a potential is something that might be used or developed, it is not something that forces its way out despite obstacles or exerts an inexorable causal impact. Also, the fact that physiological needs must be satisfied before other needs can become active does not give the physiological needs any energic contribution to the later needs or to anything else, nor does it endow them with causal significance.

Both Rogers and Miller and Dollard acknowledge the body's presence (in organismic valuing and in primary drives, respectively), and yet they relegate it to a minor role so far as personality is concerned. For Rogers it underlies the organismic valuing process, which however plays a major role only in babies and the fully functioning person, the latter being an ideal. For Miller and Dollard the body is the origin of primary drives (to avoid cold or pain, to seek food, and so on). Thus for both these theorists the body merely provides a kind of background function.

For Skinner the body plays a minimal

role. It houses effector muscles, which mediate responses. It is the responses which are of primary interest, however, and Skinner explicitly rejects the possibility of appealing to bodily functions for causal explanations. Bandura and Walters follow Skinner in this matter.

Lewin and Rotter appear to ignore the body completely. Even the need for physical comfort (in Rotter's theory) is not really attributed to the body. It simply refers to a group of *behavior potentials* (= *need potential*) associated with a group of *reinforcement values* (= *need value*) in a set of similar reinforcement circumstances of a certain kind.

Evaluation of Uses of the Body. There is obviously a range of usage of the body as a component in personality. Freud construes the body as the only source of energy in the personality; it is also an important safety device when it receives the discharges of excess tension that become symptoms of conversion hysteria or psychosomatic disorder. Also, the ego is first a *body* ego. Thus for Freud the body is an integral part of the personality.

By contrast, Lewin and Rotter ignore the body almost entirely, assuming that it has no part in personality. The range goes from inclusion of the body as an integral part of personality (Freud) to total exclusion of the body from personality (Rotter).

At what point along this range *should* a theory of personality place the body? In my judgment it should be at the Freudian end of the range, making the body an integral part of personality. If there were no body there would be nobody, no personality, no experience, no behavior. Disembodied experiences and behaviors do not exist in human form. Moreover, it seems to me that exclusive concentration upon the body as a source of independent variables is one-sided and inadequate no less than concentration upon the body solely as an envelope of dependent variables would be (which would, however, be entirely proper perhaps for a subdiscipline such as psychosomatic medicine.) Relegation of the body to the role of mediating instrumental and other forms of response is equally inadequate, although to ignore that role would be folly. Again it is not enough to summarize all these possibilities by referring to the "system as a whole" and nodding to the body while theoretical effort is directed to supposedly more important matters in experience, behavior, or the environment. If we admit that the body is totally involved in personality we must begin again to formulate its total role. Obviously that cannot be done in these pages, except to suggest some general directions. These would include the body as envelope of independent, dependent, and intervening variables; the body as vehicle of behaviors and experiences; the body as biological potentials; the body as entity with size, weight, shape, mobility, and the like. It might be a useful rule to require of every theorist dealing with a particular set of phenomena in personality that they at least consider it from the *somatic point of view*. Thus, for example, a theoretical model of stress must go beyond the body if it is to be part of a theory of personality and not simply a medical model, but equally it must at least consider the somatic point of view if it is to be part of a theory of personality and not simply a model of experience or behavior.

Psychophysical Systems

By *psychophysical systems* we mean physical and associated psychological structures together with their processes of interrelation and of causal influence upon body, experience, and behavior (chapter 2).

Theorists' Use of Psychophysical System Constructs. Most of the theorists reviewed in this book have employed constructs classified as psychophysical systems. Many of these are dispositional concepts with a structural implication: instincts, archetypes, needs, traits, drives, habits, and so on. Others are mechanism concepts such as defense mechanisms, complexes, or reactive inhibition. Others are concepts of structure or organization, such as ego and superego, sense of identity, strata, regions and tension systems, and so on. Yet some theorists (Bandura and Walters, Maslow, Rogers, Skinner) do without psychophysical system constructs, either because they assume that there is no "structure" in personality or because they assume that, additionally, any appearance of structure in personality is actually attributable to regularities in the environment, that is, the environment can have a structure which produces stability in the responses of the human organism.

Are Psychophysical System Constructs Necessary? The theorists who do not employ psychophysical system constructs assume that everything about personality which needs to be explained for scientific purposes can be explained without such constructs. This fact in itself poses a challenge to those who think otherwise. The argument in effect says that personality phenomena can be equally well understood using different kinds of constructs, such as contingencies between stimuli and responses (Skinner) or between stimuli, cognitions, and responses (Bandura and Walters). Humanistic theorists seem to assume that all crucial consistencies of personality can be understood as experiential (Rogers) or as the manifestation of biological potentials broadly conceived (Maslow). In either case *apparent stability* is not denied; the source of the stability is variously attributed to characteristics of experience, body, or the environment, or

some combination of these three. Similarly, concepts of mechanism or organization may be attributed to some component other than psychophysical systems. Clearly this might be true of some but not all such dispositional, mechanism, or organizational concepts. If it were true of all of them, then the component of psychophysical systems would not be necessary. Or would it?

Consider that it is one thing to offer a plausible explanation of surface phenomena, but quite another to make existential propositions about related entities or processes. For example, one might suppose that Skinner's demonstration of a contingency between certain discriminative stimuli, certain operants, and certain reinforcing stimuli constituted a sufficient explanation of learning by that organism of that behavior in that environment. Hence one would not need to invoke any mysterious mechanisms or structures or dispositions to account for it; and one might be tempted to propose, in conclusion, that none exist. But surely this would be incorrect. For a *contingency* must exist somewhere other than merely in the experimenter's mind if it is to have any material consequence in another organism's behavior. Where and in what form would it exist? Presumably in the learning organism. It would be remembered, presumably, and hence located in memory. The exact nature of memory storage is still a matter of debate and inquiry, but few would deny today that it has both physical (chemical, neural) aspects and also dispositional aspects for experience and behavior, as when something pops into awareness from memory or an animal goes right back to lever pressing when the red light returns. Thus the surface contingency is an appearance created by an underlying psychophysical reality. If there is any doubt, remove the animal's neural memory banks and see if the discriminative stimulus continues to elicit operants according to the "contingency." It does not.

We may conclude that acceptance of a good surface explanation does not entail the rejection of other existential propositions. Indeed arguments can be given to suggest that the surface explanation omitting reference to psychophysical systems actually contains such reference in a hidden way. We shall return to this problem in the next section, in connection with experience. But for the moment we might conclude that psychophysical system constructs are necessary for a theory of personality because the record of experience and behavior (with all its elements of stability, change, and plasticity) cannot be attributed solely to the environment and must be at least considered from the somatic point of view. It cannot be disembodied.

Experience

Theorists' Uses of Experience. Some construct in the experience component can be found in all the theories we have studied except those of Cattell, Eysenck, and Skinner. Although these three theorists may include experiential terms in their writing, as part of informal exposition, their theories strictly do not have experiential components. Among the remainder we find a great variety of experience constructs: dreams (Freud, Jung), consciousness or awareness (Freud, Jung, Murray, Erikson, Rogers), subjective probability (Rotter), fantasy (Freud, Jung, Erikson, Lewin, Rotter—the latter calling it *irreal behavior*), thinking and other higher mental processes (Freud, Jung, Miller and Dollard). Other more proprietary constructs include the beta press (Murray), conscious sense of trust (Erikson), life space and valence (Lewin), symbolic rehearsal (Bandura and Walters), peak experiences (Maslow), and experience, self-concept, and ideal self (Rogers).

The Unconscious and Unaware Experience: Unresolved Problems. The careful reader will perhaps have noticed an inconsistency in my treatment of the unconscious and of unaware experience. I have represented the unconscious in Freud's and in Jung's theories as a part of the psychophysical systems. For Freud, the preconscious was placed as a part of experience but marked off from actual conscious experience (figure 10.1). For Jung the personal unconscious was located partly in the psychophysical systems and partly in the experience component (figure 12.2). But in my treatment of Rogers's theory, we saw that all experience which is not symbolized, including that which is denied to awareness, was placed in the experience component (see figure 5.2).

I believe these placements are all consistent with what the authors have said in their theoretical statements. In Freud's theory, for example, the unconscious includes the id, and the id is a reservoir of instinctual energy including repressed drives. The mechanism of repression, however, is effected by the ego, being a withdrawal of consciousness from the idea of a drive which is threatening to the ego. This seems quite similar to Rogers's construct of denial to awareness for experiences inconsistent with portions of the self-concept which are controlled by conditions of worth. And yet Rogers's construct of unsymbolized or unaware experience was placed in the experience component, not in the psychophysical systems component. Going back to Freud's theory for a moment, the mechanism of repression is supposed to be put into effect by the unconscious part of the ego. So to be consistent between Freud and Rogers we should perhaps place repression and the repressed ideas in the experience component, where Rogers's comparable constructs are located. At present we have two comparable constructs located in two different components of the definition of personality.

An alternative solution is to place Rogers's constructs of denial to awareness and of the resulting unaware experiences in the psychophysical systems component. But that would do violence to Rogers's theory, because he explicitly disavows any dynamic unconscious. So that, although repression and denial **appear** to be comparable constructs, their location in the psychophysical systems component of one theory and in the experience component of another theory appears justified by their respective contexts in different theories.

The problem is not solved, however; it is merely shelved. For we should ask a more general question about the experience component in our definition of personality: Does it include unconscious processes? Could it be that psychophysical systems include structural aspects which are unconscious and process aspects which are unconscious, but that the unconscious process aspects may also be classified as part of the experience component of personality? Would it also be true that behavior can have unconscious process aspects associated with psychophysical structures? An example would be found in symptomatic behaviors, as in the compulsion side of obsessional-compulsive neurosis; another example would be in overdetermined errors or accidents. Such examples serve the purpose of bringing abstract questions down to actual cases. There is evidently a real theoretical problem here that must be worked out. The lead which we have uncovered above is the possibility that constructs like repression and denial, along with the matters repressed or denied, may have all three: psychophysical system aspects, experience aspects, and behavior aspects. It will take a good deal of theoretical work to clarify this matter.

Evaluation of the Uses of Experience Components. In my judgment the experience components in our definition of personality have been underutilized. Rarely do we find a personality theory which specializes in the study of experience as a function of other variables. Yet Freud and Jung undoubtedly began with basically that intention, and were impressed with the many interesting questions that were posed by anomalies of experience in their patients: The feelings associated with transference, the lack of feelings associated with mechanisms of isolation, the gaps in the experiential record (amnesia, repression proper), or intrusion into the record (such as screen memories, and so on). But the focus of both theories swiftly turned to elaboration of inner dynamics, of unconscious processes, of the complexities in psychophysical systems. Skinner sought to correct such tendencies in his call for focus upon straight description of behavior. We might call for another correction through straight description of experience. Rogers, of course, has devoted almost all of his theoretical attention to experience. But he has concentrated on variables relating constructs within the experience component, such as openness to experience, or congruence, or the match between self-concept and the ideal self.

When Rogers deals with experience variables as a function of other variables it is almost always the perceived or experienced environment which supplies those independent variables. Except in the context of therapy research little attention is paid to actual environmental variables. Experience should be not only described more fully but related more explicitly to independent variables from the body, psychophysical systems, and behavior. In particular, variables of the behavioral record should be more adequately integrated with variables of the experiential record. Erikson has begun such formulations in his proposals that identity consists in part of *accrued* confidence, *accrued* experience of drives, skilled performances, and role behaviors. His construct of a sense of identity embraces the components of experience, behavior, and psychophysical systems.

Behavior

Theorists' Uses of Behavior. The theorists studied in this book include some who pay very scant attention to behavior and some who are interested solely in behavior. The range may be viewed as from Rogers to Skinner. There are variations in type of usage, however. Some theorists (such as Freud) cover *instrumental* (or goal-seeking behavior) and also *symptomatic* behavior (such as compulsive handwashing.) Other theorists (Maslow, for instance) include *expressive* behavior, such as painting or singing for pleasure or moping, pouting, or slumping in sadness. Other theorists appear to be most interested in *repeated* behaviors, the characteristic behaviors that indicate the presence of traits or source traits. Obviously there is great variety here: instrumental, consummatory, expressive, or symptomatic responses; responses in stimulus-response chains; and even larger chunks of the behavioral record in consistent characteristics.

Evaluation of Uses of Behavior. Theorists all seem to take a one-sided view of behavior. Whenever a theory is formulated as a theory of function it invariably places behavior on the dependent variable side of its equations. Obviously it does not need to do that; it could quite well place the body or experience or even psychophysical systems on the dependent side. For example, the strength of a person's need for dominance might be studied as a function of the relative size of their body and the amount of restriction previously placed on their muscular movement. A person's conscious sense of identity can be studied as a function of graduated physical exercises. In modern research it is quite common to find dream events or dream contents studied as a function of prior or concurrent stimulation or behavior. Theories of personality should catch up with such facts and abandon preoccupation with behavior as the envelope of dependent variables. It is simply too limiting on behavior. In everyday life we know that behavior can be the cause of experience events or of bodily change. For example, feelings of shame are produced by certain behaviors; increased size and strength of biceps may be a function of regular relevant behaviors.

Summary Recommendation

All components of the definition of personality given in chapter 2 are used by one or more theorists, and some theorists use all the components (Freud, for example). It seems to me that a theory which does not use all the components is unlikely to prove satisfactory in the long run. More attention should be given also to the entire network of causal connections between and within different components.

In much personality research today there is an undue emphasis upon behavior as the component from which dependent variables are to be drawn. Yet it is obvious that the body, for example, can provide a valuable source of dependent variables. Examples include the effects of stressful life events in raising the probability of physical illness (Holmes & Rahe, 1967), or the effects of defense mechanisms on psychosomatic disorder (Alexander et al., 1968). It is also obvious that behavior can provide a useful source of independent variables, as the effects of exercise show.

Additionally, in most personality research and theory today there is undue neglect of the body. Perhaps it would be useful to add at least a brief treatment "from the somatic point of view" to theoretical work on any major topic in personality science.

Types of Theories

In chapter 8 it was suggested that the overall theory developed by a theorist may include one or more quite different types of component theory. A theory of *cause* proposes either hidden or previously unrecognized causes which make it possible to explain certain facts. A theory of *function* specifies functional relationships between constructs, sometimes but not always with mathematical expressions. A theory of *structure* proposes that objects are composed of particular parts, often including tentative laws about how the parts compose the object. A theory of *pattern* proposes that there is a certain order to be found in a previously unordered array of facts. A theory of *priority* specifies what order *ought* to be imposed on an array of facts. A theory of *system* proposes numerous constructs for a given set of phenomena and specifies that every construct has some consequential relationship with all other constructs in the theory.

Our studies in this book have included theories of all types. At this point it seems useful to evaluate the utility of the classification of types of theory.

Theories of Cause

Many theorists offer a theory of cause in personality, ranging from psychic energy (Freud, Jung) to brain functions (Cattell, Eysenck); from needs (Murray) to field forces (Lewin). Freud's theoretical model of dreams proposes that instinctual energies in conflict constitute the essential cause; Miller and Dollard's model of imitation proposes that response and drive reduction constitute essen-

tial causes. Theories of cause are found within theories of function (such as Miller and Dollard's or Eysenck's theory) and also within theories of system, as in Rogers's theory of incongruence as the cause of psychological maladjustment.

Many theories of cause are offered in conjunction with a theory of structure (Freud, Jung, Murray, Cattell, Eysenck, and others). But some theorists do not include a theory of cause where the causal influences are located within the personality. Such theorists (Skinner, for example) also do not propose a theory of personality structure. Their theory of cause locates the relevant sources of influence in the environment or in "contingencies" between environment and behavior. It seems to me that such theories would be best left in their original domain as theories of behavior, not to be confused with theories of personality. Behavior is only one component of personality. It no more deserves to be substituted for the whole than does any other component such as the body, psychophysical systems, or experience.

All of the theories we have studied are more or less incomplete in their consideration of causal relationships. This is understandable and acceptable insofar as each has sought to address some restricted range of relevant phenomena, to produce theoretical models of particular events or facts. But if we aim for a comprehensive theory of personality the constructs and causal relations must span the entire domain of body, psychophysical systems, experience, and behavior. Causal relations within and between these components will be hypothesized in a comprehensive theory.

At the present we find instances of each kind of causal relation hypothesized by one or another theory, the set as a whole being scattered among different theories. As examples of causal relations hypothesized to hold *within* major components of personality, we have seen body-body relations such as genetic inputs to brain functions (Eysenck). We have seen experience-experience relations hypothesized, such as the accrued experience (of the ego's ability to integrate identifications) which produces the conscious part of the sense of identity (Erikson). We have seen causal relations hypothesized within the psychophysical systems, such as the effect of archetypes in producing the shadow or the animus (Jung). We have seen causal relations hypothesized within the behavior component, as in reflex chains (Skinner).

Often causal relations are posited *between* components. Variations in autonomic lability are hypothesized to cause variations in neuroticism (body and psychophysical systems); repressed sexual impulses are hypothesized to cause hysterical symptoms (psychophysical systems and body and also behavior); quasi-needs cause locomotion toward positive valences (experience and behavior); and so on.

Theories of Function

Little needs to be said about theories of function; they are possibly the elite among scientific theories. Their real interest lies in the substantive models of structure, cause, pattern, or system which they subsume and which they represent in functional form. Theories of function are notable primarily for this form of representation and for their consequent amenability to mathematical treatment. But neither the form nor the mathematical treatment guarantees a theory viability: witness the fate of Lewin's theory, which had much of both, as compared with Freud's theory, which had none of either.

Theories of Structure

Before considering the matter of structure we need to examine an odd question it poses. What kinds of facts require a structural the-ory? Beyond the body there are no tangible objects in personality which could have a physical structure. But we saw in chapter 4 that a theory of structure can be properly developed for behavior, proposing for instance that complex behaviors are composed of chained component reflexes. Here the "object" in question is a complex behavior like dancing or operating an automobile. We recall from chapter 8 that a *model object* is simply a description of the facts to be explained.

One kind of fact typically explained by a theory of structure is regularities in the record of experience, behavior, or both. These regularities characterize a given individual, and individuals differ in such characteristics, giving rise to the existence of stable individual differences. The theories of Cattell and Eysenck seek to account for such differences with an appropriate number of independent, underlying psychophysical structures (indicated by factors). Murray's theory seeks to account for such regularities and individual differences by constructs of need and thematic disposition, conceived as structural features of the ego which have dispositional and causal implications for an individual's experiences and behaviors. When symptoms arise, when patients report continued anguish and unreasoned anxiety in their experience, or when they display compulsively repetitive behaviors in their record, once again some structural basis is assumed. In this case, however, the contrasts between different times or subjects of experience, or between different behavioral episode series, or between experiences and behaviors in the record, lead the theorist to propose underlying structures which are at odds with each other, which give rise to conflict. For example, the ego structure is assumed to be in conflict with the id or the superego. Warring regularities in the record give rise to explanations in terms of warring structures.

The fundamental feature of facts requiring a theory of structure, then, seems to be regularity in the record. To some extent individual differences with respect to record (different degrees of a given regularity in different people) provide a secondary manifestation of regularity. Another manifestation would be the concordances and discordances between different topical regularities within a given person. Thus regularities in the record, patterns of regularities in the record, and individual differences in regularities all seem to invite explanation in structural terms.

Can a theory that does not include a theory of structure explain regularities, patterns of regularities, and individual differences? Learning theorists have claimed to do so by proposing that crucial structures exist in the environment. For example, the environment contains repeated cues of danger, and therefore stable avoidance habits are developed. But this type of theory rests upon principles of conditioning, which we have seen are of dubious validity with respect to adult human beings. Some humanistic theorists have proposed that the structures only exist in experience (Rogers) or the body (Maslow). Neither tackles the problems of regularity, pattern, and individual differences in a comprehensive way. For example, Maslow can name self-actualizing people and describe their common regularities (see chapter 1). But his theory can do very little with the obvious differences in personality between various self-actualizers. For example, how would his theory account for differences between Lincoln, Einstein, Eleanor Roosevelt, George Washington Carver, Sholem Aleichem, Jane Addams, Florence Nightingale, Auguste Renoir, Goethe, Marie Curie, and Winston Churchill? The theory's only terms for explaining such differences would be "biological potentials."

It has no terms for describing them systematically. By contrast Cattell's theory would provide an eloquent account of such individual differences in terms of second-stratum temperament factors of extraversion, anxiety, alertness, and control, and also in terms of ergs and sentiments. As a matter of fact Cattell often provides illustrations of the meaning of factors by citing eminent people who illustrate a high degree of the trait (regularity) in question. For example, he describes Marie Curie as low in protension, Winston Churchill high in guilt proneness but low in radicalism, Eleanor Roosevelt high in premsia, Florence Nightingale and Abraham Lincoln high in superego strength (Cattell, 1973, pp. 166-174).

To be comprehensive, then, it appears that a theory of personality must include a theory of structure.

Theories of Pattern

We have studied two main kinds of pattern theory of personality, developmental and typological. Amid swirling arrays of facts, such theories propose an order along a time dimension or by classification. Examples are Erikson's theory of psychosocial development (temporal pattern) and Jung's theory of types (classification pattern).

There is an unstudied relationship between such theories and related theories of cause and structure. For example, Freud's theory of developmental pattern contains a number of points at which particular causal processes are proposed to account for characteristics of the development. An example is the role of the castration complex in motivating transition from the phallic to the latency stage. The example suggests that, after a temporal pattern theory has been proposed, a causal theory may be employed to produce a theoretical model of transitions from one to another point in the pattern.

Sometimes it seems that a theory of pattern can employ the results of a theory of structure. For example, in Jung's overall theory, one part of the component theory of structure distinguishes the conscious from unconscious domains. Then, in the theory of types (a pattern theory) each type is described by characteristics which are conscious, and also by characteristics which are unconscious. For example, the working of the inferior function in each type is typically described as unconscious.

Theories of Priority

A theory of priority can be superimposed on a theory of pattern, even as Maslow, for example, superimposes the relative desirability of self-actualization needs on his pattern theory of prepotency among the five main groups of needs. Occasionally this theory of priority appears to take precedence in the mind of the theorist, in which case the theory becomes an advocacy for personal and social change. Humanistic psychology, in fact, has embraced such advocacy as part of its considered responsibility. At present there seems to be an uneasy tension between humanistic psychologists and others, including those who specialize in personality science but not from a humanistic viewpoint. It is difficult to unravel the crucial issues here (for clarification see Rychlak, 1968).

It is possible that in certain cases the theory of priority may include testable hypotheses, such as that a commune of self-actualizing people will have less crime and less mental disorder than a commune of persons motivated primarily by esteem and safety needs. In such applied issues the theory of priority has a valuable place. But it seems questionable to me whether it strictly should be included as part of a scientific theory of personality (even though such theories have been so included in the past). My preference would be to locate them in theories of application; that would keep the books a bit straighter.

Theories of System

Maslow's theory and Rogers's theory are theories of system in the sense given to system theory by Ludwig von Bertalanffy, who writes (1968, pp. 24-25),

> System theorists agree that the concept of "system" is not limited to material entities but can be applied to any "whole" consisting of interacting "components" . . . and even if the components of a system are ill-defined, it can at least be expected that certain principles will qualitatively apply to the whole *qua* system. . . . Bearing in mind these limitations, one concept which may prove to be of a key nature is the organismic notion of the organism as a spontaneously active system. . . . It appears that internal activity rather than reaction to stimuli is fundamental.

Despite the fact that humanistic theories of personality have been named as theories of system by von Bertalanffy, they fail to show some of the marks of such theories. For example, although both Rogers and Maslow emphasize a central striving and purposiveness in human personality, neither has included any servomechanisms or feedback loops in his theory. By contrast Cattell has included such loops explicitly in his analysis of certain second-stratum factors (see chapter 15). Peterfreund and Schwartz (1971) have advanced a new "systems" formulation of Freud's theory, emphasizing feedback mechanisms. So apparently the option to develop a systems theory is not limited to humanistic psychologists. Indeed, Royce and Buss (1976) propose a systems theory of personality based almost entirely on the results of factor analysis.

It therefore seems likely that a theory of system should be relieved of the obligation to deal only with purposive systems. It can be employed usefully in further consideration of materials otherwise treated according to a theory of structure, cause, or pattern. Like a theory of function, a theory of system seeks to relate variables without specifying causal connections. However, unlike a theory of function, the theory of system treats relationships in terms of information processing, feedback mechanisms, and possibly also whole-characteristics.

Summary on Types of Theory

It seems that each type of theory can be found among the many overall theories of personality studied in this book. Different types of theories apparently accomplish different goals and have different capabilities for accomplishing particular goals. For example, the goal of explaining individual differences seems best served by a theory of structure; the goal of describing psychological types is best served by a theory of classification patterns.

Yet the various types of theory do not seem to be entirely *coordinate*. That is, the various types contain some that are apparently derived from a different level of analysis. For example, a theory of function can include a theory of cause, although a theory of cause cannot include a theory of function. Perhaps it would be better to conceive of the six types of theory as two sets of three types each. The first set contains the theories of structure, cause, and pattern. The second set contains the theories of function, system, and priority. Theories of the second set may always include or be superimposed on theories of the first set, but not vice versa. Within each set the theories are coordinate in the sense that they cannot be overlaid upon each other or include each other, but they can be put to work side by side, so to speak. For example, a theory of structure and a theory of cause can work together (and often do,

as in Freud's theory). Each tackles a somewhat different aspect or part of the problem. But a theory of function and a theory of structure can both go to work on the same aspect or part of the problem, treating it in a different way. For example, in Lewin's theory (chapter 19) the theory of function, that is, the detail of $B = f\ (P,\ E)$, is overlaid on a theory of structure (the regions and boundaries of the person, P)

Methods

Some of the most refreshing of principles ever set forth by a scientist are those given us by B. F. Skinner, listed in box 4.1. They commend lively responsiveness and pursuit of the interesting. The content of this third section takes sanction from his wisdom, and points to matters that are of interest to me, and that promise to make work easier. These will be summarized briefly under the three headings of theory development, model objects, and confrontation experiments.

Theory Development

At several points throughout the book we have come across issues in need of clarification, matters needing further research, points at which theory needs to be further developed. Are there any guidelines for such development? Some can be drawn from Mario Bunge's work to which we referred in chapters 6 and 8.

We cannot test a theory as a whole, but only portions of it that are brought to bear in a particular theoretical model of a restricted set of phenomena. The first guideline would seem to be: Get some practice in formulating and using theoretical models.

Theories change through their exercise in theoretical model applications. If the models work, the theories pass; if they don't, the theories need a check-up and a change. Sometimes such changes are disparagingly called "post hoc." But if the change is included from then on it cannot be post hoc for very long. In the next model it will be pre hoc. A recent experiment in my laboratory tested the hypothesis that increasing the number of cues will increase the vividness of imagery; the hypothesis stems from a model of image formation based upon a theory of cognitive processes which assumes that perception and imagery use common pathways or channels. The results of the experiment were uniformly opposite to those predicted. Increasing the number of sensory cues consistently decreased the vividness of imagery. The hypothesis proved to be inaccurate. This calls the model into question, and thereby the theory. A post hoc change in the theory states that the common pathways are shared most closely by perception and *memory* images; they are shared less closely by images which are constructed. The related change in the model states that increasing the number of sensory cues reduces the chance that a subject will find an idiosyncratic memory image that fits all the cues. It is easier to have an image of a dog than of a fluffy, grey spotted, big dog, because just any old dog image would do for the single cue, but not for the triple cue. At present this change in the theory is post hoc with respect to the results of the given experiment. But the next model we build will derive from the new theory as modified.

There is an interaction, then, between theory, theoretical model, and test or confirmation. If the test fails, the theory is changed to accommodate a change in the model which seems indicated by the test results. The new theory then produces a new model which is subjected to a new test or confirmation.

The example of a particular experiment is simple and may be misleading. For that reason we added the word *confirmation,* which may include observational evidence. Freud could not possibly have checked up on his theory with a simple model and experiment such as the one described. It took years of careful observation to establish the inadequacy of the original topographic theory of structure in which all ego functions were conscious.

The second guideline, however, is that models should be tested through explicit predictions of outcomes of observations or experiments. This sounds commonplace enough, but the emphasis is upon actively generating test conditions, which also involves active change of models found to have defects. In line with Skinner's principles, we should always be on the lookout for a change that makes a model work more accurately and with less effort on our part. In this light, a clearcut disconfirmation of a hypothesis is more useful than a confirmation. A related point is that a clearcut confirmation of a model can also provide support for any other model from which an identical prediction can or might be made. Hence it is important to find instances in which competing models predict *different* outcomes.

As we saw in chapter 8, changes can occur in model objects as well as in theoretical models. The model object is our representation of the facts to be explained. Changes in model objects also will produce or require changes in related theoretical models, and ultimately in their parent theories. This process too may be put to active use by more or less deliberate efforts to find appropriate changes in model objects. For example, Lazarus (1976, chapter 5) describes how the data of stress reactions were reinterpreted by Selye with the observation that *any* noxious physical agent would produce the same set of physiological stress responses as would specific toxins or injuries. Previously the model object had been that specific agents produce specific stress re-actions and hence specific illnesses. Selye's change stated that most agents are nonspe-cific and produce nonspecific stress reactions which are the same in illnesses of many dif-ferent forms. Other workers, including Laz-arus, considered the facts of nonspecific re-actions, including marked changes in color and size of various glands, and suggested that the model object should be changed further. For to this point the entire set of facts relates a physical noxious stimulus to physiological re-actions (discharge of hormones) which pro-duce the chemical and physical changes in glands and blood. But other data suggest that such changes can occur when the noxious stimulus or event is merely *anticipated* by the person or animal without actually occurring. Thus a psychological fact must be included in the model object: *Anticipation* of harm pro-duces stress reactions. Lazarus proposes that in all stress events, including frustrative, toxic, and other actual physical stress situations, the animal or person *also* makes an appraisal of threat (unless unconscious). Explanation of changes in glands must consider the possi-bility that this appraisal, not the noxious physical stimulus, is the effective cause. Ex-perimental data support such alternative hy-potheses.

Crucial to our present purpose, however, is the addition of the psychological fact to the model object of stress. Such addition could have come from thinking about the facts as previously given. The facts pertained to wak-ing organisms, whose cognitive functions would almost certainly be alerted by any nox-ious stimuli. Simply thinking about model ob-jects, then, could well result in changes. To be of real use, though, such changes must be capable of receiving assent from the body of contemporary scientists. This third guideline for developing theory takes us directly into the next topic, model objects.

Model Objects

In previous chapters we have often found that disagreements between theorists are based upon different sets of facts in the first place. An outstanding example is the differing in-terpretations of imitation offered by Miller and Dollard on one hand and by Bandura and Walters on the other, as discussed in chapter 21. Similarly, Freud and Jung dif-fered in their theoretical models of transfer-ence; the chief difference was that they also disagreed on the model object of transference, the facts in question (chapter 13).

How can we ensure that two models are really in competition and not merely giving that appearance? One approach is to devise a common language that is precise enough and refers to observable things enough so that scientists cannot easily be mistaken in think-ing they agree on the facts when they do not. Behaviorism may be seen as one such attempt. Indeed Skinner's recommendations for trans-lating everyday language into behavioral lan-guage is a direct attempt to solve the prob-lem of scientific communication. Another approach seems to be that of "modern experi-mental personality" a term that refers to an approach to personality which relies solely on laboratory experiments. When an experiment is carefully described, as to subjects, methods, and procedures, then presumably any other scientist, upon reading this description, can *replicate* the experiment—establish the same or closely similar experimental conditions in his or her own laboratory. The results of one sci-entist can then be assumed to be directly com-parable to those obtained by another scientist.

The approach of behavioral language and that of full explicit descriptions of experi-mental procedures both have merit. Both no doubt accomplish other goals as well as serve the latent function of securing better communication among psychologists. Unfor-tunately the behavioral language cannot really encompass more than behavioral facts and their relations with environments. And modern experimental personality seems to be predicated on the methodological assumption that accumulating enough facts by the experimental method will allow for new and better theories to be developed. Studies typically follow one another in a chain linked around one or two variables and a very general concept such as equity, attribution, person perception, and so on. Often it is hard to recognize a connection between these experiments and any major theory of personality. So, except for rare programs like Silverman's, on the psychoanalytic theory of psychopathology (Silverman, 1976), theory and experiment in personality science have gone their separate ways. Rotter (1975) has pointed out that this separation of ways has occurred even when experimenters are using (and misusing) a theoretical construct such as internal versus external control (chapter 20). Loosed from its theoretical moorings the construct is likely to be used in ways that give it quite new (and undefined) meanings. Limitations attending the measurement of the theoretical construct are apt to be forgotten. The result is a series of experiments which appear on the surface to be dealing with the theoretical construct but in fact are dealing with an unknown variable which has been given a familiar name. The experiments may be technically sound (design, sampling, analysis) but they present "results" which are misleading.

The many experiments purporting to demonstrate "conditioning" in adult humans offer another prime example. The "modern experimental personality" approach provides no guarantee against simulation by the subjects. Hence the model object created by this approach may contain misrepresentations of the facts of human personality. Careful theoretical work tying such experiments to major

theories capable of conceptualizing the simulation would seem to be required.

One recommendation to be made, then, is that experiments should be aimed at testing and extending or revising theoretical models derived from major theories of personality. This would mean that the experimental approach toward developing adequate model objects would be coordinated with efforts to formulate increasingly testable theoretical models drawn from major theories of personality.

There may be a third way to improve the consensus on model objects, namely, by paying more attention to documentation of the descriptive details of facts or classes of facts under study, and by placing them in a public domain. For example, an article might do nothing more than describe in detail what a given author means by "locus of control" or "anxiety" or "aggression." The intent would be to provide a statement of a model object with which other scientists could work if they agree, or to which they could write a rejoinder or addendum if they disagree.

Confrontation Experiments

It is rare to find experiments which directly pit one theory against another through the testing of models derived from each. It is not necessary that the two models predict totally contradictory results, although this is certainly the desired state of affairs for a crucial experiment. The idea here is to broaden the notion of a crucial experiment to include possibly compatible predictions or merely different predictions within the same experimental setting and with the same groups of subjects. In workshop 21 an example was provided of a setting in which models of imitation taken from Miller and Dollard's theory and from Bandura and Walters's theory could be put into confrontation. Much was learned from the mere formulation of such an experiment, even without actually carrying it out.

Specifically it was learned that the two theoretical models of "imitation" were actually directed at quite different model objects.

In the results of confrontation experiments it would be possible often to distinguish between rival interpretations. Without the confrontation it often is not possible to make such distinctions. For example, an experiment testing the psychoanalytic model of dreams might induce dreaming hypnotically and then test for amount of primary process shown in Rorschach responses to cards previously used as stimulus materials during dream induction. Results consistent with the model would be supportive of both model and parent theory. They could, however, be interpreted equally well as consistent with the model of dreaming drawn from Jung's theory. Had a confrontation experiment been devised, in which both models were used to make predictions, the results would have shown more clearly which model best accounted for the data, whether both did equally well, or whether they actually addressed somewhat different aspects of the data.

Some Thoughts for the Future

In chapter 6, Brewer's (1975) survey of studies on human conditioning was mentioned. He concluded that adult humans only appear to be conditioned. Once they become aware of the contingencies they simulate the expected results. For years this fact has been unrecognized and most psychologists (myself included) have assumed that humans can be conditioned and that the mechanisms are basically similar to those assumed in animal conditioning. Some psychologists have further assumed that everything else about human beings can be explained in terms of conditioning; others have assumed that conditioning can occur and still not provide a useful ac-count of the most important phenomena in human personality.

Rogers (chapter 5) has suggested that the self-concept might be built up from thousands of conditionings, but that its salient characteristic as a fluid but consistent gestalt could not be accounted for in the same way. The phenomenal whole which is a self-concept, he said, cannot be accounted for by conditioning. Now we have to rephrase his argument and say that a self-concept might be built up from a thousand simulated conditionings, but that the phenomenal whole which is the self-concept cannot be accounted for by simulated conditioning. If that sounds strange, it should. For the whole of our conception of human psychological capabilities is challenged by Brewer's conclusions. The phenomena of conditioning are among the best established in the science. People have for years carried out careful studies aimed at determining this and that specific optimum value for conditioning to occur or to be resistant to extinction. An example is the determination of the optimal interval of time between conditioned and unconditioned stimulus presentations (it appears to be about .5 seconds for eyelid conditioning). If Brewer's conclusions are correct, then all of these efforts have yielded results on adult humans which only appear to support (or be consistent with) the underlying theoretical model which so far has guided the research.

We may have here a prime example of the dictum that a confirmation is of less value than a disconfirmation. For the confirmations have led us to accept the theoretical model when, by all appearances at this time, it is wrong.

What is the correct model object at present so far as apparent conditioning experiments are concerned? It seems to be best described in part as it was before, with a complete statement of the experimental procedures and contingencies and outcomes as given in chapter 4 for both classical and operant conditioning. But then another part must be added, which is that the conditioning occurs only if the subject is aware of the contingencies and is willing (for whatsoever reasons) to simulate the expected outcome.

If that is the model object, then what new theoretical model shall we propose? From what theory shall we draw our constructs and hypotheses?

Yet another question can be asked. Can it be that no matter what model we devise, the human adult will be able to simulate results which support that model? Consider that the theoretical model we devise will be devised by a human brain. Perhaps any model which can be devised by a human brain can also be simulated by another human brain.

If this is true, then it has implications both for a theory of personality and for the methodology required to evaluate that theory. First, the theory must include a construct for this capacity to simulate. Second, the theory must specify under what conditions the simulation capacity is and is not likely to be in operation. For example, if awareness is necessary for simulation, then presumably conditions not entering awareness will not be likely to elicit simulated experiences and behaviors and simulated causal connections. Third, the theory must spell out some hypotheses concerning the role of the simulating capacity in normal personality development and functioning. This endeavor will likely lead to a review of relevant theoretical models in one or more of the existing theories, including those presented in this book. As assumptions, constructs, hypotheses and evidence are considered they must be examined in the light of the new knowledge of simulation. For if conditioning can be simulated by human adults surely much else can be simulated too. A theory which has rested upon clinical evidence, for example, could equally well have rested upon simulated clinical evidence. Patients may well have had experiences, behaviors, bodily manifestations, and even changes in psychophysical systems which in effect simulate the theoretical model of the clinician.

In short, all theories of personality are now suspect; perhaps *all* theories of human psychology (learning, perception, memory, social, and so on) are suspect.

The methodology that a new theory of personality must develop will have to deal first of all with the fact of simulation. Given guides by the theory concerning conditions under which simulation will likely be operative, methods must be sought which provide for control studies of hypotheses under conditions favorable and unfavorable to simulation. It seems likely that the technologies developed by Silverman (1976) for studying the effects of unconscious impulse arousal would offer useful examples of conditions unfavorable to simulation. On the other side, much may be learned from those studies referred to by Brewer (1975) which simply told subjects what the contingencies were and then found immediate "conditioning." Here we might have a way of testing the limits of simulation for any model devised: Describe it to the subjects and ask them to simulate accordingly.

I think we may be confident that the next few years of work in personality theory will be lively and full of surprises.

Appendix A

The Lie Detector: When Experience and Behavior Are Inconsistent

The lie detector or polygraph offers a good opportunity to study inconsistencies. Someone is believed to be concealing something, and it is hoped that astute questioning will trigger the person's memory or consciousness of that very thing and that this will produce a physiological reaction that can be measured by the lie detector. In the polygraph test while the subject is being questioned his or her heart rate, respiration, and GSR are recorded on a paper tracing.

Such research has been used to test the validity of a self-reported delinquent behavior questionnaire, for example (Clark and Tifft, 1966). Did the respondent, a known delinquent, lie when reporting that he had not stolen anything worth fifty dollars or more? The question is asked again while electrodes pick up his reactions: "During the past year have you taken things worth fifty dollars or more that did not belong to you?" The subject answers no, but the lie detector twitches, indicating some unusual psychophysical disturbance.

We might suppose that the respondent ac-

tually had an image of himself and other boys stripping off hubcaps from several autos one evening last April. The theft netted each boy about sixty-five bucks, but why tell about that?

Going back now to Krasner and Ullmann's challenge (1973), does this image or thought classify as behavior as defined by measurable changes in some form of corporeal activity? It would seem so; after all, there was the unusual reaction on the lie detector coinciding with the subject's verbal response. There were two forms of corporeal activity, the change in electrical resistance on the skin (and possibly other physiological reactions picked up by the lie detector's electrodes) and the vocalization. Moreover we know the total situation and the stimulus, namely the particular interview question. We conclude that the boy lied; we conclude that he has taken things worth fifty dollars or more during the past year; we conclude that he knows he has, but is concealing this fact.

The argument has rushed on too swiftly, however, for the image or thought was not actually measured at all. We must retrace the argument.

The lie detector data do not tell us the

boy's experience at that moment. They simply tell us that something happened to make the polygraph's pen deflect sharply. We infer that the boy was lying when he said no. We suppose that he remembered the events and lied about them. The detector simply suggests that he lied, which means that he had one thought that was "the truth" but he told us something different. The whole meaning of "lie" rests upon our tacit assumption that people can think the truth and tell something different.

In fact, then, not only does the lie detector *not* measure or define the boy's image experience; its use even assumes that there *was* some experience which neither the detector nor the boy's words describe. One thing that is implied by "thoughts and feelings that do not classify as behavior," then, is that they make lies possible. They make games like *Truth or Consequences* possible. They make diplomacy and intrigue possible.

Krasner and Ullman might reject this argument and say that the lie-detector is too crude an instrument. The boy's thought would have been measurable in some form of corporeal activity if we had more sensitive instruments. That is, we are now asked to believe that the boy's experience is a "covert" behavior, one that it is very difficult to see. Some remote device would so record and integrate the excitations of nervous tissue that a read-out could be obtained showing the boys removing hubcaps.

This argument will not work. It will not work because the physical basis of bodily events cannot distinguish between experience and behavior. It cannot even distinguish between overt and covert behavior. Either will be associated with some physical events. To make an argument that physical events in the nervous system are simply covert behavior is to claim that all behavior is associated with covert behavior. For example, if we put the same recording device onto a pigeon's brain while it pecks at a target, the device will give a read-out showing the pigeon's peck. Does that mean the read-out is from the covert peck? It does not. It means the read-out is from the nervous excitations associated with the actual peck.

So with the boy, the read-out from the ultimately sensitive device is a read-out from nervous excitations associated with his image of stealing the hubcaps. We cannot get rid of the distinction between behavior and experience by appealing to nervous excitations.

Appendix B

Use of Statistics Procedures for Test Analysis

A brief description of the meanings of certain terms used in statistics and in psychological test analysis may be useful to some readers at this point and at later points in the book.

We deal with a set of observations, each of which is recorded as a numerical *score*. For example, a person gets a score of 30 on a thirty-five-item test of historical knowledge. The entire class of students might get scores ranging from 23 to 35. How shall we describe these scores as a whole? We might wish to compare this class as a whole with last year's class as a whole, and therefore need some way to characterize both classes. We deal with the *distribution* of scores for a class, and we characterize that distribution by stating its central point, that is, its average score or *arithmetic mean*. Suppose we have a class of forty students. We might arrange their scores as shown at top of the opposite column. This is called a *frequency distribution* of scores, since for every score we plot the frequency of students obtaining that score. For instance, four students obtained a score of 26; only one

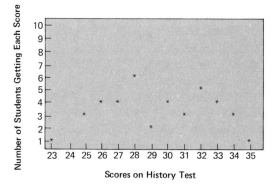

achieved a perfect score of 35. To obtain the mean of this distribution, add all the scores and divide by 40, the total number of scores. In the example, the addition yields 1,178. Divide by 40 to obtain the mean: 1,178/40 = 29.45. This number is an estimate of the average score of students in this class on this test. Students in last year's class might have received a mean of only 23.72. There are ways to test if the difference between the two classes' scores (29.45 − 23.72 = 5.73) could have occurred by chance in two random samples of students from the same general population. A small difference can probably be attributed to chance. A larger difference, relative to the variation expected in two similar

544

random samples, would have been very unlikely to have occurred by chance. If it is really unlikely that it occurred by chance, then we conclude that there was some real cause for the difference.

We estimate *how unlikely* the difference would be to occur by chance. For instance, the difference of 5.73 or more might occur only once in one hundred times by pure chance. It is very *im*probable. We would say that its probability (p) is very small, is in fact less than ($<$) .01 (one in a hundred): $p < .01$. In psychology we say that a difference with a p-value of .05 or .01 or smaller is *statistically significant*. Many results in psychological research are described as being either significant or not significant statistically, and this is what it means.

You may notice that the frequency distribution of test scores is not evenly arranged, nor is it strictly symmetrical. There are lumps in it. For instance there is a high point where six students scored 28; at another high point five students scored 32. This might suggest that the entire group is not just randomly distributed around its own mean of 29.45, but rather that there are two groups of students, one with a mean around 27 to 28, the other with a mean around 32 to 33. There is only a suggestion of this in the given distribution, and it probably is not significantly different from the case of one single group around the mean of 29.45. But following is a distribution which would be more likely to represent two distinct groups. This distribution of scores has two high points, called *modes*, at 25 and 33. The distribution with only one high point in the middle is called *unimodal;* the distribution with two high points is called *bimodal.* In one of the tests of Jung's theory it was reasoned that extraverts should fall at one end of a score distribution and introverts should fall at the other end if there really are two types. Thus a distribution of scores on a test for ex-

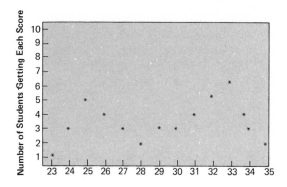

traversion-introversion should be bimodal if the pattern theory is correct, and if this particular statistical interpretation of it is correct.

We have spoken of *reliable* tests in chapter 7. A test is reliable if it tends to yield the same score for an individual if administered a second time or if the individual takes two separate forms of the same test and receives a closely similar score in each. Similarly, the test is reliable if an individual's scores on both halves of a test are roughly the same. It means that the test is measuring some real condition of the individual which shows the same on both halves, or on both forms, or on both occasions. Ordinarily the reliability is estimated by *correlating* the scores of a sample of persons on the two halves or the two forms or the two occasions. For instance, scores on the history test might be charted for the even-numbered test items and for the odd-numbered items. This is one way to split the test into halves.

Student	Score on even items	Score on odd items
A	12	11
B	14	11
C	19	16
D	18	15
.		
.		
.		
Y	16	16
Z	14	13

Notice that in each column of half scores the numbers rise and fall. If they rise and fall more or less in parallel, then the test has good reliability. For instance, student C has the highest half score in both columns, 19 and 16 respectively. Student A has the lowest in both columns. Exceptions occur when student B ties with student A on the odd items and with student Z on the even items. Thus there are irregularities in the parallelism, which means it is not perfect. To the extent that it is not perfect there is *un*reliability in the measurements yielded by this test. The range of reliability is usually expressed as a decimal value from .00 to +1.00, where .00 means total lack of parallelism, total unreliability; +1.00 means total or perfect reliability.

The notion of *validity* is also important in evaluating a psychological test. Does the test really measure what it is supposed to measure? Does the history test really measure knowledge of history? Or are the scores more related to how test-wise the student is? Does a test of extraversion-introversion really measure that construct? One way to evaluate this matter is to administer two quite different tests, both of which are supposed to measure the same construct. Scores obtained on the two tests from a single sample of subjects can then be correlated. If both tests accurately measure knowledge of history they should have parallel columns of scores; if both measure extraversion-introversion they should have closely parallel sets of scores. Once again we can estimate this degree of parallelism, or correlation, using a procedure which yields values from .00 to +1.00, where .00 means there is no relationship between the two tests—no validity—and +1.00 means perfect validity. Other ways of estimating validity include comparison of the mean scores for two groups known to differ on the construct being measured. For example, a test supposed to be measuring anxiety should show a higher mean score on a group of patients diagnosed as having an anxiety reaction than on a group of "normal" university students (see for example, Taylor, 1953).

Reliability coefficients are usually expected to be higher than validity coefficients. Values of .8 or better would be considered as representing good reliability; values of .5 or better would be considered as good validity. We need more parallelism between two halves of the same test (or two forms) before we will accept it as being reasonably reliable; we settle for somewhat less parallelism between two *different* tests in considering them to have acceptable validity.

Appendix C

The Correlation Coefficient

In Appendix B we introduced the general idea of a correlation coefficient. Now we must give an exact formula for calculating such a coefficient.

Suppose that we have two columns of numbers representing scores on two tests, A and B. In order to calculate the coefficient of correlation we must first transform those scores as follows.

Let X_{ai} be a score on A and X_{bi} be a score on B, both scores belonging to a particular person or individual called i. If there are fifty individuals there will be fifty scores on each test. As shown in Appendix B, we can calculate the mean (M) of the scores on A and the mean of the scores on B. Call them M_a and M_b respectively. Now we wish to represent every individual's score as a deviation from the group mean. Deviation scores of an individual would be shown as x_{ai} and x_{bi} for the two tests respectively, and would be obtained as follows:

$$x_{ai} = X_{ai} - M_a$$
$$x_{bi} = X_{bi} - M_b$$

The mean of the deviation scores for each test will be zero, because the sum of the raw scores less than the mean is equal to the sum of the raw scores greater than the mean. If a raw score is less than the mean the deviation score will be negative. For example, if the score is 43 and the mean is 49, the deviation score is −6. If we add up all the negative deviation scores and all the positive deviation scores the sum is zero; hence the mean is zero. This is true for all columns of test scores regardless, provided they are transformed to deviation scores. This is very convenient for calculating the correlation coefficient, which is expected to reflect the relationship between the two columns of scores in terms of varying up and down together (known as *co*variation). If the columns differ in their means then that fact tends to confuse the picture of covariation.

Another fact that tends to confuse the picture is differences between the two columns of scores in terms of range or spread. Test A might have scores going from 10 to 27, and test B might have scores from 10 to 93. In order to remove this source of confusion and make the ranges of the two tests the same we carry out another transformation. First we calculate a good measure of the range or spread in each column. This is the *standard deviation* (*SD*). Then we divide each deviation score in a column by the standard deviation of that column. The resulting transformed scores are known as *standard scores* or *z-scores*.

To calculate, first, the standard deviation for each column we first square each deviation score, then we take the mean of those squares, and finally we take the root of that mean. The standard deviation equals the root mean squared deviation score:

$$SD_a = \sqrt{Sum\ (x_{ai}{}^2)/N}$$

Then, to calculate a *z*-score we divide the deviation score by the standard deviation. Each score in the column then receives this treatment:

$$z_{ai} = x_{ai}/SD_a;\ z_{bi} = x_{bi}/SD_b$$

In place of two columns of original scores, then, we now have two columns of *z*-scores, such that the mean of each column is zero and the sum of squares is *N*; the standard deviation of each column is now exactly 1.00. In other words, there is no difference in the means of the two columns and there is no difference in the range or spread of the two columns. Means are both zero, and standard deviations (measures of spread) are both 1.00. Now we can really see what the covariation between the two tests is like. And at this point it is very simple to do so, since we simply multiply each individual's *z*-score on test A by the same individual's *z*-score on test B, then sum these products and divide by *N*. (In these calculations, *sum* is often expressed as Σ.) In other words we obtain the mean of the products of the *z*-scores:

$$r_{ab} = \Sigma\ (z_{ai} \cdot z_{bi})/N$$

where r_{ab} is the correlation coefficient between test A and test B. As discussed in the text of chapter 11, a correlation coefficient can take values from −1.00, through 0.00, to +1.00.

For the interested reader, a sound but brief elementary introduction to correlations and factor analysis is given by Child (1970); a fuller but still introductory treatment is given by Comrey (1973).

Appendix D

Estimating the Heritability of a Trait

It is known that twins born from one egg (identical twins) have an almost identical set of genetic characters, while twins born from two separately fertilized eggs (fraternal twins) have only half of their genes in common. This fact allows us to expect that, if a trait is completely determined by heredity, then identical twins should have exactly similar scores on that trait while fraternal twins should be only partially similar in their scores. Environment also plays a part in determining traits. If a trait were determined entirely by environmental features, then most probably there would be no greater resemblance between identical twins than between fraternals on that trait. These expectations allow us to develop procedures to calculate the probable degree of heritability of a trait by studying twins. If we have one set of identical twins and a set of fraternal twins who are comparable in other respects to the identicals (in age, social class, and so forth), then we may compare the extent of similarity in each group. If the identical twins tend to be much more similar than the fraternals then the trait probably has that much more contribution from heredity.

This means that differences between persons in the trait are due to differences between those persons in underlying genetic makeup.

Suppose we had test scores on five pairs of identical twins and five pairs of fraternals:

Identical twins		Fraternal twins	
Twin A	Twin B	Twin 1	Twin 2
17	14	20	12
12	13	11	15
10	11	7	13
8	8	9	6
5	4	3	6

The identical twin pairs are apparently much more similar. This can be seen readily if we calculate the difference of scores in each pair:

Difference in scores for identical twin pairs	Difference in scores for fraternal twin pairs
3	8
−1	−4
−1	−6
0	3
1	−3

Further calculations allow us to estimate how much greater the differences are among fraternal twins (or how much greater the similarity is between identicals). These estimates are also used in calculating the extent to which heredity contributes to variation in the trait. Some calculations give this result as a percentage of the trait's variation that is due to heredity. Readers interested in further study of behavioral genetics should consult McClearn and DeFries, 1973.

References

(Certain references are included for bibliographic information only and are not specifically cited in the text.)

Abraham, K. *Selected papers.* London: Hogarth, 1927.

Adler, A. *Understanding human nature.* Greenwich, Conn.: Fawcett Publications, 1927.

Adorno, T. W., Frenkel-Brunswik, E., Levinson, D. J., and Sanford, R. N. *The authoritarian personality.* New York: Harper & Row, 1950.

Alexander, F., French, T. M., and Pollock, G. H. *Psychosomatic specificity,* vol. 1. Chicago: University of Chicago Press, 1968.

Allison, J., Blatt, S. J., and Zimet, C. N. *The interpretation of psychological tests.* New York: Harper & Row, 1968.

Allport, G. W. *Personality: A psychological interpretation.* London: Constable, 1937.

———. *Pattern and growth in personality.* New York: Holt, 1961.

Allyon, T., and Azrin, N. H. The measurement and reinforcement of behavior of psychotics. *Journal of the Experimental Analysis of Behavior,* 1965, 8, 357-383.

Altman, L. L. *The dream in psychoanalysis.* New York: International Universities Press, 1969.

Altman, P. L., and Dittmer, D. S. *Growth: Including reproduction and morphological development.* Washington, D. C.: Federation of American Societies for Experimental Biology, 1962.

Amsel, A. The role of frustrative nonreward in continuous reward situations. *Psychological Bulletin,* 1958, **55,** 102-119.

Anderson, R. L., and Bancroft, T. A. *Statistical theory in research.* New York: McGraw-Hill, 1952.

Apostle, H. G. *Aristotle's physics.* Bloomington, Indiana: Indiana University Press, 1969.

Arlow, J. A., and Brenner, C. *Psychoanalytic concepts and the structural theory.* New York: International Universities Press, 1964.

Aronson, H., and Weintraub, W. Patient changes during classical psychoanalysis as a function of initial status and duration of treatment. *Psychiatry: Journal for the Study of Interpersonal Processes,* 1968, 31, 369-379.

Assagioli, R. *Psychosynthesis.* New York: Viking, 1965.

Atkinson, J. W., and Feather, N. T. (eds.) *A theory of achievement motivation.* New York: Wiley, 1966.

Axline, V. M. *Play therapy.* Boston: Houghton Mifflin, 1947.

———. *Dibs: In search of self.* Boston: Houghton Mifflin, 1964.

Bandura, A. Comments on Dr. Epstein's paper. In M. R. Jones (ed.), *Nebraska symposium on motivation.* Lincoln: University of Nebraska Press, 1962. (a)

———. The influence of rewarding and punishing consequences to the model on the acquisition and performance of imitative responses. Unpublished manuscript, Stanford University, 1962. (Cited in Bandura and Walters, 1963, pp. 57, 262). (b)

———. *Principles of behavior modification*. New York: Holt, Rinehart and Winston, 1969.

———. Analysis of modeling processes. In A. Bandura (ed.), *Psychological modeling: Conflicting theories*. Chicago: Aldine-Atherton, 1971.

———. Behavior theory and the models of man. *American Psychologist*, 1974, **29**, 859-869.

Bandura, A., Blanchard, E. G., and Ritter, B. The relative efficacy of desensitization and modeling approaches for inducing behavioral, affective, and attitudinal changes. *Journal of Personality and Social Psychology*, 1969, **13**, 173-199.

Bandura, A. and Jeffrey, R. W. Role of symbolic coding and rehearsal processes in observational learning. *Journal of Personality and Social Psychology*, 1973, **26**, 122-130.

Bandura, A., Ross, D., and Ross, S. A. Imitation of film-mediated aggressive models. *Journal of Abnormal and Social Psychology*, 1963, **66**, 3-11.

Bandura, A., and Walters, R. H. *Adolescent aggression*. New York: Ronald Press, 1959.

———. *Social learning and personality development*. New York: Holt, Rinehart & Winston, 1963.

Barker, R. G., and Wright, H. F. *One boy's day: A specimen record of behavior*. New York: Harper, 1951.

Barrett-Lennard, G. T. Dimensions of perceived therapist response related to therapeutic change. Unpublished doctoral dissertation, University of Chicago, 1959.

Barton, K., Kawash, G., and Cattell, R. B. Personality, motivation and marital role factors as predictors of life data in married couples. *Journal of Marriage and the Family*, 1972, pp. 474-480.

Battig, W. F. Within-individual differences in cognitive processes. In R. L. Solso (ed.), *Information processing and cognition: The Loyola symposium*. Potomac, Md.: Lawrence Erlbaum Associates, 1975.

Benedict, Ruth. *Patterns of culture*. Boston: Houghton Mifflin, 1935.

Benson, L. *Plant classification*. Boston: D. C. Heath and Co., 1957.

Bergin, A. E. The evaluation of therapeutic outcomes. In A. E. Bergin and S. L. Garfield (eds.), *Handbook of psychotherapy and behavior change*. New York: Wiley, 1971.

Bergin, A. E., and Suinn, R. M. Individual psychotherapy and behavior therapy. In M. R. Rosenzweig and L. W. Porter (eds.), *Annual review of psychology*, vol. 26. Palo Alto, Cal.: Annual Reviews, Inc., 1975.

Bernadin, A. C., and Jessor, R. A. A construct validation of the Edwards' Personal Preference Schedule with respect to dependency. *Journal of Consulting Psychology*, 1957, **21**, 63-67.

Berne, E. *What do you say after you say hello?* New York: Grove Press, 1972.

Bernoulli, D. On the properties and motions of elastic fluids, especially air. In S. G. Brush (ed.), *Kinetic theory*, vol. 1. *The nature of gases and heat*. New York: Pergamon Press, 1965. (Originally pub. 1738.)

Birney, R. C. Research on the achievement motive. In E. F. Borgatta and W. W. Lambert (eds.), *Handbook of personality theory and research*. Chicago: Rand McNally, 1968.

Boyle, R. The spring of the air. In S. G. Brush (ed.), *Kinetic theory*, vol. 1. *The nature of gases and heat*. New York: Pergamon Press, 1965. (Originally pub. 1660.)

Bradway, K. Jung's psychological types. *Journal of Analytical Psychology*, 1964, **9**, 129-135.

Braithwaite, R. B. *Scientific explanation*. New York: Harper Torchbooks, 1960.

Brebner, J. and Cooper, C. The effect of a low rate of regular signals upon the reaction times of introverts and extraverts. *Journal of Research in Personality*, 1974, **8**, 263-276.

Breger, L. and McGaugh, J. L. Critique and reformulation of "learning-theory" approaches to psychotherapy and neurosis. *Psychological Bulletin*, 1965, **63**, 338-358.

Brewer, W. F. There is no convincing evidence for operant or classical conditioning in adult humans. In W. B. Weimer and D. S. Palermo (eds.), *Cognition and the symbolic processes*. New York: Wiley-Interscience, 1975.

Brody, S., and Axelrad, S. *Anxiety and ego formation in infancy*. New York: International Universities Press, 1970.

Brogden, W. J. Animal studies of learning. In

S. S. Stevens (ed.), *Handbook of experimental psychology*. New York: Wiley, 1951.

Brown, L. B. (ed.) *Psychology and religion*. Baltimore, Md.: Penguin Books, 1973.

Brush, S. G. (ed.) *Kinetic theory*, vol. 1. *The nature of gases and heat*. New York: Pergamon Press, 1965.

Bugental, J. F. T. The challenge that is man. In J. F. T. Bugental (ed.), *Challenges of humanistic psychology*. New York: McGraw-Hill, 1967.

Buhler, C. and Allen, M. *Introduction to humanistic psychology*. Monterey, Cal.: Brooks/Cole, 1972.

Bunge, M. *The myth of simplicity*. Englewood Cliffs, New Jersey: Prentice-Hall, 1963.

———. *Method, model and matter*. Boston: D. Reidel, 1973.

Butler, J. M. Addendum concerning changes in relation between self-concepts and ideal concepts. In H. J. Vetter and B. D. Smith (eds.), *Personality theory: A source book*. Englewood Cliffs, N. J.: Prentice-Hall, 1971.

Butler, J. M., and Haigh, G. V. Changes in the relation between self-concepts and ideal concepts consequent upon client-centered counseling. In C. R. Rogers and R. F. Dymond (eds.), *Psychotherapy and personality change*. Chicago: University of Chicago Press, 1954.

Butler, J. M., Rice, L., and Wagstaff, A. *Quantitative naturalistic research*. Englewood Cliffs, N. J.: Prentice-Hall, 1961.

Carnap, R. *Testability and meaning*. New Haven, Conn.: Graduate Philosophy Club of Yale University, 1954.

Carrigan, P. M. Extraversion-introversion as a dimension of personality: A reappraisal. *Psychological Bulletin*, 1960, **57**, 329-360.

Cartwright, Dorwin. Lewinian theory as a contemporary systematic framework. In S. Koch (ed.), *Psychology: A study of a science*, vol. 2. New York: McGraw-Hill, 1959.

Cartwright, D. S. Self-consistency as a factor affecting immediate recall. *Journal of Abnormal and Social Psychology*, 1956, **52**, 212-218.

Cartwright, J. Personal communication, 1976.

Cattell, R. B. *Personality*. New York: McGraw-Hill, 1950.

———. *Factor analysis*. New York: Harper, 1952.

———. *Personality and motivation: Structure and measurement*. New York: World, 1957.

———. Factor analysis: An introduction to essentials. *Biometrics*, 1965, **21**, 190-215; 405-435.

———. The data box. In R. B. Cattell (ed.), *Handbook of multivariate experimental psychology*. Chicago, Ill.: Rand McNally, 1966.

———. *Structured learning theory*. Advanced publication No. 13. Laboratory of Personality and Group Analysis. Champaign, Ill.: University of Illinois, Department of Psychology, 1970. Mimeo.

———. The 16PF and basic personality structure: A reply to Eysenck. *Journal of Behavioral Science*, 1972, **1**, 169-187.

———. *Personality and mood by questionnaire*. San Francisco: Jossey-Bass, 1973.

———. Radial parcel factoring versus item factoring in defining personality structure in questionnaires: Theory and experimental checks. *Australian Journal of Psychology*, 1974, **26**, 103-119.

———. Third order personality structure in Q-data: Evidence from eleven experiments. *Journal of Multivariate Experimental Personality and Clinical Psychology*, 1975, **1**, 118-149.

———. Personal communication, 1976.

Cattell, R. B., and Bartlett, H. W. An R-dR-Technique operational distinction of the states of anxiety, stress, fear, etc. *Australian Journal of Psychology*, 1971, **23**, 105-123.

Cattell, R. B., and Cattell, M. D. *Handbook for the Jr.-Sr. High School Personality Questionnaire (HSPQ)*. Champaign, Ill.: Institute for Personality and Ability Testing, 1969.

Cattell, R. B., and Child, D. *Motivation and dynamic structure*. New York: Wiley, 1975.

Cattell, R. B., and Dielman, T. E. The structure of motivational manifestations as measured in the laboratory rat: An examination of motivational component theory. *Social Behavior and Personality*, 1974, **2**, 10-24.

Cattell, R. B., Eber, H. W., and Tatsuoka, M. M. *Handbook for the Sixteen Personality Factor Questionnaire (16PF)*. Champaign, Ill.: Institute for Personality and Ability Testing, 1970.

Cattell, R. B., and Hendricks, B. *The sensitivity of the dynamic calculus to short-term change*

in interest structure. Unpublished manuscript, 1972.

Cattell, R. B., and Horn, J. L. An integrating study of the factor structure of adult attitude-interests. *Genetic Psychology Monographs,* 1963, **67,** 89-149.

Cattell, R. B., Horn, J. L., Sweney, A. B., and Radcliffe, R. A. *Handbook for the Motivation Analysis Test.* Champaign, Ill.: Institute for Personality and Ability Testing, 1964.

Cattell, R. B., and Nichols, K. An improved definition from ten researches of second order personality factors in Q-data. *Journal of Social Psychology,* 1972, **86,** 187-203.

Cattell, R. B., and Scheier, I. *The meaning and measurement of neuroticism and anxiety.* New York: Ronald Press, 1961.

Child, D. *The essentials of factor analysis.* New York: Holt, Rinehart and Winston, 1970.

Child, I. L., and Whiting, J. W. M. Determinants of level of aspiration: Evidence from everyday life. *Journal of Abnormal and Social Psychology,* 1949, **44,** 303-314.

Chodorkoff, B. Self-perception, perceptual defense, and adjustment. *Journal of Abnormal and Social Psychology,* 1954, **49,** 508-512.

Chomsky, N. A review of B. F. Skinner's *Verbal behavior. Language,* 1959, **35,** 26-58.

Ciaccio, N. V. A test of Erikson's theory of ego epigenesis. *Developmental Psychology,* 1971, **4,** 306-311.

Clark, J. P., and Tifft, L. L. Polygraph and interview validation of self-reported deviant behavior. *American Sociological Review,* 1966, **31,** 516-523.

Cohen, J. *Operant behavior and operant conditioning.* Chicago, Ill.: Rand McNally, 1969.

Cole, D., Jacobs, S., and Zubok, B. The relation of achievement imagery scores to academic performance. *Journal of Abnormal and Social Psychology,* 1962, **65,** 208-211.

Comrey, A. *A first course in factor analysis.* New York: Academic Press, 1973.

Corcoran, D. W. J. The relation between introversion and salivation. *American Journal of Psychology,* 1964, **77,** 298-300.

Cronbach, L. J., and Meehl, P. E. Construct validity in psychological tests. *Psychological Bulletin,* 1955, **52,** 281-302.

Cummings, L. L., and El Salmi, A. M. Empirical research on the bases and correlates of managerial motivation: A review of the literature. *Psychological Bulletin,* 1968, **70,** 127-144.

Deutsch, M. Field theory in social psychology. In G. Lindzey and E. Aronson (eds.), *The handbook of social psychology,* vol. 1. New York: Addison-Wesley, 1968.

Devore, A. Personal communication, 1976.

Dixon, N.F. Apparent changes in the visual threshold as a function of subliminal stimulation. *Quarterly Journal of Experimental Psychology,* 1958, **10,** 211-215.

———. *Subliminal perception: The nature of a controversy.* Maidenhead, England: McGraw-Hill, 1971.

Doerr, H. O., and Hokanson, J. E. The relation between heart rate and performance in children. *Journal of Personality and Social Psychology,* 1965, **2,** 70-77.

Dollard, J. *Caste and class in a southern town.* New Haven: Yale University Press, 1937.

———. *Victory over fear.* New York: Reynal and Hitchcock, 1942.

Dollard, J., Doob, L. W., Miller, N. E., Mowrer, O. H., and Sears, R. R. *Frustration and aggression.* New Haven: Yale University Press, 1939.

Dollard, J., and Miller, N. E. *Personality and psychotherapy.* New York: McGraw-Hill, 1950.

Eaves, L. J., and Eysenck, H. J. Genetical and environmental components of inconsistency and unrepeatability in twins' responses to a neuroticism questionnaire. Unpublished manuscript, Department of Genetics, University of Birmingham, Birmingham, England. Mimeo. 1975. (a)

———. The nature of extraversion: A genetical analysis. *Journal of Personality and Social Psychology,* 1975, **32,** 102-112. (b)

———. A genotype-environmental model for psychoticism. *Advances in Behavior Research and Therapy,* 1977, **1,** in press.

Edwards, A. L. *Manual for the Edwards Personal Preference Schedule.* (Rev. ed.) New York: Psychological Corporation, 1959.

Edwards, A. L., and Cronbach, L. J. Experimental

design for research in psychotherapy. *Journal of Clinical Psychology*, 1952, **8**, 51-59.

Ellman, C. An experimental study of the female castration complex. Unpublished doctoral dissertation, New York University, 1970.

English, H. B., and English, A. C. *A comprehensive dictionary of psychological and psychoanalytical terms.* New York: Longmans, Green, 1958.

Epstein, S. The measurement of drive and conflict in humans: Theory and experiment. In M. R. Jones (ed.), *Nebraska symposium on motivation.* Lincoln: University of Nebraska Press, 1962.

Erikson, E. H. Configurations in play. *Psychoanalytic Quarterly*, 1937, **6**, 139-214.

——. *Young man Luther.* New York: Norton, 1962.

——. *Childhood and society.* New York: Norton, 1963. (Originally pub. 1950.)

——. *Insight and responsibility.* New York: Norton, 1964.

——. *Identity, youth, and crisis.* New York: Norton, 1968.

——. *Ghandi's truth.* New York: Norton, 1969.

——. *Dimensions of a new identity.* New York: Norton, 1974.

——. *Life history and the historical moment.* New York: Norton, 1975.

Estes, W. K., and Lewin, Kurt. In W. K. Estes, S. Koch, K. MacCorquodale, P. E. Meehl, C. G. Mueller, Jr., W. N. Schoenfeld, and W. S. Verplanck. *Modern learning theory.* Englewood Cliffs, N. J.: Prentice-Hall, 1954.

Estes, W. K., and Skinner, B. F. Some quantitative properties of anxiety. *Journal of Experimental Psychology*, 1941, **29**, 390-400.

Eysenck, H. J. *Dimensions of personality.* London: Kegan Paul, 1947.

——. The effects of psychotherapy: An evaluation. *Journal of Consulting Psychology*, 1952, **16**, 319-24. (a)

——. *The scientific study of personality.* London: Routledge and Kegan Paul, 1952. (b)

——. *Psychology and the foundations of psychiatry.* London: H. K. Lewis, 1955.

——. (ed.). *Behaviour therapy and the neuroses.* Oxford, England: Pergamon Press, 1960.

——. *The effects of psychotherapy.* New York: International Science Press, 1966.

——. *The biological basis of personality.* Springfield, Ill.: Charles C Thomas, 1967.

——. Historical introduction. In H. J. Eysenck (ed.), *Readings in extraversion-introversion,* vol. 1. *Theoretical and methodological issues.* New York: Wiley-Interscience, 1970.

——. Conditioning, introversion-extraversion and the strength of the nervous system. In H. J. Eysenck (ed.), *Readings in extraversion-introversion,* vol. 3. New York: Wiley-Interscience, 1971.

——. Primaries or second-order factors: A critical consideration of Cattell's 16PF battery. *British Journal of Social and Clinical Psychology*, 1972, **11**, 265-269.

——. Therapy unproven: A letter to the editor. *APA Monitor*, 1975, **6**, no. 6, 3.

Eysenck, H. J., and Eysenck, S. B. G. *Manual for the Eysenck Personality Inventory.* San Diego: Educational and Industrial Testing Service, 1968.

——. *Personality structure and measurement.* San Diego: R. R. Knapp, 1969.

Eysenck, H. J., and Rachman, S. *The causes and cures of neurosis.* San Diego: Educational and Industrial Testing Service, 1965.

Eysenck, S. B. G. A dimensional analysis of mental abnormality. Unpublished doctoral dissertation, University of London (England), 1955.

Fenichel, O. *The psychoanalytic theory of neurosis.* New York: Norton, 1945.

Ferster, C. B., and Skinner, B. F. *Schedules of reinforcement.* Englewood Cliffs, N. J.: Prentice-Hall, 1957.

Fisher, S. *Body experience in fantasy and behavior.* Englewood Cliffs, N. J.: Prentice-Hall, 1970.

Fiske, D. W. *Measuring the concepts of personality.* Chicago: Aldine, 1971.

——. The limits for the conventional science of personality. *Journal of Personality*, 1974, **42**, 1-11.

Fiske, D. W., Cartwright, D. S., and Kirtner, W. L. Are psychotherapeutic changes predictable? *Journal of Abnormal and Social Psychology*, 1964, **69**, 418-426.

Fitz, D. A renewed look at Miller's conflict theory. *Journal of Personality and Social Psychology*, 1976, **33**, 725-732.

Frankl, V. E. *Man's search for meaning* (Rev. ed.) New York: Simon and Schuster, 1970.

———. *The doctor and the soul.* (2nd ed.) New York: Vintage Books, 1973.

Franks, C. M. Personality and eyeblink conditioning seven years later. *Acta Psychologica*, 1963, **21**, 295-312.

Franks, C. M., and Trouton, D. Effects of ambarbital sodium and dexamphetamine sulphate on the conditioning of the eyelid response. *Journal of Comparative and Physiological Psychology*, 1958, **51**, 220-222.

French, J. W. *Toward the establishment of noncognitive factors through literature search and interpretation.* Princeton, N. J.: Educational Testing Service, 1973.

Freud, A. *Normality and pathology in childhood: Assessments of development.* New York: International Universities Press, 1965.

Freud S. *Beyond the pleasure principle.* London: Hogarth, 1948. (Originally pub. 1920.)

———. The interpretation of dreams. In J. Strachey (ed.), *Standard edition of the complete psychological works of Sigmund Freud,* vols. 4 and 5. London: Hogarth, 1953. (Originally pub. 1900.)

———. Three essays on the theory of sexuality. In J. Strachey (ed.), *Standard edition of the complete psychological works of Sigmund Freud,* vol. 7. London: Hogarth, 1953, pp. 125-243. (Originally pub. 1905b.)

———. A phobia in a five-year-old boy. In E. Jones (ed.), *Collected papers.* New York: Basic Books, 1959, pp. 149-289. (Originally pub. 1909.)

———. A religious experience. In *Collected papers,* vol. 5. New York: Basic Books, 1959, pp. 243-246. (Originally pub. 1928.)

———. Charcot. In E. Jones (ed.), *Collected papers.* vol. 1. New York: Basic Books, 1959, pp. 9-23. (Originally pub. 1893a.)

———. Fragment of an analysis of a case of hysteria. In E. Jones (ed.), *Collected papers.*

New York: Basic Books, 1959, pp. 13-146. (Originally pub. 1905a.)

———. Formulations regarding the two principles of mental functioning. In E. Jones (ed.), *Collected papers.* New York: Basic Books, 1959, pp. 13-21. (Originally pub. 1911.)

———. Freud's psycho-analytic method. In E. Jones (ed.), *Collected papers,* vol. 1. New York: Basic Books, 1959, pp. 264-271. (Originally pub. 1904.)

———. Instincts and their vicissitudes. In E. Jones (ed.), *Collected papers,* vol. 4. New York: Basic Books, 1959, pp. 60-83. (Originally pub. 1915a.)

———. On narcissism: An introduction. In E. Jones (ed.), *Collected papers,* vol. 4. New York: Basic Books, 1959, pp. 30-59. (Originally pub. 1914a.)

———. On the history of the psychoanalytic movement. In E. Jones (ed.), *Collected papers,* vol. 1. New York: Basic Books, 1959, pp. 285-359. (Originally pub. 1914b.)

———.Repression. In E. Jones (ed.), *Collected papers,* vol. 4. New York: Basic Books, 1959, pp. 84-97. (Originally pub. 1915b.)

———. The defence neuro-psychoses. In E. Jones (ed.), *Collected papers,* vol. 1. New York: Basic Books, 1959, pp. 59-75. (Originally pub. 1894.)

———. The infantile genital organization of the libido. In E. Jones (ed.), *Collected papers,* vol. 2. New York: Basic Books, 1959, pp. 244-249. (Originally pub. 1923b.)

———. The passing of the Oedipus complex. In E. Jones (ed.), *Collected papers,* vol. 2. New York: Basic Books, 1959, pp. 269-276. (Originally pub. 1924.)

———. The predisposition to obsessional neurosis. In E. Jones (ed.), *Collected papers,* vol. 2. New York: Basic Books, Inc., 1959, pp. 122-132. (Originally pub. 1913.)

———. The unconscious. In E. Jones (ed.), *Collected papers,* vol. 4. New York: Basic Books, 1959, pp. 98-136. (Originally pub. 1915c.)

———. The unconscious in psychoanalysis. In E. Jones (ed.), *Collected papers,* vol. 4. New

York: Basic Books, 1959, pp. 22-29. (Originally pub. 1912.)

———. Letter 86. In E. L. Freud (ed.), *Letters of Sigmund Freud*. New York: Basic Books, Inc., 1960. (Originally pub. 1885.)

———. The psychopathology of everyday life. In J. Strachey (ed.), *Standard edition of the complete psychological works of Sigmund Freud*, vol. 6. London: Hogarth, 1960. (Originally pub. 1901a.)

———. Some psychical consequences of the anatomical distinction between the sexes. In J. Strachey (ed.), *Standard edition of the collected works of Sigmund Freud*, vol. 19. London: Hogarth, 1961, pp. 243-258. (Originally pub. 1925.)

———. The future of an illusion. In J. Strachey (ed.), *Standard edition of the complete psychological works of Sigmund Freud*. vol. 21. London: Hogarth Press, 1961, pp. 5-56.

———. *The ego and the id*. New York: Norton, 1962. (Originally pub. 1923a.)

———. Introductory lectures on psychoanalysis. In J. Strachey (ed.), *Standard edition of the complete psychological works of Sigmund Freud*, vols. 15 and 16. London: Hogarth, 1963. (Originally pub. 1917.)

———. *The problem of anxiety*. New York: Norton, 1963. (Originally pub. 1926.)

———. New introductory lectures on psychoanalysis. In J. Strachey (ed.), *Standard edition of the complete psychological works of Sigmund Freud*, vol. 22. London: Hogarth, 1964, pp. 1-182. (Originally pub. 1933.)

———. Letter 14. In J. Strachey (ed.), *The standard edition of the complete psychological works of Sigmund Freud*, vol. 1. London: Hogarth, 1966, pp. 184-185. (Orig. pub. 1893b)

———. Project for a scientific psychology. In J. Strachey (ed.), *Standard edition of the complete psychological works of Sigmund Freud*, vol. 1. London: Hogarth, 1966. (Originally pub. 1895.)

Freud, W. E. The baby profile: Part II. *Psychoanalytic Study of the Child*, 1972, **26**, 172-194.

Friedman, S. On vegetarianism. *Journal of the American Psychoanalytic Association*, 1975, **23**, 396-406.

Friedman, S. M. An empirical study of the castration and Oedipus complexes. *Genetic Psychology Monographs*, 1952, **46**, 61-130.

Gambrill, E. D. The use of behavioral methods in a short-term detention setting. *Criminal Justice and Behavior*, 1976, **3**, 53-66.

Geiger, H. Introduction. In A. H. Maslow, *The farther reaches of human nature*. New York: Viking, 1971.

Gendlin, E. T. Research in psychotherapy with schizophrenic patients and the nature of that "illness." *American Journal of Psychotherapy*, 1966, **20**, 4-16.

Ghiselli, E. E. *Theory of psychological measurement*. New York: McGraw-Hill, 1964.

Gill, M. M. The primary process. In R. R. Holt (ed.), *Motives and thought: Psychoanalytic essays in honor of David Rapaport. Psychological Issues* **5**, no. 2-3, Monograph 18/19. New York: International Universities Press, 1967.

Glucksberg, S., and King, J. Motivated forgetting mediated by implicit verbal chaining: A laboratory analog of repression. *Science*, 1967, **158**, 517-519.

Goldman-Eisler, F. The problem of "orality" and its origin in early childhood. *Journal of Mental Science*, 1951, **97**, 765-782.

Gordon, T. *Parent effectiveness training*. New York: Peter H. Wyden, 1970.

Gorsuch, R. L. and Cattell, R. B. Second stratum personality factors defined in the questionnaire realm by the 16 P.F. *Multivariate Behavioral Research*, 1967, **2**, 211-224.

Gourevitch, V. and Feffer, M. H. A study of motivational development. *Journal of Genetic Psychology*, 1962, **100**, 361-375.

Gray, J. A. Causal theories of personality and how to test them. In J. R. Royce (ed.), *Multivariate analysis and psychological theory*. London: Academic Press, 1973, pp. 409-451.

Gray, H. and Wheelwright, J. B. Jung's psychological types, their frequency of occurrence. *Journal of Genetic Psychology*, 1946, **34**, 3-17.

Guilford, J. P. Factors and factors of personality. *Psychological Bulletin*, 1975, **82**, 802-814.

Guntrip, H. *Psychoanalytic theory, therapy, and the self.* New York: Basic Books, 1973.

Guttman, N., and Kalish, H. I. Discriminability and stimulus generalization. *Journal of Experimental Psychology*, 1956, **51**, 70-88.

Hall, C. S. *The content analysis of dreams.* Englewood Cliffs, N. J.: Prentice-Hall, 1966.

Hall, C. S., and Lindzey, G. *Theories of personality* (2nd ed.). New York: Wiley, 1970.

Hartman, H. *Ego psychology and the problem of adaptation.* New York: International Universities Press, 1958.

Hebb, D. O. What psychology is about. *American Psychologist*, 1974, **29**, 71-79.

Heider, F. On Lewin's theory and methods. *The Journal of Social Issues*, 1959, Supplement Series No. 13.

Hilgard, E. R., and Bower, G. H. *Theories of learning.* Englewood Cliffs, N. J.: Prentice-Hall, 1975.

Hillman, J. Archetypal theory: C. G. Jung. In A. Burton (ed.), *Operational theories of personality.* New York: Brunner-Mazel, 1974.

Hjelle, L. A., and Ziegler, D. J. *Personality theories: Basic assumptions, research, and applications.* New York: McGraw-Hill, 1976.

Holmes, T. H., and Rahe, R. H. The social readjustment rating scale. *Journal of Psychosomatic Research*, 1967, **11**, 213-218.

Holt, R. R. *Assessing personality.* New York: Harcourt Brace Jovanovich, 1971.

Honig, W. K. (ed.). *Operant behavior: Areas of research and application.* Englewood Cliffs, N. J.: Prentice-Hall, 1966.

Horn, J. L. Motivation and dynamic calculus concepts from multivariate experiments. In R. B. Cattell (ed.), *Handbook of multivariate experimental psychology.* Chicago: Rand McNally, 1966.

Horowitz, M. J. *Image formation and cognition.* Englewood Cliffs, N. J.: Prentice-Hall, 1970.

———. *Stress response syndromes.* New York: Aronson, 1976.

Howarth, E., and Browne, J. A. Investigation of personality factors in a Canadian context: I. Marker structure in personality questionnaire items. *Canadian Journal of Behavioral Science*, 1971, **3**, 161-173.

Howarth, E., and Eysenck, H. J. Extraversion, arousal, and paired-associate recall. *Journal of Experimental Research in Personality*, 1968, **3**, 114-116.

Hull, C. L. *Principles of behavior.* Englewood Cliffs, N. J.: Prentice-Hall, 1943.

Hull, C. L., Hovland, C. I., Ross, R. T., Hall, M. Perkins, D. T., and Fitch, F. G. *Mathematico-deductive theory of rote learning.* New Haven: Yale University Press, 1940.

Inkson, J. H. K. Achievement motivation and occupational choice. *Australian Journal of Psychology*, 1971, **23**, 225-234.

IPAT. *Psychological tests and services: Catalog order form.* Urbana, Ill.: Institute for Personality and Ability Testing, 1972.

Jackson, D. N. *Personality research form manual.* Goshen, New York: Research Psychologists Press, 1967.

Jackson, D. N., Ahmed, S. A., and Heapy, N. A. Is achievement a unitary construct? *Journal of Research in Personality*, 1976, **10**, 1-21.

Jacobson, E. *The self and the object world.* New York: International Universities Press, 1964.

James, W. *The principles of psychology*, vol. I. New York: Dover Publications, 1950. (Originally pub. 1890.)

Jeffrey, R. W. The influence of symbolic and motor rehearsal in observational learning. *Journal of Research in Personality*, 1976, **10**, 116-127.

Jensen, A. Extraversion, neuroticism, and serial learning. *Acta Psychologica*, 1962, **20**, 69-77.

Jessor, R., Graves T. D., Hanson, R. C., and Jessor, S. L. *Society, personality, and deviant behavior.* New York: Holt, Rinehart & Winston, 1968.

Jessor, S. L., and Jessor, R. The transition from virginity to nonvirginity among youth: A social-psychological study over time. *Developmental Psychology*, 1976, **11**, 473-480.

Jones, E. *The life and work of Sigmund Freud.* (abridged ed.) New York: Basic Books, 1961.

Jourard, S. M. *Healthy personality.* New York: Macmillan, 1974.

Jung, C. G. *Modern man in search of a soul*. New York: Harcourt Brace Jovanovich, 1933.

———. *Psychology and religion*. New Haven, Conn. Yale University Press, 1938.

———. *Flying saucers: A modern myth of things seen in the sky*. New York: Harcourt Brace, 1959.

———. The psychology of dementia praecox. In *Collected works of C. G. Jung*, vol. 3. Princeton, N. J.: Princeton University Press, 1960. (Originally pub. 1907.)

———. Freud and Jung: Contrasts. In *Collected works of C. G. Jung*, vol. 4. Princeton, N. J.: Princeton University Press, 1961. (Originally pub. 1929.)

———. Approaching the unconscious. In C. G. Jung (ed.), *Man and his symbols*. New York: Doubleday, 1964.

———. *Memories, dreams and reflections*. New York: Random House, 1965.

———. On the psychology of the unconscious. In *Collected works of C. G. Jung*, vol. 7. Princeton University Press, 1966. (Originally pub. 1917.)

———. The relations between the ego and the unconscious. In *Collected work of C. G. Jung*, vol. 7. Princeton, N. J.: Princeton University Press, 1966. (Originally pub. 1928.)

———. Symbols of transformation. In *Collected works of C. G. Jung*, vol. 5. Princeton, N. J. Princeton University Press, 1967. (Originally pub. 1911.)

———. A study in the process of individuation. In *Collected works of C. G. Jung*, vol. 9. Princeton, N. J.: Princeton University Press, 1969. (Originally pub. 1934.)

———. The archetypes and the collective unconscious. In *Collected works of C. G. Jung*, vol. 9. Princeton, N. J.: Princeton University Press, 1969.

———. Aion: Phenomenology of the self. In Joseph Campbell (ed.), *The portable Jung*. New York: Viking, 1971. (Originally pub. 1951.)

———. Instinct and the unconscious. In Joseph Campbell (ed.), *The portable Jung*. New York: Viking, 1971. (Originally pub. 1919.)

———. Psychological Types. In *Collected Works of C. G. Jung*, vol. 6. Princeton, N. J.: Princeton University Press, 1971. (Originally pub. 1921.)

———. Psychological types (1923). In *Collected works of C. G. Jung*, vol. 6. Princeton, N. J.: Princeton University Press, 1971. (Originally pub. 1923.)

———. The structure of the psyche. In Joseph Campbell (ed.), *The portable Jung*. New York: Viking, 1971. (Originally pub. 1927.)

———. *Mandala symbolism*. Princeton, N. J.: Princeton University Press, 1972. (Originally pub. 1955.)

———. The association method. Lectures given at Clark University, 1909. In *Collected works of C. G. Jung*, vol. 2. Princeton, N. J.: Princeton University Press, 1973. (Originally pub. 1909.)

———. Experimental observations on the faculty of memory. In *Collected works of C. G. Jung*, vol. 2. Princeton, N. J.: Princeton University Press, 1973. (Originally pub. 1905a.)

———. The associations of normal subjects. In *Collected works of C. G. Jung*, vol. 2. Princeton, N. J.: Princeton University Press, 1973. (Originally pub. 1904.)

———. The reaction-time ratio in the association experiment. In *Collected works of C. G. Jung*, vol. 2. Princeton, N. J.: Princeton University Press, 1973. (Originally pub. 1905b.)

Kelly, G. A. *A theory of personality: The psychology of personal constructs*. New York: Norton, 1963.

Kernberg, O., Burstein, E. D., Coyne, L., Applebaum, A., Horwitz, L., and Voth, H. Psychotherapy and psychoanalysis: Final report of the Menninger Foundation's Psychotherapy Research Project. *Bulletin of the Menninger Clinic*, 1972, **36**, Nos. 1 and 2.

Keynes, J. M. *The general theory of employment, interest and money*. New York: Harcourt Brace Jovanovich, 1936.

Kirtner, W. L., and Cartwright, D. S. Success and failure in client-centered therapy as a function of initial in-therapy behavior. *Journal of Consulting Psychology*, 1958, **22**, 329-333.

Klein, G. S., and Krech, D. The problem of personality and its theory. In D. Krech and G. S. Klein (eds.), *Theoretical models and personality theory*. Durham, N. C.: Duke University Press, 1952.

Kleinsmith, L. J., and Kaplan, S. Paired-associate learning as a function of arousal and interpolated interval. *Journal of Experimental Psychology*, 1963, **65**, 190-193.

Kline, P. *Fact and fantasy in Freudian theory*. London: Methuen, 1972.

Koch, S. (ed.). *Psychology: A study of a science*. New York: McGraw-Hill, 1959.

Koffka, K. *Principles of gestalt psychology*. New York: Harcourt, Brace, Jovanovich, 1935.

Kolb, L. C. *Noyes' Modern Clinical Psychiatry*. Philadelphia: Saunders, 1968.

Krasner, L., and Ullmann, L. P. *Behavior influence and personality: The social matrix of human action*. New York: Holt, Rinehart & Winston, 1973.

Krause, M. S. An analysis of Carl Rogers' theory of personality. *Genetic Psychology Monographs*, 1964, **69**, 49-99.

Kretschmer, E. *Physique and character*. New York: Harcourt Brace Jovanovich, 1926.

Kuhn, T. S. *The structure of scientific revolutions*. (2nd ed.) Chicago: University of Chicago Press, 1970.

Laplanche, L., and Pontalis, J. B. *The language of psychoanalysis*. New York: Norton, 1973.

Laverty, S. G. Sodium amytal and extraversion. In H. J. Eysenck (ed.), *Readings in extraversion-introversion*, vol. 3. New York: Wiley-Interscience, 1971.

Lazarus, R. S. *Psychological stress and the coping process*. New York: McGraw-Hill, 1966.

———. *Personality* (2nd ed.). Englewood Cliffs, N. J.: Prentice-Hall, 1971.

———. *Patterns of adjustment*. New York: McGraw-Hill, 1976.

Lefcourt, H. M. Recent developments in the study of locus of control. In B. A. Maher (ed.), *Progress in experimental personality research*, vol. 6. New York: Academic Press, 1972.

Lefcourt, H. M., Sordoni, C., and Sordoni, Carol. Locus of control and the expression of humor. *Journal of Personality*, 1974, **42**, 130-143.

Lewin, K. *A dynamic theory of personality*. New York: McGraw-Hill, 1935.

———. *Principles of topological psychology*. New York: McGraw-Hill, 1936.

———. *Field theory in social science*. New York: Harper, 1951.

Lewis, M. K., Rogers, C. R., and Shlien, J. M. Time-limited, client-centered psychotherapy: Two cases. In A. Burton (ed.), *Case studies in counseling and psychotherapy*. Englewood Cliffs, N. J.: Prentice-Hall, 1959.

Liebert, R. M., and Spiegler, M. D. *Personality: Strategies for the study of man*. (2nd ed.) Homewood, Ill.: Dorsey, 1974.

Lifton, R. J. (ed.) *Explorations in psychohistory*. New York: Simon and Schuster, 1974.

Lindner, R. M. *Rebel without a cause*. New York: Grove Press Black Cat Books, 1944.

Lippitt, B., and White, R. The "social climate" of children's groups. In R. Barker, J. Kounin, and H. F. Wright (eds.), *Child behavior and development*. New York: McGraw-Hill, 1943.

London, I. D. Psychologists' misuse of the auxiliary concepts of physics and mathematics. *Psychological Review*, 1944, **51**, 42-45.

Lowell, E. L. The effect of need for achievement on learning and speed of performance. *Journal of Psychology*, 1952, **33**, 31-40.

Lundin, R. W. *Personality: A behavioral analysis*. (2nd ed.) New York: Macmillan, 1974.

Lykken, D. T. Psychology and the lie detector industry. *American Psychologist*, 1974, **29**, 725-739.

Macdonell, W. R. On criminal anthropometry and the identification of criminals. *Biometrika*, 1902, **1**, 177-227.

MacKinnon, D. W. A topological analysis of anxiety. *Character and Personality*, 1944, **12**, 163-177.

MacLean, P. D. The limbic brain in relation to the psychoses. In P. Black (ed.), *Physiological correlates of emotion*. New York: Academic Press, 1970.

Maddi, S. R. *Personality theories: A comparative analysis*. (3rd ed.) Homewood, Illinois: Dorsey Press, 1976.

Maier, N. R. F. *Studies of abnormal behavior in the rat*. New York: Harper, 1939.

Marcia, J. E. Determination and construct validity of ego identity status. Unpublished doctoral dissertation, The Ohio State University, 1964.

———. Development and validation of ego-identity status. *Journal of Personality and Social Psychology*, 1966, **3**, 551-558.

Marrow, A. J. *The practical theorist: The life and work of Kurt Lewin.* New York: Basic Books, 1969.

Marx, M. H., and Hillix, W. A. *Systems and theories in psychology* (2nd ed.) New York: McGraw-Hill, 1973.

Masling, J., Johnson, C., and Sturansky, C. Oral imagery, accuracy of perceiving others, and performance in Peace Corps training. *Journal of Personality and Social Psychology*, 1974, **30**, 414-419.

Maslow, A. H. Personality and patterns of culture. In R. Stagner (ed.), *Psychology of personality.* New York: McGraw-Hill, 1937.

———. A test for dominance-feeling (self-esteem) in women. *Journal of Social Psychology*, 1940, **12**, 255-270.

———. Self-esteem (dominance-feeling) and sexuality in women. *Journal of Social Psychology*, 1942, **16**, 259-294. (b)

———. The dynamics of psychological security-insecurity. *Character and Personality*, 1942, **10**, 331-344. (a)

———. *Motivation and personality.* New York: Harper & Row, 1954.

———. A conversation with Abraham H. Maslow. *Psychology Today*, 1968, **2**, 35 ff.

———. *Motivation and personality* (2nd ed.) New York: Harper & Row, 1970. (a)

———. *Religions, values, and peak experiences.* New York: Viking, 1970. (b)

———. *The farther reaches of human nature.* New York: Viking, 1971.

Maslow, A. H., Birsh, E., Stein, M., and Honigmann, I. A clinically derived test for measuring psychological security-insecurity. *Journal of General Psychology*, 1945, **33**, 21-51.

Maslow, A. H., and Mittelmann, B. *Principles of abnormal psychology.* New York: Harper, 1941.

Maslow, A. H., Rand, H., and Newman, S. Some parallels between the dominance and sexual behavior of monkeys and the fantasies of psychoanalytic patients. *Journal of Nervous and Mental Diseases*, 1960, **131**, 202-212.

McClearn, G. E., and DeFries, J. C. *Introduction to behavioral genetics.* San Francisco, Cal.: Freeman, 1973.

McClelland, D. C. Measuring motivation in phantasy: The achievement motive. In H. Guetzkow (ed.), *Groups, leadership, and men.* Pittsburgh: Carnegie Press, 1951.

———. Encouraging excellence. *Daedalus*, 1961, **90**, 711-724.

McGinnies, E., and Ferster, C. B. (eds.) *The reinforcement of social behavior.* New York: Houghton Mifflin, 1971.

McGuire, W. (ed.) *The Freud/Jung letters.* Princeton, N. J.: Princeton University Press, 1974.

Mead, M. *Sex and temperament in three primitive societies.* New York: Morrow, Apollo Edition, 1963.

Messe, L. A., Arnoff, J., and Wilson, J. P. Motivation as a mediator of the mechanisms underlying role assignments in small groups. *Journal of Personality and Social Psychology*, 1972, **24**, 84-90.

Miller, J. G. Living systems: The organism. *Quarterly Review of Biology*, 1973, **48**, 92-276.

Miller, N. E. Experimental studies of conflict. In J. McV. Hunt (ed.), *Personality and the behavior disorders.* New York: Ronald Press, 1944.

———. Studies of fear as an acquirable drive: I. Fear as motivation and fear-reduction as reinforcement in the learning of a new response. *Journal of Experimental Psychology*, 1948, **38**, 89-101. (a)

———. Theory and experiment relating psychoanalytic displacement to stimulus-response generalization. *Journal of Abnormal and Social Psychology*, 1948, **43**, 155-178. (b)

———. Personal communication, 1976.

Miller, N. E., and Dollard, J. *Social learning and imitation.* New Haven: Yale University Press, 1941.

Miller, N. E., and Kraeling, D. Displacement: greater generalization of approach than avoidance in a generalized approach-avoidance conflict. *Journal of Experimental Psychology*, 1952, **43**, 217-221.

Milton, G. A., and Lipetz, M. E. The factor structure of needs as measured by the EPPS. *Multivariate Behavioral Research*, 1968, **3**, 37-46.

Mischel, W. *Introduction to personality*. (2nd ed.) New York: Holt, Rinehart & Winston, 1976.

Mitchell, K. M., Truax, C. B., Bozarth, J. D., and Krauft, C. C. Antecedents to psychotherapeutic outcome. *National Institutes of Mental Health Final Report*. MH 12306, 1973.

Morgan, C. D., and Murray, H. A. A method for investigating fantasies. *Archives of Neurology and Psychiatry*, 1935, **34**, 289-306.

Morgan, C. T., and Waldman, H. "Conflict" and audiogenic seizures. *Journal of Comparative Psychology*, 1941, **31**, 1-11.

Murray, E. J. A case study in a behavioral analysis of psychotherapy. *Journal of Abnormal and Social Psychology*, 1954, **49**, 305-310.

———. Resolution of complex decisional conflicts as a function of degree of avoidance. *Journal of Research in Personality*, 1975, **9**, 177-190.

Murray, E. J., and Berkun, M. M. Displacement as a function of conflict. *Journal of Abnormal and Social Psychology*, 1955, **15**, 47-56.

Murray, E. J., and Miller, N. E. Displacement: steeper gradient of generalization of avoidance than of approach with age of habit controlled. *Journal of Experimental Psychology*, 1952, **43**, 222-226.

Murray, H. A. What should psychologists do about psychoanalysis? *Journal of Abnormal Psychology*, 1940, **35**, 150-175.

———. *Thematic Apperception Test manual*. Cambridge, Mass.: Harvard University Press, 1943.

———. Preparations for the scaffold of a comprehensive system. In S. Koch (ed.), *Psychology: A study of a science*, vol. 3. New York: McGraw-Hill, 1959.

———. Autobiography. In E. G. Boring and G. Lindzey (eds.), *A history of psychology in autobiography*, vol. 5. Englewood Cliffs, N. J.: Prentice-Hall, 1967.

Murray, H. A., (with several collaborators). *Explorations in personality*. New York: Oxford, 1938.

Myers, I. B. *Manual for the Myers-Briggs Type Indicator*. Princeton, N. J.: Educational Testing Service, 1962.

Newman, B. M., and Newman, P. R. *Development through life*. Homewood, Ill.: Dorsey Press, 1975.

Office of Strategic Services Assessment Staff. *Assessment of men*. New York, Rinehart, 1948.

Olds, J., and Milner, P. Positive reinforcement produced by electrical stimulation of septal area and other regions of rat brain. *Journal of Comparative and Physiological Psychology*, 1954, **47**, 419-427.

Pacella, B. L. Early ego development and the *déjà vu*. *Journal of the American Psychoanalytic Association*, 1975, **23**, 300-318.

Paivio, A. *Imagery and verbal processes*. New York: Holt, Rinehart & Winston, 1971.

Pavlov, I. P. *Conditioned reflexes: An investigation of physiological activity of the cerebral cortex*. London: Oxford University Press, 1927.

Pearson, K. On lines and planes of closest fit to systems of points in space. *Philosophical Magazine*, 1901, **2**, Sixth Series, 559-572.

Penfield, W. *The mystery of the mind*. Princeton, N. J.: Princeton University Press, 1975.

Pervin, L. A. *Personality: Theory, assessment, and research*. New York: Wiley, 1970.

Peterfreund, E., and Schwartz, J. T. *Information, systems, and psychoanalysis*. New York: International Universities Press, 1971.

Phares, E. J., and Lamiell, J. T. Internal-external control, interpersonal judgments of others in need, and attribution of responsibility. *Journal of Personality*, 1975, **43**, 23-38.

Porter, L. W. A study of perceived need satisfactions in bottom and middle management jobs. *Journal of Applied Psychology*, 1961, **45**, 1-10.

Porter, R. B., and Cattell, R. B. *The IPAT Children's Personality Questionnaire*. Champaign,

Ill.: Institute for Personality and Ability Testing, 1960.

Preus, A. *Science and philosophy in Aristotle's biological works.* New York: Georg Olm, Veelag Hildesheim, 1975.

Pribram, K. H. The foundation of psychoanalytic theory: Freud's neuropsychological model. In K. H. Primbram (ed.), *Brain and behavior,* vol. 4. *Adaptation.* Baltimore, Maryland: Penguin Books, 1969, pp. 395-432.

———. Toward a neuropsychological theory of the person. In K. H. Pribram (ed.), *Brain and behavior,* vol. 1. *Mood, states, and mind.* Baltimore, Penguin Books, 1969.

Progoff, I. *The death and rebirth of psychology.* New York: McGraw-Hill, 1973.

Pylyshyn, Z. W. What the mind's eye tells the mind's brain: a critique of mental imagery. *Psychological Bulletin,* 1973, **80**, 1-24.

Raimy, V. *Misunderstandings of the self.* San Francisco: Jossey-Bass, 1975.

Rapaport, D. The structure of psychoanalytic theory: A systematizing attempt. In S. Koch (ed.), *Psychology: A study of a science,* vol. 3. New York: McGraw-Hill, 1959.

———. On the psychoanalytic theory of affects. In M. M. Gill (ed.), *The collected papers of David Rapaport.* New York: Basic Books, 1967.

Ricciuti, H. N., and Sadacca, R. *The prediction of academic grades with a projective test of achievement motivation: II. Crossvalidation at the high school level.* Princeton, N. J.: Educational Testing Service, 1955.

Roberts, T. B. Maslow's human motivation needs hierarchy. *Research in Education,* ERIC document ED-069-591, 1973.

Robertson, J. *Young children in hospitals.* New York: Basic Books, 1958.

———. *Hospitals and children.* London: Gollancz, 1962.

Rogers, C. R. *Counseling and psychotherapy.* Boston: Houghton Mifflin, 1942.

———. *Client-centered therapy.* Boston: Houghton Mifflin, 1951.

———. A theory of therapy, personality, and interpersonal relationships, as developed in the client-centered framework. In S. Koch (ed.), *Psychology: A study of a science,* vol. 3. New York: McGraw-Hill, 1959.

———. *On becoming a person.* Boston: Houghton Mifflin, 1961.

———. Sharing something of yourself. Tape no. 1, *Mental Health Info-pak Cassette Series: Dr. Carl Rogers.* Chicago, Ill.: Instructional Dynamics, 1971.

———. *Becoming partners: Marriage and its alternatives.* New York: Delacorte Press, 1972.

———. In retrospect: Forty-six years. *American Psychologist,* 1974, **29**, 115-123.

Rogers, C. R., and Dymond, R. F. (eds.) *Psychotherapy and personality change.* Chicago: University of Chicago Press, 1954.

Rogers, C. R., and Skinner, B. F. Some issues concerning the control of human behavior. *Science,* 1956, **124**, 1057-1066.

Rogers, C. R., and Wood, J. K. Client-centered theory: Carl R. Rogers. In A. Burton (ed.), *Operational theories of personality.* New York: Brunner/Mazel, 1974.

Rosen, B. C. The achievement syndrome. *American Sociological Review,* 1956, **21**, 203-211.

Rotter, J. B. *Social learning and clinical psychology.* Englewood Cliffs, N. J.: Prentice-Hall, 1954.

———. Generalized expectancies for internal versus external control of reinforcement. *Psychological Monographs,* 1966, **80**, Whole No. 609, pp. 1-28.

———. Some problems and misconceptions related to the construct of internal versus external control of reinforcement. *Journal of Consulting and Clinical Psychology,* 1975, **43**, 56-67.

Rotter, J. B., and Hochreich, D. J. *Personality.* Glenview, Ill.: Scott, Foresman, 1975.

Royce, J. R., and Buss, A. R. The role of general systems and information theory in multifactor individuality theory. *Canadian Psychological Review,* 1976, **17**, 1-21.

Rychlak, J. F. *A philosophy of science for personality theory.* Boston: Houghton Mifflin, 1968.

Sahakian, W. S. (ed.) *Psychology of personality: Readings in theory.* (3rd ed.) Chicago, Ill.: Rand McNally, 1977.

Sanford, N. *Issues in personality theory.* San Francisco: Jossey-Bass, 1970.

Saunders, D. R. The social psychology of UFOs. Address to the Social-Personality Program, Department of Psychology, University of Colorado, Spring 1973.

———. A factor analytic study of the AI and the CCI. *Multivariate Behavioral Research,* 1969, **4**, 329-346.

Schafer, R. Problems in Freud's psychology of women. *Journal of the American Psychoanalytic Association,* 1974, **22**, 459-485.

Schlesinger, K., and Groves, P. M. *Psychology: A dynamic science.* Dubuque, Iowa: Wm. C. Brown Company Publishers, 1976.

Sears, R. R. *Survey of objective studies of psychoanalytic concepts.* New York: Social Science Research Council, 1943.

Sells, S. B., Demaree, R. G., and Will, D. P., Jr. Dimensions of personality: II. Separate factor structures in Guilford and Cattell trait markers. *Multivariate Behavioral Research,* 1971, **6**, 135-186.

Shagass, C., and Kerenyi, A. B. Neurophysiological studies of personality. In H. J. Eysenck (ed.), *Readings in extraversion-introversion,* vol. 3. New York: Wiley-Interscience, 1971.

Shands, H. C. Momentary deity and personal myth. *Contemporary Psychoanalysis,* 1973, **9**, 417-444.

Shapiro, K. J., and Alexander, I. E. *The experience of introversion: An integration of phenomenological, empirical, and Jungian approaches.* Durham, N. C.: Duke University Press, 1975.

Sheldon, W. H. *The varieties of temperament.* New York: Harper, 1942.

Shlien, J. M. Cross-theoretical criteria in time-limited therapy. In *The sixth international congress of psychotherapy: Selected lectures.* New York: Karger, 1965.

Shostrom, E. *Personal Orientation Inventory Manual.* San Diego: Educational and Industrial Testing Service, 1966.

———. (ed.) *Three approaches to psychotherapy.* Orange, Cal.: Psychological Films, 1965.

Silverman, L. H. Drive stimulation and psychopathology: On the conditions under which drive-related external events evoke pathological reactions. In R. R. Holt and E. Peterfreund (eds.), *Psychoanalysis and contemporary science,* vol. 1. New York: Macmillan, 1972.

———. Psychoanalytic theory: "The reports of my death are greatly exaggerated." *American Psychologist,* 1976, **31**, 621-637.

Singer, J. L. *Daydreaming.* New York: Random House, 1966.

Skinner, B. F. *The behavior of organisms: An experimental analysis.* Englewood Cliffs, N. J.: Prentice-Hall, 1938.

———. *Science and human behavior.* New York: Macmillan, 1953.

———. *Verbal behavior.* Englewood Cliffs, N. J.: Prentice-Hall, 1957.

———. A case history in scientific method. In S. Koch (ed.), *Psychology: A study of a science,* vol. 2. New York: McGraw-Hill, 1959.

———. *The technology of teaching.* Englewood Cliffs, N. J.: Prentice-Hall, 1968.

———. *Beyond freedom and dignity.* New York: Knopf, 1971.

———. *About behaviorism.* New York: Knopf, 1974.

———. *Particulars of my life.* New York: Knopf, 1976.

Slocum, W. J. Motivation in managerial levels: Relationship of need satisfaction to job performance. *Journal of Applied Psychology,* 1971, **55**, 312-316.

Smith, M. L., and Glass, G. V. Meta-analysis of psychotherapy outcome studies. *American Psychologist,* 1977, **32**, 752-760.

Solomon, R. L., Kamin, L. J., and Wynne, L. C. Traumatic avoidance learning: The outcomes of several extinction procedures with dogs. *Journal of Abnormal and Social Psychology,* 1953, **48**, 291-302.

Spearman, C. General intelligence objectively determined and measured. *American Journal of Psychology,* 1904, **15**, 201-293.

———. *The abilities of man.* London: Macmillan, 1927.

Spence, D. P., and Gordon, C. M. Activation and measurement of an early oral fantasy: An exploratory study. *Journal of the American Psychoanalytic Association,* 1967, **15**, 99-129.

Spence, K. W. *Behavior theory and conditioning.* New Haven, Conn.: Yale University Press, 1956.

Sperry, R. W. An objective approach to subjective experience: Further explanation of a hypothesis. *Psychological Review*, 1970, **77**, 585-590.

Spitz, R. A. *The first year of life*. New York: International Universities Press, 1965.

Stagner, R. *Psychology of personality*. (4th ed.) New York: McGraw-Hill, 1974.

Standal, S. W. The need for positive regard: A contribution to client-centered theory. Unpublished doctoral dissertation, University of Chicago, 1954.

Stephenson, W. *The study of behavior*. Chicago: University of Chicago Press, 1953.

Stern, G. G. *Activities Index—College Characteristics Index—preliminary manual*. Syracuse: Psychological Research Center, 1958.

———. *People in context*. New York: Wiley, 1970.

Stevens, S. S. Mathematics, measurement, and psychophysics. In S. S. Stevens (ed.), *Handbook of experimental psychology*. New York: Wiley, 1951.

Stricker, L. J., and Ross, J. An assessment of some structural properties of the Jungian personality typology. *Journal of Abnormal and Social Psychology*, 1964, **68**, 62-71. (a)

———. Some correlates of a Jungian personality inventory. *Psychological Reports*, 1964, **14**, 623-643. (b)

Suinn, R. M., Osborn, D., and Page, W. The self-concept and accuracy of recall of inconsistent self-related information. *Journal of Clinical Psychology*, 1962, **18**, 473-474.

Suppe, F. (ed.). *The structure of scientific theories*. Urbana, Ill.: University of Illinois Press, 1974.

Sweney, A. B. Objective measurement of dynamic structure factors. In R. B. Cattell and F. W. Warburton (eds.), *Objective personality and motivational tests: A theoretical introduction and practical compendium*. Urbana, Ill.: University of Illinois Press, 1967.

Tarpy, R. M. *Basic principles of learning*. Glenview, Ill.: Scott, Foresman, 1975.

Taylor, J. T. A personality scale of manifest anxiety. *Journal of Abnormal and Social Psychology*, 1953, **48**, 285-290.

Technical recommendations for psychological tests and diagnostic techniques. *Psychological Bulletin Supplement*, 1954, **51**, no. 2, part 2, 1-38.

Tharp, R. G., and Wetzel, R. J. *Behavior modification in the natural environment*. New York: Academic Press, 1969.

Thrasher, F. M. *The gang: A study of 1,313 gangs in Chicago*. (abridged ed.) Chicago: University of Chicago Press, 1963. (Originally pub. 1927.)

Thurstone, L. L. *Multiple factor analysis*. Chicago: University of Chicago Press, 1947.

Toder, N. L., and Marcia, J. E. Ego identity status and response to conformity pressure in college women. *Journal of Personality and Social Psychology*, 1973, **26**, 287-294.

Tolman, E. C. Principles of purposive behavior. In S. Koch (ed.), *Psychology: A study of a science*, vol. 2. New York: McGraw-Hill, 1959.

Tosi, D. J., and Lindamood, C. A. The measurement of self-actualization: A critical review of the personal orientation inventory. *Journal of Personality Assessment*, 1975, **39**, 215-224.

Toulmin, S. Postscript: The structure of scientific theories. In F. Suppe (ed.), *The structure of scientific theories*. Urbana, Ill.: University of Illinois Press, 1974.

Toynbee, A. *A study of history*. (abridged ed.) New York: Oxford University Press, 1946.

Truax, C. B. and Mitchell, K. M. Research on certain therapist interpersonal skills in relation to process and outcome. In A. E. Bergin and S. L. Garfield (eds.), *Handbook of psychotherapy and behavior change*. New York: Wiley, 1971.

Turner, C. W., and Layton, J. F. Verbal imagery and connotation as memory-induced mediators of aggressive behavior. *Journal of Personality and Social Psychology*, 1976, **33**, 755-763.

Vaillant, G. E. Natural history of male psychological health. V. The relation of choice of equal mechanism of defense to adult adjustment. *Archives of General Psychiatry*, 1976, **33**, no. 5, 535-545.

(Continued from copyright page)

Pages 30-31: from *Behavior Influence and Personality: The Social Matrix of Human Actions* by L. Krasner and L. P. Ullman. Copyright © 1973 by Holt, Rinehart and Winston, Inc. Reprinted by permission of Holt, Rinehart and Winston and the authors.

Pages 31-32: from William James, *The Principles of Psychology.* Published by Dover Publications, Inc., by special arrangement with Henry Holt and Company.

Page 34: from R. M. Liebert and M. D. Spiegler, *Personality Strategies for the Study of Man* (2nd ed.), p. 7, Dorsey Press, 1974. Reprinted by permission of the author and the publisher.

Page 36: from R. G. Barker and H. P. Wright, *One Boy's Day: A Specimen Record of Behavior,* Harper & Row, 1951. Reprinted by permission of the authors and the publisher.

Page 36: from F. M. Thrasher, *The Gang* (abridged ed.), 1963, pp. 86, 71. Reprinted by permission of The University of Chicago Press.

Pages 36-37: from *The Collected Works of C. G. Jung,* ed. Herbert Read, Michael Fordham, Gerhard Adler, and William McGuire, trans. R. F. C. Hull. Bollingen Series XX, vol. 5, *Symbols of Transformation,* p. 458. Copyright © 1961 by Bollingen Foundation. Reprinted by permission of Princeton University Press.

Page 37: from M. J. Horowitz, *Image Formation and Cognition,* p. 11, Appleton-Century-Crofts, 1970. Reprinted by permission of the author and the publisher.

Pages 37-38: from Margaret Mead, *Sex and Temperament in Three Primitive Societies,* Morrow, 1935. Reprinted in paperback 1963 (with new Preface), Apollo editions, Morrow, New York. Reprinted by permission of the author and the publishers.

Page 50: from H. A. Murray, "What Should Psychologists Do About Psychoanalysis?" In *Journal of Abnormal Psychology,* vol. 35, 1940, pp. 150-175. Copyright 1940 by the American Psychological Association. Reprinted by permission of the author and the publisher.

Page 59: from Joel Allison, Sidney J. Blatt, and Carl N. Zimet, *The Interpretation of Psychological Tests,* pp. 115-116. Copyright © 1968 by Joel Allison, Sidney J. Blatt, and Carl N. Zimet. Reprinted by permission of Harper & Row, Publishers, Inc., and the authors.

Page 65: from M. H. Marx and W. A. Hillix, *Systems and Theories in Psychology* (2nd ed.), p. 434, McGraw-Hill, 1973. Used by permission of the author and the publisher.

Page 95: from B. F. Skinner, *Science and Human Behavior,* pp. 112-113. Copyright 1953 by Macmillan, Inc. Reprinted by permission of the author and the publisher.

Pages 119-120: from M. S. Krause, "An Analysis of Carl Rogers's Theory of Personality." In *Genetic Psychology Monographs,* 1964, vol. 69, pp. 49-99. Reprinted by permission of the author.

Page 132: from D. Rapaport, "The Structure of Psychoanalytic Theory: A Systematizing Attempt." In S. Koch, ed., *Psychology: A Study of a Science,* vol. 3, pp. 112-113, McGraw-Hill, 1959. Reprinted by permission.

Page 133: from Dorwin Cartwright, "Lewinian Theory as a Contemporary Systematic Framework." In S. Koch, ed., *Psychology: A Study of a Science,* vol. 2, p. 21. McGraw-Hill, 1959. Used by permission of the author and the publisher.

Page 133: from James F. T. Bugental, ed., "The Challenge That Is Man," in *Challenges of Humanistic Psychology,* pp. 5-12, McGraw-Hill, 1970. Reprinted by permission of the author and the publisher.

Pages 133-34: from Charlotte Buhler and Melanie Allen, *Introduction to Humanistic Psychology,* pp. 1-2, published by the Association for Humanistic Psychology, 1972. Reprinted by permission of the publisher.

Page 153-54; 164: from Neal E. Miller and John Dollard, *Social Learning and Imitation,* pp. 97; 86-87, Yale University Press, 1941. Reprinted by permission of the authors and the publisher.

Page 157: from N. E. Miller, "Theory and Experiment Relating Psychoanalytic Displacement to Stimulus-Response Generalization." In *Journal of Abnormal and Social Psychology,* 1948, vol. 43, pp. 155-178. Copyright 1948 by the American Psychological Association. Used by permission of the author and the publisher.

Page 158: from E. J. Murray and M. M. Berkun, "Displacement as a Function of Conflict." In *Journal of Abnormal and Social Psychology,* 1955, vol. 51, pp. 47-56. Copyrighted by the American Psychological Association, 1955. Used by permission of the authors and the publisher.

Page 165: from J. Dollard and N. E. Miller, *Personality and Psychotherapy,* p. 158, McGraw-Hill, 1950. Reprinted by permission of the author and the publisher.

Page 182: from M. J. Horowitz, *Stress Response Syndromes,* pp. 82-85, Aronson, 1976. Reprinted with permission of author and publisher.

Page 188: from Clark L. Hull, *Principles of Behavior,* p. 178, Prentice-Hall, 1943. Used by permission of author and publisher.

Pages 193-94: Reproduced by permission from Walter Buckley, editor, *Modern Systems Research for the Behavioral Scientist.* Aldine Publishing Company, Chicago. © 1968 by Walter Buckley.

Page 197: from M. Bunge, *Method, Model and Matter,* p. 113, D. Reidel, 1973. Used with permission.

Page 202: from D. W. Fiske, *Measuring the Concepts of Personality,* p. 98, Aldine Publishing Co., 1971. Used by permission of author and publisher.

Page 211: from L. L. Altman, *The Dream in Psychoanalysis,* International Universities Press, 1969. Used by permission of the publisher.

Page 214: from "Project for a Scientific Psychology." In James Strachey, (Ed.), *The Standard Edition of the Complete Works of Sigmund Freud,* vol. I. London: The Hogarth Press, 1966. Reprinted by permission of Sigmund Freud Copyrights, Ltd., and The Hogarth Press, Ltd.

Page 217: from "The Unconscious," in *Collected Papers,* Sigmund Freud, edited by Ernest Jones, M. D., vol. 4, authorized translation under the supervision of Joan Riviere, published by Basic Books, Inc., by arrangement with The Hogarth Press, Ltd. and The Institute of Psycho-Analysis, London.

Page 220: from "The Ego and the Id." In James Strachey, (Ed.), *The Standard Edition of the Complete Psychological Works of Sigmund Freud,* vol. XIX. London: The Hogarth Press, 1961. Reprinted by permission of Sigmund Freud Copyrights, Ltd., The Hogarth Press, Ltd., and Norton and Co.

Page 226: from E. H. Hilgard and G. H. Bower, *Theories of Learning,* Prentice-Hall, 1975. Used by permission of the author and the publisher.

Page 247: from "Repression," in *Collected Papers,* Sigmund Freud, edited by Ernest Jones, M. D., vol. 4, authorized translation under the supervision of Joan Riviere, published by Basic Books, Inc., by arrangement with The Hogarth Press, Ltd. and The Institute of Psycho-Analysis, London.

Page 254: from G. W. Allport, *Personality: A Psychological Interpretation,* p. 188, Constable & Company, Ltd. Used by permission.

Page 270: from "The Infantile Genital Organization of the Libido," in *Collected Papers,* Sigmund Freud, edited by Ernest Jones, M. D., vol. 2, authorized translation under the supervision of Joan Riviere, published by Basic Books, Inc., by arrangement with The Hogarth Press, Ltd. and The Institute of Psycho-Analysis, London.

Pages 271 and 277: from "Three Essays on the Theory of Sexuality" by Sigmund Freud (1905), translated and newly edited by James Strachey, published by Basic Books, Inc., Publishers, New York. Copyright © 1962 by Sigmund Freud Copyrights, Ltd. Reprinted by permission.

Pages 271 and 277: from "Three Essays on Sexuality." In James Strachey, (Ed.), *The Standard Edition of the Complete Works of Sigmund Freud,* vol. VII. London: The Hogarth Press, Ltd., 1953. Reprinted by permission of Sigmund Freud Copyrights, Ltd., and The Hogarth Press, Ltd.

Page 273: from Robert M. Lindner, *Rebel Without a Cause,* pp. 193-194, Grune & Stratton, Inc., 1944. Copyright 1944 by Grune & Stratton; renewed. Reprinted by permission of Harold Ober Associates Incorporated and the publisher.

Page 281: from A. Bandura and R. H. Walters, *Social Learning and Personality Development,* p. 25, Holt, Rinehart and Winston, 1963. Used by permission of the author and the publisher.

Pages 303, 305, 306, 308, 329 330, 404: reprinted from the *Collected Works of C. G. Jung,* ed. Herbert Read, Michael Fordham, Gerhard Adler, and William McGuire, trans. R. F. C. Hull. Bollingen Series XX. Vol. 4, *Freud and Psychoanalysis,* pp. 338-339, © 1961 by Bollingen Foundation. Vol. 5, *Symbols of Transformation,* pp. 64-65; 124; 458, © 1956 by Bollingen Foundation; vol. 7, *Two Essays on Analytical Psychology,* pp. 53-54; 190, © 1966 by Bollingen Foundation; vol. 9, part I, *The Archetypes and the Collective Unconscious,* p. 307, © 1969 by Bollingen Foundation. Reprinted by permission of Princeton University Press.

Page 305: from C. G. Jung, "Approaching the Unconscious." In C. G. Jung, ed., *Man and His Symbols,* p. 69. © 1964 Aldus Books, Ltd. and reprinted with their permission.

Page 323: from "On the History of the Psychoanalytic Movement," *Collected Papers,* Sigmund Freud, edited by Ernest Jones, M. D., vol. 1, authorized translation under the supervision of Joan Riviere, published by Basic Books, Inc., by arrangement with The Hogarth Press Ltd., and The Institute of Psycho-Analysis, London.

Page 331: from "A Religious Experience," in *Collected Papers,* Sigmund Freud, edited by Ernest Jones, M. D., vol. 5, edited by James Strachey, published by Basic Books, Inc., by arrangement with The Hogarth Press, Ltd. and The Institute of Psycho-Analysis, London.

Page 383: from John L. Horn, "Motivation and Dynamic Calculus Concepts from Multivariate Experiment," in Raymond B. Cattell, *Handbook of Multivariate Experimental Psychology,* © 1966 by Rand McNally & Company, Table 20-1, pp. 617-18. Reprinted by permission of Rand McNally College Publishing Company.

Page 388: from R. B. Cattell and D. Child, *Motivation and Dynamic Structure.* London: Holt-Blond, Ltd., 1975. New York: Wiley & Sons, 1975. Reprinted by permission of authors and publisher.

Page 405: from R. B. Cattell, *Personality,* pp. 654 and 657, McGraw-Hill, 1950. Reprinted by permission of author and publisher.

Page 379: from R. B. Cattell, *Personality and Mood by Questionnaire,* page xii, Jossey-Bass, 1973. Used by permission of author and publisher.

Page 411: from A. B. Maslow, *Motivation and Personality* (2nd ed.), p. 46, Harper & Row, 1970. Used by permission of the publisher.

Page 411: from *The Farther Reaches of Human Nature* by A. H. Maslow, Introduction by Henry Geiger. Copyright © 1971 by Bertha G. Maslow. An Esalen Book, reprinted by permission of The Viking Press.

Page 426: from H. J. Eysenck, *Psychology and the Foundations of Psychiatry,* p. 5, H. K. Lewis, London, 1955. Reprinted with permission of the author and the publisher.

Page 473: from M. Deutsch, "Field Theory in Social Psychology." In G. Lindzey and E. Aronson, eds., *The Handbook of Social Psychology,* vol. 1, pp. 412-487, Addison-Wesley, 1968. Used with permission of author and publisher.

Page 477: from K. Lewin, *Field Theory in Social Science,* p. 323, Harper & Row, 1951. Used with permission of the publisher.

Pages 494-95: from E. C. Tolman, "Principles of Purposive Behavior." In S. Koch, ed., *Psychology: A Study of a Science,* vol. 2, pp. 92-157, McGraw-Hill, 1959. Used by permission.

Page 515: from Joseph Wolpe, "Reciprocal Inhibition as the Main Basis of Psychotherapeutic Effects." *A.M.A. Archives of Neurology and Psychiatry,* 1954, vol. 72, pp. 205, 206. Copyright 1954 by the American Medical Society and used with their permission and the permission of the author.

Name Index

Abraham, K., 210, 551
Adler, A., 3, 13, 483, 551
Adorno, T.W., 257, 551
Ahmed, S.A., 558
Alexander, F., 41, 531, 551
Alexander, I.E., 313, 564
Allen, M., 6, 18, 108, 134, 553
Allison, J., 59, 551
Allport, G.W., 29, 33, 39-41, 225, 253, 280, 392, 551
Allyon, T., 95, 551
Altman, L.L., 211, 551
Altman, P.L., 551
American Association of Humanistic Psychology, 5, 133
American Humanist Association, 5
American Psychological Association (APA), 5, 50, 150, 164, 202
Amsel, A., 507, 551
Anderson, R.L., 179, 551
Apostle, H.G., 551
Appelbaum, A., 559
Archimedes, 131
Aristotle, 186
Arlow, J.A., 551
Arnoff, J., 561
Aronson, E., 554
Aronson, H., 255, 551
Assagioli, R., 314, 551
Atkinson, J.W., 63, 551
Avogadro, 189
Axelrad, S., 279, 552
Axline, V.M., 115, 551
Azrin, N.H., 95, 551

Bancroft, T.A., 179, 551
Bandura, A., 149, 168, 169, 280, 500, 503-22, 526, 528, 529, 539, 551, 552
Barker, R.G., 36, 552
Barrett-Lennard, G.T., 114, 552
Bartlett, H.W., 451, 553
Barton, K., 390, 552
Battig, W.F., 200, 552
Benedict, R., 4, 190, 552

Benson, L., 190, 552
Bergin, A.E., 114, 200, 226, 552
Berkun, M.M., 158-61, 167, 169, 562
Bernadin, A.C., 61, 552
Berne, E., 273, 553
Bernheim, H., 209
Bernoulli, D., 130, 131, 133, 552
Binzwanger, H., 315
Birney, R.C., 63, 552
Birsh, E., 561
Black, P., 560
Blanchard, E.G., 514, 552
Blatt, S.J., 59, 551
Bleuler, E., 209, 376
Borgatta, E.F., 552
Boring, E.G., 562
Bowen, N.V., 566
Bower, G.H., 168, 516, 558
Boyle, R., 129, 135, 139, 552
Bozarth, J.D., 562
Bradway, K., 313, 552
Braithwaite, R.B., 129, 134, 552
Brebner, J., 436, 552
Breger, L., 170, 171, 518, 552
Brenner, C., 551
Breuer, J., 209
Brewer, W.F., 99-101, 172, 441, 518, 540, 541, 552
Brill, A.A., 210
Brody, S., 279, 552
Brogden, W.J., 76, 552
Brown, L.B., 333, 552
Browne, J.A., 393, 457, 558
Brucke, E., 207
Brush, S.G., 65, 129-31, 552, 553
Buckley, W., 566
Bugental, J.F.T., 5, 133, 553
Buhler, C., 6, 18, 108, 134, 553
Bunge, M., 65, 127, 129, 139, 140, 181, 197, 536, 553
Burstein, E.D., 559
Burton, A., 558, 560, 563
Buss, A.R., 194, 535, 563
Butler, J.M., 115, 553

Carnap, R., 137, 138, 553
Carrigan, P.M., 457, 553
Cartwright, C.I., 190
Cartwright, D., 133, 553
Cartwright, D.S., 117, 118, 307, 553, 555, 559
Cartwright, J., 129, 553
Cattell, M.D., 392, 553
Cattell, R.B., 142, 361-96, 399-420 passim, 439, 440, 444, 447, 460, 525, 526, 529, 533, 534, 552-56, 557, 562, 564, 565
Charcot, J., 208, 209, 556
Child, D., 387, 388, 548, 553, 554
Child, I.L., 474, 554
Chodorkoff, B., 117, 121, 132, 142, 554
Chomsky, N., 98, 99, 170, 518, 554
Ciaccio, N.V., 279, 350, 554
Clark, J.P., 542, 554
Clore, G.L., 566
Cohen, J., 554
Cole, D., 63, 554
Comrey, A., 548, 554
Cooper, C., 436, 552
Corcoran, D.W., 430, 434, 554
Corsini, R., 566
Coyne, L., 559
Cronbach, L.J., 139, 554
Cummings, L.L., 19, 554

Dalton, J., 189
De Fries, J.C., 550, 561
Demaree, R.G., 564
Deutsch, M., 473, 554
De Vore, A., 292, 327, 554
Dielman, T.E., 553
Dittmer, D.S., 551
Dixon, N.F., 35, 225, 227, 256, 258, 554
Doerr, H.O., 432, 554
Dollard, J., 132, 136, 149-76, 179, 181, 186, 192, 195, 497, 500, 503, 506, 513, 514, 517, 519, 521, 526, 529, 538, 539, 554, 561
Doob, L.W., 554

Douglas, J.D., 566
Dymond, R.F., 119, 553, 563

Eaves, L.J., 437, 438, 440, 554
Eber, H.W., 380, 386, 405, 449, 553
Edwards, A.L., 61, 62, 554
Einstein, A., 135, 138
Ellman, C., 257, 555
El Salmi, A., 19, 554
English, A.C., 209, 555
English, H.B., 209, 555
Epstein, S., 166-69, 171, 551, 555
Erikson, E.H., 191, 279, 283, 339-58, 399-420 passim, 526, 529, 530, 534, 554, 555
Estes, W.K., 91, 477, 478, 533, 555
Eysenck, H.J., 40, 101, 185, 186, 196, 198-200, 255, 312, 374, 423-44, 447, 460, 525, 526, 529, 533, 553-55, 558, 560, 564
Eysenck, S.B.G., 429, 430, 455, 555

Feather, N.T., 63, 551
Feffer, M.H., 22, 557
Fenichel, O., 274-77, 280, 555
Ferenczi, S., 209
Ferster, C.B., 89, 91, 95, 555, 561
Fisher, S., 258, 555
Fiske, D.W., 118, 119, 128, 202, 399, 555
Fitch, F.G., 558
Fitz, D.A., 165, 556
Fluegel, J.C., 423
Frankl, V.E., 192, 556
Franks, C.M., 439, 556
French, J.W., 457, 556
French, T.M., 41, 551
Frenkel-Brunswik, E., 551
Freud, A., 210, 279, 283, 556
Freud, E.L., 557
Freud, Martha (Bernays), 207, 208
Freud, S., 50, 57, 67, 131, 150, 155, 156, 163, 185, 195, 197, 205, 207-86, 321-36, 399-420 passim, 441, 447-60, 525, 526, 529, 531, 533, 535, 536, 556, 566
Freud, W.E., 279, 280, 557
Friedman, S., 278, 559
Fromm, E., 4

Galen, 453
Galileo, G., 131, 478
Galton, F., 429
Gambrill, E.D., 95, 557
Garfield, S., 565
Geary, P.S., 566
Geiger, H., 21, 557
Gendlin, E., 118, 119, 557
Ghiselli, E.E., 459, 557
Gill, M.M., 557, 563
Glass, G.V., 226, 227, 564
Glucksberg, S., 256, 553
Goldman-Eisler, F., 278, 557
Gordon, C.M., 278, 564
Gordon, T., 116, 557
Gorsuch, R.L., 457, 557
Gourevitch, V., 22, 557
Graves, T.D., 558
Gray, H., 312, 557
Gray, J.A., 196, 439, 440, 557
Greenhouse, H.B., 566
Groves, P.M., 213, 214, 557

Guetzkow, H., 561
Guilford, J.P., 392, 457, 558, 564
Guntrip, H., 352, 558
Guttman, L., 558
Guttman, N., 85, 558

Haigh, G.V., 553
Hall, C.S., 194, 260, 477, 558
Hall, G.S., 210
Hall, M., 558
Hanson, R.C., 558
Hart, J.T., 565
Hartman, H., 282, 558
Heapy, N.A., 558
Hebb, D.O., 21, 134, 558
Heider, F., 473, 558
Hendricks, B., 391, 553
Hilgard, E.R., 118, 226, 516, 558
Hillix, W.A., 65, 128, 184, 561
Hillman, J., 305, 558, 566
Hjelle, L.A., 180, 558
Hochreich, D.J., 484-86, 489, 490, 563
Hokanson, J.E., 432, 554
Holmes, T.H., 531, 558
Holt, R.R., 40, 557, 558
Holzer, T.E., 196, 197, 566
Honig, W.K., 95, 558
Honigmann, I., 561
Hoppe, F., 474
Horn, J.L., 383, 385, 404, 554, 558
Horowitz, M.J., 37, 182, 183, 200, 558
Horwitz, L., 559
Hovland, C.I., 558
Howarth, E., 198-200, 393, 457, 558
Hull, C.L., 65, 135, 136, 150, 169, 173, 188, 434, 505, 558
Hunt, J. McV., 561

Inkson, J.H.K., 64, 558
Institute for Personality and Ability Testing (IPAT), 362, 392, 558, 563

Jackson, D.N., 62, 64, 558
Jacobs, S., 554
Jacobson, E., 558
James, W., 30, 381, 558
Jeffrey, R.W., 513, 517, 552, 558
Jensen, A., 432, 558
Jessor, R., 61, 493, 494, 552, 558
Jessor, S.L., 493, 494, 558
Johnson, C., 561
Jones, E., 207, 209, 210, 556, 558
Jones, M.R., 551, 555
Jourard, S.M., 6, 559
Jung, C.G., 37, 50, 209, 289-336, 395, 399-420 passim, 441, 444, 447, 460, 525, 526, 529, 533, 534, 538, 539, 545, 552, 559, 566

Kalish, H.I., 85, 558
Kamin, L.J., 507, 564
Kant, I., 453
Kaplan, S., 199, 560
Kaufmann, Y., 308, 309, 311, 566
Kawash, G., 390, 552
Kelly, G.A., 32, 559
Kerenyi, A.B., 439, 564
Kernberg, O., 224, 559
Keynes, J.M., 193, 559
King, J., 256, 557

Kirtner, W.L., 118, 555, 559
Klein, G.S., 186, 560
Kleinsmith, L.J., 199, 560
Kline, P., 132, 225, 227, 258, 278, 560
Knight, G., 149
Koch, S., 65, 81, 82, 107, 131-33, 553, 555, 560, 562-64
Koffka, K., 463, 465, 560
Kohler, W., 108, 463
Kolb, L.C., 208, 560
Kounin, J., 560
Kraeling, D., 158, 561
Kraepelin, E., 425
Krasner, L., 30, 34, 542, 560
Krauft, C.C., 562
Krause, M.S., 119-21, 560
Krech, D., 186, 560
Kretschmer, E., 40, 560
Kuhn, T.S., 135, 137, 560

Lambert, W.W., 552
Lamiell, J.T., 492, 562
Laplace, P.S. de, 65
Laplanche, L., 218, 560
Laverty, S.G., 440, 560
Layton, J.F., 333, 565
Lazarus, R.S., 182, 183, 191, 258, 537, 538, 560
Leat, M., 513, 566
Lefcourt, H.M., 491, 560
Levey, A., 435, 436
Levinson, D.J., 551
Lewin, K., 50, 51, 65, 133, 188, 463-81, 483, 484, 488, 489, 496, 526, 529, 536, 555, 560, 561
Lewis, M.K., 115, 560
Liebert, R.M., 29, 34, 180, 560
Lifton, R.J., 351, 560
Lindamood, C.A., 22, 565
Lindner, R.M., 273, 560
Lindzey, G., 194, 477, 554, 558, 562
Linnaeus, C., 190
Lipetz, M., 61, 562
Lippitt, B., 467, 560
London, I.D., 477, 560
Lowell, E.L., 63, 560
Lundin, R.W., 30, 560
Lykken, D.T., 35, 560

MacCorquodale, K., 555
MacDonnell, W.R., 560
MacKinnon, D.W., 478, 560
MacLean, P.D., 431, 550, 560
Maddi, S.R., 29, 560
Maher, B.A., 560
Maier, N.R.F., 200, 560
Marcia, J.E., 350, 561, 565
Marrow, A., 464, 561
Marx, M.H., 65, 128, 184, 561
Masling, J., 278, 561
Maslow, A.H., 3-25, 33, 41, 67, 73, 116, 117, 124, 134, 136, 137, 142, 180, 191-94, 201, 399-420 passim, 525, 528, 533-35, 557, 561
Maslow, B., 5
McClearn, G.E., 550, 561
McClelland, D.C., 62, 63, 561
McGaugh, J.L., 170, 171, 518, 552
McGinnies, E., 95, 561
McGuire, W., 289, 322, 323, 327, 561

Mead, M., 37, 38, 561, 566
Meehl, P.E., 139, 554, 555
Messe, L.A., 22, 561
Mezei, L., 513, 566
Miller, J.G., 194, 561
Miller, N.E., 132, 136, 149-76, 179, 181,
    186, 192, 195, 497, 500, 503, 505-9,
    513, 514, 517, 519, 521, 526, 529, 538,
    539, 554, 556, 561, 562
Milner, P., 266, 562
Milton, G.A., 61, 562
Mischel, W., 516, 562
Mitchell, K.M., 114, 562, 565
Mittelman, B., 5, 561
Morgan, C.D., 58, 562
Morgan, C.T., 200, 562
Mowrer, O.H., 554
Mueller, C.G., Jr., 555
Murray, E.J., 158-61, 165, 167-69, 171,
    562
Murray, H.A., 49-70, 73, 124, 136, 142,
    180, 181, 186, 191, 192, 194, 226, 465,
    526, 529, 533, 562
Myers, I.B., 312, 562

Newman, B.M., 350, 562
Newman, P.R., 350, 562
Newman, S., 4, 561
Newton, I., 130, 131, 187
Nichols, K., 457, 554

Office of Strategic Services Assessment
    Staff, 50, 58, 562
Olds, J., 266, 562
Osborn, D., 565

Pacella, B.L., 562
Page, W., 565
Paivio, A., 189, 434, 562
Palermo, D.S., 552
Parke, R.D., 566
Pasteur, L., 185
Pavlov, I.P., 73, 75, 562
Pearson, K., 370, 374, 424, 562
Penfield, W., 35, 562
Perkins, D.T., 558
Pervin, L.A., 29, 562
Peterfreund, E., 183, 225, 535, 562
Phares, E.J., 492, 562
Pollock, G.H., 41, 551
Pontalis, J.B., 218, 560
Porter, L.W., 18, 19, 137, 562
Porter, R.B., 392, 562
Preus, A., 186, 563
Pribram, K.H., 200, 215, 563
Prince, M., 50
Progoff, I., 312, 563
Pylyshyn, Z.W., 189, 190, 563

Rachman, S., 254, 255, 438, 555, 566
Radcliffe, R.A., 385, 554
Rahe, R.H., 531, 558
Raimy, V., 478, 563
Rand, H., 4, 561
Rapaport, D., 131, 132, 557, 563
Raynor, R., 514, 566
Renner, K.E., 566
Reyher, J., 258, 566

Ricciuti, H.N., 63, 563
Rice, L., 115, 553
Ritter, B., 514, 552
Roberts, T.B., 23, 563
Robertson, J., 279, 563
Rogers, C.R., 6, 32, 97, 107-24, 134, 137,
    142, 180, 399-420 passim, 441, 526,
    528-30, 534, 540, 553, 560, 563
Rose, R.J., 566
Rosen, V.C., 63, 563
Rosenzweig, M.R., 552
Ross, D., 510, 522, 552
Ross, J., 312, 565
Ross, R.T., 558
Ross, S.A., 510, 522, 552
Rotter, J.B., 149, 479, 483-99, 503, 526,
    529, 539, 563
Royce, J.R., 194, 227, 535, 563
Rychlak, J.F., 186, 535, 563

Sadacca, R., 63, 563
Sahakian, W.S., 180, 563
Saint Paul, 193
Sanford, N., 194, 551, 564
Saunders, D.R., 62, 128, 564
Schafer, R., 210, 282, 564
Scheier, I., 404, 553
Schlesinger, K., 213, 214, 557
Schoenfeld, W.N., 555
Schwartz, J.T., 183, 535, 562
Sears, R.R., 258, 554, 564
Sells, S.B., 392, 393, 457, 564
Selye, H., 538
Shagass, C., 439, 564
Shands, H.C., 37, 564
Shapiro, K.J., 313, 564
Sheldon, W.H., 40, 564
Shlien, J.M., 115, 560, 564
Shostrom, E., 22, 564
Silverman, L.H., 257, 539, 564
Singer, J.L., 42, 564
Skinner, B.F., 30, 73-104, 124, 131-34,
    136, 142, 149, 172, 179, 187, 192, 195,
    201, 505-7, 518, 526-29, 533, 536-38,
    554, 555, 563, 564
Slocum, E.J., 19, 564
Smith, B.D., 553
Smith, M.L., 226, 227, 564
Solomon, R.L., 507, 564
Solso, R.L., 552
Sordoni, C., 560
Sordoni, Carol, 560
Spearman, C., 423, 429, 564
Spence, D.P., 278, 564
Spence, K.W., 108, 432, 564
Sperry, R.W., 35, 565
Spiegler, M.D., 29, 34, 180, 560
Spitz, R.A., 279, 565
Stagner, R., 29, 561, 565
Standal, S.W., 111, 565
Stein, M., 561
Stephenson, W., 313, 565
Stern, G.G., 61, 62, 565
Stevens, S.S., 130, 552, 565
Strachey, J., 556, 557
Stricker, L.J., 312, 565
Sturansky, C., 561
Suinn, R.M., 114, 117, 552, 565

Suppe, F., 127, 565
Sweney, A.B., 385, 554, 565
Tarpy, R.M., 85, 565
Tatsuoka, M.M., 380, 386, 405, 449, 553
Taylor, J.A., 546, 565
Tharp, R.G., 75, 102, 565, 566
Thrasher, F.M., 36, 565
Thurstone, L.L., 370, 565
Tifft, L.L., 542, 554
Toder, N.L., 350, 565
Tolman, E.C., 494, 495, 565
Tomlinson, T.M., 565
Tosi, D.J., 22, 565
Toulmin, S., 197, 565
Toynbee, A., 190, 565
Trouton, D., 439, 556
Truax, C.B., 114, 562, 565
Turner, C.W., 333, 565

Ullman, L.P., 30, 34

Vaillant, G.E., 258, 565
Van der Veen, F., 114, 566
Verplanck, W.S., 90, 555, 566
Vetter, H.J., 553
Von Bertalanffy, L., 193, 194, 535, 566
Von Franz, M.L., 300, 315, 566
Von Wright, G., 186, 187, 566
Voth, H., 559

Wagstaff, A., 115, 553
Waldman, H., 200, 562
Walters, R.H., 149, 168, 169, 280, 281,
    503-22, 526, 528, 529, 539, 552, 566
Warburton, F.W., 565
Waskow, I.E., 209, 566
Waterman, A.S., 350, 566
Waterman, C.K., 350, 566
Watson, D.L., 102, 566
Watson, J.B., 73, 514, 566
Weimer, W.R., 552
Weintraub, W., 255, 551
Weisz, G., 454
Wertheimer, M., 4, 463
Wetzel, R.J., 75, 565
Wheelwright, J.B., 312, 557
Whipple, E.C., 195, 196, 566
White, R.W., 66, 350, 467, 560, 566
Whiting, J.W.M., 474, 554
Whitmont, E.C., 308, 309, 311, 566
Wickens, D.D., 35, 333, 566
Wiggins, J.S., 180, 566
Will, D.P., 564
Wilson, J.P., 561
Wiseman, R.J., 258, 566
Wolfenstein, M., 278, 566
Wolpe, J., 254, 255, 514, 515, 518, 566
Wood, J.K., 563
Woods, R.L., 260, 566
Wright, H.F., 36, 552, 560
Wundt, W., 453
Wynne, L.C., 507, 564

Young, W., 36, 566

Ziegler, D.J., 180, 558
Zimet, C.M., 59, 551
Zubok, B., 554

Subject Index

Ability, 194, 226, 374
Abstraction, 29
Acceptance of self and others, 13, 24, 119
Accuracy of a theory, 22, 66, 118, 121,
    127, 136-42, 172, 173, 181, 196, 197,
    226, 227, 258, 282, 283, 314, 355,
    356, 393, 431, 433, 441, 478, 479,
    496, 518
  degrees of, 138
  and depth, 139
  determining the, 138
  of models and, 184, 185
  and power, 140, 258
Achievement
  motivation, 63
  need for. See Need, achievement
Acquisition
  of conditioned reflexes, 76
  curve of, 77
  of imitation habits, 154, 155
  of new behavior pattern, 77, 508, 509
  rate of, 77
Action, 219, 221, 236, 339, 466
Activities Index (AI), 61
Actones, 57, 58, 69
Actualizing tendency, 111, 120, 121
  analysis of construct, 120
  as motive, 111, 121
  and self-actualization, 121
Adaptiveness, 62
Adjustment and maladjustment, 29, 31,
  112, 113, 489, 490
Adolescence, 271, 272, 346-49
Affect, 35, 235-37, 243, 280
Affectia, 376-79
Affiliation, 128
  need for. See Need, affiliation
Agencies, in Freud's theory, 208-86
  passim, 340
Aggression, 168, 270, 504, 509
  conflicts involving, 257
  frustration and, 150
  instinct of, 223, 241, 258
  as measured erg, 384-86

models of, 150, 161, 165, 504
  need for. See Need, aggression
  targets of, 158-61, 168, 169, 280, 504
  turned against self, 238, 241, 247
Aggressive energy, 237, 238, 280, 329
Aggressive feelings, 158
Airline hostesses and pilots, 16 PF pro-
  files, 391
Alcohol, 258, 434, 493, 516
Alpha press, 56, 180, 465
Ambition, 276
Amnesia, 327, 328
Anal stage
  and character formation, 275, 276
  in Erikson's theory, 342-46
  in Freud's theory, 269
Analytical (Jungian) psychotherapy, 308,
  309, 327, 425
Anger, 115, 155, 342, 431
Anima and animus, 305, 306
Anticipation, 38, 91, 240
Anxiety
  Cattell's model, 361, 379, 380, 385,
    386, 390, 458, 459
  Eysenck's model, 431-34, 458, 459
  Freud's model, 210, 235-62 passim,
    387, 411
  MacKinnon's model (based on Lewin's
    theory), 478
  Miller and Dollard's model, 161-65
  moral, 240
  neurotic, 240
  and phobia, 38, 254, 255
  and reality, 240
  Rogers's model, 112, 113
  in stress reaction, 183
  in syndrome of insecurity, 11
Anxiety reaction, 240, 423, 515
Approach tendencies, 156, 157, 469-71
  gradients in, 156, 157
Archetypes, 294, 295, 304-8, 326, 327, 403
Arousal, 199, 257
Articulation of theory, 135, 150
Ascendance, 53, 61, 68

Assertion, as measured erg, 384-89
Assessment, 57-62, 66, 505
Assumptions, 2, 3, 64, 117, 119, 127-46
  passim, 181, 183, 184, 199, 254-57,
  363, 425, 437-40, 517, 541
  compared with hypotheses and laws,
    130
  empirical, 98, 130, 132, 149-76 passim,
    185, 186, 188, 230, 281, 361, 374,
    505
  Freud's basic and special, 131, 212,
    267, 280
  humanistic, 134
  Lewin's basic, 133
  methodological, 130-33, 281, 456, 473,
    484, 504-6, 539
  Skinner's basic, 131
  workshop in, 202, 203
Attention, 162, 432
Attitude, 108, 118, 383
  ergs and, 385
  measurement of, 383-85
  sentiment and, 385
Attitude types, 295-300
Audiogenic seizures, 200
Authority, attitude toward, 257, 273, 342,
  467
Autia, 377-81, 392
Autobiographical material, 67
Autoerotism, 41, 267
Autonomic nervous system, 90, 214, 240,
  378, 429, 432
Autonomy, 191, 343
  need for. See Need, autonomy
  versus doubt stage, 342-44
Avoidance tendencies, 156, 157, 469-71
  gradients in, 156, 157
Awareness, 109-12, 214, 218, 343
  availability to, 110, 113, 119, 216, 239,
    257, 529
  memory and, 119, 183, 216
  periphery of, 109
  symbolization and, 110, 119, 132, 529
  therapist's, 114

Bandura: brief biography, 503
Bandura and Walters's theoretical models
  of acquisition of behavior patterns, 508, 509
  of imitation, 507-13, 519, 520, 539
  of socialization, 505, 506
Bandura and Walters's theory, 149, 503-22
  accomplishments, 513-15
  critique, 515-19
  of function, 503-22
Barrier, 466, 469
Bedwetting, 75, 142, 251-53, 276
Behavior
  abnormal, 27
  body and, 39-42, 45, 215, 431
  causal properties of, 38
  change, 33, 101
  characteristic, 30, 118, 191, 265, 454, 455, 531
  complex, 84, 86, 92, 195
  construct of, 98
  control of, 89, 97
  covert, 98
  defined by Rogers, 121
  defined by Skinner, 75
  in definition of personality, 29, 40, 41, 73, 104, 171, 531
  determinants of, 29-38, 72, 73, 97, 186, 188, 194, 209, 235, 239, 257, 342, 363, 387, 429, 440, 456
  discriminative, 93
  emotional, 90, 92, 201, 484
  as envelope of dependent variables, 531
  experience and, 34-46 passim, 191, 479
  expressive, 531
  frequency of, 75, 80, 82
  as function of person and environment, 188, 464-67
  as a function of traits, 361
  goal-directed, 121, 347, 484, 531
  individual control of own, 94
  influence, 30
  integration of, 84
  maintenance of, 83
  matched-dependent, 152-55
  out of control, 90
  overt, 3, 98, 133, 186
  as part of personality, 41, 171, 353
  pattern of, 73, 119, 504, 505, 508
  potential, 484, 527
  potentials for, 324, 508
  problem, 493, 494
  psychophysical systems and, 29, 33, 479
  record of. See Record, of behavior
  relation to stimuli, 73
  same behaviors, 152, 519
  science of, 30, 92, 98
  self-directed, 108
  social, 92, 281, 282
  stimulus control of, 30, 33, 34, 84, 95
  therapy, 11, 94, 200, 255, 429
  unemitted, 98
  values and, 111
  variables, 93-95, 98
  verbal, 94, 95, 99
  workshop in, 42, 43
Behavior modification, 33, 75, 95, 101, 503, 504, 514-18

self-directed, 102
workshop in, 102, 103
Behaviorism, 4, 6, 96-98, 193, 517
  language of, 92, 96, 538
  radical, 30-35
Beta press, 34, 40, 465
"Black holes," 187
Body
  behavior and, 40-45, 215, 279, 281, 431, 527
  causal properties of, 40, 41, 121, 238, 267, 271, 293, 527
  in definition of personality, 29, 40, 41, 121, 525-27
  discharge of energy in, 235
  experience and, 40, 41, 96, 221, 258, 267, 270, 293, 527
  influences on, 40, 41, 209, 269, 273, 274, 363, 527
  -mind problem, 214
  as part of personality, 44, 121, 221, 239, 240, 266, 267, 270, 282, 341, 431, 525
  psychophysical systems and, 39, 40, 44, 45, 171, 239, 266, 267, 431
  shape, 44
  structures and processes of, 39-42, 73, 74, 240, 267, 269, 429
  workshop in, 44, 45
Brain
  and behavior, 35, 186, 294, 434
  and consciousness, 35, 214
  and experience, 35, 208, 214, 294
  midbrain, 108, 196, 432-34
  and psychological structures, 39, 266, 294, 365, 377, 429, 432
  and simulation, 541
Breast, 57, 238, 267, 344, 512

Canonical variates, 427, 428
Cases
  Anne, a truant, 75, 78, 94, 101
  Bobby, matched-dependent learning, 153
  boy with symbolic masturbation, 216
  Dora, a case of hysteria, 210, 244, 248-53
  Earnst, an engineering student, 52, 60
  girl with obsession, 246
  girl with symptoms symbolic of sexual movements, 216, 244
  Harold, a case of nystagmus due to unresolved oedipal conflicts, 273
  Hartley Hale, becomes productive only when someone shows interest, 66, 67
  hungry guest, a behavioral analysis, 95
  Instructor's dilemma, thinking through a personal problem, 164
  Little Hans, a case of childhood phobia, 242-45, 254, 270
  Martin Luther, identity formation in a creative person, 351, 352
  Mrs. T., a hospitalized patient, 59
  neurodermatitis, 41
  patient's dreams dealing with sexual conflicts, 211
  patient's dreams early in treatment, 211
  patient's dreams late in treatment, 211

patient's dreams with "broken heart" symbol, 304
patient's dreams with "world clock" symbol, 306
patient with hysterical deafness, 293
Peter, a case of anal retention, 343
phobia in a pilot, 164, 165
a physician's religious experience, 331
a prosperous business collapses: effects of compensation, 298
psychotherapy patient showing displaced hostility, 158
Rick, a bed-wetter, 75, 94, 101
systematic desensitization of an acute anxiety reaction, 515
young man on a date, a case of spontaneous self-study, 166
young woman, a case of change in an entire syndrome, 10, 11
Castration, 216, 242, 245, 282
  anxiety, 242, 270, 276, 278, 345
  complex. See Complex, castration
  symbols of, 216, 243
Catharsis, 209
Cathexis, 218, 222, 227, 236, 245, 246, 332, 505
Cattell: brief biography, 362, 363
Cattell's theoretical models
  anxiety, 380-82
  conflict, 387, 388
  ego, self, and superego, 377-92 passim, 399-420 passim
  extraversion, 376-80
  inner control, 382
Cattell's theories
  accomplishments, 389-92
  of cause, 387-89, 532
  critique of, 392-94
  of function, 361-96
  of structure, 377-87, 448-51
Causal forces, 3, 73, 74, 121
Causal inference, 73
  from dependent and independent variables, 187
Causal relations, 180, 187, 506
  inner systems of, 31, 33, 186, 504, 517
  in personality, 29, 32-39, 186
  in theories of cause, 185-87, 235-62
  in theories of function, 187
Causation (or causal action), 133
  experimental manipulation, 187, 505, 506
  "natural," 187
  physical, 39
  psychological, 39, 184, 187, 212, 504
  Skinner's model, 91, 92, 187
  structure and process in, 39, 136
Cause, 72, 188
  acting, 186
  hidden, 73, 136, 185, 235, 255, 442
  meanings of, 186
  mechanisms of, 136, 137, 496
  stream of, 97
  theory of. See Theory, of cause
  uncaused, 94
  unrecognized cause, 186, 235, 356, 442
Cerebral cortex, 186, 196, 200, 432, 434
  balance of excitatory and inhibitory potentials, 186, 196, 199, 434-36

Chain or sequence
of discriminative stimuli and responses, 79, 84-86, 92, 505
of fractional anticipatory cue-producing responses, 163, 170
of reinforcements, 486
Characteristics, 194, 243
core (in self-actualizing people), 13-25, 201
dynamic, 11, 29
pattern of, 3, 10, 191, 453, 454
of self or ego, 110, 222, 347
static, 11
structural, 29
Children's Personality Questionnaire (CPQ), 392
Classification, 162, 180, 190, 201
workshop in, 144-46
Clitoris, 271
Cognition, 35
experience and, 35
need for. See Need, cognition
in Skinner's theory, 86-88, 92, 94
Cognitive
appraisals, 182, 183
processes or processing, 183, 188, 432, 516
theory, 100, 101
Collective unconscious. See Unconscious, collective
College Characteristics Index (CCI), 61
Community feeling, 13, 24
Comparisons of theories, 321-36, 353-55, 447-60
workshop in, 394, 395, 459
Compensation, 4, 272, 297, 298, 308-10, 357
Competing theories, 185, 321-36, 353, 503-22
models, 185, 200, 332, 399-420, 504-6, 519, 537
requirements for, 196, 321, 332, 537
workshop in, 520
Complex
castration, 270
claustral, 58, 142, 180, 186
in Freud's theory, 222, 255, 505
in Jung's theory, 300, 301, 307
in Murray's theory, 57, 58, 66, 67, 180, 186, 191
Oedipal, 222, 255, 270, 273, 326, 345, 351
Complexity of a theory, 64, 65, 313, 314, 431
Composite score, 427
Condensation, 244, 245, 249
Conditioning, 7, 80, 99, 429
acquisition and, 77
of anxiety responses, 254
in Bandura and Walters's theory, 504, 507, 514, 518
cognitive theoretical model of, 101
ease of, 101
extinction and, 77, 100
in Eysenck's theory, 433-44 passim
in Miller and Dollard's theory, 149-76 passim
operant, 30, 43, 78-104, 514
reinforcement and, 78, 82, 99

respondent, 75-78
in Skinner's theory, 75-104
Type R, 75, 78-104 passim, 507
Type S, 75-78, 84-87, 93, 507, 516
verbal, 99
with and without awareness in adult humans, 99-101, 172, 440, 441, 518, 539-41
Conditions of worth, 111, 112, 114, 120-22, 400-420 passim
Confirmation and disconfirmation of hypotheses, 127, 131, 181, 258, 278, 283, 537, 540
Conflict, 136, 155-61, 181, 200, 209, 226, 239, 256, 258, 301, 323, 328, 333, 345, 387, 388, 392
line, 158
maximum point, 158
models of, 155-61, 166-68, 256-58, 387, 388, 469-71
neurosis and, 38, 163-65, 265, 274
workshop in, 479, 480
Congruence, 112, 114, 117, 132
Conjunctivity, 55
Conscience, 222, 240, 351
Consciousness, 6, 31, 35, 96, 110, 214-86 passim
contents of, 34, 35, 120
Freud's model of, 215-18, 227-31, 323
Jung's model of, 291-93, 324
in Maslow's theory, 3
in Rogers's theory, 109, 110, 119
stream of, 31
withdrawal of, 163-65, 246, 293
workshop in, 227-31
Consequences of behavior, 94
Constants (scientific), 135, 137
Constructs, 66, 67, 73, 98, 119, 127-46 passim, 151, 181, 184-87, 197, 312, 394, 399-420 passim, 473, 484, 496, 517, 539, 541
compared with concepts, 128, 199
comparisons of, 400-420, 496, 529, 530
defined, 128
full meaning of, 139
mediational, 171, 189, 504
mental, 208
neurological, 74, 208, 212
psychodynamic, 280, 504, 505
psychophysical system, 527-29
types of, 195
workshop in, 356, 357, 419, 420
Contingency, 89, 92, 97
awareness of, 100, 101
and environment, 30, 281, 528
response-reinforcement, 100, 168, 201, 528
stimulus-response, 33, 79, 86, 97, 281
workshop in, 173, 174
Control group, 229, 230, 258, 335, 510
Controls
of behavior, 33, 34, 94, 240
in Cattell's theory, 379, 382, 386, 390
in Freud's theory, 182, 274, 345
by higher mental processes, 163
in Jung's theory, 325, 328, 330
social, 92
stimulus control, 34, 94, 517
of variables, 141

Copying, 152, 181, 508, 519
Correlation, 73, 78, 79, 92, 94, 128, 129, 364-74
Correlation coefficient, 365-70, 547-48
Cortertia, 379-82, 386, 390
Creativity, 6, 13, 23, 44, 117, 134, 306, 348, 351
Crime, 246, 429, 440
Cues, 149-76 passim, 181, 504
response-produced, 161, 181
Culture, 4, 6, 38, 190, 224, 227, 269, 297, 322, 339, 340, 346, 348
Cumulative recorder, 81
Curiosity, 55, 253, 269, 345, 385

Data, scientific nature of, 74, 75, 79, 137-42, 506
workshop in, 143
Daydreams, 93, 241, 466
Death instinct, 220, 221, 238, 242, 329
Defecation or elimination, 58, 90, 238, 269, 275, 276, 343
Defense mechanisms, 120, 182, 236, 244, 246, 256, 258, 274, 283-85, 326
condensation, 244
denial, 112, 113, 117, 132, 142, 183, 529
displacement, 136, 155, 156, 244
distortion in awareness, 112, 113, 117
failure of, 120
projection, 247, 258, 326
reaction formation, 248, 274, 276, 326
repression, 163, 182, 221, 224, 235-62 passim, 293-318 passim, 322, 529
reversal, 248
sublimation, 247, 280
suppression, 258
workshop in inferring, 283-85
Defensiveness, 132
Deference. See Need, deference
Definitions, 64, 376, 377
Definitions of personality, 3, 28-46 passim, 41, 44, 72, 107, 171, 172, 479, 525-32
diagrams illustrating, 25, 40, 41, 69, 104, 123, 176, 231, 262, 318, 358, 444, 481, 499, 521
Delusions, 191, 426
Democratic character, 13, 24
Dependency, 61, 275, 385, 467
Depression, 140, 141, 223, 275, 423
Deprivation, 61, 92, 219, 506
Depth of theory, 97, 127, 136-42, 173, 227, 258, 283, 315, 356, 393, 394, 441, 479, 497, 519
meaning of, 136, 142
risks associated with greater, 137
Description, 135, 201, 505
of behavior, 73, 79, 98, 505
of contingencies, 79, 99
quantitative, 145
as a response, 98
Detachment, quality of, 13, 24
Diagnostic testing, 59, 425
Differentiation, 221, 222, 243, 471, 476-78
Dimension, 423-44 passim
of cue-relevance, 167

of stimulus-dissimilarity, 157-60, 166, 181
See also Factors
Diplomacy, 34
Discrimination, 86, 151, 153, 432, 504, 507
  training, 86, 504
Disgust, 244, 250, 274
Disjunctivity, 55
Displacement, 136, 155, 156, 181, 244, 249, 504
Dispositions, 49, 73, 171, 363, 494
Dollard: brief biography, 150
Dominance, 53, 54, 62, 128, 191, 330
  need for. *See* Need, dominance
Dreams, 37, 210-12, 218, 221, 246, 282, 289, 308, 466
  Freud's model of, 235, 241, 244, 248-53, 326, 333
  interpretation of, 209, 210, 224, 250-53, 259, 260, 310, 311
  Jung's model of, 309-11, 333, 403
  manifest and latent content of, 249, 250-53, 258, 333
  representation in, 250
  Skinner's model of, 93
  substitutions in, 251-53
  -work, 250
  workshop in, 259-60
Drives
  in Bandura and Walters's theory, 504
  Epstein's definitions of, 166
  in Eysenck's theory, 432, 433
  in Freud's theory, 243, 257, 258
  measurement of, 166
  in Miller and Dollard's theory, 150-76 passim, 181
  Skinner's model of, 88, 92
  strength of, 89, 156, 167
Drugs, 258, 429, 439, 440
Dualism, 34
Dynamic calculus, 387
Dynamics
  group. *See* group dynamics
  of personality, 13, 186, 237

Early School Personality Questionnaire (ESPQ), 392
Education, 92, 94, 96, 137, 340, 345, 429
Edwards' Personal Preference Schedule (EPPS), 61
Ego, 74, 399-420
  and anxiety, 237, 240, 241, 248
  in Cattell's theory, 380
  -defense, 237, 246, 248
  described by Freud, 221, 222
  development, 339-41
  in Erikson's theory, 339-41, 346
  in Freud's theory, 208-86 passim, 324, 328, 340, 527
  in Jung's theory, 293-318 passim, 324, 326
  psychology, 226, 282
  strength of, 224, 377-81, 390, 448, 449
Ego identity, 340, 346
Embarrassment, 94
Emotion, 183, 199, 219, 221
  and affect, 239
  in Bandura and Walters's theory, 507

in Cattell's theory, 377, 378
conditioned emotional reaction, 507, 514
in Freud's theory, 182, 214, 215, 219, 235-62 passim
in Jung's theory, 294, 301
in Lewin's theory, 464
in Miller and Dollard's theory, 165, 171
and physiological responses, 239, 432, 433
in Rotter's theory, 484
Skinner's model of, 90-92
Watson's model of, 514
Empathic understanding, 113, 114, 118
  workshop in, 122
Empirical basis, 127, 137, 142, 181, 426
  and criterion of accuracy, 139
  and criterion of depth, 139
  and criterion of fruitfulness, 140
  defined, 137
  further meaning of, 138
Encoding, 35, 516
Energic components of personality, 57
Energy, 182
  discharge, 236, 238, 241, 271, 297
  emotional, 240, 244, 301
  physical energy, 44, 212-15, 235, 236, 302
  in physics, 195
  psychological or mental energy, 132, 218, 235, 238, 239, 256, 303, 325, 326, 495
  sources of, 237, 238, 240, 249, 302
  spiritual, 303
Environment, 6, 188
  action on, 221, 267
  in definition of behavior, 75, 98
  as envelope of causes or determinants, 32, 39, 73, 84, 188, 194, 377, 378, 429, 437, 438
  feedback from, 99
  geographic, 479
  meaningful, 50, 483
  perceived or psychological, 73, 468-77, 479, 530
  physical, 31
  pressures from, 55, 73
  relation of, to definition of personality, 30, 32, 41, 51, 84, 267
  responses to, 29
  similarity of two or more, 437
  social or cultural, 31, 94, 341
Erg, 384-89, 526
Ergic tension. *See* Tension, ergic
Erikson: brief biography, 339-41
Erikson's theoretical model of identity, 346-48, 399-420 passim
Erikson's theory
  accomplishments of, 350-52
  critique of, 352-56
  of pattern, 339-58
  research on, 350
Erogenous zones, 266-70, 274, 279, 525
Erotism
  excitation of, 267, 269
  in Erikson's theory, 342
  in Freud's theory, 266-86
  skin, 267
Excitatory potentials, 186, 196, 434-36

Exhibitionism, 41, 247, 270
  need for. *See* Need, exhibition
Expectancy
  in Rotter's theory, 484, 485, 496
  in Tolman's theory, 494, 495
Experience, 133, 215, 243, 247, 324, 331, 339-41, 529-31
  affective or emotional, 35, 214, 239, 341
  awareness and, 109, 110, 119, 132, 529
  behavior and, 34, 35, 38, 42-45, 191, 339, 479
  body and, 40, 41, 45, 110, 215, 282
  causal properties of, 35, 38, 121, 272
  characteristic, 29, 265
  childhood, 219, 265-86, 339, 358
  conscious, 3, 109, 110, 113, 119, 214, 215, 342, 456
  considered as behavior, 34, 92-94, 484
  construct of, 109, 119
  defined by Rogers, 109
  in definition of personality, 31, 40, 41, 122, 479, 529-31
  determinants of, 29, 35, 118, 235, 244, 257, 363
  divisions of, 122
  environment and, 110, 122
  evidence of direct, 109
  imaginative, 37
  inner, 29, 36-38, 91, 99, 101, 289, 375
  in Lewin's theory, 464-81 passim, 483
  openness to, 110, 111, 132
  as part of personality, 35, 267, 353
  peak, 16, 18, 24
  potentially conscious, 109, 215
  potentials for, 324
  psychophysical systems and, 29, 479
  record of. *See* Record, experience
  in Rogers's theory, 107-24 passim
  in Rotter's theory, 483-99 passim
  self-experiences, 110-12, 120, 122
  subjective, 5, 6, 31, 32, 45, 72, 96, 107-25, 171, 496
  symbolized, 110, 112, 529
  unaware, theoretical problem of, 529-31
  workshop in, 42, 43
Experiencing, 109, 117, 133
Experiment
  clinical compared with cognitive, 141
  confrontation, 520, 529, 540
  crucial, 139, 333-35, 539
  demand characteristics of, 468
  design, 100, 173, 174, 199, 333-35, 520
  dissociation, 99
  independent and dependent variables in, 187
  instances of, 85, 91, 117, 154, 160, 167, 185, 198-200, 256, 257, 363, 364, 432-44 passim, 467, 471-73, 509, 510-12, 540
  replication, 538
  results of as model object, 198, 199, 202, 442, 537-39
  subjects' guesses in, 100, 101, 441, 518
  workshop in, 173, 174, 228-32, 333-35, 520
Experimental analysis of behavior, 79-104 passim

Explanation, 73, 95, 128, 133, 214, 529
  of general facts as goal of scientific
    theories, 128, 129, 181, 201
  mentalistic or psychodynamic, 473
  task of theoretical models, 183, 199,
    201
Extinction
  in Bandura and Walters's theory, 504,
    507, 514
  of conditioned operants, 83, 85, 89
  of conditioned respondents, 77
  curve of, 77, 83, 89, 100
  in Miller and Dollard's theory, 151
  in Skinner's theory, 77, 83, 88
  spontaneous recovery from, 83, 151,
    504
  of undesired behavioral responses, 514
Extraversion and introversion, 141, 198
  and brain function, 196, 434, 440, 452
  Cattell's model of, 376-80, 386, 387,
    390
  and conditionability, 435, 436
  and cultural pressures, 297
  as defined by Eysenck, 431
  as defined by Jung, 296
  and drug effects, 439, 440
  Eysenck's model of, 185, 196, 198, 431,
    434-36
  Gray's model of, 196
  heritability of, 297, 376-78, 436
  Jung's model of, 295-300
  measurement of, 312, 313, 376-78, 430
  and memory, 141, 198
  second-stratum source trait of, 379
Extravert, 186, 198-200, 295-98, 423-44
    passim
Eysenck: brief biography, 423, 424
Eysenck Personality Inventory (EPI),
    430-44 passim
Eysenck's theoretical models, 186
  anxiety, 431-34
  drug effects, 439, 440
  extraversion-introversion, 436-38
  genetic effects on psychoticism, 436-38
  neuroticism, 432-34
Eysenck's theories, 199
  accomplishments of, 438-40
  of cause, 432-39, 532
  critique of, 440-42
  of function, 423-44
  research on, 430-36 passim
  of structure, 429-32

Factors and factor analysis, 194, 364-74,
    424, 429-32, 456-59
  Cattell's method of, 371-74, 456-58
  Eysenck's method of, 374, 424, 456-58
  meaning of factors in, 365, 395, 454
  number of factors problem in, 367-70,
    440, 456-59
  number of personality factors in Cat-
    tell's model of, 377-87, 456
  number of personality factors in Eysen-
    ck's model of, 429-30, 454, 456
  order of factoring in, 376-80, 456-58
  order of factors and strata of personal-
    ity in, 378-80, 404-7, 456
  Pearson's method of, 370, 371, 424,
    456

purpose of, 364, 365
relationship of, to correlation coefficients, 367-70, 395, 454
rotation of factors in, 371-74, 392
theory of personality structure and,
  374-80, 429-32, 451-55
theory of system and, 535
Facts, 127, 254, 279, 425, 442
  accounted for by theory, 181
  as basis for theory, 425
  clinical, 221
  experimental, 127, 128, 199, 200, 442,
    538, 539
  general, 127-29
  as model object, 198, 199, 201, 533
  new, discovered by scientists, 128, 201,
    212
  new, predicted by theory, 135, 426, 442
  particular, 127, 128
  sets of, in tests of competing models,
    195
Faith, 303, 342, 347, 352, 418
Family influences, 437, 438, 506
  See also Parental influences
Fantasy, 63, 93, 241-44, 267, 282, 466,
  497
  unconscious, 209, 276, 278, 294, 308,
    326
Father, image of, 271, 326, 332
Fear, 142, 219, 240, 251-53, 294, 431, 464
  as acquirable drive, 161, 165, 507
  as measured erg, 384-87
  of snakes, 514
Feeling, 32, 36, 38, 44, 50, 114, 171, 212,
  243, 246, 332, 409
  of acceptability, 111
  of adequacy, 111
  ambivalence of, 219
  of anger, 114
  of anxiety, 111, 240
  awareness of, 114
  discussion of, 118
  and emotion, 239
  in Freud's theory, 219, 239, 243
  of guilt, 223
  of happiness, 240, 302, 303
  of hate, 219
  incongruent, 114
  of inferiority, 4, 475
  in Jung's theory, 291-318 passim, 324,
    456
  of love, 219, 240
  mixtures of, 219
  of pain, 240
  of pleasure, 268, 269
  of rejection, 219, 363
  in Rogers's theory, 108, 109
  of shame, 38, 342, 531
  of sorrow, 219
  of worth, 111, 342
Field
  converging, 470
  as experienced or perceived, 121, 464,
    467
  of force, 135, 470, 471
  physical, 135
  theory. See Theory, field
  workshop in, 479, 480
Fixation, 271-75, 283, 326

Force
  in biology, 268
  driving and restraining, 469
  in physics, 130, 187, 188, 235
  in psychology, 132, 188, 235, 238, 239,
    281, 438, 464, 468, 476-78, 505
  and valence, 469, 484
  workshop in, 479, 480
Formalism of theories, 64, 65, 131
Free association, 209, 220, 224
Free will, 94, 97, 292
Freedom of movement
  in Lewin's theory, 488
  in Rotter's theory, 487, 488, 492-94
Freshness of appreciation, 15, 24
Freud: brief biography, 207-12
Freud's theoretical models
  anxiety, 235-62 passim, 387, 411
  consciousness, 215-18, 227-31, 321-36
    passim
  dreams, 248-53
  the ego, 220-23, 399-420 passim
  neurosis, 163, 185, 246, 265, 272, 274,
    327, 426-29
  reaction to stress, 182
  the unconscious, 163, 321-36 passim
Freud's theories, 131, 150, 185, 197
  accomplishments of, 224, 248-53,
    277-80
  of cause, 185, 186, 195, 235-62, 326-32,
    532
  critique of, 224-27, 253-59, 280-83
  of pattern, 186, 195, 265-86
  research on, 225-27, 256-59, 278-80
  of structure, 186, 195, 207-32, 323-26,
    447
Fruitfulness of a theory, 66, 121, 127,
  137-42, 173, 227, 257, 283, 314, 356,
  393, 441, 479, 496, 518, 519
Frustration, 55, 241, 274, 342, 433, 475
  tolerance, 280
Frustrative nonreward, 507
Fully functioning person, 109, 112, 117,
  180, 192
Function, theory of. See Theory, of function
Functional relationship, 187, 188
  antecedent-consequent, 505
Fusion of needs or instincts, 52, 239, 268

Generalization as inferential process, 119,
  128, 184, 189, 253, 426, 431, 441,
  442
Generalization of learning, 151, 154, 504,
  507
  curve of, 86
  of expectancies, 485, 494, 495
  of gradients of approach and
    avoidance, 157, 161
  stimulus and/or response, 85, 99, 151,
    154
Generation gap, 277
Generativity versus stagnation stage, 349
Genetics, 377-82, 440
  biometrical, 437
  twin studies and, 436-38
Genital stage
  in Erikson's theory, 346-49
  in Freud's theory, 271, 272

in relation to identity and intimacy, 346-49
in relation to mental health, 277
Genitals, 216, 242-45, 250, 254, 256, 267, 269-71, 276, 278, 340, 344, 512
Genuineness of therapist, 114, 118
Gestalt psychology, 4, 463, 464
Glands, 42, 43, 74, 90, 91, 213, 215, 235, 237-39
Goal, 52, 244, 347, 466, 484
distance from, 156, 158
objects, 73, 243
psychological distance from, 188, 347
valence of, 188, 468-72
God, 302, 303, 327, 328, 331, 351, 352
Grades, 63, 475, 487
Group dynamics, 22, 473
Guilt, 191, 250, 256, 294, 344, 351, 352
and the ego, 237, 240
feelings of, 41, 45, 223, 246, 345
as a form of anxiety, 240
and the superego, 222, 223, 240, 272
Guilt proneness, 377-81

Habit, 23, 39, 44, 133, 149-75 passim, 181, 195, 281
strength, 188
Hallucinations, 191, 241, 243, 245, 426
"Hard" versus "soft" science, 140-42
related to accuracy, 142
Hate, 219, 242, 247, 323
Heart-rate, 90, 100, 161, 433
Heredity, 429, 505, 549, 550
Hierarchy of needs
Maslow's theory of, 6
model of, 7, 9
prepotency in, 7, 9
High School Personality Questionnaire (HSPQ), 392
Higher mental processes, 161-65, 169, 238, 516
Hostility, 158, 219, 238, 242, 247
Humanistic psychologists, 5, 117, 133, 517
Humanistic psychology, 5, 108, 117
as science, 21
systems theory and, 535
tenets of, 5, 535
Humor, 248, 492
philosophic, 15
Hunger, 109, 155, 236, 238, 266, 269, 495
Hypnosis, 208, 216, 218, 258, 272, 515
Hypothalamus, 431, 436
Hypothesis, 64, 99, 127-46 passim, 181, 182, 184, 185, 197, 199, 321, 425, 541
basic client-centered, 108, 118, 119
causal, 129, 185, 196
confirmation of, 131, 158
deduced from explicit empirical assumptions, 156-59, 199, 436-38, 473
instances of, 108, 115-19, 129, 131, 185, 214, 235, 249, 256, 272, 278, 282, 297, 356, 377, 430-40, 466, 471-73, 508-12
illustrated, 129
of inner structures and processes in personality, 30, 86, 91, 98, 99, 149, 256, 271, 374-80, 431, 504, 516, 517

scientific, 119, 129, 425
testable, 130, 142
tests of, 127, 129, 130, 154, 181, 185, 278, 282, 425-27, 471-73, 539
theoretical models and, 156-61, 196, 197, 431, 539, 541
validity of, 108, 161
varying in importance, 138
workshop dealing with, 143-45, 202, 203, 520
Hysteria versus dysthymia, 424
See also Neurosis, hysterical

I (myself), 31, 94, 418, 419
Id, 74, 208-86 passim, 324, 533
described, 220, 221
thought processes and, 221, 225, 243
Idea, 208, 212, 216-18, 221, 239, 243, 247, 323, 324, 409
association of, 250-53
Identification
in Freud's theory, 221, 222, 270, 392
in identity elements, 346-48
Identity, 399-420 passim
as composite image, 348
elements of, 346-48
Erikson's model of, 346-48, 408-10
formation of, 191, 346
inner sense of, 31
psychosocial moratorium and, 347, 348
versus identity confusion stage, 346-48
Imagery, 63, 94, 333
creative, 37
in Jung's theory, 301, 312
in Murray's theory, 57, 58
in new account of identity, 348
in planning, 37, 38
Skinner's model of, 92-95
visual, 183, 218, 515
Images, 37, 50, 57, 67, 72, 171, 183, 188, 218, 222, 236, 271, 324, 346, 409, 537
archetypal or primordial, 303-6, 323-26, 333, 402-4
hypnagogic, 37
intrusion of, 183
Imitation
Bandura and Walters's model, 507-13, 519, 520
children's, 99
Miller and Dollard's model, 150, 152-55, 506, 507, 519, 520
workshop in, 173, 174, 520
Impulse, 6, 188, 238, 240
dangerous or destructive, 163, 220, 237, 258
instinctual, 155, 210, 219, 221, 237, 244, 247, 258, 292
sensory, 200
sexual or erotic, 41, 45, 220, 251-53, 258, 271, 345
unconscious, 6, 163, 283-85, 333, 541
Impulsiveness, 430, 431, 454, 455
Incentive value, 63, 509
negative, 63
Incongruence, of self-concept, 112, 114, 121
Incongruent behaviors, 121
Incorporation, 269, 341

Individual differences, 197, 227, 281, 363, 533
in behavioral characteristics, 186
in conditioning phenomena, 101
in functioning of the nervous system, 186
in therapy clients, 118, 119, 121
Individuation, 308, 309, 413, 414
Industry versus inferiority stage, 345, 346
Inferiority, feelings or sense of, 4, 345
Information, 182, 213, 214, 384
and computer models, 189
and imagery, 189, 516
Information processing, 189, 194, 516, 536
Inhibition
hypothesis for extraversion, 434, 439
learning theory and, 157, 434, 507
psychoanalytic theory and, 210, 236, 240
reactive, 434
reciprocal, 254, 514, 515
Inhibitory potentials, 186, 196, 434-36
Initiative versus guilt stage, 344, 345, 356
Insecurity, 11, 142
innate, 39
Instincts, 219, 221, 222, 236-38, 241, 295, 324, 325, 329, 525
aim, 238, 248, 266, 271
destructive, 163, 220, 237, 238, 266
impetus, 238, 239
integration of partial sex-, 272, 274
object, 238, 247, 266
self-preservative, 221, 222, 237, 238, 240, 266, 326
sex, 133, 235, 238, 251-53, 266, 326
source, 238
Integrity versus despair stage, 349
Intellectual ability, 63
Intelligence, 429, 440
Intentions, 97, 98
Internal frame of reference, 113, 114, 180
Interview, 65, 66, 107, 115, 116, 142, 350
Intimacy versus isolation stage, 348, 349
Introversion. See Extraversion
Introvert, 4, 186, 198-200, 295-98, 423-44 passim
compensation in, 4
Intuition, 291-318 passim, 324, 456

Jealousy, 220, 253, 271
Joy, 21, 250, 431
Jung: brief biography, 289-91
Jung's theoretical models
consciousness, 291-93, 321-36 passim, 455, 456
dreams, 309-11
ego, 293, 399-420 passim
research on, 312-13
the unconscious, 293-95, 321-36
Jung's theories
accomplishments of, 308-11
of cause, 300-308, 326-32, 452, 453, 532
critique of, 311-15
of pattern, 295-300, 452, 453
of structure, 291-95, 323-26

Kymograph, instrument to record behavior, 81, 82

Language, 163, 170
  acquisition, 94, 99, 170
  community, 94, 99, 170
  English sentences, 99
  everyday, 92, 93
  grammar, 99
  Miller and Dollard's model, 163, 170
  psychological, 133
  Skinner's model, 94, 99
Latency stage, 270, 278, 345, 346
Law, scientific, 29, 127-46 passim, 181,
    195, 321
  causal, 187
  compared with assumptions and
    hypotheses, 130
  of composition, 84, 189
  defined, 129
  instances of, 77, 78, 84-86, 93, 99, 129,
    135, 195, 309, 310, 432, 483
  quantitative, 135
Leadership, 44, 63, 467
Learning, 151, 182, 188, 237, 429, 483,
    503
  paired-associate, 198-200, 256, 333-35,
    433
Lemon test, 431, 435, 454, 455
  workshop in, 442, 443
Level of aspiration, 474-76, 483, 496
Lewin: brief biography, 463, 464
Lewin's theoretical models
  aspiration, 188, 474-76
  conflict, 188, 469-71
  mental retardation, 473
  needs, 468-72
  success and failure experiences, 474
Lewin's theory, 133, 496
  of cause, 468-72, 532
  of function, 188, 463-81
  of structure, 471, 472
Libido, 235-62 passim, 266, 269, 270, 274,
    303, 322, 326, 329
Lie-detector, 35, 542, 543
Life space, 464-69, 477
Love, 7, 11, 55, 219, 323, 330, 348
  need for. See Need, love
  object, 219, 222, 270, 271, 277
  fear of loss of, 155
Lying, 35

Maladjustment and adjustment, 112, 113,
    117, 489, 490
Mandala, 306, 402, 403
Maslow: brief biography, 4-6
Maslow's theoretical models
  needs, 6-9
  self, 411-14
  self-actualization, 5, 12, 399-420
  syndrome of insecurity, 11
Maslow's theory
  accomplishments of, 18-21
  of cause, 3-25, 194
  critique of, 21-22
  of pattern, 3-25, 194
  of priority, 3-25, 194
  research on, 11, 12, 19, 22
Masochism, 242, 247
Masturbation, 216, 242, 245, 246, 267,
    271, 272

Matched-dependent learning, 153-55, 181,
    519, 520
  workshop in, 173, 174, 520
Mathematical analysis, 142
Mathematical topology, 476-78
Meaning, 35, 192, 214, 259, 260
Meaningful, 42, 43, 50, 133
Measurement, 135, 427
  in personality research, 142, 312, 505
  workshop in, 145
Melancholia, 240
Memory, 38, 42, 43, 93, 108, 141, 183,
    208, 209, 213-15, 218, 236, 237, 245,
    271, 278, 301, 388, 537
  active, 183
  awareness and, 113, 215, 216
  consolidation, 199
  experience and, 109, 215
  failure, 117
  forgetting as defense, 117, 247, 256
  immediate, 117, 199
  importance of for theory of personality,
    214
  long-term, 183, 199
  recall, 117, 198, 199
  recognition, 93
  retrieval and, 199, 516
  schemata, 183
  short-term, 183
  storage, 199, 516
  trace, 199, 218
Men, 299, 329, 493, 494
Mental functioning, 237, 295, 455, 456
Mental or psychological disorder, 191,
    376, 426
Metamotivation, 17
Miller: brief biography, 150
Miller and Dollard's theoretical models
  conflict, 150, 155, 179, 181
  displacement, 156-58, 179, 181, 504
  frustration and aggression, 150
  imitation, 150, 152-55, 506, 519, 520
  neurosis, 163-65, 181
Miller and Dollard's theory, 149-76, 181
  accomplishments of, 165-68
  of cause, 149-76 passim, 181, 186, 195,
    532
  critique of, 168-73
  of structure, 149-76 passim, 195
Mind, 34, 57, 92, 96, 108, 214, 216, 221,
    243, 244
Modality and mode in Erikson's theory,
    341, 344
Model object, 181, 197-205 passim, 212,
    255, 340, 538-41
  change in, 199, 200, 340, 537
  meaning of, 197, 198, 201, 533
  possibilities for consensus on, 539
Models (to be imitated), 516
  aggressive, 509-12
  characteristics of, 152, 511, 513
  in copying, 152
  or leaders in matched-dependent learn-
    ing, 153-55
  in observational learning, 507-13, 516
  symbolic, 513, 516
Models (as representations), 179-205
  passim

comparisons of theoretical, 321-36, 394,
    395, 445-61, 520
  competing, 195, 196, 282, 309, 310,
    332, 399-420 passim, 520
  instances of, 179-205 passim
  mathematical, 99, 179, 199, 386-88,
    437, 438, 476-78
  model objects, 181, 197-205 passim,
    212, 313
  theoretical models, 156-60, 170, 179-205
    passim, 249, 254, 291-95, 309-11,
    321-36, 376-78, 392, 433, 434, 437,
    438, 468-76, 502-3 passim, 536-41
  workshop in, 143-45, 202, 203, 520
  various meanings, 179, 197
Mood, 333-35, 426
Moral development, 246
Mother
  archetype of, 294
  image, 271, 279
  in personality development of child, 279
Motivation, 88, 92, 182, 184, 253
  achievement. See Need, achievement
  to approach success, 63
  to avoid failure, 63
  deficiency, 15
  drive and, 6, 150
  growth, 15
  homeostasis, 194
  instinct and, 6, 150, 219
  metamotivation, 17
  need and, 7, 121
  structure of, 383-87
  and temperament, 386, 387
  theory of, 88, 109, 111, 121, 180, 254,
    383-88
  traits of, 375, 383-86
Motivation Analysis Test (MAT), 384,
    385, 390
Mouth, 265, 266, 269, 283, 341, 495
Murray: brief biography, 49-52
Murray's theoretical models
  environmental pressures, 55-57
  needs, 51-70 passim, 180
  personal characteristics in the record,
    57-61
Murray's theory, 49-70
  accomplishments of, 57-63
  of cause, 181, 186, 532
  critique of, 63, 67
  of pattern, 181, 186
Muscles, 39, 42, 74, 95, 208, 213, 215,
    221, 255, 269, 272, 343, 531
Narcissism, as measured erg, 384-88
Need
  abasement, 53, 54, 61
  achievement, 52-54, 61-64
  activation of, 9, 73, 88, 188
  affection, 8
  affiliation, 52, 55
  aggression, 53-55, 59-62
  autonomy or independence, 53, 55
  belongingness, 8
  biological, 6
  cognition, 55
  cognizance, 66
  comfort, physical, 487
  construct of, 88, 180, 533
  construction, 54

deference, 53, 54, 62
dependence, 487
dominance, 53, 61, 62, 487
endurance, 61
esteem, 8
exhibition, 53, 55, 62
frustration of, 275
groups of needs, 53-70 passim, 61, 62
harmavoidance, 58
hierarchy of, 6
instinctoid nature of, 6, 526
integrate, 58, 67
latent, 53
Lewin's model, 188, 464, 468-72
love, 7, 88, 487
manifest, 52-70 passim
Maslow's model, 6-9, 192
Murray's model, 51-70 passim, 180
nurturance, 53, 55, 61, 68
order, 53, 54
physiological, 7
play, 53
potential, 487, 527
recognition, 487
reduction, 188
Rotter's model, 487
safety, 8
satisfaction, 57, 121, 201, 275, 471
seclusion, 58
self-actualization, 8, 193, 201, 526
sentience, 53, 61
sex, 53, 55, 56, 61, 236
Skinner's model, 88, 89
spiritual, 6, 526
subsidiation of, 52
succorance, 58, 61
syndrome formation and, 10
value, 487-89, 527
Nerve
motor, 74, 208
sensory, 74, 208
Nervous system, 24, 39, 42, 74, 199, 215, 424
Neurodermatitis, 41
Neurology, 74, 440
Neurones, 186, 212-14, 236
Neurosis, 39, 140, 323, 426-29
anxiety, 426
Freud's model, 163, 185, 246, 265, 272, 274, 327, 426-29
hysterical, 185, 208, 209, 216, 239, 244, 246, 423, 426
Jung's model, 297, 308, 309
Miller and Dollard's model, 163-65, 181
obsessional-compulsive, 239, 240, 246
symptoms of, 164
Neuroticism
defined, 431
Eysenck's biological model, 432-34
heritability of, 436
measurement of, 430
Nonreward, 507
Nuclear system (in Freud's theory), 213, 214, 236
Nurturance. See Need, nurturance

Object cathexis, 222, 277, 332
Objectivity, 134
Observation, 265, 279, 375, 425, 426, 508
background function of, 508

by children, 99, 339, 340, 507, 509
difference from experiment, 138
scientific, 130, 138, 142, 181, 279
workshop in, 356, 357
Observational learning, 507-13
disinhibitory effect, 510, 512
eliciting effect, 510, 512
inhibitory effect, 510, 512
modeling effect, 510-12
Observer, 42, 43, 98, 516
Obsession. See Neurosis, obsessional-compulsive
Occupation and occupational opportunity, 340, 346, 347
Oedipus complex. See Complex, oedipal
Openness to experience, 110-12
Operant
conditioning, 78
control of, 91
defined, 78
Operations, experimental, 85, 86, 88, 333-35, 506
Opposites (in Jung's theory), 329, 330
Oral stage
in Erikson's theory, 341, 342, 346
in Freud's theory, 269, 275
Orderliness, 54, 61, 62, 275
Organism, 111, 194, 240, 340, 516
Organismic valuing process, 111, 112, 120, 121
Organization in personality, 28, 31, 51, 57, 194, 378-80
Orgasm, 271

Pain, 41, 158, 217, 219, 220, 222, 236, 240, 243, 247, 340, 342, 507
Parental influences, 168, 274, 278, 343, 351, 504, 505
Parmia, 377-81
Parsimony, 128
Pattern
classification, 180, 191, 192, 201
of personality characteristics, 3, 180, 191
temporal, 191, 192, 265, 339-58
theory of. See Theory, of pattern
Peak experience, 16, 18, 19, 24, 142
Peeping Tom, 55, 247
Penis, 161, 242, 245, 254, 256, 269-71, 276, 282, 344
Perception, 27, 93, 214, 216, 218, 221, 295
awareness and, 113, 216
brain functions and, 213
efficiency of in self-actualizing people, 15, 24
experience and, 109
Gestalt theory of, 463, 464
of own body, 221, 222, 236
of self, 110
subliminal, 35, 227, 256, 257, 278
Perceptual conscious, 221, 324
Perceptual wholes, 466
Performance, 516
distinguished from acquisition of responses, 508, 510
novel response, 509
Periodic reconditioning, 83, 84
Permeability of boundaries, 471-73

Person, as technical term, 188, 464, 471-73
Persona, 305, 324, 326, 400-20 passim
Personal unconscious. See Unconscious, personal
Personality, 26
an abstraction from behavior, 29
acquisition by imitation, 154, 155
assessment of, 57-59, 66, 390, 505
as behavior, 29, 33
characteristics, 3, 180, 191, 194, 201
compared with character and temperament, 28, 247
components in definition of, 32ff, 39, 171
development of, 5, 112, 113, 155, 191, 265-86, 340-58, 402-4, 504
dynamics, 141, 161, 186
everyday meanings, 28
healthy, 6, 117, 119, 272, 277
as inner experience, 31
integrative definition of, 40
as learned habits, 150, 155
as organization of systems within the individual, 28, 74, 150, 226, 281, 378-80
paranoid, 247, 258
as pattern of behaviors, 72
relationships with other branches of psychological science, 27
science of, 33, 141, 201, 202, 429
structure, 3, 141, 207-32, 321, 323-25, 365
Personality Research Form (PRF), 62
Personnel selection, 57, 389
Phallic stage, 270, 274, 344-46
Phobia, 38, 241, 254, 519
Physiological needs. See Needs, physiological
Pleasure, 40, 41, 45, 192, 217, 240, 241, 243, 255, 271, 340, 346
centers, in brain, 266
infantile, 57, 266, 280
principle, 219, 237, 241, 243, 249
Positive feedback, 235, 236
Positive regard, 111, 120, 121
conditional, 111, 112
need for, 111, 120, 121
satisfaction, 120
Postulates, 64, 120
Potentials, 5, 6, 19, 44
actualization of, 111, 120, 134
and humanistic psychology, 5, 134
Power, 192, 330
as field of forces, in Lewin's theory, 469-71, 495
of a theory, 140-42, 173, 181, 187, 227, 258, 283, 314, 356, 393, 441, 479, 496, 518
Praise, 75, 91, 92
Preconscious, 216, 218, 323
Prediction, 135, 139, 181, 190
degrees of importance of, 139
as function of theory, 135, 138, 436, 477, 537
instances of, 117, 118, 135, 160, 167, 185, 199, 257, 433-44 passim, 494
opposite, 100
Premsia, 377-81, 388
Pre-School Personality Questionnaire, 392

Press, 51, 55, 57, 67, 180
  aggressive person, 55
  alpha, 56, 180, 465
  beta, 34, 40, 56, 73, 465
  coercion, 55, 60
  dominance, 60
  inferior person, 55
  opposition, 55
  superior person, 55
Primary process thinking, 237, 243, 244, 246, 249, 258-60
Priority, theory of. See Theory, of priority
Private events, 98
Problem-centering, 16, 24
Problem-solving, 93, 101, 164, 165
Problems, 92, 93, 118
Proceedings, 56
Process, 39
  cognitive, 189
  mental, 243
  psychophysical, 39, 45, 239
  underlying, 29
Projection
  in Freud's theory, 219, 242
  in Jung's theory, 314, 315
Projective techniques, 58-61, 425
Propositions, 189
Protension, 377-81, 392
Psyche (psychic or mental), 332, 505
  apparatus, 182, 183, 241
  energy, 303
  trauma, 182
Psychoanalysis, 50, 425
  as treatment procedure, 5, 209, 210, 224, 226, 227, 243, 254, 255
  theory of personality, 6, 41, 58, 67, 182, 183, 257, 339, 392, 505
Psychohistory, 339
Psychological tests, 139, 141, 142, 186, 194, 202, 227, 314, 342, 394, 427, 505
  objective or miniature situation tests, 375, 429
Psychophysical systems, 29, 35, 38, 51, 171, 238, 265, 267, 281, 282, 353, 363, 432
  causal properties of, 29, 33, 527
  defined, 39, 527
  in definition of personality, 29, 41, 49, 121, 171, 527, 528
  workshop in, 44, 45
Psychosexual development, 265-86, 340-58
  erotism in, 266, 267
  stages of, in Erikson's theory, 340-58
  stages of, in Freud's theory, 265-86, 525
Psychosis, 246, 376, 377, 426-29
Psychosocial development, 191, 279, 339-58
  moratorium in, 347-52
Psychosomatic disorders, 41, 227
  theory of, 41, 247
Psychotherapy, 96, 107, 113-19, 136, 137, 158, 165, 200, 224, 226, 227, 424, 429
Psychoticism, 429, 436
  heritability of, 436-38
  measurement of, 427, 437

Punishment, 91, 92, 94, 155, 223, 351, 352, 377, 378, 466, 467, 470, 506, 507
Purposive striving, 116, 193, 333, 484, 535

Q-sort, 110
Quasi-needs, 472
Quasi-stellar radio sources (quasars), 130, 195, 196
Questionnaires, 61, 64, 186, 312, 313, 375, 376, 437, 454, 455
  workshop in, 315-17, 356, 357

Ratings, 365-67, 375, 376, 427, 454, 455
  workshop in, 357
Reaction formation, 248, 274, 276, 326
Reaction time, 301, 436
Reality, 216, 219, 241, 246, 258, 340
  level of, 466
  principle, 237, 241, 243
  testing, 218, 243
  and unreality, 466
Record
  of behavior, 35-46 passim, 74, 80-84, 280, 529, 531, 533
  cumulative, 79-83, 87, 89
  definition, 35
  determinants of, 38, 529
  determinants within, 38
  of experience, 35-46 passim, 74, 180, 202, 529, 530, 533
  interview transcription, 107
  regularity in, 533, 534
  workshop in, 44, 45, 283-85
Red shift, 195, 196
Reflex, 73-104 passim, 133, 201, 237
  after-discharge of, 76
  chain of, 84, 86
  change in strength of, 91
  conditioned, 78, 133
  dynamic laws, 77
  eye-blink, 73
  groups of, and motivation, 88
  integration of, 84, 86
  knee-jerk, 73
  latency, 76
  static properties of, 77
  strength of, 76-79, 88
  threshold, 76
Regions
  boundaries and, 471-73, 476-78
  of life space, 469
  of person, 471, 477
Regression, 280, 327, 345
Rehearsal, symbolic, 517
Reinforcement, 51, 82, 83, 87, 88, 99, 152, 188, 201, 242, 281
  in Type R conditioning, 78
  in Type S conditioning, 78, 435
  positive, 94, 100
  value, 485, 486, 527
  vicarious, 507, 512, 516
  See also Conditioning
  See also Schedules of
Reliability of measurements, 61, 135, 202, 457, 458
Religious experience, 328-32
Repetition compulsion, 229, 237, 243

Repression
  in Freud's theory, 221, 224, 237, 241-44, 247, 251, 265, 271, 273, 322, 529
  in Jung's theory, 293, 303-7
  in Miller and Dollard's theory, 163, 164
Resistance, 244, 323
  in analytical psychotherapy, 332
  in psychoanalysis, 220, 243, 255, 332
Response
  anticipatory, 151, 152, 161, 169
  approach, 79, 158
  autonomic, 100, 161
  avoidance, 107, 158, 507
  in Bandura and Walters's theory, 504
  chained, 84
  conditioned (CR), 76, 86, 87, 93, 94, 435, 507
  conformity, 95
  construct of, 98
  cue-producing, 161-63, 181
  displaced, 157, 158, 181
  emotional, 94, 507
  frequency, 79, 80, 435
  inhibition, 157, 507
  labeling, 163-65
  magnitude, 76
  maintenance of rate, 83
  in Miller and Dollard's theory, 149-75 passim, 181
  novel, 509
  rate of, 80, 82, 84, 89, 91, 95, 280
  reduced form of, 98
  in Skinner's theory, 73-101 passim
  strength of, 157
  unconditioned (UR), 75, 87, 93
  unemitted, 93
  verbal, 99, 163, 171
Reward, 75, 91, 151
  in Bandura and Walters's theory, 504
  in Miller and Dollard's theory, 149-76 passim, 181
Rogers: brief biography, 107-9
Rogers's theoretical models
  personal development, 112, 113
  psychotherapy, 113, 114, 425
  research on, 114, 117-19
  self-concept, 110, 399-420 passim
Rogers's theory, 107-24, 132, 180
  accomplishments, 113-16
  of cause, 110-12
  critique, 116-22
  of priority, 112, 113
  of structure of experience, 109, 110
Role, 339-58 passim
Rotter: brief biography, 483
Rotter's theoretical models
  internal-external control, 490-92
  need, 487
  research on, 490-94
Rotter's theory, 149, 483-99
  accomplishments, 489-94
  critique, 494-97
  of function, 483-99
  workshop in, 497, 498

Sadism, 247, 343
Salivation, 75-78, 86, 90, 95, 163, 267, 431, 435

Schedules of reinforcement, 83, 90, 91, 95, 507, 516
  awareness and, 100
  defined, 89
  fixed-interval, 83, 89, 142
  fixed-ratio, 89, 90
  variable-interval, 89
  variable-ratio, 89
Schizophrenia, 140, 191, 257, 258, 365
School attendance, 75
Scoptophilia, 247, 248
Scratching, 41, 45, 267, 270
Secondary process thinking, 237, 245, 246
Security, 57
Self, 31, 92, 110
  changes in, 120
  construct of, 180, 399-420
  control, 92, 94, 343
  -experiences, 112, 120, 122
  ideal, 110, 112, 400-20 passim
  Jung's model, 306-8, 326, 399-420
  Maslow's model, 399-420
  perception of, 110
  physical, 31, 407
  -reproach, 222, 223
  Rogers's model, 109
  social, 399-420 passim
  spiritual, 31
  -study, 165, 166
  subjective view of, 117
  -understanding, 108, 119
Self-actualization
  Krause's critique, 120, 121
  in Maslow's theory, 5, 201, 399-420 passim
  in Rogers's theory, 108-24
  syndrome of, 12-17
Self-actualizing individuals, 5, 12, 24, 134, 180, 201, 258
  workshop in, 23, 24
Self-actualizing tendency, 111, 121
Self-concept, 109-12, 117, 399-420 passim
  change, 112, 113
  congruence of, 112
  experiences inconsistent with, 111
  incongruence of, 112, 122
  wholeness of, 117
Self-description, 64, 110, 132, 347
Self-preservative instincts, 221, 222, 237, 240
Self-ratings, 64
Self-regard, 120
Self-sentiment, 386, 402-20 passim
  strength, 376-82
Self-structure, 110, 117
Self-sufficiency, 377-81, 390, 392
Sensation, 42, 58, 93, 222, 244, 267
  awareness and, 113
  conditioned, 94
  in Jung's theory, 291-318 passim, 324, 456
Sense of, in Erikson's theory, 342
Sense organs, 42, 73, 213, 341, 432
Sensuous expression, 54, 55, 62
Sentiment, 384-86
Sex
  component or part instincts of, 258, 265, 274, 326
  genital organization of, 268

impulses, 41, 45, 251-53
instincts, 133, 235, 271
instincts in Freud's theory, 155, 235, 238
as measured erg, 384-88
need for. See Need, sex
objects of instinct, 238, 267, 269, 271
perversions, 55, 265, 271, 277
pregenital organization, 268, 270
stages in development of instinct, 265-72
symbols of in dreams, 250, 251
Sexuality
  adult, 271, 274, 322, 346
  infantile, 209, 210, 254, 270, 278, 340, 346
Shadow, 305, 324, 326
Shame, 38, 274, 276, 344
Shock, 91, 156, 157, 160, 256
Simplicity of theories, 65, 431
Simulation by human subjects, 101, 539-41
Situations, 30, 31, 86, 388, 389, 484
  concrete, Lewin's concept of, 465, 468
Sixteen Personality Factor Questionnaire (16PF), 376, 377, 380, 386, 392
Skin resistance (GSR), 90, 100, 167
Skinner Box, 78, 79
Skinner: brief biography, 73, 74
Skinner's principles of scientific method, 81, 536, 537
Skinner's theoretical models
  causation, 91, 92, 187
  drive, 88, 92
  emotion, 90-92
  imagery, 92-95
  language, 94, 99
  need, 88, 89
  Type R conditioning, 78-104 passim
Skinner's theory, 73-104, 201, 506, 516
  accomplishments, 92-95
  of cause, 73-104 passim, 195
  critique, 95-101
  of structure, 73-104 passim, 195
Slip of the tongue, 244, 248
Sociability, 430, 431, 454, 455
Social learning theory. See Theory, social learning
Social position, 340, 346
Socialization, 505, 506
Sociocultural factors, 339, 340, 356, 492-94
Somatic point of view, 527
Source trait, 361-96 passim
Spirit, 74, 214, 311, 322, 330, 332
Spiritual rebirth, 294, 327-33
Spontaneity, 13, 24, 535
Stage theories of development, 265-86, 339-58
States contrasted with traits, 450, 451
Statistical terms (mean, standard deviation, etc.), 365-74, 544-46
Stimulation, 182, 215, 236, 245
  excessive, 182, 236, 432
Stimulus
  ambient, 389
  aversive, 91, 92, 94, 507
  barrier, 182
  conditioned (CS), 75, 87, 93, 435, 514

construct of, 98
discriminative, 29, 79, 84, 86-88, 90-92, 94, 95
dissimilarity dimension, 157-60, 166, 181
eliciting, 75-78, 84, 507
environmental, 30, 150, 172, 213, 267, 280, 281, 295, 340, 505
focal, 389
internal, or drive stimuli, 151, 238, 239, 271
in operation of personality traits, 362, 363
reinforcing, 78, 82, 84, 91, 92, 281
in S-R or Skinner's theory, 33, 51, 73-105 passim, 188, 194, 441
strength of, 161
in Tolman's theory, 494, 495
triggering, 257, 362, 389
unconditioned (US), 75, 87, 93, 435, 514
Strata in personality structure, 376-82
Stream of consciousness, 31
Stress reactions
  Freud's model, 182
  Horowitz's model, 183
  Lazarus's model, 182, 183, 537, 538
Structure
  of behavior, 84
  conceptions of, 451
  of experience, 109
  hypothesized internal, 30, 281, 394
  laws of composition and, 84, 189
  of personality, 3, 31, 221, 291-95, 323-26, 376-87, 533, 534
  physical, 39
  and process, 39
  psychological, 39
  psychophysical, 39, 41, 45, 171, 281
  and regularities in the record, 534
  in theories of personality, 29, 30, 33, 533
  theory of, in personality. See Theory, of structure
  theory of in various fields of science, 189
  underlying, 29, 370, 505, 533
Structured learning, 391
Stuttering, 257
Subject matter of theories, 180, 181
Subjective experience. See Experience, subjective
Subjective judgment, 63
Subjective probability, 63, 485, 496
Sublimation, 248, 259, 274, 332
Subsidiary need, 58
Subsidiation, 52
Succorance. See Need, succorance
Sucking, 57, 236, 238, 239, 266, 269, 279, 342
Suffering, 272
  need for, 41
Suicide, 241, 258
  16PF profiles for attempted, 390
Superego, 74, 219
  in Cattell's theory, 377-82, 400-420 passim

in Freud's theory, 219, 221-24, 235, 237, 324, 345, 392, 400-420 passim, 528, 533
in Erikson's theory, 408-11
strength of as source trait, 377-82, 449, 450
Surface trait, 365, 367
Surgency, 377-81
Symbolic processing, 516, 517
Symbolization of experience, 110, 112, 114, 529
Symbols, 110, 216, 221, 243, 244, 250, 259, 260, 289, 303, 333, 505
Sympathetic nervous system, 432
Symptoms, 164, 181, 183, 185, 208-10, 216, 218, 239, 243, 244, 248, 254-57, 272, 274
Syndrome, 10, 180, 191
defined, 10
insecurity, 6, 11, 142, 191
self-actualization, 6, 13, 180, 191
statics and dynamics, 11
System
of categories, 115, 144-46
classification, 190
cognitive, 29
conscious, 213, 236
emotional, 29
explanatory, 181
feedback mechanisms and, 535
general systems theory, 193, 194, 535
hypothetico-deductive, 99
in inner personality, 28, 33
logical, 119
models, 193
motivational, 29
nervous, 39
nuclear, 213, 214, 236
perceptual, 29, 213
preconscious, 218
psychophysical, 29, 35, 38, 39, 49
theory of. See Theory, of system
Systematic desensitization, 514, 515

Tachistoscope, 257, 427
Temperament, 346, 347
defined, 374
traits, 374
Tension, 188, 238, 267, 271, 471, 477
ergic, 377-81, 450, 451
and incompleted tasks, 471-73
Testability, 138, 142, 181, 196, 440, 473
Thema, 57
Thematic Apperception Test (TAT), 58-61, 64, 66, 67, 167, 171, 313
Thematic dispositions, 49, 66, 73, 180, 533
assessment of, 57, 59, 66
defined, 57
workshop in, 68, 357
Theoretical model
meaning of, 181, 199, 201
See also Model, theoretical
Theory
axioms, 127
of cause, 122, 180, 181, 185, 186, 194-205 passim, 235-62, 300-308, 321-36, 387-89, 432-39, 441, 532, 533

change or development of, 197, 215, 220, 536-38
cognitive, 100, 101, 169, 172
comparison of theories, 321-36, 353-55
competition between theories, 195, 196, 321-36, 353-66
conditioning or learning, 100, 188, 255, 281, 441, 516
in criminal investigation, 184
criteria for evaluating, 127, 134, 136, 137-41, 181, 541
disproving a, 197
essential components of scientific, 127, 201, 426
field, 464-73 passim, 483
formal, 64, 65, 127, 134
of function, 73-104, 149-76, 185, 187, 188, 194-205 passim, 361-96, 423-44, 463-81, 483-99
functions of in science, 135
general or overall, 179-82, 197, 289, 441
liberalized S-R-R, 168, 169, 172
mathematical models and, 65
meanings of word "theory," 179, 180
of mechanics, 182
mechanistic, 133, 134, 194
mentalistic, 94-96, 171
nature of scientific, 127-46 passim, 179, 426, 441, 442
neurophysiological, 235, 432-36, 459
of pattern, 144, 181, 185, 190-205 passim, 265-86, 295-300, 321, 339-58, 441
phenomenological, 180
of priority, 20, 21, 112, 113, 185, 192-205 passim, 321, 532, 535
psychodynamic, 171, 172, 186, 194, 257
psychological, 64, 65, 99, 134
simplicity of, 127
social learning, 149-76, 483-99, 503-22
statistical, 179
of structure, 84, 109-11, 122, 185, 188, 194-205 passim, 207-32, 235, 291-95, 321-25, 376-87, 429-32, 441, 532-34
sub-, or component, or special theories, 179-81
of system, 185, 193-205 passim, 441, 532, 535, 536
theoretical models related to, 181, 182, 195-205 passim, 392, 519, 541
types of, 179-205, 532, 536
workshop in, 202, 203, 497, 498
Thinking and thoughts, 31, 32, 43, 57, 58, 92, 94, 108, 114, 189, 191, 246, 324, 426
determinants of, 29
and experience, 109
Freud's model, 209, 215, 221, 237, 240, 241, 244
in Jung's theory, 291-318 passim, 324, 456
Miller and Dollard's model, 163-65, 170
Skinner's model, 92-95
Thirst, 133, 238
Threat, 111, 112, 117, 132, 142, 182, 219, 222, 240
Thumbsucking, 266, 269, 270
Time, 190, 191, 216, 218, 219, 246

Training, 99, 114, 276, 504, 507
Parent Effectiveness, 114, 116
Traits, 186, 505
concept of, 363
heritability of, 377-82, 436-38, 505
interaction, 382
kinds of, 374
learning and, 155
measurement of, 186, 364-76
organization of, 378-80
psychophysical dispositions as, 363
source, 365-96
surface, 365, 367
theory of, 194, 505
Transcendence, 16
Transference, 219, 255, 332
Transmitters, 57
Truancy, 75
Trust
in infant, 191
versus mistrust stage, 341
Truth-values, 98, 181
Type
anal character, 275, 276, 326
feeling types, 299, 315, 316, 395
genital character, 277
intuitive types, 300, 315, 316
in Jung's theory, 298-315 passim, 395, 452, 453
oral character, 275
pattern theory of, 190-94, 298-315 passim
as pattern of traits, 190, 453
phallic character, 276
physique and, 41
sensation types, 299, 300, 315, 316
thinking types, 298, 299, 315, 316, 395
various theories of, 453
workshop in, 315-17

Unconditional positive regard, 112-14, 118, 120
Unconscious
collective, 294, 295, 324
in Erikson's theory, 342
in Freud's theory, 185, 208-86 passim, 321-36, 529, 541
in Jung's theory, 293-318 passim, 321-36, 529
in Murray's theory, 53, 57, 60, 61
in a new theory, 541
personal, 293, 294, 324
psychological processes, assumption of, 131, 505
in Rogers's theory, 529
wish, 185, 219, 242, 244, 249
Unidentified flying objects (UFO's), 128, 129, 314, 315
Unity-thema, 51, 61, 65, 67
Unpleasure, 236, 240
Urination, 58, 90, 239, 242, 252, 267, 269, 275, 276
nocturnal enuresis, 253, 276
relation to sex organs, 242, 269

Vagina, 244, 271
Valence, 468-72, 484
Validity of tests and measurements, 61, 202

construct, 139
  predictive, 139
Values, 110-12
  B-values, 17
  introjected, 111, 112
Vascular system, 39
Visions, 295, 300
Vulva, 269, 276

Walters: brief biography, 503
Warmth, as a personality variable, 114
Whole person concepts, 5, 27, 108, 117, 180, 477, 535
Wisdom, 6, 328, 349
Wish, 244, 292
  fulfillment, 244, 249-51, 333
  incestuous, 254, 326, 332

Womb, 57, 282
Women, 9, 282, 299, 355, 389, 449, 450, 493, 494
Word-association test, 300, 301